A SUFI COMMENTARY ON THE QUR'ĀN

ʿABD AL-RAZZĀQ AL-KĀSHĀNĪ

A SUFI COMMENTARY ON THE QUR'ĀN

Ta'wīlāt al-Qur'ān

Volume II

Translated by
Khalid Williams

THE ROYAL AAL AL-BAYT INSTITUTE
FOR ISLAMIC THOUGHT
and
THE ISLAMIC TEXTS SOCIETY

Copyright © The Royal Aal al-Bayt Institute for Islamic Thought 2021

This first edition published 2021 by
THE ROYAL AAL AL-BAYT INSTITUTE FOR ISLAMIC THOUGHT &
THE ISLAMIC TEXTS SOCIETY
MILLER'S HOUSE
KINGS MILL LANE
GREAT SHELFORD
CAMBRIDGE CB22 5EN, UK.

British Library Cataloguing-in-Publication Data.
A catalogue record for this book is
available from the British Library.

ISBN: 978 1911141 44 0 VOL I
ISBN: 978 1911141 45 7 VOL II

The Royal Aal al-Bayt Institute for Islamic Thought and
The Islamic Texts Society hold no responsibility for the persistence
or accuracy of URLs for external or third-party internet websites
referred to in this publication, and do not guarantee that any
content on such websites is, or will remain,
accurate or appropriate.

CONTENTS

Editor's Introduction   IX

A SUFI COMMENTARY ON THE QUR'ĀN
Volume II

Contents

EDITOR'S INTRODUCTION

I. SUFI APPROACHES TO QUR'ĀNIC COMMENTARY

The discipline of Qur'ānic commentary (*tafsīr*) has been described by Walid Saleh as 'one of the most voluminous of Islamic literary genres, second only to the legal tradition'. Generations throughout the lands in which Muslims reside have attempted this art. The early works of *tafsīr* displayed a limited diversity, but they also possessed a certain commonality, as Sunni exegetes afforded the highest authority to commentaries from the Prophet, and then his Companions and their Followers. In addition, the dictates of philology and the works of Arabic grammarians came to be a central hermeneutic tool in commentaries, but without being given an open-ended authority to explain the revelation. After the initial phase of exegetical activity, there emerged Sufi commentaries on the Qur'ān that discussed the 'inner meaning' (*bāṭin*) of the Qur'ān, which was to differ from the 'outer meaning' (*ẓāhir*) explained in conventional commentaries.[1]

Pieter Coppens argues that the acceptance of a separate 'Sufi genre' within the *tafsīr* tradition seems to be 'a modern invention'. He states that pre-modern biographical dictionaries on Qur'ānic commentators (*ṭabaqāt al-mufassirīn*) would include works of Sufis like Sulamī and Qushayrī, but they would simply identify the authors as 'Sufi' rather than regarding that identity as a specific methodology. However, he cites the contemporary Muḥammad Ḥusayn al-Dhahabī as clearly identifying two strands of Sufi commentary: firstly, the methodology based on 'speculative philosophy' (*naẓarī*); secondly, an exposition founded on 'allusion' (*ishārī*). The former is considered to be a type of eisegesis, whereby the Sufi commentator reads a preconceived system of thought into the Qur'ān. The latter is a form of interpretation based on 'hidden allusions that appear to the masters of the path (*arbāb al-sulūk*)', which differ from the outer meanings, yet might still conform to them in a broad sense. Moreover, Coppens shows that scholars identify a commentary as 'Sufi' if its hermeneutic methodology centres on 'allusion' (*ishāra*), 'unveiling' (*kashf*) and the 'inward' (*bāṭin*), and can be seen to be 'experiential'.[2]

In *Ṣūfī Commentaries on the Qur'ān in Classical Islam*, Kristan Zahra Sands points out that 'Ṣūfī interpretations are more suggestive than declarative; they are "allusions" (*ishārāt*) rather than explanations (*tafāsir*), to use the Arabic terms. They therefore indicate possibilities as much as they demonstrate the insights of each writer.' Sufis also described their interpretative craft as 'understanding' (*fahm*) or 'striking similitudes' (*ḍarb al-mithāl*). Sands identifies 'several basic premises' which inform Sufi exegetes of the Qur'ān on the basis of their reading of verses of the scripture and on the interpretations attributed to ʿAlī b. Abī Ṭālib and Jaʿfar al-Ṣādiq, both of whom are particularly revered by Sufis. She explains that Abū Ḥāmid al-Ghazālī—in response to those who would restrict Qur'ānic commentary to 'exoteric exegesis' (*ẓāhir al-tafsīr*) and the transmitted interpretations of authorities like Ibn ʿAbbās and Mujāhid—mounted a defence of alternative commentary, whereby he noted that one cannot reject all such interpretation as the 'exegesis by personal opinion' (*tafsīr bi'l-ra'y*) condemned by the Prophet. As summarized by Sands, Ghazālī explained 'personal opinion' in two ways: firstly, 'sound personal effort (*al-ijtihād al-ṣaḥīḥ*), which is praiseworthy'; secondly, 'opinion biased by inclination (*hawā*), which is not'.[3]

As to ʿAbd al-Razzāq al-Kāshānī, the author of the Sufi commentary that is the subject of this translation, the preferred term he uses for his approach to commentary—as can be seen from the Arabic title *Ta'wīlāt al-Qur'ān*—is *ta'wīl*. Sands writes,

> The terms *tafsīr* and *ta'wīl* have a complicated history. In the first few centuries of Islam, they were used interchangeably to refer to any commentary on the Quran. Over time, however, the word *tafsīr* began to be applied only to those works that relied heavily on the transmitted interpretive traditions from the first few generations of Muslims, while *ta'wīl* became a term used to describe other types of interpretations. In the fourteenth century both al-Nīsābūrī and al-Kāshānī used the word *ta'wīl* to describe their interpretative activity.[4]

Sands explains that Kāshānī's introduction to *Ta'wīlāt al-Qur'ān*[5] makes it clear 'that the process of *ta'wīl* is unending, while that of *tafsīr* is limited', so 'while it is prohibited to alter the external sense of the Qur'ān, this prohibition does not extend to understanding its additional meanings'.[6]

Kāshānī states in the introduction, 'Now, they say that he who explains (*fassara*) [the Qur'ān] on the basis of opinion (*ra'y*) has truly become a disbeliever (*kāfir*), and as for [esoteric] interpretation (*ta'wīl*) that "it neither spares nor leaves behind", for it varies in accordance with the [different] states and moments of the listener along the stages of his wayfaring (*sulūk*) and by the variation of his degrees (*daraja*).' For Kāshānī, the outer meaning purifies souls, but the inner meaning replenishes their thirst.

II. KAMĀL AL-DĪN ABŪ AL-FAḌL ʿABD AL-RAZZĀQ AL-KĀSHĀNĪ[7]

A. Life, Work and Sectarian Affiliation

Historians have established the broad details of Kāshānī's life, although his actual name is alternatively spelt Kāsānī, Qāshānī, Qāshī and Kāshī.[8] He is likely to have been born in the Persian province of Kāshān, around 650–60/1252–61, and died between 730–6/1329–35.[9] This was a period when the Mongolian Īlkhānid dynasty (r. from around 1253–1258 until about 1335–1353 CE) came to rule large parts of the Eastern Islamic lands.[10] Over the span of Kāshānī's life, the dynasty went through tumultuous events, with creedal flux, as well as fierce military encounters with the Mamlūks who ruled the neighbouring territories. In relation to the latter, it is noted that the Īlkhānids launched six attacks on the Mamlūks between 1260 and 1312.[11]

The dynasty's initial rulers were Buddhist, starting with the founder Hūlāgū (d. 1265).[12] The third ruler, Aḥmad Takūdār (r. 1282–4), converted to Islam and honoured the Sufis, and had a Muslim supervise the endowments (*awqāf*) and act as his chief envoy to the Mamlūk sultan, with whom he tried to reconcile.[13] However, Takūdār did not make Islam the state religion. This did not happen until the reign of the seventh ruler, Ghāzān (r. 1295–1304), who converted to Islam just prior to assuming the throne.[14] Although Ghāzān patronised and revered the Prophet's family (*ahl al-bayt*), and is said to have utilized Shiʿi symbols of leadership to justify his own rule, he is identified as a Sunni.[15] Uljāytū (r. 1304–16), Ghāzān's successor as ruler, became a Shiʿi some time between 1308 and 1310, although this move was not followed by everyone in the 'military aristocracy', nor senior ministers. His conversion led to rebellions in the Sunni-majority region under his control (he is alleged to have re-converted to Sunni Islam; however, this is doubted by historians). Uljāytū's assault upon Damascus in 1312 led Ibn Taymiyya to issue his legal edict that the Tatars were 'apostates' (*murtaddūn*).[16] Yet, Uljāytū's son and successor, Abū Saʿīd (r. 1317–35), returned to the Sunni creed, and immediately overturned the Shiʿi decrees of his father (such as performing the Friday prayer sermon in the Shiʿi method or printing coins with the images of the Twelve Shiʿa Imams).[17]

Kāshānī's life, therefore, coincided with momentous upheavals in the region. His early life is described by him in an important letter on the doctrine of Ibn ʿArabī that he wrote to the Kubrawī master ʿAlāʾ al-Dawla al-Simnānī;[18] this letter has been preserved along with Simnānī's response by a number of scholars, including Jāmī in his *Nafaḥāt al-uns*. Kāshānī's letter mentions his advanced traditional studies, covering Sacred Law, logic and philosophy, which did not provide him with spiritual contentment. After suffering a spiritual crisis, Kāshānī turned to Sufism.[19] Hādīzāda has opined that this entry into Sufism occurred when Kāshānī was aged between twenty-five and thirty-five.[20] On his entry into Sufism, he became a disciple of the Suhrawardī master Nūr al-Dīn ʿAbd al-Ṣamad Naṭanzī, and visited other Sufi masters in the region, especially in Shiraz. After Naṭanzī passed away, Kāshānī is reported to have travelled extensively in Persia and to have journeyed to the holy cities in the Hijaz, as well as to Egypt and Konya.[21] He lived in Shiraz for approximately two decades (roughly 1281–1300), moved to Baghdad after 1300 and finally settled in Tabriz for the remainder of his life from around 1321 until 1335.

In Tabriz, Kāshānī was patronised by Rashīd al-Dīn (chief minister under both Ghāzān and Uljāytū, and author of the grand history of the Mongols entitled *Jāmiʿ al-tavārīkh*[22]), and then by Rashīd al-Dīn's son Ghiyāth al-Dīn (chief minister under Abū Saʿīd). This patronage of Kāshānī by Rashīd al-Dīn and then Ghiyāth al-Dīn indicates that Kāshānī was not a reclusive Sufi detached from social life. In fact, it is recorded that he occupied certain official government positions and was the 'Sufi laureate' to Uljāytū; as such, he was one of the four 'royal escorts' on military offensives. Indeed, Kāshānī was to become a favourite of Abū Saʿīd.[23]

Kāshānī's influence and legacy, however, lie in the contribution that he made to the school of Ibn ʿArabī. Kāshānī studied under Muʾayyid al-Dīn al-Jandī, who himself had studied with Qūnawī,[24] the stepson of Ibn ʿArabī and leading exponent of Akbarian doctrine. James Winston Morris writes that Kāshānī 'has almost certainly been the most widely read (and cited) of these early interpreters of Ibn ʿArabī, to such an extent that much of the subsequent discussion of "Ibn ʿArabī's" thought and doctrine, whether in the Eastern Islamic world or in the modern West, can best be understood as in fact a reference to Kāshānī's writings—especially where writers are expounding what they take to be Ibn ʿArabī's "system" or philosophic "doctrine" (e.g., of *waḥdat al-wujūd*).'[25] In this regard, Kāshānī authored one of the most popular commentaries on Ibn ʿArabī's *Fuṣūṣ al-ḥikam*.[26]

Kāshānī wrote in both Arabic and Persian, and is best known for his works of 'philosophical Sufism'.[27] His most important work is *Ta'wīlāt al-Qur'ān*. This Qur'ānic commentary may in fact be a part of a larger Qur'ānic work entitled *Ḥaqā'iq al-ta'wīl fī daqā'iq al-tanzīl*, which focuses on grammar and syntax in a conventional manner and exists in manuscript form in the Süleymaniye Library in Istanbul. In this manuscript of the *Ḥaqā'iq al-ta'wīl*, the *Ta'wīlāt al-Qur'ān* comprises the Sufi section of the work.[28] Kāshānī is also well known for producing a popular glossary of Sufi nomenclature, entitled *Iṣṭilāḥāt al-ṣūfiyya*, which has been published in both short and long versions (see the Bibliography for details of an English translation). In addition, he composed a commentary on Anṣārī's *Manāzil al-sā'irīn*; a work on chivalry (*futuwwa*) in both Arabic and Persian, entitled *Tuḥfat al-ikhwān fī khaṣā'iṣ al-fityān*;[29] an Arabic treatise on predestination and destiny entitled *Risāla fī'l-qaḍā' wa'l-qadar*, which ends with a discussion of the life after death; and a number of smaller works on a variety of subjects, including matters of eschatology, meditations and aphorisms, such as the Persian work on eschatology entitled *al-Mabda' wa'l-maʿād*.

Although Kāshānī can easily be identified as a Sufi (who would quote Sufis like al-Ḥasan al-Baṣrī, al-Junayd, al-Fuḍayl, Abū Yazīd and al-Ḥallāj, with a discernible influence of Abū Ṭālib al-Makkī and Abū Ḥāmid al-Ghazālī[30]), and more specifically as a proponent of the school of Ibn ʿArabī, it is a greater challenge to place him within strictly Sunni or Shiʿi terms. Kāshānī's practice of citing from prominent members of the Prophet's family, in particular ʿAlī b. Abī Ṭālib and Jaʿfar al-Ṣādiq, has led to him being identified as Shiʿi. However, the evidence is not so decisive. Proof for his Sunnism comes from a number of instances: his praise of the Companions Abū Bakr (see commentary on Q. 18:16 below; and *Iṣṭilāḥāt al-ṣūfiyya*, under the entry for *al-ṣiddīq*), and his citing from and praying over other Companions like ʿUmar (see commentary on Q. 10:62 and 11:11 below) and ʿĀ'isha (see commentary on Q. 2:199, 2:285 and 17:73 below); his *Ḥaqā'iq al-ta'wīl* cites Sunnis like Abū Ḥanīfa, Shaybānī, Abū Yūsuf, Saʿīd b. al-Musayyab, ʿIkrima, Shaʿbī, Ibrāhīm al-Nakhaʿī, Qatāda, Sufyān al-Thawrī, Sufyān b. al-ʿUyayna, whilst he utilises *ḥadīth* sources that are distinctly Sunni in *al-Mabda' wa'l-maʿād*; one of his foremost students, Dāwūd al-Qayṣarī, was a Sunni; and his principal Sufi shaykh,

Naṭanzī, was a leading guide in the Suhrawardī spiritual order, which is Sunni. On the Shiʿi side, in addition to his attachment to the Prophet's family, which is also a traditional Sunni virtue, one of his major students, Saʿīd al-Qūnawī, was a Shiʿi. Moreover, the fact that Kāshānī remained popular in the courts of Uljāytū (who fluctuated between the Sunni and Shiʿi creeds) and Abū Saʿīd (a staunch Sunni) also provides no clues for determining Kāshānī's allegiance to either of the two groups.[31] And while Lory states that Kāshānī's 'Shīʿī inclinations are apparent throughout his writings', he nonetheless concedes that he 'did not express opinions incompatible with Sunnī orthodoxy'.[32]

B. The *Ta'wīlāt al-Qur'ān*

SALIENT FEATURES OF THE WORK

Ta'wīlāt al-Qur'ān has been described by Pierre Lory as Kāshānī's 'magnum opus', a complete commentary of the Qur'ān, which is 'one of the masterpieces of Ṣūfī exegesis';[33] however, it does not cover every verse, but comments on each *sūra*, whether in whole or in part. The work exhibits such Akbarian qualities that in Arabic it is published under the title *Tafsīr Ibn ʿArabī*. Osman Yahia did find some later manuscripts attributing the work to Ibn ʿArabī (in contrast with Pierre Lory, following Brockelmann, who only found manuscripts attributing it to Kāshānī), but Morris states that this mistake is 'unfortunately as symptomatic as it is historically unfounded'.[34] In addition, an autographed copy of Kāshānī's *Ta'wīlāt al-Qur'ān* has led Lory and Yahia to conclude that Kāshānī only wrote up to *Sūra* 32 (a point also made by Hermann Landolt).[35] If this is the case, there is no indication of who completed the work, and no great discrepancy has been identified between the two parts.

The present translation into English of *Ta'wīlāt al-Qur'ān* has been divided into two volumes. Volume I, translated by Feras Hamza, covers the introduction until the end of *Sūra* 18 (The Cave, *al-Kahf*); Volume II, translated by Khalid Williams, comprises the commentary from *Sūra* 19 (Mary, *Maryam*) to the final *Sūra*.

KĀSHĀNĪ'S AKBARIAN AND AVICENNIAN METHODOLOGY

Lory argues that the *Ta'wīlāt al-Qur'ān* 'follows roughly the doctrines of Ibn ʿArabī, but he introduces many personal interpretations'.[36] Yet, Morris puts forth a comprehensive description of the nature of *Ta'wīlāt al-Qur'ān*, and how it ought to be regarded as a didactic manual for spiritual aspirants:

Kāshānī is *not* at all representative of Ibn ʿArabī's 'style' or 'method' of exegesis, and only to a very limited extent (for reasons outlined below in this section) of Ibn ʿArabī's 'thought.' More important, far from 'representing Sufi thought at its highest level of esoteric exegesis' […], it is—as Kāshānī himself explicitly brings out in his Introduction […]—an elementary work, for beginners on the spiritual Path, with very limited pedagogical aims, and therefore is completely different in style and content from what one usually finds (to take only examples in the framework of this article) in either the works of Ibn ʿArabī or the more intimate passages in ʿAbd al-Qādir's *Mawāqif*.[37]

Ibn ʿArabī infrequently used the term *ta'wīl* for his exegesis and tended to use the term *tafsīr* for his 'spiritual understanding', whereas *ta'wīl* can be seen to be used by him in 'a pejorative sense of an "esoteric" interpretation arbitrarily attached to a Koranic expression, with no essential inner connection to the actual meaning of the text'.[38] In broad terms, Morris has provided the following summation:

> For him [Ibn ʿArabī], in general, what we would ordinarily call the 'spiritual' meaning *is* precisely the 'literal' meaning (as typified in his characteristic linguistic, 'etymological' approach to key Koranic terms), indeed *is* the 'Reality' of the Koran itself—in a sense which *includes*, but is in no way reducible to, the sort of historicist and legalistic viewpoints (themselves 'interpretations') that are unthinkingly accepted as the 'obvious' meaning of the text most of the time. This 'Platonic' understanding of the Koran (and of revelation in general) is in no way reducible to the sort of *ẓāhir/bāṭin* or *tafsīr/ta'wīl* schema implicit in Kāshānī's approach (and in the philosophic, Sufi, and Shiite perspectives he ultimately draws on), and cannot really be 'taught'—precisely because that would imply that the 'meaning' were somehow reducible to a system or set of concepts somehow separable from the triad Koran-reader-Reality which alone is the matrix within which, for Ibn ʿArabī, that meaning is necessarily both manifested and perceived.[39]

As such, Morris argues that Kāshānī's work is a departure from the norm in Sufi Qurʾānic 'hermeneutics', as the method of such 'interpretation' (*ta'wīl*) was characterised by 'a profound and inevitably quite personal awareness of the immediate spiritual implications of particular Koranic verses'; but Kāshānī's work is the 'the *application* to the Koran of a coherent metaphysical system, elaborated in all of his works, based on elements from both Ibn ʿArabī's writings and the prevalent Avicennian school of philosophy in which Kāshānī himself was originally trained.'[40]

The 'personal interpretations' of Kāshānī that Lory speaks of 'are applications of Qurʾānic verses to the spiritual evolution of a Ṣūfī, a process he calls *taṭbīq* ("adaptation"), intending something like the application of revelation to human microcosmic experiences'.[41] Sands states that 'Al-Kāshānī is not the first commentator to use this technique [*taṭbīq*], but he is the first to use it so extensively and exclusively, and the first to apply it to entire passages of the Qurʾān. It is this method that invites the charge of allegorical reductionism, and yet, however one judges the results, this does not appear to have been al-Kāshānī's intention.'[42]

By way of exemplifying the Avicennian influence, Sands adds that Kāshānī makes extensive use of allegories throughout his interpretation of the Qurʾānic story of Moses and al-Khaḍir (or pronounced al-Khiḍr)—discussed below from Q. 18:65–18:82—where he combines 'the terminology and concepts' of Ibn Sīnā and the Sufis. Here, Kāshānī begins by explaining Moses' search for al-Khaḍir as being for the 'holy intellect' (*al-ʿaql al-qudsī*), which is necessary for the 'ascent to perfection'; and the allegories continue throughout the explanation of the passage. Sands notes that Ibn ʿArabī would adopt and adapt some of Ibn Sīnā's ideas, but Kāshānī utilises a distinctly Avicennian interpretation of 'the soul and knowledge' in this section; and so he is here more in 'allegiance' to Ibn Sīnā than Ibn ʿArabī. Furthermore, Kāshānī's discussion of *the orphan boys* (Q. 18:82) as 'the twin rational faculty of the considerative and the practical' is, in the words of Sands, an acceptance of 'Ibn Sīnā's conception of the practical and theoretical intellects'.[43]

THE INFLUENCE OF IBN ʿARABĪ

(a) *'Oneness of Being'* (waḥdat al-wujūd)

From the beginning of his commentary, in the introductory comments, Kāshānī makes clear his adherence to the doctrine of 'Oneness of Being':

> As for the innermost hearts (*asrār*), when their hearing is hit by those striking verses, they become attentive and aware through these [striking verses] of the risings of [His] Attributes, whereby they become perplexed by their beauty upon seeing them, bewildered and confused at their self-disclosure. They [their innermost hearts] begin to come apart until their spirits have reached their collar-bones [Q. 75:26] whereupon there

rises afterwards the beautiful appearance of His enduring countenance; and that witnessing decrees the negation of their existence, obliging them to affirm [the truth of the witnessing itself].

The Akbarian concept of 'Oneness of Being' or 'Unity of Existence' (*waḥdat al-wujūd*) is one of the most well-known facets of the school. Although Ibn ʿArabī is said to be the founder of the school of the Oneness of Being, William C. Chittick argues that he never actually used the term himself, albeit 'the idea permeates his works'.[44] Indeed, it is a point that has drawn stern criticism as some have understood it in pantheistic terms. Nevertheless, Chittick explains Ibn ʿArabī's thought in the following way:

> [H]is main concern is not with the mental concept of being but with the experience of God's Being, the tasting (*dhawq*) of Being, that 'finding' which is at one and the same time to perceive and to be that which truly is. No doubt Ibn al-ʿArabī possessed one of the greatest philosophical minds the world has ever known, but philosophy was not his concern. He wanted only to bask in the constant and ever-renewed finding of the Divine Being and Consciousness. He, for one, had passed beyond the veils, though he was always ready to admit that the veils are infinite and that every instant in life, in this world and for all eternity, represents a continual lifting of the veils.[45]

Chittick goes on to say, 'Simply stated, there is only one Being, and all existence is nothing but the manifestation or outward radiance of that One Being. Hence "everything other than the One Being"—that is, the whole cosmos in all its spatial and temporal extension—is non-existent in itself, though it may be considered to exist through Being.'[46]

In light of these explanations, one further example of Kāshānī's understanding of the concept is worth repeating for its emphasis on the divide between the Creator and the creation, as he writes in the commentary on Q. 6:91:

> Had they known Him as He ought to be known, they would have realised that His servants have no existence nor does anything else [for that matter] except through Him. All exists through His existence: there is no existence except His. The entirety of the world of the visible is His exoteric aspect and [the entirety of] the world of the Unseen is His esoteric aspect, and for every esoteric aspect there is an exoteric one. So what inhibition is there against certain of His Attributes manifesting

themselves in a human locus? Indeed, there is no [better] locus
for the manifestation of His perfect esoteric knowledge and
wisdom than the perfect man. Therefore the Prophet, in terms
of form, represents His exoteric aspect; and in terms of meaning,
represents His esoteric aspect: His knowledge descends onto his
heart and manifests itself on his tongue, wherewith he calls His
servants to His Essence. There is no dualism here, except when
considering the differentiation of His Attributes. However,
when considering the union, there is no existent other than Him,
neither the Prophet nor anyone else.

In addition, Kāshānī makes the following commentary on Q. 53:11, which
serves as a further elaboration:

[53:11] The heart (*fu'ād*) did not deny what he saw in the station of
unification. The *fu'ād* is the heart that has ascended to the station
of the spirit in witnessing: the witness of the Essence with all the
Attributes, existing with veridical existence. This unification is
the unification of existence (*jamʿ al-wujūd*), not the unification of
Unity (*jamʿ al-waḥda*) in which there is neither heart nor servant
because all is annihilated therein, which is what they call 'the
source of unification of the Essence'.

Such distinctions in Kāshānī's thought are further emphasised in his
commentary on Q. 112:2:

[112:2] *God, the Self-Sufficient, Besought of all*: the Essence in the
presence of Oneness, from the perspective of the Names, is the
absolute support for all things, because of how every contingent
being needs It and exists through It. He is the Absolutely
Independent on which all things depend, as He says, *For God is
the Independent, while you are the needy* [Q. 47:38]. Since everything
but Him exists through His existence, it is not a thing in itself,
because the contingency that is necessary for quiddity does not
entail existence. Thus, there is nothing that shares His genus or
likeness in existence.

(b) *Sainthood* (walāya) *and prophethood* (nubuwwa)

In *Ta'wīlāt al-Qur'ān*, Kāshānī adheres to the doctrines of sainthood and
prophethood found in the Akbarian school. For instance, in commentary
of Q. 4:64, he writes,

As for prophethood, this is to inform of spiritual knowledge
and realities that have to do with the differentiated aspects of

[God's] Attributes and acts. Prophethood is the exoteric aspect of sainthood, which is to be absorbed in the source of the union and the annihilation in the Essence. The knowledge of these two is the knowledge of the affirmation of the unity of the Essence and the effacement of the acts and Attributes [in the Essence]. Thus, every messenger is a prophet and every prophet is a saint (*walī*), but not every saint is a prophet, nor is every prophet a messenger, even if the rank of sainthood is nobler (*ashraf*) than prophethood and prophethood [nobler] than messengership. It was said [by the poet], 'The station of prophethood is in an interstice (*barzakh*): slightly below that of the saint and just above that of the messenger.'

Regarding sainthood being 'nobler' than prophethood, Michel Chodkiewicz has conducted a study of Ibn ʿArabī's doctrine on the matter and he states, 'This does not in the least mean that the *awliyā'* [His saints] are superior to the prophets and the messengers: every *rasūl* [messenger] and every *nabī* [prophet] is above all and by definition a *walī*. *Walāya* is superior to *nubuwwa* or *risāla* in the persons of the prophets and messengers.' Ibn ʿArabī states, 'When you see a prophet expressing himself in words which do not arise from his legislative authority, it is because he is a *walī* and an *ʿārif* (a gnostic or knower); and the station which he occupies by virtue of being *ʿalīm* (wise) is more complete and more perfect than the station he occupies by virtue of being a messenger or a legislative prophet.' Chodkiewicz argues that Ibn ʿArabī's (and also Kāshānī's) 'demarcation' between *walāya* and *nubuwwa* is 'clear' in the 'strict sense' (as the saints 'are no more than the heirs' of the prophets), but that it can be 'tenuous, and it is easy to understand how Ibn Taymiyya and many after him found it a cause for alarm'.[47]

(c) Eschatology and the 'Hermeneutics of Mercy'

Kāshānī's commentary on Q. 11:108 attempts to navigate between the literal and the esoteric meanings of the verses pertaining to the length of punishment in Hell. For Kāshānī, there is a distinction between *eternally condemned* and *eternally punished*. He writes in commentary of Q. 11:108,

> *An unending gift* [for the believers]: that is, one that is not interrupted. The same is true of the opposite [case of the wretched] given that it is a very severe punishment (*waʿīd*), even though His Words (Exalted is He)—[that He is] *Doer of what*

He desires [Q. 11:107]—suggest that it [might be otherwise]. But that [restraint on our part in relation to that clause] is the tongue of refined manners and [the way of] being mindful of the manifest senses in verifying esoteric meanings. As for the reality [of the case], it dictates that because the wretched one belongs in the various aforementioned levels of the Fire, he will not exit from it but will move from one layer to another and from one grade to another and is thereby eternally (*khulūd*) condemned. Consequently, what is meant by the exception [in his case] is something else and that is that from the perspective of the exclusive unity [of God] he is with his Lord and the Lord leads him by his forelock along a straight path: the barren west winds (*al-dabūr*), which is the vain desire of the soul, drives him to Gehenna. There he finds himself at the source of propinquity (*qurb*) alongside the vain desire of his soul, and takes pleasure in (*yataladhdhadhu*) that which is appropriate for him so that it becomes [for him] the source of bliss (*ʿayn al-naʿīm*). And in his case that which is called the Fire (*musammā al-nār*) disappears and becomes a Garden by virtue of his enjoyment of pleasures therein, even if he should be distant from the bliss of the fortunate one, as related in the *ḥadīth*: 'Watercress will grow forth from the bottom of Gehenna,' and it is also [stated] therein, 'There will come a time when Gehenna's gates will be closed shut when there no longer remains anyone in it.'

The metaphysical argument put forward by Kāshānī is part of what Chittick calls Ibn ʿArabī's 'hermeneutics of mercy'. For Chittick, the latter's 'Qurʾānic interpretations—and all his writings are Qurʾānic interpretations—are permeated by the idea of the divine mercy. His metaphysics, theology, cosmology and spiritual psychology are rooted in the good opinion that God's mercy predominates over his wrath. Where this stress on mercy comes out with special clarity is on the issue of hell.'[48] In relation to the disbelievers, Ibn ʿArabī argues that they will spend eternity in Hell, but the 'punishment' (*ʿadhāb*) of the inhabitants of Hell will eventually become a pleasurable 'sweetness' (*ʿudhūba*); yet that perpetuity in *ʿudhūba* will be without ever experiencing the beatific vision (*ruʾya*) of the Divine, which shall only be for the believers in Paradise.[49] Ibn ʿArabī writes in the *Futūḥāt*, 'No chastisement will remain in the Fire except imaginal chastisement within the presence of imagination, in order that the properties of the divine names may subsist.'[50] Chittick writes, 'In several places Ibn ʿArabi insists that the pleasure of hell is precisely the removal of suffering and pain.'[51] Moreover, this eventual bliss for the disbelievers in Hell, as Pagani explains, is not 'sublime' but 'is whatever is appropriate (*mulāʾim*) to the "nature" (*ṭabʿ*) or "temperament" (*mizāj*) of each man'.[52] So whilst Ibn ʿArabī might seem, on occasion, to extol the bliss of the disbelievers in Hell—comparing it to the peace that Abraham experienced when he was thrown into the fire—he is also clear that the bliss is, as Pagani says, 'relish in wretchedness, quite simply "natural perversion"';[53] or as Qayṣarī stated in commentary on the *Fuṣūṣ*, '[B]liss for corrupt (*khabītha*) souls comes only from vile things, like a dung beetle relishes filth and cannot abide good things.'[54]

The centrality of mercy in the thought of Ibn ʿArabī and Kāshānī is in accordance with Q. 6:12: [*God*] *He has prescribed for Himself mercy.* Kāshānī says in explanation of this verse, 'He has obligated His Essence to it in the sense that it [mercy] is the effusion of goodness and perfection, in a manner commensurate with the preparedness [for it] of the recipient entities.' In other words, each person seeks the intimate connection between *Being* (*wujūd*) and *mercy* (*raḥma*). Ibn ʿArabī often quotes God's words in Q. 7:156, *My mercy embraces all things*, which our commentator explains in the following terms:

> [The mercy] is not singled out for any one person to the exclusion of another or any one thing to the exclusion of another. So contained in this chastisement is a mercy whose quintessence cannot be known and whose worth cannot be estimated, the mercy of the pleasure of arrival, regarding which He has said, 'No soul knows what has been hidden for it [of reward] that delights the eye,' being also delightful in a way that cannot be approximated by any other pleasure. [It is] as one of them once said, 'Every pleasure I have attained from Him, except the pleasure of the ecstasy of my chastisement.' By God, this chastisement is dearer than red sulphur, and as for [that] mercy it is not excluded from anyone's share!

For Ibn ʿArabī, and for Kāshānī too, the whole cosmos (*ʿālam*) must return to mercy because 'the cosmos has no escape from returning to God, for He is the one who says, "To Him the whole affair is returned" [Q. 11:123]. When its return reaches Him, the affair goes back to the beginning, the origin, the originator. The beginning is a mercy that "embraces all things," and the originator "embraces all things in mercy and knowledge." Hence, in going back, the affair is immersed in mercy.'[55]

Ibn ʿArabī contends that the essential indication of mercy overriding wrath is the Divine's *basmala*—*In the Name of God, the Compassionate, the Merciful* (Q. 1:1)—which begins all but one of the Qurʾān's chapters, and so it is 'a statement of good news'. He goes on to say, 'Thus His mercy is all-inclusive, and hope is great for everyone.'[56]

THE SPIRITUAL PATH: LAW AND PRACTICE TOWARDS EXPERIENTIAL KNOWLEDGE

Under his commentary for Q. 2:38, Kāshānī writes, '"Guidance" is the Law, and whoever follows it will be secure from evil consequence and will not fear any punishment or annihilation. Moreover, [by adhering to the Law] he would have found solace in things other than the passions and [carnal] pleasure, grieving not for what he will have missed of the ephemeral things of this world or its bliss.' He then states in the commentary on Q. 2:199, '*Then press on from where the people press on*: then press on towards the outer forms of devotion and obedience, and all of the duties ordained by the obligations and transactions of the Law; and *from where* means from the station from which all people press on [to engage in these devotions] and be like any one of them.' Kāshānī's firm adherence to the Sacred Law is also a distinctive feature of Ibn ʿArabī's spiritual methodology.[57] Thereafter, the seeker of the Divine is to engage in dedicated spiritual exertion in conformity with the Sacred Law until the heart becomes illuminated. In this way, Kāshānī says in the commentary on Q. 18:70,

> '*If you follow me* in the wayfaring along the path of perfection, *then do not question me concerning anything*. In other words, you must follow [my] lead and persevere along the journey with works, acts of self-discipline, [noble] character traits and exertions, and not demand realities or significations, *until* the moment for that comes along and then *I* [*myself*] *make mention of it*—that is, of that knowledge—*to you,*' and inform you about the Unseen realities upon your disengagement through interactions belonging to the mould and to the heart.

As Kāshānī then highlights in his commentary on Q. 2:152, the path of obedience and remembrance is the attainment and increase of gnosis (*maʿrifa*):

> *So remember Me*, by responding [to the call], through obedience and out of [a positive] will, *and I will remember you*, by granting you more and successive wayfaring and the effusion [from Me] of the light of certainty, *and be thankful to Me*, for the grace of sending a messenger and guidance by wayfaring along the path to Me out of love, and I will increase you in gnosis from Me and

love of Me, *and be not ungrateful towards Me*, by being indifferent and veiling yourselves by the grace of religion from the Grace-giver, as this is ingratitude, nay disbelief [itself].

In fact, it could be argued that the central theme of Kāshānī's commentary on the Qur'ān is gnosis or direct experiential knowledge of God. In other words, expounding on the essential truth and realization of Divinity, whether in experiencing Essential Unity (*al-dhātī al-aḥadī, al-dhātī al-aḥadiyya, al-waḥda al-dhātiyya, al-waḥdāniyya al-dhātiyya* and *waḥdatahu al-dhātiyya*), or Essential Oneness (*al-tawḥīd al-dhātī* and *al-dhātī al-wāḥidiyya*) or the Unity of the Essence (*aḥadiyyat al-dhātī*).

III. ON THE TRANSLATION OF *TA'WĪLĀT AL-QUR'ĀN*

The translation of the main text for this volume was produced by Feras Hamza, with me giving the text a final edit, as well as adding this introduction, some notes and producing an appendix of the persons cited in the text and a bibliography of works referred to by Hamza and by me. Footnotes added to the main text are by Hamza unless indicated by '[Ed.]', whereby the latter refer to my notes. Some of the terms in the original translation, such as the choice for *walāya* and *awliyā'*, were amended in agreement with the publishers. The translation of the Qur'ān used in this publication was Hamza's translation for The Royal Aal al-Bayt Institute for Islamic Thought, which has been slightly amended by me in places. During my edit, I have been helped by referring to M. A. S. Abdel Haleem's *The Qur'an: A New Translation*, Muhammad Marmaduke Pickthall's *The Meaning of the Glorious Koran* and Seyyed Hossein Nasr et al. (eds.), *The Study Quran: A New Translation and Commentary*. In Volume II numerous translations of Qur'ānic verses not included by Kāshānī have been added at the beginning and middle of certain *sūra*s, and are indicated by being enclosed within square brackets. However, when Kāshānī ends a *sūra* before the verses have been completed, then these have not been added. Footnotes added to Volume II are by the translator Khalid Williams unless indicated by '[Ed.]', whereby the latter refer to my notes.

I must express my great appreciation to Fatima Azzam at the Islamic Texts Society for inviting me onto this project and supporting me through it, especially in her detailed advice on my introduction. I am also grateful to Khalid Williams and Eric Winkel for clarifying some queries in the translation of Volume I, although any ultimate mistakes are mine because I modified their suggestions on occasions. Furthermore, I thank my dear friend Mike Best, for benefiting me with discussions on language; Salman Younis, for providing me with Pierre Lory's article on Kāshānī; and Ismail Lala, for allowing me to see a pre-print version of his *Knowing God*. *Wa'l-ḥamdu li-Llāh*.

Andrew Booso
27 April 2021

NOTES TO EDITOR'S INTRODUCTION

1 See Walid Saleh, 'Quranic Commentaries', in Seyyed Hossein Nasr et al., eds., *The Study Quran: A New Translation and Commentary* (*SQ*), San Francisco: HarperOne, 2015, pp. 1645 and 1651–2.

2 See Pieter Coppens, *Seeing God in Sufi Qur'an Commentaries: Crossings between This World and the Otherworld*, Edinburgh: Edinburgh University Press, 2018, p. 17.

3 See Kristen Zahra Sands, *Ṣūfī Commentaries on the Qur'ān in Classical Islam*, Abingdon, UK and New York: Routledge, 2006, pp. 3, 7–8, 10, 12, 33, 35, 39, 42, 47–56 and 67.

4 See Sands, *Ṣūfī Commentaries*, p. 42.

5 This is the name of the work preferred by Ismail Lala, *Knowing God: Ibn ʿArabī and ʿAbd al-Razzāq al-Qāshānī's Metaphysics of the Divine*, Leiden & Boston: Brill, 2020, p. 25; Sands, *Ṣūfī Commentaries*, p. 76; Pierre Lory, s.v. 'ʿAbd al-Razzāq al-Kāshānī', in Kate Fleet, Gudrun Krämer et al., eds., *Encyclopaedia of Islam*, 3ʳᵈ ed. (*EI³*), 6 vols., Leiden: Brill, 2007–. The editors of *SQ* prefer to call the work *Taʾwīl al-Qurʾān*; see *SQ*, pp. LVIII and 1923.

6 Sands, *Ṣūfī Commentaries*, pp. 42–3.

7 After listing the variations given for his name, Ismail Lala affirms this option; see Lala, *Knowing God*, p. 18.

8 Ḥājī Khalīfa refered to Kāshānī as ʿAbd al-Razzāq al-Samarqandī; see ibid., p. 17.

9 Majīd Hādīzāda and ʿAbd al-Khāliq Maḥmūd argued that he died in 736/1335. See Lory, *EI³*, s.v. 'Kāshānī'; Lala, *Knowing God*, p. 27–8.

10 See John L. Esposito, ed., *The Oxford Dictionary of Islam*, New York: Oxford University Press, 2003, p. 167; Christiane Gruber, *The Ilkhanid Book of Ascension: A Persian-Sunni Devotional Tale*, London & New York: Tauris Academic Studies, 2010, p. 3; Michael Hope, *Power, Politics, and Tradition in the Mongol Empire and the Īlkhānate of Iran*, Oxford: Oxford University Press, 2016, pp. 1 and 112.

11 Under Ghāzān, during the winter of 1299–1300, the Īlkhānids defeated the Mamlūks and occupied Damascus for three months, before fleeing the city upon news of the Mamlūks reforming with a huge army. The Īlkhānids set out to attack Damascus again in 1301, but abandoned the venture; a 1303 attack was thwarted by the Mamlūks before it reached Damascus; and a 1312 attempt on the city by the Īlkhānids under Uljāytū came to nothing for the Īlkhānids. See Jon Hoover, 'Ibn Taymiyya between Moderation and Radicalism', in Elisabeth Kendall and Ahmad Khan, eds., *Reclaiming Islamic Tradition: Modern*

Interpretations of the Classical Tradition, Edinburgh: Edinburgh University Press, 2016, pp. 178–9; Denise Aigle, 'The Mongol Invasions of Bilād al-Shām by Ghāzān Khān and Ibn Taymīyah's Three "Anti-Mongol" Fatwas', *Mamlūk Studies Review*, vol. XI, no. 2, 2007, p. 89.

12   There were reports that Hūlāgū had converted to Islam, and these were even included in Dhahabī's *Ta'rīkh al-Islām*; see Peter Jackson, *The Mongols and the Islamic World: From Conquest to Conversion*, New Haven & London: Yale University Press, 2017, p. 376.

13   See Judith Pfeiffer, 'Reflections on a "Double Rapprochement": Conversion to Islam among the Mongol Elite During the Early Ilkhanate', in Linda Komaroff, ed., *Beyond the Legacy of Genghis Khan*, Leiden & Boston: Brill, 2006, pp. 371–2, 375 and 385–8; Aigle, 'The Mongol Invasions of Bilād al-Shām', p. 90; Jackson, *Mongols and the Islamic World*, p. 367.

14   Ghāzān's rule is often noted as the 'real beginnings of Islamization' as future rulers would all be Muslim. Nonetheless, he is noted for having maintained a certain religious 'syncretism' between his pre-Islamic past and his Islamic faith until at least 1302. See Jackson, *Mongols and the Islamic World*, pp. 362–4.

15   Hoover, 'Ibn Taymiyya between Moderation and Radicalism', p. 178; Hope, *Power, Politics, and Tradition in the Mongol Empire*, pp. 177–8; Aigle, 'The Mongol Invasions of Bilād al-Shām', pp. 89–93.

16   Hope, *Power, Politics, and Tradition in the Mongol Empire*, p. 188; Lala, *Knowing God*; Hoover, 'Ibn Taymiyya between Moderation and Radicalism', pp. 179–180; Aigle, 'The Mongol Invasions of Bilād al-Shām', p. 118; Yahya Michot, *Ibn Taymiyya: Mardin: Hégire, fuite du péché et demeure de l'Islam*, trans. Jamil Qureshi as *Ibn Taymiyya: Muslims Under Non-Muslim Rule*, Oxford & London: Interface Publications, 2006, p. 162; Jackson, *Mongols and the Islamic World*, pp. 377–380.

17   P. Jackson, *Encyclopædia Iranica*, s.v. 'Abū Saʿīd Bahādor Khan'; Lala, *Knowing God*, pp. 23–4; Judith Pfeiffer, 'Conversion Versions: Sultan Öljeytü's Conversion to Shiʿism (709/1309) in Muslim Narrative Sources', *Mongolian Studies*, vol. XXII, 1999, p. 47. Jackson notes that Abū Saʿīd was the first ruler of the dynasty who was born a Muslim and given an ostensibly Muslim name; Jackson, *Mongols and the Islamic World*, p. 371.

18   In his youth, Simnānī had been close to the second Īlkhānid ruler, Abāqā (r. 1265–82), and the fourth, Arghūn (r. 1284–91), who was a committed Buddhist who opposed Islam; and the latter lavished him with gifts. He turned to Sufism in 1284 after experiencing a spiritual crisis when he was in the army of Prince Arghūn on the battlefield against Aḥmad Takādār or the latter's son-in-law ʿAlīnāq. He left the service of Arghūn and gave his gifts from the latter away in charity. See Hope, *Power, Politics, and Tradition in the Mongol Empire*, p. 112; Pfeiffer, 'Reflections on a "Double Rapprochement"', pp. 380–1; Jamal J. Elias, *The Throne Carrier of God: The Life and Thought of ʿAlāʾ ad-dawla as-Simnānī*, Albany, NY: SUNY Press, 1995, pp. 18–9.

19 Lory, *EI³*, s.v. 'Kāshānī'

20 Hādīzāda, cited in Lala, *Knowing God*, p. 19.

21 Lory, *EI³*, s.v. 'Kāshānī'; Lala, *Knowing God*, pp. 20–1; Hope, *Power, Politics, and Tradition in the Mongol Empire*, pp. 9–10 and 16.

22 Peter Jackson called Rashīd al-Dīn's work 'official history', as it was ordered by Ghāzān and its second part was completed upon the instruction of Uljāytū. Rashīd al-Dīn, a convert from Judaism, would have his faith vehemently scrutinized by Ibn Taymiyya as the 'heretical and hypocritical rogue of a wazir (*wazīr hādhā l-khabīth al-mulhid al-munāfiq*)'. See Jackson, *Mongols and the Islamic World*, pp. 26–7 and 379–380.

23 See Lala, *Knowing God*, p. 21.

24 On Qūnawī, see William C. Chittick, 'Rūmī and *waḥdat al-wujūd*', in Amin Banani et al., eds., *Poetry and Mysticism in Islam: The Heritage of Rūmī*, Cambridge: Cambridge University Press, 1994, pp. 77–9.

25 James Winston Morris, 'Ibn ʿArabī and His Interpreters Part II (Conclusion): Influences and Interpretations', *Journal of the American Oriental Society*, vol. cvii, no. 1, 1987, p. 101. The term *waḥdat al-wujūd* is not actually from Ibn ʿArabī, but is likely to have originated with Ibn Sabʿīn, who lived around the time of Qūnawī. See William Chittick, 'Rūmī', pp. 72 and 82.

26 See Sands, *Ṣūfī Commentaries*, pp. 76–7; Lory, *EI³*, s.v. 'Kāshānī'.

27 *SQ*, p. 1923. 'Philosophical Sufism' can be understood as a translation of *al-taṣawwuf al-naẓarī* or

al-ʿirfān al-ʿnaẓarī, which pertain to *maʿrifa*, defined in the sense of gnosis or esotericism, rather than simply a profound recognition of and faith in God. *Philosophical Sufism* differs with essential Sufism (*al-taṣawwuf al-ʿamalī* or *al-ʿirfān al-ʿamalī*). See Saeed Zarrabi-Zadeh, *Practical Mysticism in Islam and Christianity: a Comparative Study of Jalal al-Din Rumi and Meister Eckhart*, Abingdon, Oxon and New York: Routledge, 2016, pp. 9 and 20 n62; Mark Sedgwick, 'Islamic and Western Esotericism', *Correspondences*, vol. vii, no. 1, 2019, p. 278; Seyyed Hossein Nasr, *The Garden of Truth: The Vision and Promise of Sufism, Islam's Mystical Tradition*, New York: HarperOne, 2007, pp. 209–234.

28 Personal correspondence with Ismail Lala, 19 April 2019.

29 For a study of this work, see Fatemeh Tayefeh Aghakhan Hashtroodi, 'Concept of Chivalry (*Futuwwah*) According to Abd al-Razzaq Kashani: Analysis of His Tuhfah al-Ikhwan Fi Khasais al-Fityan', PhD thesis, University of Malaya, 2015.

30 See Lala, *Knowing God*, p. 27.

31 Ibid., pp. 22–4.

32 Lory, *EI³*, s.v. 'Kāshānī'.

33 Ibid.

34 Morris, 'Ibn ʿArabī and His Interpreters Part II', p. 101.

35 See Morris, 'Ibn ʿArabī and His Interpreters Part II', p. 101, for references to the opinions of Lory (following Brockelmann), Yahia and Landolt.

36 Lory, *EI³*, s.v. 'Kāshānī'. For a discussion of Ibn ʿArabī's 'method of allusion (*ishāra*)', including his rejection

of 'rational interpretation (ta'wīl ʿaqlī)', together with a 'hyperliteralism' based on 'close attention to the etymological and grammatical possibilities of the text', as well as 'a more purely symbolic or allegorical approach', see Sands, Ṣūfī Commentaries, pp. 39–41.

37 Morris, 'Ibn ʿArabi and His Interpreters Part II', p. 102. The author of the Mawāqif is Emir ʿAbd al-Qādir al-Jazā'irī, the nineteenth-century Algerian Sufi-warrior, and not ʿAbd al-Qādir al-Jīlānī who famously founded the Qādirī spiritual order and died in the twelfth century CE. For the life and thought of Jazā'irī, see Tom Woerner-Powell, Another Road to Damascus: An Integrative Approach to ʿAbd al-Qādir al-Jazā'irī (1808–1883), Berlin & Boston: De Gruyter, 2017. For a survey of Jīlānī's life, see S. Abul Hasan Ali Nadwi, Ta'rīkh-i-daʿwat awr ʿazīmat, trans. Mohiuddin Ahmad as Saviours of the Islamic Spirit, 4 vols., Lucknow: Academy of Islamic Research and Publications, 1986–1997, vol. 1, pp. 177–202.

38 Morris, 'Ibn ʿArabi and His Interpreters Part II', p. 102.

39 Ibid. Chittick notes that Ibn ʿArabī's 'works are based not on rational analysis of the Qur'an but on the direct "unveiling" (kashf) of its meanings, a visionary knowledge of its varied senses given by God'. See William C. Chittick, 'Ibn al-ʿArabī's Hermeneutics of Mercy', in Steven T. Katz, ed., Mysticism and Sacred Scripture, Oxford: Oxford University Press, 2000, p. 154.

40 Morris, 'Ibn ʿArabi and His Interpreters Part II', pp. 102–4. See also Sands, Ṣūfī Commentaries, pp. 76–7.

41 Lory, EI³, s.v. 'Kāshānī'.

42 Sands, Ṣūfī Commentaries, pp. 77, 92 and 138.

43 Ibid., pp. 92–3 and 165–6 (notes 57 and 64).

44 William C. Chittick, The Sufi Path of Knowledge: Ibn al-ʿArabi's Metaphysics of Imagination, Albany, NY: SUNY Press, 1989, p. 79.

45 Ibid., p. 3.

46 Ibid., p. 79.

47 See Michel Chodkiewicz, Le Sceau des Saints, Prophétie et Sainteté dans la doctrine d'Ibn ʿArabî, trans. Liadain Sherrard as Seal of the Saints: Prophethood and Sainthood in the Doctrine of Ibn ʿArabî, Cambridge: Islamic Texts Society, 1993, pp. 114–5. For Ibn Taymiyya on Ibn ʿArabī, see Alexander D. Knysh, Ibn ʿArabi in the Later Islamic Tradition: The Making of a Polemical Image in Medieval Islam, Albany, NY: SUNY Press, 1999, in particular chapter 4. The complex relationship of Ibn Taymiyya and his group to Sufism has been thoroughly explored in a number of works, including Hikmet Yaman, 'Ḥanbalīte Criticism of Sufism: Ibn Taymiyya (d. 795/1328), a Ḥanbalīte Ascetic (Zāhid)', Ekev Akademi Dergisi, vol. XIII, no. 43, 2010, pp. 37–56; Arjan Antonius Johannes Post, 'The Journey of a Taymiyyan Sufi: Sufism Through the Eyes of ʿImād al-Dīn Aḥmad al-Wāsiṭī (d. 711/1311)', PhD thesis, Utrecht University, 2017. Thanks to Arnold Mol, Imran Iqbal and Arjan Post for guiding me to the latter thesis, and to Rezart Beka for the article by Yaman.

48 See Chittick, 'Ibn al-ʿArabī's Hermeneutics of Mercy', p. 156.

49   See William C. Chittick, *Imaginal Worlds: Ibn al-'Arabi and the Problem of Religious Diversity*, Albany, NY: SUNY Press, 1994, pp. 113–7; Gregory A. Lipton, *Rethinking Ibn 'Arabi*, New York: Oxford University Press, 2018, pp. 7–9.

50   Ibn ʿArabī, *Futūḥāt*, cited in Chittick, *Imaginal Worlds*, p. 115.

51   See William C. Chittick, *Ibn ʿArabi: Heir to the Prophets*, Oxford: Oneworld, 2005, pp. 136–8.

52   Samuela Pagani, 'Ibn ʿArabī, Ibn Qayyim al-Jawziyya, and the Political Functions of Punishment in the Islamic Hell', in Christian Lange, ed., *Locating Hell in Islamic Traditions*, Leiden & Boston: Brill, 2016, pp. 187–192.

53   Ibid.

54   Qayṣarī, cited ibid.

55   Ibn ʿArabī, *Futūḥāt*, cited in Chittick, 'Ibn al-ʿArabī's Hermeneutics of Mercy', p. 159.

56   Ibn ʿArabī, *Futūḥāt*, cited in Chittick, 'Ibn al-ʿArabī's Hermeneutics of Mercy', p. 160.

57   See Chittick, *Sufi Path of Knowledge*; Michel Chodkiewicz, *Un Océan sans rivage. Ibn 'Arabī, le Livre et la Loi*, trans. David Streight as *An Ocean Without Shore: Ibn ʿArabī, the Book and the Law*, Albany, NY: SUNY Press, 1993; Eric Winkel, *Islam and the Living Law: The Ibn al-Arabi Approach*, Karachi: Oxford University Press, 1997; Omar Edaibat, 'Muḥyī l-Dīn Ibn ʿArabī's Personalist Theory of the *Sharīʿa*: An Examination of His Legal Doctrine', *Journal of Sufi Studies*, vol. XI, 2017, pp. 1–46.

19
MARY
SŪRAT MARYAM

In the Name of God, the Compassionate, the Merciful

[19:1] *Kāf. Hā. Yā. ʿAyn. Ṣād.*

[19:2] [*A mention of your Lord's mercy to His servant Zachariah,* [19:3] *when he called out to his Lord a call in secret:*] it has been stated before that the one who calls upon his Lord only deserves a response if he calls upon Him with the voice of his true condition, and if he calls to Him with that Name of His which is the source of his desire (*maṣdar maṭlūbihi*). This depends on the petitioner's preparedness (*istiʿdād*) for this, whether he is aware of it or not, since the divine grace and emanation only come according to one's preparedness, and that preparedness pertains only to the implications of that Name. God then answers by manifesting that Name, healing the petitioner's blemishes and fulfilling his needs by granting his desire. Thus, when the sick man cries 'O Lord,' he really means 'O Healer,' since it will be through that Name that the Lord heals him. Likewise, when the poor man calls upon Him, He answers him with His Name the Rich, for He is his Lord. Zachariah (may God grant him peace) called upon his Lord pleading that He grant him an heir to inherit his religious station; and he invoked two matters—two extenuating circumstances—to support his plea. The first was his weakness and old age, which made him unable to continue his religious duties.

[19:4] [*He said, 'My Lord!*] *Indeed, the bones within me have become feeble, and my head is alight with grey hair*: He responded to him with His Name the All-Sufficient, compensating him for his weakness and giving him strength, and aiding him with a son. He then invoked the nurture which God had shown him in the past: *and I have never been in my supplications to You, my Lord, unsuccessful*: He answered this with His Name the Guide, and guided him to his desire with glad tidings and a sure promise. The felicitous nurture born of success to which Zachariah alluded with these words was a reference to God's pre-eternal knowledge of a then-inexistent entity whose engendering would bring felicity: that is, His will of perfection for that thing upon its eventual arrival into existence. Thus, it was necessary that it be guided to him; and guidance requires grace, which means the arrangement of the means required for the desired thing to reach its target. Yet Zachariah did not observe those means to be in place, and so expressed his fear that his kinsfolk were not up to the task:

[19:5] [*And truly I fear my kinsfolk after me:*] God answered this with His Name the Protector, and protected him from their potential harms. Zachariah then invoked the apparent impossibility of an heir due to the absence of the necessary means: *and my wife is barren.*' God answered this with His Name the Knower, for He knew well of the absence of worldly causes that Zachariah invoked to the Causer Himself, and He knew well that this thing would come to pass even without them; and what He knows must surely come to pass, as the angels said to the wife of Abraham (may God grant him peace): *So has your Lord said. Indeed, He is the Wise, the Knower* [Q. 51:30]. Then, when He gave him tidings of the child and guided him to the object of His knowledge, he was incredulous at this because of his attachment to the material world of causality, and repeated his argument about the absence of the required means:

Q. 19:5

[19:8] [*He said, 'My Lord,*] *how shall I have a son when my wife is barren and I have reached infirm old age?*' This is because he was pleading for a true son to be his heir and follow in his footsteps along his path, upholding the affairs of the faith, even if that heir was not from his own loins because of the unsuitability of his kinsfolk for such a task. The Lord then repeated the tidings to him and guided him to the truth of how easy such a matter was to Him given His omnipotence. Zachariah requested a sign of this, and He guided him to one and kept His promise through His Name the Truthful. Then, in His mercy, He gifted him John; for those four conditions in the moment of that promise and glad tidings required a response of mercy through the sum of those five Names. *Kāf Hā Yā ʿAyn Ṣād* in that case [entail the following]: the *Kāf* represents the Divine Name *al-Kāfī* ('the All-Sufficient'), as was required by Zachariah's weakness, old age and infirmity; the *Hā* represents the Divine Name *al-Hādī* ('the Guide'), as was required by God's nurture of him and His will to grant his desire; the *Yā* represents the Divine Name *al-Wāqī*[1] ('the Protector'), as was required by Zachariah's fears about his kinsfolk; the *ʿAyn* represents the Divine Name *al-ʿĀlim* ('the Knower'), as was required by his declarations about the lack of apparent means; and the *Ṣād* represents the Divine Name *al-Ṣādiq* ('the Truthful'), as was required by the promise. The sum of those five names is the Merciful, Who gifted him the son and granted his desire in the midst of all these circumstances. The invocation of these letters, and their arrangement in this sequence, is an allusion to how the manifestation (*tajallī*) of these Attributes, and consequently the actualisation of these Names, was in essence the manifestation of His mercy to His servant Zachariah when he called upon Him. In turn, this mercy was in essence the existence of John (may God grant him peace). Therefore, Ibn ʿAbbās said (may God be pleased with him), '*Kāf* refers to *al-Kāfī*, *Hā* to *al-Hādī*, *Yā* to *al-Wāqī*, *ʿAyn* to *al-ʿĀlim*, and *Ṣād* to *al-Ṣādiq*.' And God knows best.

On the level of spiritual correspondence (*taṭbīq*), one can say that Zachariah called upon the spirit in the station of the preparedness of the primordial intellect, with a call in secret, and complained of his weakness, appealed to its nurture, and complained of his fear of the kinsfolk of egocentricity and how the wife of the soul was barren and bereft of the child of the heart. '*So grant me from Yourself a successor, who may inherit from me and inherit from the House of Jacob*—the active intellect—*and make him, my Lord, acceptable*': adorned with the required perfections. Then came the response: *Indeed, We give you good tidings of a boy*—the heart—*whose name is John* because he is ever-living.[2]

[19:10] *He said, 'Lord, appoint for me some sign'*: by means of which I might reach him. '*Your sign is that you shall not speak*' to the hosts of the senses by occupying yourself with sensory distractions and involving yourself in natural matters.

[19:11] *So he emerged before his people from the sanctuary and signalled to them, 'Make glorifications'*: that is, 'Be about your own personal worship, each one of you, and devote yourselves to it and forsake your curiosity.'

[19:12] '*O John*—O heart—*hold on to [the Book firmly]*': the book of knowledge called 'the discriminating intellect'. *And We gave him judgement*—meaning wisdom—*while still a child*: while still fresh from the spiritual birth. [19:13] *And compassion from Us*, meaning mercy with the

---

1 *Al-Wāqī* begins with the letter *wāw*, but the letters *wāw* and *yā* are often considered to be identical or interchangeable since they both represent the same root letter under different morphological circumstances.

2 The Arabic name for John, *Yaḥyā*, means 'he lives'.

3

perfection of the manifestations (*tajaliyyāt*) of the Divine Attributes, *and purity*, meaning sanctification and purity by isolation; *and he was God-fearing*: he avoided the attributes of the ego.[19:14] *And dutiful to his parents*: the spirit and the soul.

[19:15] *And peace be upon him*: he was purified and sanctified from the garb of materiality; *the day he was born, and the day he dies* by annihilation in Unity, *and the day he shall be raised* by subsistence after annihilation, *alive in God.*

[19:16] *And mention in the Book Mary when she withdrew from her family to an easterly place*: the easterly place was the realm of the holy, because of her connection to the Holy Spirit when she isolated herself and withdrew from the plain of nature and the locus of the ego; her family were the impulses of I-ness (*anā'iyya*) and nature.

[19:17] [*Thus, she veiled herself from them*:] the veil she adopted was the protecting wall of holiness that barred the way to the folk of the realm of ego—the veil of the heart, which is the limit of the reach of material knowledge and its farthest extent. The Holy Spirit could only be sent to her when she entered the realm of the holy by isolating herself, as He says, *We sent to her Our Spirit,* [*and he assumed before her the likeness of a well-proportioned human*]. The reason he took on this form was so that her soul would be influenced and feel at ease, and she would be stirred in the natural way, and this vision would rouse her natural appetite (*shahwa*) as happens in a passionate dream (*al-manām min al-iḥtilām*), so that her drop of fluid (*nuqta*) would be awakened in the womb and from it the child would be formed.[1] As was noted earlier, revelation (*waḥy*) is similar to true dreams in how the body's strength is frozen while receiving it, so that it is unable to act just as it is when asleep. When images appear during inspiration to the sapient soul (*al-nafs al-nāṭiqa*)—which in our convention is called 'the heart'—and it connects to the holy spirits, they flow through the animal (*ḥayawāniyya*) and natural (*ṭabīʿiyya*) soul and cause the body to react.

Q. 19:15

---

1 Whilst it is common for commentators to interpret Mary's encounter with the angel in the form of *a well-proportioned human* 'so that she would not be overcome with fear and recoil from him' (*SQ*, p. 768, paraphrasing Zamakhsharī), Kāshānī's sensual-biological explanation has some precedent in conventional *tafsīr* literature. For example, Qurṭubī spoke of how Gabriel's blowing of the Spirit into Mary 'aroused her appetite' in order for the 'two waters' of child conception to mix in her. In recent times, this explanation has been rejected as being in opposition to the Sacred Law and intellectually deficient. See Abū ʿAbd Allāh Muḥammad b. Aḥmad al-Qurṭubī, *al-Jāmiʿ li-aḥkām al-Qurʾān*, ed. ʿAbd Allāh b. ʿAbd al-Muḥsin al-Turkī et al., Beirut: Muʾassasat al-Risāla, 2006, vol. v, p. 142 (commentary of Q. 3:47, together with Turkī's footnote). [Ed.]

The only reason the child could be formed from a single drop of fluid was that, in natural science, it is established that the male fluid plays the role in the creation of the child that rennet does in the production of cheese, while the female fluid plays the role of the milk.[1] In other words, the male fluid has a greater propensity to cause coagulation, while the female's fluid has a greater propensity to be coagulated—it is not that the male fluid is entirely coagulating and the female fluid entirely coagulated, but that the male side is more active and the female side more receptive, because otherwise they could not be united into one thing.

The male fluid is not coagulated until it becomes a part of the child. What this means is that if the woman's constitution is particularly strong and masculine—as is the case with noble women with strong souls—and the constitution of her liver is hot, then the fluid that comes from her right kidney will be hotter than what comes from her left kidney. When they meet in the womb and the womb has a powerful grasp and attraction, the fluid from the right kidney will fulfil the role of the male fluid with respect to its coagulating propensity; and the fluid from the left kidney will fulfil the role of the female fluid with respect to its propensity to be coagulated, and the embryo will be formed. Now in the special circumstance that the soul of the woman in question is aided and strengthened by the Holy Spirit, the influence of her connection to it will flow into her physical body and alter its constitution, linking all of its active power to this spiritual aid, so that it will become capable of doing extraordinary things for which no suitable analogy can be found. And God knows best.

Q. 19:21

[19:21] *And so that We may make him a sign for people*: a sign of the Resurrection; *and a mercy from Us* to them in how he will perfect for them their Divine Laws, wisdoms and knowledge, and guide them; for this reason have We done it, and he will be the embodiment of the spirit of divine mercy. *And it is a thing [already] decreed*: in the Preserved Tablet, ordained from pre-eternity. Ibn ʿAbbās is related to have said, 'She became at ease when he said, *I am only a messenger of your Lord, that I may give you a boy [who shall be] pure* [Q. 19:19], and he approached her and blew into her sleeve'—that is, into her body. This is why she experienced her emission, as we described before, in the same way as lustful feelings or embraces can cause premature emissions. It has been said that the spirit which appeared to her was the spirit of Jesus himself (may God grant him peace), and that

---

1 The 'cheese analogy' of conception was a widespread belief discussed by Aristotle in *The Generation of Animals*. See Sandra Ott, 'Aristotle Among the Basques: The "Cheese Analogy" of Conception', *Man* (New Series), vol. XIV, no. 4, 1979, pp. 699–700.

he descended and became attached to her and conceived within her. The truth, however, is that it was the Holy Spirit because he was the active cause of Jesus' existence, which is why he said *that I may give you a boy* [*who shall be*] *pure*. The spirit of Jesus only attached to the drop of fluid after it was conceived in the womb and settled there, which was when it was engendered and united such that it was able to accept the spirit.

[19:22] [*Thus, she conceived him*] *and then withdrew with him to a distant place*: that is, far away from the aforementioned eastern place, because she gave birth to him in the western place which represents the world of nature and the physical realm. This is why He said,

[19:23] *And the birth pangs brought her to the trunk of the palm-tree*: the palm-tree of the soul.

[19:24] *Then he called her from below her*: Gabriel called her from a lower place relative to her station in the heart: that is, from the world of nature that was the cause of her woe, namely the pregnancy which had caused her such shame and disgrace. *Do not grieve. Your Lord has made below you a rivulet*: that is, a stream of wondrous knowledge of nature and Oneness of the acts with which God has singled you out and distinguished you, as is evident from the creation of a child from your fluid alone.

Q. 19:22

[19:25] *And shake the trunk* [*of the palm-tree towards you*]: the palm-tree of your soul, which has climbed to the heights of the spirit-heavens though your connection to the Holy Spirit, and which now blooms with true life after having been dried out through toil and deprived of the water and life of desire, and which now bears the fruit of gnostic sciences and meanings. Shake that tree, and inspire it to reflect; *there will drop on you*, from the fruit of gnostic sciences and realities, *dates fresh and ripe*.

[19:26] *So eat* from above you the fresh dates of gnostic sciences and realities and the knowledge of the self-disclosures of the Divine Attributes, gifts and states; *and drink* from beneath you the water of natural knowledge, the marvels of creation, the wonders of the divine acts, the science of reliance, and the self-disclosures of the divine acts, natures and causes. God says, *They would surely have received nourishment from above them and from beneath their feet* [Q. 4:66]; *and* [*let*] *your eye be comforted* by this perfection and the blessed child, by the power granted by the divine nurture. *And if you* [*happen to*] *see any human being*, meaning any of the outward-looking folk who are veiled from realities by the surface images of means, and from the divine design and power by creation and wisdom; folk who would not understand your words or believe you about your condition, because they cannot see beyond the norm and are veiled by their turbid minds and delusions from the light of the Real, *then say, 'I have vowed to the Compassionate a fast'*: do not speak to them about anything, nor present them with something that they could not accept, until he can speak for himself.

[19:33] *And peace be upon me* at the same three stations as was said about John before, because my entity has been detached and sanctified and cannot be veiled by the material, even in my infancy. The meaning of peace is to be freed from the blemishes that occur as a result of attachment to the material.

[19:34] *That is Jesus, son of Mary, a statement of truth*: that is, the Word of the Real representing a pre-eternally detached entity, as has been discussed before.

[19:35] *It is not [befitting] for God to take to Himself a son* because nothing else can exist alongside Him. *Glory be to Him* above the notion of anything existing alongside Him. *When He decrees a thing, He only says to it 'Be!' and it is*: that is, He brings it into being by the mere attachment of His will to it, instantly.

Q. 19:33

[19:40] *Indeed, We shall inherit the earth and all who are on it*: at the Major Resurrection, through absolute annihilation and the essential presential vision. Sincerity is the root of every virtue, the foundation of every perfection, the base of every station, and the preparation for every gift.

[19:42] *Why do you worship that which neither hears nor sees*: something other than God whom you seek and to which you attribute power; *and is of no avail to you in any way*: in reality because it is powerless?

[19:43] *Indeed, there has come to me knowledge*: that is, knowledge of the Essential Oneness.

[19:47] *Peace be to you*: that is, may God purify your entity from the material that has veiled it! *I shall ask forgiveness of my Lord for you*: I shall ask Him to cover your entity with His light and erase the turbidity of your attributes with His Attributes, and the lowliness of your soul's condition with His acts, if it is possible.

[19:51] *Indeed, he was devoted*: this can be read as *mukhliṣan* in the active voice, meaning 'devoted'; he dedicated his being and his conduct to God's countenance, and never allowed himself to be distracted by anything other than Him, even His Attributes, which he did not consider apart from His Essence, for his sight did not waver nor stray when he said, *Show me that I may behold you* [Q. 7:143]. It can also be read as *mukhlaṣan* in the passive voice, meaning 'made devoted'; God cleansed him of his own self-regard and annihilated every remnant of him, so that he was purified from that

7

blasphemy by the total self-disclosure of the Divine, and became upright by the mastery that God bequeathed him, as He says, *And when his Lord revealed Himself to the mountain, He levelled it to the ground, and Moses fell down senseless. And when he recovered his senses, he said, 'Glory be to You! I repent to You'* [Q. 7:143] from the sin of displaying self-regard.

And he was a messenger, a prophet: the station of messenger is lower than the station of prophet because it is concerned with rulings such as the lawful and unlawful, and enjoining prescriptions such as prayer and fasting; it pertains to communicating codes (*aḥkām*) to human beings of legal age. Prophethood, on the other hand, means to be informed of unseen spiritual realities such as the states of the afterlife and divine gnostic sciences such as the identity of the Divine Attributes and Names, and what pertains to God in terms of praises and glorifications. Sainthood is above them both because it means to be annihilated in the Essence of God without any regard for creation. It is the noblest of all stations because it precedes them; if there is not first sainthood, then there cannot be prophethood or messengership because it forms their basis. This is why the Qur'ān affirms here first of all that Moses was devoted, which is to say made devoted, in the passive voice. The reason He delayed mention of his prophethood until after his messengership was that it is nobler and more clearly indicative of praise and reverence. He did not place sainthood after them both to emphasise its nobility because, although it is nobler, it is hidden so that its nobility and virtue is unknown except to those few folk endowed with true gnosis and blessed with keen perception. Thus, it would be of no use to single it out for praise and reverence. Nor would it have been appropriate to speak only of his sainthood by calling him devoted and then saying no more, even though it is nobler than either of them, because it is possible for a person to be a saint without being either of the others, but not vice versa. Therefore, the only appropriate way to describe him was in this manner and this order.

Q. 19:52

[19:52] *And We called him from the right side of the Mount*: the mountain of his existence, which is the end of the mountain of the heart in the station of mystery, which is the venue of intimate discourse; hence, His Words *and We brought him near in communion*, and why Moses was called the One Who Spoke with God (*kalīm Allāh*). He described it as the right side, which is the nobler, stronger and more blessed side, to distinguish it from the left side, which is the breast, because revelation comes from the realm of the spirit, which is the Blessed Valley.

[19:57] *And We raised him to a high station*: if this refers to his metaphorical station, then it means nearness to God and his rank in the station of sainthood from the source of unification. If it refers to a physical place, then it means the fourth celestial sphere, which is the abode of Jesus (may God grant him peace), because of how it is the locus of his spirit and the source of its effusion; it emanated from the motion of the solar sphere as the object of its love.

[19:58] *When the signs of the Compassionate were recited to them*: they heard the exterior of every sign with their souls, and the interior with their hearts, and understood the limit with their inner mysteries, and ascended to the look-out points with their spirits.[1] They would behold the Speaker adorned with the Attributes through which He manifested Himself in the signs, and so *they would fall down prostrating [and weeping]*: annihilated in the Name by which He manifested through the Attribute revealed in that sign, weeping in their longing to behold Him through all His other Attributes as encompassed by His Name the Merciful, or God. This is the weeping of the heart, if it is not the weeping of the soul in fear of remoteness (*buʿd*) [from the Divine], as the poet said, 'He weeps when they approach, longing for them; / He weeps when they withdraw, fearing separation (*firāq*).'

Q. 19:58

[19:59] [*But there succeeded after them a posterity who neglected the prayer and followed [their] lusts*:] they neglected the prayer of presence because they were in the station of the soul, and presence can only be with the heart, and there can be no prayer without it. As a consequence of being veiled by the attributes of the soul from the station of the heart, it was inevitable that they would follow their lusts. *So they shall [soon] encounter perdition*: evil and error; for the further they follow those lusts, the more they are veiled and the further they stray, so that they pile sins upon sins and become mired in them, as he (may God bless him and grant him peace) said, 'The sin that follows another is penalty for it.'

[19:60] *Whereas those who repent* from the first sin and return to the station of the heart, *and believe* with certitude, *and act righteously* by attaining virtue, *such shall enter Paradise* in an absolute sense according to their merit and their ranks in faith and action, *and shall not be wronged in any way*: nothing will be taken from them that their condition and station merits.

[19:61] *Gardens of Eden* arranged according to their ranks in the station of the soul, the heart and the spirit, *which the Compassionate, Who bestows*

---

1 A reference to the *ḥadīth* cited by the author in the introduction, 'No verse of the Qurʾān has been sent down except that it has an exterior (*ẓāhir*) and an interior (*bāṭin*), with every letter (*ḥarf*) having a limit (*ḥadd*), every limit a look-out point (*muṭṭalaʿ*).'

9

the glories of favour and its roots and branches, *has promised to His servants in the Unseen*: at a time when they were oblivious to them.

[19:62] [*Therein they shall not hear anything that is trifling, but only* [*a greeting of*]] *'Peace!'* which will cleanse them of their faults and free them from matter with gnostic sciences and wisdoms. *And therein they will have their provision morning and evening*: that is, at all times, or morning in the garden of the heart when the sun of the spirit rises, and evening in the garden of the soul when it sets.

[19:63] *That is Paradise*—the absolute Garden whose name can stand for any one of the many gardens it contains—*which We shall give as inheritance to those of Our servants who are God-fearing*: in a way commensurate to the level of their God-fearing. If one avoided base things and sins, We shall give him the garden of the soul, which is the garden of objects. If he was God-fearing with his deeds through reliance, he shall have the garden of the heart and the presence of the self-disclosures of the divine acts. If he was God-fearing with his attributes in the station of the heart, he shall have the garden of the Attributes. If he was God-fearing with his essence and his being through annihilation in God, he shall have the garden of the Essence.

Q. 19:62

[19:64] *'And we do not descend except by the commandment of your Lord'*: the descent of the angels and the soul's connection to the High Council can only occur by means of two things: either a primordial preparedness and innate purity that would make the essence of the spirit fit to enter the supreme realm, or else a provisional preparedness born of purification, which is not sufficient on its own but rather must depend on the angels. Consider God's Words, *Truly those who say, 'Our Lord is God!' and then remain upright, the angels descend upon them* [Q. 41:30], and how the descent is dependent on the uprightness, which means mastery that implies a natural disposition. Then consider His Words [about the devils], *They descend upon every sinful liar* [Q. 26:222], using the emphatic term *affāk*, which means 'someone who is a liar by nature'. Likewise, the angels descend only on one who is a person of true faith. When this second type of aptitude coincides with the first, it is a sign of the permission and command of the Real; for the emanation is universal, complete and uninterrupted, and if it delays it is only because the aptitude is missing. Therefore, when the revelation was slow in coming and his patience faltered, this verse came down to say, 'We do not descend of our own accord, but only by His command.'

'To Him belongs all that is before us' of the realms' divine power above us, ahead of the realms towards which our faces are turned and outside

the sphere of our knowledge, *and all that is behind us* of the realms of the dominion on earth, below our own realms, *and all that is between those* [*two*] of the realms of the dominion in which we reside, all of which are within the sphere of His domination, under His authority, and encompassed by His knowledge. *And your Lord is never forgetful*: He does not forget anything that has the aptitude for a perfection by declining to grant it, nor does He neglect the right of any deserving party. He encompasses all aptitudes with His knowledge and bestows perfection upon them, and sends down what is ordained for them at the right moment. So if the revelation seems late in coming, it is only so on your end, not on His.

[19:65] *'The Lord of the heavens and the earth and all that is between them*: He is Lord to each of them through a Name that suits it, and directs them and grants them whatever their condition requires; He is Lord over all through all of His Names. *So worship Him* with your worship as dictated by your condition until you are prepared to receive His grace and for the revelation to descend. It is not enough for there to be worship to bring about preparedness through purification once or twice, but rather it must be perpetual; so remain constant in that purity which brings about acceptance, *and be steadfast in His worship* by turning to Him constantly. *Do you know* [*of*] *anyone who could be His namesake'*—anything that resembles Him such that you might be distracted by it and turn your face towards it, that it might grace you with your desire?

Q. 19:65

[19:67] [*Does not man then remember that We created him before,*] *when he was nothing* tangible in the realm of witnessing, or nothing significant, as He says *a period of time in which he was a thing unmentioned* [Q. 76:1], for an entity endowed with existence when compared to the time before creation is like nothing at all, absorbed as it is into the source of unification.

[19:68] *We will surely gather them and the devils*: that is, We will gather the veiled deniers to be resurrected alongside the devils who deluded them and led them astray from the truth, because in their turbidity and distance from the light the souls of the veiled ones resemble the souls of the devils, and so naturally they will be resurrected alongside them, especially if they followed them in their beliefs. *Then We shall bring them around Hell*: the hell of nature in the lower world, because of how they are veiled by material coverings and dark clouds in the prison of corporeality, chained and fettered, *crouching* because of how their bodies are bent due to their twisted souls, so that they are unable to stand.

[19:69] *Then We shall pluck out from every party* [*whichever of them was most hardened in disdain of the Compassionate*]: that is, We shall single out that one for a harsher chastisement because of what We know of his condition, since We know him better than he does, and We shall subject him to whatever chastisement is most apt for him.

[19:71] *There is not one of you, but he shall come to it*: at the Resurrection, every one of you will have to come through the realm of nature because it is the route to the realm of holiness. *That is an inevitability [already] decreed by your Lord*: a firm ruling which has already been rendered. Everyone who is called forth to have his spirit returned to his body will have to pass over Hell in order to cross the Bridge, because when the believer goes over it his light will put out its flames so that he does not feel them. It is related that Hell itself will say, 'Pass, believer, for your light has extinguished my flames.' Were you to ask him after his entrance into Paradise what his experience with Hell was like, he would answer that he was altogether unaware of it. Al-Ṣādiq (may God grant him peace) was asked, 'Will even you have to come to it?' He replied, 'It will be cool when we pass over.' Ibn ʿAbbās is related to have said, 'They will pass over it as though it were melted butter.' Jābir b. ʿAbd Allāh is reported to have asked the Messenger of God (may God bless him and grant him peace) about this and he replied, 'When the inhabitants of Paradise enter it, they will say to one another, "Did our Lord not promise us that we would have to come to Hell?" The answer will come, "You did come to it, but it was cool."' It was also related that he was asked about this verse and replied, 'I heard the Messenger of God (may God bless him and grant him peace) say, "To come to it means to enter it. Everyone, whether righteous or wicked, will enter it; but it will be cool and safe for the believers, just as it was for Abraham (may God grant him peace). The fire will even make a sound as it cools."' Thus, when God said, *Indeed, those to whom [the promise of] the best reward went beforehand from Us, they will be kept away from it [Hell] [Q. 21:101]*, this means they will be kept from its torment.

Q. 19:71

[19:72] *Then We will deliver those who were wary* because of their detachment, and permit them to pass over the Bridge, which represents following the path of justice to Oneness, *and leave those who did wrong* who squandered the light of their preparedness in the darkness, or put it in the wrong place, *crouching therein*, motionless because they are stuck fast in the mire of dark materiality, as he (may God grant him peace) said, 'Injustice will be darkness on the Day of Resurrection.'

[19:76] *And God increases in guidance those who found [right] guidance*: that is, just as He leads on the people of misguidance in their error so that they become ever more misguided and veiled the more they persist in their ignorance and foulness, so too God increases the guided folk with grace. Every time they act upon what they know, they become prepared to receive new knowledge and so they are bequeathed it, as he (may God grant him peace) said, 'When someone acts on what he knows, God bequeaths him knowledge that he did not have.' Therefore, when they act in accordance with certain knowledge, He increases them with the eye of certitude; and when they act upon that, He grants them the reality of certitude. *And the enduring things, the righteous deeds* of knowledge and virtue *are better in your Lord's sight in [terms of] reward* because of how they lead to divine self-disclosures and paradisiacal gardens of the heart, *and better in [terms of the] return* through the return to the Essential Unity.

[19:83] *Have you not regarded that We unleash the devils against the disbelievers to urge them impetuously?* In the discussion of the descent of the angels, we saw that the goodly soul draws aid from the realm of the dominion and the heavenly angels because of its connection to them in purity, detachment and illumination. Likewise, evil souls draw from the terrestrial souls of darkness because of their correspondence to them and their common elements of darkness, turbidity and foulness. The Messenger of God (may God bless him and grant him peace) was astounded by the extent of their darkness and their insistence in error and delusion, such that the devils would constantly visit them and urge them: that is, goad them and sabotage them by incessantly casting misgivings and evil whisperings into their hearts.

Q. 19:83

[19:84] *We are only counting for them, carefully*: counting their breaths as they pass by leading them nearer and nearer to the final fate of their unbelief and their deeds, and the chastisement for their states and their beliefs; for everyone has an appointed time at which they will soon arrive.

[19:85] *The day on which We shall gather those who fear God, to the Compassionate, with honour*: He mentioned the Name the Compassionate because of the universality of His mercy according to the degrees of their God-fearing, as He said before, *Those of Our servants who are God-fearing* [Q. 19:63]. One of the gnostics said upon hearing this verse, 'If someone is with the Compassionate, then with whom will he be gathered?' Another answered him, 'From the Compassionate to the Compassionate, and from the Conquering One to the Kind One.' The one who is wary of sin, iniquity and the attributes of the soul, which is the first level of God-fearing, might be gathered to the Compassionate in the garden of the acts, and then of the Attributes; and then after reaching God in the garden of the Attributes, he will be able to travel with God according to the self-disclosures of His Attributes; and when his journey reaches the Essence, it will be a true journey to God, *with honour*.

[19:86] *And drive the guilty*, because of their foul deeds, *into Hell* of nature, *a thirsty herd*, as though they are thirsty camels led into Hell to drink.

[19:87] *They will not have the power to intercede, save him who has made a covenant with the Compassionate*: this covenant is the one that God made with the people of faith to adhere to the previous covenant, by repenting and turning to Him at the second purification after the first one. This means to shed the veils of the soul and take on the attributes of the Compassionate and become connected with the realm of the holy, which is the presence of the Divine Attributes. Thus, again, He mentioned the Name the Compassionate, which means the Giver of all favours from first to last, encompassing all the attributes of kindness. In other words, no one can intercede with Him for heavenly supports and holy illuminations unless they are prepared to receive the mercy of the Compassionate and to connect to the Divine through the true covenant. Ibn Masʿūd related that the Prophet (may God bless him and grant him peace) said to his Companions one day, 'Is it beyond any one of you to say this, each morning and evening? "Lord God, Creator of heaven and earth, Knower of the Unseen and the visible, I pledge to You that I will testify that there is no god but You, alone without partner, and that Muḥammad is Your servant and messenger; and that if You were to leave me to my own devices, I would certainly stray near to evil and far from good, and that I trust only in Your mercy. Make a covenant for me that You may present to me on the Day of Resurrection, for You do not break Your promises."'

Q. 19:86

[19:93] *There is none in the heavens and the earth but he comes to the Compassionate as a servant*, because they are constrained by the realm of contingency and the possibility of non-being, and can have no existence or perfection save through Him. Through the Name the Compassionate, He granted their existences and their perfections, and they are nothing in and of themselves. Had they not worshipped Him with true servitude through the potentialities of their essences in non-being, they would never have been brought into existence, even if they did not worship Him after coming into existence by fulfilling the duties they owed in return for the blessings He gave them when they were perfected. Thus, they are forever His subjects, bound to remain under His power and dominion.

[19:94] *Verily He knows their number* from pre-eternity when He ordained their entities and potentialities from His holy emanation, and decreed them in His knowledge, *and has counted them precisely*; their quiddities and realities are nothing but the forms of information that emerged in non-being through His knowledge and came into existence by the emanation of His mercy, exactly as was ordained.

[19:95] *And each one of them will come to Him on the Day of Resurrection*—the Minor Resurrection[1]—alone and detached from all means and aids, just as they were at the first creation, and also at the Intermediate Resurrection, [*each one*] *alone*, detached from physical connections and removed from all egocentric attributes and natural powers. As for [when they are] at the Major Resurrection, *Everyone who is on it will perish, yet there will remain the countenance of your Lord, [the countenance] of majesty and munificence* [Q. 55:26–27].

[19:96] *Indeed, those who believe* with true faith, whether based on knowledge or certitude, *and perform righteous deeds* that purify them and prepare them to receive the self-disclosures of the Attributes of God by detaching from their own garb, *for them the Compassionate shall appoint love*, as He said, 'The servant continues to draw nearer to Me with voluntary deeds until I love him; and when I love him, I become his hearing with which he hears, and his sight with which he sees, and his hand with which he grasps.' In reality, this love is the effect and result of the primary nurture described in His Words, *He loves them, and they love Him* [Q. 5:54]. If He loved someone before they came into existence in the possibility of the Unseen realm with the love of selection, then they will inevitably love God when they come into existence and are moved to hold faithfully to the first covenant, and renew that covenant with the later one, the covenant with God, through adherence to that and by following the Absolute Loved One, as He said, *Say: 'If you love God, follow me, and God will love you, and forgive you your sins; God is Forgiving, Merciful'* [Q. 3:31]. If this following is sincere in the person's deeds and states, then God will love him with the love of purification, above the love that was the fruit of the first love, because the first was essential and hidden while the second

Q. 19:95

---

1 According to Kāshānī's *Kitāb Iṣṭilāḥāt al-Ṣūfiyya* (s.v. *qiyāma*): 'Resurrection into eternal life after death may be divided into three types. The first is the resurrection, following physical death, into a life within either the higher or the lower Intermediate Worlds, depending on the state of the dead person during life on earth [...] [t]his is the Minor Resurrection [...] The second is the resurrection, after voluntary death, into the eternal life of the Heart of in the Holy world [...] This is the Intermediate Resurrection [...] The third is the resurrection, after annihilation in God, into the life of reality, whilst enduring within Truth. This is the Major Resurrection.' 'Abd al-Razzāq al-Kāshānī, *Kitāb iṣṭilāḥāt al-ṣūfiyya*, trans. Nabil Safwat as *A Glossary of Sufi Technical Terms*, London: Octogan Press, 1991, p. 98.

is perfect and open. When this happens, the person will become beloved to his fellow people and the people of innate faith will naturally accept him. The Messenger of God (may God bless him and grant him peace) is reported to have said, 'When God loves a servant, He says, "O Gabriel, I love so-and-so, so love him too!" So Gabriel loves him, and then he calls out to the folk of heaven, "God loves so-and-so, so love him too!" So the folk of heaven love him. Then He places love for him on earth.' Qatāda is related to have said, 'Whenever a servant approaches God, God makes the hearts of His servants approach him.' This is the meaning of His Words *for them the Compassionate shall appoint love.* And God knows best.

Q. 19:96

20
ṬĀ HĀ
SŪRAT ṬĀ HĀ

In the Name of God, the Compassionate, the Merciful

[20:1] *Ṭā. Hā:* the *Ṭā* alludes to the Pure One (*Ṭāhir*), the *Hā* to the Guide (*Hādī*). On account of his great compassion and love for his people, due to his being the embodiment of mercy and the depiction of love, the Prophet (may God bless him and grant him peace) was despondent at how the revelation had not had any effect on their faith, and he felt that this was due to some sort of remnant within himself, as God described: *Yet it may be that you will consume yourself with grief in their wake if they should not believe in this discourse* [Q. 18:6]. So he increased his devotion, spending all night in prayer and standing for so long that his feet became swollen with blisters. Therefore, he was told that their lack of faith was not on his account, but only on theirs because of the density of their veil and their unpreparedness. Hence, it was not due to any remnant of the attributes of his soul, or any remnant of I-ness in him, or any deficiency or flaw in his guidance, as he may have worried; so he need not wear himself out. He was called with two of the Names of God to indicate his innocence of those two things: any remnant of the ego, or any flaw in his guidance. Thus, he was told, 'O you who are purified from the pollution of remnants, O guide!'

[20:2] *We have not revealed the Qurʾān to you so that you should be miserable* or wear yourself out with exertion, but rather for it to be a reminder for those whose hearts are softened and prepared to receive it, after your purification and refinement. Both of these have been attained— praise be to God! You have become perfect and perfected, which are the only two goals of spiritual exertion, and they have been achieved in you. We have manifested to you with those two Names, so you need not trouble yourself further. That some have not been guided by your guidance is due only to hardness of heart, the opposite of the humility and softness that are required to attain guidance; it is not your fault.

The letters could also be taken as an oath rather than a call: I swear by the two Names through which the Lord manifests to impart purification and adornment; for the purpose of revelation is for the effect of them both to be attained within you, not for you to wear yourself out and suffer, and this has been achieved so you need not exert yourself further. For this reason, the family of Muḥammad are called the House of Ṭā Hā, due to how these two meanings have been achieved in them and how these two Names have been manifested through them.

[20:4] *A revelation from Him Who created the earth* to His Words *To Him belong the Most Beautiful Names* [Q. 20:8]: We revealed it as revelation from Him Who is endowed with all the Attributes of beauty and majesty, of which you have a certain share in all, since otherwise you would not be capable of receiving it and bearing it. When an effect is passed on, it must be suited to the recipient just as it is to the source; and if the source is the Essence endowed with all the Most Beautiful Names, the recipient, which is your own essence, must also be endowed with them. So just as He created the high heavens and the earth, meaning the realm of spirits and the realm of bodies which is the absolute body, and made them veils of His majesty and the coverings of His beauty, likewise He also veiled you with the heavens of the levels of your mystery, from the seven aforementioned veils which are your spirit-being, the degrees of your perfection, and the earth of your visible form which is your body.

Q. 20:4

[20:5] *The Compassionate [presided upon the Throne]*: that is, your Lord is the Majestic, veiled by the veils of created being because of His majesty; and He is the Beautiful, manifesting through the beauty of His mercy to all things, for nothing is bereft of the mercy of the Compassionate, since otherwise it would not exist. This is why He chose to mention the Name the Compassionate (*al-Raḥmān*) rather than the Merciful (*al-Raḥīm*), because it is only from it that the universal emanation reaches all. Just as He presided over the Throne of all being by the disclosure of His undiscriminating compassion therein and the manifestation of its effect, which is the universal emanation from Him to all beings, likewise He presided over the throne of your heart by the disclosure of all His Attributes therein and the spread of their effect from Him to all of creation. Thus, you became a mercy to all the worlds, and your prophethood became universal and final. The meaning of this presiding was His manifestation in him fully and completely, since no part of his being could be a locus for anything else, and so this manifestation could only preside over him in totality. This is why he (may God grant him peace) did not cast a shadow, since no remnant of his attributes remained with his essence without being subsumed in this realisation in the Real through subsistence after total annihilation.

[20:6] *To Him belongs whatever is in the heavens* to His Words *and whatever is beneath the soil*: this illustrates the encompassment of His overwhelming power and dominion over all; it is all beneath His dominion, power, authority and influence, and there can be no being, motion, stillness, change or constancy except by His command. Just so, you have become annihilated in totality, overwhelmed by His Unity and the annihilation of His overwhelming power, so that you do not hear, see, grasp or walk except through Him and by His command.

[20:7] *And should you be loud in your speech, then indeed He knows the secret and [that which is] yet more hidden*: this illustrates the perfection of His subtleness. His knowledge penetrates all things, and He knows their exteriors and interiors, and their secrets and most secret mysteries. Whether you speak out loud or keep silent, He is aware of it. Now since the Attributes mentioned are the Primary Attributes that encompass all others, and the Names that include all other Names, although the Essence still remains unitary and is not made plural by them, He says:

Q. 20:6

[20:8] *God*: that is, the One Who reveals whilst endowed with all these Attributes is God—*there is no god save Him*: His Essential Unity, which is the reality of His Ipseity, is not rendered plural or countable by them, for He is He through all eternity just as He was in pre-eternity; He is nothing but He, and there exists nothing but He with regard to His Unity and source because of this. *To Him belong the Most Beautiful Names*, which are His Essence considered with the effects of His Attributes.

[20:10] *When he caught sight of a fire*—the fire was the Holy Spirit, which kindles light in human souls; He saw it with the eye of his insight thanks to the light of guidance—*and said to his family*, meaning his egocentric faculties, '*Wait*: be silent and still, for one can only travel to the holy realm and attach to it when one restrains these human faculties from the external and internal senses which distract it. *Indeed, I see a fire [in the distance]. Perhaps I [can] bring you a brand from it*: that is, a form of connective light from which you will all benefit with illumination, so that your essence becomes pure virtue; *or find at the fire some guidance*': someone to guide me with the knowledge and gnosis required for guidance to the Real; by connecting to it, I might attain an illuminating state or some illustrative images.

[20:11] *And when he reached it*—that is, connected with it—*he was called [by name], 'O Moses!* [20:12] *Indeed, I am your Lord*, veiled with the image of fire, which is one of the coverings of My majesty in which I am manifested. *So remove your sandals*: that is, your soul and your body, or the two worlds, because to detach yourself from them is to detach yourself from the two worlds; just as you detached your spirit and mystery from their attributes and states in order to connect with the Holy Spirit, detach your heart and your breast from theirs by cutting the ties, erasing the effects, and becoming annihilated from the attributes and acts. He referred to them as *sandals* rather than 'garments' because had he not detached from wearing them he would not have been connected to the realm of the holy; and at this point, he was already connected, so He commanded him to fully devote himself to it, as He said elsewhere, *And devote yourself to Him with complete devotion* [Q. 73:8]. It seems, then, that he still retained a remnant of connection and attachment to them that restrained his foot, which represents the lower part of the heart called 'the breast', and prevented him from moving further towards the holy with his spirit and his mystery, even after orienting them towards it. Therefore, He commanded him to detach from them in the station of the spirit, which is why He explained the necessity of removing the sandals by saying, *For, lo and behold, you are in the holy valley of Ṭuwā*: that is, the realm of the spirit purified from the effects of attachment and the states of material connections and relations. It is called Ṭuwā because of how the realms of the dominion and the bodies of heaven and earth are folded up (*ṭayy*) beneath it. A truthful man said that he was told to remove them because they were made from untanned carrion donkey hide. It was also said that when he was called, Satan whispered to him, 'That is Satan calling you!' He replied, 'Away with you! I hear the call from all six directions with every part of my body, and only the Compassionate calls that way.'

[20:13] *And I [Myself] have chosen you, so listen to what is being revealed*: this is a promise of election, made after the total essential manifestation that crumbled the mountain of his existence into dust through annihilation in Him, and made him fall down unconscious and then awoke him with veridical divine existence, as He says, *And when he recovered his senses he said, 'Glory be to You! I repent to You, and I am the first of the believers.' He said, 'O Moses, I have elected you from among people for My Messages and My Speech'* [Q. 7:143–144]. This self-disclosure is the manifestation of the Attributes before that of the Essence. Therefore, He sent him off and did not give him tidings of the Prophetic Message yet, but rather

Q. 20:11

commanded him to engage in spiritual exertion, presence and contemplation, and promised him that the Major Resurrection would soon come. This selection was close to the fundamental choosing of which He said, *Thereafter his Lord chose him, and relented to him, and guided him* [Q. 20:122]: between it and the election. He then repeated:

[20:14] *Indeed, I am God (Allāh)*, with emphasis and with mention of *God* rather than 'Lord' this time, so that he did not stop at the Attributes in the presence of the Names and thereby be veiled from the Essence. Lord was the Name through which He manifested to him, for He would not direct him in his search for guidance and the firebrand by anything other than that Name, the Knower, the Guide, acting through Gabriel. In other words, I am the One endowed with all Attributes, and *there is no god but Me*; I am neither plural, nor is My Unity and identity made numerous by My many manifestations and Attributes. *So worship Me*: devote your worship to My Essence, rather than My Names and Attributes, with essential worship, and prepare your I-ness for annihilation in My reality and absolute essential glorification; *and establish prayer [in order to make remembrance of Me]*: the prayer of spirit-witnessing for the invocation of My Essence, beyond the prayer of heart-presence for the invocation of My Attributes.

Q. 20:14

[20:15] *The Hour*—the Major Resurrection of total annihilation in Unity—*is assuredly coming. [But] I will to keep it hidden* by veiling Myself with Attributes in order to separate the ranks and display the souls and deeds, *so that every soul may be requited* according to its efforts for good or evil, and a distinction can be made between perfection and deficiency, salvation and damnation. I shall not reveal this to any but a select few of My elite, one after another, because if I were to reveal it everything would be annihilated and there would be no souls, deeds, requitals or anything else.

[20:16] *So do not let him bar you from it* so that you remain in the veil of Attributes, *who believes not in it* because of his lack of preparedness, so that he remains in a given rank veiled by the Attributes, acts, effects or rivals, which is the hidden or open idolatry, *but follows his own caprice* in the station of the soul or the heart, for caprice remains as long as I-ness remains, and it will ruin you just as it ruined the one who barred you.

[20:17] *And what is that in your right hand, O Moses?* This was an allusion to his soul: that is, the thing in the hand of his intellect, for the intellect is the right hand with which a man grasps what God bestows and applies it to himself.

[20:18] *He said, 'It is my staff. I lean upon it*: that is, I rely on it in the realm of the visible, the attainment of perfection and the journey to God and adoption of His character traits (*akhlāq*), and I cannot do these things without it; *and I beat down [leaves] with it for my sheep*: that is, I beat down the leaves of the beneficial sciences and practical wisdoms from the tree of the spirit, by stirring them with contemplation for the sheep of my animal faculties; *and I have uses for it in other ways,'* such as acquiring stations and seeking states, gifts and self-disclosures. The reason He asked him this was to calm the awe that was stricken in him by the manifestation of His might and to replace it with security; and the reason he answered with more than he was asked was due to how enraptured he was by the communion, and how dearly he longed to prolong that intimacy.

[20:19] *He said, 'Cast it down, O Moses!'* In other words, remove the control of the intellect from it.

[20:20] *And he cast it down*: he let it go its way after it was illuminated by the manifestation of the Attributes of divine power; *and lo and behold, it was a serpent moving swiftly*: the snake moved because of its rage. The soul of Moses (may God grant him peace) was powerfully angry and wrathful, and when he reached the station of the manifestations of the Attributes, it was necessary for him to be further prepared for the manifestation of power, as was discussed in [*sūrat*] *al-Kahf* [Q. 18]. So at his moment of annihilation, his anger was replaced by the divine anger and the lordly power, and so became a serpent which swallowed up everything it found.

Q. 20:19

[20:21] *He said, 'Take hold of it*: control it with your intellect, as before, *and do not fear* that it might emerge and overcome you, thus changing your state for the worse, for your anger has been annihilated and it will only move by My command; it is not merely hidden by the light of the heart in the station of the soul, ready to emerge again later. *We will restore it to its former state*: that is, dead and annihilated, moved on to the level of the vegetative faculty wherein it is senseless and unmoving. Moses (may God grant him peace) had killed it through the tutelage of Shuʿayb (may God grant him peace). His transformation of it into the vegetative faculties explains why it was called 'a staff', and this is why it is said that Shuʿayb (may God grant him peace) gifted it to him.

[20:22] *'And thrust your hand into your flank*: that is, thrust your intellect to the side of your spirit, which is your right flank, so that it can be illuminated by the light of veridical guidance. When the intellect allies with the soul and is clutched to its side on the left flank to govern matters of ordinary life, it is sullied thereby so that it becomes turbid and cannot be illuminated or receive lordly gifts and divine realities. Therefore, he was commanded to thrust it to the side of the spirit, so that it would be purified to receive the light of holiness. *It will emerge white*, illuminated by the light of veridical guidance and the rays of holy light, *without any fault*: that is, without any blight, flaw or ailment born of estimation and fancy. [*That is*] *yet another sign*, one attribute added to another.

[20:23] '*That We may show you of Our greatest signs*: of the signs of the manifestations of Our Attributes, the greatest sign being annihilation in Unity. In other words, so that by your vision you can be in the station of the manifestation of the Attributes, that through them and by them We might show you Our Essence at the essential manifestation; and you might behold Us, through Us, at the Major Resurrection.

[20:24] '*Go to Pharaoh. He has indeed transgressed*': by manifesting his I-ness and thereby being veiled, and straying beyond the limits of servitude. This indicates that prophethood and messengership do not depend on essential annihilation, since Moses had not experienced the forty nights in which God manifested to him with His Essence until after Pharaoh's destruction. Therefore, this Message was only at the station of the manifestation of the Attributes. This supports what we have said several times about how the greater portion of the Prophet's journey (may God bless him and grant him peace) was after his prophethood, revelation and guidance by inspiration had begun.

Q. 20:23

[20:25] '*My Lord, expand my breast for me*: with the light of certitude and mastery in the station of the manifestation of the Attributes, that it is not constricted by their persecution, and that my soul does not suffer pain from their tyranny and mindless villainy. Grant that when I speak to them with Your Words, I might hear their words with Your hearing so that I recognise them as Your own words, and that I see their persecution with Your sight so that I recognise it as Your own act; grant that I see and hear all that with which they meet me as coming from You, so that I can bear Your test through You. Do not expose my soul by making it perceive all of that to be from them, so that it is veiled by its attributes and theirs from Yours.

[20:26] '*And make easy for me my affair*: that is, my call, by giving them the good grace to accept Your religion, and aid me against the adversaries with Your support and holy aid.

[20:27] '*And undo the knot* [*upon my tongue*]: the knots of intellect and reflection that restrain my tongue from being loosened by Your Speech, and keep from me the courage and boldness to speak openly to convey Your Message, manifest Your Word and uphold Your religion against theirs with arguments and proofs to counter their pharaonic tyranny, for the sake of respecting the divine authority.

[20:28] *'So that they may understand what I [shall] say*: by Your softening their hearts and instilling humility and reverence in them, and by the support You extend to me from the realm of holiness and aid.

The rest of the story does not bear any allegorical interpretation; but if you would like a spiritual correspondence for it, then know that the Moses of the heart asks God with the voice of its true condition to appoint the Aaron of the intellect, its elder brother from their father the Holy Spirit, as its minister to strengthen it, give it counsel regarding its affairs, and aid it with its opinions, and be a partner and assistant to it in attaining its perfections. It justifies this plea by saying:

[20:33] *'So that we may glorify You*: by detaching from the attributes and states of the soul, *over and over again;* [20:34] *and remember You over and over again*: by acquiring gnostic sciences and realities and being present for unveilings and the station of the manifestations of Attributes.

[20:35] *'Indeed, You are ever Seeing us'*: that is, seeing our preparedness to receive perfection, and our aptitude for it; so aid us and make us allies in the cause of that which You desire from us.

[20:36] *'You have been granted your request* and given the grace to attain your desire.

[20:37] *'And certainly, We have done you a favour [already] another time,* even before your desire and request for Our aid, [20:38] *when We revealed to your mother*, the animal soul, *that which was revealed*: that is, when We inspired her to:

[20:39] *'"Cast him in the chest* of the body or corporeal nature, *then cast him into the river* of material nature, *and then the river shall throw him up*, when the light of discrimination and guidance emerges, *onto the shore* of salvation; *[there] an enemy*, the tyrannical evil-enjoining pharaonic soul, *shall take him."* And I cast upon you a love from Me*: that is, I loved you and made you beloved to hearts and to everything, even the evil-enjoining soul and its faculties, for the one I love is loved by all. I did this in order *that you might be reared* and raised under My protection and care.

[20:40] *'When your sister*, the active intellect, *walked up*, when it emerged and was stirred, *and she then said* to the evil-enjoining soul and the faculties sympathetic to it, *"Shall I show you*, with courtesy and beautiful conduct with its kinsfolk the reproaching soul and its compartmentalised faculties, on the occasion of the loss of their joy, *someone who will take care of him?"* for you, by raising him with reflection, nursing him with the milk of practical wisdom and beneficial knowledge, which will counsel him and help him in the acquisition of perfection, guide him to righteous deeds, and prepare him to ascend to a lofty rank. *Thus, We restored you to your mother* who was pining for you, the reproaching soul that reproaches itself for the squandering of its joy, so that it could find solace in the light of certitude, and you could be refined by practical wisdom and nurse on its milk, and be raised in its care by means of compartmentalised perceptions, physical instruments and purifying acts; *that her eyes might rejoice,* illuminated by your light, *and not grieve* for the loss of her joy.

Then you slew a soul: that is, the image of wrathfulness that controlled you, by means of spiritual exertion and self-slaying, *whereupon We delivered you* from the distress of the control of the evil-enjoining soul and the ruin it was wreaking upon you; *and We tried you* with many tribulations by the emergence of the soul and its attributes, and the spiritual exertion needed to repel them, slay them and purify them.

Then you stayed for several years among the people of Midian: the Midian of knowledge from the spiritual faculties with Shuʿayb, the active intellect. *Then you came [hither] as ordained* according to the ordained perfection commensurate with your preparedness, or for the sake of something I ordained for you: that is, some of the total perfection that was ordained to you, namely the essential manifestation that would be given to you after the perfection of the attributes.

Q. 20:41

[20:41] *'And I chose you for Myself*: that is, I selected you for Myself and made you one of My elites among the people of the city of the body, because of your noble character traits and your worthiness to be My vicegerent.

[20:42] *'Go, you and your brother*, and so on to the end of the story. If you would like a spiritual correspondence for it, then it is as follows: Moses of the heart, go with your brother the intellect *with My signs*, My arguments and proofs, *and do not flag in remembrance of Me.*

[20:43] *'Go the two of you to Pharaoh*: the tyrannical evil-enjoining soul that has transgressed its bounds by overpowering and ascending above the spiritual faculties.

[20:44] *'And speak to him gentle words'* with mercy and sensitivity when inviting it to surrender to the command of the Real and yield to the rule of the Divine Law, and perhaps it will soften, be admonished and yield. Yet when they feared its pharaonic tyranny because of how accustomed it was to its ascendancy, God encouraged them by promising aid, assistance, protection, nurture and encompassment of all the strife that they would encounter from it. Furthermore, He commanded them to convey the Message to make it yield and obey, and to make it desist from its idolisation of the animal faculties and to stop enabling them. [This was] so that He could send it along with them to the divine presence and the emanation of holy spiritual illuminations and gnostic realities, rather than tormenting it with the pursuit of physical pleasures and worldly delights.

[20:47] *'We have verily brought you a sign*: a proof showing how you are obliged to follow us; *and may peace*, meaning freedom from faults and salvation from attachments, and the illuminating emanation from the spirit realm, *be upon him who follows* this proof and holds fast to the divine light.

[20:48] *'Indeed, it has been revealed to us that the chastisement'* in the hell of nature and the pit of matter shall befall those who reject and oppose this.

[20:49] *'So who is your Lord?'* This is an allusion to the veiling of the soul from the Lord's presence.

[20:50] *'Our Lord is He Who gave'* it guidance with evidence, and insight with arguments: that is, He gave it a constitution that was for its own good, and instruments that suited its needs, benefits and aims, and guided it to attaining them.

Q. 20:47

[20:51] *'So what of the generations of old?'* This alludes to how it is veiled from the Resurrection and the states of the afterlife, salvation and damnation, and from God's encompassing knowledge of it. Since the first obligation is to know God by His Attributes, and knowledge of the afterlife depends on this, he answered by invoking God's knowledge of it and its many states, and how this knowledge is affirmed in the Preserved Tablet for all eternity, and how He cannot err or forget.

[20:53] *The One Who made for you*, O corporeal faculties, *the earth* of the body *a cradle, and threaded for you therein ways* in the form of limbs and body parts, such as the eye, the ear, the nose and so on, *and sent down from the heaven* of the spirit *water* of perception and spiritual strength. *And therewith We brought forth various kinds* of perceptions, actions, characteristics, states and special properties for every power among you.

[20:54] *Eat* and nourish yourselves from the states, characteristics, supports and gifts that are meant for you, such as contentment, patience, knowledge of names, character traits, and numbers, and all the other perceptions, desires and stations; *and pasture your cattle*: the animal faculties, with the characteristics and traits they require.

[20:55] *From it We created you*: We formed you according to the varying constitutions of the body parts that form their outer shell; *and into it We shall restore you* with death through exertion until it penetrates and infiltrates it entirely, so that it is motionless and does not seek to transgress its bounds or overwhelm anything else, through the erasure of the soul until annihilation; *and from it We shall bring you forth a second time* at the station of subsistence through the gift of true life, whereupon its motions will become just, and its dispositions sound.

[20:56] *And verily We showed him all Our signs* of the arguments and proofs guiding the way to detachment from materiality and the presence of illuminations; *but he denied* because of their material nature *and refused* to accept because of its incomprehension of detachments, and declined to wrest it from its bodily abode. Therefore, he said:

[20:57] *'Have you come to us so that you may expel us from our land by your sorcery?'* He accused the proof of being sorcery because it was beyond the limits of his perception and he was incapable of accepting it, deluded as he was by the faculties of estimation and fancy and thus given to obstinate arguing and debate. It is rare for the soul to yield to obvious proof and plain truth without spiritual exertion and self-slaying; whenever they visit it, it is spurred by estimation and fancy into nitpicking and criticism.

[20:59] [*'Your tryst shall be the Day of Adornment*:] the tryst is the time when the arguments are formed and the stations are ordained, which is the time when the sapient soul is adorned with perceptions, and the intellectual and spiritual faculties are mustered to bring forth their information and treasures; *at forenoon,'* when the light of the sun of the active intellect shines, since this is where the soul refuses to accept it and musters its plots in the form of various fallacies and delusions, which the heart suppresses with certainties, exposing its lies and deceptions.

[20:62] [*So they disputed their matter among themselves*:] the battle that rages among the egocentric faculties is caused by their refusal to obey the heart and the attraction of each of them to their various contradictory passions; [*and kept secret their private counsel*:] all of them attempted to hide their motivations for opposing the heart, which were also the cause of their internal opposition to one another.

[20:63] [*They said, 'These two men are indeed sorcerers who intend to expel you from your land by their sorcery, and do away with your excellent tradition'*:] they accused them of sorcery because they were incapable of grasping their meanings and perceiving their proofs. The tradition they deemed excellent was the attainment of physical pleasures and the indulgence of bodily lusts.

[20:65] [*They said, 'O Moses, either cast or we shall be the first to cast.'* [20:66] *He said, 'Nay, you cast!'*] That they cast first is an allusion to the precedence of delusions and fancies in the human being over rationalities and certainties when first travelling the path, since otherwise there would

Q. 20:56

27

be no need for sure proofs and plain evidence. It also alludes to how the one who calls to the truth must first repudiate falsehood and do away with doubts by means of sound arguments, in order to put paid to the false belief so that the truth can replace it. [*And lo and behold, their ropes and their staffs appeared to him by* [*the effect of*] *their sorcery as though they were gliding swiftly:*] the ropes and staffs represent the fallacies and sophistries of unsound arguments that threaten to bewilder and overwhelm the heart, were it not for the aid of the Real by the light of the spirit and the intellect, which is the meaning of His Words.

[20:68] '*Do not be afraid! Indeed, you shall have the upper hand.* [20:69] *And cast that which is in your right hand*, the rational intelligent hand, which must cast its reliable proof in order to obliterate their deceptive contrivances and delusional falsehoods so that they vanish into nothing. *For what they have produced is only a sorcerer's trick*': a deception with no basis in reality, not akin to what I produced, as they claimed.

[20:70] '*Thereat the sorcerers cast* [*their heads*] *down prostrating,*' and the faculties of estimation, imagination, suggestion and sensation yielded when it became clear that they were outmatched. But the evil-enjoining soul persisted in its pharaonic tyranny, because it had not yet been broken and trained out of its customs and its ascendancy and control over the faculties. Clinging obstinately to its stubborn refusal to yield, it declared:

[20:71] '*I shall assuredly cut-off* [*your hands and feet on opposite sides and I shall assuredly crucify you on the trunks of palm trees*]': this is an allusion to how it banished and threatened the faculties, when they yielded and accepted to cease pursuing their usual lives of chasing bodily pleasures and passions, by resisting them and obeying the heart. Their crucifixion on palm trunks represents how they were stopped by self-slaying from spiritual exertion at the bounds of the vegetative faculties, and fixed in their places there. Their growth began at the highest levels of the vegetative faculties, without being permitted to roam to the other levels where they might usurp other roles and acquire other controlling powers, or at the limbs which represent their influences and outward extensions. When interpreted this way, this threat is an example of the soul's private dialogue and thoughts because of satanic influences meant to discourage efforts. [It is] as God says, *That is but Satan instilling fear through his partisans* [Q. 3:175], in order to dissuade them from obeying the heart and serving it dutifully.

If it is taken to mean an outward debate as described in God's Words, *Dispute with them by way of that which is best* [Q. 16:125], after belief in the obvious and faith in what is clearly an unanswerable proof, then everything between *Go the two of you* [*to Pharaoh*] [Q. 20:43] and *So they disputed their matter among themselves* [Q. 20:62] could be taken literally to mean that they discussed the matter privately, arguing over what possible counter-argument they could give to what they had been shown. It has been said that by *These two men are indeed sorcerers* [Q. 20:63], they meant, 'Their arguments, eloquence and reasoning are too powerful, and no one could hope to answer them.'

[20:64] *So summon up your guile*: that is, agree on whatever you will use to challenge us, so that you can be agreed and united.

[20:66] *Then, lo and behold, their ropes and their staffs*—meaning their estimations and fancies— *appeared to him by* [*the effect of*] *their sorcery*, in the form of phrasing, rhetoric, eloquence and the employment of fallacy, sophistry and analogy, [*as though they were gliding swiftly*].

[20:67] [*And Moses sensed*] *fear* that the ignorant would triumph and misguidance would be ascendant, as the Commander of the Believers ʿAlī (may God grant him peace) said, 'Moses did not fear for himself, but he feared that the ignorant would triumph and misguidance would be ascendant.'

Q. 20:64

[20:68] *We said, 'Do not fear!* We encouraged him and aided him with the Holy Spirit.

[20:69] '*And cast that which is in your right hand*: in other words, that which is in the control of your intellect: the soul harmonised by the rays of holiness and illuminated by the light of truth. *It shall swallow up that which they have produced*: that is, the doubts and falsehoods they have fabricated, with illuminating arguments and clear proof. *For what they have produced is only a sorcerer's trick*': a deception and an illusion.

[20:70] *Thereat the sorcerers cast* [*their heads*] *down prostrating*, sincerely yielding and acknowledging that he was in the right, when they realised the truth of his arguments and witnessed his unanswerable and miraculous proofs. *They said, 'We* [*now*] *believe* [*in the Lord of Aaron and Moses*]' with certain faith, for the truth was unveiled to them and they recognised His lordship over all. The reason they attributed the Lord to Moses and Aaron alone, though they could have called Him the Lord of the Worlds, was that they had an extra claim to him and His lordship had an extra merit for them. He lords over all with whatever Name is appropriate for them and reflects their preparedness; and He was the Lord of those two with the greatest of His Most Beautiful Names, according to the perfection of their preparedness, and because of how He manifested in them with the perfections of His Attributes and showed Himself to the people through them by His signs. Thus, they recognised that it was only by the plea of those two that they had been shown all this, and it was only by their means that they had arrived to it, and only by following them had they found it, not by their independent means.

Know also that the sorcerer is the best prepared person to recognise a prophet, because the foundations of supernatural occurrences consist of three things: first, there are those which pertain to the composition and constituency of material things and forms, and the mixing of differing compositions and substances, which is the province of magic (nayranjāt). Secondly, there is the mustering of the heavenly and earthly faculties by enumerating the lower forms and primordial materials, in order to summon emanations of the heavenly souls and connect them with earthly bodies, which is the province of talismans (talsamāt). Thirdly, there is the influencing of souls and their states drawn from the higher realm, which is the province of the perfected ones sent for prophethood and given unanswerable miracles (muʿjizāt) to assist their call, and also the province of the realised ones who reach the end of the path of sainthood without being prophets, to whom are granted miraculous gifts (karāmāt). The difference between them is that the miracle is accompanied by a challenge and a confrontation, while the miraculous gift is not.

Q. 20:71

The third kind described above is also the province of the one who seeks this world and disregards the higher realm, in which case it is called 'sorcery' (siḥr). The soul of the sorcerer in the beginning of its innate disposition was powerful and gifted with influences over this world and its bodies. But it turned away from its origin by leaning towards the lower world, and becoming removed from the root of the faculties and the source of influence and power by inclining towards the natural world. This caused the continuous weakening of the illumination and holy rays that were within it, which, on the contrary, continue to grow within the soul of the prophet and the saint, as they turn towards the Real and bathe in the light of holiness, aided by the power of dominion, and reach towards the divine presence. So when a sorcerer encounters a prophet, it is natural that he will be quick to yield and give himself over to him, since he is better equipped than anyone to recognise a prophet once he reveals his miraculous challenge. Moreover, he will be the most eager of them to welcome his call and his illuminations, and the quickest of them to acknowledge him, since he is the best prepared of all of them—as long as his initial preparedness has not been erased entirely and the religion of lower nature has not completely overwhelmed him.

[20:72] '*We will not choose you*: these words issue from the might of aspiration, which the soul attains by the power of certitude; for the power of certitude in the heart bequeaths the soul the might of aspiration, which is its lack of concern for worldly happiness, bodily discomfort, ephemeral immediate pleasures and physical pains, overshadowed as they are by the felicity of the afterlife and the eternal intellectual pleasures. Consequently, they scorned and belittled such things by saying, *What you decree is only [relevant] in the life of this world.*

[20:73] '*[And] that He may forgive us our sins*: in other words, that His light might cover the dark forms and base attributes that blighted our souls, because of inclination towards natural pleasures and love for worldly delights; *and the sorcery to which you forced us*': that is, in opposition to Moses, for when they recognised him by the light of their preparedness and knew that he was in the right, they renounced their opposition to him, so the cursed one forced them.

[20:74] *Indeed, whoever comes to his Lord* at the Minor Resurrection *as a criminal* burdened by corporeal forms that incline to natural crime, *[for him there shall be Hell] wherein he shall neither die* the natural death that brings an end to pain, *nor live* the true life that brings salvation from the consequences of sin.

Q. 20:72

[20:75] *And whoever comes to Him a believer* with true faith, *having performed righteous deeds* of personal virtue that purify the soul, *for such shall be the highest degrees* of the [20:76] *gardens* of the Attributes, according to the degrees of their ascendance in the perfections.

[20:77] '*Lead My servants [on a journey by night]* in the darkness of the attributes of the soul and the night of corporeality, *and strike for them a dry path* of detachment *in the sea* of the world of primordial matter, dry and untouched by the damp of material forms or the moisture of corporeal matter. *Do not fear to be overtaken* by the materialistic ones who are sunk in the abysses of natural desire, *and do not be afraid*' of their victory or ascendancy over you, for they are confined and imprisoned there, unable to reach you.

[20:78] *Then He [Pharaoh] pursued them* to destroy their religion by immersion in natural desires, *and there engulfed them what did engulf them of the sea*: eternal destruction and perpetual torment. We have already seen the spiritual correspondence for this.

[20:80] *We made a tryst with you on the right side of the Mount* of the heart, beside the Holy Spirit, which is the seat of the revelation that they call 'the inner-heart' (*rūʿ* and *fuʾād*), *and We sent down to you* the *manna* of states and stations of sensorial experiences and the *quails* of knowledge and gnosis of certainties.

[20:81] *Eat of the good things We have provided you*: that is, be nourished on those goodly gnostic teachings and accept them into your hearts, for they shall give them life; *but do not transgress regarding it* by allowing the soul to emerge and exult in itself when it rises, or to behold its own splendour, perfection and beauty, *lest descend upon you [of My wrath]*: the wrath of deprivation and the blight of failure. *And he [on whom My wrath descends] certainly perishes*: falling from the station of nearness to the pit of the soul, veiled from the light of the manifestation of the Attributes of beauty in the shadows of veiling and the coverings of majesty.

[20:82] *And indeed I am Forgiving*, covering the attributes of the transgressing soul and its self-adoration and aggrandising with the lights of My Attributes, *toward him who repents* of its aggrandisement and ascendancy and asks for forgiveness by breaking the soul and making it yield, holding it to the humility of its neediness and poverty, *and believes* in the lights of the heart-attributes and the manifestations of the divine illuminations, *and acts righteously* in acquiring stations such as reliance and contentment and the dispositions that prevent disturbances, with presence and purity, *and then follows guidance* to the light of the Essence and the state of annihilation.

Q. 20:81

[20:83] *'And what has hurried you [to depart] from your people, [O Moses?'*

[20:84] *He said, 'They are close upon my track, and I hastened to You, my Lord, that You may be pleased.'*

[20:85] *He said, 'Indeed, We tried your people after you, and the Samaritan led them astray.'*

[20:86] *Thereupon Moses returned to his people, angry and sad. He said, 'O my people, did not your Lord promise you a fair promise? Did the period seem too long for you, or did you desire that wrath should become incumbent against you from your Lord, and so you broke your tryst with me?'*

[20:87] *They said, 'We did not break our tryst with you of our own accord, but we were laden with the burdens of the people's ornaments, and we cast them, and so did the Samaritan cast.'*

[20:88] *Then he produced for them a calf, a [mere] body with a low. And they said, 'This is your God and the God of Moses: so he forgot.'*

[20:89] *Did they not see that it did not reciprocate their words, nor did it have any power over hurt for them or any benefit?*

[20:90] *And Aaron had certainly said to them beforehand, 'O my people, you are only being tested thereby! But truly your Lord is the Compassionate, so follow me and obey my command.'*

[20:91] *They said, 'We will not cease to cling to it until Moses returns to us.'*

[20:92] *He said, 'O Aaron, what held you back when you saw them going astray,* [20:93] *that you did not follow me? Did you then disobey my command?'*

[20:94] *He said, 'O son of my mother, do not clutch my beard or my head! Indeed, I feared that you would have said, "You have caused division among the Children of Israel and you did not wait for my word."'*

[20:95] *He said, 'And what have you to say, O Samaritan?'*

[20:96] *He said, 'I perceived what they did not perceive, so I seized a handful from the track of the messenger and threw it* [in]. *Thus my soul prompted me.'*

[20:97] *Said he, 'Begone! It shall be yours* [as your lot] *throughout life to say, "Do not touch* [me]*!" And indeed there will be a tryst for you, which you will not fail to keep. Now look at your god to whom you remained clinging! We will surely burn it and then into the waters scatter* [the ashes].]

The meaning of all this on the literal level is that when Moses (may God grant him peace) was honoured with the station of communion with the Almighty and granted the unveiling of the Attributes, and sent to free the Israelites and guide them to the truth, he was promised a Divine Law by which he could rule his people. Therefore, he placed Aaron in charge of his people and went off to meditate in solitude, [but this was] before they had become firm in their faith and attained the certitude required for their total adherence to the truth. The affair of the golden calf was his chastisement for this, despite how he was motivated purely by a yearning to see God, because it was not the right time for him to leave the perfecting of his people to another. [This was so] since the task of perfecting them with gnostic certitude and intellectual perfection would be an affirmation of his solid footing in obedience and deference to the divine command, which was necessary for his ascent. Moses proffered the excuse that his people were following him in the religion, although their conduct was not yet based on the foundations of certitude, and that he had only been hasty in order to seek the station of divine contentment, meaning total annihilation in the Attributes: that is, mastery of the station of manifestation by the Attributes, wherein takes place the communion with God.

Q. 20:91

The reason God tested them with the Samaritan was to differentiate those who were ready for the perfection of detachment from those who were unprepared because of their immersion in materiality, such that they could perceive only tangible things and had no cognisance of detached intellectual matters. Thus, they said, *'We did not break our tryst with you of our own accord'*: that is, 'It was not that our disposition commanded us so that we left off freely based on our own opinion.' They were slaves by nature with no opinions or dispositions of their own; they did not choose, but rather were led by nature, shackled by their own materialism with no path to follow other than blind imitation and action, bereft of realisation and knowledge. The Samaritan was able to enthral them with a talisman of precious metal because of how the love of gold was such a fundamental part of their nature, as their souls were base and attracted to the gold-nature. This archetypal form manifested in it because of the natural correspondence, and this was an instance of the intermixing of the heavenly and terrestrial faculties. Hence, he said, '*I perceived what they did not perceive*,' referring to the sciences of nature and mathematics on which are based the sciences of talismans and symbols, '*so I seized a handful from the track of the messenger*.' This is said to refer to the dust in the tracks left by Ḥayzūm, the horse of life upon which Gabriel rides. In other words, from that which connected with the tracks of the universal heavenly animal soul, tamed for the active intellect and under its control, carrying its attributes and serving as its mount. [This is] so that it can ascend upon it and its influence can reach the elemental natures, lower celestial bodies and those other places by means of which its influences reach material things, which react to it according to their propensities and receive the unusual states which are akin to the dust in the tracks of its mount; '*and threw it*': that is, 'I threw it onto the molten substance cast into the configuration of the calf.' This was from the temptations of the evil satanic soul.

Q. 20:97

So, in his anger, Moses exclaimed to him, '*Begone!*' The reason why divine chastisement is occasioned by the angering of the prophets and saints is that they are the manifestations of the Attributes of God, so anyone who angers them will incur the wrath of God and be damned in this life and the next, and punished with everlasting torment, and suffer the consequences of their actions. The particular nature of the Samaritan's chastisement—namely that he was never again to be touched—was the consequence of how he distanced himself from the truth by inviting others to falsehood, and the result of the curse Moses laid upon him when he thwarted his plot and did away with his scheme.

On the level of spiritual correspondence, the meaning of this passage is that when the heart is granted unveiling and attracted by the spiritual struggle and journey, and attains perfection of knowledge by unveiling and not by acquisition, it lays itself open to rebuke from the Real when it is too hasty in seeking direct witnessing and presence, and thereby overlooks the dictates of the Divine Law and the spiritual struggle. It must then be redirected towards work and effort in order to preside over the faculties so that the station of rectitude can be attained; for the Aaron of the intellect, which is its vicegerent, is not strong enough to govern its people—the spiritual and corporeal faculties—and guide them, support them and bolster them without effort, struggle and consistent adherence to obedience and correct action. In such a situation, the Samaritan of the egocentric faculties will stir up the senses and kindle in them the flame of love for passions, and then cast upon this fire something of the assistances of fate, according to the particular circumstances: that is, those which have been affected by the influence of the animal soul, which is the horse of life. Through this, its nature will take on the form of the calf cast in the mould of materiality, whose only desires are eating and drinking and whose only interests are pleasure and passion, with no concern for the aforementioned work, effort and selflessness. Thus, the spirit of caprice will be breathed into it and it will come to life, gain strength and cry out with a low, and all the faculties will worship it and take it as a god. Every time the intellect aided by the light of the heart attempt to alert it to its error and delusion, and call it back to the truth and to adherence and obedience to intellectual reason, it will disobey.

Q. 20:97

This will go on until finally the heart returns to it enlightened by the light of truth and aided by the assistance of holiness, angered for the sake of God and aghast at its error and its religious confusion. The heart will rebuke it and chastise it with the tongue of the self-reproaching soul, and remind it of God's promises and warnings and of the long-held covenant with the Lord according to the dictates of creation, and of how it has fallen from its innate disposition. It will inspire it with fear for how it has incurred the wrath of God by forsaking this covenant and breaking its promise, after it acknowledged His lordship at the covenant of innate disposition. Yet these words will have no effect on it because by then it will be a captive of caprice, obedient only to the power of delusion, heading willingly to its own ruin. The only way to save it will be to break the materialistic nature with the hammer of spiritual struggle, and burn it with the fire of effort; and then blow away its ashes with the winds of divine mercy which, when they blow upon it, scatter it into the waters of primordial matter and render it lifeless and motionless.

This occurs after the intellectual power changes upon following the heart and accompanying it to the secret of correct orientation, by guiding the faculties towards nature and grasping them by the head to turn them to their usual direction which follows the spirit by the influence of the light upon it, until they react and are influenced by the rays of holiness and the light of divine guidance. The beard by which it grasps them is their masculine nature, which was turned downwards towards its lower aspect, towards the animal faculties. It pulls them towards itself, upwards in the direction of the presence of truth and the realm of holiness in which it resides. Strengthened by divine aid and lordly power, it influences them and brings them back to obedience of the command of the Real and the authority of the heart, and rescues them from the domination of estimation and fancy.

Aaron's excuse symbolises how the intellect that is not enlightened by the light of guidance and aided by the rule of the Divine Law is not powerful enough to protect the faculties and resist delusion and caprice, and only leads them further into confusion, and hence to ruin. When the light of the heart and the intellect becomes ascendant and totally overpowers the nature so that rectitude on the path is attained, the faculty of estimation is defeated and banished so that it is rendered unable to touch any of the faculties with its deluding influence, nor does any faculty accept its temptations. It becomes accursed and banished and cries out, 'Do not touch me!' There will assuredly be a tryst for it, a limit and a station beyond which it cannot transgress. It seeks to dominate and overpower, planting its lies and deceits in minds and seeking to poison desires. This is the station of rectitude for God and the upholding of the duties of servitude to God. It is utterly essential for the affirmation of Oneness (*tawḥīd*) and the attainment of the stations of detachment and inner solitude, which is why He then said:

Q. 20:98

[20:98] *Indeed, your God is the One God, than whom there is no other god*: for until this point is reached the spiritual wayfarer is praying towards two *qiblas*, and his worship is a constant back-and-forth between two directions, and he holds to two gods. *He embraces all things in [His] knowledge*: upon this, affirmation of Oneness is realised in a practical sense and His knowledge's encompassing of all things and their bounds and limits becomes manifest, so that every faculty stands by the light and power of the Real in its proper place of worship and obedience to Him, seeking refuge with Him from its own strength and power, worshipping Him to the utmost of its ability, witnessing Him, and acknowledging His lordship according to the knowledge of Him which He has granted it.

[20:99] *Thus, We relate to you some stories of what is past* of the states and stations of the wayfarers who went before you, to strengthen your heart and make you all the firmer in the station of rectitude, as you were commanded; *and We have given you from Ourselves a Reminder* of something greater still: a reminder of the Essence that whelms all the levels of the affirmation of Oneness.

[20:100] *Whoever turns away from it* by turning to the side of baseness and the influence of crude nature and I-ness, *he shall indeed on the Day of* the Minor *Resurrection bear a burden* of these heavy material forms and the sins of attachments to primordial substrata.

[20:101] [*Therein abiding. And evil for them on the Day of Resurrection is that burden!*]

[20:102] *The day the Trumpet is blown,* the day life is breathed into the trumpet of corporeality when the spirits are restored to their bodies, *and We shall assemble the criminals (mujrimīn),* those who clung to material forms (*ajrām*), *on that day bruised:* that is, blind with milky eyes, or with bruised and ugly appearances that would make pigs and apes look seemly in comparison.

[20:103] [*They will whisper to one another, 'You have tarried only ten nights.'*

[20:104] *We know very well what they will say, when the most just of them in the way will say, 'You have tarried only a day':*] they will whisper because of their extreme fear, or because they are unable to speak, and they will deem the life of this world to have been so short because of how quickly it was over. The more intelligent among them will be the ones who deem it the shortest.

Q. 20:100

[20:105] *They will question you concerning the mountains:* that is, the physical beings. *Say: 'My Lord will scatter them [as ashes]* with the winds of temporal happenings, ashes and scraps, and then dust scattered about the earth with no remnants or traces. Or it may refer to temporal beings, in general, in which case it means that He will scatter them with divine breezes from the source of Unity.

[20:106] *'Then He will leave them* at the Major Resurrection *a level hollow* of pure unitary being.

[20:107] *'You will see therein neither [crookedness nor any curving]':* there is no duality or otherness to impinge on its straightness.

[20:108] *On that day,* when the Major Resurrection arrives, *they will follow the Summoner,* meaning the Real, without Whom they have neither motion nor life; *there will be no deviation therein:* that is, there will be no straying from Him or moving out of His control, since He will have hold of their forelocks and lead them down a straight path. They will go along with the Real according to His will. *Voices will be hushed [before the Compassionate]* because His voice is the only voice, *so that you hear nothing but a faint shuffle* comparative to outward appearances. Or, when the Minor Resurrection

37

arrives, *they will follow the Summoner*, meaning Isrāfīl, the director of the fourth celestial sphere from which life emanates, and none whom he summons will deviate from him to anything other than what the divine wisdom dictates of attachment to him. *Voices will be hushed* that summon to anything other than that to which the Compassionate summons, *so that you hear nothing but a faint shuffle* of corrupt thoughts and hopes.

[20:109] *On that day intercession will not profit*: that is, the intercession of those whom they followed and loved in the world, taking them as exemplars and adhering to their guidance; *except* [*intercession*] *from him whom the Compassionate permits* with the propensity to receive it. The emanation of the perfect souls to which imperfect souls turn with desire and hope is dependent on their propensity to receive it with purity, which is the meaning of divine permission; *and whose word He approves*: that is, for whom He approves an influence that is suited to those for whom they intercede. Thus, intercession depends on two things: the power of the intercessor to influence, and the ability of the person interceded for to receive it and be influenced.

Q. 20:109

[20:110] *He knows* both sides: *what is before them* of the ability to receive with intrinsic preparedness and the illuminating influence of the intercessor, *and* [*what is*] *behind them* of the obstacles that arise from the side of the body and its faculties and the wicked forms that remove intrinsic receptiveness, or the preparations that are attained by its means through self-purification according to the practical intellect.

[20:111] *And faces*—meaning all beings in their entirety—*shall be humbled before the Living, the Eternal Sustainer*, all of them subjects of His domain dwelling beneath His power and might, given life and sustenance by Him alone, not by themselves or anything else; *and he will certainly have failed* and fallen from the light of His mercy and the intercession of the intercessors [*who carries* [*the burden of*] *evildoing*]: doing evil against himself by failing to be prepared for it and by sullying the purity of his innate disposition, so that his receptiveness to illumination is erased by the blackening and darkening of his face.

[20:112] *But whoever does righteous deeds* by self-purification and adornment, *being a believer* with true faith, [*shall fear neither wrong, nor injustice*]: he shall not fear the loss of any of the attendant perfections, nor the denial of any of his rights as merited by his intrinsic preparedness of that level.

[20:113] [*Thus, We have revealed it as an Arabic Qur'ān, and We have distributed in it* [*statements*] *of threats,*] *so that they may fear* by self-purification, *or it may arouse in them a remembrance* by adornment.

[20:114] *So exalted be God, [the King, the Truth:]* infinitely sublime and magnificent such that none can know His true measure or thwart His command in His kingdom, which is ascendant over all things, directing them by His will and power and according to His justice which affords each person their right, according to His wisdom.

And do not hasten [with the Qur'ān] before [its revelation is completed for you, and say, 'My Lord, increase me in knowledge']: do not hasten when the yearning stirs up within you to experience the reception of intimate divine knowledge from the treasure-trove of unification, before He has ordained that it be sent to you and reach you, for the descent of knowledge and wisdom is determined by your ascent through the levels of preparedness. Never stop seeking and hoping for emanations, for they are infinite, and search for more of it by increased self-purification, ascent and adornment. Increase is sought only through the prayer of the state and the expression of personal preparedness, and cannot be hastened by requests and petitions before it can be received. Whenever you learn something new, your preparedness will rise to what is higher and more hidden than it.

Q. 20:114

[20:115] *[And We made a covenant with Adam before, but he forgot, and We did not find in him any constancy.*

[20:116] *And when We said to the angels, 'Prostrate before Adam!' so they prostrated, except Iblīs: he refused.*

[20:117] *Then We said, 'Adam, indeed this is an enemy of yours and of your wife. So do not let him cause you both to be expelled from the Garden, so that you then toil:]* the story of Adam and its interpretation has been discussed several times already.

[20:118] *'It is indeed [assured] for you that you will neither be hungry therein nor go naked*: for becoming detached from the adornment of the material in the spiritual world prevents one from being exposed to the clash of opposites (*aḍdād*), and from adorning oneself in a way that leads to corruption, so that the soul can enjoy the attainment of its true desire, safe from loss and deprivation.

[20:119] *['And it is indeed [assured] for you neither to be thirsty therein, nor to suffer the sun.'*

[20:120] *Then Satan whispered to him, saying, 'O Adam, shall I guide you to the Tree of Immortality, and a kingdom that does not waste away?'*

[20:121] *So both of them ate of it, and their shameful parts were exposed to them, and they began to piece together onto themselves leaves of the Garden. And Adam disobeyed his Lord and so he erred.*

[20:122] *Thereafter his Lord chose him, and relented to him, and guided him.*

[20:123] *He said, 'Go down both of you from it all together, some of you being enemies of others. Yet if there should come to you guidance from Me, then whoever follows My guidance shall not go astray, neither shall he be miserable.*]

[20:124] *But whoever disregards My remembrance* by directing himself towards the lower world through the inclination of I-ness, [*his shall be a straitened life*] because of his dominant avarice and selfishness. The one who turns away from the Real does so because his soul strays and is attracted towards worldly delights and material wants, due to how seemly they appear to it. Hence, he becomes inordinately engrossed and infatuated with them, because of the strength of his love for them through natural affinity and participation in darkness and inclination towards the lower world. Thus, he becomes more and more obsessed with them and protective of them; and the more he gets, the more avaricious he is for them. This is the meaning of 'a straitened life'. One of the Sufis said that whenever someone turns away from the remembrance of his Lord, he becomes darkened and suspicious about his own provision. The one who is mindful of Him, on the contrary, is always certain about his provision and reliant on Him, and so is comfortable in his life, spending what he has and relying on his Lord for what he does not have. *And on the Day of* the Minor Resurrection, *We shall bring him to the assembly, blind* to the light of the Real, as He says elsewhere: *And whoever was blind in this* [life] *will be blind in the Hereafter* [Q. 17:72].

[20:125] [*He shall say, 'My Lord, why have you brought me to the assembly blind, though I used to see?'*

[20:126] *He will say, 'So it is. Our signs came to you, but you forgot them; and so today you will be forgotten'*:] his denial of his own blindness will be voiced by his intrinsic preparedness and the primordial light in him, which will deny his blindness caused by his ingrained love for baseness and his soul's passion for material iniquity and disregard of the clear signs and shining lights that will cause God to turn away from him and leave him in that state.

[20:127] [*And so We requite him who is prodigal and believes not in the signs of his Lord.*] *And the chastisement of the Hereafter is more terrible and more enduring* than the straitened life in this world, because it is spiritual and eternal.

[20:128] [*Is it not a guidance to them how many We destroyed before them of generations amid* [the ruins of] *whose dwelling-places they walk? Surely in that there are signs for people of sense.*]

[20:129] *And but for a decree that had already preceded from your Lord,* [*it would have been an inevitability and a specified term*]: that is, had there not been a decree that this community would never be subjected to mass extinction or chastisement in this world because their prophet was the Prophet of Mercy, as He says, *But God was not about to chastise them, while you were among them* [Q. 8:33].

[20:130] *So be patient* through God *with what they say*: for you can see that they are only acting out what God has destined for them, trapped in the prison of His omnipotence and His plot for them; *and make glorifications [by praising your Lord].* Purify your soul by detaching it from its attributes and taking on the Attributes of your Lord, for their manifestation upon you is the true praise, *before the rising of the sun* of the Essence in the state of annihilation, *and before its setting* by being veiled when the attributes of the soul reappear in the station of the heart when the Attributes manifest, for glorifying God there erases the attributes of the heart, *and in the watches of the night*, the times when the darkening and variegating attributes of the soul are dominant, *and make glorifications* by self-purification *at either side of the day* of the spirit's shining forth upon the heart with purity, *that perhaps you may [be pleased and] reach the station of contentment*, which is the perfection and culmination of the station of the manifestation of the Attributes.

Q. 20:130

[20:131] *And do not extend your glance [towards what We have given to some pairs among them to enjoy, [as] the flower of the life of this world that We may try them thereby]*: do not turn your eyes towards the soul's variegations and manifestation through inclination towards worldly delights, for they are the images of the tribulation of the worldly folk. *And your Lord's provision* of realities, other-worldly mysteries and spiritual illuminations *is better and more enduring*.

[20:132] *And bid your family*—the spiritual and egocentric faculties—*to prayer* of presence, meditation, submission and obedience, *and be steadfast in [the maintenance of] it* through spiritual struggle and unveiling. *We do not ask [of you any provision]* from the lower realm, such as sensory perfections and egocentric experiences. *We provide you* from the higher realm with spiritual mysteries and holy realities, *and the [best] ending*, the one that truly matters and is worthy of being called 'an ending', because it is detached of bodily adornments and egocentric forms, *[will be in favour of God-fearing]*.

[20:133] *[And they say, 'Why does he not bring us a sign from his Lord?']* *Has there not come to them the clear proof of what is in the former scrolls* of realities, wisdoms and matters of certain gnosis recorded in the heavenly tablets and the sublime spirits? And God (Exalted is He) knows best.

41

21
THE PROPHETS
SŪRAT AL-ANBIYĀ'

In the Name of God, the Compassionate, the Merciful

[21:1] *Nigh has drawn for people their reckoning* at the Minor Resurrection. Indeed, if they recognised the Resurrection, they would be certain of their reckoning right now; *yet they are heedless, disregardful.*

[21:2] [*There does not come to them any new reminder from their Lord, but they listen to it as they play* [21:3] *with their hearts preoccupied. And they are secret in* [*their*] *conference,* [*they*] *the evildoers: 'Is this other than a* [*mortal*] *human being like yourselves? Will you then take* [*to*] *sorcery, even though you are able to see?'*

[21:4] *He said, 'My Lord knows the words in the heavens and the earth, and He is the Hearer, the Knower.'*

[21:5] *Nay but they say, 'A muddle of nightmares. Nay, he has fabricated it; nay, he is a poet! So let him bring us a sign, such as was sent to the ancients.'*

[21:6] *No town before them ever believed of those that We destroyed. Would they then believe?*

[21:7] *And We sent none before you other than men to whom We revealed. Ask the People of the Remembrance if you do not know.*

[21:8] *And We did not make them bodies that did not eat food, and they were not immortal.*

[21:9] *Then We fulfilled to them the promise. So We delivered them and whomever We would, and We destroyed the prodigal.*

[21:10] *Now We have sent down* [*as revelation*] *to you a Book in which there is the remembrance that is yours. Will you not understand?*

[21:11] *And how many did We destroy of towns that had been wrongdoing, and brought forth another people after it!*

[21:12] *And when they felt Our might, behold, they ran away from it.*

[21:13] *'Do not run* [*away*]! *Return to the opulence which you were given to enjoy and your dwelling-places, that perhaps you might be asked.'*

[21:14] *They said, 'O woe to us! We have indeed been doing wrong.'*

[21:15] *So that remained their cry until We made them as reaped [crops], stilled.*

[21:16] *And We did not create the heaven and the earth and all that is between them in play.*

[21:17] *Had We desired to find some diversion, We would have found it with Ourselves, were We to do [so]*: that is, had We wanted to create beings that simply blinked in and out of existence, as was said, *We die and we live, and nothing but time destroys us* [Q. 45:24], We would have easily done so, but this would have been contrary to wisdom and reality, and so We did not create them.

[21:18] *Nay, but We hurl the truth* with certitude based on proof and inspiration *against* belief based on *falsehood, and it obliterates it, and behold, it vanishes. And for you, there shall be woe*, perdition, *for what you ascribe*, meaning the denial of the Resurrection. Or it means: We hurl the essential manifestation at the Major Resurrection, which is the affirmed unchanging truth, against the falsehood of these ephemeral beings; and it overpowers it and makes it into pure nothingness, so that it is utterly annihilated. Thus, it is made plain that everything is real, and His affair is serious, and there is no falsehood or diversion; and you shall come to ruin and total annihilation *for what you ascribe* of the affirmation of the existence of other-than-God and the attribution of quality, act and influence to it.

Q. 21:14

[21:19] *[And to Him belongs whoever is in the heavens and the earth, and those who are near Him do not disdain to worship Him, nor do they weary.*

[21:20] *They glorify [Him] night and day, and they do not falter.*

[21:21] *Or have they chosen gods from the earth who resurrect?*

[21:22] *Had there been in [either of] them gods other than God,] the two would have surely deteriorated*, because Unity (*waḥda*) ensures that things endure, while multiplicity ensures that they deteriorate. Consider how everything that has a particular distinction that makes it unique among all other things is defined by that distinction, such that if it did not possess it, it would not exist. This attests to His Unity (*waḥdāniyya*), as a poet said, 'In everything there is a sign of Him, / Showing how He is the One (*Wāḥid*).' The balance by which the heavens and the earth were brought into existence is the shadow of Unity in the world of multiplicity. Were there not a configuration of Unity in composite beings, such as the balance of humours, they would not exist; and if that form were removed, they would deteriorate immediately. *So glory be to God, the Lord of the Throne*: that is, may He be declared transcendent in the emanation upon all things by His lordship of the Throne from which this emanation descends upon all beings, *above what they ascribe* to Him of the possibility of multiplicity.

[21:23] [*He shall not be questioned about what He does, but they shall be questioned.*

[21:24] *Or have they chosen besides Him gods? Say: 'Bring your proof. This is the Remembrance of those with me and the Remembrance of those before me. Nay, but most of them do not know the truth, and so they are disregardful.'*

[21:25] *And We did not send any messenger before you but We revealed to him that 'There is no god except Me, so worship Me.'*

[21:26] *And they say, 'The Compassionate has taken a son.' Glory be to Him! Nay, but they are [merely] servants who are honoured.*

[21:27] *They do not [venture to] speak before Him and they act according to His command.*]

[21:28] *He knows what is before them*: that is, what is ahead of them from the universal knowledge affirmed in the Mother of Books, which contains all knowledge of detached entities from the inhabitants of the realms of power and dominion; *and what is behind them* of the knowledge of individual beings and events affirmed in the lowest heaven; so how could their knowledge go beyond the extent of His, or their actions precede His command? *And they do not intercede except for him with whom He is satisfied*, meaning him whom He knows to be worthy of intercession by receiving it, because of the purity of his preparedness and his soul's preparedness for the light of divine domination; *and they, [for awe of Him, are apprehensive]*: in awe of the glories of His countenance and in fear, apprehension and submission to the lights of His grandeur.

Q. 21:23

[21:29] [*And should any of them say, 'I am a god besides Him', such a one We will requite with Hell. Thus We requite wrongdoers.*]

[21:30] *Have they not realised,* [those who disbelieve,] being veiled from the truth, *that the heavens and the earth were closed together,* fused in the single primordial substratum and material body, *and then We parted them* with the differentiation of forms, or that the heavens of the spirits and the earth of the body were fused together in the form of a single droplet, and then We parted them with the differentiation of bodies and spirits; *and We made, of water every living thing?* In other words, We created every animal from a single droplet. [*Will they not then believe?*]

[21:31] *And We set in the earth* of the body *firm mountains* of bones, *lest it should shake with them,* lest they conflict with each other, going and coming without harmony, so that you would not be able to stand independently with them; *and We set in them ravines,* veins and nerves *as roads* to facilitate the senses and all the faculties, *that perhaps they may be guided* by those senses and roads to the signs of God and so recognise Him.

[21:32] *And We made the heaven* of the intellect *a roof raised above them, preserved*: from change, forgetfulness and error; *and yet of the signs thereof*, their proofs and arguments, *they are disregardful.*

[21:33] *And He it is Who created the night* of the soul *and the day* of the intellect, which is *the sun* of the spirit *and the moon* of the heart, *each in an orbit*, a lofty position, boundary and level in the heavens of the spiritual beings (*rūḥāniyyāt*), *swimming*, travelling towards God.

[21:34] [*And We did not assign to any human being before you immortality. What, if you [are fated to] die, will they be immortal?*

[21:35] *Every soul shall taste death, and We will try you with ill and good as an ordeal. And then unto Us you shall be brought back.*

[21:36] *And whenever the disbelievers see you, they only take you in derision: 'Is this the one who mentions your gods?' And yet when it comes to the mention of the Compassionate, they are disbelieving.*]

[21:37] *Humanity was created of haste*, for the soul, which is the root of this creation, is always swinging and crashing around and is never constant in any one state, and so it is naturally hasty. If it were not, it would be unable to travel and ascend from one state to another, for the spirit is always constant; it is by its connection to the soul that the heart exists, and by the two of them it is given balance in its movement. As long as a man is in the station of the soul and the light of the spirit and the heart has not overcome him to impart tranquillity and peace, he will always be hasty by nature. [*Assuredly, I shall show you My signs, so do not demand that I hasten.*

Q. 21:32

[21:38] *And they say, 'When will this promise be [fulfilled], if you are truthful?'*]

[21:39] *If those [who disbelieved]*, veiled from the Compassionate of universal emanation and from the total resurrection of all, [*only knew of the time when they shall not [be able to] ward off the Fire from their faces, nor from their backs,*] when the chastisement will whelm them from all sides by the command of the Compassionate of encompassing knowledge and unified command, and they will not be able to prevent it from in front of them in the direction facing the soul tormented with the fire of divine power and total deprivation from spiritual lights and human perfection, nor from in front of them in the direction of the body tormented by the fire of physical forms, egocentric scorpions and serpents, material pollutants and bodily pains, *nor shall they be helped* by compassionate assistances, because of the denseness of their veil and the severity of their doubts when they were hasty.

[21:40] [*Nay, but it shall come upon them suddenly, dumbfounding them, and they shall not be able to ward it off, nor shall they be granted any respite.*

[21:41] *And verily messengers before you were derided, but those who mocked them were encircled by that which they used to deride.*

[21:42] *Say: 'Who can guard you by night and day from the Compassionate?' Nay, but of the Remembrance of their Lord they are disregardful.*

[21:43] *Or is it that they have gods to defend them besides Us? They cannot help themselves, nor shall they be protected from Us.*

[21:44] *Nay, but We provided [comforts] for these and their fathers until life lasted long for them.] Do they not see*—[in other words,] is their heedlessness so wanton that they do not see—*how We visit the land* of the body with old age, *diminishing it at its edges*, such as hearing, sight and the other faculties, or the earth of the waking soul directed towards the Real and mindful of the lights of the Attributes as We lessen its own attributes and faculties? *Are they the ones who will prevail*, or will it be Us?

[21:45] *Say: 'I warn you only by the Revelation.' But the deaf do not hear the call when they are warned.*

[21:46] *And if a whiff [of the chastisement of your Lord were to touch them they would indeed say, 'O woe for us! Indeed, we were doing evil'*: this means] a whiff of the lordly breezes in the form of chastisement: that is, from the hidden subtleties, as the Commander of the Believers [ʿAlī] (may God grant him peace) said, 'Glory be to Him Whose wrath upon His enemies is severe despite the vastness of His mercy, and whose mercy to His allies is vast despite the severity of His wrath.' He lifts from them the veil of heedlessness that built up over their long indulgence, which was a curse in the guise of a blessing, a subtle overpowering to wake them up and alert them to their wrongdoing in how they turned away from truth and wallowed in falsehood.

[21:47] *And We shall set-up the just balances*: the balance of God is His justice, which is the shadow of His Unity and its necessary Attributes, by means of which the heavens of spirits and the earth of bodies came into being and were sustained; if not for it, existence would not remain intact. When it enveloped all things, every being was marked by its justice according to its state and its possibilities and became, relative to every individual and indeed to everything, a distinct balance so that there were as many balances as there were things. All of them are parts of the absolute balance, which is why He referred to the *balances* (mawāzīn)[1] as *just* (qisṭ),[2] by way of

---

1 In the plural.
2 In the singular.

alluding to it; for they are all the single absolute justice, and reality is not multiple even though outward appearances are. He made this an expression of the manifestation of its implication, which will occur *on the Day of* the Minor *Resurrection* for the veiled one and the Major Resurrection for those who experience it.

And no soul shall be wronged in any way, because all the good that it has done will be represented in the scale of good deeds, which is the position of the spirit relative to the heart, and all the evil that it has done will be placed in the scale of bad deeds, which is the position of the soul relative to it. The heart is the beam of the scale. It is said that the scale of good deeds will be loaded with bright white stones, while the scale of bad deeds will be loaded with dark black stones; but at the Reckoning the heavy side will go up and the light side down, the reverse of how it works with a physical scale, because there the heavy side is the victorious and important one which endures with God, while the light side is the defeated ephemeral one which has no value with God and no importance. Nothing that a soul has done will be omitted, *and even if it be the weight of a [single] mustard seed, [We shall produce it]*. This is what is meant by the saying, 'God will reckon His creatures more swiftly than the bleat of a lamb.' *[And We suffice as reckoners.]*

Q. 21:48

[21:48] *And verily We gave the Moses* of the heart *and the Aaron* of the intellect, or according to their literal meanings, *the Criterion*, the discriminating unveiling knowledge which is called 'the discerning intellect', *and an illumination*, a perfect light of spiritual visions, *and remembrance*, a reminder and a counsel, *for those who are wary of God*: those whose souls have been purified from pollutants and veiling attributes, so that the lights of the goodly things of magnificence shine forth from their hearts upon their souls to cleanse and purify them, which engenders fear in times of solitude before arriving at the station of heart-presence:

[21:49] *[Those who fear their Lord in concealment,] and who, on account of the Hour, [are apprehensive]*: that is, who view the Major Resurrection with apprehension and expectation of its arrival because of the power of their certitude; for apprehension is only felt by someone who is expecting something to happen. This means: We gave them [Moses and Aaron], in the station of the heart, the knowledge to discern between truth and falsehood from the universal realities and gnostic truths; and in the station of the spirit, We gave them the guiding light that outshines all other lights; and in the station of the soul and the level of the breast, We gave them a reminder of the counsels, teachings and Divine

47

Laws from the particular sciences which benefit those travellers who are prepared to receive them.

[21:50] *And this is a [blessed] Remembrance*: filled with goodness and blessing and encompassing all three matters, and also adding to them essential unveiling and true witnessing in the station of Ipseity, the source of the Unification of Unity (*jamᶜ al-aḥadiyya*) and the summation of the totality of elegant speech, surrounding all witnessing and wisdom; for the meaning of 'blessing' (*baraka*) is 'growth and addition'.

[21:51] *And verily We had given the Abraham* of the spirit *his rectitude* that was specific to him and that suited his kind, namely guidance to the affirmation of Essential Oneness (*al-tawḥīd al-dhātī*) and the station of witnessing and intimate friendship, *before*: that is, before the level of the heart and the intellect, having precedence over them in honour and glory; *and We were Aware of him*: that is, none but Us know his perfection and virtue because of how lofty his stature is.

Q. 21:50

[21:52] *When he said to his father*, the universal soul, *and his people*, the rational souls both heavenly and otherwise, *'What are these images*, these intelligible forms (*al-ṣuwar al-maᶜqūla*) from the realities of minds and things, and the identities of beings dwelling within them, *to which you [constantly] cleave?'* insisting on imagining them. This was when he ascended from the station of the Holy Spirit and passed through the veils of light to the field of Essential Oneness, as he (may God grant him peace) said elsewhere: *'I am innocent of what you associate. Verily I have turned my face to Him Who originated the heavens and the earth; a ḥanīf*¹ [Q. 6:78–79]. It was also in this station that he said to Gabriel (may God grant him peace), 'For you I have no need.'

[21:53] *They said, 'We found our fathers*, our causes from the realms that preceded all souls from the inhabitants of the realm of divine power, *worshipping them'* by maintaining their presence in their beings and never being distracted from them.

[21:54] *[He said, 'Truly you and your fathers have been] in manifest error'*: veiled from the truth by a veil of light, falling short of reaching the Essence Itself and stopping in the isthmuses of the Attributes, not guided to the reality of Unity and not immersed in the sea of Ipseity.

[21:55] *[They said,] 'Do you bring us the truth, [or are you being frivolous]?'* In other words: was your coming to us in this way occasioned by the Real, so that the true speaker of your words was the Almighty Real, or did you

---

1 For a succinct explanation of a *ḥanīf*, see Kāshānī's commentary on Q. 16:120. [Ed.]

come of your own accord so that your words came only from yourself, and hence were mere frivolity with no reality to them? If you are upheld by the Real, walking His path and speaking His Words, then you have spoken the truth, and your words are real, and you have surpassed us, and we have fallen behind you. If you are only here of your own accord, then the opposite is true.

[21:56] *He said, 'Nay, but your Lord*—the one who came and spoke through Me, your Lord Who nurtures you with creation, sustenance, life, detachment, knowledge and teaching—*is the Lord of the heavens and the earth,* [*the One*] *Who originated them,* the Lord of all things Who brought them into existence, *and to that* fact—the fact that these are the Words of the Real, the Lord of all—*I am a witness.* In addition, this witnessing was the witnessing of lordship (*shuhūd al-rubūbiyya*) and creation, for otherwise he would not have said 'I', since essential witnessing (*shuhūd dhāti*) is pure annihilation wherein there is no recognition of the 'I' nor any duality. This duality, after the declaration that the One Who had come and spoken was the Real Himself Who created all things, indicates that this was a figurative substitution of identity.

Q. 21:56

[21:57] [*And, by God,*] *I shall devise* [*a stratagem*] *against your idols*: I shall erase the images of things and the substances of beings to whose creation, protection and control you have cleaved, and whose existence you have asserted, after you have gone away, [*with your backs turned'*] to the source of Essential Unity by turning to the multiplicity of attributes by the light of Oneness.

[21:58] *And so he reduced them,* with the awe of essential omnipotence and eye-witnessing, *to fragments,* ephemeral decaying pieces, [*all*] *except the principal one among them,* namely its essence which remained on the primordial certitude because of which the Friend of God was given that name, *that they might return to it* to receive the emanation from it and bathe in its light and knowledge, just as he had already done.

[21:59] *They,* the souls besotted with their minds, *said, 'Who has done this* act of insult and degradation *to our gods?* [who are] the objects of our passion and worship, by attributing them to veiled delusion and portraying them as being ephemeral as dust in the wind. In their horror at him and at what he had done, they said, *Indeed, he is an evildoer'*: one of those who violates the rights of plain objects of worship and their qualities and perfections, denying them and attributing them instead to the Real; or one of those who violates the rights of their own selves by effacing and overpowering them.

[21:60] *They said, 'We heard a young man* possessing all the chivalry and courage needed to overcome everything other than God, and [who was] generous with his soul and his possessions, *making [ill] mention of them*, speaking of their lack of power and perfection and attributing to them non-being and annihilation—*[he is called Abraham].'*

[21:61] *They said, 'Then bring him [before the people's eyes]*, in front of all the souls, *that they may testify'* and bear witness to his perfection and virtue, and learn from it.

[21:62] [*They said,*] *'So is it you who has done this [to our gods, O Abraham]?'* They meant this accusingly, for they had not yet recognised his perfection; for everything that souls can recognise is below the perfection of the minds with which they are besotted, and so they are veiled from his divine perfection, which ennobles him above them.

[21:63] *He said, 'Rather, it was this principal one among them who did it:* that is, I did not do it with my own individuality which makes me better than them, but rather with my reality and my ipseity which is nobler and greater than it. *So question them, if they can speak'* independently: that is, they have no speech, knowledge or existence in and of themselves, but only through God, besides whom there is no other god.

Q. 21:61

[21:64] *So they turned [thinking] to themselves*: with acknowledgement and surrender, recognising that a possibility has no being of its own, never mind any perfection; *and they said, 'Indeed, it is you who are the evildoers'* by attributing being and perfection to other-than-God, and not to Him.

[21:65] *Then they were turned on their heads* in shame at his own perfection and their deficiency, humiliated and yielding to him, [*and said*], *'You are certainly aware* with true God-gifted knowledge *that these [idols] cannot speak'* because they are annihilated; and as for us, we know only what God has allowed us to know. They acknowledged their deficiency just as they acknowledged Adam after first objecting to him, saying, *We know not except what You have taught us* [Q. 2:32].

[21:66] [*He said,*] *'Do you then worship, besides God*, and venerate in addition to Him, that which cannot benefit you in any way, nor harm you?* For only He can bring benefit and do harm.

[21:67] *'Fie on you [and what you worship besides God]! I* spurn your existence and the existence of your idols, and the existence of anything at all besides God. *Do you not comprehend* how there is no influencer, and no deity, besides God?'*

[21:68] [*They said,*] *'Burn him*: leave him to burn in the fire of passion that you first kindled by throwing those realities and gnostic sciences to him, which served as the kindling for that fire when he beheld the dominion of the heavens and the earth when God showed it to him, as He said, *And so We show Abraham the kingdom of the heavens and the earth* [Q. 6:75], and the radiation of the lights of Attributes and Names with the manifestation of beauty and majesty upon him behind the veils of your substances, which was the spark that lit that fire; *and stand by your gods*, the objects of your passion and worship in the emanation of those lights and the lighting of that fire, *if you are to do anything*': by the command of the Real.

[21:69] [*We said,*] *'O fire, be coolness* [*and safety for Abraham*]*!'* [Meaning] by the arrival to the state of annihilation, for the bliss of that arrival brings total divine peace and safety from the deficiency of temporality and the blight of imperfection and contingency in the substance of the fire of passion.

[21:70] *And they sought to outwit him*: by annihilating him and burning him; *but We made them the greater losers*: set below him in perfection and rank.

[21:71] *And We delivered him as well as* the *Lot* of the intellect by subsistence after annihilation through the gift of veridical existence, [and brought them] *to the land* of corporeal nature *which We have blessed* with practical fruitful perfections, beneficial beautiful character traits, Divine Laws and virtuous aptitudes, *for all peoples*: that is, for those who are ready to receive His emanation, nurture and guidance.

Q. 21:69

[21:72] *And We gave him* the *Isaac* of the heart to return to his station by perfecting his creation when he returned from the Real, *and* the *Jacob* of the soul approved and tested with tribulation, made tranquil with certitude and purity, *as a gift* illuminated with the light of the heart and born from it; *and each of them We made righteous* with rectitude and fixity in guidance.

[21:73] *And We made them leaders* of all the faculties and imperfect prepared souls, *guiding by Our command*, while the spirit guides by states, visions and lights, and the heart by mysteries, unveilings and secrets, and the soul by sublime character traits, interactions and courtesies. This is the meaning of His Words, *And We inspired in them the performance of good deeds and the maintenance of prayers and the payment of* zakāt, *and they used to worship Us* with affirmations of Oneness and true servitude in the station of detachment and solitude. That was the application of the outward Abraham onto its inner meaning, but it could also be interpreted another way which befits the words of the Prophet (may God grant him peace), 'I and ʿAlī were two lights, glorifying God and hymning His praises and His Unity. The angels glorified Him following our own glorification, and praised Him following our own praise, and extolled His Oneness following our own extolling. Then when Adam (may God grant him peace) was created, we moved to his brow, and from his brow to his loin, and then to Seth...' and so on. This interpretation is that the Abrahamic spirit (may God sanctify him) was perfected in the first level of the ranks of spirits, emanating their perfections to the farthest reaches of the dominion, healing their faults, breaking the idols of the substances of beings and the gods of essences and possibilities from matter and detached forms by the light of Oneness, unfolding the degrees of perfections, healing those who stopped with the Attributes and were veiled by other-than-God from the Essence; and so the Nimrod of the disobedient tyrannical soul and his people, its faculties, cast him with the trebuchet of the remembrance of power into the fire of the heat of the womb-nature. God made that fire cool and safe for him: that is, He made it a place of divine peace and freedom from blights. In other words, they placed the atom of his existence—the manifestation of his spirit—into the fire, and God saved him and bore him to the land of the body, which He had blessed for all peoples by His guidance to them and His perfecting care and nurture of them therein, by means of the knowledge and deeds which constituted their true provisions and their perfect attributes.

Q. 21:74

[21:74] *And to the* Lot *of the heart* We gave judgement and knowledge; and We delivered him from *the inhabitants of* the town *of the body* which had been committing *the* vileness *of errant passions.* Indeed, they were a folk of evil [people], immoral: by how they approached things from other than the commanded direction and did things contrary to how the Divine Law and the intellect prescribed them.

[21:75] *And We admitted him into Our mercy* of mercifulness and the station of the manifestation of the Attributes. *He was indeed one of the righteous* who act according to knowledge and adhere to rectitude.

[21:76] *And* the Noah *of the intellect* when he called before: from the direction of the foot of the heart, and requested from God the perfection he required. *And We responded to him*: as a consequence of the exhaustiveness of his perfection necessitated by his preparedness and his setting out to act; *and We delivered him* [*and his people*]: We delivered the faculties of holiness, contemplation, praise, and all the other intellectual faculties, *from the* [*great*] agony which was the existence of their perfections by power, for everything that is latent in a thing by power is agonising for it and it wishes for release by the manifestation and appearance of that thing through action. The stronger the preparedness, and the more complete the perfection of the latent thing, the greater the agony.

[21:77] *And We helped him against the people [who denied Our signs]*: the egocentric and corporeal faculties which denied the signs of rational matters and forbidden things. *They were indeed an evil people* who prevented him from attaining perfection and detachment and veiled him from lights by their denial, *so We drowned them* in the waters of the primordial ooze and the bottomless material ocean, *all of them*.

[21:78] *And the David* of the discursive intellect (*al-ʿaql al-naẓarī*), which is the station of the inner-heart, *and the Solomon* of the cognitive intellect (*al-ʿaql al-ʿilmī*), which is the station of the breast, *when they gave judgement concerning the tillage*: that is, concerning the perfections that were placed in the earth of preparedness, stored there in pre-eternity, planted in the innate disposition and destined to sprout at the emergence into manifestation and existence. *They gave judgement* with knowledge, action, contemplation and spiritual exertion to make it bloom and ripen, and to harvest it, *when strayed into it*, with corrupting influence in the dark of the night of the dominance of corporeal nature and egocentric attributes, *the sheep of a [certain] people*: the appetitive animal faculties; *and We were [witnesses] to their judgement* according to their states, for the judgement was by Our command, before Our sight, and according to Our will.

Q. 21:77

The David of the inner-heart judged according to the dictate of taste, ruling that the sheep of the base animal faculties be returned to the owners of the tillage from the spiritual faculties by right of ownership, so that they could slaughter them and deal death to them by conquering and overwhelming them, and then consuming them. The Solomon of the cognitive intellect judged according to the dictate of knowledge, ruling that the spiritual faculties be given charge of them so that they might benefit from their milk of beneficial knowledge, particular cognitions, and virtuous character traits and dispositions, and that they might nurture them with refinement and education, and that the owners of the sheep turn their efforts towards the soul and its animal faculties, such as anger, impulse, imagination, estimation and their ilk, by tilling and rectifying the earth of preparedness with acts of obedience, worship and spiritual discipline, according to Divine Laws, sublime character traits, courtesies, and all other manner of righteous deeds. By this, the tillage will flourish and reach the limits of perfection. Then the sheep can be returned to their owners when this perfection is attained, so that they can be protected, shepherded, led and refined in their animalistic actions by the virtue of temperance, and the tillage can be returned to its owners, the spirit and its faculties, in a state of verdure, flourishing with knowledge and wisdom, blooming with the flowers of gnostic sciences and realities and the lights of manifestations and witnessings. Thus, He then says:

[21:79] *And We gave understanding of this to Solomon*: for acting with piety and spiritual discipline according to the Divine Law and practical wisdom is a more direct way to attain perfection and put it into action than universal knowledge, contemplation, consideration, experiential realisation and unveiling. *And to each We gave judgement and knowledge*: for both of them were correct in their opinion, and practical and discursive wisdom and unveiling are both complementary in the pursuit of perfection, and together lead to the attainment of nobility. *And We disposed the mountains* of the body *to glorify* [*God*] *with* the *David* of the heart, with the tongues of their special natures by which they were commanded; and they were directed with him in their own particular way so that they did not disobey him or refuse him, or object to his commands, but rather went along with him and followed his instructions, subservient and obedient, having been trained and tamed to assent to his commands, and coached in the ways of obedience and worship; *and the birds* of the spiritual faculties *also* glorified with invocations and contemplations, flying in the air of the spirits of lights. *And We were* [*doers*], with the power to effect that subduing.

Q. 21:79

[21:80] *And We taught him the art of making garments for you*: garments of piety and God-fearing; for the strongest chain mail is piety, *to protect you against* the violence of the wild irascible faculties, and against the ascendancy of avarice, natural impulses and the satanic estimative faculties. *Will you then be thankful* and honour the right of this favour, by turning to the lordly presence with your entire being?

[21:81] *And for Solomon*: We subdued for the Solomon of the practical intellect, settled on the throne of the soul in the breast, *the wind* of caprice *to blow strongly—making its way* obediently *at his command, to the land* of the body trained with obedience and courtesy, *which We have blessed* with the blossoming of goodly character traits, virtuous dispositions and righteous deeds; *and We have knowledge of all things* regarding the means of perfection.

[21:82] *And* [*we subdued*] *of the devils* of estimation and imagination *some that dived for him* into the sea of primordial matter to extract the pearls of particular meanings, *and performed tasks other than that*: acts of composition, differentiation, construction, inflaming acquired inspirations, and the like. *And We were watchful over them*: protecting them from deviation, error, false insinuations and lies.

[21:83] *And the Job* of the tranquil soul which endured all manner of tribulations in spiritual discipline until it reached the perfection of self-purification through struggle, *when he called out to his Lord* in the midst of the intense suffering of total exertion and striving, '*Indeed, harm has befallen me*—namely weakness, exhaustion and incapacitation—*and You are the Most Merciful of the merciful*': in the giving of ease and relief.

[21:84] *So We responded to him* with relief of states after the toil of actions, heralding the perfection of tranquillity and the descent of divine peace, *and removed the harm* of spiritual discipline *that had befallen him* with the light of guidance, and We removed from him the darkness of suffering by allowing the radiant light of the heart to shine forth; *and We gave him [back] his family*, the egocentric faculties which We first conquered and slew with discipline and then revived with true life, *along with them [other children] the like of them*, the assistances of the spiritual faculties and the lights of the heart-attributes, showering them with the means of virtue of character and the states of beneficial particular knowledge, *as a mercy from Us and a reminder to worshippers*.

[21:85] [*And Ishmael and Idrīs and Dhū al-Kifl*—*all were of the patient.*

[21:86] *And We admitted them into Our mercy. Indeed, they were among the worthy.*]

Q. 21:84

[21:87] *And Dhū al-Nūn*, which is the spirit that has not yet reached the rank of perfection, *when he went off* by parting from physicality, *enraged* at his people—the egocentric faculties—because of how they were veiled and insisted on defying him and arrogantly refusing to obey him, *thinking that We had no power over him*: that is, that We would not use Our power on him by testing him with the tribulation that was meted out to him, or that We would not constrict him. So the whale of mercy swallowed him up because it was necessary that he connect to the body in order to fulfil Our wise purpose for him. *Then he cried out in the darknesses* of the three levels—namely physical nature, the vegetative soul and the animal soul—with the voice of preparedness: '*There is no god except You!* He proclaimed the affirmation of Essential Oneness, which was planted in him at the forming of the ancient covenant and the pledge of innate disposition, and then the declaration of transcendence that was attained at the first detachment in pre-eternity, saying, *Glory be to You!* Thereafter he confessed his deficiency and his unjust treatment of his people, saying, *I have indeed been one of the wrongdoers.*'

[21:88] *So We responded to him* with the grace of direction and illumination by the light of guidance towards arrival, *and delivered him [from the distress]* of being deficient and veiled, by the light of manifestation and the lifting of the veil; *and thus We deliver the believers* who have true and certain faith.

[21:89] *And the* Zachariah *of the guileless spirit removed of all knowledge, when he cried out to his Lord,* [*'My Lord, do not leave me without an heir,*] pleading for perfection with the voice of preparedness, and so was granted the John of the heart to invigorate him with knowledge, and complained about how he was alone and bereft of the heart's help in receiving knowledge and fulfilling his legacy, while still acknowledging that annihilation in God is better than practical perfection by saying, *And You are the best of inheritors,'* including the heart and all others.

[21:90] *So We responded to him, and gave him the* John *of the heart after healing his spouse, the soul which was barren because of its poor character traits and the domination of the darkness of nature over it, by beautifying its traits and dispelling the darkness that had rendered it barren,* [*and We restored* [*fertility to*] *his wife for him*]*. Indeed, they*—those perfected prophets—*would hasten to good works,* rushing towards the witnessings that constitute absolute goodness with their spirits, *and supplicate Us* to plead for unveilings with their hearts, *out of desire* for perfection *and in awe* and fear of deficiency, or out of desire for divine kindness and mercy in the station of the manifestations of the spirit, and in awe of divine omnipotence and might; *and they were submissive before Us* with their souls.

[21:91] *And the one who guarded* [*her virginity*]: the pure chaste soul prepared for worship, who guarded the virginity of her preparedness and the part of her inner being where the spirit influenced, by protecting it from the touches of the corporeal faculties within it; *so We breathed into her* [*of Our spirit*], of the influence of the Holy Spirit with the breath of true life, so that the Jesus of the heart could be born. *And We made her* [*and her son*], the heart, a clear sign (ʿalāma) and a plain guidance *for all the worlds* of the spiritual faculties and the prepared insight-seeking souls, to guide them to the truth and a straight path.

[21:92] *'Indeed, this is* [*your community, one community*]: the path leading to reality, the special path of Oneness reserved for those aforementioned prophets and your own path, O realised seekers, is one path wherein there is no crookedness, swerving or straying from the truth to any other, nor any inclination; *and I alone am your Lord,* so worship Me; single Me out for your worship and direction, and look not towards any other.

[21:93] *But they fragmented* [*their affair*]: those who were veiled and oblivious to the truth became divided, heedless to the affair of their religion, and made their religion into a fragmented thing *among themselves,* choosing the divergent paths that branched out in accordance with their various caprices; *all shall return to Us* regardless of what intent, path or direction they choose, and We shall requite them according to their deeds and their paths.

[21:94] *And whoever* [*performs righteous deeds* and] *is characterised by practical perfections*, *while he is* [*a believer*] with certain knowledge—his endeavour will be appreciated, not rejected, at the Intermediate Resurrection and the arrival at the station of innate disposition; *and We will indeed* [*write it down for him*]: We will depict the form of that endeavour in the book of his heart, so that when he is detached the lights of the Attributes will show upon him.

[21:95] [It is] forbidden (*mumtaniʿ*) *for any town* [*which We have destroyed*], whose destruction and ruin We have ordained in pre-eternity, that they should return to innate disposition after being veiled by the attributes of the soul at creation.

[21:96] *Until when* the *Gog* of the egocentric faculties *and the Magog* of corporeal faculties *are let loose* by the corruption of balance and the breakdown of order, *and they slide down* with ruin and erasure *from every slope* of the parts of the body which are their loci and established seats.

Q. 21:94

[21:97] *And the true promise* of the coming of the Minor Resurrection draws near with death, [*and behold the gaze of the disbelievers will be fixed:* '*O woe to us! Verily we were oblivious to this. Nay, but we were doing wrong*']: the gaze of the veiled ones will be frozen in terror and panic, and they will cry out with woe and anguish, confessing their wrongdoing and deficiency.

[21:98] '*Indeed, you and what you worship* [*besides God shall be fuel for Hell; and you shall come to it*']: those of you who worship aught but God are veiled by that thing from the truth, and shall be cast with the object of their worship, with which they stood, into one of the levels of Hell, made distant and deprived according to the level of that which they worshipped.

[21:99] [*Had these been gods, they would never have come to it, and they will all abide therein.*]

[21:100] *For them there will be groaning therein* of the pain of being veiled, the agony of the torment, the domination of the fires of passions, and the long length of the deprivation and separation; *and they will not hear in it* the Words of the Real and the angels, because of the denseness of the veil and the intense blockage of the heart's ears by the power of ignorance, just as they will not see the lights because of the intense obstruction of darkness and blindness of insight.

[21:101] *Indeed, those to whom [the promise of] the best reward* of felicity *went beforehand from Us,* and whose felicity We ordained in the primordial decree, *they will be kept away from it* because they are detached from ego-centric garbs and natural coverings.

[21:102] *They will not hear the faintest sound from it* because they will be on such a higher level than it, *and they will abide in what their souls*—their essences—*desired* of the three gardens, particularly witnessings in the gar-den of the Essence.

[21:103] *The Supreme Terror* of death at the Minor Resurrection *shall not grieve them,* nor will the manifestation of might and majesty at the Major Resurrection, *and the angels shall receive them* upon death with glad tidings, or at the awakening of the soul with peace and salvation, or at the Intermediate Resurrection and the true awakening with approval, or at the return to subsistence after annihilation in the state of rectitude with total felicity. [*'This is your day, the one which you were promised.'*]

Q. 21:101

[21:104] *The day when We shall roll up the heaven*: that is, they shall not be grieved by the day when We shall roll up the heaven of the soul and all that it contains of images of deeds and configurations of sublime character traits at the Minor Resurrection, *as the Scribe rolls up* the written scroll in order to keep what is written upon it preserved; or the heaven of the heart and what it contains of knowledge, attributes, and gnostic and rational sciences at the Intermediate Resurrection; or the heaven of the spirit and what it contains of knowledge from witnessings and self-disclosures at the Major Resurrection. *As We began the first creation, We shall repeat it* by the awakening at the second creation for the Minor, or by returning to innate disposition for the Intermediate, or by subsist-ence after annihilation for the Major.

[21:105] *Certainly, We wrote in the Psalms* of the heart *after the Remembrance* in the Tablet: *'The land* of the body *shall be inherited by My righteous servants'*: the righteous faculties illuminated with the light of divine peace after the destruction of the wicked faculties by spiritual discipline. Or it means: We wrote in the Psalms of the Preserved Tablet after the remembrance in the Mother Book: *The land shall be inherited by My righteous servants,* meaning the spirit, the inner-heart, the heart, the intellect, the soul, and all the faculties, with rectitude after the destruction of the righteous by annihilation in Unity.

[21:106] [*Indeed, there is in this*] *a proclamation for* all *people* [*who are devout*], worshipping God by travelling to Him.

[21:107] [*We did not send you, except as*] *a* tremendous *mercy* [*to all the worlds*], encompassing discriminating mercifulness (*raḥīmiyya*) by guiding them to absolute perfection, and also undiscriminating compassion (*raḥmāniyya*) by guaranteeing their safety from obliterating chastisement for as long as he was among them, because of how His mercy outstrips His wrath.

Q. 21:107

22
THE PILGRIMAGE
SŪRAT AL-ḤAJJ

In the Name of God, the Compassionate, the Merciful

[22:1] *O people, fear your Lord*: beware of His wrath by detaching from material veils and egocentric attributes. *Indeed,* [*the earthquake of the Hour*], the disturbance of the earth of the body at the Minor Resurrection for those who are reckoned at it, *is a tremendous thing*.

[22:2] *On the day when you behold it, every nursing female will neglect* [*her suckling*]: everything that nourishes the body parts will cease to nourish them; *and every pregnant female* of the faculties that protect its perceptions, such as imagination, fancy, memory and intellect, *will deliver her burden* of perceptions because of their drunkenness, confusion, bewilderment and panic. Or it means that every faculty that carries a body part will deliver its burden and its control and independence because of weakness, or that every body part that carries the power it contains will deliver it by abandoning it; or that all of the perfections that are possible within it by its power will be delivered by corruption and miscarriage; or that every soul carrying its conditions and attributes, whether virtuous or base, will deliver them by manifesting and displaying them; *and you will see people* [*as though*] *drunk* from the throes[1] of death, bewildered and unconscious, *yet they will not be drunk* on wine in a literal sense, but rather on the severity of the chastisement: [*but God's chastisement is severe*].

[22:3] [*And among people are those who dispute about God without any knowledge and* [*those who*] *follow every rebellious devil,* [22:4] *about whom it has been decreed that whoever takes him for a friend, he will make him go astray and will lead him to the chastisement of the Blaze*.

[22:5] *O people, if you are in doubt about the Resurrection, then, lo and behold,*

---

1 A play on the words *sukārā* ('drunken') and *sakarāt* ('death-throes').

[*consider that*] *We have created you from dust, then from a drop, then from a clot, then from a* [*little*] *lump of flesh, partly formed, and partly unformed, that We may make clear to you. And We establish in the wombs whatever We wish for a specified time, then We bring you forth as infants, and then that you may come of age. And there are some of you who are taken away, and there are some of you who are relegated to the most abject time of life, so that after* [*having had*] *some knowledge, he no longer knows anything.*] *And you see the earth* of the soul *torpid*, dead through ignorance and bereft of the vegetation of virtues and perfections. *Yet when We send down* the *water* of knowledge from the sky of the spirit *upon it, it stirs* with real life, *and swells* with ascension through the stations and ranks, *and grows* [*plants of*] *every delightful kind* of the perfections and virtues that beautify it.

[22:6] *That is because God is the* constant enduring *Truth*, and all besides Him is ephemeral and changing, *and because He revives the dead* of ignorance by the emanation of knowledge at the Intermediate Resurrection, just as He will revive the dead of nature at the Minor Resurrection, [*and has power over all things*].

[22:7] *And because the Hour*, in both meanings, *will come,* [*whereof there is no doubt,*] *and because God will resurrect those who are in the graves*: that is, He will revive the dead of ignorance from the grave of the body at the Intermediate Hour by resurrection in the locus of the heart, the return to innate disposition and the life of knowledge, just as He will resurrect the dead of nature at the second creation and the Minor Resurrection.

[22:8] [*And among people there are some who dispute about God*] *without* [*any*] *knowledge*, meaning reasoning, *or guidance*, meaning unveiling and experience, *or an enlightening Book*, meaning revelation and discerning inspiration.

[22:9] [[*They are*] *turning aside to go astray from the way of God. For him there will be ignominy in this world, and on the Day of Resurrection We shall make him taste the chastisement of the burning.*

[22:10] '*That is* [*the chastisement*] *for what your hands have sent ahead, and because God is not unjust to His servants.*'

[22:11] *And among people there are those who worship God with unsteady faith: if good* [*fortune*] *befalls him, he is reassured by it; but if an ordeal befalls him, he makes a turnabout, losing both this world and the Hereafter. That is the manifest loss.*]

[22:12] *He calls on besides God that which could not hurt him, and that which could not profit him*, whatever it may be. *Such* a state of being veiled by other-than-God *is extreme error* from the truth.

[22:13] [*He calls on him whose harm is likelier than his benefit. Truly an evil patron and an evil friend!*] Its harm is likelier than its benefit because calling upon it and stopping with it can only veil one from the truth.

[22:14] [*Truly God shall admit those who believe and perform righteous deeds into gardens underneath which rivers flow. Indeed, God does whatever He desires.*

[22:15] *Whoever supposes that God will not help him in this world and the Hereafter, let him extend a rope to the ceiling, and let him hang himself. Then let him see whether his strategy dispels that which enrages him.*

[22:16] *So We revealed it as clear signs, and indeed God guides whomever He desires.*

[22:17] *Truly those who believe, and those of Jewry, and the Sabaeans, and the Christians, and the Magians and the polytheists—God will indeed judge between them on the Day of Resurrection. Assuredly, God, over all things, is Witness.*

[22:18] *Have you not seen that to God*] prostrate *whoever is in the heavens and whoever is in the earth* of the heavenly and earthly dominions and all other things, those that exist now and those that will come to exist later, with submission, obedience and deference to the acts and qualities that God wants of them? Their adherence to His command, lack of disobedience to His will and yielding to His power is represented by prostration, which is an expression of total subservience, [*together with the sun and the moon, and the stars and the mountains, and the trees and the animals, as well as many of humankind*]. Disobedience is not possible for any of them except for those human beings who follow Satan, outwardly if not inwardly, who are the exception to the multitude of humankind who are doomed to chastisement and damnation as decreed in pre-eternity. They are the ones in whom the satanic nature is dominant, and thus are destined for deviance and damnation. [*And for many the chastisement has become due.*] *And he whom God abases* by making him the vessel of His all-conquering power and wrath, and the locus for His vengeance and anger, *there is none to give him honour. Indeed, God does whatever He wishes.*

Q. 22:13

[22:19] [*These twain are two contenders who contend concerning their Lord. As for those who disbelieve,*] *garments of fire will be cut out for them*: garments of the fire of God's wrath and overwhelming power, which are configurations and bodies that correspond to the attributes of their twisted souls, tormenting them immensely; *and boiling water will be poured over their heads*: the boiling water of caprice and love for the world that dominates them, or the boiling water of compounded ignorance and corrupt beliefs, poured over the higher part of them which sits beside the spirit, in the form of overwhelming divine power and deprivation from the One to Whom they truly owe their love and belief.

[22:20] *By which will be melted*, [meaning] made to dwindle and fade away, *that which is in* [*their bellies and their skins*]: the powerful meanings contained in the bellies of their aptitudes, and the human images and configurations contained in their external forms, so that their meanings and forms are changed; and whenever their skins are consumed, they are replaced with other skins.

[22:21] *And there will be hooked rods*, meaning scourges, *of iron for them*: the iron of the influences of dominion in the hands of the *Zabāniya*[1] of heavenly bodies that influence material souls, with which they scourge them and turn them from the realm of holiness to the chasms of defilement.

[22:22] *Whenever they desire* with the instincts of human disposition and the claim of primordial preparedness *to exit from it*, from those fires back to the space of the human levels, *on account of* the *anguish* of those dark and blackened configurations and the woe of those unavoidable depths, *they are* beaten with those painful scourges and *made to return into* those ruinous pits, *and* [*it will be said to them*]: '*Taste the chastisement of the burning!*'

Q. 22:20

[22:23] [*Indeed, God shall admit those who believe and perform righteous deeds into*] the *gardens* of the hearts *underneath which* the *rivers* of knowledge *flow, adorned therein with bracelets of* noble character traits and virtues, fashioned from the *gold* of intellectual knowledge and practical wisdom *and the pearl* of heart-centred gnostic sciences and unveiled realities, *and their raiment therein will be silk* of the rays of the lights of Divine Attributes and manifestations of divine subtlety.

[22:24] And He guided them *to wholesome words* of remembrance of the Attributes in the station of the heart, *and* [*they shall be guided*] *to the path* [*of the Praised*]: the path of the One endowed with those Attributes, meaning the Oneness of the Essence which is praised by being described with those Attributes. This is nothing other than the path of the Essence and the ladder of arrival to It by means of annihilation.

[22:25] [*Indeed, those*] *who disbelieve*, covered as they are by the veils of nature, *and who bar from the way of God and the Sacred Mosque*, which is the breast of the courtyard of the Kaʿba of the heart, *which We have assigned for people*, the human faculties in an absolute sense, *equally for the dweller therein*, the intellectual and spiritual faculties, *and the visitor*, the egocentric faculties because of the possibility that they can reach it and circumambulate it when the heart ascends to the station of the secret; *and whoever* arrives

---

1 The guardians of Hell (cf. Q. 96:18).

at it and then *seeks [to commit] sacrilege therein* by inclination to nature and caprice *by doing wrong*, which means taking matters of the knowledge and worship of the heart and putting them in the place of the I-ness—such as by using them to attain worldly aims and displaying them to achieve physical pleasures by seeking fame, wealth and power; or on the contrary, indulging in physical musts and egotistical pleasures while imagining them to be beneficial for this life and the next, or turning them from their proper purpose by ostentation or hypocrisy, or committing sacrilege and evil—*We shall make him taste a painful chastisement* in the hell of nature.

[22:26] *And when We settled for* the *Abraham* of the spirit *the site of the House* of the heart, which is the source consulted for all actions and sublime character traits. It is said that God showed Abraham its site, after it had been raised to heaven in the time of the Flood, by sending a wind to uncover the area around it so that he could rebuild it on its original foundations: that is, He guided him to its site after raising it to heaven in the time of the flood of ignorance and the waves of the dominating forces of nature, by means of the winds of mercy which uncovered the human configurations, natural pollutants and material debris that lay around it, so that he could build it on its original foundations of primordial human disposition. *'Do not ascribe any partner [to Me]*: that is, We made it a reference for the building of the house with the stones of deeds, the clay of wisdoms and the plaster of sublime character traits, and We said, 'Dot not associate': that is, We commanded him to uphold the Oneness; *and [purify My House]*: purify the house of the heart from those pollutants, *for those who circumambulate it*, [meaning] the faculties of the soul that circle around it to attain illumination and personal virtue, *and those who are resident*, the faculties of the spirit that uphold it by transmitting gnostic sciences and teachings of wisdom, *and those who bow and prostrate*, the corporeal faculties that learn from it forms of legal and intellectual worship and courtesy. Or it means: for the guidance of the seekers of insight and knowledge, the struggling wayfarers, and the humble worshippers.

Q. 22:26

[22:27] *'And announce among the people [the [season for] Pilgrimage]* with the summons to visit the station of the heart. *And they shall come to you on foot*, detached from the attributes of the soul, *and on every [lean camel]*, on every soul emaciated by lengthy spiritual discipline and struggle. *They shall come [from every deep ravine]*, from every distant path sunk deeply in the mire of nature.

[22:28] *'That they may witness things that are of benefit to them*, teachings of knowledge and action gleaned from the station of the heart, *and mention*

God's Name by proclaiming His Attributes *on appointed days* of the lights of manifestations and unveilings, *the livestock which He has provided them*: the cattle of the souls, slaughtered in offering to God with the spears of self-denial and the knives of spiritual struggle. *So eat thereof*, and benefit from the meat of their sublime character traits and dispositions to aid and support the traversal of the path, *and feed [the wretched poor]*: benefit the seekers with strong souls who suffer from the domination of their attributes and the prevalence of their configurations by their refinement and training, and benefit the poor with weak souls and dated knowledge who are weakened by lacking the learning and education they require.

[22:29] *'Then let them do away [with their self-neglect]*: let them rid themselves of the dirt of superfluities and the excesses of polluting states, by trimming the moustache of avarice and trimming the nails of anger and rancour: in sum, the remaining pollutants of the soul; *and let them fulfil their vows* by undertaking to manifest with action the meanings and perfections that were stored in them when they accepted them at the primordial covenant. The way to do away with this self-neglect is self-purification and the removal of the barriers to it, fulfilling their vows, and adorning themselves with virtue and gnosis; *and perform the circumambulation* by following the path to the higher dominion around the mighty throne of God, *the* Ancient (*qadīm*) *House.'*

Q. 22:29

[22:30] *[That is]* that: meaning that is the command. *And whoever venerates the sacraments of God*, which are the things whose sanctity may not be violated, by purification, self-sacrifice and all the other rites, such as adorning the self with virtues and avoiding vices, exposing oneself to the lights of manifestations, adopting attributes and ascending through stations—*that shall be better for him [with his Lord]*, in the presence of his Lord and the seat of His nearness. *And* the cattle of goodly souls *are lawful for you* by benefitting from their sublime character traits and actions on the path, and enjoying justified desires (*ḥuqūq*) but not wanton ones (*ḥuẓūẓ*), *except for that which has been recited to you* in *sūrat al-Mā'ida* [Q. 5]. The latter describes the vices that can be mistaken for virtues, namely those which the soul produces in forms other than their own or in incorrect modes so that in fact they are pure vices, which are forbidden for those travelling the path to God. *So avoid the abomination of* the *idols* of worshipped desires and indulged caprices, as God says: *Have you then seen him who has taken as his god his [own] desire* [Q. 45:23]; *and avoid false speech* of deceptive teachings and delusional doubts drawn from imagination and fancy and employed in debates, arguments and quarrels.

[22:31] *Being ḥanīfs to God*: inclining away from corrupts paths and false knowledge, turning away from everything that might impair their perfections and deeds—even from the adornment of perfection itself, since it is a veil; *not ascribing partners to Him*: by regarding anything other than Him or looking to anything but Him on His path. *For whoever ascribes partners to God* by stopping with anything or inclining to it, *it is as though he had fallen from the heaven* of the spirit *and been snatched away by [vulture] birds* of egocentric impulses and satanic caprices, which tear him to shreds, *or [as though] the wind* of the soul's caprice *had blown him into a far-off place* from the truth, ruining, blinding and destroying him.

[22:32] *[That [is his state]]. And whoever venerates the sacraments of God*, being souls prepared and directed with grace along the path of God, guided therein towards His countenance, *then that* veneration and the attainment of their perfection *derives from the piety of the hearts*, from the deeds of those with pious hearts detached from egocentric attributes and evil configurations.

Q. 22:31

[22:33] *You may benefit from them* with deeds, sublime character traits and perfections of knowledge and action, *until a specified time*, which is annihilation in God through reality. *Thereafter its lawful sacrifice*, the limit to which it is driven and the place where it must be sacrificed, *[is by the Ancient House]* upon arrival at the sanctuary of the breast, at the Kaʿba of the heart, by the station of the inner mystery. This is where the soul ascends to its station, annihilated from its life and its attributes.

[22:34] *And for every community* of the faculties, *We have appointed a [holy] rite* specific to it, *that they might mention God's Name* by adopting His Attributes which are their manifestations in orienting towards Oneness, *over what He has provided them* of perfection by means of the *livestock* of the soul, which is one of the cattle, meaning the goodly souls. *For your God is One God, [so submit to Him]*: declare His Oneness by turning towards Him and not looking to anything but Him, devote to Him your submission and obedience, and surrender to Him alone. *And give good tidings [to the humbly obedient]*: those who humble themselves to receive His emanation.

[22:35] *Who, when God is mentioned* with presence, *their hearts tremble* in response to receive His emanation, *and who endure [patiently]* and steadfastly *whatever may befall them* of self-denial and struggle, *and who observe prayer* of witnessing, *and who, from that which We have provided them* of virtues and perfections, *expend* with annihilation in God and His emanation to the prepared.

[22:36] *And [as for] the sacrificial camels*, meaning the noble and great souls, *We have appointed them [for you as one of God's sacraments]*, the gifts that point to God. *There is good for you in them*: felicity and perfection. *So mention God's Name over them* by adopting His Attributes and annihilating your own attributes in them, which is the meaning of sacrifice in God's cause, *when they are lined up* standing to uphold what God has obliged them to uphold, fettered with the chains of the Divine Law and the courtesies of the path, refraining from their own motions and agitations. *Then, [when their flanks have collapsed,]* when they have fallen from their caprice, which is their life and power by which they agitate and seek independence, by slaying them in God's cause, *eat [of them, and feed the [self-contained] beggar and the suppliant]*: benefit from their virtues, and share the benefit with the prepared and the seekers who come to ask of the disciples. *So We have disposed them for you* with spiritual discipline, *that perhaps you might be thankful* for the blessings of preparedness and grace by employing them in God's cause.

[22:37] *Neither their flesh*, meaning their virtues and perfections, *nor their blood*, meaning their annihilation through the draining of their caprices, *shall reach God, rather it is [your piety]*, your detachment from them and their attributes, *[that shall reach Him,]* for the cause of arrival is detachment and annihilation in God, not merely attaining virtues in the place of vices. *Thus,* by this disposal through spiritual discipline *has He disposed them for you, [that you may magnify God]* by annihilation in Him from them and from everything else, *for His guiding you* by detachment, isolation and treading the path to reality. *And give good tidings to the virtuous* who bear witness in servitude apart from subsistence and annihilation, in the state of uprightness and stability.

Q. 22:36

[22:38] *Indeed, God protects those who believe*: He protects the spiritual faculties from the injustice of the egocentric faculties, by grace. *Indeed, God does not love the treacherous* faculties which do not honour the trust of God regarding the perfections He placed in them by employing them for obedience, thereby betraying the heart perfidiously and violating their covenant, *the ungrateful* who use God's blessings to disobey Him.

[22:39] *Permission is granted to those who fight* against delusion, imagination and others: the spiritual faculties which struggle with the egocentric faculties, *because they have been wronged* by the dominance and ascendancy of the attributes of the soul. *[And God is truly able to help them]*.

[22:40] *Those* wronged ones are those *who were expelled [from their homes]* from their proper places and ranks by being enslaved and put in the service of the pursuit of appetites and physical pleasures, *without right, [only because they said, 'Our Lord is God']*: they only did this to them because of their upholding of Oneness, which necessitates veneration, stability and turning towards truth and away from falsehood. *Were it not for God's causing [some people]*, the people of the egocentric faculties, *to drive back others*, such as driving back the appetitive faculties with the irascible and vice versa; or the people of the faculties in a general sense, such as the egocentric being driven back by the spiritual, or the estimative with the intellectual, or some egocentric faculties with others, as has been described—*destruction would have befallen the monasteries* of the monks of the inner mystery and their cells, *and the churches* of the Christians of the heart and the halls of their manifestations, *and the synagogues* of the Jews of the breast and their temples, *and the mosques* of the faithful of the spirit and the stations of their witnessing and annihilation in God, *in which God's* Supreme *Name is mentioned [greatly]* by adornment with His character traits, adoption of His Attributes, realisation of His mysteries, and annihilation in His Essence. *Assuredly God will help [those who help Him]*, conquering with His light those who stand against Him and challenge His Being and manifestation. *[God is truly Strong,] Mighty*, and overwhelms those who defy Him with His omnipotent power and dominion.

Q. 22:41

[22:41] *Those who, if We empower them in the land* with uprightness through veridical divine existence, maintain the prayer of awareness and witnessing, *and pay* zakāt of true knowledge and certain gnostic sciences drawn from the *niṣāb*[1] of unveiling, to its worthy recipients among the seekers, *and enjoin* upon the egocentric faculties and imperfect souls *decency* in lawful actions and good character traits in the station of witnessing, *and forbid* them *indecency* in corporeal appetites, physical pleasures, vices and interactions. *And with God rests the outcome of all matters*, as all will return to Him.

[22:42] *[And if they deny you, the people of Noah denied before them, and ʿĀd, and Thamūd,* [22:43] *as well as the people of Abraham, and the people of Lot,* [22:44] *and the folk of Midian, and Moses was also denied. And I granted the disbelievers respite, then I seized them, and how [terrible] was My abhorrence!*

[22:45] *How many a town I have destroyed, while it was doing wrong, but now it lies fallen down on its roofs, and a neglected well, and a lofty palace.*

[22:46] *Have they not travelled in the land so that they may have hearts with*

---

1 The minimum amount of wealth that must be owned by an individual before *zakāt* is required from them.

which to comprehend, or ears with which to hear? Indeed, it is not the eyes that turn blind, but it is the hearts that turn blind within the breasts.

[22:47] *And they ask you to hasten the chastisement, even though God would never break His promise. And truly a day with your Lord is like a thousand years of your counting.*

[22:48] *To how many a town did I give respite while it was doing wrong; [but] then I seized it, and with Me lies the journey's end.*

[22:49] *Say: 'O people, I am only a manifest warner to you.'*

[22:50] *And so those who believe and perform righteous deeds—for them there shall be forgiveness and a glorious provision.*

[22:51] *But those who strive against Our signs, seeking to incapacitate— those—they shall be the folk of Hellfire.*

[22:52] *And We did not send before you any messenger or prophet:]* the differ- ence between the prophet and the messenger is that the prophet is the one who reaches annihilation in the station of sainthood and then returns with gifted existence to the station of uprightness, having attained realisation and gnosis of the Real, to act as a prophet for Him and for His Essence, Attributes, acts and Divine Laws by His command. He is sent to call oth- ers to Him according to the Divine Law of the messenger who was sent before him, rather than establishing his own Divine Law or founding a new dispensation or religion. He performs miracles and issues warn- ings and tidings to the people. Such were the prophets of the Children of Israel, all of whom called to the religion of Moses (may God grant him peace), rather than founding religions and Divine Laws of their own. Those of them who were given Books, such as David (may God grant him peace), were given Books containing gnostic sciences, realities, counsels and proverbs, not codes and Divine Laws. Thus, the Prophet (may God grant him peace) said, 'The scholars of my community are like the proph- ets of the Children of Israel,' meaning the saints of gnosis and stability. The messenger is the one who, in addition to all this, also founds a Divine Law and a code (*taqnīn*). Thus, the prophet is between the saint and the messenger.

[And We did not send before you any messenger or prophet] but that when he hoped[1]—meaning that his soul manifested with a hope in the station of variegation (*talwīn*)—*Satan cast into his hope* something that corresponded to it, because the manifestation of the soul creates darkness and blackness

Q. 22:47

---

1 *Tammanā* is here translated as 'hoped' rather than 'recited', as this better reflects the author's interpretation.

in the heart with which Satan veils it, in order to make it a venue for his insinuations and a mould in which to cast it by corresponding to it. *Thereat God abrogates whatever Satan had cast*: by shining the light of the spirit onto the heart with divine assistance and removing the darkness of the soul's manifestation and tames it, thereby showing the corruption of what Satan cast into it and rendering it distinct from the angelic inspiration, so that it melts away and the angelic inspiration remains; *then God confirms His revelations*: with stability. *And God is Knower*: He knows the satanic impulses and how to erase them from the midst of His revelation; *Wise*: He ordains His revelations with His wisdom.

[22:53] [*That He may make what Satan has cast a trial for those in whose hearts is a sickness and those whose hearts are hardened. Indeed, the evildoers are [steeped] in extreme defiance*:] it is from His wisdom that He makes the satanic inspiration a test for the doubters and hypocrites who are too veiled and hard of heart to accept the truth, and puts them to trial so that their doubts and veils only worsen. With their darkened souls and blackened hard hearts, they accept only what Satan casts, as God says: *Shall I inform you upon whom the devils descend? They descend upon every sinful liar* [Q. 26:221–222]. In their obstinacy, they are distant from the truth, so how should they accept it?

Q. 22:53

[22:54] *And that those who have been given knowledge*, the folk of certitude and realisation, *may know that it*, meaning Satan's ability to cast *is* a decree of wisdom and *the truth from your Lord*, according to justice and correspondence, *so that they may believe therein* by seeing that it is all from God, *and their hearts may find reassurance* and tranquillity *in it* by the light of divine peace and uprightness that allows one to differentiate between satanic and divine inspirations. *Indeed, God guides [those who believe to a straight path]*: the path of truth and uprightness, so that their feet do not slip from it by accepting what Satan casts, and their hearts accept only what the Compassionate casts because of its purity and intense brightness and brilliance.

[22:55] *And those [who disbelieve]*—those who are veiled—*will not cease to be in doubt of it, until [the Hour]* of the Minor Resurrection [*comes upon them unawares], or there comes upon them the chastisement [of a day of desolation]*: a terrible moment that cannot be defined or described because of its horror, or a time that is terrible beyond compare, or a time in which there will be no goodness at all.

[22:56] *The kingdom on that day*, when the chastisement comes and the Resurrection arrives, *will be God's*, and nothing will keep Him from them for there will be no strength, power or authority for anyone but Him.

[*He will judge*] between them. [*Then those who believed and performed righteous deeds,*] those who had certitude and acted with uprightness and justice, *will be in gardens* [*of Bliss*]: the gardens of the Attributes wherein they will dwell in bliss.

[22:57] [*While those who disbelieved and denied Our signs,*] those who were veiled from the Essence and who belied the Attributes by attributing them to other than God, *for them will be a humiliating chastisement* of the attributes of the souls and configurations, because of how they were veiled from the glory and majesty of God, and so were brought under the humiliation of His domination.

[22:58] *And those who emigrated* from the realms of the souls and their lower regions *in the way of God, and then were slain* with the sword of spiritual discipline and yearning, *or died* by seeking and tasting, *God shall provide them* from the sciences of unveilings and the teachings of manifestations, *with a good provision.* [*Indeed, God is the best of providers.*]

Q. 22:57

[22:59] *Assuredly, He will admit them into* [*a place that is pleasing to them*]: the station of contentment. *Indeed, God is Knowing* of the stages of their preparations and aptitudes, and what perfections need be granted to them; [and] *Forbearing*: He does not punish them immediately for their mistakes in their variegations or their neglect of their disciplines, thereby denying them what their states merit, in order to make them able to receive it.

[22:60] [*That* [*is so*]. *And whoever retaliates with the like of what he was made to suffer, and then is* [*again*] *made to suffer aggression, God will surely help him*:] when someone responds to an injustice by adhering to the way of fairness, and then inclines to being wronged rather than to wrong another, God's wisdom dictates that He help him with assistances of the dominion and support him with lights of divine power. Prudence in matters of justice means to prefer being wronged than wronging another. The Prophet (may God grant him peace) said, 'Rather be the servant of God who is wronged than the servant of God who wrongs others.' *Indeed, God is Pardoning*: He enjoins clemency and abstaining from punishing; but He is *Forgiving* of those who are unable to pardon.

[22:61] *That* forgiveness when the soul manifests with retaliation, or that aid and succour when the person acts justly and then prefers to be wronged the second time, *is because God makes the night* of the soul's darkness *pass into the* light of the *day* of the heart by moving it and making it ascendant over it so that it is stirred to retaliate, *and makes the* light of the *day* of the heart *pass into the night* of the soul's darkness so that it pardons, each by His ordainment and the direction of His decree, *and because God is*

71

Hearer of their intentions, *Seer* of their deeds, and He treats them according to their states.

[22:62] [*That is because God, He is the Truth, and what they call on besides Him, that is false, and because God, He is the High, the Great.*

[22:63] *Have you not seen that God sends down water from the heaven whereupon the earth turns green. Indeed, God is Subtle, Aware.*

[22:64] *To Him belongs all that is in the heavens and all that is in the earth. Indeed, God, He is Independent, Praiseworthy.*

[22:65] *Have you not seen that God has disposed for you all that is in the earth, and* [*that*] *the ships run upon the sea by His command, and He holds back the heaven lest it should fall on the earth, save* [*when it may do so*] *by His leave. Indeed, God is, with people, Gentle, Merciful.*

[22:66] *And He it is Who gave you life, then He will cause you to die, then He will give you life* [*again*]. *Indeed, humanity is very ungrateful.*

Q. 22:62

[22:67] *For every community We have appointed a* [*holy*] *rite which they are to observe. So do not let them dispute with you about the matter, but summon* [*people*] *to your Lord. Indeed, you follow a straight guidance.*

[22:68] *And if they dispute with you, say: 'God knows best what you do.*

[22:69] *'God will judge between you on the Day of Resurrection concerning that wherein you used to differ.'*

[22:70] *Do you not know that God knows all that is in the heaven and the earth? Truly that is* [*recorded*] *in a Book. Indeed, that is easy for God.*

[22:71] *And they worship besides God that for which He has never revealed any warrant, and that of which they have no knowledge. And those who do evil shall have no helper.*

[22:72] *And when Our signs are recited to them,* [*though they are*] *clear signs, you perceive on the faces of those who disbelieve denial. They would almost pounce upon those who recite Our signs to them. Say: 'Shall I inform you about something worse than that? The Fire! God has promised it to the disbelievers. And it is an evil journey's end!'*

[22:73] *O people, a similitude is being struck, so listen to it: truly those on whom you call besides God will never create a fly, even if they rallied together to do so. And if a fly should take away something from them, they would not be able to recover that from it. Feeble is the seeker and the* [*thing*] *sought.*]

[22:74] *They do not esteem God with the esteem He deserves*: that is, they do not know Him as He ought to be known, for they attribute influence to things other than Him, and affirm existence for things other than Him. The one who truly knows Him knows only what he finds within himself of His Attributes; and if they knew Him as He ought to be known,

72

they would be annihilated in Him, witnessing His Essence and Attributes, knowing that all things but Him can exist only through His Being and by His power, not their own. So how could they have existence and influence of their own? *Indeed, God is Strong*: dominating everything besides Him with the strength of his overwhelming power and annihilating them so that they have neither existence nor strength; [and] *Mighty*: overcoming everything so that they are rendered powerless.

[22:75] [*God chooses from the angels messengers and [also chooses] from people. Indeed, God is Hearer, Seer.*

[22:76] *He knows that which is before them and that which is behind them, and to God all matters are returned.*]

[22:77] *O you who believe* with certain faith, *bow down* with the annihilation of Attributes *and prostrate yourselves* with the annihilation of the Essence, *and worship your Lord* in the station of uprightness with the existence that is gifted to you, for no one can worship God as He ought to be worshipped if they have any remnant of I-ness left, since worship is commensurate with gnosis; *and do good* with perfection and rectitude, *that perhaps you may be prosperous* with salvation from the remnant of I-ness and variegation.

Q. 22:75

[22:78] *And struggle in the way of God, a struggle worthy of Him*: that is, strive in servanthood to the furthest extent until it transcends your I-ness and selfhood. This is a stern warning against the presence of variegation, because as long as a person retains a trace of selfhood he is not struggling in the way of God with a struggle that is worthy of Him. The worthy struggle is total annihilation so that neither essence nor trace remains. This is the meaning of struggling in His way. *He has elected you* by veridical existence and nothing else, so do not pay heed to anything but Him by manifesting your selfhood, *and has not laid upon you in [your religion, which is]* His religion, *any hardship* of toil and difficulty in worship: for as long as the soul remains or the servant feels any remnant of the heart and spirit, and does not settle in the light of Oneness or give himself over to the station of isolation, the vitality and taste of the worship will be incomplete, and so it will involve some hardship, constriction, toil and difficulty. Once the person becomes stable in uprightness and ascends in purity until he reaches complete love, he will find tranquillity and vitality. [Such is] *the creed of your true father Abraham*, namely pure Oneness. The meaning of his fatherhood is that he was a forerunner in affirming Oneness, and all who uphold it inherited it from him and thus are his children.

He, meaning Abraham or God, *named you Muslims*—people who submitted their beings to God with annihilation in Him—and made you knowers of Islam first and last. This is the meaning of His Words *Before, and in this, so that the Messenger might be a witness against you* in the matter of Oneness, a guardian to watch over you in its station and assist you so that no remnant of you would manifest, *and that you might be witnesses against humankind* by perfecting them and overseeing their stations and ranks, and passing onto them the lights of Oneness, if they accepted them. *So maintain* the *prayer* of essential witnessing, for you are at risk because of the nobility of your station and the glory of your goal, *and pay* zakāt by passing this grace on to those who are prepared for it and training the seekers of insight, for that is the way to give thanks for your state and to worship in your station, *and hold fast* in this guidance *to God* by not seeing it as coming from yourselves, and by adorning yourselves with His character traits. *He is your Patron* in the station of uprightness by reality, and your Helper in guidance by continuous assistances. *An excellent Patron and an excellent Helper*, and He is the Giver of grace.

Q. 22:78

23

THE BELIEVERS
SŪRAT AL-MU'MINŪN

In the Name of God, the Compassionate, the Merciful

[23:1] *Indeed, prosperous*—having attained the greatest victory—[*are the believers*]: the folk of certitude:

[23:2] *Those who* [*in their prayers*]—the prayer of the heart's presence—*are humble*, overwhelmed by dread and reverence of the light of magnificence that is manifested before them; [23:3] *and from vain talk*—namely the redundant [speech]—*turn away*: renouncing curiosity because of their absorption in the Real; [23:4] *and who fulfil payment of* zakāt by becoming detached from their attributes; [23:5] *and with regards to their private parts* and the means of their lusts and passions, *they are guardful*: by renouncing their desires and confining themselves to their duties, [23:6] [*except from their spouses, and what* [*slaves*] *their right hands possess, for then they are not blameworthy*].

[23:7] *But whoever seeks* [*anything*] *beyond that* by inclining to desires, *those*—*they are* [*transgressors*] who transgress against themselves.

[23:8] *And who are keepers of their trusts*, the secrets which God bequeathed to them in their inner mysteries, *and their covenants* which God made with them at the origin of innate disposition—these they keep by fulfilling them and reviving them.

[23:9] *And who are watchful* [*of their prayers*]: the prayer of their spirit-witnessing.

[23:10] *Those* who possess these qualities, *they are the inheritors* [23:11] *who shall inherit* the *Paradise* of the garden of the spirit in the holy enclosure, [*wherein they will abide.*

[23:12] *And We certainly created man from an extraction of clay.*

[23:13] *Then We made him a drop in a secure lodging.*

[23:14] *Then We transformed the drop* [*of semen*] *into a clot. Then We trans-*

formed the clot into a [little] lump of flesh. Then We transformed the lump of flesh into bones. Then We clothed the bones with flesh.] Then We produced him as [yet] another creature distinct from the one that passed through these stages of creation, by blowing Our Spirit into him and forming him in Our Image. Thus, in reality, it was creation, but also something other than creation. [*So blessed be God, the best of creators!*

[23:15] *Then indeed after that] you die* natural deaths.

[23:16] *Then on the Day of* the Minor *Resurrection you shall surely be raised* for the second creation. Or it means: you shall die the voluntary death of spiritual seeking (*irāda*), and then on the day of the Intermediate Resurrection you shall be raised in reality. Or it means: you shall die the death of annihilation, and then on the day of the Major Resurrection you shall be raised in subsistence.

[23:17] [*And verily We created] above you,* above your images and bodies, *seven paths* from the seven aforementioned Unseens;[1] *and We are never unmindful of* its *creation,* for the Unseen is visible to Us.

[23:18] *And We sent down* out of the heaven of the spirit the water of certain knowledge *out of the heaven* of the spirit [*in measure*]*, and We lodged it [within the earth]* as tranquillity in the soul; *and We are indeed able to take it away* by means of veiling and covering.

[23:19] *Then We produced for you therewith gardens of* the *date palms of* states and gifts, *and the vines of* character traits and acquisitions, *wherein is abundant fruit for you* of the fruits of the pleasures of souls, hearts and spirits, *and whereof [you eat]* to gather your nourishment and your God-fearing.

[23:20] *And a tree* of meditation *that grows on Mount [Sinai],* the mountain of the brain, or the mountain of the true heart, by the power of the intellect, *that produces* what it produces in the guise of the *oil* of preparation for the lighting of the fire of the active intellect, *and seasoning* of illuminating colouring or experiential realisation (*dhawq ḥālī*), [*for those who eat*]: those who wish to see, learn and partake of spiritual meanings.

[23:21] *And indeed in the cattle* of the animal faculties *there is for you a lesson* on which you may reflect in this life and the next. *We give you to drink of what is in their bellies* of phenomena and beneficial sciences, *and you have many uses in them* for wayfaring, *and you eat of them* and are nourished with goodly character traits.

[23:22] *And on them and on the ships* of the Divine Law, which bear you

Q. 23:15

---

1 The Unseen of the jinn, the soul, the heart, the mystery, the spirit, the hidden, and the Unseen of Unseens. See Kāshānī's comments on Q. 16:77.

on the sea of primordial matter, *you are carried* to the realm of holiness by the power of grace.

[23:23] [*And verily We sent Noah to his people, and he said, 'O my people, worship God. You have no [other] god besides Him. Will you not then fear?'*

[23:24] *But the council of his people, who disbelieved, said, 'This is just a human being like you who desires to gain superiority over you. And had God willed, He would have sent down angels. We never heard of such among our forefathers.*

[23:25] *'He is just a man possessed by madness. So bear with him for a while.'*

[23:26] *He said, 'My Lord, help me because they deny me.'*]

[23:27] *So We revealed to him* [*saying*], *'Build the Ark* of practical wisdom and Prophetic Law *under Our watch*, with Our protection to you from any errors in the craft, *and* [*by*] *Our revelation* with knowledge and inspiration. *Then, when Our command comes* that the corporeal faculties and souls engrossed in materiality be destroyed, *and the oven* of the body *gushes* with the ascendance of corrupt matter and foul contaminants, *bring into it of every kind* [*of animal*] *two mates*: that is, two types of everything from the universal and particular images, by which I mean two images, one universal and typical and the other particular and personal, *together with your family* of the spiritual faculties and detached human souls who followed your Divine Law, *except for those against whom the Word has already gone forth* that they be destroyed, namely your spouse the animal soul and corporeal nature. *And do not plead with Me concerning those who have done wrong*, of the egocentric faculties and souls engrossed in primordial materiality, which seek to ascend over the spiritual faculties and detached human souls and usurp their roles. *They shall indeed be drowned* in the sea of primordial matter.

Q. 23:23

[23:28] *'And when you have settled* [*in the Ark*] with constancy in the journey to God, [*together with those with you, say: "Praise be to God Who has delivered us from the wrongdoing folk,"* then] adopt the Attributes of God in the form of heart-centred praise in thanks for the blessing of salvation from the darkness of the satanic forces.

[23:29] *'And say: "My Lord, cause me to land in a blessed landing*, which refers to the station of the heart which God blessed with the unification of the realms and perception of the universal and particular meanings, and made safe from the flood of the sea of primordial matter and the deluge of its waters, [*for You are the best of all who bring to land*].'"

[23:30] *Indeed, in that there are signs*: indications and testimonies to those endowed with insight; *and surely We were putting them to the test* with the tribulations of the attributes of the soul and detachment from them through spiritual discipline; or putting the intellects to the test by reflecting on their states upon the unveiling of their states and chronicles.

[23:31] *Then, after them, We brought forth another generation*: at the second creation.

[23:43] [*No community can precede its term, nor be deferred.*

[23:44] *Then sent We Our messengers successively. Whenever there came to a community its messenger, they denied him; so We made them follow one another, and We turned them into folktales. So away with a people who do not believe!*

[23:45] *Then We sent Moses and his brother Aaron with Our signs and a manifest warrant* [23:46] *to Pharaoh and his council; but they disdained, and they were a tyrannical folk.*

[23:47] *And they said, 'Shall we believe two humans like ourselves, while their people are servile to us?'*

[23:48] *So they denied them [both] and became of those who were destroyed.*

[23:49] *And verily We gave Moses the Book that perhaps they might be guided.*]

Q. 23:31

[23:50] *And We made the son of Mary,* the heart, *and his mother,* the tranquil soul, *a sign*—one sign, for they were united in turning and travelling to God and in how the soul emerged from her upon its ascension. *And We gave them refuge on a height level,* a place elevated by the heart's ascension to the station of the spirit and the soul's ascension to the station of the heart, *and watered by springs*: a place of stability, constancy and permanence wherein repose can be found in its verdure, and a place of certain knowledge that is uncovered and laid bare.

[23:51] [*'O messengers, eat of the good things and perform righteous deeds. Indeed, I know what you do.*

[23:52] *Verily this, your community, is one community and I am your Lord, so fear Me.'*

[23:53] *But they split into sects regarding their affair.*

[23:54] *So leave them in their error for a while.*]

[23:55] *Do they suppose that, in the wealth and children with which We provide them,* [23:56] *We are hastening to [provide] them with good things?* In other words, the granting of the enjoyment of worldly pleasures and ephemeral desires to them does not signify that We are hastening to provide them with good things, as they imagine. The true meaning of hastening for goodness is the grace to receive the good things that endure: namely the grave of responsiveness and receptiveness with intense God-fearing at the self-disclosure of the divine magnificence, and first-hand certitude of the signs of the manifestation of lordly Attributes and Essential Oneness through annihilation in the Real; and then the undertaking to guide creation and grant them their perfections in the station of subsistence—all this accompanied by fear of the appearance of any remnant of I-ness during the return to the realm of lordship from the Essential Unity. This is the true meaning of hastening with, to, and for good things. [*Rather, they are not aware.*

[23:57] *Indeed, those who, for fear of their Lord, are apprehensive,* [23:58] *and who believe in the signs of their Lord,* [23:59] *and who do not associate others with their Lord,* [23:60] *and who give what they give, while their hearts tremble* [*with awe*], *because they are going to return to their Lord*—[23:61] *those* [*are the ones who*] *hasten to* [*perform*] *good works, and they* [*are the ones who*] *shall come out ahead in them.*]

[23:62] *And We do not task any soul beyond its capacity*: We do not hold everyone to the standards of those who shall come out ahead, since their stations can only be attained by precious few. It has been said that the road to the presence of the Real is too narrow to be trodden by everyone, and that those who reach its end must do so one at a time. Every person is tasked with what befits his personal aptitude, according to the perfection that pertains to it, which is the limit of his capacity. *And with Us is a Record*—the Preserved Tablet or the Mother Book—*that speaks* [*the truth*] according to the levels of each soul's aptitude and the bounds of its perfections and limits, and what is rightfully due to them; *and they will not be wronged* by being deprived of it or prevented from it if they strive for it and earnestly seek it through spiritual discipline. Each will be given what he is able to reach and what he yearns for by journeying towards it.

Q. 23:57

[23:63] *Nay,* [*but their hearts,*] *the hearts of the veiled ones, are in ignorance*, deluges of primordial matter and ignorant obliviousness *of this* precedence and this search for the truth, *and they have other deeds* [*that they will perpetrate*] which are contrary to this and will cause them to be distanced from this door and veiled even further. Just as the deeds of the foremost will cause them to ascend in illumination and become unveiled, with [the consequence] that they reach the Real, so too will the actions of these others cause them to descend and become polluted and more coarsely veiled, leading to them being expelled from the door of the Real, for their deeds are concerned with seeking the world and its passions, and the caprice of the soul and its pleasures. [Thus,] *besides which they are doing* [such actions] constantly and consistently.

[23:64] [*Indeed, when We seize their affluent ones with chastisement, behold! They are supplicating loudly.*

[23:65] *'Do not supplicate* [*out loud*] *on this day! Truly you will not receive help against Us.*

[23:66] *'Verily My signs used to be recited to you, but you used to take to your heels,* [23:67] *disdainful because of it, while in* [your] *night sessions you talked nonsense':*] whenever they heard mention of these signs and perfections, they became all the more obstinate and dedicated to their delusions, and proudly engrossed in their falsehood; thus, turning on their heels and heading into the pits of the hell of nature.

[23:68] [*Have they not contemplated the discourse, or has there come upon them that which has not come upon their forefathers?*

[23:69] *Or is it that they do not recognise their* [own] *Messenger and so they reject him?*

[23:70] *Or do they say, 'There is a madness in him'? Nay, he has brought them the truth; but most of them are averse to the truth*:] when they ruined their aptitudes and extinguished their lights by the rusting of their hearts according to the faculties of the soul and nature, and became ever more veiled by deluges of primordial matter and benighted configurations from the light of guidance and intellect, they became unable to contemplate the discourse and did not understand the realities of Oneness and justice. Therefore, they accused him of madness and did not recognise him, because of the contrast between light and darkness and the opposition of falsehood and truth; and so they rejected him and the truth which he brought.

Q. 23:66

[23:71] *And if the truth had followed* [*their desires, indeed the heavens and the earth and whoever is in them would have been corrupted*: if the truth,] which is Oneness and justice—meaning the call to the Essence and the Attributes— had followed *their desires* which were dispersed in falsehood, arising from their unjust darkened souls, veiled by multiplicity from Unity, it would have transformed into falsehood, because of the absence of the justice by which the heavens and the earth are upheld, and the Oneness by which all detached essences are sustained. It is through Unity that the realities of things are preserved, and through its shade, which is justice and the arrangement of multiplicities, that heaven and earth are sustained. Thus, all would be corrupted. [*Nay, We have brought them their Remembrance, but they are disregardful of their* [own] *Remembrance.*

[23:72] *Or do you ask them for any recompense? Yet the recompense of your Lord is better and He is the best of providers.*

[23:73] *Indeed, you summon them to a straight path*:] the straight path to which he summons them is the path of Oneness required for attaining justice in the soul, love in the heart, and the witnessing of Unity in the spirit. Those who are veiled from the realm of light by darkness, and from the intellect by the senses, and from holiness by profanity, do nothing but cling to darkness, hatred, enmity and reliance on multiplicity; and so, of course, they are astray from the path and wandering in the opposite direction. The path is in one valley, and they in another.

[23:74] [*Indeed, those who do not believe in the Hereafter are deviating from the path.*

[23:75] *And had We shown them mercy and relieved them of the harm afflicting them, they would surely persist in their insolence, bewildered.*

[23:76] *And We have already seized them with chastisement, yet they did not humble themselves to their Lord, nor did they devote themselves to prayer.*

[23:77] *Until when We opened on them the gate of a severe chastisement, behold! they are aghast thereat.*

[23:78] *And He it is Who made for you hearing, and eyes, and hearts. Little thanks do you show.*

[23:79] *And He it is Who dispersed you on earth, and to Him you shall be gathered.*

Q. 23:74

[23:80] *And He it is Who gives life and brings death, and due to Him is the alternation of night and day. Will you not then comprehend?*

[23:81] *Nay, but they say the like of what the ancients said.*

[23:82] *They said, 'What, when we are dead and have become dust and bones, shall we then be raised?*

[23:83] *'Already We and our fathers have been promised this before: these are nothing but the fables of the ancients.'*

[23:84] *Say: 'To whom does the earth and whoever is in it belong, if you [truly] knew?'*

[23:85] *They will say, 'To God.' Say: 'Will you not then remember?'*

[23:86] *Say: 'Who is the Lord of the seven heavens and the Lord of the Great Throne?'*

[23:87] *They will say, 'God.' Say: 'Will you not then be God-fearing?'*

[23:88] *Say: 'In whose hand is the dominion of all things and who protects, while from Him there is no protection, if you know?'*

[23:89] *They will say, 'God.' Say: 'How then are you bewitched?'*

[23:90] *Nay, but We have brought them the truth, and they are indeed liars.*

[23:91] *God has not taken any son, nor is there any god along with Him; for then each god would have taken away what he created, and some of them would surely rise up against others. Glorified be God above what they ascribe.*

[23:92] *Knower of the Unseen and the visible, and exalted be He above what they associate!*

[23:93] *Say: 'My Lord, if You should show me what they are promised,*
[23:94] *my Lord, then do not put me among the evildoing folk.'*

[23:95] *Indeed, We are able to show you what We promise them.*]

[23:96] *Ward off with that which is better than the evil [deed]*: if someone does you an ill deed, stand firm in the station of the heart and consider which good deed would be best to reply to it, so that the soul of the other is tamed and pacified, and renounces the ill deed and feels remorse for it. Do not allow your soul to react and return the ill deed in kind, so that his soul becomes all the sharper and more violent, and persists in the ill deed. If you repay it with the best of good deeds, you will exert control over your soul, defeat your personal demon and strengthen your heart. You will uphold what God has commanded you to do, and attain the virtue of forbearance, and put your knowledge into action, and become firm in obedience to the Merciful and defiance of Satan. In addition to your own good deed, you will also rectify the soul of your fellow and win it over if there is the least bit of hope in him, and you will set his soul straight and give it strength. This will constitute another good deed for you, so that you will attain two good deeds, while if you had retaliated you would have incurred two sins. *We know best what they allege*: leave the sinner to God's knowledge, and know that God is aware of him and will requite him on your behalf if he deserves a penalty, since He is better able to do it than you are, or pardon him if He has made him able to repent and knows that he can be rectified. Seek refuge with God from the violence of anger and the stirring of the soul by Satan's goading and insinuations, and from his presence and proximity. Turn to your Lord and seek refuge with Him:

[23:97] [*And say:*] '*My Lord, I seek protection in You [from the promptings of devils:*] devote yourself to turning towards Him with your heart, tongue and body, and seek shelter at His door from the insinuations, invitations and presence of the accursed one, so that he is conquered, cursed and banished.

[23:98] [*'And I seek protection in You, my Lord, lest they visit me.'*

[23:99] *Until when death comes to one of them, he says, 'My Lord, send me back,* [23:100] *that I might act righteously in that which I have left behind'*:] if the one who is evil and accuses you of evil and speaks ill of you remains that way until he dies, and witnesses the portents of chastisement and begins to perceive the terrible configurations of his sins, he will wish that he could go back; and he will express remorse, and vow to do righteous deeds for the faith that he forsook. Yet he will attain only woe and remorse, and speak only platitudes of woe and remorse, and make useless claims to no avail or response. [*By no means! It is merely a word that he speaks,*] *and behind them*—that is, in the way of their return—[*there is a barrier*] composed of dark and evil configurations, corresponding to the configurations of their sins in suspended forms. These prevent them from returning to the truth as well as to the lower world, and constitute the barrier between the seas of light and darkness, and the worlds of incorporeal spirits and compound bodies. They will be tormented there with the most grievous forms of torment and cruel kinds of retribution [*until the day when they are raised*], at the time of the bodily gathering when the Trumpet is blown and the Resurrection commences, and the bodies are summoned forth.

[23:101] [*And when the Trumpet is blown,*] *there will be no more ties* [*of kinship*] *between them* [*on that day*] because they will be veiled from one another by the structures that correspond to their characters, deeds and configurations which were rooted in their souls and ordained for them. Therefore, they will not recognise one another *nor will they question one another* because of the enormity of the terrors in which they find themselves and their obliviousness to their former connections. The relationships and kinship that existed among them before will be severed because of their dispersal through these varied torments and causes of veiling. Their forms and skins will be changed and their images and faces replaced according to what is dictated by their faults and the attributes of their souls. This is the meaning of His Words *The Fire will scorch their faces, while they glower therein* [Q. 23:104], which describe the dominance of wretchedness and foul ending that will bring ruin, banishment, rejection and damnation, when they are driven away like dogs.

Q. 23:101

[23:102] [*Then those whose scales are heavy, they are the successful,* [23:103] *and those whose scales are light, they are the ones who have lost their souls, abiding in Hell.*

[23:104] *The Fire will scorch their faces, while they glower therein:*

[23:105] *'Were not My signs recited to you, and you used to deny them?'*

[23:106] *They will say, 'Our Lord, our wretchedness overcame us, and we were an erring folk.*

[23:107] *'Our Lord, bring us out of it! Then, if we revert, we will indeed be evildoers.'*

[23:108] *He will say, 'Begone in it, and do not speak to Me.*

[23:109] *'Indeed, there was a party of My servants who would say, "Our Lord, we believe; therefore, forgive us, and have mercy on us, for You are the best of the merciful."*

[23:110] *'But then you took them as an object of ridicule until they made you forget My remembrance, and you used to laugh at them.*

[23:111] *'Indeed, I have rewarded them this day for the endurance they showed. They are indeed the winners.'*

[23:112] *He will say, 'How long did you tarry in the earth in years?'*

[23:113] *They will say,] 'We tarried a day, or part of a day. [Yet ask those who keep count!]'* Ibn ʿAbbās said, 'The torment they will endure between the two blasts of the Trumpet will cause them to forget how long they were veiled in that barrier.' These forms will cause them to forget how long they tarried; and they will forget because by then it will all be over, and what is over is of no consequence. God Himself will then confirm that what they say is true:

[23:114] *[He will say,] 'You tarried but a little, if only you knew*: you thought that it was a long duration and so were deluded by it and infatuated with its pleasures and delights; but had you known how short it really was you would have prepared yourselves and detached yourselves from it.

[23:115] *[Did you suppose that We created you aimlessly and that you would not be returned to Us?'*

[23:116] *So exalted be God, the King, the Truth! There is no god except Him, the Lord of the Noble Throne.*

[23:117] *And he who calls on another god along with God has no proof thereof; his reckoning will indeed be with his Lord. Truly the disbelievers will not be successful.*

[23:118] *And say:] 'My Lord, forgive* the configurations of attachments, *and have mercy* by granting perfections, *and You are the best of the merciful.'*

24
LIGHT
SŪRAT AL-NŪR

In the Name of God, the Compassionate, the Merciful

[24:1] [*A* sūra *which We have revealed and prescribed and wherein We have revealed manifest signs that perhaps you might remember.*

[24:2] *As for the fornicatress and the fornicator, strike each of them a hundred lashes. And do not let any pity for them overcome you in God's religion, if you believe in God and the Last Day. And let their chastisement be witnessed by a group of the believers.*

[24:3] *The fornicator shall not marry anyone but a fornicatress or an idolatress, and the fornicatress shall be married by none except a fornicator or an idolator, and that is forbidden to believers.*

[24:4] *And those who accuse honourable women* [*in wedlock*], *and then do not bring four witnesses, strike them eighty lashes, and do not accept any testimony from them ever; and those—they are the immoral,* [24:5] *except those who repent thereafter and make amends, for God is indeed Forgiving, Merciful.*

[24:6] *And those who accuse their wives, but have no witnesses, except themselves, then the testimony of one of them shall be to testify* [*swearing*] *by God four times that he is indeed being truthful,* [24:7] *and a fifth time that God's wrath shall be upon him if he were lying.*

[24:8] *And the chastisement shall be averted from her if she testify* [*swearing*] *by God four times that he is indeed lying,* [24:9] *and a fifth time that God's wrath shall be upon her if he were being truthful.*

[24:10] *And were it not for God's bounty to you and His mercy, and that God is the Relenting, Wise...!*

[24:11] *Indeed, those who initiated the slander are a band from among yourselves. Do not suppose that it is bad for you; rather, it is good for you. Upon every man of them shall be the* [*onus of the*] *sin which he has earned; and as for him who bore the greater share thereof, there will be an awful chastisement for him.*

[24:12] *Why, when you [first] heard about it, did the believing men and women not think good of themselves, and say, 'This is a manifest calumny?'*

[24:13] *Why did they not produce four witnesses to it? And since they did not produce the witnesses, those, in God's sight, they are liars.*

[24:14] *And were it not for God's bounty to you and His mercy in the life of this world and the Hereafter there would have befallen you, for what you engaged in, an awful chastisement,* [24:15] *when you were receiving it [welcomingly] with your tongues, and were uttering with your mouths that whereof you had no knowledge, supposing it to be a light matter, while with God it was grave.*

[24:16] *And why, when you heard it, did you not say, 'It is not for us to speak about this. Glory be to You! This is an awful calumny?'*

[24:17] *God admonishes you, lest you should ever repeat the like of it, if you are [in truth] believers.*

[24:18] *And God clarifies for you the signs, and God is Knower, Wise.*

Q. 24:12

[24:19] *Indeed, those who love that indecency should be spread, concerning those who believe, theirs will be a painful chastisement in the life of this world and the Hereafter, and God knows, and you do not know.*

[24:20] *And were it not for God's bounty to you, and His mercy and that God is Gentle, Merciful…!*

[24:21] *O you who believe, do not follow in the steps of Satan. For whoever follows in the steps of Satan, assuredly he enjoins indecency and what is reprehensible. And were it not for God's bounty to you and His mercy, not one of you would ever have grown pure. But God purifies whom He will, and God is Hearer, Knower.*

[24:22] *And do not let those of you who possess bounty and those who are affluent swear not to give to the near of kin and the poor and those who emigrate in the way of God. Let them forgive and excuse. Do you not love that God should forgive you? And God is Forgiving, Merciful.*

[24:23] *Indeed, those who make accusations against honourably married women, who are unaware and who believe, shall be cursed in this world and the Hereafter; and there will be an awful chastisement for them* [24:24] *on the day when their tongues and their hands and their feet shall testify against them concerning what they used to do.*

[24:25] *On that day God will pay them in full their just due, and they shall know that God is the Manifest Truth.*

[24:26] *Vile women are for vile men, and vile men for vile women. Good women are for good men, and good men for good women—such are absolved of what they say. For them will be forgiveness and a glorious provision.*

Regarding His Words *Indeed, those who initiated the slander* [Q. 24:11] up to His Words *a glorious provision* [Q. 24:26], the reason He spoke so severely

about the matter of slander and issued such a stern warning about it, in a
way that He did not do with other sins, describing a consequence for it
that is even more severe than the consequences for adultery or murdering
an innocent, was because the severity of a vice and the enormity of a sin is
determined by the faculty which is its source. The measure of a vice depends
on how veiled the sinner is from the divine presence and the holy lights, and
how far steeped he is in calamities of primordial matter and ruinous chasms
of darkness, according to their differing levels. The nobler the faculty that
constitutes its source and origin, the fouler the resulting vice will be, and
the inverse is also true. This is because vices are the opposite of virtues; and
so the nobler a virtue is, the fouler the opposing vice is. Slander is the vice
of the faculty of speech, which is the noblest of the human faculties, while
adultery is the vice of the appetitive faculty and murder is the vice of the
irascible faculty. The greater nobility of the former compared to the latter
two necessitates that its vice be fouler also. This is because the former faculty is what makes the human being human, and raises him into the higher
realm and directs him towards the divine presence, allowing him to attain
knowledge and perfections and to acquire goodness and felicity. If, then, it
is corrupted by the dominance of the satanic nature over it and is thereby
veiled from the light by the domination of darkness, it will suffer the most
wretched damnation and incur the chastisement of the fire, which means
the rusting of the heart and total veiling, as He says, *Nay, indeed! Rather, upon
their hearts is the rust of that which they earned. Nay, they, on that day, will be veiled
from their Lord* [Q. 83:14–15]. This is why the chastisement and torment for
corrupt doctrine must be perpetual, while that for corrupt action need not
be: *God forgives not that anything should be associated with Him. But He forgives
other than that to whomever He wills* [Q. 4:48].

Q. 24:26

As for the other two [sins], the vice of each of them relates to how
they overwhelm the faculty of speech. But they can then be erased if this
faculty reigns them in and controls them after their passion dies down and
their power fades, when the light ascends to overwhelm and dominate
them by nature. This is the situation of the self-reproaching soul when
it inspires repentance and remorse. Or it could be that these sins remain
because the person persists in them and declines to ask forgiveness for
them. But either way, their vice does not reach as far as the station of
the inner mystery and the locus of presence and intimate discourse with
the Lord, but go no further than the limit of the breast. Innate disposition does not become veiled by them, nor does reality become perverted,
unlike the case for the other.

It is obvious that the satanic impulse that seeks to tempt humanity is further from the divine presence than the predatory and bestial impulses, and as far away from it as can be. The vice of speech turns man into a devil, while the other two vices turn him into an animal like a beast or a predator; and there is more hope that an animal can be rectified and saved than that a devil can be. Thus, God says, *Shall I inform you upon whom the devils descend? They descend upon every sinful liar* [Q. 26:221–222]. He then forbids following in the footsteps of Satan, for such indecencies are only committed when Satan is followed and obeyed. Hence, the sinner becomes one of his hosts and his followers, and so is even more despicable and wretched than he is: deprived of God's grace, which is His light and guidance; veiled from His mercy, which is the emanation of perfection and felicity; cursed in this life and the next; and reviled by God and His angels. His own limbs will testify against him, and their forms will be altered and disfigured. He is vile in essence and in soul, steeped in foulness. Such vile deeds arise only from vile people, and therefore God says, *Vile women are for vile men.* As for the good people who are innocent of these vices, they produce only goodly things and virtues. *For them will be forgiveness* in the form of the divine lights which will cover their soul's attributes, *and a glorious provision* of meanings and gnostic teachings inspired in their hearts.

Q. 24:27

[24:27] [*O you who believe, do not enter houses other than your houses until you have [first] asked permission and greeted their occupants. That is better for you, that perhaps you might remember.*

[24:28] *And if you do not find anyone in them, [still] do not enter them until permission has been given to you. And if it is said to you, 'Go away,' then go away, for this is purer for you. And God knows what you do.*

[24:29] *You would not be at fault if you enter [without permission] uninhabited houses wherein is comfort for you. And God knows what you disclose and what you hide.*

[24:30] *Tell believing men to lower their gaze and to guard their private parts. That is purer for them. Indeed, God is Aware of what they do.*

[24:31] *And tell believing women to lower their gaze and to guard their private parts, and not to display their adornment, except for what is apparent; and let them draw their veils over their bosoms and not reveal their adornment, except to their husbands or their fathers, or their husbands' fathers, or their sons, or their husbands' sons, or their brothers, or their brothers' sons, or their sisters' sons, or their women, or what their right hands own, or such men who are dependant, not possessing any sexual desire, or children who are not yet aware of women's private parts. And do not let them thump with their feet to make known their hidden ornaments. And rally to God in repentance, O believers, so that you might be prosperous.*

[24:32] *And marry off the spouseless among you and the righteous ones among your male slaves and your female slaves. If they are poor, God will enrich them out of His bounty. God is Embracing, Knowing.*

[24:33] *And let those who cannot find the means to marry be content, until God enriches them out of His bounty. And those who seek a written contract [of emancipation], from among those whom your right hand owns, contract with them accordingly, if you know in them any good, and give them out of the wealth of God which He has given you. And do not compel your slave-girls to prostitution when they desire to be chaste, that you may seek the transient things of the life of this world. And should anyone compel them, then surely God, after their compulsion, will be Forgiving, Merciful.*

[24:34] *And verily We have revealed to you clear verses and an example of those who passed away before you, and an admonition for those who fear God.*]

[24:35] *God is the Light of the heavens and the earth*: light is that which is intrinsically visible, and makes other things visible. In an absolute sense, it is one of the Names of God, symbolising the intensity of His manifestation and how He makes all other things manifest. A poet said, 'He is hidden by how intensely manifest He is, / So that the eyes of blind folk strain to see Him. / To be graced with the light of His countenance / Is the greatest fortune for blurry eyes.' So since they exist by His existence, and are manifested by His manifestation, He is *the Light of the heavens and the earth*: that is, the One Who makes manifest the heavens of the spirits and the earth of the bodies. He is absolute existence through which all beings are given existence and illuminated.

Q. 24:32

The likeness of His Light—the description of His existence and manifestation in the worlds and how they are manifested through Him—*is as a niche wherein is a lamp*: this alludes to the body that is intrinsically dark, but illuminated by the light of the spirit, which is represented by the lamp. It is enclosed by the grille of the senses, through which the light glistens, like the niche with the lamp. [*The lamp is in a glass, the glass as it were a glittering star kindled from a blessed olive tree*:] the glass alludes to the heart illuminated by the spirit, which illuminates all around it by shining upon it, just as the lamp is illuminated by the fire within it, and lights up all that is around it. He likens *the glass* to a *glittering star* because of its simplicity, bright light, high position and constant shining, just as is true of the heart. The tree from which this lamp is kindled is the holy purified incorrupt soul, likened to it because of how its spreading branches resemble the soul's varied faculties. It grows from the earth of the body, and its

89

branches reach through the sky of the heart into the heaven of the spirit. The tree is called *blessed* because of its many benefits and boons, which are the fruits of good characteristics, deeds and cognitions; its tremendous growth in the form of the ascent in perfections, and the achievement of felicity in this life and the next; the perfection of the worlds by it; and how the manifestation of lights, mysteries, gnostic teachings, realities, stations, acquisitions, states and gifts depend on it. The tree is called *olive* specifically because of how its cognitions are particular and exist side by side with material attachments, much like an olive, which is not all kernel; and because of its abundant preparedness to be ignited and illuminated by the light of the fire of the active intellect, which reaches it through the medium of the spirit and the heart, much like the abundance of oil in the olive tree makes it predisposed to catch fire. The meaning of it being *neither of the east nor of the west* is that it is in the middle between the west of the world of bodies where the divine light sets and is concealed by the veil of darkness, and the east of the world of spirits where the light rises and emerges from the veil of light, because it is subtler and lighter than the body yet denser than the spirit. *Its oil* of preparedness from the holy primordial light stored within it *would almost glow forth [of itself]* by emerging into action and reaching perfection by itself, and thus shine *though no fire* of the active intellect *touched it*, nor did the light of the Holy Spirit reach it, because of the power of its preparedness and the intensity of its purity.

Light upon light! This means that the light which shines forth from the acquired perfection is another light in addition to the light of stable preparedness that originally shines, as though the light is multiplied. *God guides to His Light*, which is manifested by His Essence and manifests all things with grace and guidance, *whom He will* of the folk of nurture so that they attain felicity. *[And God strikes similitudes for people;] and God is Knower of all things*: He knows similitudes and their application, and He reveals their true meaning to His saints.

[24:36] *In houses*—that is, God guides to his light whom He will in stations—*God has allowed to be raised*, [by] allowing them to be built and their steps to be made high, *and wherein His Name is remembered* with the tongue, spiritual discipline and the adoption of sublime character traits in the station of the soul; presence, vigilance and the emulation of Attributes in the station of the heart; intimate discourse, communion and realisation of mysteries in the station of the inner mystery; tender communion through witnessing and dazzling rapture in lights in the station of the spirit; and immersion, extinction and annihilation in the station of the Essence. *Therein* [*they*] *make glorifications to Him* with self-purification, the extolling of Divine Transcendence and Oneness, and detachment and seclusion, *in the mornings* of manifestation *and the evenings* of concealment.

[24:37] *People* who are the peerless foremost, detached and secluded to uphold the truth, *whom neither trading,* in the form of exchanging the good of the Hereafter for worldly things in their asceticism, *nor selling* their souls and their possessions, in return for Paradise in their struggle, *distracts from the remembrance of God,* remembrance of the Essence, *and the observance of* the *prayer* of witnessing through annihilation, *and payment of* zakāt of guiding and perfecting others in the state of subsistence. *They fear a day when hearts and eyes will be tossed about*: when hearts will be transformed into mysteries, and eyes into insights. Indeed, [it is the day] when their realities will be transformed by being annihilated and then granted existence through the Real, as He said [in the *ḥadīth qudsī*], 'I become his hearing and his sight.' [In fact,] what they fear is that any remnant of their egos might remain after that.

Q. 24:37

[24:38] *So that God may reward them* with true existence *for the best of what they did* with the gardens of deeds, souls and works, *and give them more out of His bounty* of the gardens of hearts and attributes; *and God provides whomever He will* of the gardens of spirits and witnessings, *without* [*any*] *reckoning* because they are manifold beyond all counting or measuring.

[24:39] *And as for those who disbelieve* and so are veiled from the religion, *their works* which they do in hope of reward *are like a mirage in a plain* because they are produced from empty configurations and upheld by an animalistic soul, *which the thirsty man supposes to be water,* which symbolises how the doer of those deeds in hope of reward imagines them to be enduring, delightful, permanent things that will conform to his expectations, *until he comes to it* at the Minor Resurrection *and finds it to be nothing* that exists, but only a thing that is empty, corrupt, nothing but a false notion, as God says: *And We shall attend to the works they did and turn them into scattered dust* [Q. 25:23]. *And he finds God there,* [*Who pays him his account in full*]: that is, he finds the angels of God, the Hell-guardians of the faculties and heavenly and earthly souls there at that fanciful delusion, leading him into the fires of deprivation and the woe of loss, and give him what his corrupt doctrine and false deeds merit: the hell of ignorance and the deluge of darkness; [*and God is swift at reckoning*].

[24:40] *Or as the manifold darkness on* the *deep sea* of primordial matter, whose depths swallow up the corpse of every ignorant soul veiled by corporeal configurations, enveloping all of the egocentric faculties connected to it, *covered by* the *billow* of corporeal nature, *above which there is [another] billow* of the vegetative soul, *above which there are clouds* of the animal soul and its benighted configurations, *manifold [layers of] darkness, one on top of another.* *When he*—meaning the one who is veiled—*holds out his hand,* the intellectual contemplative faculty, by reflection, *he can scarcely see it* because of its darkness and the blindness of his own insight and how he has not been guided to anything. How can a blind person see a black object in the dead of night? *And he whom God has not granted any light,* by shining the lights of the spirit upon him through holy aid and intellectual support, *has no light.*

[24:41] *Have you not seen that God is glorified by all who are in* the realm of *the heavens* of the spirits by extolling His holiness and manifesting His Attributes of beauty, *and* the realm of *the earth* of the bodies by praising and magnifying Him and manifesting His Attributes of majesty, *and the birds* of the faculties of the heart and the inner mystery by both, *with wings spread* and flocking together arranged in their levels in the sky of the mystery, directed by the light of divine peace, none of them straying beyond their bounds, as He says, *And there is not one of us, but he has a known station* [Q. 37:164]. *Each [one of them] knows its prayer*: its specific form of obedience and how it yields to Him and submits to His power and authority, whether it be intellectual or practical, and how it keeps to His teachings and is sincerely devoted to Him in all that He commands it; *and its glorification*: its expression of the particular trait innate to it which bears witness to His Unity. *And God knows what they do*: their deeds and their obedience.

Q. 24:41

[24:42] [*And to God belongs the kingdom of the heavens and the earth, and with God is the journey's end.*]

[24:43] *Have you not seen how God drives the clouds* of the intellect with the winds of insights and inspirations into scattered branches of particular images, *then composes them* into all manner of compositions, *then piles them up* into arguments and proofs, *whereat you see the rain* of conclusions and certain matters of knowledge *issuing from the midst of them? And He sends down from the heaven* of the spirit *out of the mountains* of the lights of divine peace and certitude, which bring dignity, tranquillity and stability, *wherein,* in those mountains, *is the hail* of realities, unveiled gnostic teachings and experiential meanings. Or it means out of the mountains in heaven, wherein are mined the minerals of sciences and discoveries and all their types; for every science and craft has a mine in the spirit where it is rooted according to innate disposition, from which that science is extracted. This is why some people take to certain sciences easily but not to others, and why some people take to most of them while others do not take to any of them at all. All are directed towards that for which they were created. So He sends down from the heaven of the spirit, out of the mountains therein, the hail of gnostic teachings and realities *and smites with it whom He will* from the spiritual faculties, *and turns it away from whom He will* of the egocentric faculties and the veiled souls. *The brilliance of its lightning*—meaning the glimmers of that hail, representing the flashing lights He sends which do not remain for long, but only flash and then disappear until they become stable—*would almost take away the eyes* of insight with bewilderment and astonishment; and the more it increases, the more their bewilderment grows. Therefore, he (may God grant him peace) said, 'Lord, increase me in bewilderment!'—meaning knowledge and light.

[24:44] *God alternates the night* of the soul's darkness *and the day* of the spirit's light, by sometimes allowing the light of the spirit to dominate so that it illuminates the heart and soul, and other times allowing the dark of the soul to emerge so that it becomes turbid and exposes the heart to variegations. *Indeed, in that there is a lesson* to be contemplated [*for those who see*]—those who have heart-vision, or those who have insight—so that they seek God's aid with these variegations and the darkness of the soul, and take refuge in the Real and the source of light, and pass into the station of the inner mystery and the spirit, and the veil is lifted for them.

Q. 24:44

[24:45] *And God has created every beast*, the beasts of the impulses that tread over the lands of the souls and stir them to actions, *from* a certain *fluid*, namely an item of knowledge which corresponds to the impulse that gives birth to it. The origin of every impulse is a given perception. *Among them are some that creep upon their bellies*, crawling about in nature and instigating natural corporeal actions, *and among them are some that walk on two feet*, the human impulses that instigate human actions and practical perfections, *and among them are some that walk on four*, the animal impulses that provoke predatory and bestial actions. *God creates whatever He wishes* of these impulses from the source of His immense perfect power which originates actions. [*Indeed, God has power over all things.*

[24:46] *And verily We have revealed manifest signs, and God guides whomever He will to a straight path*:] He guides whom He will with these signs, composed of wisdoms, meanings, gnostic teachings and realities from the source of His total comprehensive wisdom, which manifests sciences and states to the path of Oneness that leads straight to Him.

[24:47] *And they say, 'We believe in God and the Messenger*: they claim to uphold Oneness in unification (*jamʿ*) and differentiation (*tafṣīl*), and to act in accordance with it; *and we obey'. Then a party of them turn away* by failing to act in accordance with this unification and differentiation through indulging in licentiousness and heresy; *and those—they are not believers* possessing the true faith, as they claim to, which is knowledge of God in unification and differentiation.

[24:48] [*And when they are summoned to God and His Messenger, that he may judge between them, behold, a party of them are averse.*

[24:49] *But if right be on their side, they would come to him willingly.*

[24:50] *Is there a sickness in their hearts? Or are they in doubt, or do they fear that God and His Messenger will be unjust to them? Rather, those—they are the wrongdoers.*

[24:51] *All that the believers say, when they are summoned to God and His Messenger, that he may judge between them, is that they say, 'We hear and we obey.' And those are the successful.*]

Q. 24:47

[24:52] *And he who obeys God* inwardly by the witnessing of unification, *and His Messenger* outwardly by the rule of differentiation, *and fears God* with the heart by vigilantly observing the manifestations of the Attributes, *and has awe of Him* with the spirit by keeping his I-ness under control while witnessing the Essence, *those—they are the winners* of the supreme triumph.

[24:53] [*And they swear by God solemn oaths that if you order them, they will surely go forth. Say: 'Do not swear! Acknowledged obedience [is better]. Indeed, God is Aware of what you do.'*

[24:54] *Say: 'Obey God, and obey the Messenger. But if you turn away, [know that] he is only responsible for that with which he has been charged, and you are responsible for that with which you have been charged. And if you obey him, you will be [rightly] guided. And the Messenger's duty is only to convey [the Message] clearly.'*]

[24:55] *God has promised those of you who believe* with certitude *and perform righteous deeds* by acquiring virtues *that He will surely make them successors in the earth* of the soul, if they strive for God's sake as He deserves, *just as He made those who were before them*—His saints who reached the station of annihilation in Oneness before them—*successors; and He will surely establish for them* with subsistence after annihilation *their religion*, the approved path of uprightness *which He has approved for them, and that He will give them in exchange after their fear* in the station of the soul *security* by reaching uprightness. *'They worship Me*—declaring My Oneness—

[*without associating anything with Me*]: without paying regard to anything other than Me or acknowledging it.' *And whoever is ungrateful after that* by committing the tyranny of letting his I-ness loose and straying from uprightness and mastery into variegation, *those—they are the immoral* who have strayed outside the religion of Oneness.

Q. 24:55

25

THE CRITERION
SŪRAT AL-FURQĀN

In the Name of God, the Compassionate, the Merciful

[25:1] *Blessed*, endowed with manifold goodness, *is He Who revealed the Criterion* and ever increased it, for the revelation of the Criterion (*Furqān*) was the manifestation of the discerning intellect (*ʿaql furqānī*) meant solely *for His* special *servant*, who was singled out from the rest of the worlds by his perfect preparedness, in a way that was not possessed by anyone but him. His discerning intellect is the encompassing intellect which is called the 'universal intellect' (*ʿaql al-kull*), which embodies the perfections of all intellects. This only happened when He manifested his self in his Muḥammadan manifestation, through which all His Attributes were emanated to all creatures in all their different states of preparedness. This manifestation is the multiplication and increase of goodness that could not be multiplied or increased any further. Therefore, He said, *That he may be to all the worlds a warner*: that is, to the masses. The Message of every other prophet was meant only for those creatures who had the appropriate level of preparedness, whereas his Message (may God grant him peace) is universal for all. This is the very meaning of the 'seal of prophethood', and explains why his community is the best of communities.

[25:2] *He to Whom belongs the kingdom of the heavens and the earth,* which He rules in His dominion. He engendered each thing with a brand, marking it with the sign of possibility, and testifying to its non-existence; *and Who has not taken a son, nor has He any partner in the kingdom; and He created everything, and then determined it in a precise measure* according to the recognition of some of His Attributes and the manifesting of some of His perfections, but not others: that is, He ordained their levels of preparedness, as He willed, from their perfections, which are His own Attributes.

[25:3] [*Yet they have taken besides Him gods, who create nothing but have* themselves been created, and who possess no harm for themselves, nor any benefit, nor do they possess [any power over] death or life, or resurrection.

[25:4] *And those who disbelieve say, 'This is nothing but a calumny that he has invented, and other folk have helped him with it.' Verily they have committed wrong and [spoken] falsehood.*

[25:5] *And they say, 'Fables of the ancients which he has had written down so that they are read to him morning and evening.']*

[25:6] *Say: 'It has been revealed by Him Who knows [the secret] hidden* from the veiled ones in the worlds *of the heavens and the earth. Indeed, He is ever Forgiving* by covering the attributes of the soul which veil secrets with the lights of His Attributes, *Merciful'* by bestowing perfections upon hearts when they are purified according to their preparedness. One manifestation of His forgiveness and mercy is this very revelation in which you doubt, O veiled ones!

[25:7] *And they also say, 'What is it with this Messenger that he eats food and walks about in the marketplaces? Why has an angel not been sent down to him so as to be a warner along with him?*

Q. 25:4

[25:8] *'Or [why is not] a treasure thrown down to him, or [why has he not] a garden for him to eat from?' The wrongdoers say, 'You are just following a man bewitched!'*

[25:9] *See how they strike similitudes for you, so that they go astray and are unable to find a way.*

[25:10] *Blessed is He Who, if He wishes, will give you better than that—gardens underneath which rivers flow, and will give you palaces.]*

[25:11] *Nay, but they deny [the Hour]:* the Major Resurrection. This denial is due only to their excessive veiling or lack of preparedness, both of which necessitate the chastisement of torment, because of how the fires of corporeal nature and configurations of primordial matter will inevitably overwhelm the darkened souls:

[25:11] *[Nay, but they deny the [coming of the] Hour, and We have prepared for those who deny the Hour a blaze.*

[25:12] *When it sees them from a distant place, they will hear it raging and roaring:]* the effect and power of the Hell-guardians of the heavenly and earthly souls upon them, which will affect them only from afar, if they are prepared to receive it because of how they will reside in the deepest depths, will appear to them as the effects of its power and the dominating rage of its influence.

[25:13] *And when they are flung* from all of the locations of the fire of depriving nature *into a narrow place,* to confine them in an isthmus that befits

97

their configurations and is balanced according to their preparedness, *thereof bound together* with chains of the love of base things and passions which will prevent them from moving to attain their desires, and fetters of images of primordial matter that restrain their limbs and devices and keep them from engaging in any motions in pursuit of their lusts, kept together with their corresponding devils who tempted them from the path of righteousness and beckoned them into error, *they will at that point pray for [their own] annihilation*: hoping for death and mourning what they have lost, because they will be in such a dire state that death will be preferable.

[25:14] [*'Do not pray for a single annihilation on this day, but pray for many annihilations!'*]

[25:15] *Say: 'Is that better, or the Garden of Immortality*, the garden of the realm of holiness, which has been promised [*to the God-fearing*], those who are detached from the raiment of bodies and the attributes of the souls, [*which will be their requital and journey's end*]?'

Q. 25:14

[25:16] *In it they shall have what they wish* of spiritual delights, [*abiding*] for all eternity—[*it is a promise binding on your Lord, [a promise] much besought.*]

[25:17] *And on the day when He will assemble them] and that which they worship besides God*—this applies universally to everything that is worshipped besides God—[*and will say, 'Was it you who misled these servants of Mine, or did they go astray from the way?'*

[25:18] *They will say,*] speaking with the voice of their state, because everything besides the veiled person testifies with its being and existence to God and His Unity, glorifies Him by manifesting His distinction and perfection, and obeys Him in all that He desires of its actions. This is the meaning of His Words, *'Glory be to You! It was not for us to take any guardians besides You.* Their state speaks and declares them innocent of misguidance while affirming the misguidance of those who stand with them and are veiled by them, because of their engrossment in sensory pleasures and absorption in worldly good things, which engendered heedlessness and caused them to neglect remembrance and fall into perdition. [*But You gave them and their fathers ease [of living] until they forgot the Remembrance and became a lost folk.'*

[25:19] *Thus, they will deny you in what you allege, and they will neither be able to circumvent, nor help. And whoever of you does evil, We shall make him taste an awful chastisement.*

[25:20] *And We did not send before you any messengers but that they ate food and walked in the marketplaces. And We have made some of you a trial for others: Will you be steadfast? And your Lord is ever Seer.*

[25:21] *And those who do not expect to encounter Us say, 'Why have the angels not been sent down to us, or why do we not see our Lord?' Assuredly, they are full of arrogance within their souls and have become terribly insolent.*]

[25:22] *The day when they see the angels, there will be no good tidings on that day for the guilty,* because that day is the time of the Minor Resurrection and the destruction of the body, when the heavenly and earthly spiritual forces will influence them with overwhelming power and affliction; and they will be compelled into isthmus-configurations (*al-hay'āt al-barzakhiyya*) that will be at odds with what the nature of their spirits originally was, though at that time they will befit them exactly. *And they will say, 'A forbidding ban!'* They will hope that God will keep this from them and prevent it.

[25:23] [*And We shall attend to the works they did and turn them into scattered dust:*] the reason their deeds will be turned to dust is that they were not built on sound doctrines. The basis for action is faith that expresses sound innate disposition; and if that is lacking, then every good deed is really a sin, because it comes from a corrupt intention and is dedicated to something other than God.

Q. 25:21

[25:24] [*Those who will be the folk of Paradise on that day will be in a [far] better abode, and a [far] better resting place.*]

[25:25] *And on the day when the heaven* of the animal spirit *will be split asunder with the clouds* of the human spirit when they open for it. This is why the works of exegesis say that these clouds will be fine and white. It is symbolised by clouds because of how it acquires the corporeal configuration and subtle psychic image from the body and is veiled by them, and because of how it is the source of knowledge just as clouds are the source of water. This image contains reward and retribution before the corporeal resurrection; *and the angels will be sent down [in a [majestic] descent]* by connecting to it, either to reward it or to punish it, because they are either manifestations of kindness or manifestations of overwhelming power.

[25:26] *The kingdom*—meaning that which is form and unchanging, [i.e.] *the true kingdom*—*on that day will belong to the Compassionate* endowed with all the Attributes of kindness and overwhelming power, Who bestows to all what they deserve. Every false kingdom will be abolished, and no one will be able to save the chastisement from Him, nor find refuge with anyone but Him, because all connections and relations will be severed, and the kingdom of the Compassionate will be absolutely manifest. Or it means the day when the heaven of the heart will be split asunder with the clouds of the light of divine peace, and the angels of the spiritual faculties will descend with divine supports and illuminations of the

99

attributes—this is at the Intermediate Resurrection, when the authority over the heart will be for the Compassionate ascended upon His Throne and manifesting to it with all His Attributes.

And either way, *it will be a hard day for the disbelievers*: in the first case because of how, when the body is destroyed, they will be tormented by benighted configurations and the overwhelming power of the heavenly faculties; and in the second case because of the manifestation of their torment at the witnessing and beholding of the Master of this Resurrection, when there is no other independent being that can influence alongside Him, nor any other dominating power to share in His mastery over their state. Alternatively, [it will be a hard day for them] in the sense that they represent the egocentric faculties, which will be overwhelmed at that time and tormented by spiritual discipline. And God knows best.

[25:27] [*And* [*it will be*] *a day when the wrongdoer will bite his hands, saying,* '*O would that I had followed a way with the Messenger!*

Q. 25:27

[25:28] '*O woe to me! Would that I had not taken so and so as a friend!*

[25:29] '*Verily he has led me astray from the Remembrance after it had come to me: And Satan is ever a deserter of humanity.*'

[25:30] *And the Messenger says,* '*O my Lord. Indeed, my people consider this Qur'ān as something to be shunned.*'

[25:31] *So We have appointed to every prophet an enemy from among the guilty, but your Lord suffices as a Guide and a Helper.*

[25:32] *And those who disbelieve say,* '*Why has the Qur'ān not been revealed to him all at once?*' *Thus,* [*it is*], *that We may strengthen your inner-heart with it, and We have arranged it in a specific order:*] the strengthening of his inner-heart (may God grant him peace) by the Qur'ān was that, when he was returned—at the station of subsistence after annihilation—to the veil of the heart in order to guide humankind, from time to time his soul would overcome his heart with its attributes and he would consequently experience variegation. [It is] as God says, *And We did not send before you any messenger or prophet but that, when he hoped, Satan cast into his hope* [Q. 22:52]; and as He says, *He frowned and turned away* [Q. 80:1]. Then God would correct him by sending revelation and attraction, and educate and admonish him; and he would always return to Him and repent. He (may God grant him peace) said, 'My Lord educated me, and educated me well.' He (may God bless him and grant him peace) also said, 'Sometimes a shadow falls on my heart, and I ask God's forgiveness seventy times in a day.' This went on until he became firm and upright. It was the means by which God put him to the test through the preaching of the Message, which led people to persecute him and show him enmity and hostility.

The wisdom of this tribulation lay in two things. The first [wisdom] pertained to himself, whereby his soul manifested with all its attributes in response to the ascendancy of those opposing enemies, in [relation to] their souls and their attributes, preparedness and ranks. Thus, God would educate him with the wisdom of the existence of each attribute and the virtue of each faculty. In this way, he would attain all the noble character traits and the perfections of all the prophets, as he (may God grant him peace) said, 'I have been sent to complete the noble character traits, and I have been given the sum of all [excellent] speech.' His manifestation with every attribute was necessary in order for him to receive their virtues and wisdoms, since, were it not for the different directions [brought about] in the heart by means of the attributes of the soul, he would not have been prepared to receive the diverse wisdoms and virtues that pertained specifically to each of them. The second wisdom pertained to the community, whereby he was a messenger to all people with all their different states of preparedness and the varied attributes of their souls. Therefore, it was necessary that he be endowed with the sum of all wisdoms, speech, virtues and sublime character traits, so that he could guide all of them with the necessary wisdoms, purify them with the appropriate sublime character traits, and teach them the knowledge from which they could benefit, according to their states of preparedness and their attributes. Otherwise, he would not have been able to call them all. Thus, the revelation was distributed piece by piece according to the differing attributes of the soul and how they appeared at different times, in order to strengthen his heart and keep it firmly upright on the path to God, and in God by adopting His Attributes, and from God in guiding humankind. This is the true meaning of uprightness, so that his example could be followed by wayfarers, arrivals and perfected spiritual guides, as they travelled and kept the company of the Real and were perfected. The arrangement (*tartīl*) was that between each piecemeal revelation there would be an interval, wherein the previous one could firmly sink into his heart and become a permanent trait, rather than an ephemeral state. This makes clear the meaning of His Words:

Q. 25:33

[25:33] *And they do not bring you any similitude*—meaning any unusual attribute—*but that We bring you the truth* to curb the falsehood of that attribute, as He says, *Nay, but We hurl the truth against falsehood, and it obliterates it* [Q. 21:18], which refers to the virtue that opposes that particular vice. *And [what is] better [as] exposition*: that is, a disclosure by means of a Divine Attribute which is manifested to you to fulfil its role and disclose

101

it. In reality, this disclosing Divine Attribute is an exposition and a rebuttal of that false attribute. Every egocentric attribute is the dark shadow of a luminous Divine Attribute in the stages of descent, causing it to be veiled, diminished and sullied—consider passion as opposed to love, anger as opposed to omnipotence, and so on.

[25:34] *Those who will be gathered on their faces*, because of the intensity of their souls' inclination towards the lower direction, so that their innate disposition was perverted, they will be resurrected in forms with faces against the ground and dragged *toward* the Fire (*nār*) of nature: *they will be in the worst place* to receive the truth that would annul the falsehood of their attributes, *and furthest astray from the way* to be guided to the Attributes of God, which would expose and unveil their attributes.

[25:35] [*And verily We gave Moses the Book, and made Aaron, his brother, [go] with him as a minister.*

Q. 25:34

[25:36] *Then We said, 'Go both of you to the people who have denied Our signs.' Then We destroyed them utterly.*

[25:37] *And the people of Noah, when they denied the messengers—We drowned them and made them a sign for people. And We have prepared for the evildoers a painful chastisement.*

[25:38] *And [We destroyed] ʿĀd and Thamūd, and the dwellers at Rass, and many generations in between.*

[25:39] *For each [of them] We struck similitudes, and each [of them] We ruined utterly.*

[25:40] *And verily they will have passed by the town on which an evil shower was rained upon. Can it be that they have not seen it? Nay, but it is that they do not expect resurrection.*

[25:41] *And when they see you, they take you in mockery only: 'Is this the one whom God has sent as a messenger?*

[25:42] *'Indeed, he was about to lead us astray from our gods, had we not stood by them.' And soon they will know, when they behold the chastisement, who is further astray from the way.*]

[25:43] *Have you seen him who has taken as his god his own desire?* Everyone who is veiled by something will stand by that thing because he loves it and associates with it, and therefore in reality he worships his own caprice by worshipping the thing he loves. The thing that inspires his caprice to love something other than God is Satan; and so anyone who loves something other than God, except for the sake of God and through love for God, is a worshipper of that thing, his caprice and Satan too. [Such a person] worships many things, and is split in many directions. *Will you be a guardian over him* after all that, by calling him to the Oneness when he is as distant as can be and veiled by one of its shadows?

[25:44] [*Or do you suppose that most of them listen or comprehend? They are but as the cattle—nay, but they are further astray from the way.*]

[25:45] *Have you not seen your Lord, how He extends the [twilight] shadow* with relative existence (*wujūd iḍāfī*)? Know that the quiddities of things and the realities of essences are all a shadow of the Real and a universal attribute of absolute existence. Their extension is their manifestation through His Name the Light, which denotes the outward external existence through which all things are manifested and which brings the hidden secret of non-being into the open plain of existence, meaning relative existence. *For had He willed, He would have made it still*: that is, firm in the non-being that is the storehouse of its existence, the Mother Book or the Preserved Tablet wherein the existence of all things is affirmed inwardly. Its reality is not pure non-being in the sense of nothingness, since then it would not be able to exist at all, for that which has no existence inwardly in the storehouse of the Real's knowledge and His Unseen can never exist outwardly. The act of creation and erasure is nothing other than manifesting that which is affirmed in the Unseen and then concealing it. He is the Outwardly Manifest and the Inwardly Hidden, and He has knowledge of all things. *Then We made the sun* of the intellect *an indicator of it*, [i.e.] the shadow, guiding to the fact that its reality is not the same thing as its existence, since otherwise there would be no difference between them outwardly and there would be nothing other than the existence alone; for if its existence were not possible, it would not be anything at all, and therefore nothing indicates that it is anything other than its existence except for the intellect.

Q. 25:44

[25:46] *Then We retract it to Us* by annihilating it *by gentle retraction*, because everything that is annihilated from existent things at any time is gentle compared to what precedes it, and everything that is retracted will be manifested again shortly afterwards in a different manifestation. The term 'retraction' (*qabḍ*) shows that the annihilation is not a total erasure, but only a prevention from spreading beyond His grasp (*qabḍa*), which is the intellect that protects its form and its reality from pre-eternity to sempiternity.

[25:47] *And He it is Who made for you the night* of the darkness of the soul *as a garment* to cover you from being overwhelmed by the witnessing of the Real and His Attributes, and the Essence and its shadow, so that you are veiled, *and the sleep* of heedlessness in the life of this world *for repose* so that you rest oblivious to the true eternal life, as he (may God grant him peace) said, 'The people are asleep; and when they die, they awaken.' *And He made the day* of the light of the spirit *for rising* to revive your hearts, so that you spread out into the expanse of holiness after the sleep of the senses.

[25:48] *And He it is Who sends forth the winds* of lordly fragrances *dispersing* life and glad tidings *before* [*His mercy*], the mercy of perfection by the manifestation of the Attributes; *and We send down from the heaven* of the spirit *purifying water* of knowledge to cleanse you of the pollution of impurities and the dross of natures, corrupt doctrines and corrupting ignorance.

[25:49] *That We might revive a dead land*, a heart dead by ignorance, *and give it as drink to the many cattle* of egocentric faculties by means of beneficial practical sciences, *and humans* of spiritual faculties by means of discursive sciences, [*which*] *We have created.*

Q. 25:48

[25:50] *And verily We have distributed it*, this revealed science, *among them* in various forms and images, *so that they may remember* their realities and their true homes, and the covenant, connection and goodly origin which they have forgotten. *But most people are only intent on ingratitude* towards the gift of veridical guidance, and thanklessness towards the mercy of mercifulness (*raḥīmiyya*), because of how they are veiled by the forms of mercy in the coverings of majesty from murky depths of primordial matter.

[25:51] *And had We willed, We could have sent forth in every town a warner*: that is, We could have distributed among several people your absolute perfection by which you call all of humankind to the truth, and measured it out according to the classes of people and their varying levels of preparedness for the prophets, as He says *for every folk there is a guide* [Q. 13:7], so that We sent a prophet to each class of people who suited them. This is how it was before He sent Muḥammad, so that Moses was exclusive to the Israelites, Shuʿayb to the people of Midian, and so on. With this We would have lessened your struggle, since struggle is commensurate with perfection, and the greater the perfection, the harder the struggle. God rules over each group with one of His Names; and since the perfect messenger manifests all of His Attributes and realises all of His Names, he is obliged to struggle with all groups and communities with all the Attributes. But We did not do this, because of the immensity of your value and your status as the absolutely perfect, the supreme pole, the seal. This was expounded upon further in the commentary on His Words, *Thus,* [*it is,*] *that We may strengthen your inner-heart with it* [Q. 25:32].

104

[25:52] *So do not [obey the disbelievers]* who are veiled because of how they stop at certain veils and lack certain attributes; *but struggle against them therewith*, since you have been sent to all humankind, *with a great endeavour*, the greatest of all struggles. [It is] as he said, 'No prophet was abused as much as I have been': which means that no prophet was perfected as much as he was.

[25:53] *And He it is Who merged the two seas*, mixing the seas of body and spirit through engendering: *this one*, the sea of the spirit, *palatable, sweet*, pure and delicious, *[and the other,]* the sea of the body, *saltish, bitter*: putrid and turbid and unpalatable; *and He set between the two an isthmus*, which is the animal soul that acts as a barrier between them, so that they cannot mix and the spirit is not sullied by the body and made dense, nor is the body illuminated by the spirit and made detached, *and a forbidding ban*: a sanctuary where each of them can seek refuge from the assault of the other, and an obstruction to prevent it.

[25:54] *[And He it is Who created man from water, and made for him ties of blood and ties of marriage. For your Lord is ever Powerful.*

Q. 25:52

[25:55] *And they worship besides God that which neither benefits them, nor harms them; and the disbeliever is ever a partisan against his Lord.*

[25:56] *And We have not sent you except as a bearer of good tidings, and as a warner.*

[25:57] *Say: 'I do not ask of you in return for this any reward, except that whoever wishes to follow a way to his Lord [should do so].'*

[25:58] *And put your trust in the Living One Who does not die*: observe how all things die, and are unable to move themselves, as He says, *You will indeed die, and they [too] will indeed die* [Q. 39:30]. They only move because of instigators which God created in them. Witness this through the annihilation of your deeds and the deeds of all in the acts of the Real, and the lifting of their veils from His acts; for the station of trust is annihilation in the divine acts. His Words *in the Living One Who does not die* indicate that the foundation of trust is the witnessing of the Attribute of His life through which every living thing lives, for anything that will die does not live in and of itself.

The station of trust is realised by the ascent from the station of the annihilation of the acts to annihilation in the attribute of life. The Sufis say that a station is only truly realised when one ascends to the station above it. If every living thing will die, then it only lives through the life of the Essentially Living Whose life is one with His Essence, and it is through Him that they move. So be not concerned with their deeds, for even if

105

they were to apply all of their efforts jointly to harm you, they would not be able to harm you unless God destined it for you, as the *ḥadīth* says.

And make glorifications in His praise and extol Him by detaching yourself from your attributes and erasing them with His own, for no one besides Him can possess an independent attribute that could be a source of their action. Adorn yourself in His praise by taking on His Attributes, for true praise is to adorn oneself with His Attributes of perfection for which He is praised. This is the culmination and realisation of the station of trust, by negating the attributes that are the foundations of deeds from the other. When you detach yourself from your attributes and adorn yourself with His, you will witness how His knowledge encompasses all things. Hence, you will have no further need to ask Him to protect you from their crimes against you or to requite them for their abuse of you; and you will witness His power to requite them. As Abraham (may God grant him peace) said, 'His knowledge of my state means that I have no need to ask Him.' This is the meaning of His Words, *And He suffices as One Aware of the sins of His servants.*

Q. 25:59

[25:59] *Who created the heavens and the earth*: that is, He Who was veiled by the heavens of the spirits and the earth of the bodies, *and all that is between them* of faculties, in six days which are the six thousand from the beginning of the time of Adam until Muḥammad (may God grant them peace); for creation is nothing other than the veiling of the Real by things, and the days are the days of the Hereafter, not the days of this world. For there was no world then, nor any sun or daytime: *And truly a day with your Lord is like a thousand years of your counting* [Q. 22:47]. *And then He presided upon the Throne* of the Muḥammadan heart on the seventh day, which is Friday, the day of congregation, when all Attributes and Names meet. This is the meaning of presiding through uprightness with total manifestation and universal emanation, which is the mercy of undiscriminating compassion. This is why He chose to mention the Name *The Compassionate* in the context of this presiding, rather than any other Name, since presiding means total manifestation only in the context of this Name. One could also interpret the days as the six months wherein the creation of the heavens of the spirit of the embryo, the earth of its body and the faculties that lie between them were completed, and the presiding as the total manifestation upon the throne of its heart, which was upon the water of the droplet before the creation of what He created in the seventh month, wherein He established it in another creation by making it a human being. Or one could take the compassion to mean the universality of His supra-sensory or formal emanation from its heart to all the parts of its being. *So ask about Him anyone who is well aware*: ask a gnostic of Him, and he shall tell you about His state, and ask him about how He knows all things.

[25:60] *And when it is said to them, 'Prostrate yourselves [before the Compassionate,' they say, 'And what is the Compassionate? Should we prostrate ourselves to whatever you bid us?' And it increases their aversion]*: when you command them to become annihilated in all His Attributes and in obedience to Him, they refuse to obey your command because they are unprepared to receive this emanation and lack the knowledge of this Name, for they have not had the success to attain all of the Names, or are veiled from them.

[25:61] *Blessed is He Who has placed in the heaven* of the soul the *constellations* of the senses, *and has placed in it a lamp and a shining moon*: the lamp of the sun of the spirit, and the moon of the heart shining with the light of the spirit.

Q. 25:60

[25:62] *And He it is Who made the night* of the darkness of the soul, *and* the *day* of the light of the heart, *[to appear] in succession for him who desires to remember* the forgotten covenant in the daylight of the heart, and reflect on the meanings and gnostic sciences, *or desires* in the night of the darkness of the soul *to be thankful* by doing deeds of obedience and acquiring sublime character traits and dispositions.

[25:63] *And the [true] servants of the Compassionate*, those who are chosen to receive the emanation of this Name because of their ample preparedness, *are those who walk upon the earth modestly*, those whose souls are tranquil with the light of divine peace, so that they refrain from trampling around as their nature would otherwise dictate. They are modest in their physical motions because their limbs have been trained with the demeanour of tranquillity; *and who, when the [ignorant address them, say [words of] peace]*: when the people of foolishness address them, they let their words go by peacefully without objecting to them, because they are filled with mercy and distanced from foolish displays of I-ness. Their souls have grown, nourished by the light of the heart, so that they are unaffected and undisturbed by harassment.

[25:64] *And who spend the night [before their Lord]*, dead to the station of the soul by their own volition, *prostrating* with spiritual discipline *and standing* upright through the attributes of the heart, alive through its life for God's sake, saying with the voice of their states whose prayers are never long in the answering:

[25:65] [*And who say,*] '*Our Lord, avert* [*from us the chastisement of Hell. Indeed, its chastisement is abiding.*

[25:66] '*It is truly a wretched abode and residence!*'

[25:67] *And who, when they expend, are neither prodigal nor parsimonious; but between such lies moderation.*

[25:68] *And* [*those*] *who do not call on another god along with God, nor slay the soul which God has forbidden, except with due cause, and who do not commit fornication—for whoever does that shall meet with retribution:*] He first describes them as being completely purified and annihilated from all the attributes of the soul, the vices that plunge one into the torment of the hell of nature, the evil abode and the wretched fate. He then describes them as being completely adorned with all four genera of virtue. This describes their life through the heart after their death from the soul, as is said, 'Die by volition, and you shall live by nature.' Finding the balance between prodigality and parsimony when spending is the virtue of justice. The upholding of Oneness described in His Words *and* [*those*] *who do not call on another god along with God* is the foundation of the virtue of wisdom. When it is attained, its shadow, which is justice, falls over the souls so that it is characterised by all the virtues. Refraining from slaying the forbidden soul alludes to the virtue of courage, and refraining from fornication is the virtue of chastity. He then speaks of those who are on their opposite, veiled from the emanation of divine mercy, which is within the divine compassion whose universal emanation they are unprepared to receive, so that they are not marked by it even though they are included in its manifest emanation which includes all things. Therefore, He says *for whoever does that*—[meaning] whoever commits all the types of vices including associating partners with God—*shall meet* [*with retribution*]: in requital for the great absolute sin:

[25:69] It will be spiritual and physical *chastisement that is doubled for him* in the form of complete veiling and the configurations of lower matter *on the Day of* the Minor *Resurrection,* and he will abide therein [*abased*] with utter debasement.

[25:70] *Except for him who repents* by returning to God and renouncing sin, so that he exchanges idolatry for faith, and vices for virtues, [*and believes, and acts righteously:*] *for such, God will replace their evil deeds with good deeds* by erasing those configurations from their souls and establishing the others; *for God is ever Forgiving,* covering the attributes of their souls with His light, *Merciful,* emanating perfections upon them in His grace. This is true repentance.

Q. 25:65

[25:71] [*And whoever repents and acts righteously, indeed turns to God with due repentance:*] then after speaking of true repentance, He describes the condition of the spiritual wayfarers, saying:

[25:72] *And those who do not give false testimony* that is, they do not indulge the people of falsehood who are engrossed with objects of delusion; for the people of this world are people of falsehood who think ephemeral things are eternal, vile things are beautiful, non-existent things are real, and evil things are good. They are false, astray and errant, and so they steer clear of them by keeping to seclusion and preferring deeds of obedience and worship. *And, when they come across senseless talk* and idle curiosity, *they* turn away from it and pass by with dignity, and do not sully their honour by engaging with it, content as they are with their needs and not chasing after luxuries. They are truly ascetic, renounced and detached. Then after describing true asceticism and detachment, He then connects this with true worship and realisation, saying:

Q. 25:71

[25:73] *And those who, when they are reminded of the revelations of their Lord*—that is, when gnostic mysteries, realities, manifestations of Attributes and witnessings are unveiled to them—*do not fall on* the knowledge of those revelations *deaf and blind*; but rather receive them with attentive ears—the ears of the heart, not the soul—and witness them with keen eyes lined with the light of guidance. He then describes how they seek to ascend from the station of the heart to the level of the foremost, and ask God's protection from the variegation of the soul and its attributes, that they might follow the path of those who are drawn near:

[25:74] *And those who say, 'Our Lord, grant us in* the *spouses* of our souls, *and* the *offspring* of our faculties [*a joyful sight*] that brings joy to our eyes in the form of their obedience and willing surrender, and their illumination with the light of the heart, and make them lowly so that they do not seek to ascend and dominate with pride and tyranny, *and make us paragons for the God-fearing,'* the detached folk, by our arrival at the station of the foremost.

[25:75] *Those—they will be rewarded with the sublime abode* of Paradise and the garden of the spirit *forasmuch as they were steadfast* with God and in God, from everything but God; *and they will be met therein with a greeting* of eternal life,[1] *and* [*words of*] *peace* and freedom from all blights. God will give them life by sustaining them perpetually through His own subsistence, and grant them peace by lending His perfection to them, as He says, *Their*

---

1 A play on the common lexical root of *taḥiyya* ('greeting') and *ḥayāt* ('life').

greeting on the day they encounter Him will be 'Peace' [Q. 33:44]; *their greeting therein: 'Peace!'* [Q. 14:23].

[25:76] [*Abiding therein. Excellent is it as an abode and station.*

[25:77] *Say:*] '*My Lord would not be concerned with you were it not for your supplication.* [*But you have denied, and so that will remain binding*':] were it not that you seek God and have aspiration, you would be something unremarkable and of no account, like the insects and scurrying beasts. A man is only a man, and something of account, if he is a person of aspiration and seeking. And God (Exalted is He) knows best.

Q. 25:76

26
THE POETS
SŪRAT AL-SHUʿARĀʾ

In the Name of God, the Compassionate, the Merciful

[26:1] [*Ṭā. Sīn. Mīm.*

[26:2] *Those are the signs of the Manifest Book:*] *Ṭā* alludes to the Pure One (*ṭāhir*), *sīn* to Peace (*salām*), and *mīm* to the One Who encompasses all things with knowledge (*muḥīṭ*). The Manifest Book whose revelations are these Names and Attributes is the perfect Muḥammadan being endowed with elucidation and wisdom, as the Commander of the Believers (may God grant him peace) said, 'Within you is the Manifest Book / By whose letters the hidden is made plain.' Thus, the meaning is similar to what was said about *Ṭā Hā*: when the Prophet saw that they were not being guided by his light nor heeding his call, he felt as though this were his failing rather than theirs, and so he increased his spiritual discipline and effort and became further annihilated in witnessing. So God revealed to him: These attributes —purity from the pollution of remnants of I-ness that might prevent you from influencing the souls of others, freedom from deficiencies in preparedness, and perfection that covers all levels with knowledge—are the attributes of the book of your essence, which makes manifest every perfection and level by being adorned with all the Divine Attributes and incorporating the meanings of all His Names.

[26:3] [*Perhaps, you might kill yourself that they will not become believers:*] do not destroy yourself for their sake by engaging in excessively difficult disciplines because they do not believe in it and reject it, for this is their own failing, whether because they are too heavily veiled or because they are not prepared for it. His Words *Perhaps, you might kill yourself* are meant to express compassion: be kinder to yourself, lest you destroy yourself with disciplines because of their lack of faith and rejection.

[26:4] *If We wish We will send down to them [a sign] from the heaven* from the higher realm with Our assistance to you, whereby *their necks will remain bowed in humility* and they will yield and surrender outwardly, even if faith has not yet entered their hearts, as it was on the day of the Conquest of Mecca. Though their faith is not yet present, since it is a matter of the heart, they will still be made to submit by force and necessity.

[26:5] [*And there would never come to them from the Compassionate any remembrance that is new, but that they used to disregard it.*

[26:6] *Verily, then, they have denied; but soon there will come to them the news of that which they used to deride.*

[26:7] *Have they not contemplated the earth: how many We have caused to grow therein of every splendid kind [of vegetation]?*

[26:8] *Indeed, in that there is a sign, but most of them are not believers.*

[26:9] *And truly your Lord, He is the Mighty, the Merciful.*

[26:10] *And when your Lord called to Moses*: the Moses of the heart refined with practical wisdom, trained with intellectual sciences, inflamed by the remembrance of holy lights and intimate perfections, and the description of realities disengaged and detached from all but the divine presence. This heart overcomes the appetitive faculty by striving to seek spiritual provisions from gnostic teachings of certitude and meanings of reality, after slaying the tyrant of appetite which served the Pharaoh of the evil-enjoining soul, and fleeing from its oppression to the Midian of the city of knowledge on the spiritual horizon. There it entered the service of the Shuʿayb of the spirit in the station of the inner mystery, which is the venue of communion and intimate discourse, by an intellectual traversal of the path of wisdom, thereby acquiring sublime character traits by temperance, before travelling with God on the path of Oneness and spiritual discipline by renunciation and detachment.

Yet if the soul remains, after being strengthened by knowledge and gnosis and beautified by virtue, it will become proud of its own beauty and perfection; and in the midst of its noblest state, it will begin to transgress and vie with its Lord for the Attributes of magnificence and greatness, delighting in its glory and splendour, veiled by its egocentricity and its attempt to usurp the perfection of the Real because of His regard for it. Thus, it will become the most evil of people, according to the words of the Prophet (may God grant him peace), 'The most evil of people will be those still alive when the Resurrection begins.' If it were to die and then experience the Resurrection, it would be the best of people.

'*Go to the wrongdoing folk,* [26:11] [*Pharaoh's folk*]: the egocentric pharaonic faculties who aid the Pharaoh of the evil-enjoining soul and

Q. 26:5

take it as their lord, attributing the perfection of the Real to it, which is the most heinous kind of wrongdoing. *Will they not show fear* of My might and My power to destroy them and annihilate them?'

[26:12] [*He said, 'My Lord,*] *I fear they will deny me* and my call to Oneness, and that they will not obey my efforts to engage in spiritual discipline, renunciation and detachment.

[26:13] *'And that anguish will constrain my breast* because I lack the ability to compel them, and I know that they will refuse to accept the commandments of the Divine Law and the secrets of revelation, and anything that is outside the bounds of their usual mental sphere, since they are accustomed to this and to their pharaonic tyranny; *and that my tongue will not utter clearly* these meanings to them, because they contradict that to which they have become accustomed and upon which they have been raised, namely the practical wisdoms that call for maintaining balance in character rather than becoming totally annihilated. *So send for* the *Aaron* of the intellect, that he might train them with logic and direct them in a manner which they will find easy to accept, and which takes into consideration the welfare of both this life and the next and the happiness of both abodes. Their disposition will be softened and their obstinacy weakened by his amiability and tact, and how he treats them with his knowledge and forbearance.

Q. 26:12

[26:14] *'And I have sinned against them* by slaying the tyrant of appetite. *And I fear* that if I call them to Oneness and command them to become detached and renounce luxuries so as to suffice with needs, *they will slay me'* with domination and force. This represents the situation of the one whose soul is veiled by wisdom and has not yet found his feet on the path of Unity, although he is certainly prepared for it and unwilling to stop at the perfection he has already attained. It is very rare for such a person's soul to accept something that contradicts his beliefs and to yield to following the Divine Law based on the authority of another, unless the divine nurture has been destined for him and grace aids him by attracting him.

[26:15] [*Said He,*] *'Certainly not!* assuaging his fears by encouraging him and promising him support. *Go both of you* [*with Our signs*]: He commanded him to take the intellect with him because it was well suited to the task of affirming Oneness through proofs that would overcome the opposition of pharaonic tyranny. *We will indeed be with you, hearing*: He promised shelter, protection and strengthening of certitude, for when the Real is with someone, nothing can defeat him.

[26:16] [*'So the two of you approach Pharaoh and say, "Indeed, We are the*

113

Messenger of the Lord of the Worlds,] [26:17] *that you should let go forth with us the Children of Israel"'*: the spiritual faculties that have been weakened and enslaved in the pursuit of corporeal pleasures.

[26:18] [*He said, 'Did we not rear you among us as a child, and did you not stay with us for years of your life?*] This represents the state of childhood and youth up until the time of detachment and the search for perfection, which takes hold at the age of forty. In this time, the heart is engaged in rearing the soul and serving as its guardian instinctively.

[26:19] [*'And you committed that deed of yours being an ingrate'*:] the deed was the blameworthy movement of the soul when it sought to dominate through appetite. The ingratitude of which he accused him was the snubbing of the duties of his childrearing.

[26:20] [*He said, 'I did that then,*] *when I was astray*: that is, I was not an ingrate because it was right to be so, but because I was one of those who are not guided to the path of Unity.

Q. 26:18

[26:21] [*'So I fled from you, as I was afraid of you.*] *Then my Lord gave me judgement*, a wisdom (*ḥikma*) more sublime than the path of rational argument, beyond the bounds of acquisition and logic, *and made me one of the messengers* to convey it to you.

[26:22] [*'That is a favour with which you now reproach me, that you have enslaved the Children of Israel'*:] the enslaving of the Children of Israel, the faculties which are my people, was not a favour that you did for me, that you might expect my gratitude; but it was an act of transgression and tyranny. Had you not enslaved them, my mother—physical nature — would not have cast me into the river of primordial matter in the box of the body, and I would have been raised by my own folk, my people, the spiritual faculties.

[26:23] *Pharaoh said, 'And what is "the Lord of the Worlds"?'* It is said regarding this story that Pharaoh was a proponent of logical enquiry and so asked about the reality of God. So Moses (may God grant him peace) answered him:

[26:24] [*He said,*] *'The Lord of the heavens and the earth and all that is between them*: thereby explaining that His reality cannot be known with exactitude because of its simplicity, and cannot be known to the intellect because of the power of its light and subtlety. Instead, he described it by referring to an external attribute and a necessary quality, and then objected to his ignorance and lack of certitude by saying *should you have conviction'*: in other words, 'Were you a person of conviction, you would know that there is no way for the intellect to know Him except by ascertaining His existence by the evidence of His acts which are His alone. As for His reality, no one but Him can know it. What you have asked is something that the rational mind cannot reach.' When Moses said this, Pharaoh mocked him and invited his people to witness his weak intellect and how his answer did not fit the question, by way of expressing his incredulity and inviting his people to mock him:

[26:25] [*He said to those who were around him, 'Did you not hear?'*

[26:26] *He said, 'Your Lord and the Lord of your forefathers.'*

[26:27] *He said, 'Indeed, this messenger of yours sent to you is a madman!'*] When Moses repeated his attempt to explain, by mentioning another special divine quality, Pharaoh called him a madman.

[26:28] [*He said, 'The Lord of the east and the west and all that is between them:*] Moses attempted a third time, and then added *should you comprehend'*: in other words, 'If I am mad, then where is your own mind, that it might recognise its own bounds and not stray beyond its limits?' This statement alludes to how when the soul is veiled by the objects of its own comprehension, it cannot be guided to gnosis of the Real and the wisdom of the Message and the Divine Law, nor will it deign to follow or yield to obey. Instead, it will manifest its self-regard, seek knowledge and lordship, and attempt to dominate the Divine Message, which is the meaning of His Words:

Q. 26:25

[26:29] [*He said,*] '*If you choose any god other than me, I will surely make you a prisoner!*'

[26:30] [*He said, 'What if I bring you something manifest?'*

[26:31] *He said, 'Then bring it, if you are truthful.'*

[26:32] *So he threw down his staff, and, lo and behold, it was a manifest serpent.*

[26:33] *Then he drew out his hand and, lo and behold, it was white before the onlookers*:] the manifest thing that prevented him from dominating, and turned him back from his ascendancy and tyranny, was the blinding holy light and the illuminating Throne-proof, which captured the heart on the spiritual horizon, and confounded the soul and the faculties which indicated the truthfulness of his claim. This took the form of the strengthening of his two intellectual faculties—the discursive and the cognitive—for the configuration of light and the power of omnipotence. The first became a holy faculty aided by far-reaching wisdom, upon which it leaned for support in the subduing of the rival in debate as well as the repelling of the enemy in combat. The second became an angelic faculty aided by perfect omnipotence, that it might confound anyone who attempted to overwhelm it with power or challenge it with force. When he threw down the staff of holy power, by means of the invocation of the heart, it became a serpent manifesting the serpent-nature of powerful domination; and when he drew out the hand of angelic nature from the pocket of the heart, the onlooker was dazzled by the brilliance and the light.

[26:34] [*He said to the council around him, 'Indeed, this man is a cunning sorcerer,* [26:35] *who seeks to expel you from your land by his sorcery. So what do you advise?'*

[26:36] *They said, 'Put him and his brother off for a while and send gatherers into the cities* [26:37] *to bring you every cunning sorcerer'*:] when the pharaonic soul and its faculties were dazzled and confounded, and feared that he would expel them from the land of the body and drive away the evil of their corruption and power therein, preventing their domination and tyranny, they sent out satanic impulses to rouse the egocentric inclinations to the cities where resided the delusional and imaginative faculties.

Q. 26:34

[26:38] [*So the sorcerers were assembled at a fixed time of a known day*:] they gathered their sorcerers to cast misgivings and insinuations with the instruments of deceit and nagging doubt, and assembled them at the time of gathering when all of the egocentric, corporeal and spiritual faculties came together to direct the inner mystery towards the presence of holiness.

[26:39] [*And it was said to the people, 'Will you assemble!'*

[26:40] *Maybe we will follow the sorcerers, should they be the victors'.*

[26:41] *So when the sorcerers came, they said to Pharaoh, 'Shall we indeed have a reward if we were to be the victors?'*

[26:42] *He said, 'Yes* [*of course*]*! And you shall then be among those closest* [*to me*]*'.*

[26:43] *Moses said to them, 'Cast what you have to cast'.*

[26:44] *So they cast their ropes and their staffs, and said, 'By the power of Pharaoh we shall surely be the victors!'*] They cast the ropes of delusion and imagination and the staffs of misgivings and insinuations, to make it seem that by the power of Pharaoh the evil-enjoining soul and its power would be triumphant, hoping to be rewarded with respect, status and closeness to the heart of power and authority.

[26:45] [*Thereat Moses cast his staff and, lo and behold, it was swallowing what they had faked*:] the serpent of holy power snatched them up by the power of Oneness, and swallowed their calumnies by the light of realisation.

[26:46] [*So the sorcerers fell down prostrating.*

[26:47] *They said, 'We believe in the Lord of the Worlds,* [26:48] *the Lord*

of Moses and Aaron':] when they lost their instruments, the sorcerers of delusion, imagination and fancy yielded and believed, by the light of certitude and the guidance of the Moses of the heart and the Aaron of the intellect, in their Lord.

[26:49] *[Pharaoh] said, 'Do you believe him, though I have not given you leave? He is indeed your chief, the one who has taught you sorcery. Soon you will know I will assuredly cut-off your hands and legs on opposite sides, then I shall surely crucify you all.'*

[26:50] *They said, 'There is no harm [in that]. Surely to our Lord we shall return.*

[26:51] *'Indeed, We hope our Lord will forgive us our iniquities, for being the first to believe':*] their hands and legs were amputated, rendering them unable to roam around the land of the body spreading all manner of trickeries, machinations and plots and seeking comfort and the slaking of lusts and appetites, and to exercise authority and power over the estates of the corporeal faculties. By disobeying the soul and obeying the heart, they were crucified upon the trees of the vegetative soul, kept from moving by means of discipline, power and authority, turned towards their Lord by following the heart and conformity to the inner mystery when it set out towards the Real, forgiven for their sins of calumny and deceit by the light of holiness.

Q. 26:49

[26:52] *[And We revealed to Moses, [saying], 'Journey with My servants by night, for indeed you will be pursued':*] He revealed to the Moses of the heart how the spiritual faculties would have to journey forth, in the night of the calm of the senses and the stillness of the egocentric faculties, to the presence of Unity, passing through the sea of primordial matter.

[26:53] *[Then Pharaoh sent to the cities gatherers, [saying]:*

[26:54] *'Indeed, these are but a small gang.*

[26:55] *'And indeed they have enraged us.*

[26:56] *'And indeed we are all on our guard.'*

[26:57] *So We made them go forth from gardens, and springs, [26:58] and treasures, and splendid places.*

[26:59] *So [it was], and We made the Children of Israel to inherit these.*

[26:60] *Then they pursued them at sunrise.*

[26:61] *And when the two hosts sighted each other, the companions of Moses said, 'We have been caught!'*

[26:62] *He said, 'Certainly not! Indeed, I have my Lord with me. He will guide me.'*

[26:63] *Thereupon We revealed to Moses: 'Strike the sea with your staff,' whereupon it parted, and each part was as a mighty mountain:*] the Pharaoh of the soul pursued them with variegations, mustering his forces from the cities of the natures of the limbs, afraid that he would lose his authority and kingship, filled with rage at the impudence of the heart and how it had amassed followers and overcome his domain and his allies. When they had almost caught up with them and were about to meet and face one another, the Moses of the heart, by the command of the Real, brought down the staff of holy power onto the sea of primordial matter, and it was divided into needs (*ḥuqūq*) and luxuries (*ḥuẓūẓ*).

[26:64] [*And there We brought near the others.*

[26:65] *And We delivered Moses and all those who were with him.*

[26:66] *Then We drowned the others*:] Moses and his people were saved by following the path of detachment. Furthermore, by their renunciation of luxuries and insistence on needs, they saw that their enemies were expelled from the paradisiacal gardens of egocentric pleasures, and the springs of their experiential realisation and caprices, and the treasures of their hoards and means, and the station of dependence on their appetites. Then Moses and his people emerged from the sea by this parting, and the Pharaoh of the soul and his people were all drowned.

Q. 26:64

[26:67] [*Indeed, in that there is a sign, but most of them are not believers.*

[26:68] *And surely your Lord, He is the Mighty, the Merciful.*

[26:69] *And recite to them the tiding of Abraham,* [26:70] *when he said to his father and his people,*] '*What do you worship?*'

[26:71] [*They said, 'We worship idols and remain cleaving to them.'*

[26:72] *He said, 'Do they hear you when you supplicate?*

[26:73] *'Or do they bring you benefit or harm?'*

[26:74] *They said, 'Rather, we found our fathers so doing.'*

[26:75] *He said, 'Have you considered what you have been worshipping,* [26:76] *you and your ancestors?*

[26:77] *'They are indeed hateful to me*:] when someone clings to a thing and loves it, adores it and is loyal to it, he is a worshipper of that thing, and veiled by it from his Lord, prevented from reaching His perfection. Such a thing is hateful to a monotheist, for to him nothing but God exists, except in delusions. The instigator of such worship is Satan, and such a worshipper is dominated by darkness and enmity. Yet the monotheist knows that none but the Real can cause harm or benefit, nor does he see or hear by his own power, for he sees that the Real is with every soul in all that it does, and that the hands that perform all actions are in the presence of His Names, from whence they come. Thus, he (may God grant him peace) said:

[26:78] *'[He] Who created me, and it is He Who guides me, [26:79] and provides me with food and drink,* to the end: [26:80] *[and when I am sick, it is He Who cures me; [26:81] and Who will make me die, then give me life]*: He is the Creator, the Guide, the Giver of Food and Drink, the Healer, the Dealer of Death, the Bringer of Life. He affirms this elsewhere when He says, *And it will be said to them, 'Where is that which you used to worship besides God? Do they help you, or do they help one another?'* [Q. 26:92–93]; *'So [now] we have no intercessors, nor any sympathetic friend'* [Q. 26:100–101]. Since this station was the station of annihilation, wherein the only sin is for any remnant of the ego to remain, he feared the sin of his state and therefore hoped for forgiveness from Him by the light of His Essence, and said:

[26:82] *'And Who, I hope, will forgive me my iniquity on the Day of Judgement* at the Major Resurrection, and not punish me with deprivation for the emergence of any remnant of my ego. He then requested uprightness in his realisation of Him in the station of subsistence, saying:

Q. 26:78

[26:83] *'My Lord, grant me [unerring] judgement and unite me with the righteous*: that is, wisdom and judgement in the Real, that I might be one of those whom You have made a means for the righteousness of the world and the perfection of Your creation.

[26:84] *'And confer on me a worthy repute among posterity*: make me beloved to You, that by Your love the rest of creation will always love me, and I will attain a worthy repute among them; for when someone loves something, he will frequently speak of it well, and the one will become linked with the other.

[26:85] *['And make me among the inheritors of the Garden of Bliss.*

[26:86] *'And forgive my father, for indeed he is one of those who are astray.*

[26:87] *'And do not disgrace me on the day when they are resurrected; [26:88] the day when neither wealth nor children will avail,]* [26:89] *except him who comes to God with a heart that is sound'*: the soundness of the heart is in two things: its freedom from a lack of preparedness in innate disposition, and its liberty from the veils of the soul's attributes in creation.

[26:90] *[And Paradise will be brought near for the God-fearing, [26:91] and Hell will be revealed [plainly] for the perverse.*

[26:92] *And it will be said to them, 'Where is that which you used to worship [26:93] besides God? Do they help you, or do they help one another?'*

[26:94] *Then they will be hurled into it, they and the perverse, [26:95] and the hosts of Iblīs, all together.*

[26:96] *They shall say, as they wrangle therein, [26:97] 'By God, we had indeed been in manifest error, [26:98] when we equated you with the Lord of the Worlds.*

[26:99] 'And it was none other than the sinners that led us astray.

[26:100] 'So [now] we have no intercessors, [26:101] nor any sympathetic friend.

[26:102] 'If only we had another turn, we would have been among those who believe!'

[26:103] Indeed, in that there is a sign; but most of them are not believers.

[26:104] And truly your Lord, He is the Mighty, the Merciful.

[26:105] The people of Noah denied the messengers, [26:106] when Noah, their brother, said to them, 'Will you not fear [God]?

[26:107] 'Indeed, I am a trusted messenger [sent] to you.

[26:108] 'So fear God and obey me.

[26:109] 'I do not ask of you any reward for it; for my reward lies only with the Lord of the Worlds.

[26:110] 'So fear God and obey me.'

[26:111] They said, 'Shall we believe in you, when it is the lowliest people who follow you?'

Q. 26:99

[26:112] He said, 'And what do I know of what they may have been doing?

[26:113] 'Their reckoning is only my Lord's concern, if only you were aware.

[26:114] 'And I am not about to drive away the believers.

[26:115] 'I am just a plain warner.'

[26:116] They said, 'If you do not desist, O Noah, you will assuredly be among those assailed.'

[26:117] He said, 'My Lord, my people have denied me, [26:118] so judge conclusively between me and them, and deliver me and the believers who are with me.'

[26:119] So We delivered him and those who were with him in the laden Ark.

[26:120] Thereafter We drowned the rest.

[26:121] Indeed, in that there is a sign; but most of them are not believers.

[26:122] Truly your Lord, He is the Mighty, the Merciful.

[26:123] ʿĀd denied the messengers, [26:124] when Hūd, their brother, said to them, 'Will you not fear God?

[26:125] 'Indeed, I am a trusted messenger [sent] to you.

[26:126] 'So fear God and obey me.

[26:127] 'I do not ask of you any reward for this; for my reward lies only with the Lord of the Worlds.

[26:128] 'Do you build on every prominence a monument so that you may hurl abuse?

[26:129] 'And you set-up structures that perhaps you might last forever.

[26:130] 'And when you assault, you assault like tyrants.

[26:131] 'So fear God, and obey me.

[26:132] 'And fear Him Who has provided you, in a way that you know,

[26:133] *provided you with cattle and sons,* [26:134] *and gardens, and springs.*

[26:135] *'Indeed, I fear for you the chastisement of a tremendous day.'*

[26:136] *They said, 'It is the same to us whether you admonish [us] or are not one of those who admonish.*

[26:137] *'This is merely the fabrication of the ancients,* [26:138] *and we will not be chastised.'*

[26:139] *So they denied him, whereupon We destroyed them. Indeed, in that there is a sign; but most of them are not believers.*

[26:140] *Truly your Lord, He is the Mighty, the Merciful.*

[26:141] *Thamūd denied the messengers,* [26:142] *when Saleh, their brother, said to them, 'Will you fear God?*

[26:143] *'Indeed, I am a trusted messenger [sent] to you.*

[26:144] *'So fear God and obey me.*

[26:145] *'I do not ask of you any reward for this; for my reward lies only with the Lord of the Worlds.*

[26:146] *'Will you be left secure in that which is here,* [26:147] *amid gardens and springs,* [26:148] *and farms and date palms with slender spathes?*

Q. 26:132

[26:149] *'And you hew dwellings out of the mountains arrogantly.*

[26:150] *'So fear God and obey me,* [26:151] *and do not obey the command of the prodigal,* [26:152] *who cause corruption in the earth. And act righteously.'*

[26:153] *They said, 'You are indeed one of the bewitched.*

[26:154] *'And you are just a human being like us. So bring [us] a sign, if you are sincere.'*

[26:155] *He said, 'This is a she-camel; she shall drink, and you shall drink [each] on a known day.*

[26:156] *'And do not cause her any harm, for then you shall be seized by the chastisement of an awful day.'*

[26:157] *But they hamstrung her, and then became remorseful.*

[26:158] *So they were seized by the chastisement. Indeed, in that there is a sign; but most of them are not believers.*

[26:159] *Truly your Lord, He is the Mighty, the Merciful.*

[26:160] *The people of Lot denied the messengers,*

[26:161] *when Lot, their brother, said to them, 'Will you not fear God?*

[26:162] *'Indeed, I am a trusted messenger [sent] to you.*

[26:163] *'So fear God and obey me.*

[26:164] *'I do not ask of you any reward for this; my reward lies only with the Lord of the Worlds.*

[26:165] *'What! Of all people you come unto males [to fornicate],* [26:166] *and forsake the wives your Lord has created for you? Nay, but you are a transgressing folk.'*

[26:167] *They said, 'If you do not desist, O Lot, you will assuredly be of those expelled.'*

[26:168] *He said, 'Indeed, I abhor what you do.*

[26:169] *'My Lord, deliver me and my family from what they do.'*

[26:170] *So We delivered him and all his family,* [26:171] *except an old woman among those who stayed behind.*

[26:172] *Then We destroyed [all] the others,* [26:173] *and We rained on them a rain, and evil was the rain of those who were warned!*

[26:174] *Indeed, in that there is a sign; but most of them are not believers.*

[26:175] *Truly your Lord, He is the Mighty, the Merciful.*

[26:176] *The dwellers in the wood denied the messengers,* [26:177] *when Shuʿayb said to them, 'Will you not fear God?*

[26:178] *'Indeed, I am a trusted messenger [sent] to you.*

[26:179] *'So fear God and obey me.*

Q. 26:167

[26:180] *'I do not ask of you any reward for this; my reward lies only with the Lord of the Worlds.*

[26:181] *'Give full measure and do not be of those who give short measure,* [26:182] *and weigh with an even balance,* [26:183] *and do not defraud people in their goods, and do not be degenerate in the earth, seeking corruption.*

[26:184] *'And fear Him Who created you and the former generations.'*

[26:185] *They said, 'You are indeed one of the bewitched.*

[26:186] *'You are just a human being like us. And we indeed think that you are one of the liars.*

[26:187] *'Then make fragments of the heaven fall upon us, if you are of the truthful.'*

[26:188] *He said, 'My Lord knows best what you are doing.'*

[26:189] *But they denied him, so they were seized by the chastisement of the day of the shade. Assuredly it was the chastisement of a tremendous day.*

[26:190] *Indeed, in that there is a sign; but most of them are not believers.*

[26:191] *Truly your Lord, He is the Mighty, the Merciful.*

[26:192] *Verily it is the revelation of the Lord of the Worlds,* [26:193] *brought down by the Trustworthy Spirit,* [26:194] *upon your heart, that you may be [one] of the warners,* [26:195] *in a clear Arabic tongue.*

[26:196] *And truly it is in the scriptures of the ancients.*

[26:197] *Is it not a sign for them that the learned of the Children of Israel recognise it?*

[26:198] *For had We revealed it to some non-Arabs,* [26:199] *and had he recited it to them, they would not have believed in it.*

[26:200] *So We have caused it to penetrate the hearts of the criminals.*

[26:201] *They will not believe in it until they behold the painful chastisement,* [26:202] *so that it will come upon them suddenly while they are not aware.*

[26:203] *Thereupon they will say, 'Shall we be granted any respite?'*

[26:204] *So do they [seek to] hasten Our chastisement?*

[26:205] *Consider [this] then: If We were to let them enjoy [life] for [many] years,* [26:206] *then there were to come on them that which they have been promised,* [26:207] *in what way would that enjoyment which they were given avail them?*

[26:208] *And We have not destroyed any town but it had warners,* [26:209] *as a reminder, for We were never unjust.*]

Every prophet mentioned in this passage can be interpreted to signify the spirit or the heart, and the rejections of his people to signify the refusal of the egocentric faculties to conduct themselves with the conduct of the spiritual folk and adorn themselves with the character traits of the perfected ones. The words of each prophet (may God bless them and grant them peace), *Will you not fear God*, mean: will you not keep away from vices? *Indeed, I am a trusted messenger [sent] to you* to convey to you the wisdoms and meanings of certitude I have received from the Real, unadulterated with delusions and fancies. *So fear God* through detachment and self-purification, *and obey me* through illumination and self-adornment. *I do not ask of you any reward for it* from the particular pleasures and cognitions you possess, as I have no need for them; *for my reward lies only with the Lord of the Worlds*, Who grants me universal meanings and wisdoms and shines the blissful lights of holiness upon me.

Q. 26:201

[26:210] *It has not been brought down by the devils.*

[26:211] *[Neither would it behove them, nor are they capable.*

[26:212] *Indeed, they are barred from the hearing:]* devils only descend when souls are prepared for their descent by being plunged in foulness, depravity, treachery, deceit and all other vices. The cognitions of devils are forms of delusion and fancy. If a person detaches from the attributes of the soul and rises above the horizon of delusion into the presence of holiness, and his soul is illuminated by spiritual lights and the lamps of meteors of divine glory, and his intellect is enlightened through its connection to the active intellect, and he receives gnostic teachings and realities in the higher realm, it is neither appropriate nor possible for demons to descend upon him, nor for them to gain access to universal realities, meanings and Divine Laws. They are banished from the heaven of the spirit and prevented from hearing the speech of the higher realm of dominion, pelted with meteors of holy lights and intellectual proofs. The sphere of delusion cannot rise above the horizon of the heart and the station of the breast, nor can it pass into the boundary of the inner mystery. How, then, could it hope to reach the one who *was on the highest horizon, then he drew near and drew closer still* [Q. 53:7–8]?

[26:213] *So do not invoke any other god with God*: do not pay heed to the existence of the other by manifesting your own soul, nor be veiled from Unity by multiplicity in the course of your mission, *lest you be among the chastised* by means of the casting of devils, since although they are prevented from descending by conformity and vigilance, God says, *Satan cast into his hope* [Q. 22:52]. This means that it is not impossible for them to descend to the objects of the minds and souls of the divine warners and cast into them, though it is impossible for them to descend upon them to accompany and delude them while they are receiving the revelation.

[26:214] *And warn the nearest of your kinsfolk*: those whose preparedness is close to your own and whose states are similar to your own by natural predisposition; for reception is determined by the nature of what is in the soul and what is close to the spirit.

[26:215] *And lower your wing to*, by descending to the level of, *the believers who follow you*: so that you can address them with language they understand, and lift them up from their own station so they can ascend. And if they are not able to follow you:

[26:216] *But if they disobey you* because their hearts are rusted and the veil covering them is dense, [*say, 'I am absolved of what you do.'*

[26:217] *And put your trust in the Mighty, the Merciful*:] absolve yourself from their power and authority, and your own power and authority, through trust and annihilation in His acts. Neither they nor you are able to do anything that God does not will, nor can anything come to pass except what He desires. In your reliance and annihilation from your own deeds, witness the sources of His acts from the might with which He overcomes whomever of the sinners He will, veiling them and barring them from faith and the mercy and light which He bestows upon whomever of the people of guidance He will. He veils the veiled ones with His overwhelming power and majesty, and guides the guided ones with His kindness and beauty. You have nothing to do with it: *You cannot guide whomever you like, but [it is] God [Who] guides whomever He will* [Q. 28:56].

[26:218] *Who sees you* and is with you, protecting you, *when you stand* among creation at the Minor Resurrection, and with innate disposition at the Intermediate Resurrection, and with Unity at the time of uprightness at the Major Resurrection; [26:219] *and your movements [among those who prostrate]*: your turning and traversal through the realms of those who are annihilated in His acts, Attributes and Essence with the soul, the heart, and the spirit in their ranks, as well as before the first creation in the loins of your forefathers, the prophets, annihilated in God from all of these.

[26:220] *Indeed, He is the Hearing* Who hears what you say, *the Knower* Who knows what you know, and knows that it is not from the speech and casting of the devils.

[26:221] *Shall I inform you upon whom the devils descend?*

[26:222] *They descend upon every sinful liar.*

[26:223] *They report the heard [sayings], but most of them are liars.*

[26:224] *As for the poets, [only] the perverse follow them.*

[26:225] *Have you not noticed that in every valley they rove* [26:226] *and that they say what they do not do?*

[26:227] *Save those who believe and perform righteous deeds and remember God frequently and vindicate themselves after they have been wronged. And those who are wrongdoers will soon know the reversal with which they will meet*: this is an affirmation of His Words, *Neither would it behove them, nor are they capable* [Q. 26:211], because calumny and sin are inherent to souls which are turbid, impure, dark and base, who draw aid from devils because of this correspondence, inviting them to descend to them and cast inspiration upon them according to their affinity. Their ranks include the poets who compose works of fancy and embellishment, poetic analogies and false lies, whether they are set in metre or not. Then the errant perverse folk follow them and accept their fabrications and calumnies. However, they are set apart from those who compose poems of gnostic teachings and realities, ethics, admonishments, morals, virtues and other things that benefit their fellow humans and arouse their passion for seeking the Divine. And God knows best.

Q. 26:220

27
THE ANTS
SŪRAT AL-NAML

In the Name of God, the Compassionate, the Merciful

[27:1] *Ṭā. Sīn.* Those tremendous attributes contained in *Ṭā Sīn*, whose root is purity (*ṭahāra*) from the attributes of the soul and the innate security (*salāma*) of the person's preparedness from deficiency, *are the signs of the Qurʾān*, meaning the Qurʾānic intellect, which is the Muḥammadan preparedness that includes all perfections inwardly; and when it is manifested and emerges into action at the Major Resurrection, it becomes a *furqān* ('discerning criterion'): [*and a Manifest Book*].

[27:2] *A guidance and good tidings* [*for the believers*: the words] *a guidance and good tidings* stand in for the *Mīm* in *Ṭā Sīn Mīm*, because guidance to the Real and good tidings of arrival cannot come until after cognitive perfection. Guidance of the other, which means the imparting of perfection, is the requirement of knowledge, which is perfection, and thus can stand in for it. Both of these are covered by the word *Those*, which alludes to the aforementioned attributes symbolised by *Ṭā Sīn Mīm*. In other words, he is a guide and a deliverer of good tidings to the believers, those who have certain knowledge of the Oneness.

[27:3] *Those who observe* the *prayer* of presence and vigilance, *and give* zakāt on behalf of the attributes of the soul: that is, they purify themselves with detachment and spiritual discipline; *and who are certain of the Hereafter*, the station of witnessing: that is, in the state of unveiling, they are certain because they see first-hand, and the messenger guides them to it and gives them glad tidings of the garden of the Essence and the supreme triumph.

[27:4] *Indeed, those who do not believe in the Hereafter,* [*We have adorned their deeds for them*]: they are veiled by how their souls have exulted in their own perfections and the configurations of their deeds, *and so they are bewildered* and their insights are unable to perceive the Attributes of the Real and the manifestations of their lights. Otherwise, they would not have become veiled by their deeds and attributes, but would have been annihilated from them.

[27:5] *Those are they for whom there is an awful chastisement* with the fires of veiling and deprivation from the pleasures of the manifestation of the Attributes; *and in the Hereafter* and the station of the unveiling of the Essence at the Major Resurrection, *they will be the greatest losers* because of how densely veiled they are by their own attributes and essences, and so they will have no share of the two gardens and their delights.

[27:6] *And truly you are receiving the Qur'ān*—namely the Qur'ānic intellect—*from One*: that is, from the origin of the unification of Unity in the Attributes, which has no veil between it and the presence of Unity. Indeed, it is itself the holiest veil which emanates to all the states of preparedness from the discriminating intellects upon their masters from the human immutable entities (*aʿyān thābita insāniyya*). [He is] *Wise, [Knowing,]* One of complete infinite wisdom and universal encompassing knowledge.

Q. 27:5

[27:7] *Remember*, from the teachings and wisdoms of the Real, the time [*When*] the *Moses* of the heart *said to his family*, the soul and the outward and inward senses, *Wait*[1] and hold fast here, and do not disturb me with movement. *'Assuredly I notice*, with the eye of insight, *a fire* —and what a tremendous fire, the fire of the active intellect! *I will bring you news from there*: knowledge of the path to God, for he had lost the path to God while preoccupied with tending to the sheep of the bestial faculties and his spouse the animal soul; *or bring you a firebrand*, a flame of light to shine upon you when I connect to the fire and become illuminated by it, *that perhaps you might warm yourselves'* from the cold of reliance on the body and satisfaction with it, and the caprice of its pleasures, that by the motion of that fire you might yearn for my garden and travel with my love to the station of the breast.

[27:8] *But when he reached it, he was called [with the following words]: 'Blessed*, endowed with plentiful goodness, *is he who is in the fire*, meaning the Moses of the heart who reached the fire by the manifestations of the Divine Attributes, and the discovery of the perfections of reality, and the station of communion, born of prophethood, *and who is around it*, the spiritual faculties and heavenly angels with the lights of unveiling, the secrets of knowledge and wisdom, holy aids, and secret experiential states; *and*

---

1 This word does not occur in this verse, but does occur in the similar verses 20:10 and 28:29.

Glory be to God, the Lord of the Worlds: witness the transcendence of God's Essence by detaching yourself from egocentric attributes, corporeal veils, flaws and deficiencies.

[27:9] ['*O Moses. Indeed, it is*] *I, God, the Mighty* Who has overpowered your soul and everything else through annihilation in Him, *the Wise* Who has taught you wisdom and guided you with it to the station of communion.

[27:10] '*Throw down* the *staff* of your holy being, made whole by the rays of holiness. Do this now that it has been corrected by spiritual discipline; let it go free and do not hold it back, for now it is illuminated. *And when he saw it wriggling* and moving *like a serpent* alive[1] and made ascendant by manifestation, *he turned his back* to face the Real *in flight*, fearing the re-emergence of the soul, *and did not come back*, remaining disturbed by the thought that a remnant of his soul still remained. '[*O Moses,*] *do not fear* the ascendancy of the soul and the emergence of the veil, for when the soul is revived after its voluntary death and its annihilation by spiritual discipline, if it then becomes independent and insists on its own command, it will be a veil and a tribulation; yet if it moves by My command, alive with the light of the spirit and real divine love rather than by its own caprice, it will not be a veil.

'*Indeed, in My presence the messengers do not fear*, for I sent them forth with subsistence after annihilation, and revived their souls with My own life, [27:11] *except him who has wronged* by manifesting the soul before becoming upright and mastering the station of subsistence, which is an existential sin for which there must be repentance by seeking forgiveness, and fear by tribulation, *but then changed* [*his wrong*] *for good after* by fear and self-correction though taming the soul and fleeing to the presence of the Real from its evil, *after* [*having done*] *evil* in whichever of its attributes it manifested. *Then truly I am Forgiving* and will cover its darkness with My light, *Merciful* and will have mercy after forgiveness by My own Attribute, by which that attribute of the soul was manifested.

[27:12] '*And insert your hand*, the cognitive intelligence, *into your bosom* beneath the garb of the soul, connected to the heart in your left armpit where the breast lies, *and it will emerge white*, illuminated and empowered, *without any blemish* of variegation or manifestation with any of its attributes, but rather illuminated by the light. [*This will be one*] *among nine signs*: take these two signs between the holy soul and the cognitive intel-

---

1 A play on the dual meaning of the word *ḥayya*, which can mean 'snake' or 'alive'.

ligence: one of which is alive with the life of the heart and the other of which is illuminated by its light. They are two among nine signs; the other seven are the ones known among the theologians as the 'seven ancients', [which are] the Divine Attributes through which the Real manifests to the heart so that they become its own attributes: life, power, knowledge, will, hearing, sight and speech. [These signs shall be presented] *to the Pharaoh* of the evil-enjoining soul veiled by egocentricity *and his folk*, its faculties. Whenever they manifest with their pharaonic tyranny, and with whatever attribute they manifest, and wherever they are found, go to them with these attributes. *Indeed, they are an immoral lot'* who have strayed from the religion of the Real and obedience to Him into the religion of caprice, denying the Oneness by their very appearance.

[27:13] *But when Our* illuminating *signs came to them* from him *plain to see, they* were bewildered [and *said, 'This is manifest sorcery'*].

[27:14] *And they denied them* through how they manifested with their attributes and opposed them, [*though their souls had been convinced*] via the path of knowledge and intellect, *wrongfully and arrogantly* because of their pharaonic tyranny and how they were accustomed to dominance and lacked the disposition of justice. *So behold how was* their *sequel* [*for agents of corruption*], and how they were drowned in the sea of pitch because of how they sowed corruption in the earth of the body through their tyranny.

Q. 27:13

[27:15] *And verily We gave* the *David* of the spirit *and the Solomon* of the heart *knowledge*, and they were adorned with the collective lordly attributes, *and* they expressed this when *they said, 'Praise be to God Who has favoured us over many of His believing servants.'*

[27:16] *And the Solomon* of the heart *inherited from the David* of the spirit the kingdom to rule and prophethood for guidance, *and he said, 'O people*—he called to the corporeal faculties when he ruled over them, saying—*we have been taught the speech of the birds*, the spiritual faculties, *and we have been given of all things*: of universal and particular cognitions and acquired and bequeathed perfections. *Indeed, this is the manifest favour'*: the clear perfection that lifts a person above others.

[27:17] *And Solomon's hosts of the jinn* of estimative and imaginative faculties and impulses, *and the humans* of outward senses, *and the birds* of the spiritual faculties, *stood assembled for him* through his subdual and domination of the wind of caprice by the rule of the active intellect, seated upon the throne of the breast, atop the stairs of balanced temperament, *as they were being arrayed*, arranged in order from first to last according to the judgement of the active intellect, none of them going ahead with excess or lagging back with negligence.

[27:18] *When they came to the Valley of the Ants*: the ants of avarice for amassing wealth and material means by travelling the path of practical wisdom and the suppressing of base dispositions; *an ant said*: it was the disposition of greed, the queen of the impulses of avarice. It is said that this ant was crippled because the intelligence had broken its leg and restrained it by impeding its natural speed. *'O ants*, the impulses of avarice previously enumerated, *enter your dwellings, lest Solomon and his hosts crush you while they are unaware!'* In other words, hide in your homes and nests, lest the heart and the spiritual faculties crush you with death and annihilation. This is the logical path for acquiring goodly dispositions and sublime character traits, for otherwise the ant queen and her brood would have vanished without a trace through annihilation in the manifestation of the Attributes.

[27:19] *Whereat he smiled, amused at its words*: he rejoiced at the fading of base dispositions and the attainment of virtuous ones; and asked his Lord for the grace to give thanks for the favour He had bestowed on him, by allowing him to adorn himself with His Attributes and acts and be annihilated from his own; and [that God] grant the same to his parents the spirit and the soul, by the perfection and illumination of the former and the acceptance and influence of the latter. [*And he said,*] *'My Lord, inspire me to be thankful for Your grace wherewith You have favoured me and my parents, and to do good that will please You*: by uprightness in adhering to the rights of the manifestation of Your Attributes, and heart-rooted acts of worship dedicated to Your countenance and the light of Your Essence; *and include me, by Your mercy, among Your righteous servants'*: by the perfection of Your Essence, among the ranks of the perfected ones who are the cause of the soundness of the world and the perfection of creation.

[27:20] *And he reviewed the birds* of the spiritual faculties, [*then he said, 'Why is it that I do not see the hoopoe? Or is he among the absent?'*]: he noted the absence of the hoopoe of the reflective faculty, because if the reflective faculty is in the service of estimation, it will be imaginative and its reflective nature will be absent, indeed non-existent. It can only be reflective when it obeys the intellect.

[27:21] *'Assuredly I will chastise him with a severe chastisement* of strenuous spiritual discipline, barring him from serving estimation and forcing him to serve intelligence; *or I will slaughter him* by making him die, *unless he brings me a clear warrant'* or becomes obedient to the intellect because of the purity of its substance and the illumination of its essence, so that it brings forth a clear argument with its motions.

Q. 27:18

[27:22] *But he did not remain long*: its spiritual discipline did not take long because of its holiness, and it did not need to be slain for purification before it returned with a clear warrant and was trained in the art of constructing arguments according to the soundest method; *and he said, 'I have discovered something of which you have no knowledge*: of the circumstances of the city of the body and the perception of particulars and their composition with universals. The heart itself perceives only universals, so it is only the reflective faculty that can connect them to particulars by the composition of analogies and the formation and deduction of opinions. By means of reflection, it can encompass the states of all the worlds and attain the good things of both lives. *I have brought you from Sheba*—the city of the body—*a verified report* based on first-hand eye-witnessing.

[27:23] *'I found a woman ruling over them*: she was the animal spirit, which the Sufis call 'the soul'; *and she has been given [an abundance] of all things*: of the means which the body controls and by which its dominion is completed; *and she possesses a great throne*, which is the corporeal nature that it reclines on, by the configuration of its elevation from the natures of the simple elements, namely the balanced temperament. Or one could interpret the city of Sheba to represent the physical world, and the throne to represent the body.

Q. 27:22

[27:24] *'I found her and her people prostrating to the sun* of the veiled worldly intellect *instead [of God]* the Real, by yielding to it and surrendering to its rule rather than yielding to the rule of the spirit, following the way of Oneness and obeying the command of the Real; *and the Satan* of estimation *has adorned for them their deeds* of acquiring desires, bodily lusts and physical perfections, *and he has barred them from the way* of the Real and following the path of virtue by justice, *so that they are not guided* to Oneness and the straight path.

[27:25] *'So they do not prostrate themselves to God*—he has barred them from the way so that they do not yield and surrender by donating their perfections to the intellect—*Who brings forth the hidden* possible perfections *in the heavens* of the spirits *and the earth* of the body; *and He knows what they conceal* of the perfections inside them by obstructive actions that prevent the preparedness from passing over to the intellect, *and what they proclaim* of benighted configurations and base character traits.

[27:26] *'God—there is no god except Him*, and so worship and submission are permitted to none but Him, *the Lord of the Mighty Throne'* which

131

encompasses all things. The throne of the Bilqīs[1] of the soul was tiny compared to its might, so why would she not obey Him? She was veiled by love for her own throne from obedience to Him.

[27:27] [*He said,*] '*We shall see whether you have spoken the truth* about your knowledge of their errors and their circumstances by intellectual means, *or whether you are of the liars* who follow conjecture and fabricate corrupt fantasies.

[27:28] '*Take this letter of mine*, which is practical wisdom and the Divine Law, *and deliver it to them, then turn away from them and see what* [*response*] *they shall return*': will they agree to yield and obey, or will they refuse?

[27:29] [*She said, 'O council. Indeed, a noble letter has been delivered to me.*]

[27:30] '*It is from Solomon*, having emerged from the heart and then delivered via reflection to the soul, *and, lo and behold, it is,* "*In the Name of God, the Compassionate, the Merciful*: in the Name of the Essence which emanates preparedness and its instruments to the intellect, and emanates the perfection it requires in the form of sublime character traits and attributes.

Q. 27:27

[27:31] '"*Do not rise up against me* [*in defiance*]: do not seek ascendancy or dominance; *but come to me in submission*"': yielding and surrendering.

[27:32] [*She said,*] '*O council, give me an opinion* [*in this matter of mine. I never decide on a matter until you are present.*'

[27:33] *They said, 'We possess force and we possess great might. The matter is for you* [*to decide*]. *So see what you will command*']: this alludes to the receptiveness of the soul and the nobility of its substance, and how it can disobey the commands of its faculties to seek dominance and to become deluded with configurations of power and supremacy, although it can only accept something after consulting them and seeking their counsel.

[27:34] [*She said, 'Indeed, kings, when they enter a town, ruin it, and reduce the mightiest of its inhabitants to the most abased. That is what they too will do*:] the ruination of the town and abasement of its mighty folk symbolises how it is denied its luxuries and pleasures, and restrained from dominating the faculties by spiritual disciplines.

[27:35] '*Indeed, I will now send them a gift* of the riches of sensory cognitions, egocentric desires and estimative and imaginative pleasures, and the support of primordial matter, which I will make seemly to them with the use of suggestions, insinuations and instigations; *and wait to see* [*with what* [*response*] *the envoys return*]': to see whether he will accept them

---

1 The given name of the Queen of Sheba in the Islamic tradition.

and soften and incline towards the soul, or reject them and be firm in his inclination towards the Real.

[27:36] [*But when he came to Solomon, he said, 'Are you supplying me with wealth?*] What God has given me* of gnostic certainties, holy realities, intellectual pleasures and luminous witnessings *is better than what He has given you* of sensory, imaginative and estimative trivialities. *Nay, but it is you who exult in your gift*, not we, for we only exult in what is with God, not those things.

[27:37] *'Go back to them*: this is addressed to the imaginary envoy who was sent to bear the gifts to them to seduce them; *for we shall assuredly come to them with* the *hosts* of spiritual faculties and the supports of divine lights, *which they will not be able to face and we shall expel them from there* with compulsion, domination and subdual, *humiliated*, [*and they shall be utterly abased'*] by nature and stature because of the lowliness of their rank in their clay origin, before they were illuminated by refined manners.

[27:38] [*He said, 'O council, which of you will bring me her throne*] *before they come to me in submission?'* In other words, before the soul and its faculties approach with sublime character traits and obedience, for it is easier to tame the natural faculties by deeds and refined manners than to tame the animal soul and its faculties by sublime character traits and habits.

Q. 27:36

[27:39] [*An* afreet *from among the jinn*]—the *afreet* was the faculty of estimation, which subdues the soul with fear and hope and encourages it to do deeds by means of estimative suggestions and agreeable hopes—[*said, 'I will bring it to you*] *before you rise from your place*: that is, while you remain in the station of the breast before you ascend to the station of the inner mystery, when the faculty of estimation withdraws from action by guidance and conformity. [*Indeed, I have the strength for it and I am trustworthy.'*

[27:40] *The one who had knowledge of the Book*—referring to] the active intellect that possesses knowledge, namely practical and legal wisdom from the book of the Preserved Tablet. It tames the soul and guides it towards obedience by inspiring in it love for perfection, nobility, beautiful acclaim and honour—[*said: 'I will bring it to you*] *before your glance returns to you'*: before you regard your own essence and how it must ascend to your realm, which is the realm of holiness, to perceive universal realities, gnostic truths and first-hand eye-witnessings; for perfection of deed comes before perfection of experiential realisation and unveiling. *Then, when he saw it standing before him*, firm in the midst of his connection to it, trained in the way of obedience and unchanged by appetitive temptations and satanic

133

impulses, *he said, 'This is of my Lord's bounty, that He may try me, whether I give thanks*: by obedience and adherence to the Divine Law *or am ungrateful* by disobedience and contravention of the Divine Law; or whether I will give thanks for the grace to obey by following the path, approaching the [divine] presence, adopting the attributes and witnessing the manifestations, or be ungrateful by veiling myself by observing my own deeds and turning away from the Real by delusion and self-satisfaction, and stopping entranced at the intelligible (*maʿqūl*) and the intellect (*ʿaql*). [*And whoever gives thanks, gives thanks only for his own sake; and whoever is ungrateful,* [*should know*] *then my Lord is surely Independent, Generous.'*]

[27:41] [*He said,*] *'Disguise her throne for her* by changing habits and renouncing blameworthy things, and wearing down the natural faculties with spiritual disciplines, and curbing them by confronting them with that which occupies a higher level than them, namely the corporeal configurations and the pleasures and delights of the body; and by making lower those things that are on the side of excess in matters of eating, drinking, sleep and the like, and the dominating natural faculties; and by making higher those things which are lower, such as spiritual effort and discipline, asceticism, sleeplessness, and all other neglected aspects of corporeal matters and dominated spiritual faculties. *That we may see whether she will be guided* to the virtues and the ways of perfection by spiritual discipline, for the salvation of her substance, the nobility of her core, and the goodness of her preparedness and receptivity, *or be of those who cannot be guided'* to it because of the inverse.

[27:42] *So when she came* to ascend to the station of the heart, illuminated by its lights, adorned with its sublime character traits, yielding and submitting to its hosts, *it was said, 'Is your throne like this?'* Does your throne have this altered appearance, or has it retained its original appearance? *She said, 'It looks like the one'*: compared to my current state, it seems to be the one, compared to its original state. When I was directed towards the lower, my throne was like that in correspondence to my state; but now that I am directed towards the higher, it has this appearance, equal to and corresponding to my current state. *'And we were given the knowledge* [*before her*]: before this state: we were given it in pre-eternity, at the covenant of innate disposition; *and we had* [*submitted*] before this creation, although we forgot and have only just now recalled it.

[27:43] *'And what she worshipped* [*besides God*], the sun of the worldly intellect, *barred her* from Oneness, *for she belonged to* [*disbelieving*] *folk'* veiled from the Real.

Q. 27:41

[27:44] *It was said to her, 'Enter the palace [hallway]'*: the station of the breast, which is a plastered hallway smoothed out by the challenging of opposites and the contradiction of natural impulses, flattened by detachment from matter, composed from bottles of the lights of the pure heart, resembling glass in its purity and luminescence. *And when she saw it, she supposed it to be a pool* of the sea of Unity, because that was the aim of her spiritual stage of detachment and ascension, and the culmination of her perfection in drawing near and receiving. Her glance did not stray to anything higher than it, nor to the impossible perfections above it, because it already seemed to contain the utmost expression of Oneness, the beauty of the Divine and the ultimate goal; *and so she bared her legs*: she uncovered her lower aspect, which sat closest to the body and carried her within it, divided into the irascible and appetitive faculties, from the corporeal coverings and garments of primordial matter, by severing the ties to them. Yet she was still covered with the hair[1] of residual configurations composed of her deeds and the blackening remnants of her contaminations; and for this reason it is said that Solomon will enter Paradise five hundred years after the other prophets, and will go in crawling upon his knees. [*He said, 'It is a hallway paved with crystal.' She said, 'My Lord, indeed,*] *I have wronged myself* by being veiled and adopting the intellect sullied with estimation, drunk upon caprice, as my god; *and I submit* by yielding to the command of the Real and following the path of Oneness, *with Solomon to God, the Lord of the Worlds.'* This interpretation also fits with the reading of the throne as representing the body.

Q. 27:44

There is also another interpretation, which is that it means that she was bound to be veiled by her intelligibles (*maʿqūlāt*) for as long as her throne remained, and she only yielded to the Solomon of the heart at the second creation. In that case, *The one who had knowledge of the Book* [Q. 27:40] would mean the active intellect, and his bringing of the throne before the glance returned would mean the engendering of the second body in an instant. In this case, the meaning of *before they come to me in submission* [Q. 27:38] would be that the material of the body comes before the soul's attachment to it.

Ibn al-ʿArabī[2] (may God have mercy on him) said that he brought the throne by annihilating it in its original position and recreating it

---

1 An allusion to the popular account, found in many works of exegesis and also in some Jewish texts, of the Queen of Sheba's legs being covered with hair.
2 The text here has 'Ibn al-Aʿrābī', but Kāshānī appears to be alluding to the *Fuṣūṣ al-ḥikam* where an almost identical statement is found (Muḥyī al-Dīn Ibn ʿArabī, *Fuṣūṣ al-ḥikam*, Beirut: Dār al-Kutub al-ʿIlmiyya, n.d., p. 155).

in the presence of Solomon, and then it was disguised by altering its appearance; and by *It looks like the one* [Q. 27:42], she meant that it resembled it. The palace hall was the material of the second body, and so in this reading the entrance to the hall would have come before the disguising of the image. The baring of the legs represents the detachment from the first body without the removal of the corporeal configurations, which are represented by the hair. This is based on the fact that deficient veiled souls must have some attachments. And God knows best.

[27:45] *And verily We sent to Thamūd*, the people of scanty water,[1] which represents worldly things, [*their brother*] the *Saleh* of the heart with the call to Oneness: [*'Worship God!'*] *And lo and behold, they* [*then*] *became two parties*, the party of the spiritual faculties and the party of the ego-centric faculties, *quarrelling with one another*. The first said that what Saleh had brought was true, while the second said that it was false and that their own way was true.

Q. 27:45

[27:46] [*He said, 'O my people,*] *why do you* [*seek to*] *hasten on evil*, dominating the heart with baseness, *before* [*seeking good* and] *acting with virtue? Why do you not ask God to forgive you* by illuminating you with the light of Oneness, and disavow the dark corporeal configurations, *so that you might be shown mercy?'* by the emanation of perfection.

[27:47] [*They said,*] *'We augur evil of you* because of how you seek to bar us from luxuries and comforts, [*and of those who are with you.' He said,*] *'Your evil augury is with God*: the cause of both your good and your evil is from God. [*Nay, but you are a people being tried.'*

[27:48] *And there were in the city a band of nine men, who were causing corruption in the land and did not reform* [*their ways*].

[27:49] *They said, 'Swear to one another by God that we will attack him by night together with his folk. Then we will surely say to his heir that we did not witness the destruction of his folk and* [*that*] *indeed we are being truthful'*.

[27:50] *So they plotted a plot, but We* [*also*] *plotted a plot, while they were not aware*.

[27:51] *So behold how was the consequence of their plot! For lo and behold, We destroyed them and all their people*:] the mischief-making band were the senses: ire, appetite, estimation and imagination. Their plot was to destroy him in the darkness of the night of the soul. His heir was the spirit. God's plot with them was to destroy them by bringing the mountains of the

---

1 The name Thamūd is said to come from the word *thamad*, meaning 'little water'.

limbs down upon them and destroying them in the cave of their dwelling, and destroying their people with the Cry, which was the first blowing of the Trumpet.

[27:52] [*So those then are their houses [lying] deserted because of the evil which they did. Indeed, in that there is a sign for a people who have knowledge.*

[27:53] *And We delivered those who believed and were fearful.*

[27:54] *And Lot, when he said to his people, 'What! Do you commit [such] abomination while you watch?*

[27:55] *'What! Do you come unto men in lust instead of women? Nay, but you are truly a people in ignorance':*] the abomination of the people of Lot was that they went unto males, which in this spiritual correspondence means that the egocentric faculties went behind the spiritual faculties and removed them from their position of influence: choosing instead to be influenced from the lower direction and to dominate them for the sake of attaining carnal pleasures and corporeal desires.

Q. 27:52

[27:56] [*But the only response of his people was that they said, 'Expel Lot's family from your town. They are indeed a folk who [prefer to] remain pure!'*

[27:57] *So We delivered him and his family, except his wife—We decreed [for] her to be of those who remained behind.*

[27:58] *Then We rained on them a rain. And evil indeed was the rain of those who were warned.*

[27:59] *Say [O Muḥammad]:*] '*Praise be to God* for the emergence of His perfections and the manifestations of His Attributes upon the outward forms of His creations, *and peace be on His servants whom He has chosen*' by purifying their preparednesses (*istiʿdādāt*) and absolving them of deficiencies and blights. Praise be to Him and Him alone, for all perfections which manifest upon the outward forms of things are His Attributes of beauty and majesty, and no other being plays any role in this. The purification of the essences of the chosen ones from His servants, and the cleansing of their entities from deficiencies of preparedness and the blight of the veil, is from His peace upon them. The active attainment of both in the perfect prophetic manifestation is attained by his utterance of these words, commanded to do so from the source of unification in the station of differentiation, and then transported from the station of differentiation to the source of unification, beginning from it and returning to it. *Is God*, unto Whom belongs all praise and all peace, *better* in an absolute and essential sense, *or the partners which they ascribe*, the beings to which they attribute existence and influence? Nothing remains, after the absolute perfection and absolute acceptance which is the name of absolute peace according to the holiest emanation, except pure non-being and absolute total evil, which is opposed to absolute total good. How, then, could it be better?

[27:60] *Or He Who created the heavens and the earth,* [*and sends down for you water from the heaven, whereby We cause to grow splendid gardens whose trees you could never cause to grow?* In other words,] is the absolute influencer and Creator of all possible entities and their attributes better in influence and creation, or that which has no existence of its own, never mind any influence or creative power? *Is there a god with God* who can influence and create? *Nay, but they are a people who ascribe equals* and stray from the Real and cling, deluded, to falsehood.

[27:61] [*Or He Who made the earth an abode* [*of stability*] *and made rivers* [*to flow*] *throughout it and set firm mountains for it, and set an isthmus between the two seas. Is there a god with God? Nay, but most of them have no knowledge.*

Q. 27:60

[27:62] *Or He Who answers the desperate one when he calls to Him and Who removes* [*his*] *distress and makes you successors in the earth. Is there a god with God? Little do you remember.*]

[27:63] *Or He Who guides you* to the light of His Essence *in the darkness of the land,* the veils of beings and acts, *and the sea,* the veils of Attributes, *and Who sends forth the winds* of grace to give life to hearts *as harbingers of His mercy* of manifestations. [*Is there a god with God? Exalted be God* [*high*] *above what they associate* [*with Him*]*!*]

[27:64] *Or He Who originates creation* by concealing Himself in their entities and veiling Himself with their essences, *then brings it back again* by annihilating them in the source of unification and destroying them in His Essence by erasure, or by manifesting them at the creation and then returning them to innate disposition, *and Who provides for you from the heaven* with spiritual nourishment *and* [*from*] *the earth* with material nourishment, for gnostic teachings and realities come from heaven, while wisdoms and sublime character traits come from earth. [*Is there a god with God? Say: 'Produce your proof if you are truthful.'*

[27:65] *Say: 'No one in the heavens or the earth knows the Unseen, except God, and they are not aware when they will be resurrected.*

[27:66] *Nay, has their knowledge come to comprise the Hereafter? Nay, for they are in doubt of it. Rather, they are blind to it.*

[27:67] *And the disbelievers say, 'What! When we and our fathers are dust shall we indeed be brought forth* [*again*]*?*

[27:68] *'Already we and our fathers have been promised this before.* [*But*] *these are just the* [*legendary*] *fables of the ancients.'*

[27:69] *Say: 'Travel in the land and see how was the sequel for the criminals.'*

[27:70] *And do not grieve for them, and do not be distressed by their schemes.*

[27:71] *And they say, 'When will this promise be, if you are truthful?'*

[27:72] *Say: 'It may be that part of what you seek to hasten on is close behind you.'*

[27:73] *And indeed your Lord is bountiful to people, but most of them are not thankful.*

[27:74] *And surely your Lord knows what their hearts conceal and what they proclaim.*

[27:75] *And there is not a thing hidden in the heaven and the earth but it is in a manifest Book.*

[27:76] *Indeed, this Qur'ān recounts to the Children of Israel [the means to resolve] most of that concerning which they differ.*

[27:77] *And truly it is a guidance and a mercy for believers.*

[27:78] *Surely your Lord will decide between them by His judgement. And He is the Mighty, the Knower.*

[27:79] *So rely on God, for you are indeed upon the manifest truth.*

[27:80] *Indeed, you cannot make the dead hear, nor can you make the deaf hear the call when they have turned their backs [upon you]; [27:81] nor can you lead the blind out of their error. You can only make those hear who believe in Our signs and have therefore submitted.]*

Q. 27:70

[27:82] *And when the word [of judgement] falls upon them*—when the perpetual damnation that was decreed in Our judgement is realised—*We shall bring forth for them a beast*: from the image of the soul of every damned person, with altered configurations and horrific shapes, the proportions of its limbs and body parts huge and distorted according to the narrations about it, as determined by its character traits and dispositions. It will arise *from the earth* of the body shortly before the Minor Resurrection, of which it is a portent; [and] *which shall speak to them* in the language of its life and attributes, [*saying,*] '*Indeed, people had no faith in Our signs*': Our ability to resurrect them.

[27:83] *[And the day when We shall gather from every community a group of those who denied Our signs, and they will be set in array, [27:84] until, when they arrive, He shall say, 'Did you deny My signs without comprehending them in knowledge, or what was it that you did?'*

[27:85] *And the word [of judgement] shall fall upon them because of the evil they committed, and they will not speak.*

[27:86] *Do they not see that We made the night that they may rest in it, and the day for sight? Indeed, in that there are signs for a people who believe.]*

[27:87] *And on the day when the Trumpet will be blown*: the first death-dealing blast at the Minor Resurrection, *everyone in the heavens and the* earth—the detached intellectuals and materialistic ignorant folk, or the spiritual and corporeal faculties—*will be terrified, except whom God wishes* of the monotheists who are annihilated in God and the witnesses who live in God. *And all will come to Him* at the gathering place for the Resurrection, [*in [utter] humility,*] abased, with no power or will; or they will come to Him in surrender and submission to His command to die.

[27:88] *And you see the mountains* of the bodies, *supposing them to be still* and fixed to their places, *while they drift* and disappear, dissolving *like passing clouds* until their parts are gathered on the long day of the Resurrection. *The handiwork of God Who has perfected everything*: He made this blast of the Trumpet as well as this death and revival to judge the servants for their deeds, with the exacting handiwork that befits Him. *Indeed, He is aware of what you do.*

[27:89] *Whoever brings a good deed*, by erasing one of the attributes of his soul through repenting to God of it, *shall have good for it* by a Divine Attribute replacing it; [*and they shall be secure from the terror of that day*].

Q. 27:88

[27:90] *And whoever brings an evil deed* by being veiled with one of the attributes of his soul, *their faces shall be thrust* by the collapse of their edifice, because of their strong inclination toward the lower direction, *into the Fire* of nature. *'Are you requited [except for what you used to do]* by the forms of your deeds being made into the configurations of your own forms?'

[27:91] [Say:] *'I have been commanded* to not regard anything other than the Real, and *only to worship the Lord of this land*, the heart, *which He has made inviolable*, protecting it from the domination of the attributes of the soul and preventing the folk of impurity from entering it, securing it and those within it, that my soul not be thrust into the fire of nature; *and to Whom all things belong* beneath His dominion and lordship. He gives to His servant as He pleases, and withholds from him as He pleases, and wards off those who seek to dominate him. *And I have been commanded to be of those who submit* and who surrender their beings through annihilation in Him.

[27:92] *'And to recite the Qur'ān'*: deferring to the sum of perfections by manifesting them and bringing them out by action in the station of subsistence. [*So whoever is guided, he is guided only for his own sake; and whoever goes astray, say: 'I am just one of the warners.'*]

[27:93] *And say: 'Praise be to God*: adorning yourself with His praiseworthy Attributes. *He will show you [His signs]*: His Attributes in the station of the heart; *and you will recognise them.* [*And your Lord is not oblivious of what they do.'*] Or He will show you the signs of His acts and their influence by compulsion in the station of the soul, and you will recognise them when you are tormented by them.

Alternatively, [Q. 27:87–88 refers to]: *on the day when the Trumpet will be blown* by the manifestation of the Essence at the Major Resurrection, *everyone in the heavens and the earth will be terrified* by the swoon of annihilation and total conquest, *except whom God wishes* of the folk of subsistence who are given life through His life, and awaken after the swoon of annihilation in Him. *And all will come to Him in [utter] humility,* fallen from the level of life and existence, utterly conquered. *And you see the mountains* of existing beings, *supposing them to be still* and fixed in their state, *while* in reality *they drift like passing clouds,* fading away.

Q. 27:93

28
THE STORY
SŪRAT AL-QAṢAṢ

In the Name of God, the Compassionate, the Merciful

[28:1] [*Ṭā. Sīn. Mīm.*

[28:2] *Those are the signs of the Manifest Book.*

[28:3] *We will recount to you [something] of the tale of Moses and Pharaoh truthfully, for a people who believe.*]

[28:4] *Indeed, Pharaoh*, the evil-enjoining soul, *had exalted himself* with tyranny *in the land* of the body, *and reduced its people* into sects (*firaq*) who differed and warred with one another, because of how they followed diverse paths and strayed from the way of justice, Oneness and the straight path, *oppressing a group of them*, the spiritual faculties, *slaughtering [their sons]*, the kin of the spirit in influence and exaltedness from its progeny, by slaying it and refusing to obey its impulses and authority, *and sparing [their women]*, the kin of the soul in receiving influence and lowliness, by strengthening it and giving it free rein to act. [*Indeed, he was of those who cause corruption.*]

[28:5] *And We desired to show favour to those who were oppressed [in the land]* by debasement, humiliation, and being used to perform natural acts and in the service of attaining bestial and predatory pleasures, and to slaughter the sons and spare the women; and so We chose to save them from torment *and to make them [exemplars]*, foremost leaders, *and to make them [the inheritors]*: kings of the earth, by annihilating Pharaoh and his folk.

[28:6] *And to establish them in the land* by aid, *and to show* the *Pharaoh* of the evil-enjoining soul *and the Haman* of the intellect sullied by estimation, known as the worldly intellect, *and their hosts*, the egocentric faculties, *from them that of which they were apprehensive*, namely the emergence of the Moses of the heart and the end of their kingdom and power at his hands.

[28:7] *And We revealed to the mother of Moses*, the innocent wholesome soul that retains its innate disposition, which is the self-reproaching soul,

'*Suckle him* with the milk of particular perceptions and primordial beneficial sciences; *then, when you fear for him* that the evil-enjoining soul and its
assistants might subjugate it, *cast him into* [*the waters*] of primordial intellect
and original preparedness, or into the waters of corporeal nature by concealment; *and do not fear* his demise *or grieve* for his parting, *for We will restore
him to you* after the emergence of discernment and the light of maturity,
and make him one of the messengers' to the Children of Israel.

[28:8] *Then Pharaoh's folk*—the egocentric faculties—*picked him up*: sub-
jugating and dominating him; for it is not possible to reach discernment and
maturity, nor to become cautious, without the aid and support of imagination, estimation and the other means of outward and inward perception; *so
that he would become an enemy and a* [*cause of*] *grief to them* in the end, and also
for him to know that the worst of all his enemies was the soul between his
sides, and thus subjugate it and its allies by means of spiritual discipline, and
annihilate it by blocking, breaking and slaying it. [*Indeed, Pharaoh and Haman
and their hosts were sinners.*]

Q. 28:8

[28:9] *And Pharaoh's wife*, the tranquil gnostic soul by the light of
certitude and divine peace, whose purity inspired her with love for him,
making her overcome the evil-enjoining soul and influence it with variegation, *said, 'A joyous sight for me* by nature due to correspondence, *and you*
by the mediation and connection of spousal kinship and continuity. Some
say that Pharaoh replied, 'For you, but not for me'; and that when they
tried to open the box, it would not open until Āsiya opened it, after she
saw a light inside it which made her love him. [*Do not slay him.*] *Perhaps
he will be of benefit to us* in obtaining the means of livelihood and looking
after our affairs and managing things by reason; *or we will adopt him as a
son,'* if he corresponds to the soul rather than the spirit and follows caprice
and serves the interests of the body, thereby strengthening us. *And they
were not aware* that this would not be the course that events would follow.

[28:10] *And the inner-heart of Moses's mother*—the innocent self-
reproaching soul—*became empty* of the intellect because of Pharaoh's
domination of her and her fear of him because of his subjugation of her.
Indeed, she was about to expose him: she was about to obey the evil-enjoining
soul inwardly and outwardly, by ceasing to resist it with her inner mystery
and what she harboured of the light of preparedness and the state of the
concealed Moses, because of how he had been forcibly distanced, *had We
not fortified her heart* by granting her forbearance and strength by spiritual
aid and divine inspiration, *that she might be of the believers* in the Unseen by
the purity of preparedness.

[28:11] *And she said to his sister*, the reflective faculty, *'Follow him'* and keep up with his state by examining his intelligible meanings and cognitive and practical perfections. *So she watched him from afar*: she perceived his state from afar because she had not ascended to his level, nor could she see his unveilings and secrets or the lights of his attributes which he attained; *while they were not aware*: they did not know that his sister was watching him, because the egocentric faculties cannot reach the level of the reflective faculties.

[28:12] *And We had forbidden him to [take to the breasts of] foster mothers*: We had prevented him from deriving energy and nourishment from the pleasures and desires of the egocentric faculties, and from accepting their caprices and preparations, *from before* the employment of reflection by the light of preparedness and the purity of innate disposition. *So she said, 'Shall I show you a household who will take care of him for you*, by raising him with sublime character traits and ethics, and nursing him with the milk of principles via witnessings, intuitions and experiences, rather than the path of sensation and conjecture; *and who will act in good faith towards him?'* Thus, bolstering him with practical wisdoms and righteous deeds and refining him, rather than misleading him with delusions and errors and corrupting him with vileness and ugliness.

Q. 28:11

[28:13] *Thus, We restored him to his mother* the self-reproaching soul, by inclining towards her and approaching her, *so that her eyes might delight*, illuminated by his light, *and not grieve* for the loss of the delight of her eyes and her splendour and support, *and that she might know* by attaining certitude through his light *that God's promise* of connecting every prepared person to His perfection which is hidden within them, and of returning every reality to its origin, *is true; but most of them do not know*, and therefore they do not search for the perfection hidden within them, because of the veil and the cover of doubt and uncertainty.

[28:14] *And when he came of age* and reached the station of chivalry and perfect innate disposition, *and [then] was [fully] mature* and upright by attaining his perfection and then becoming detached from the soul and its attributes, *We gave him judgement and knowledge*, meaning discursive and practical wisdom. *And so do We reward those who are virtuous*: those who are adorned with the virtues and travel the path of temperance.

[28:15] *And he entered the city* of the body *at a time when its people were oblivious*, when the egocentric faculties were calm and quiet, lest they overwhelm and subjugate him, *and found therein two men*, the intellect and caprice, *fighting—one of his own faction*, meaning the intellect, *and the other*

of his enemies, meaning caprice, one of the followers of the Satan of estimation and the Pharaoh of the evil-enjoining soul. *So the one [who was
of his faction] called to him [for help against the one who was of his enemies]:* the
intellect called to him for help against caprice. *So [Moses] punched him,*
striking him with one of the configurations of practical wisdom, with
the power of divine aid, wielded in the hand of practical intellect, *and
did away with him. He said, 'This* antagonism and fighting *is of Satan's doing,*
for he goaded caprice into aggression and enmity. *Indeed, he is a manifest,
misleading enemy.'* Or one could read it as: this murder was of Satan's doing,
because meeting belligerence with excess is not the way of the virtue of
temperance emanated from the Compassionate, but rather stems from the
corresponding vice of negligence, such as meeting gluttony with atrophy,
or miserliness with waste, or profligacy with parsimony. In each case,
both are from Satan.

[28:16] *[He said, 'My Lord,] I have indeed wronged myself* with excess
and negligence, *so forgive me!'* Cover for me the vice of my wrongdoing,
by the light of Your justice. *So He forgave him* for the attributes of his
soul inclining to excess and negligence, by His light, and so he attained
temperance. *Truly He is the Forgiving* Who covers the configurations of
souls with His light, *the Merciful* Who emanates perfection when the soul
is purified from vices.

Q. 28:16

[28:17] *He said, 'My Lord, forasmuch as You have been gracious to me,* by
the blessings of knowledge and practice You have given me, protect me
so that *I will never be a partisan,* a helper, *of the criminals':* the egocentric
faculties which indulge in the vices.

[28:18] *In the morning he was in the city* of the body, *fearful* of the subjugation of the egocentric faculties, *[vigilant]* of the impulses, misgivings and
chattering of the soul in the station of vigilance; *when behold, the one who
had sought his help [the day before cried out to him for help]:* once again, the intellect called to him for help from the faculties of the soul, namely estimation
and imagination, because they despoil the station of vigilance and provoke
misgivings and qualms and stir up impulses and inclinations. They never tire
or pause in any of the stations of presence of the heart except for annihilation in God. Therefore, when Moses challenged him, he argued with him
in response: *[Moses said to him, 'Clearly you are a trouble-maker!'*

[28:19] *But when he was about to strike the man who was an enemy to both
of them, he said, 'O Moses,] do you want to slay me just as you slew a soul yesterday? You merely want to be a tyrant in the land, and you do not want to be of
the reformers':* the reason he accused his companion, the intellect, of being

a trouble-maker was that he was captivated by estimation and unable to repel it or respond to its challenge to the heart. He only wanted to strike out, but when he was about to strike him, he challenged him and upbraided him, saying, *Do you want to slay me just as you slew a soul yesterday?* As long as the heart has not reached the station of the spirit and become annihilated in the station of sainthood, or taken on the Divine Attributes, the Satan of estimation will not yield to it, because it awaits the day of the Major Resurrection. As long as the heart is in the station of chivalry and adorned with its perfections at the Intermediate Resurrection, it will seek to delude it; and it will not be subjugated or desist from seeking to dominate it simply because of cognitive and practical perfection.

[28:20] *And a man came from the outskirts of the city*: he was the love that inspires one to travel to God, which they call spiritual will (*irāda*). His coming from the outskirts of the city symbolises how he was sent from the hidden place of preparedness when the soul's caprice is slain; *hastening*, for there could be no swifter motion than his. [*He said, 'O Moses. Indeed, the council are conspiring to slay you*:] he came to warn him of their subjugation of him and alert him to how they were plotting to move against him when the authority of estimation overcame him, and to challenge him and debate him until they destroyed him through misguidance. *So leave* their city and the boundaries of their authority, and head for the station of the spirit. *Indeed, I am speaking to you in good faith.'*

Q. 28:20

[28:21] *So he departed [from it]* by resolving to struggle for God's sake and maintain presence and vigilance, *fearful* of their domination, seeking refuge with God for salvation from their evil, [*vigilant. He said, 'My Lord, deliver me from the evildoing people'*].

[28:22] *And when he turned his face towards Midian*, the station of the spirit, [*he said, 'Perhaps my Lord will show me the right way'*]: his hope trumped his fear because of the chivalry of spiritual will, and he sought veridical guidance, through spiritual lights and self-disclosures of the Attributes, to the straight path of Oneness and the road to God.

[28:23] *And when he arrived at the water of Midian*, the waterhole of unveiled knowledge and the pool of secret knowledge and discourse, *he found a group of people there*, saints and wayfarers to God and those in the midst of the path, who drank from the pool of unveiling, *watering* their faculties and disciples from it. Or it represents the sanctified intellects and incorporeal spirits of the people of the realm of divine power, who in reality are the folk of that pool, from which they water the sheep of heavenly and human souls and the dominion of the heavens and the earth.

And *he found besides them*, on the level lower than theirs, *two women*—the discursive and practical intelligences—*holding back [their flock]* of faculties from it, because they had drunk from intellectual knowledge and practical wisdom, before the Moses of the heart arrived to the waterholes of unveiling and the pools of experiential realisation, and they had no share of unveiled knowledge. [*He said, 'What is your business?' They said,*] '*We do not water [our flock] until the shepherds have moved on*: that is, we drink from the leftovers of the shepherds of the spirits and sanctified intellects, when they move on from the pool and head to us and pass onto us their leftover water; *and our father*, the spirit, *is a very old man'*: too old to do the watering himself.

[28:24] *So he watered [their flock] for them*: from the waterhole of his experiential realisation and the pool of his unveiling, by sharing his bounty with all the faculties; for when the heart comes to a waterhole and drinks, its bounty is shared among all the faculties, and they are illuminated by its light. *Then he retreated* from his station *to the shade* of the soul in the station of the breast, disdaining its intelligible knowledge when compared to the unveiled knowledge drawn from the grace of the Real and its holy station, and knowledge unveiled directly from God; *and said, 'My Lord! Indeed, I am in utter indigence of whatever good You send down to me'*: 'I need, and beg for, the tremendous good which You have sent down to me in the form of this unveiled knowledge.' This is the station of ecstasy and yearning, which is a fleeting state; but he was asking for it to be made a permanent disposition for him.

Q. 28:24

[28:25] *Then one of the two women came to him*: she was the discursive intelligence, illuminated by the light of holiness so that it could then be called 'the holy faculty'; *walking bashfully* because of how moved she was by him and his light, [*and she said,*] '*My father invites you*: this alludes to the spiritual attraction by the light of the holy faculty and the angelic suggestion; *that he may pay you a wage for watering [our flock] for us'*: that is, a reward for watering the distracting and veiling faculties from your bounty and illuminating them with your light; for when they reacted to this holy thunderbolt and were watered by this secret bounty, it became easy to ascend to the holy presence, and the heart's preparedness was strengthened to connect with the spirit, for the veils were torn down, or at least their darkness and denseness was dispelled. *So when he came to him* and connected with him and ascended to his station, in order for him to witness the spirit in its own state, [*and recounted to him the story,*] *he* [their father] *said, 'Do not be afraid. You have escaped from the evildoing people'*: this was the image of his state.

[28:26] *One of the two women said, 'O my father, hire him*: employ him to struggle for God's sake and be vigilant about tending to the sheep of the faculties, so that they do not wander off and spoil our company and sow confusion in our group, and to engage in the invocation of the heart in the station of the manifestations of the Attributes and the journey through them, in return for the wage of the reward of manifestations and knowledge of unveilings. *Indeed, the best [man] you can hire* for this work *is the strong* in acquiring perfection, *the trustworthy man'* who will not betray God's covenant, but he will stay true to it by living up to the preparedness gifted to him; or who will not betray the spirit by inclining to its daughters and thereby being veiled by the intelligible.

It is said that the shepherds would cover the opening of the well with a boulder that took seven men to lift, or some say ten men, but Moses was strong enough to move it by himself. There is an allusion in this to how divinely-inspired knowledge (*ʿilm ladunī*) can only be attained by one who adorns himself with the Seven or Ten Divine Attributes.

Q. 28:26

[28:27] *He said, 'I desire to marry you to one of these two daughters of mine*: to make her your spouse, that she might enjoy holy light and unveiled knowledge in your company, and obey your judgement and command, and not veil herself from you when she speaks; *on condition that you hire yourself to me for eight years*: work for me by struggling until you pass through eight stages, the stages of the Seven Divine Attributes, by becoming annihilated from your own attributes in God's, the last of which is the station of divine communion, and then the stage of witnessing wherein is the culmination of the request you made when you said, *'My Lord, show me that I may behold You!'* [Q. 7:143]. *And if you complete ten* by ascending through two more stages, namely annihilation in the Essence and subsistence with realisation afterwards, *that shall be of your own accord*, from the perfection and strength of your preparedness, the particularity of your essence, and the dictate of your ipseity. These are the ten perfections with which Abraham's Lord tested him, making him a leader of humankind in the station of Oneness when he passed them. And God knows best. *I do not want to be hard on you*, or burden you with more than you can bear, or more than your preparedness can accommodate. *God willing, you shall find me to be one of the righteous'* guardians who provide their charges with the favours and teachings they need to arrive, and guide them to the perfection stored in the core of the essence at the root of preparedness, by divine illumination, not one of those who would charge you with more than you can bear.

[28:28] [*He said*,] '*That is* [*settled then*] *between me and you*: the covenant you made with me shall stand between us, according to our strength, preparedness and effort, and no one but us shall be involved in it. *Whichever of the two terms I complete, there shall be no injustice* [*done*] *to me*: whichever of the two ends I reach, I shall not be blamed, for my only duty is to strive. As for reaching the end, it only depends on the preparedness I was granted in pre-eternity, and this will determine my strength to strive. [*And God is Guardian over what we say*':] our affair is entrusted to God, and He will bear witness over it. God has undertaken to provide us with the perfection that was destined for us, and it comes to us from His holiest emanation, and no one can change it, nor can anyone observe it but He. Until I arrive, no one can know the level of perfection that has been stored in my preparedness, for it is a matter of the Unseen whose knowledge God has claimed for Himself alone.

[28:29] *So when Moses had completed the term* and reached the limit of perfection, which was the shorter of the two terms, *and was travelling with his family*, the faculties in their entirety, journeying to the presence of holiness in the company of all of them so that none of them resisted him or fell behind him, and he had attained the disposition of training in spiritual discipline and vigilance without any affectation, *he saw in the distance on the side of the Mount* [*Ṭūr*], the mountain of the inner mystery which is the perfection of the heart in ascension, *a fire* of the Holy Spirit, the clear horizon through which revelation was transmitted to the prophets who received it. [*He said to his family*, '*Wait, I see a fire in the distance. Maybe I will bring you news from it or a brand from the fire, that you may warm yourselves.*'

Q. 28:28

[28:30] *And when he reached it, a call came from the right bank of the valley*] *at the blessed spot*, the station of the heart called 'the inner mystery', *from the tree* of his sanctified soul, [*saying*,] '*O Moses! Indeed, I am God, the Lord of the Worlds*': this is the station of divine communion and annihilation in the Attributes, so that both the Speaker and the Hearer were God, as he said, 'I become his hearing with which he hears, and his tongue with which he speaks.'

[28:31] [*And:* '*Throw down your staff.*' *And when he saw it quivering, as if it were a serpent, he turned his back, and did not look back:* '*O Moses, come forward, and do not be afraid. Indeed, you are safe:*] the interpretation of the throwing down of the staff and the hand appearing white was given in *sūrat al-Naml*.[1]

---

1 See the commentary on 27:8–12 above.

[28:32] *'Insert your hand into your bosom and it will emerge, white, without any blemish;] and draw your arm [back] to your side [as a precaution] against fear*: do not fear veiling or variegation upon the return from God, and steel yourself with my aid, secure and realised in God.

I heard our master (*shaykh*) Mawlā Nūr al-Dīn ʿAbd al-Ṣamad (may God sanctify his dear spirit) say, while speaking about the witnessing of Oneness and the station of annihilation, that his father related that there was once a certain dervish in the service of the great master Shihāb al-Dīn al-Suhrawardī who experienced tremendous first-hand experiential realisations of them. One day his master saw him weeping and lamenting, and asked what was wrong. He replied, 'I became veiled from Unity by multiplicity; and when I tried to go back, I could not recapture my state.' The master told him that this was the beginning of the station of subsistence, which is better and higher than his previous state, and reassured him. *These then shall be two proofs from your Lord* of the aforementioned respite, [*to Pharaoh and his council; for surely they are an immoral people.'*

Q. 28:32

[28:33] *He said, 'My Lord, I have indeed slain a soul among them and so I fear that they will slay me.]*

[28:34] *'And my brother* the Aaron of the intellect *is more eloquent than me in speech*, because the intellect is the spokesman for the heart, and without it the states of the heart would not be understood. If matters of experiential realisation are not expressed in an intelligible form, contextualised in the configuration of knowledge and the known, and explained by allegory and interpretation so that they can reach the ken of minds and souls, it will not be possible to understand them. [*So send him with me] as a helper to confirm me*, and as an assistant to explain what I mean in the form of knowledge accompanied by confirming proof, *for I truly fear that they will deny me'* because of how far my state is from their understanding, and how far they are from my station and state. There must be an intermediary.

[28:35] [*He said,]* *'We will strengthen your arm by means of your brother* and aid you with his support, *and We will give you both* victory (*ghalaba*), by granting you influence over them through the power of the dominion and aiding you with the intellect by the holy power; and the intellect will manifest your perfection in a practical image and an analogical proof, [*so that they will not be able to touch [either of] you because of Our signs: the two of you, and those who follow you [two], will be the victors.'*

[28:36] *But when Moses brought them Our clear signs they said, 'This is nothing but concocted sorcery. And we never heard of such [a thing] among our forefathers.'*

150

[28:37] *And Moses said, 'My Lord knows best who brings guidance from Him and whose will be the sequel of the [Blissful] Abode. Indeed, the evildoers will not be successful.'*

[28:38] *And Pharaoh said, 'O council, I do not know of any god for you other than me.]* So kindle for me, O Haman, a fire of caprice *over the clay* of wisdom, mixed from the water of knowledge and the soil of material configurations; *and make me [a tower]*: a lofty stage of perfection, such that anyone who climbs it shall become a gnostic. This was an allusion to how he was veiled by his own soul and incapable of detaching his intellect from material configurations, because of the deluding influence of estimation. In other words, the soul veiled by its own egocentricity from the worldly intellect, itself veiled by its own comprehension (*maʿqūl*), attempted to build an edifice from knowledge and action—both tainted by delusions of estimation—and a high station of perfection attained by study and learning, rather than by divine inheritance and direct transmission, such that anyone who climbed it would suppose himself a perfected gnostic. As was noted in [*sūrat*] *al-Shuʿarāʾ* [Q. 26], they were a people veiled by the intelligible from the Divine Law and prophethood, trained in logic and wisdom and absorbed in them, seeing philosophy as the sum of all perfection, denying gnosis, spiritual wayfaring and arrival. *That I may take a look at the god of Moses* by means of philosophy, *[for truly I consider him to be a liar']*: he deemed him a liar because he was below the level of gnosis and Oneness, and veiled by his attributes of egocentricity, transgression and pharaonic tyranny. Nor was their pride attained alongside annihilation, such that they could be proud through the Real, rather than falsehood, and so rise above the attributes of their souls.

 Q. 28:37

[28:39] *[And he and his hosts acted arrogantly in the land without right, and thought they would not return to Us.*

[28:40] *So We seized him and his hosts, and flung them into the waters. So behold how was the sequel for the evildoers.*

[28:41] *And We made them leaders who invite to the Fire, and on the Day of Resurrection they will not be helped.*

[28:42] *And We made a curse pursue them in this world, and on the Day of Resurrection they will be among the spurned.*

[28:43] *And verily We gave Moses the Book after We had destroyed the former generations, [containing] eye-openers for people, and as guidance, and mercy, that perhaps they might remember.]*

[28:44] *And you were not on the western side*: the side where the sun of the Essential Unity set in the being of Moses and became veiled by his being in the station of divine communion, because he heard the call from the tree of his soul. Therefore, his prayer-direction (*qibla*) was to the west, and his call was to the outward manifestations which were the setting-places of the sun of reality, unlike Jesus (may God grant him peace). [*You were not there*] *when We decreed to Moses the commandment*, revealing it to him by direct communion, *nor were you among the witnesses* to his station in the ranks of his deputies and the saints of his time who did witness it.

[28:45] [*But We brought forth generations, and life was prolonged in their case:*] but your generation is long after his, and during the many generations between them the people forgot it. So We showed you his station and state during your Ascension and the route of your path, that they might remember. *And you were not a dweller among the people of Midian*, the station of the spirit, *reciting to them* [*Our revelations*]: the knowledge of our Attributes and witnessings. On the contrary, you were on your own path, by which you rose from the highest horizon and approached the presence of Unity to the station of *the length of two bows away or nearer* [Q. 53:9]; [*but truly We are the senders*:] you told them of this when We sent you to return to the station of the heart after annihilation in the Real.

Q. 28:45

[28:46] *And you were not on the side of the Mount*, standing in the station of the inner mystery, [*when We called out,*] but [it is] *as a* perfect all-encompassing *mercy from your Lord* that visited you and raised you to the station of annihilation in Unity, in which are incorporated the stations of all the prophets; and your attribute and the image of your essence rose, by realisation in Him, to the station of subsistence, and you were sent forth so that your prophethood would be the universal seal of all prophethood; *that you may warn a people* whose preparedness for receiving has reached a level of perfection that their forefathers, who lived in the time of the previous prophets, did not reach, and that you might call them to the perfection of the station of the loved ones to which no one before ever called his people; *to whom no warner came before you* calling them to that to which you call them, *and that perhaps they may remember* by reaching the perfection of love.

[28:47] [*Otherwise, if an affliction should befall them because of what their own hands have sent before them, they might say, 'Our Lord, why did You not send a messenger to us, that we might have followed Your signs and been of the believers?'*]

[28:48] *But when the truth came to them from Us, they said, 'Why has he not been given the like of what Moses was given?' And did they not disbelieve in what was given to Moses before? They said, 'Two sorcerers abetting each other'. And they said, 'We indeed disbelieve in both.'*

[28:49] *Say: 'Then bring some Book from God that is better in guidance than these two, that I may follow it, if you are truthful.'*

[28:50] *Then if they do not respond to you, know that they are only following their desires. And who is more astray than he who follows his desire without any guidance from God? Indeed, God does not guide the evildoing folk.*

[28:51] *And now verily We have brought them the Word, that perhaps they might remember.*]

[28:52] *Those to whom We gave* [*the Book*], the Qur'ānic and discerning intellect, *before this, they believe in it* because of the perfection of their preparedness, while others do not.

[28:53] [*And, when it is recited to them, they say, 'We believe in it. It is indeed the Truth from our Lord. Indeed, even*] *before it we had submitted'* our faces to God, with faith in Oneness and surrender to His command.

[28:54] *Those will be given their reward twice over* [*for the patience they showed*]: first at the Intermediate Resurrection with deeds and attributes before annihilation in the Essence, and then at the Major Resurrection upon subsistence after annihilation from the three gardens; *and they ward off* absolute *evil* from their own deeds, attributes and essences *with* absolute *good* from witnessing the acts, Attributes and Essence of the Real; *and expend of that which We have provided them*, by guiding others to perfection and sharing their perfections with those who are prepared to receive them.

Q. 28:49

[28:55] *And when they hear vanity* aimed at diverting them from accepting this, *they disregard it* and are unmoved by it because they are monotheist saints, though not prophets, [*and say, 'To us* [*belong*] *our deeds and to you* [*belong*] *your deeds.*] *Peace to you*: may God give you security from the blights that prevent the acceptance of the truth! *We do not desire* companionship with *the ignorant'* who are lost because of foolishness and compounded ignorance, for they will not benefit from our company nor accept our guidance.

[28:56] *You cannot guide whomever you like* to be guided simply because of your concern for their condition, since you cannot truly know their level of preparedness. Your kinship of nation or family with them is merely a tie of blood, not true origin, and your passing friendship with them does not reveal the truth of their spiritual reality; *but God guides whomever He will* from the recipients of His nurture, *and He knows best those who will be guided*: those who will accept guidance, since He knows their level of preparedness and how their hearts are not sealed.

[28:57] *And they say, 'If we were to follow the Guidance with you, we will be deprived from our land.' Have We not established for them a secure Sanctuary to which are brought fruits of all kinds as a provision from Us? But most of them do not know.*

[28:58] *And how many a town We have destroyed whose lifestyle was one of arrogant ungratefulness! Those are their dwellings, which have not been dwelt in after them except a little. And it was We Who were the [sole] inheritors.*

[28:59] *And your Lord never destroyed the towns until He had raised up in their mother-town a messenger to recite Our signs to them. And We never destroyed the towns unless their inhabitants were committing evil.*

[28:60] *And whatever things you have been given are [only] the [short-lived] enjoyment of the life of this world and an ornament thereof; and what is with God is better and more lasting. Will you not understand?*

[28:61] *Is he to whom We have given a fair promise, which he will receive, like him to whom We have given the enjoyment of the life of this world, then on the Day of Resurrection he will be of those arraigned?*

[28:62] *And on the day when He will call to them and say, 'Where are My partners, those whom you used to claim?'*

Q. 28:58

[28:63] *Those against whom the Word [of punishment] will have become due, shall say, 'Our Lord, these are the ones whom we led astray. We led them astray, even as we went astray. We declare our innocence before You; it was not us that they worshipped.'*

[28:64] *And it shall be said, 'Call [now] to your associates!' So they will call to them, but they will not answer them, and they will see the chastisement: [they will wish] if only they had been guided!*

[28:65] *And on the day when He will call to them and say, 'What response did you give to those [messengers] who were sent?']*

[28:66] *The tidings will be obscured to them on that day*: realities will be unclear and muddied to them at the Minor Resurrection because they will be veiled, halting with things other than God like a blind person. Their total ignorance was instilled in them at the times of the two creations, as He says, *And whoever was blind in this [life] will be blind in the Hereafter* [Q. 17:72], because of their inability to speak and the seal set upon their mouths.

[28:67] *But as for him who repents*, breaking away from the attributes of the soul which covered his sight and enveloped his heart and preparedness, *and believes* in the Unseen by means of knowledge, *and acts righteously* by adorning himself with goodly attributes and acquiring merits and virtues, *maybe he will be among the successful* who triumph by detaching from the station of the soul and entering the station of the heart, and returning to innate disposition from the veil of creation.

[28:68] *And your Lord creates whatever He will* of veiled and unveiled folk, *and chooses* by the dictate of His will and His nurture for them as He desires. *They do not have the choice* about this. *Glory be to God [and exalted be He above what they associate with Him]*: above any other being having any choice alongside His, thus being a partner to Him.

[28:69] [*And your Lord knows what their breasts conceal and what they proclaim.*

[28:70] *And He is God;*] *there is no god except Him*: He has no partner in existence. *To Him belongs [all] praise* absolutely [*in the former and in the latter*], for all outward perfections in the outward appearances of things, as well as all hidden perfections within them, are from Him. Every beautiful, wealthy, strong and mighty person in this world is beautiful, wealthy, strong and mighty by His beauty, wealth, strength and might. Every perfected knower and gnostic of Him in the Hereafter is perfected, knowing and gnostic by His perfection, knowledge and gnosis. *And to Him belongs the judgement*: He overwhelms all things according to His desire and judges them by the dictate of His will, so that all who are ugly, poor, humble and weak in this world are thus by His judgement and decree, and all who are veiled, debased, captivated and rejected in the Hereafter are thus by His overwhelming power and judgement. *And to Him you will be returned*: by annihilation in His Being, His Attributes and acts, or His Essence.

Q. 28:69

[28:71] [*Say: 'Have you considered*] *if God were to make the night* of the darkness of the soul *everlasting over you until the Day of* Minor *Resurrection, what god other than God could bring you light* from the light of the spirit? *Will you not then listen* while you are in the veil, and thereby understand these meanings and wisdoms and come to have faith in the Unseen?

[28:72] [*Say: 'Have you considered*] *if God were to make over you the day* of the light of the spirit *perpetual* with the everlasting manifestations [of the Real] *until the Day of* Minor *Resurrection, what god other than God could bring you night* from the moments of obliviousness, the triumph of the attributes of the soul and the coverings of nature, *wherein you rest* until [you attain] the rights of your souls and repose for your bodies? *Will you not then see* by the light of the spirit of the manifestations of the Real?

[28:73] *And of His mercy He has made for you night and day* through obliviousness and presence in the station of the heart, and concealment and manifestation in the station of the spirit, *that you may rest therein* in the darkness of the soul and find solace in the light of the body and the rhythm of worldly existence; *and that you may seek* the *bounty* of the radiance of His unveilings and the manifestations of His Attributes and witnessings, *that perhaps you might give thanks'* for His favours both outward and inward, material and spiritual, from your beginnings to your ends by utilising them for God's sake to fulfil your obligations to Him in every station, by Him, in Him, and for Him.

[28:74] [*And on the day when He will call to them and say, 'Where [now] are My associates whom you used to claim?'*]

[28:75] *And We shall draw from every community a witness*: on the Day of Resurrection when the Mahdī comes forth, We shall bring out the prophet of every community, who knows them best; *and We shall say*, through the lips of that witness who testifies to the truth on behalf of all of them and is not veiled by them from it, '*Produce your evidence*' to show whether what you follow is true or false. *Then* they will fail to do it, and the proofs of the prophets will show true, and *they will know that the right is God's*, as the testimony of the witness will show. *And that which they used to invent*—their different schools of thought and divergent branching paths—[*will fail them*]. Alternatively, We shall say to the witnesses, '*Produce your evidence*' by proclaiming Oneness [of God], and they will do so, and all will recognise that the right is God's.

Q. 28:74

[28:76] *Indeed, Korah belonged to the people of Moses*, and was a scholar like Balaam the son of Beor,[1] *but he became insolent towards them* because he was veiled by his soul and his knowledge through arrogance and haughtiness towards them, and so became dominated by avarice and love for this world. This was a tribulation from God because of his delusion and regard for his own soul and its perfections, which veiled him, and thus his caprice inclined towards the lower direction, and the earth swallowed him up, veiled and cursed: [*For We had given him so many treasures that [the number of] their keys would verily have burdened a group of strong men. When his people said to him, 'Do not exult! Indeed, God does not love those who exult.*

[28:77] '*But seek, in that which God has given you, the Abode of the Hereafter. And do not forget your share of this world, and be good just as God has been good to you. And do not seek to cause corruption in the earth. Truly God does not love the agents of corruption.*'

[28:78] *He said, 'In fact, I have been given it because of knowledge I possess.' Does he not know that God had already destroyed before him generations of men stronger than him in might and greater in the amassing? The guilty will not be questioned about their sins.*

[28:79] *So he emerged before his people in his finery. Those who desired the*

---

1 The story of this scholar from among the Israelites is traditionally appended to the exegesis of Q. 7:175 (see the commentary of the *Jalālayn* and that of Ibn Kathīr thereto), as having been given great knowledge by God but misused it, so that it turned against him.

*life of this world said, 'O would that we had the like of what Korah has been given!
Indeed, he enjoys great fortune.'*

[28:80] *But those to whom knowledge had been given said, 'Woe to you! God's
reward is better for him who believes and acts righteously; and none will obtain it,
except those who are steadfast.'*

[28:81] *So We caused the earth to swallow him and his dwelling, and he had
no host to help him besides God, nor was he of those who can rescue themselves.*

[28:82] *And those who had longed to be in his place the day before were saying,
'Alas! God expands provision for whomever He will of His servants and straitens
[it]. Had God not been gracious to us, He would have made us to be swallowed too.'
And lo and behold, indeed those who are ungrateful never prosper.]*

[28:83] *That is the Abode of the Hereafter,* in the enduring holy realm,
which We shall grant to those [*who do not desire to be haughty in the earth, nor [to
cause] corruption:* those] who are not veiled by their souls and their attributes, so that their innate desire for advancement and ascent in the heaven
of the spirit is not twisted into an egocentric desire for dominance and
supremacy over people on earth, nor is their righteous search for gnostic
realities, virtues and lofty goals corrupted into the urge to amass material
means and wealth and to unjustly usurp the rights of others. *And the sequel
will be for [those who fear]:* the detached ones whose souls are purified from
ruinous vices and deluding caprices.

Q. 28:80

[28:84] [*Whoever brings a good deed shall have better than it; while whoever
brings an evil deed, those who commit evil deeds shall only be requited for what they
used to do.*]

[28:85] *Indeed, He Who has prescribed for you the Qur'ān*—obliging it for
you in pre-eternity at the beginning, along with the perfect preparedness, which is the gathering Qur'ānic intellect (*al-'aql al-Qur'ānī al-jāmi'*)
that combines all perfections and the sum of all excellent speech and wisdom—*will surely restore you to a place of return* of tremendous magnificence
which can barely be known or appreciated: annihilation in God in the
Unity of the Essence, and subsistence through realisation of Him through
all the Attributes.

Say: 'My Lord knows best him who brings guidance: no one knows my
state, nor the nature of my guidance and the divinely-inspired knowledge
granted specially to me, except for my Lord, not I nor any other, because
I am annihilated in Him from my own self, and all others are veiled from
my state; *and him who is in manifest error':* veiled from the truth because
of a lack of preparedness and dense veiling. Others besides me are veiled
from the state of my preparedness; even I do not know it, but only He

knows it, because of my annihilation in Him and my realisation of Him.

[28:86] *And you never expected that the Book would be conferred on you*: the book of the discerning intellect that differentiates what has been combined within you, for you were covered by the curtains of creation, and veiled from what had been placed within you; *but it was* conferred upon you *as a mercy from your Lord*, so that the Attribute of all-merciful mercy could be manifested upon you and its emanation could whelm you little by little until it became your own character. *So never be a supporter of the* veiled *disbelievers* by becoming veiled by it from annihilation in the Essence, lest your I-ness emerge by regarding its own perfection.

[28:87] *And never let them bar you from God's signs* and the manifestations of His Attributes [*after they have been revealed to you*], lest you halt with your own I-ness just as they halt with things other than God, thus becoming one of the idolaters through regarding yourself and treating it as God's fellow being. *And summon to your Lord* through Him, not to your own self through it; for you are the beloved, and the beloved does not summon to himself nor live through himself, but rather summons to his beloved through his beloved; [*and never be of the idolaters.*

[28:88] *And do not call on another god with God;*] there is no god except Him: do not call on anything besides Him, whether your own self or anything else. It was [the Prophet's] obedience to the command *summon to your Lord* that attained for him the attribute of *nor has he erred* [Q. 53:2], just as his adherence to *do not call on another god with God* attained for him the attribute of *the eye did not swerve* [Q. 53:17]. *Everything will perish except His countenance*, which is His Essence, for there is nothing besides Him. *His is the judgement* by His conquering of all things beneath His Attributes, *and to Him you will be brought back* through annihilation in His Essence.

Q. 28:86

29
THE SPIDER
SŪRAT AL-ʿANKABŪT

In the Name of God, the Compassionate, the Merciful

[29:1] *Alif. Lām. Mīm.*

[29:2] [*Do people suppose that they will be left to say, 'We believe,' and they will not be tried?*] The Divine Essence, and the Real Attributes whose source and origin with respect to other things is knowledge, and the Relative Attributes whose origin and source is principality (*mabdaʾiyya*), have dictated that people not be left with their deficiency, heedlessness and veiledness simply because they utter words and do deeds that outwardly conform to the truth. Rather, they will be tried with all manner of tribulations and tested with hardships and spiritual disciplines, until what was hidden in their preparedness and stored in their natural dispositions comes to light. The Divine Essence desired that the perfections it stored in the source of unification be manifested, and therefore It secreted them within the essences of humankind and placed them in the realm of witnessing, as the Real said [in the well-known *ḥadīth qudsī*], 'I was a hidden treasure...' and so on.[1] Hence, He made Himself beloved to them by trying them with blessings and misfortunes, so that they would recognise Him when His Attributes were manifested upon them, and thus become themselves manifestations of Him leading to Him in the end, just as they had been stores and treasuries for Him in the beginning. He is the beginning, which means that He must also be the end.

[29:3] *And certainly We tried those who were before them*: the folk of insight and preparedness, with all manner of misfortunes, trials, disciplines and tribulations, in order to differentiate those who are sincere in their seeking and ready to receive perfection by the manifestation of His perfection,

---

1 '...And I loved to be known, and so I created the world.'

from those who are insincere, confounded and ill-prepared. [*So God shall surely know those who are sincere, and He shall surely know those who are liars.*

[29:4] *Or do those who commit evil deeds suppose that they can elude Us? Evil is that which they judge!*]

[29:5] *Whoever expects to encounter God* in one of the realms—whether it be the realm of rewards and traces, the realm of act, the realm of character traits, the realm of the Attributes, or the realm of the Essence—[*should know that*] God's [*appointed*] *term* in one of the three stations *will indeed come*: they should be certain that the meaning will take place according to their states and their expectations when the appointed term comes, and they should do good works in order to find grace in the garden of the soul by means of traces and deeds at the moment of natural death. Or they should strive for self-effacement, with spiritual discipline and vigilance in order to witness, in the garden of the heart, manifestations of the Attributes and the stations of the character traits, in order to be inspired and moved by them at the moment of voluntary death. Or they should struggle for God as befits Him, through annihilation in Him, to experience the fragrance of witnessing and the experiential realisation of beauty in the garden of the spirit at the moment of major death and the great catastrophe. [*And He is the Hearer, the Knower.*]

Q. 29:4

[29:6] *And whoever struggles*, in whichever station and for whatever realm he desires, *struggles only for his own sake*. [*Indeed, God is Independent of* [*the creatures of*] *all the Worlds.*]

[29:7] *And those who believe* with any one of the aforementioned types of faith, *and perform righteous deeds* commensurate with their faith, *We will surely absolve them of their misdeeds*, their bad deeds and character traits, or their attributes, or their essences, with the lights of His Essence, *and We will indeed requite them with the best of what they used to do*, with Our acts, which comes from Our Attributes, in place of their deeds.

[29:8] *And We have enjoined on humanity kindness to his parents; but if they urge you to ascribe to Me as partner that of which you do not have any knowledge, then do not obey them. To Me will be your return whereat I will inform you of what you used to do*: He decreed that noble character traits begin with kindness to one's parents, since they are the locus for the manifestation of the two attributes of creation and lordship, and thus their right is next to God's right, and obedience to them is next to obedience to Him. Justice is the shadow of Oneness, and so the one who believes in God's Oneness must be just; and the beginning of justice is to fulfil the rights of the parents, since of all people they are the most deserving. Hence, their rights must be put ahead of everyone else's, except for God's. This is why it is obligatory to obey them in all things except for associating partners with God.

[29:9] [*And those who believe and perform righteous deeds, assuredly We shall admit them among the righteous.*

[29:10] *And among people there are those who say, 'We believe in God,' but if such [a person] suffers hurt in God's cause, he takes people's persecution to be [the same] as God's chastisement. Yet if there comes help from your Lord, they will assuredly say, 'We were indeed with you.' Does God not know best what is in the breasts of all creatures?*

[29:11] *And God shall surely ascertain those who believe, and He shall surely ascertain the hypocrites.*

[29:12] *And those who disbelieve say to those who believe, 'Follow our path and we will bear [responsibility for] your sins.' But they will not [be able to] bear anything of their sins. Indeed, they are liars.*

[29:13] *And they shall certainly bear their [own] burdens and other burdens along with their [own] burdens, and on the Day of Resurrection they shall surely be questioned concerning what they used to invent.*

Q. 29:9

[29:14] *And verily We sent Noah to his people and he remained among them a thousand-less-fifty years; so the Flood engulfed them, for they were wrongdoers.*

[29:15] *Then We delivered him and the occupants of the ship, and We made this a sign for all peoples.*

[29:16] *And Abraham, when he said to his people, 'Worship God and fear Him; that is better for you, if you only knew.*

[29:17] *'What you worship besides God are only graven images and you fabricate a calumny. Indeed, those whom you worship besides God have no power to provide for you. So seek your provision from God, and worship Him, and be thankful to Him; to Him you shall be returned.*

[29:18] *'But if you deny, then [many] communities have denied before you; and the messenger's duty is only to communicate [the Message] clearly.'*

[29:19] *Have they not seen how God originates creation, then restores it? Truly that is easy for God.*

[29:20] *Say: 'Travel in the land and observe how He originated creation. Then God shall bring about the other genesis. Indeed, God has power over all things.*

[29:21] *He chastises whomever He wishes, and has mercy on whomever He wishes, and to Him you shall be returned.*

[29:22] *And you will never be able to thwart [Him] on earth, or in the heaven; and you do not have besides God any guardian, or any helper.*

[29:23] *And those who disbelieve in God's signs and the encounter with Him, they have despaired of My mercy, and for those there shall be a painful chastisement.*

[29:24] *But the only answer of his people was that they said, 'Slay him, or burn him!' Then God delivered him from the fire. Indeed, in that there are signs for a people who believe.*

[29:25] *And he said,] 'You have adopted mere idols besides God [for the sake of [mutual] affection between you in the life of this world']*: that is, 'You have adopted something which you worship and hold beloved among yourselves in the life of this world.' Or, 'All that you have adopted besides God is something held beloved among yourselves in the life of this world.' Or, 'All that you have taken as idols are held beloved among you in this life,' or 'for the sake of affection between you in this life', according to the two canonical readings.[1] The meaning is that affection is of two kinds: worldly and other-worldly. Worldly affection comes from the soul from below, while other-worldly affection comes from the spirit from above. Everything that is loved and held in affection other than God, and neither for God's sake nor through love for Him, is loved with the affection of the soul, which is a passing caprice that ends whenever the physical connection is severed. It does not endure unto any of the Resurrections, because it arises from the composition of the body and the balance of the temperament. When the composition breaks down and the temperament becomes unbalanced, it disappears and all that remains is opposition and resistance, according to the individual's natures, as He says, *Then on the Day of Resurrection you will disown one another, and you will curse one another, [and your abode will be the Fire, and you will have no helpers']*. Therefore, He likens it to the dwelling of the spider in its weakness:

Q. 29:24

[29:41] *The likeness of those who choose besides God [other] patrons is as the likeness of the spider that makes a home. And truly the frailest of homes is the home of the spider, if they only knew*: as for other-worldly affection, it comes from the Essential Unity and divine love. This is the affection that exists among the pure ones and the saints because of the correspondence of their attributes and kinship of their essences. It does not become completely pure and detached from any cover until the composition breaks down, and the veils of the soul and body are rent asunder in the station of the heart and the spirit, because of its proximity to its source there. Thus, on the Day of Resurrection, it becomes pure unadulterated love, unlike the other.

[29:26] *[And Lot believed in him, and he said, 'Indeed, I am migrating toward my Lord. Indeed, He is the Mighty, the Wise.'*

---

1 The word *mawadda* ('affection') can be read in the nominative as a *khabar* denoting the predicate, or in the accusative as a *mafʿūl lah* denoting 'for the sake of'.

[29:27] *And We gave him Isaac, and Jacob, and We ordained among his descendants prophethood and the Book. And We gave him his reward in this world. And in the Hereafter he shall truly be among the righteous.*

[29:28] *And Lot, when he said to his people, 'Indeed, you commit lewdness, such as none in [all] the worlds has committed before you.*

[29:29] *'What! Do you come unto men, and cut-off the way, and you discuss in your gatherings indecency?' But the only answer of his people was that they said, 'Bring us the chastisement of God, if you are truthful.'*

[29:30] *He said, 'My Lord, help me against the people who work corruption.'*

[29:31] *And when Our messengers came to Abraham with the good tidings, they said, 'We shall indeed destroy the people of this town, for truly its people are evildoers.'*

[29:32] *He said, 'Indeed, Lot is in it.' They said, 'We know very well who is in it. Assuredly We shall deliver him and his family, except his wife: she is of those who will stay behind.'*

[29:33] *And when Our messengers came to Lot, he was distressed on their account, and he was constrained [unable] to help them. But they said, 'Do not be afraid, nor grieve. We shall surely deliver you and your family, except your wife: she is of those who will remain behind.*

Q. 29:27

[29:34] *'We are indeed going to bring down upon the people of this town a scourge from the heaven because of their immorality.'*

[29:35] *And verily We have left of that a clear sign for a people who understand.*

[29:36] *And to Midian [We sent] their brother Shuʿayb. He said, 'O my people, worship God and anticipate the Last Day, and do not be degenerate in the earth, working corruption.'*

[29:37] *But they denied him, and so the earthquake seized them, and they ended up lying lifeless prostrate in their habitations.*

[29:38] *And ʿĀd, and Thamūd, it is indeed evident to you from their [former] dwellings. For Satan adorned for them their deeds, and thus barred them from the Way, though they had been discerning.*

[29:39] *And Korah, and Pharaoh, and Haman! And verily Moses brought them clear signs, but they acted arrogantly in the land; and they could not thwart Us.*

[29:40] *So each We seized for his sin; and among them were some upon whom We unleashed a squall of stones, and among them were some who were seized by the Cry, and among them were some whom We made the earth swallow, and among them were some whom We drowned. And God never wronged them, but they wronged themselves.*

[29:41] *The likeness of those who choose besides God [other] patrons is as the likeness of the spider that makes a home. And truly the frailest of homes is the home of the spider if they only knew.*

[29:42] *Indeed, God knows whatever thing they call on besides Him. And He is the Mighty, the Wise.*

[29:43] *And such similitudes, We strike them for [the sake of] people; but none understands them, except those who know.*

[29:44] *God created the heavens and the earth with truth. Indeed, in that there is a sign for believers.]*

[29:45] *Recite what has been revealed to you of the Book, and maintain prayer*: discern what has been collected within you from the book of the Qurʾānic intellect by means of revelation and the descent of the book of discerning knowledge, and maintain absolute prayer according to all the instructions of recitation and learning. Combine perfection of knowledge with absolute action, for each bit of knowledge has a corresponding prayer. Knowledge can be of several kinds: first there is beneficial knowledge, which pertains to etiquette, actions and matters of worldly value, which are the sciences of the faculties from the Unseen realm of terrestrial dominion. Then there is noble knowledge, which pertains to sublime character traits, virtues and matters of other-worldly value, which are the sciences of the soul from the Unseen realm of the breast and the cognitive intellect. Then there is universal knowledge of certitude, which pertains to the Attributes and itself is of two kinds: that which is drawn from intellectual consideration, and that which is drawn from secret unveiling, both of which are from the Unseen realm of the heart and inner mystery. Then there is real knowledge, which pertains to manifestations and witnessings and is from the Unseen realm of the spirit. Then there is knowledge of experiential realisation and direct divine inspiration, which pertains to matters of passion and communication and comes from the Unseen realm of the hidden. Then there is true knowledge, which is from the Unseen of Unseens.

For every kind of knowledge, there is a prayer. The first is the prayer of the body with all its necessary motions and pillars. The second is the prayer of the soul with humility, concentration, submission, and a tranquil balance between fear and hope. The third is the prayer of the heart with presence and vigilance. The fourth is the prayer of the inner mystery with intimate discourse and communion. The fifth is the prayer of the spirit with witnessing and direct beholding. The sixth is the prayer of the hidden secret with tenderness and intimacy. There is no prayer in the seventh station, for it is the station of annihilation and pure love: annihilation in the source of Unity. Just as ritual prayer comes to an end with death, which is the outward image of certitude—as has

Q. 29:42

been said in a commentary on God's Words, *Worship your Lord until certitude comes to you* [Q. 15:99]—likewise the end of real prayer comes with absolute annihilation, which is the reality of certitude. As for the station of subsistence which comes after annihilation, all of the six prayers are renewed therein, along with a seventh, which is the prayer of truth with love and detachment from self.

Indeed, prayer prevents against lewd acts and indecency: the prayer of the body prevents against sins and illicit acts. The prayer of the soul prevents against vices, base character traits and benighted configurations. The prayer of the heart prevents against curiosity and heedlessness. The prayer of the inner mystery prevents against regard of other-than-God and distraction, as he (may God grant him peace) said, 'If the person in prayer knew with Whom he was speaking, he would not be distracted.' The prayer of the spirit prevents against the tyranny of the emergence of the heart with its attributes, just as the prayer of the heart prevents against the emergence of the soul therein. The prayer of the hidden secret prevents against duality and the emergence of I-ness. The prayer of the Essence prevents against the emergence of any remnant of the soul with variegation, and the presence of opposition in Oneness.

Q. 29:46

And the remembrance of God is surely greater: the remembrance of the Essence in the station of total annihilation, and the prayer of truth after stability in the station of subsistence, is greater than all invocations and prayers; *and God knows what you do* in all stations, states and prayers.

[29:46] *And do not dispute with the People of the Book unless it be in the most virtuous way*: He forbade disputing with the People of the Book unless it be in the most virtuous way because they are not veiled from the Real, but rather from the religion; they are people of preparedness and subtlety, not people of ruin and compulsion. They have only strayed from the path to their goal, which is the Real, because of certain obstacles, customs and external phenomena. Therefore, it is only wise to accompany them to the goal, which is Oneness—as He says [*except [in the case of] those of them who have done wrong, and say, 'We believe in that which has been revealed to us and revealed to you.] Our God and your God is One [and the same]*—and to accompany them on the path, as long as it is straight and true and does not deviate from the common ground we share, such as surrender and submission to the One True Absolute God, as He says *and to Him we submit.'* Thus, they will become certain that they are on the right path towards to their goal and heading His way, and their hearts will find tranquillity. The way to follow the path should be kindly explained to them, approving of what is correct in their approach and what is false and must be corrected, because of how they are veiled from it by worship. [It is as] He says, *'We believe in that which has been revealed to us and revealed to you. Our God and your God is One [and the same], and to Him we submit,'* because of the common ground between them, so that they would feel at ease with them and accept their words and be guided by their guidance, except for those of them whose hearts had become covered with darkness because of what they had acquired, and who had therefore been rendered ill-prepared and veiled from their Lord. They were the ones who had wronged themselves by ruining their own preparedness and denying their own souls their due perfections by sullying and blackening them, and preventing them from accepting because of their manifold indulgences. Such are the people of compulsion, with whom nothing but compulsion has any effect and with whom kindness is of no use, because of the great disparity between the two qualities.

Q. 29:47

[29:47] [*Thus have We revealed to you the Book. And so those to whom We have given the Book believe in it, and of these there are some who believe in it; and none denies Our signs, except disbelievers.*

[29:48] *And you did not use to recite before this any [other] Book, nor did you write it with your right hand, for then those who follow falsehood would have had doubts.*]

[29:49] *Nay, but it is clear signs in the breasts of those who have been given knowledge*: the Qur'ān is composed of pieces of real, clear experiential realisation, which are held in the breasts of the realised scholars. They are the meanings that descended from the Unseen of Unseens to the breast, not the words and letters that are enunciated by the tongue in remembrance; [*and none denies Our signs except wrongdoers*:] none deny them but the disbelievers who are veiled because of their lack of preparedness, or the wrongdoers who ruin their own preparedness with vices and allegiance to opposites.

[29:50] [*And they say, 'Why has not some sign been sent down to him from his Lord?' Say: 'Signs are only with God and I am only a plain warner.'*

[29:51] *Is it not sufficient for them that We have revealed to you the Book which is recited to them? Indeed, in that is mercy and a reminder for a people who believe.*

[29:52] *Say: 'God suffices as a witness between me and you.' He knows whatever is in the heavens and the earth. And those who believe in falsehood, and [who] disbelieve in God, those—they are the losers.*

[29:53] *And they ask you to hasten the chastisement. Yet were it not for an appointed term, the chastisement would have come upon them, but it shall assuredly come upon them suddenly while they are unaware.*

[29:54] *And they ask you to hasten the chastisement.*] Indeed, Hell shall encompass the disbelievers who are veiled from the Real, due to being so totally immersed in coverings of nature and veils of primordial matter, that there is no longer any gap through which they could escape to the world of light and gain insight and illumination from it, and breathe in its air and take their repose in it.

[29:55] *On the day when the chastisement shall envelop them from above them,* because of how they are deprived of the Real and veiled from the light, burning beneath the divine overwhelming power, *and from under their feet,* because of how they are deprived of pleasures and passions and veiled from them by the loss of material means and instruments, and tormented by the pain of configurations and the fires of traces. Thus, they exist between two grievous torments and two powerful desires: one to the higher direction because of their primordial innate disposition, and the other to the lower direction because of the firmness of the configuration that became branded upon them, while being deprived of both and suspended in an isthmus between them. We seek God's refuge from such a fate! [*And We shall say, 'Taste now what you used to do!'*

Q. 29:54

[29:56] *O My servants who believe, My earth is indeed vast. So worship [only] Me.*

[29:57] *Every soul shall taste death. Then to Us you shall be returned.*

[29:58] *And those who believe and perform righteous deeds, We shall surely lodge them in lofty abodes of Paradise, underneath which rivers flow, to abide in them—excellent is the reward of the toilers:*

[29:59] *Those who are steadfast, and who put their trust in their Lord.*

[29:60] *And how many an animal there is that does not bear its own provision! Yet God provides for it, and for you. And He is the Hearer, the Knower.*

[29:61] *And if you were to ask them, 'Who created the heavens and the earth and disposed the sun and the moon?' they would assuredly say, 'God.' So how, then, are they turned away?*

[29:62] *God extends provision for whomever He wishes of His servants and He straitens [it] for him. Indeed, God has knowledge of all things.*

[29:63] *And if you were to ask them, 'Who sends down water from the heaven, and therewith revives the earth after its death?' they would assuredly say, 'God.' Say: 'Praise be to God!' Nay, but most of them do not realise.*

[29:64] *And the life of this world is nothing but diversion and play. But surely the Abode of the Hereafter is indeed the [true] life, if they only knew.*

[29:65] *And when they board the ship, they call on God, making their supplications purely to Him; but when He delivers them to land, behold! they ascribe partners [to Him].*

[29:66] *That they may be ungrateful for what We have bestowed on them, and that they may seek enjoyment, for they will soon know!*

[29:67] *Or is it that they have not seen that We have appointed a secure Sanctuary, while people are snatched away all around them? Is it that they believe in falsehood, and are [wont to be] ungrateful for God's grace?*

[29:68] *And who does greater wrong than he who invents a lie against God, or denies truth when it comes to him? Is there not in Hell a lodging for the disbelievers?*]

[29:69] *But as for those* people of the path *who struggle for Our sake* by journeying through Our Attributes, which is the journey of the heart—for the novice in the station of the heart travels by struggling for God's sake, and the struggle of this journey is accomplished by presence, vigilance and uprightness for God by adhering to the rule of manifestations—*We shall assuredly guide them in Our ways* to the paths that lead to the Essence, which are the Attributes, since they are the veils of the Essence. Following them by adorning oneself with them leads one to the reality of the Name that is His by the Attribute with which He is described, which is the source of Essential Oneness, the door to the Unitary Presence. *And truly God is with the virtuous* who worship God with witnessing, as he (may God grant him peace) said, 'Virtuousness [*iḥsān*] is to worship God as though you see Him.' The virtuous are those who journey through the Attributes and adorn themselves with them, because they worship with vigilance and witnessing. He only said 'as though you see Him' because vision and eye-witnessing can only be attained by annihilation in the Essence after the Attributes.

Q. 29:66

30
THE BYZANTINES
SŪRAT AL-RŪM

In the Name of God, the Compassionate, the Merciful

[30:1] *Alif. Lām. Mīm.*

[30:2] *The Byzantines have been vanquished* [30:3] [*in the nearer* [*part of the*] *land*]: the Essential Unity, with the two aforementioned Attributes of knowledge and principality, has decreed that the Byzantines of the spiritual faculties be vanquished in the closest point of the land of the soul, which is the breast. The effusion of the principle (*mabda'*) necessitates the manifestation of creation and the veiling of the Real by it, and so that which is closer to the Real is vanquished by that which is closer to creation. This is the dictate of the Name the Beginner (*al-Mubdi'*) in the fulfilment of origination and His manifestation by it and by His Name the Outwardly Manifest, His Name the Creator, and all the other Names pertaining to His essential principality.

But they, after their vanquishing, shall be the victors over the Persians of the barbarous veiled egocentric faculties, by the return to God and the emergence of victory, [30:4] *in a few years* of the states wherein there is ascension to perfection, and the moments of presence, stations and manifestations. *To God belongs the command, before* by the dictate of His Name the Beginner, *and after* by the dictate of His Name the Restorer, Who *directs the command from the heaven to the earth, and then it ascends to Him* [Q. 32:5]; *and on that day*—the day of the victory of the Byzantines of the spiritual beings over the egocentricities—*the believers shall rejoice* [30:5] *in God's help* and assistance from the heavenly dominions and the holy graces He sends them. *He helps whomever He will* of the folk of His nurture who are prepared by it; *and He is the Mighty*, the strong vanquisher of the veiled Persians, *the Merciful* by the emanation of perfect graces and aiding holy lights upon the victorious Byzantines.

[30:6] *The promise of God* is to perfect the prepared folk of His nurture. *God does not fail His promise, but most people are not aware* because they are veiled and so imagine that this victory is by their own strength and acquisition, and that the person to whom it was granted would not have attained it without his own hard work. They do not understand that the prepared person was made so by His grace, and that this is a sign of His nurture, and the absence of work is the result of His forsaking and a sign that the person was not granted His nurture. Our deeds are acknowledgements, not demands.

[30:7] *They know [merely] an outward aspect of the life of this world* and how success therein depends on the efforts and plans of people; *but they, concerning the inward aspect and the states of the spiritual world, they are oblivious.* They do not understand that behind this ephemeral life there is an eternal life, as He says, *But surely the Abode of the Hereafter is indeed the [true] life, if they only knew* [Q. 29:64], and that behind the planning and work of people are the decree and dictate of God.

Q. 30:6

[30:8] *Have they not contemplated themselves? God did not create the heavens* of the Seven Unseens,[1] *and the earth* of the body, *and what is between them* of the natural faculties, the earthly and spiritual dominions, the heavenly dominion, the attributes, the character traits and so on, *except with* wisdom, justice and the manifestation of *the truth*, in their loci through the Attributes, according to their levels of preparedness to receive His manifestation, *and an appointed term*, which is the utmost perfection of each of them and their annihilation in God according to the ipseity of their primordial preparedness, until they witness on the level of their preparedness, and God inspires them with His Attributes and Essence. *But indeed many people disbelieve in the encounter with their Lord* because they are veiled from Him, and so imagine that it will be nothing more than a formal meeting in another world by the transference of one ipseity into another.

[30:9] [*Have they not travelled in the land and beheld how was the consequence for those before them? They were more powerful than them, and they effected the land, and developed it more than these have developed it; and their messengers brought them clear signs, for God would never wrong them, but they used to wrong themselves.*

[30:10] *Then the consequence for those who committed evil was evil, because they denied the signs of God and made a mockery of them.*]

---

1 Namely those of the jinn, the soul, the heart, the mystery, the spirit, the hidden, and the Unseen of Unseens. See Kāshānī's commentary on Q. 16:77.

[30:11] *God originates creation* by granting the Persians victory over the Byzantines, *and then returns it* by granting the Byzantines victory over the Persians, *then to Him you shall be returned* by annihilation in Him.

[30:12] *And on the day when the Hour comes* with the occurrence of the Minor Resurrection, *the sinners will be dumbfounded* to the mercy of God, confounded by the torment so that they cannot receive the mercy. Or at the Major Resurrection with the emergence of the Mahdī and their vanquishing under his authority and their deprivation of his mercy, when the people will divide and the believer will become distinct from the disbeliever:

[30:13] [*And none from among those partners of theirs shall be intercessors for them and they shall disavow these partners of theirs.*

[30:14] *And on the day when the Hour comes, that day they shall be separated.*

[30:15] *As for those who believed and performed righteous deeds, they shall be made happy in a garden [of Paradise].*

[30:16] *But as for those who disbelieved and denied Our signs and the encounter of the Hereafter, those—they shall be arraigned into the chastisement.*]

Q. 30:11

[30:17] *So glory be to God* above anyone but Him possessing existence, Attribute, act or influence, *when you enter the [time of the] night* as the darkness of the Persians overwhelms the light of Byzantines, *and when you rise in the morning* when their light overwhelms the darkness of the Persians.

[30:18] *And to Him belongs [all] praise [in the heavens and the earth]*: by the emergence of the Attributes of His perfection and the manifestation of His beauty in the heavens of the Seven Unseens at the time of the dawn, when the light of spiritual beings overwhelms the darkness of egocentricities, and shortly before the rising of the sun of the spirit, and by the emergence of the Attributes of His majesty in the earth of the body in the evening, when the darkness of egocentricities overwhelms the light of spiritual beings; *and as the sun declines*: the time of their annihilation and the disappearance of the sun of the spirit into the Essence, *and when you enter noontime* in subsistence after annihilation upon attaining uprightness and stability.

[30:19] *He brings forth the living* of the heart *from the dead* of the soul by returning it at dawn, *and He brings forth the dead* of the soul *from the living* of the heart by originating it in the evening; *and He revives the earth* of the body thereafter, [*after it has died*]. *And in such [a manner], you shall be brought forth* at the second creation.

[30:20] [*And of His signs is that He created you of dust, then, lo and behold, you are human beings, spreading.*]

[30:21] *And of His signs*—from His acts and Attributes via which one connects to His Essence with gnosis and wayfaring—*is that He created mates for you from yourselves*: He created souls for you as mates for your spirits, *that you might find peace by their side* and incline towards them with affection, influence and receptivity; *and He ordained between you*, on both sides, *affection and mercy*, so that the soul loves the light and influence of the spirit with acceptance and receptivity, and its agitation is calmed, and it becomes pure. Then in His mercy, God graces it with the child of the heart in the womb of preparedness, which is dutiful to it; and so it is guided by His blessing and adorns itself with His character traits, and finds success. In turn, the spirit loves the soul by influencing it and emanating light upon it; and so in His mercy, God graces it with the blessed child, which is dutiful and tender to it; and so by His blessing, it ascends and manifests His perfection. *Indeed, in that there are signs*—attributes and perfections—*for a people who reflect*: on themselves and their essences and the nature upon which they were created and which was placed within them.

Q. 30:21

[30:22] [*And of His signs is the creation of the heavens*] *and the earth and the differences of your tongues*: the tongues of the soul, the heart, the mystery, the spirit and the hidden, with each statement in each station; for there is no limit to the differences of these tongues; *and your colours*: your colouring and variegations in the seven heavens and the earth. [*Indeed, in that there are*] *signs* of the manifestations of Attributes and acts *for all peoples* of knowledge and gnosis in the ranks of their learning.

[30:23] [*And of His signs is*] *your sleep* [*by night and day*]: your heedlessness in the night of the soul and the day of the heart by the manifestation of its attributes, *and your seeking of His bounty* by ascending in perfections and acquiring character traits and stations. [*Indeed, in that there are signs*] *for people who listen* to the speech of the Real with the ear of the heart, and so understand its meaning according to their stations of development.

[30:24] [*And of His signs is*] *His showing you* the *lightning* of flashes and glimmering inspirations in the beginnings, *to arouse fear and hope*: their briefness and irregularity makes you fear that they will end and you will be left in darkness, and you hope that they will return and you will have more of them. *And He sends down* the *waters* of inspirations and unveilings *after* them *from the heaven* of the spirit and the clouds of divine peace, *and with it He revives the earth*—the barren lands of souls and preparednesses—*after it has died* of ignorance. [*Indeed, in that there are signs for people*] *who understand*, by directing their souls to heed the impulses of the intellect, the meanings of these inspirations and the wisdoms and intelligibles that are good for them.

[30:25] [*And of His signs is that the heaven and the earth remain standing by His command; then, when He calls you [to come] out of the earth, lo and behold, you shall come forth.*

[30:26] *And to Him belongs whoever is in the heavens and the earth. All are obedient to Him.*

[30:27] *And He it is Who initiates the creation, then brings it back, and that is [even] easier for Him.] His is the loftiest description [in the heavens and the earth. And He is the Mighty, the Wise]*: His is the loftiest description: the most sublime Attribute, which is uniqueness in existence and Essential Unity. A fine explanation of this phrase was the one offered by Mujāhid, who said that it simply means, 'There is no god but He.'

[30:28] [*He has struck for you a similitude from yourselves: do you have among those whom your right hands own any partners, [who may share] in what We have provided for you, so that you are equal therein, fearing them as you fear your own [folk]? So We detail the signs for people who understand.*

[30:29] *Nay, but those who do evil follow their own desires without any knowledge. So who will guide he whom God has led astray? And they have no helpers.*]

Q. 30:25

[30:30] *So set your purpose for* the *religion* of Oneness, which is the path of the Real; hence, He spoke of it in absolute terms without qualification. It is *religion* in an absolute sense, and all besides it are not truly religions because they are cut-off and do not lead all the way to the goal. The *purpose*[1] means the essence with all of its concomitants and accidents, and setting its purpose for religion means to detach it from everything but the Real and to uphold Oneness and stand with the Real, without regarding one's own self or anything else. Then one's journey will be the journey of God, and one's religion and path will be the religion and path of God, since one will not see anything but Him to exist; *as a ḥanīf*: one who inclines away from false religions, which are the paths of others and opposites, followed by those who affirm the existence of other-than-God and thereby associate partners with Him. *A nature given by God, [upon which He originated humankind]*: adhere to the nature given by God, which is the condition of purity and detachment in which the human reality was established in pre-eternity: it *is the upright religion*, from time immemorial unto eternity, its original purity unchanging and irreplaceable, the pure primordial doctrine of Oneness. This primordial disposition comes only from the holiest emanation, which is the Essence of Being, and the one who cleaves to it cannot stray from Oneness or be veiled from the Real.

---

1 *Wajh*, literally 'face'.

Straying and veiling only occur because of the coverings of creation and the accidents of nature, whether because of natural character, upbringing or culture. The first is because as he (may God grant him peace) said in the sacred (*rabbānī*) *ḥadīth*, 'I created all of My servants as *ḥanīfs*, but then Satan diverted them away from their religion and commanded them to associate others with Me.' The second is because, as he (may God bless him and grant him peace) said, 'Every child is born upon the innate disposition, until it is his parents that make him a Jew or a Christian.' Nonetheless, it is not that this reality changes in itself from its essential nature, for that is impossible. This is the meaning of His Words, *There is no changing God's creation. That is the upright religion, but most people do not know.*

[30:31] *Turn to Him*: this refers back to the previous command: that is, adhere to that special innate disposition by God, turning to Him from all others you might imagine to exist because of the devils of estimation and imagination and their false religions. Detach from material coverings, physical accidents, natural configurations and egocentric attributes, and turn to the Real and His religion. *And fear Him*, after turning to Him, by the detachment of innate disposition by annihilation in Him; *and establish prayer* of essential witnessing; *and do not be among the idolaters* by retaining the innate disposition but allowing I-ness to emerge in its station, [30:32] [*of*] *those who have divided up their* true *religion* by falling from innate disposition and being veiled by the coverings of creation and culture, *and have become* [*dissenting*] *factions*: differing groups because of how each one stands with its own veil, and their veils differ. Satan has divided them and dispersed them throughout the valleys of the soul's attributes: some of them follow the religion of dumb beasts, others the religion of predators, others the religion of caprice, others the religion of Satan himself. There are countless types of devils, and hence countless religions—*each party rejoicing in what they have*: having departed from the true religion and divided into different sects, after the sullying of innate disposition and the increasing density of the veil, each sect rejoices in the particular veil which its preparedness dictates because that is the dictate of the nature of its veil, and thus it befits its general state of preparedness. Joy is the result of a favourable perception inasmuch as it is favourable, and this is favourable in the moment because of the individual's transitory preparedness, though in reality it is not favourable at all for their primordial preparedness. This is why it leads to torment when the transitory preparedness comes to an end.

Q. 30:31

31
LUQMĀN
SŪRAT LUQMĀN

In the Name of God, the Compassionate, the Merciful

[31:1] [*Alif. Lām. Mīm.*

[31:2] *Those are the signs of the wise Book,* [31:3] *a guidance and a mercy for the virtuous,* [31:4] *who maintain prayer and pay* zakāt *and who are certain of the Hereafter.*

[31:5] *Such follow guidance from their Lord and it is they who are the successful.*

[31:6] *And among people there is he who buys the diversionary talk that he may lead [people] astray from the way of God without knowledge and take it in mockery. For such there will be a humiliating chastisement.*

[31:7] *And when Our signs are recited to such [a one] he turns away disdainfully as though he never heard them, as though there were a deafness in his ears. So give him tidings of a painful chastisement.*

[31:8] *Indeed, those who believe and perform righteous deeds, for them there shall be gardens of Bliss,* [31:9] *abiding therein—a promise of God in truth, and He is the Mighty, the Wise.*

[31:10] *He created the heavens without any pillars that you can see and cast high mountains into the earth, lest it shake with you, and He dispersed therein all kinds of beasts. And We sent down water from the heaven and We caused to grow in it every splendid kind.*

[31:11] *This is God's creation. Now show me what those [you worship] besides Him have created. Nay, but the evildoers are in manifest error.*

[31:12] *And verily We gave Luqmān wisdom: 'Give thanks to God. Whoever gives thanks gives thanks only for his own sake and whoever is ungrateful, then indeed God is Independent, Praised.'*

[31:13] *And when Luqmān said to his son, when he was admonishing him, 'O my son, do not ascribe partners to God: idolatry is truly a tremendous wrong.'*

[31:14] *And We have enjoined humanity concerning his parents—his mother bears him in weakness after weakness, and his weaning is in two years. Give thanks to Me and to your parents. To Me is the journey's end.*

[31:15] *But if they urge you to ascribe to Me as partner that whereof you have no knowledge, then do not obey them. And keep them company in this world honourably, and follow the way of him who returns to Me* [in penitence]. *Then to Me will be your return, and I will inform you of what you used to do.*

[31:16] *'O my son, even if it should be the weight of a grain of mustard-seed, and* [even if] *it be in a rock, or in the heavens, or in the earth, God will bring it forth. Indeed, God is Subtle, Aware.*

[31:17] *'O my son, establish prayer and enjoin decency and forbid indecency. And be patient through whatever may befall you. Truly that is true constancy.*

[31:18] *'And do not turn your cheek disdainfully from people and do not walk upon the earth exultantly. Indeed, God does not like any swaggering braggart.*

[31:19] *'And be modest in your bearing and lower your voice. Truly the most hideous of voices is the donkey's voice.'*

Q. 31:14

[31:20] *Do you not see that God has disposed for you whatever is in the heavens and whatever is in the earth, and He has showered His favours upon you,* [both] *outwardly and inwardly? Yet among people there are those who dispute concerning God without any knowledge or guidance or an illuminating Book.*

[31:21] *And if it is said to them, 'Follow what God has revealed,' they say, 'We will rather follow what we found our fathers following.' What! Even though Satan is calling them to the chastisement of the Blaze?*]

[31:22] *And whoever surrenders his purpose to God*: surrenders his being to God by annihilation in His acts, Attributes or Essence, *and is virtuous* by worshipping Him as though he witnesses Him, according to his station—acting first with the deeds of reliance by witnessing His acts, and then secondly with the deeds of the station of contentment by witnessing His Attributes, and thirdly by uprightness in realisation in Him by witnessing His Essence—*has certainly grasped* [the firmest handle]: the religion of Oneness; *and to God belongs the sequel of all matters*: by annihilation in Him, for all things end in Him.

[31:23] [*And whoever disbelieves, then do not let his disbelief grieve you. To Us shall be their return and We shall inform them of what they did. Indeed, God knows* [best] *what is in the breasts.*

[31:24] *We will give them comfort for a little* [while], *then We will drive them to a harsh chastisement.*

[31:25] *And if you were to ask them, 'Who created the heavens and the earth?' they will surely say, 'God.' Say: 'Praise be to God.' Nay, but most of them do not realise.*

[31:26] *To God belongs whatever is in the heavens and the earth. Indeed, God, He is the Independent, the Praised.*

[31:27] *And if all the trees on earth were pens, and the sea was replenished with seven more seas, the Words of God would not be spent. Truly God is Mighty, Wise.*

[31:28] *Your creation and your resurrection are only as [that of] a single soul. Truly God is Hearer, Seer.*

[31:29] *Have you not seen that God makes the night pass into the day and makes the day pass into the night, and He has disposed the sun and the moon, each running to an appointed term, and that God is Aware of what you do?*

[31:30] *That is because God, He is the Truth, and whatever they call on besides Him is falsehood, and because God is the High, the Great.*]

[31:31] *Have you not seen that the ships* of the body *run upon the sea* of primordial matter by the emanation of the traces of His Attributes of life, power and perception upon it, and its preparation with instruments, *by the grace of God*, to receive the perfections sent to it, *that He may show you* with this flow and preparation *some of His signs* of the manifestation of His acts and Attributes? *Indeed, in that there are signs* of the manifestation of His acts and Attributes, for they can only be seen in this locus, *for every [servant who is] steadfast* with God, by struggling against the rise of the actions and attributes of his own soul, according to the rules of the station of reliance and contentment, *grateful* for the blessings of these manifestations by fulfilling their dues and acting according to the rules of the station of reliance in the manifestation of the acts, and the rules of the station of contentment in the manifestation of the Attributes, so that he may receive more and more of His majesty.

Q. 31:26

[31:32] *And if waves* of the overwhelming impulses of the soul's attributes and nature's dictates *cover them like awnings*, like veils covering the lights of the manifestations, *they call on God, sincere before Him in their faith*: they seek refuge with God with sincerity and fulfilment of His due in their station, so that the veils can be lifted from them by the blessing of stability in action through sincerity. When the wayfarer is veiled from the higher station by variegation, he must be firm in the lower station which he already possesses, such as sincerity with respect to reliance. *But when He delivers them* by active manifestation *to the land* of the station of reliance and security, from drowning in the sea of primordial matter because of the overwhelming impulses of the soul, *some of them compromise* by adhering to justice, through fulfilling the dues of reliance and voyaging in His acts with stability. *And none denies Our signs* by recognising the dues of his station in manifestations, while being veiled from them in variegations, *except every perfidious* one who betrays the covenant of innate disposition with God when he is tried with lassitude, and every *ingrate* who does not utilise the blessings of God in ways that please Him, nor fulfils the dues of his station with regard to manifestations, nor performs the deeds of the folk of reliance and contentment when the lights of the acts and Attributes appear. Or one can interpret it as symbolising the ships of the Divine Law, running on this sea to the shore of the land of salvation and the garden of effects, to show you the signs of the manifestations of the acts.

[31:33] [*O people,*] *fear your Lord*: beware of manifesting your own acts, attributes and essences by becoming annihilated in Him from them; *and fear a day when no parent shall avail a child* [*and no child shall avail its parent in any way*], because those ties will be severed when you are mustered before God, manifesting in His Unity and overwhelming power, when there will no longer be any parents or children to avail one another. [*Indeed, God's promise is true.*] *So do not let the life of this world deceive you* from the life of the heart, which is closer to you because it is real and abiding, and there will be no other life for anyone then; *and do not let the Deceiver deceive you concerning God*: so that you display I-ness and become veiled by his insinuations and fall into tyranny.

Q. 31:33

[31:34] *Indeed, God, with Him lies knowledge of the* Major *Hour*, because all shall be annihilated in Him then, along with their knowledge; *and He sends down the rain* of this, according to levels of preparedness before annihilation; *and He knows what* perfection *is in the wombs* of preparedness, and whether they are complete or not. *And no soul knows what it will earn* [*tomorrow*]: what knowledge and stations it will acquire in the future, since it is veiled from this in its preparedness; *and no soul knows in what land* of the lands of stations *it will die* and its preparedness will be annihilated, because the perfections within it are finished; for the knowledge of preparednesses and their limits is part of that which God has reserved for Himself alone in the Unseen of Unseens. [*Indeed, God is Knower, Aware.*] And God (Exalted is He) knows best.

32
PROSTRATION
SŪRAT AL-SAJDA

In the Name of God, the Compassionate, the Merciful

[32:1] *Alif. Lām. Mīm*: the manifestation of Essential Unity and the Attributes and presences of Names is:

[32:2] *The revelation of the Book* of the absolute discerning intellect upon the Muḥammadan being, [*whereof there is no doubt,*] *from the Lord of the Worlds* by His manifestation upon his locus in the form of total mercy.

[32:3] [*Or do they say, 'He has invented it'? Nay, but it is the truth from your Lord, that you may warn a people to whom no warner came before you, that perhaps they may find [right] guidance.*]

[32:4] *God is He Who created the heavens and the earth and whatever is between them* by veiling Himself with them *in six days*: the six divine days which were the duration of the passing of the hidden secret from the turn of Adam (may God grant him peace) to the turn of Muḥammad (may God bless him and grant him peace); *then He presided upon the Throne* of the Muḥammadan heart to appear on that final day, the Friday of those days, to manifest with all of His Attributes. The presiding (*istiwā'*) of the sun at noon is the perfection of its manifestation and the fullness of its radiance. Thus, he (may God grant him peace) said, 'I was sent just as the breeze of the Hour began to blow.' The time of his sending was at the rising of the sun, and the noon of that day will be the time when the Mahdī (may God grant him peace) emerges. (Note that it is recommended to recite this *sūra* in the dawn prayer on Fridays.) *You do not have besides Him*, when He manifests, *any protector or intercessor* because all shall be annihilated in Him. *Will you not then remember* the primordial pledge at the covenant of innate disposition, when Unity was manifested?

[32:5] *He directs the command* of obliteration and creation *from the heaven* of the manifestation of Unity *to the earth* of its concealment and setting in the six days, *then it ascends to Him* by manifestation *on* the seventh *day, whose measure is a thousand years by your reckoning.*

[32:6] *That is* the Director, *the Knower of the Unseen* and the wisdom of concealment in the six days, *and the visible* of manifestation on this day, *the Mighty* barrier concealing His majesty in the veil, *the Merciful* Who unveils it and reveals His beauty, [32:7] *Who perfected everything that He created* by making it a locus for His Attributes, since perfection is reserved solely for the Attributes, and all things are loci for His Attributes, except for the perfect person. [The latter is he] who is reserved for the beauty of the Essence, hence why He singled him out for proportion (*taswiya*), which means a perfect balance of temperament and uprightness, so that he would be prepared to receive the spirit that was uniquely His (Exalted is He): [*And He began the creation of humanity from clay,* [32:8] *then He made his progeny from an extract of a base fluid,* [32:9] *then He proportioned him,*] *and breathed into him of His spirit.* [*And He made for you hearing, and sight and hearts. Little thanks do you give.*

Q. 32:6

[32:10] *And they say, 'When we are lost beneath the earth, shall we be indeed created anew?' Nay, but they disbelieve in the encounter with their Lord.*

[32:11] *Say:*] *'The angel of death,* [*who has been charged with you, shall receive you* [*in death*]*, then to your Lord you shall be returned.'*

[32:12] *And if you could but see the guilty hanging their heads* [*low*] *before their Lord: 'Our Lord, we have seen and heard. So send us back so that we may act righteously, for indeed we are convinced'*:] the angel of death is the universal human soul, which is the returning-place of particular souls, as long as they do not completely fall from innate disposition. However, they may be veiled by benighted configurations and egocentric attributes, as long as they do not reach the point of the total rusting-over of the heart and the closing of the door of forgiveness. If so, they will be received by the soul, which is akin to the heart with respect to the world. If they do reach that point, then it will only be the angels of torment who receive them. So since they did not reach that point, despite being veiled from the meeting with the Lord and inclining to the lower direction—which is why they will hang their heads because of the tenacity of the configurations of their crimes—He describes them as possessing sight, hearing and the wish to return; for if no trace of the light of innate disposition remained in them and it were completely snuffed out, they would not say, *'Our Lord, we have seen and heard,'* nor would they express the wish to return. These are the ones who will not remain in Hell perpetually, but rather will be corrected for as long as the configurations remain, and then allowed back.

[32:13] [*'And had We [so] wished,*] *We could have given every soul its* [*means to*] *guidance* by the grace to travel [to God] and equal preparedness. However, this would contradict wisdom because they would all remain in a single nature, and all possible levels would remain only theoretically possible without ever being actualised, and most of the ranks of this world would be perpetually uninhabited. The low and base things which are needed in the world for the sake of the people of veiling, debasement, hard-heartedness and darkness, far from love, mercy, light and dignity, would not exist. The world would be set out of order, and likewise it would not be possible for the righteous to be guided either, since this requires all the other levels. The order can only exist with loci of both concealment and manifestation; if all people were loci of manifestation, prophets and saved folk, the order would be disturbed by the absence of sinful folk and human devils who thrive throughout the world. Consider God's words [in the *ḥadīth qudsī*], 'I made the sin of Adam the cause for the population of the world.' Thus, true wisdom dictates that there be differing degrees of preparedness, according to strength and weakness, purity and turbidity, and that people be judged as saved or damned, so that all the attributes can be manifested in all the levels. This is the meaning of His Words, *but My Word became due* in the primordial decree: *"Verily I shall fill* the Hell of nature *with jinn,* meaning the terrestrial souls hidden from sight, *and humankind all together."*

Q. 32:13

[32:14] *'So taste [now], for your having forgotten the encounter of this day of yours,* because of how you were veiled by the coverings of nature and garments of matter. *We [too] shall forget you* by withholding mercy from you, because of how you refused to accept it and turned away from it. *And taste [now] the everlasting chastisement for what you used to practise':* according to this interpretation, the word *everlasting* here is a figure of speech denoting merely a long time. Or it could be that these words are addressed to those people and jinn upon whom the Word of the primordial decree became due.

[32:15] *Only those* truly *believe in Our signs*—the signs of Our Attributes—*who, when they are reminded of them, fall down* because of their immediate acceptance of them by the purity of their innate disposition, *in prostration,* annihilated in them, *and make glorifications in praise of their Lord:* detaching their essences and adopting the Attributes of their Lord, which is the true nature of their glorifications and praises of Him; *and they do not disdain* by allowing the attributes of their souls and egos to emerge.

[32:16] *Their sides withdraw* with detachment from natural coverings, and they stand *from their* physical *lying places* and go beyond directions by effacing all configurations, *to supplicate to their Lord* by directing themselves towards Oneness in the station of the heart, *in fear* of being veiled by the attributes of the soul through variegation, *and in hope* for the meeting with the Essence; *and they expend* upon the folk of preparedness *of what We have provided them* of gnostic secrets and realities.

[32:17] *For no* noble *soul* among them *knows what has been kept hidden for them* [*in the way of joyous sights*] of the beauty of the Essence and the meeting with the light of lights, which will delight their eyes so that they experience such pleasure and joy as cannot be known or described, *as a reward for what they used to do* by detachment and effacement in purity and action in accordance with the laws of manifestations.

[32:18] [*Is he who is*] *a believer* in Oneness, according to the religion of innate disposition, *like him who is a transgressor* by straying from that upright religion in obedience to the impulses of creation? [*They are not equal.*

[32:19] *As for those who believe and perform righteous deeds, for them shall be*] *the gardens of the Abode* according to their stations in the three gardens—[*a hospitality for what they used to do.*

[32:20] *But as for those who transgressed, their abode shall be the Fire.*] *Whenever they seek to exit from it* by the inclination of innate disposition, *they shall be brought back into it* because the lower inclination is stronger and the earthly dominion more powerful, due to the tenacity of the natural configurations; [*and it shall be said to them, 'Taste the chastisement of the Fire which you used to deny'*].

[32:21] *And We shall surely make them taste the nearer chastisement*, which is the torment of effects and the fires of affronts to the soul and nature in the form of tribulations, hardships and horrors, *before the greater chastisement*, which is to be veiled by darkness from the lights of the Attributes and the essence, *that perhaps they may return* to God when their innate disposition is purified by the strength of the nearer chastisement, before their hearts are totally rusted-over because of the density of the veil.

[32:22] [*And who does greater wrong than he who is reminded of the signs of his Lord, but then turns away from them? Indeed, We shall take vengeance upon the criminals.*]

[32:23] *And verily We gave Moses the Book* of the discerning intellect, *so do not be in doubt concerning the encounter* of Moses when you reach his level during your ascension. It is related in the stories of the Ascension that he [the Prophet] met Moses in the fifth heaven, at the point when he ascended from the station of the secret, which is the station of intimate

Q. 32:17

discourse, to the station of the spirit, which is the Sacred Valley. [*And We appointed him a guidance for the Children of Israel.*

[32:24] *And We appointed among them leaders who guided by Our command, when they had endured [patiently] and had conviction in Our signs.*

[32:25] *Indeed, your Lord will judge between them on the Day of Resurrection concerning that wherein they used to differ.*

[32:26] *Or is it not an indication for them how many generations We destroyed before them amid whose dwellings they walk? Surely in that there are signs. Are they not able to hear?*

[32:27] *Or have they not seen how We drive the water to barren land and therewith bring forth crops whereof their cattle and [they] themselves eat? Can they not see?*

[32:28] *And they say, 'When will this [decisive] judgement be, if you are truthful?'*

[32:29] *Say:] 'On the day of [this] Absolute Judgement*, which is the day of the Major Resurrection when the Mahdī emerges, [*their [newly-found] faith [then] shall not benefit those who had been disbelievers, nor shall they be given respite*]: the faith of the veiled ones will be of no use then, because it will be mere words, and the torment will not be lifted from them. And God (Exalted is He) knows best.

Q. 32:24

33
THE CLANS
SŪRAT AL-AḤZĀB

In the Name of God, the Compassionate, the Merciful

[33:1] *O Prophet, fear God*: by total annihilation from your own essence, without any remnant persisting; *and do not obey the disbelievers*, by accompanying them in some veils because of the emergence of I-ness, *and the hypocrites*, by regarding anything other than God and thus becoming two-faced. It was because he obeyed these two prohibitions that he deserved to be described by God's Words, *The eye did not swerve, nor did it go beyond* [Q. 53:17]. *Indeed, God is Knower* of the sins of states, *Wise* in trying you with variegations, for they benefit your mission of calling to and rectifying the condition of the community; for if he never experienced variegation, he would not recognise it in his community and so would be unable to guide them.

[33:2] *And follow*—in the manifestation of variegations—*what is revealed to you from your Lord*, of corrections and forms of rebuke and reprisal, according to differing stations, as had been discussed several times previously regarding His Words *And if We had not made you [stand] firm...* [Q. 17:74] and similar verses. *Indeed, God is Aware of what you do*: He knows the sources of deeds and from which attributes they come, whether the egocentric, satanic or merciful, and He guides you towards them and purifies you from them, and teaches you the way of imparting purity and wisdom regarding this.

[33:3] *And put your trust in God* for the repelling of those variegations and the lifting of those veils and coverings; *and God suffices as Guardian*, for they can only be lifted and unveiled by His hand, not by your own soul, knowledge or act. Do not be veiled by seeing annihilation as you experience it, for it is not your own deed, whether it is in the divine acts, Attributes or Essence. Nor consider the dispelling of variegations as your own achievement, for it is all by God's deed and you play no part in it, since otherwise you would not truly be annihilated.

[33:4] [*God has not placed two hearts inside any man, nor has He made your wives whom you repudiate by* ẓihār *your mothers. Nor has He made those whom you claim as* [*adopted*] *sons your sons. That is a mere utterance of your mouths. But God speaks the truth and He guides to the way.*]

[33:5] *Attribute them to their* [*true*] *fathers. That is more equitable in the sight of God. If you do not know their* [*true*] *fathers, then they are your brethren in religion and your associates. And you would not be at fault for any mistake you make, except what your hearts may premeditate. And God is Forgiving, Merciful.*]

[33:6] *The Prophet is closer to the believers than their* [*own*] *souls*, because he is the origin of their true existences and the origin of their perfections, and the source of the two emanations: the holiest emanation of preparedness first, and the sanctified emanation of perfection second. He is their true father, which is why his wives were considered as inviolable to them as their own mothers: [*and his wives are their mothers*]. The honouring of this inviolability was an expression of fealty to reality. He is the intermediary between them and the Real in the origin of their innate disposition, and the returning point for their perfections. The emanation of the Real could not reach them without him, for he is the holiest veil and the first certitude, as he said, 'The first thing God created was my light.' If he were not more beloved to them than their own selves, they would be veiled from him by their own selves; hence, they could not possibly find success. Their only way to succeed is to be annihilated in him, for he is the supreme locus of manifestation.

Q. 33:4

And those related by blood are more entitled [*from*] *one another in the Book of God than the* [*other*] *believers and the Emigrants*: they were closer to one another than to anyone else, because of the spiritual and physical connection, religious brotherhood and formal kinship between them. Kinship does not lack correspondence to reality, for there is a connection of spiritual emanation according to temperamental preparedness. Just as the temperaments and physical forms of kinsfolk correspond to one another, so too do their spirits and suprasensory states. *Nonetheless, you may do a favour to your friends* whom you love for God's sake because of spiritual correspondence and essential familiarity, as a kindness based on love and mutual goodwill in addition to that which exists between kin. *This is written in the Book*: the Preserved Tablet.

[33:7] *And when We took from the prophets their pledge* [*and from you, and from Noah and Abraham and Moses and Jesus son of Mary. And We took from them a solemn pledge*]: He mentions these five in particular because they were singled out for an additional rank and eminence. The pledge was the doctrine of Oneness and the imparting of perfection and guidance to others, which was made at the instilling of innate disposition. This was the solemn pledge, an emphatic promise of perfection of the self and others, which is why He referred to it as *their pledge*, meaning the pledge that befitted them and was especially theirs. He singled out our own Prophet (may God grant him peace) for first mention by saying *from you*, because of his precedence over the others in rank and prestige.

[33:8] [The pledge stipulated, in part,] *that He may question*, by means of their pledge and covenant and the intermediary of their guidance, *the truthful*—who believed in the first pledge and the primordial covenant when He said, *'Am I not your Lord?' They said, 'Yea, indeed we testify'* [Q. 7:172]—*about their truthfulness*: by fulfilling the pledge and reaching the Real by bringing out the perfection existent in their preparedness in the presence of the prophets, as He says, *Among the believers are people who are true to the covenant they made with God* [Q. 33:23]. The question was only occasioned by the pledge of the prophets, since He will ask them through their tongues, and they will be witnesses for them in the end just as they were witnesses over them in the beginning. [*And He has prepared for those who disbelieve a painful chastisement.*

Q. 33:8

[33:9] *O you who believe, remember God's favour to you when hosts came against you, and We unleashed against them a [great] wind and hosts you did not see. And God is ever Seer of what you do.*

[33:10] *When they came at you from above you and from below you, and when the eyes turned away [in fear], and the hearts leapt to the throats, while you entertained all sorts of thoughts concerning God.*

[33:11] *There the believers were [sorely] tried, and were shaken with a mighty shock.*

[33:12] *And when the Hypocrites, and those in whose hearts is sickness, were saying, 'What God and His Messenger promised us was [nothing] but delusion.'*

[33:13] *And when a party of them said, 'O people of Yathrib, there is not a stand [possible] for you [here], so turn back.' And a group of them [even] sought the permission of the Prophet, saying, 'Our homes are exposed,' although they were not exposed. They only sought to flee.*

[33:14] *And had they been invaded in it from all sides and had they been exhorted to treachery, they would have committed it and would have hesitated thereupon but a little.*

[33:15] *Though they had assuredly pledged to God before that, that they would not turn their backs [to flee]; and a pledge given to God must be answered for.*

[33:16] *Say: 'Flight will not avail you should you flee from death or being slain, and then you would not be extended comfort, except a little.'*

[33:17] *Say: 'Who is it that can protect you from God should He desire [to cause] you ill, or should He desire for you mercy?' And they shall not find for themselves besides God any protector or helper.*

[33:18] *Indeed, God already knows the hinderers among you and those who say to their brethren, 'Come to us,' and they do not engage in the battle except a little,* [33:19] *grudging to you. And when there is a panic, you see them looking at you, their eyes rolling like one fainting at death; but when the panic subsides, they scald you, with [their] sharp tongues, in their greed for the riches. Those—they never believed. Therefore, God has invalidated their works, and that is easy for God.*

[33:20] *They suppose that the clans have not [yet] departed; and if the clans do come, they would wish that they were in the desert with the Bedouins asking about your news. And if they were among you, they would fight but a little.]*

[33:21] *Verily there is for you a good example in the Messenger of God for whoever hopes for [the encounter with] God and the Last Day, and remembers God often:* it is obligatory for every believer to emulate the Messenger of God (may God bless him and grant him peace), in an absolute sense, so that his hope can be realised and his work completed; for he is the intermediary through which they arrive and the means by which they travel the path, because of the precious bond between him and them by the law of affinity. He mentions the hope that goes hand-in-hand with faith in the Unseen in the station of the soul, and links it to frequent remembrance, which is the act of that station, to show that the one who is at the beginning of the path must emulate him in deeds, character traits, effort, and the sacrifice of person and property; for if he is not correct in the beginning, he will not succeed at the end. Then when he detaches and becomes purified from the attributes of his own self, he must emulate him in the waterholes of the heart, which are truthfulness, sincerity, surrender and reliance, just as he emulated him in the way-stations of the soul; so that by the blessing of emulating him he can receive spiritual gifts, states and manifestations of Attributes in his station, just as he received acquisitions, stations and manifestations of the acts in the station of the soul. Then he must do the same in the stations of the mystery and the spirit, until annihilation. One aspect of sound emulation is to believe in all that he related so that one is not sullied by doubt regarding any of his reports; otherwise, one's resolve will falter and the emulation will fail. The source and foundation of action is firm belief, which is why He praised them by saying:

Q. 33:16

[33:22] *And when the believers saw the clans, they said, 'This is what God and His Messenger promised us, and God and His Messenger were truthful'* when he warned them of the trial and tribulation, so that they would sacrifice their bodies and become detached by turning to Him and away from themselves, as He said, *Or did you suppose that you should enter Paradise without there having come upon you the like of those who passed away before you? They were afflicted by misery and hardship and were so convulsed that the Messenger and those who believed with him said, 'When will God's help come?'* [Q. 2:214]. *And that* tribulation from the clans *only increased them in faith and submission* because of the power of their belief at the beginning and the soundness of their emulation in submission. They succeeded in the station of chivalry and self-sacrifice through tribulation, and broke free of the fetters of the soul because of the soundness of their innate disposition. Thus, He described them as having fulfilled their pledge, which is the perfection of the station of chivalry, and called them true men:

Q. 33:23

[33:23] *Among the believers are people who are true to the covenant they made with God*: that is, true people of tremendous quality, because of how they were true to the primordial covenant they made with God in the time of innate disposition, by the power of their certitude and their lack of panic when the clans came. Despite the numbers and strength of their enemies, they were not swayed from Oneness and the witnessing of the manifestation of the acts, and so did not fall into doubt, nor fear their might and power. *Some of them have fulfilled their vow* by being true to their pledge and reaching the perfection of their innate disposition, *and some are still waiting* in their journey by the strength of their resolve; *and they have not changed in the least*: by becoming veiled by the coverings of creation and committing violations of innate disposition, by loving the self and the body and its pleasures and inclining towards the lower direction and its passions, thereby betraying their pledge.

[33:24] [These trials occur so] *that God may reward the truthful for their truthfulness* with the garden of the Attributes, *and chastise the hypocrites* who went along with the believers by the light of innate disposition and loved them because of the innate inclination towards Unity, yet also loved the disbelievers because of the coverings of creation and their immersion in passions; they went back and forth between the two directions, neither staying with one nor the other, because of the benighted configurations of their souls. [He will punish them] *if He wishes*, if their souls are stubborn, *or relent to them*, if they are not. [Indeed, God] *is Forgiving* and can cover the configurations of souls with His light, *Merciful* in His emanation of perfection when it can be received.

[33:25] [*And God repulsed those who were disbelievers in their rage, without their attaining any good. And God spared the believers from fighting. And truly God is Strong, Mighty.*

[33:26] *And He brought down those of the People of the Book, who had supported them from their strongholds, and He cast terror into their hearts, [so that] some you slew and some you took captive.*

[33:27] *And He made you inherit their land and their homes and their possessions, and a land you had not trodden. And God has power over all things.*]

[33:28] *O Prophet, say to your wives: 'If you desire the life of this world and its adornment, come [now], I will provide for you and release you in a gracious manner.*

[33:29] *'But if you desire God and His Messenger and the Abode of the Hereafter, then God has indeed prepared for the virtuous among you a great reward'*: the test of his wives was one of the character traits of detachment and the qualities of chivalry which must be emulated in him (may God grant him peace). Despite his inclination towards them—whereby he said, 'Three things of your world have been made beloved to me'—when they disturbed his time with their inclinations towards the life of this world and its lures, he gave them the choice and detached himself from them, and invited them to choose between the world and him. If they chose by the power of their faith, they could remain with him without disquieting him and disturbing his time with demands for worldly delights and inclinations towards them, but rather with detachment and devotion to the Real, like the faculties of his soul. Or, if they chose the world and its delights, he would provide for them and release them, and empty his heart of them, just as the usurping faculties of the soul must be vanquished.

Q. 33:25

[33:30] [*O wives of the Prophet, whoever of you commits manifest indecency, the chastisement shall be doubled for her, and that is easy for God.*

[33:31] *But whoever of you is obedient to God and His Messenger, and acts righteously, We shall give her a twofold reward. And We have prepared a noble provision for her.*

[33:32] *O wives of the Prophet, you are not like any other women. If you fear [God], then do not be soft in your speech, lest he in whose heart is a sickness aspire [to you]; but speak honourable words.*

[33:33] *And stay in your houses and do not flaunt your finery in the [flaunting] manner of the former Time of Ignorance. And maintain prayer and pay zakāt, and obey God and His Messenger. Indeed, God wishes but to rid you of sin, People of the House, and to purify you with a thorough purification.*

[33:34] *And remember that which is recited in your houses of the revelations of God and wisdom. Truly God is Kind, Aware.*

[33:35] *Indeed, the men who have submitted [to God] and the women who have submitted [to God], and the believing men and the believing women, and the obedient men and the obedient women, and the men who are truthful and the women who are truthful, and the patient men and the patient women, and the humble men and the humble women, and the charitable men and the charitable women, and the men who fast and the women who fast, and the men who guard their private parts and the women who guard their private parts, and the men who remember God often and the women who remember God often—for them God has prepared forgiveness and a great reward.]*

[33:36] *And it is not [fitting] for any believing man or believing woman, when God and His Messenger have decided on a matter, to have a choice in their matter. And whoever disobeys God and His Messenger has certainly strayed into manifest error*: this is another of the character traits which must be obeyed and emulated, which is the station of contentment and annihilation in the divine will. When he (may God grant him peace) became annihilated with his essence and attributes in the Essence and Attributes of God, he was granted the Attributes of the Real in place of his own when he attained realisation of the Real in the station of subsistence by gifted existence. Thus, his decree and will was the very decree and will of the Real, as with all his other attributes. Consider how God says, *Nor does he speak out of [his own] desire. It is but a revelation that is revealed* [Q. 53:3–4]. Therefore, one essential aspect of emulating him is to become annihilated in the will of the Real; and since his will was the will of the Real, it is essential to become annihilated in his will and to renounce one's own free choice in deference to his. Anything else is disobedience and *manifest error*, for it contradicts the explicit decree of the Real.

[33:37] *And when you said to him to whom God had shown favour, and to whom you [too] had shown favour, 'Retain your wife for yourself and fear God.' But you had hidden in your heart what God was to disclose, and you feared people, though God is worthier that you should fear Him*: this is one of the divine reproaches that descended in the midst of his variegation and the emergence of his soul, to keep him firm. Those variegations were the occasions for the revelation of these reproaches, which is why his very character was the Qur'ān itself. [*So when Zayd had fulfilled whatever need he had of her, We joined her in marriage to you so that there may not be any restriction for the believers in respect of the wives of their adopted sons, when the latter have fulfilled whatever wish they have of them. And God's commandment is bound to be realised.*

[33:38] *There is no restriction for the Prophet in what God has ordained for him: [that is] God's precedent with those who passed away before—and God's commandment is inexorable destiny—*[33:39] [*and with those] who deliver the*

Q. 33:35

Messages of God and fear Him, and fear no one except Him. And God suffices as Reckoner.

[33:40] *Muḥammad is not the father of any person among you, but the Messenger of God and the Seal of the Prophets. And God has knowledge of all things.*]

[33:41] *O you who believe, remember God* with the tongue in the station of the soul, with presence in the station of the heart, with intimate discourse in the station of the mystery, with witnessing in the station of the spirit, with connection (*muwāṣala*) in the station of the hidden, and with annihilation in the station of the Essence, [*with much remembrance*].

[33:42] *And glorify Him* with detachment from the acts, the Attributes and the Essence; *morning*: at the time of the dawn of the light of the heart and the withdrawal of the darkness of the soul; and [*evening*]: at night (*layl*) at the time of the setting of the sun of the spirit with annihilation in the Essence: that is, perpetually from that time until the eternal annihilation.

[33:43] *It is He Who blesses you* according to your glorifications with the manifestations of the acts and Attributes, but not the Essence, since the glory of it would have burned them up, as Gabriel (may God grant him peace) said, 'If I went any closer, I would be burned'; [*and His angels,*] *that He may bring you forth* with the aid of the dominion and the manifestation of Names *from the darkness* of the deeds of souls *into the light* of the manifestations of His acts in the station of reliance, and from the darkness of the attributes of the souls into the light of the manifestations of His Attributes, and from the darkness of I-ness into the light of the Essence. *And He is Merciful to the believers*: gracing them with the mercy their state requires and the perfections their preparedness necessitates.

[33:44] *Their greeting* [*on the day they encounter Him will be 'Peace'*]: God's greeting to them at the time of the meeting by annihilation in Him will be to perfect them and give them peace from their flaws, by healing their imperfections with His own acts, Attributes and Essence. Or His greeting to them will be the emanation of these perfections at the time of their meeting with Him by annihilation and erasure, which will grant them security[1] from the blights of their own attributes, deeds and essences. Or the greeting will be the manifestations and the security from blights together. The first interpretation corresponds to the absolute meaning of His Name Peace. *And He has prepared for them a noble reward*: by affirming these gardens in return for their deeds of glorifications and remembrances.

Q. 33:40

---

1 *Salāma*, closely related to *salām* ('peace').

[33:45] [*O Prophet!*] *Indeed, We have sent you as a witness* to the truth, sent to humankind without being veiled by multiplicity from Unity, to all of them in all their differing states and perfections, by the light of the Real; *and as a bearer of good tidings*: for those who are prepared and fit for the triumph of arrival; *and as a warner*: to those who are veiled and who halt with other-than-God, warning them of chastisement, deprivation and veiling; [33:46] *and as a summoner to God* to every prepared person according to their state and station, *by His leave* according to what God has facilitated for them according to their preparedness, *and as a illuminating lamp* which illuminates with the light of the Real souls darkened by the coverings of ignorance and the configurations of matter and nature.

[33:47] *And give good tidings to the believers* who see by the light of innate disposition *that there will be for them*, according to the purity of their preparedness, *a great* [*bounty from God*]: of the gardens of the Attributes, by the emanation of perfections after the gifts of preparednesses.

Q. 33:45

[33:48] *And do not obey the disbelievers and the hypocrites* in variegations, as was mentioned at the beginning of this *sūra*, lest the light of your lamp be sullied, *and disregard their injuriousness* to your person so that you evade the blight of variegation and the regard of the deeds of others, for they do not do what they do independently of their own means. *And put your trust in God* by seeing that their deeds and yours are all from Him; *and God suffices as Guardian*, Who does with you and with them what He wills. If He should harm them through your outer being, then He is well able to do so—and you are innocent of the sin of variegation—just as He did to give you stability; and if not, then He knows his affairs best.

[33:49] [*O you who believe, if you marry believing women and then divorce them before you have touched them, there shall be no* [*waiting*] *period for you to reckon against them. But provide for them and release them in a gracious manner.*

[33:50] *O Prophet! Indeed, We have made lawful for you your wives whom you have given their dowries and what your right hand owns, of those whom God has given you as spoils of war, and the daughters of your paternal uncles and the daughters of your paternal aunts, and the daughters of your maternal uncles and the daughters of your maternal aunts who emigrated with you, and any believing woman if she gift herself* [*in marriage*] *to the Prophet and if the Prophet desire to take her in marriage—a privilege for you exclusively, not for the* [*rest of the*] *believers. Indeed, We know what We have imposed upon them with respect to their wives, and what their right hands own, so that there may be no* [*unnecessary*] *restriction for you. And God is Forgiving, Merciful.*

[33:51] *You may put off whomever of them you wish and consort whomever you wish, and as for whomever you may desire of those whom you have set aside, you would not be at fault. That makes it likelier that they will be comforted and not grieve, and that they will be satisfied with what you give them, every one of them will be well pleased with what you give her. And God knows what is in your hearts. And God is Knower, Forbearing.*

[33:52] *Women are not lawful for you beyond that, nor [is it lawful] for you to change them for other wives, even though their beauty impress you, except those whom your right hand owns. And God is Watcher over all things.*

[33:53] *O you who believe, do not enter the Prophet's houses unless permission is granted you to [share] a meal without waiting for the [right] moment. But when you are invited, enter, and, when you have had your meal, disperse, without any [leisurely] conversation. Indeed, that is upsetting for the Prophet, and he is [too] shy of you, but God is not shy of the truth. And when you ask anything of [his] womenfolk, ask them from behind a screen. That is purer for your hearts and their hearts. And you should never cause the Messenger of God hurt; nor ever marry his wives after him. Assuredly that would be very grave in God's sight.*

[33:54] *Whether you disclose anything or keep it hidden, truly God has knowledge of all things.*

Q. 33:52

[33:55] *They [the Prophet's wives] would not be at fault with regard to [socialising with] their fathers, or their sons, or their brothers, or their brothers' sons, or their sisters' sons, or their own women, or what their right hands own. And fear [O women] God. Surely God is Witness to all things.]*

[33:56] *Indeed, God and His angels bless the Prophet* with assistance, aid and the emanation of perfections. [*O you who believe, invoke blessings on him and invoke peace upon him in a worthy manner:*] the giver of blessings in reality is God, generally and particularly, whether through an intermediary or without one. Thus, the invocations of blessings and peace upon him on the part of the believers are from the sphere of particulars, and the true nature of their blessings upon him is that they accept his guidance and have perfect love for his essence and attributes. Their invocations are an assistance to him, perfecting and universalising his emanation, since if they had not accepted his perfections they would not have been manifested, nor would he have been characterised by guidance and the perfecting of others. Assistance comes not only from above by influencing, but also from below by being influenced. The same is true for the acceptance of love. Purity is the reality of the supplication in their invocation of blessings when they say, 'Lord God, bless Muḥammad'; and their invocation of peace is their declaring him innocent of flaws and blights regarding the perfecting and influencing of their souls. This is the meaning of their supplication for peace for him.

[33:57] [*Indeed, those who are injurious to God and His Messenger,*] *God has cursed them in this world and the Hereafter*, because the Prophet was as close as can be to Him, having attained realisation of the annihilation of his I-ness so that there was no duality left through the sincerity of his love, and therefore to attack him was tantamount to attacking God. The one who attacks God is the one who manifests his I-ness for the sake of opposing God, which makes him as far away from God as can be, which is the true meaning of being cursed. This is true in both this life and the next, outwardly and inwardly, and it is opposed to the presence of glory, so that such a person will be in the utmost state of degradation in the torment of veiling: [*and He has prepared for them a humiliating chastisement.*

[33:58] *And those who cause hurt to believing men and believing women, without the latter's having done anything, have verily borne* [*the guilt of*] *calumny and* [*the burden of*] *manifest sin.*

Q. 33:57

[33:59] *O Prophet, tell your wives and daughters and the women of the believers to draw their cloaks closely over themselves. That makes it likelier that they will be known and not be molested. And God is Forgiving, Merciful.*

[33:60] *If the Hypocrites do not desist, and likewise those in whose hearts is a sickness, as well as the scaremongers in the city, assuredly We will urge you* [*to take action*] *against them, then they will not be your neighbours in it except for a little* [*while*]*.

[33:61] *Accursed* [*shall they be*]*, wherever they are found they shall be seized and slain violently.*

[33:62] *This has been God's precedent with those who passed away before, and you will find that there is no changing God's precedent.*

[33:63] *People question you concerning the Hour. Say: 'Knowledge thereof lies only with God—*] *and what do you know, perhaps the Hour is near'* for the one who is prepared for it.

[33:64] [*God has indeed*] *cursed the disbelievers* with veiling, because of their distance from Him, [*and prepared for them a blaze* [33:65] *to abide therein forever. They shall not find any protector or helper.*

[33:66] *On the day when their faces are turned about in the Fire*, by the changing of their forms in all manner of torments and the manifestation of the veil, [*they shall say, 'O would that we had obeyed God and obeyed the Messenger!'*

[33:67] *And they shall say, 'Our Lord, we obeyed our leaders and elders, and they led us astray from the way.*

[33:68] *'Our Lord, give them a double chastisement and curse them with numerous curses!'*

[33:69] *O you who believe, do not behave as did those who harmed Moses, where-at God absolved him of what they alleged. And he was distinguished in God's sight.*

[33:70] *O you who believe,] fear God* by avoiding vices [*and speak words of integrity*], which means to say what is true and right. Truthfulness is the basis of every felicity and the root of every perfection, because it comes from the purity of the heart, which leads to the acceptance of all perfections and the lights of manifestations. Although it was already included in the God-fearing enjoined before it, since it means to avoid the vice of deceit and is part of the self-purification that is meant by God-fearing, He chose to single it out for mention again because of its great virtue, as though it were a separate thing in and of itself. This is akin to how He singled out Gabriel and Michael for mention among the angels.

[33:71] *He will rectify your deeds for you* by emanating perfections and virtues: that is, purify yourselves to receive adornment from God with the emanation of perfections upon you; *and will forgive you your sins*: the sins of your attributes by the manifestation of His own. *And whoever obeys God and His Messenger*—in self-purification and the erasure of attributes—*has verily achieved a [supreme] success*: by becoming adorned with the Divine Attributes, which is the supreme triumph.

Q. 33:69

[33:72] *Indeed, We offered the Trust to the heavens and the earth and the mountains*—the trust of the instilling of the reality of ipseity in them, thereby veiling them with individuations—*but they refused to bear it*: lest it manifest upon them in all its great enormity, because of their lack of preparedness to receive it; *and were apprehensive of it* because its tremendousness was beyond their capacity, and they were too weak to bear it and receive it. *But humanity undertook it* because of the strength of his preparedness and his ability to bear it, and so he took it and claimed it for himself. *Truly he is a wrongdoer* in how he denied God's due by manifesting himself and claiming it, *ignorant* and bereft of knowledge of it because he is veiled from it by his I-ness.

[33:73] *God will chastise the hypocrites, men and women* who did wrong by preventing the manifestation of the light of their preparedness through the darkness of physical configurations and egocentric attributes, placing it in the wrong place and thereby ignoring its due, *and the idolators, men and women* who were ignorant through being veiled by I-ness and allegiance to other-than-God, because of the heavy rust upon their hearts and the density of the veil of creation. Their wrongdoing was heinous because of the total extinguishing of their light, and their refusal to honour the Divine Trust.

God will relent to the believing men and believing women who repented from wrongdoing, by avoiding the egocentric attributes which prevent fealty, and brought the due of God which they had previously concealed into the open when they fulfilled it, and repented of ignorance of His due when they acknowledged it and honoured His Trust through annihilation in Him. *And God is Forgiving* and so concealed the sins of their wrongdoing and their ignorance of self-purification, detachment, erasure and darkness with the light of His manifestations, *Merciful* and so graced them with the mercy of veridical existence at the time of subsistence through His acts, Attributes and Essence. Or We offered the Divine Trust by manifesting to them and instilling in them the attributes which they were able to bear, by making them loci for their manifestation. Or they refused to bear it lest they treacherously hold onto it and refuse to discharge it, and were apprehensive of bearing it for this reason, so We discharged it by manifesting the perfections that had been instilled within them. Then humanity undertook it by concealing it with devilry and the manifestation of I-ness, and refused to discharge it by manifesting the perfection that had been instilled within him, instead withholding it so that the soul could manifest with darkness, refusing to ascend in the station of gnosis. And God knows best.

Q. 33:73

34
SHEBA
SŪRAT SABA'

In the Name of God, the Compassionate, the Merciful

[34:1] *Praise be to God to Whom belongs whatever is in the heavens and whatever is in the earth*: by making them loci for His outward Attributes and magnificent perfections, that He might manifest in them with veils of majesty. *And to Him belongs [all] praise in the Hereafter*: by His manifestation to the spirits with inward perfections and Attributes of beauty. In other words, praise be to Him with the Attributes of mercifulness in this world outwardly, and praise be to Him with the Attributes of compassion in the Hereafter inwardly. *And He is the Wise* Who ordained the composition of the world of witnessing by the decree of His wisdom, *the Aware* Whose knowledge penetrates the inner parts of the world of the Unseen by its subtlety.

[34:2] *He knows what penetrates the earth* of the terrestrial dominions and natural faculties, *and what issues out of it* by detachment from human souls and creational perfections, *and what comes down from the heaven* of gnostic truths and spiritual realities, *and what ascends into it* of the configurations of righteous deeds and virtuous character traits; *and He is the Merciful* by the emanation of heavenly luminary perfections, *the Forgiving* by the concealment of dark earthly configurations.

[34:3] [*And those who disbelieve say, 'The Hour will never come to us.' Say: 'Yes indeed, by my Lord, it shall come to you—[by] the Knower of the Unseen. Not [even] the weight of an atom escapes Him in the heavens or in the earth, nor [is there] anything smaller than that or greater, but it is in a Manifest Book,* [34:4] *that He may requite those who believe and perform righteous deeds—for such there will be forgiveness and a fair provision.*

[34:5] *'And those who strive against Our signs, seeking to incapacitate, for such there will be a chastisement of an awful punishment'.*]

[34:6] *And those who have been given knowledge see [that what has been revealed to you from your Lord is the truth]*: the truly realised knowers see the veracity of what has been revealed to you with their own eyes, for the veiled one cannot recognise the gnostic and his words, since the one who knows something only knows it because its meaning is instilled within him. The one who has no share of knowledge or gnosis cannot recognise the gnostic knower and his knowledge, since he is bereft of the thing that would allow him to recognise them. *And [that] it guides to the* path (*ṭarīq*) of arrival at God, *the Mighty* Who overpowers the veiled ones and restrains them with His overwhelming power and might, *the Praised* Who blesses the believers with all manner of kindnesses. Such an interpretation is a reading of the two Attributes with application to the previous passage *That He may requite those who believe* [Q. 34:4], and so on. If they are interpreted as applying to His Words *And those who have been given knowledge see…*, then it would mean *the Mighty* Who overwhelms those who arrive at Him with annihilation, and *the Praised* who blesses them with His Attributes in the station of subsistence.

[34:7] [*And those who disbelieve say, 'Shall we show you a man who will inform you that when you have been utterly torn to pieces you shall indeed be created anew?'*

[34:8] *Has he invented a lie against God, or is there a madness in him? Nay, but those who do not believe in the Hereafter will be in the chastisement and in far error.*

[34:9] *Have they not observed what is before them and what is behind them of heaven and earth? If We will [it], We can make the earth swallow them or let fall on them fragments from the heaven. Indeed, in that there is a sign for every penitent servant.*]

[34:10] *And verily We bestowed on the* David *of the spirit a [great] favour from Us* in the form of raised stature, the glorification of witnessing, and tender love, along with increased worship, reflection, and cognitive and practical perfections. [This was] by Us saying, '*O mountains* of the limbs, *repeat with him [in praise]* the glorifications that are particular to you, in the form of submission and dutifulness in acts of obedience by the motions, stillnesses, actions and reactions which We enjoined upon you, *and the birds* of the spiritual faculties [*too*],' with holy glorifications of invocations, perceptions, meditations, praises and illuminations from the incorporeal spirits and separated essences, each as it was commanded. *And We made the iron* of elemental bodily nature *malleable for him.*

[34:11] '*Fashion long coats of mail* from the configurations of piety and

God-fearing, for the most protective piety in reality is the garment of piety, which guards against the threats of the impulses of malevolent souls and the arrows of satanic temptations; *and measure [well the links]'*: employing practical wisdom and exacting intellectual and legislative craft, in the encouragement of purifying acts and the acquisition of configurations that prevent the influence of egocentric impulses. *And act*, O you people who work for God with concentration in the lower direction towards the higher, [*righteously:*] with righteous deeds that cause you to ascend to the divine presence and prepare you to receive the holy lights. These words were addressed to the David of the spirit and his family from the spiritual and egocentric faculties and body parts. [*Indeed, I am Seer of what you do.*]

[34:12] *And unto the* Solomon *of the heart* [*We gave*] *the wind* of egocentric caprice; *its morning course was a month's journey*: in the morning of the dawn of the light of the spirit—the shining of the rays of the heart and the coming of the day—it followed its course for the acquisition of sublime character traits, virtues, obedience, worship, and all other righteous matters pertaining to the welfare of the Hereafter; *and its evening course* [*was a month's journey*]: in the evening of the setting of spiritual lights in the attributes of the soul and the dimming of their shining rays, and the passing of the day of light, it followed another course for the arrangement of the needs of life, such as nourishment, provision, clothing, procreation and other matters pertaining to the welfare of worldly order and the body's sustenance. *And We caused a fount of the copper* of physical corporeal nature, by diligence in obedience and worldly transactions, *to flow for him. And of the jinn* of the faculties of estimation and imagination [*there*] *were those who worked before him* in his presence on judgements pertaining to the welfare of the world, the thriving of the nation and the comfort of the citizens, and on arrangements and decisions pertaining to the rectitude of the soul and the acquisition of knowledge, *by the leave of his Lord* and His facilitation of them for him and His guidance of matters through their hands. *And such of them as deviated from Our command* by the dictate of their jinn-nature, straying from what is right and from sound intellectual reasoning by inclining towards egocentric luxuries and bodily pleasures, *We would make them taste the chastisement of the Blaze*: by means of powerful spiritual discipline and the unleashing of the angelic faculties upon them, with the blazing scourges of overpowering intellectual impulses that contradicted the satanic nature.

Q. 34:12

[34:13] *They fashioned for him whatever he wished: lofty shrines*, noble stations, *and statues*, geometric forms, *and basins like cisterns*: for the containing

of supra-sensory provisions and spiritual nourishments, by carving meanings into physical images, representing realities with formal structures,
and incorporating universal perceptibles and inspirations of the Unseen
into verbal garments and broad particular configurations, which resembled pools because of how they were stripped of primordial substrata,
although they made use of material qualities and corporeal accidents;
and cauldrons built into the ground of the configuration of preparedness, for
the composition of sound analogies and the preparation of sources of
knowledge and gnostic truths, through the blending of correct opinions
and strong firm convictions. *'Work, House of* the *David* of the spirit, with
what We have facilitated for you, and the blessings of perfections We have
emanated upon you, *in thankfulness* by utilising these blessings for the sake
of spiritual wayfaring and turning to Me, and the fulfilment of the dues
of servitude by annihilation in Me, rather than the direction of worldly
kingship and the rectifying of physical perfections. *And few indeed of My
servants are thankful'*: by utilising their blessings for the obedience of God
with righteous deeds for His sake.

Q. 34:14

   [34:14] *And when We decreed for him death* by annihilation in Me in the
station of the mystery, *nothing indicated to them that he had died except a termite
[that gnawed away at his staff]*: they were only guided to his annihilation in
the station of the spirit and his movement towards the Real, in the state
of mystery, by a motion of earthly nature and its weak physical faculties,
which overwhelmed the animal soul which was his staff; for they had no
way of arriving at the station of the mystery, and one cannot remain in the
state of the heart therein. Nor did they have any sense that he was in a stage
beyond their own except by the link of the connection of physical nature
to him, which in its weakness was overwhelmed by the natural faculties,
through spiritual discipline and the severing of the aid of the heart from
it at that time. In other words, they were only aware of the state of the
creature that gnawed at his staff by overpowering it, because when
the heart rises, the animal soul weakens and its faculties falter, and all that
remains is the natural faculty which governs them. *And when he fell down*
in his Mosaic swoon and fainted into absorption in the divine presence,
rather than using it for deeds and employing it for discipline, *the jinn realised that had they known the Unseen* of the station of the mystery by having
awareness of the unveilings—had they been so detached—*they would not
have continued in the humiliating chastisement* of the strenuous discipline
that denied them their desires and wants, and the requirements of nature
and caprice, by contravening them and compelling them to do arduous

deeds of spiritual wayfaring, and to suffice with nothing but their rights.

[34:15] *Verily there was for Sheba,* the folk of the city of the body, *in their dwelling-place,* their residence and locus, *a sign* showing them the Attributes and acts of God: *two gardens [to the right and to the left]:* the garden of the Attributes and witnessings to their right, on the side of the heart and the isthmus, which is the stronger and nobler of the two sides; and the garden of traces and acts to their left, on the side of the breast and the soul, which is the weaker and baser of the two sides. *'Eat of your Lord's provision* from both sides, as He says, *They would surely have received nourishment from above them and from beneath their feet* [Q. 5:66]; *and give thanks to Him:* by employing the blessings of its fruits for works of obedience and travelling to Him with devotions. *A good land* because of the balance of temperament and health, *and a forgiving Lord'* Who covers the configurations of vices and the darknesses of souls and natures with the light of His Attributes and acts. You are granted stability on the side of preparedness, means and instruments, and the grace of divine assistance and the emanation of lights.

[34:16] *But they were disregardful* of giving thanks and using it as a means to reach God, and even of the eating of its fruits, which were the beneficial sciences of reality, through being mired in pleasures and passions and immersed in the darknesses of natures and configurations; *so We unleashed upon them the flood of* primordial nature by breaking *the dam* of the waters of sweet-tempered elemental natures, which the Bilqīs of the soul, their queen, had constructed. *And We gave them, in place of their two gardens, two gardens* of the thorns of harmful configurations and the roots of evil, bestial, predatory and satanic attributes, *bearing bitter fruit,* as He says elsewhere: *Its spathes are like the heads of devils* [Q. 37:65], *[and tamarisk] and sparse lote-trees,* which were the remnants of the human attributes.

[34:17] *That* retribution *is what We requited them with for their ingratitude* to Our blessings; *and is anyone but the ingrate* who utilises the blessings of the Merciful in obedience to Satan *ever [so] requited?*

[34:18] *And We set between them and the towns which We had blessed,* with the presence of heart, mystery, spirit and divinity by the manifestations of acts, Attributes, Names and Essence and the lights of unveilings and witnessings, *prominent towns:* visible interconnected stations and halting-places, such as patience, reliance, contentment and the like. *And We facilitated [for travellers] the journeying through them* to God and in God through degrees, so that the traveller journeys and ascends from station to station: *'Travel [through them],* through the halting-places of the souls, *night and day* in the stations and waterholes of the hearts, *safely'* among the satanic

Q. 34:15

obstacles and threatening egocentric attributes, by the power of certitude and sound viewpoint, upon the path of the manifest Divine Law.

[34:19] *But they said* with the voice of their state, turned towards the lower direction distant from the holy presence, inclined to physical abysses and travelling towards natural desires and satanic calamities, '*Our Lord, make far apart the stages of our travel,*' *and they wronged their souls*: by becoming veiled from the lights of the blessed towns by the darknesses of ill-fated isthmuses; *and so We made them bywords* and parables among the people, symbols of destruction and ruin, *and We caused them to disintegrate totally* by drowning and dispersion (*tafrīq*). [*Indeed, in that there are signs for every* [*servant who is*] *steadfast, grateful.*]

[34:20] *And verily Iblīs proved true his opinion of them*: of the people. This refers to his words, '*And I will surely lead them astray…And surely I will command them and they will change God's creation*' [Q. 4:119], and the like. *So they followed him*—[*all*] *except a group of the believers*, namely the sincere ones.

[34:21] *And he did not have any warrant over them,* [*but that We might know him who believed in the Hereafter from him who was in doubt thereof*]: We only allowed him to overcome them in order to manifest Our knowledge in the loci of the sincere folk of realised knowledge, and to distinguish them from the veiled doubters. The knowledge of the pure-hearted prepared person flows forth from the treasure-trove of preparedness, and springs from his heart when Satan approaches with his whisperings, and he pelts him with the lamps of illuminated arguments and expels him by seeking refuge with God when his corrupting temptations arise. This is not so for those whose hearts are blackened with the attributes of souls and whose ignorance corresponds to Satan's plots. [*And your Lord is Preserver of all things.*]

[34:22] *Say:* '*Call on those whom you have asserted besides God. They do not possess* [*even*] *so much as the weight of an atom in the heavens or in the earth, and they do not have any share in either of them, nor has He among them any auxiliary.*'

[34:23] *And intercession will not avail with Him, except for him to whom leave is given. Yet, when fear is banished from their hearts, they will say, 'What has your Lord said?' They will say, 'The truth.' And He is the Exalted, the Great.*

[34:24] *Say:* '*Who provides for you from the heavens and* [*from*] *the earth?*' *Say:* '*God!*' *And indeed either we or you are rightly guided or in manifest error.*

[34:25] *Say:* '*You will not be questioned about the sins we committed, nor shall we be questioned about what you do.*'

[34:26] *Say:* '*Our Lord will bring us together, then He will judge between us with truth. And He is the Judge, the Knower.*'

[34:27] *Say: 'Show me those whom you have joined to Him as associates. No, indeed! Rather, He is God, the Mighty, the Wise.'*

[34:28] *And We did not send you except to all of humankind [both] as a bearer of good tidings and a warner, but most people do not know.*

[34:29] *And they say, 'When shall this promise be [fulfilled], if you are being truthful?'*

[34:30] *Say: 'Yours is the tryst of a day which you can neither defer nor advance by a single hour.'*

[34:31] *And those who disbelieve say, 'We will not believe in this Qur'ān, nor in that which was [revealed] before it.' But if you were to see when the evildoers are brought to stand before their Lord, bandying arguments against one another. Those who were oppressed will say to those who were arrogant, 'Had it not been for you, we would have been believers.'*

[34:32] *Those who were arrogant will say to those who were oppressed, 'Was it us who barred you from guidance after it had come to you? Rather, you were guilty.'*

Q. 34:27

[34:33] *And those who were oppressed will say to those who were arrogant, 'Nay, but [it was your] scheming night and day, when you used to command us to disbelieve in God and set-up partners with Him.' And they will conceal their remorse when they see the chastisement, and We will place fetters around the necks of the disbelievers. Shall they be requited except for what they used to do?*

[34:34] *And We did not send a warner to any town without its affluent ones saying, 'Indeed, we disbelieve in that [Message] with which you have been sent.'*

[34:35] *And they say, 'We possess more wealth and children, and we shall not be chastised.'*

[34:36] *Say: 'Indeed, my Lord extends provision for whomever He will and restricts [it], but most people do not know.'*

[34:37] *Nor is it your wealth or your children that will bring you near to Us in closeness, except for those who believe and act righteously: those—they shall have a twofold reward for what they did, and they shall be in the lofty abodes, secure.*

[34:38] *And those who strive against Our signs, seeking to incapacitate, those—they will be arraigned into the chastisement.*

[34:39] *Say: 'My Lord extends provision for whomever He will of His servants, and restricts [it] for him, and whatever thing you may expend, He will replace it. And He is the best of providers.'*

[34:40] *And on the day when He will gather them all together, He will say to the angels, 'Was it these who used to worship you?'*

[34:41] *They will say, 'Glory be to You! You are our Supporter, not they. Nay, rather, they used to worship the jinn; most of them were believers in them.'*

[34:42] *'So today none among you has any power over another, either to benefit*

203

or to hurt.' And We shall say to those who did wrong, 'Taste the chastisement of the Fire which you used to deny!'

[34:43] *And when Our signs are recited to them, [being] clear signs, they say, 'This is just a man who desires to bar you from [worshipping] what your fathers used to worship.' And they say, 'This is nothing but a calumny that has been invented.' And those who disbelieve say to the truth when it comes to them, 'This is nothing but plain sorcery.'*

[34:44] *And We did not give them any Books for them to study, nor did We send them any warner before you.*

[34:45] *And those who were before them [also] denied, and they have not received [even] a tenth of what We gave those [others]. Yet they denied My messengers, so how was My abhorrence!*

[34:46] *Say: 'I will give you just one [piece of] admonition: that you rise up for God in twos and individually, and then reflect: there is no madness in your companion. He is just a warner to you before [the befalling of] a severe chastisement.'*

[34:47] *Say: 'I have not asked you any reward, since it is for [the benefit of] you. Indeed, my reward lies only with God, and He is Witness over all things.'*

[34:48] *Say: 'Indeed, my Lord hurls the truth. [He is] the Knower of the Unseen.'*

[34:49] *Say: 'The truth has come. And falsehood neither originates nor restores [anything].'*

[34:50] *Say: 'If I go astray, I will be going astray only to my own loss; and if I am rightly guided, it will have been by what my Lord reveals to me. Indeed, He is Hearer, Nigh.'*

[34:51] *If you could but see when they are stricken with terror, and so there is no escape, and they are seized from a close quarter.*

[34:52] *And they will say, 'We believe in him [now].' But how can they attain [it] from a place that is far away, [34:53] when they disbelieved in it before? And they throw guesses at the Unseen from a far-off place.*

[34:54] *And a barrier is set between them and what they crave, just as was done with their counterparts formerly. Indeed, they used to be in grave doubt:]* the states of the Major Resurrection—unification and differentiation (*faṣl*), the differentiation between the upholders of truth and falsehood, and the statements of the wrongdoers—will all be manifested with the emergence of the Mahdī (may God grant him peace).

35
THE ANGELS
SŪRAT AL-MALĀ'IKA

In the Name of God, the Compassionate, the Merciful

[35:1] [*Praise be to God, Originator of the heavens and the earth,*] *Appointer of the angels as messengers, having wings* [*in* [*sets of*] *two or three or four*] : representing the directions of the influence that exists in the heavenly and earthly dominions. God has appointed them as messengers, sent to the prophets bearing revelation, and to the saints bearing inspiration, and to ordinary people and all other things to ordain and destroy them. Whenever their influence reaches its target, it does so by means of a wing, and every direction of influence is a wing. For example, the two intellects—the cognitive and the discursive—are two wings of the human soul; perception, impulsive motion and active motion are three wings of the animal soul; nourishment, growth, reproduction and formation are four wings of the vegetable soul. Their wings are countless; there are as many wings as there are types of influences. Thus, the Messenger of God (may God bless him and grant him peace) related that he saw Gabriel (may God grant him peace) on the night of the Ascension bearing six hundred wings. He then alludes to their multiplicity with His Words, *He multiplies in creation what He will.* [*Indeed, God has power over all things.*

[35:2] *Whatever mercy God unfolds for people, none can withhold it; and whatever He withholds, none can release it after Him. And He is the Mighty, the Wise.*

[35:3] *O people, remember God's grace to you. Is there any creator other than God who provides for you from the heaven and earth? There is no god except Him. So how, then, do you deviate?*

[35:4] *And if they deny you, verily* [*other*] *messengers before you were denied, and to God all matters are returned.*

[35:5] *O people! Indeed, God's promise is true. So do not let the life of this world deceive you, and do not let the Deceiver deceive you concerning God.*

[35:6] *Truly Satan is an enemy to you. So treat him as an enemy. He only summons his party so that they may be among the folk of the Blaze.*

[35:7] *Those who disbelieve, theirs will be a severe chastisement; but those who believe and perform righteous deeds, theirs will be forgiveness and a great reward.*

[35:8] *Is he, the evil of whose deeds is made [to seem] fair to him so that he deems it good, [like the one who is rightly guided]? Indeed, God leads astray whomever He will and guides whomever He will. So do not let your soul expire for their sake out of regret. Indeed, God is Knower of what they do.*

[35:9] *And it is God Who unleashes the winds and they raise clouds, then We drive them to a dead land, and therewith revive the earth after it has been dead. Such will be the Raising.]*

[35:10] *Whoever desires glory [should know that] all glory belongs to God*: glory is one of the Attributes of God that are His alone, and anyone who wants it must become annihilated in the Attributes of God instead of his own.

Q. 35:6

He then refers to the path of detachment and the erasure of attributes by saying, *To Him ascends good words*: meaning goodly souls cleansed from the impurities of natures that remained on the light of their innate disposition, who remember their covenant of Oneness; *and as for righteous action* by self-purification and adornment, *He exalts it*: He raises that goodly kind to His presence and no other, so that it adopts the attribute of glory and the other attributes. Or to him ascends true knowledge from the goodly primordial innate affirmation of Oneness, from the impurities of estimative delusions and imaginative fantasies, and therefore He raises righteous action and no other. The Commander of the Believers (may God grant him peace) said, 'Knowledge is accompanied by action. The knowledge speaks to the action, and it must answer; if it does not, the knowledge departs.' The ladder of ascent to the divine presence is knowledge and action, and one cannot ascend without both of them. Affirmation of Oneness alone, though it is the foundation, is not sufficient on its own to become adorned with His glory and all His other Attributes, because the Attributes are the sources of acts. As long as the deeds of the soul, whose sources are the attributes of the soul, are not renounced by asceticism and reliance, and as long as one does not detach oneself from their configurations by worship and devotion, one will not be prepared for adornment with His Attributes. Thus, true knowledge, which is affirmation of Oneness, is like the two stiles of the ladder, and action is like the rungs which allow one to ascend. *But those who plot evil* by manifesting their souls, even if they might be folk of knowledge, *theirs shall be a severe chastisement* of the configurations of evil harmful deeds, [*and their plotting shall come to nothing.*

[35:11] *And God created you from dust, then from a drop of [seminal] fluid, then He made you pairs. And no female bears or brings forth except with His knowledge and no long-living person is given long life, nor is anything diminished of his life, but it is [recorded] in a Book. Indeed, that is easy for God.*

[35:12] *Nor are the two [kinds of] seas alike: this one is extremely sweet, pleasant to drink, and that one is salty, extremely bitter. Yet from each you eat fresh meat, and obtain ornaments which you wear. And you see the ships therein ploughing through that you may seek of His bounty, and that perhaps you may give thanks.*

[35:13] *He makes the night pass into the day, and He makes the day pass into the night, and He has disposed the sun and the moon, each moving to an appointed term. That is God, your Lord; to Him belongs the kingdom. As for those on whom you call besides Him, they do not possess [even] so much as the husk of a date-stone.*

[35:14] *If you call on them, they will not hear your call; and [even] if they heard, they would not [be able to] respond to you; and on the Day of Resurrection they will disown your [idolatrous] associations. And none can inform you like One Who is Aware.*

[35:15] *O people, you are the ones who are indigent to God. And God, He is the Independent, the Praised.*

Q. 35:11

[35:16] *If He wishes, He can take you away and bring about a new creation.*

[35:17] *And that is not an arduous thing for God.*

[35:18] *And no burdened soul shall bear the burden of another [sinful soul]. And should one burdened heavily call for its burden to be borne, nothing of it will be borne, even if [he] be a relative. You can only warn those who fear their Lord in secret and observe prayer. For whoever purifies himself is purifying himself only for [the sake of] his own soul. And to God is the [end of the] journeying.*

[35:19] *Nor are the blind and the seer equal,* [35:20] *nor darkness and light;* [35:21] *nor shade and torrid heat;* [35:22] *nor are the living equal to the dead. Indeed, God makes to hear whomever He wishes. But you cannot make those who are in the graves to hear.*

[35:23] *You are but a warner.*

[35:24] *Indeed, We have sent you with the truth, as a bearer of good tidings, and a warner. And there is not a community but there has passed in it a warner.*

[35:25] *And if they deny you, those before them also denied: their messengers brought them manifest signs, and [came] with Books, and with the illuminating Book.*

[35:26] *Then I seized those who disbelieved, and how was My abhorrence!*

[35:27] *Have you not seen that God sends down water from the heaven, wherewith We bring forth fruits of diverse hues? And in the mountains are streaks white and red, of diverse hues, and [others] pitch-black?*

[35:28] *And of humans and beasts and cattle, there are diverse hues likewise.]*

Indeed, only those of God's servants who have knowledge fear Him: none fear God but those who have knowledge and gnosis of Him, because 'fear' (*khashya*) here does not merely mean dread of retribution, but rather refers to the configuration of humility and meekness in the heart when one envisions and calls to mind the Attribute of divine magnificence. The one who cannot envision His magnificence cannot possibly fear him, while the one to whom God manifests with His magnificence will fear Him as He ought to be feared. There is a vast gulf between the envisioning of the one who has knowledge but not gnosis, and the immutable divine manifestation of the one who has both knowledge and gnosis. The ranks of fear are countless, because so are the ranks of knowledge and gnosis. *Truly God is Mighty*, overwhelming all things by His magnificence, *Forgiving*, covering the attribute of the soul's self-magnifying and the configuration of its pride with the light of the manifestation of His might.

Q. 35:29

[35:29] *Indeed, those who recite the Book of God* which He gave them at the onset of innate disposition—namely the Qur'ānic intellect, by manifesting it and bringing it into the open to become a discriminating intellect—*and observe* the *prayer* of heart-presence upon the emergence of innate knowledge, *and expend of what We have provided them* of the attributes of knowledge and action required for it to be manifested upon them, *secretly* by detaching from attributes *and openly* by renouncing deeds, *anticipate* in the station of the heart by renunciation and detachment *a commerce that will never be ruined* by the replacing of the acts and Attributes of the Real with their own.

[35:30] *That He may pay them in full their rewards* in the gardens of the soul and the heart with the fruits of reliance and contentment, *and enrich them out of His bounty* in the gardens of the spirit with witnessings of His countenance in manifestations. *Indeed, He is Forgiving*, covering for them the sins of their deeds and attributes, *Appreciative*, repaying their efforts by substituting His own acts and Attributes.

[35:31] *And that which We have revealed to you of the* absolute discriminating *Book is the* absolute immutable *truth* which can bear no addition or subtraction, *confirming what was [revealed] before it* because it contains the entirety of it. *Indeed, with regard to His servants, God is truly Aware* of their states of preparedness, *Seeing* their deeds, and He grants them perfection according to their preparedness, according to the merit of their deeds.

[35:32] *Then We bequeathed from you the Book to those of Our servants whom We chose*: the Muḥammadans singled out by God for additional nurture and the perfection of preparedness compared to all the other communities, because they only inherit it and reach it from you and by your mediation, for you are the one who gives them preparedness and perfection. Their place among the communities is as your place among the prophets.

Yet some of them are those who wrong themselves by failing to live up to the rights of their preparedness and preventing it from emerging into action, and betraying the trust that was left with them by holding onto it and refusing to discharge it because they are immersed in physical pleasures and egocentric desires; *and some of them are moderate*: following the path of the right hand and choosing righteous works and good deeds, recording virtues and perfections in the station of the heart; *and some are those who take the lead in [performing] good works*, which are the manifestations of the Attributes until annihilation in the Essence, *by the leave of God*: by His facilitation and grace. *That is the greatest favour.*

[35:33] *Gardens of Eden*, of the three gardens, *into which they will be admitted, therein they will be adorned with bracelets of gold and pearls*: forms of perfections of sublime character traits, virtues, states and gifts smelted with deeds of the gold of spiritual knowledge and the pearls of gnostic truths and realities of unveiling and experiential realisation; *and their garments therein will be of* the *silk* of the Divine Attributes.

Q. 35:33

[35:34] *And they will say* with the voice of their states and expressions when they become adorned with all the praiseworthy attributes upon subsistence after annihilation, *'Praise be to God Who has removed from us grief* at the loss of possible perfections determined by preparedness, by gifting them to us in this veridical existence. *Indeed, our Lord is Forgiving, Appreciative*, and our reward from Him is ampler and more enduring than anything we could have merited by our efforts.

[35:35] *'Who out of His favour has made us to dwell in the Abode of [everlasting] Stay* from which there is no leaving, in this gifted existence from His pure generosity and absolute grace, *wherein no toil* of effort or transference *shall touch us, nor shall we be touched by any fatigue'* of travelling or moving.

[35:36] *And as for those who disbelieve* and are veiled from you by denial, who neither accept the Book nor inherit it because of their distance from you in reality, so that there is no proximity or connection between you and them, *there will be for them the fire of* the *Hell* of nature, in which they will be chastised perpetually with all manner of deprivation and suffering. *They will neither be done away with, so that they may die* and be free of it, *nor will any [aspect] of its chastisement be lightened for them* that they might have respite from it. And God (Exalted is He) knows best.

36
YĀ SĪN
SŪRAT YĀ SĪN

In the Name of God, the Compassionate, the Merciful

[36:1] *Yā. Sīn*: here He swore on two Names indicating the perfection of his preparedness, as was discussed in *Ṭā Hā*.

[36:2] *By the Definitive Qur'ān* which is the complete perfection commensurate to his preparedness. He swore that because of these things, he was one of those sent on the path of Oneness characterised by its straightness. *Yā* alludes to His Name the Protector (*al-Wāqī*), and *Sīn* to His Name Peace (*al-Salām*). [In other words,] by the Protector of the security of your sound innate disposition from flaws in pre-eternity, and from the blights of the veils of creation and custom, and by the Peace which is its source and origin, and by the Definitive Qur'ān which is the form of its perfection which encompasses all perfections and contains all wisdoms.

[36:3] *You are*, because of these three things, *indeed of those sent [by God]*, [36:4] *on a straight path*.

[36:5] *A revelation from the Mighty, the Merciful*: the gathering Qur'ān—which embodies wisdom, whereby the latter is the form of the perfection of your preparedness—is a revelation to manifest it separately from the hidden trove of unification upon your locus: in order that it become a discriminating intellect from the Mighty Who overwhelmed your I-ness and the attributes of your creation, and conquered them with His power, to prevent them from emerging and blocking the emergence of the Qur'ān hidden within you on the locus of your heart, and its becoming a discriminating intellect. He is the Merciful, Who brought it to light upon you by the manifestations of His Attributes of perfection in their entirety.

[36:6] *That you may warn a people [whose fathers were not warned]*: a people who reached a level of perfection whose preparedness was not reached by their fathers, so that they were not warned of that which you warn of, *so they are oblivious* of the preparedness that they have been granted, which has reached a level that was not reached by any others before them, which is why He called them *those of Our servants whom We chose* [Q. 35:32].

[36:7] *The word has already proved true for most of them* in the prior decree that they are damned, *for they will not believe*, because just as preparednesses became stronger when you emerged, so too did the damned become even more evil, just as the saved became even more virtuous.

[36:8] *Indeed, We have put fetters*—chains of physical nature and love for lower bodies—*around their necks, such that they are up to the chins*: preventing their heads from nodding in assent, since they cover the necks' joints which allow the head to move, and hold them in place at their highest point so that they reach beyond the starting point of the heads, rendering them powerless to assent or be influenced by reaction and inclination to bowing or prostrating in submission and annihilation. Yet human perfections are reactive, and can only be attained by humility and surrender. *So that their heads are upturned* and prevented from receiving them by lowering the head.

Q. 36:7

[36:9] *And We have set before them* from the divine side *a barrier* of the veil of the emergence of the soul and the attributes which overwhelm the heart, preventing them from looking upwards in yearning for the true meeting upon beholding the lights of beauty, *and behind them* from the physical side *a barrier* of the veil of corporeal nature and its pleasures, which prevent them from obeying commandments and prohibitions. Hence, they are thereby held back from the righteous action which would prepare them to receive goodness and the Attributes of majesty. Thus, the path of knowledge and action is closed to them and they remain with the idols of the body, worshipping them in a deluded state without moving forward or backward. *And We have covered them* with immersion in coverings of primordial matter and envelopment in corporeal garments, *so they do not see* because of the density of the veil that surrounds them on all sides; and if they cannot see, then they will not be influenced, and it will make no difference whether they are warned or not:

[36:10] [*And it is the same to them whether you warn them or do not warn them, they will not believe.*]

[36:11] *You can only warn*, meaning that the warning is only effective on, *him who follows the Remembrance* by the illumination and purity of his preparedness, so that he is influenced by it and accepts the guidance, because of the innate affirmation of Divine Oneness and original gnosis that exists in his preparedness. Hence, he takes heed *and fears the*

Compassionate [*in secret*] by envisioning His magnificence, despite being absent from His manifestation; and so he follows the guidance along the path to the presence of that which is secret to him, to witness what has been illuminated by His light. *So give him the good tidings of* tremendous *forgiveness* with the covering of the sins of the veils of his acts, attributes and essence, *and a noble reward* of the gardens of the acts, Attributes and Essence of the Real.

[36:12] [*Indeed, it is We Who bring the dead to life, and record what they have sent ahead and their vestiges. And everything We have numbered in a clear register.*]

[36:13] *And strike for them as a similitude the folk of the town, when the messengers came to it.*

[36:14] *When We sent to them two men, and they denied them both, so We reinforced* [*them*] *with a third, and they said, 'We have indeed been sent to you* [*by God*].'

[36:15] *They said, 'You are nothing but humans like us, and the Compassionate has revealed nothing. You are only lying!'*

[36:16] *They said, 'Our Lord knows that we have indeed been sent to you* [*by Him*]!

[36:17] *'And our duty is only to communicate in clear terms'*: one could interpret *the folk of the town* [Q. 36:13] as representing the residents of the city of the body, and the three messengers as the spirit, the heart and the intellect. Initially, He sent two to them, but they denied them both, because of the lack of correspondence between the two messengers and them, and how they contrasted in light and darkness. So they were reinforced by the intellect, which corresponded to the soul through their common interests and welfare; and it could call to them and their people with the same message as the heart and spirit had, and have an effect on them.

[36:18] [*They said, 'We augur ill of you. If you do not desist, we will surely stone you and there shall befall you, at our hands, a painful chastisement.'*

[36:19] *They said, 'May your augury of ill be with you! What!* [*Even*] *if* [*it be that*] *you are being reminded? Nay, but you are a profligate people!'*] Their augury of them was that they were averse to them because they were presenting them with spiritual discipline and struggle, and forbidding them from pleasures and desires. Their stoning of them was that they pelted them with natural impulses and physical demands; and their chastisement of them was that they overwhelmed them, and used them for the attainment of their bestial predatory desires.

[36:20] *And there came a man from the furthest part of the city*: that is, from the furthest place away from it. The *man* represents ardent love (ʿishq)

Q. 36:12

inspired from the highest and most sublime height, guided by the intellect, making manifest the religion of Oneness, the call to the first Beloved, and the confirmation of the messengers. He was *hastening* because of the swiftness of his movement, calling to all with overwhelming power and compulsion to follow the messengers in [affirming] Oneness: [*He said, 'O my people, follow the messengers!*

[36:21] *'Follow them who do not ask you for any reward and who are rightly guided.*]

[36:22] *'And why should I not worship Him Who originated me and to Whom you shall be returned?* His name was Ḥabīb, and he was a carpenter, who in his early days used to carve idols—images meant as loci for the Attributes—because he was veiled by their beauty from the beauty of the Essence.

[36:23] [*'Shall I take besides Him [other] gods, whose intercession, if the Compassionate should wish me any harm, will not avail me in any way, nor will they [be able to] save me?*

[36:24] *'Indeed, I would then be in manifest error.*

[36:25] *'Indeed, I believe in your Lord. So listen to me!'*

[36:26] *It was said, 'Enter Paradise!'*] He was commanded to enter the garden of the Essence. [*He said,*] *'O would that my people,* who are veiled from my station and state, *knew* [36:27] *with what* [*munificence*] *my Lord has forgiven me* for the sin of worshipping idols and loci for the Attributes, and carving them, *and made me of the honoured ones'* because of my extreme nearness in the presence of Unity. A *ḥadīth* says, 'Everything has a heart, and the heart of the Qurʾān is *Yā Sīn*.' Perhaps this is because Ḥabīb, the well-known hero of *Yā Sīn*, believed in him six centuries before his coming, and understood the secret of his prophethood. The Prophet (may God bless him and grant him peace) said, 'There were three who were the foremost of their communities, who did not disbelieve in God for the blink of an eye: ʿAlī b. Abī Ṭālib (may God grant him peace), the hero of *Yā Sīn*, and the believer of the folk of Pharaoh.'

[36:28] [*And We did not send down on his people after him any host from heaven, nor do We [ever] send down.*

[36:29] *It was but one Cry and, lo and behold, they were extinguished.*

[36:30] *Ah, the anguish for servants, never did a messenger come to them but they mocked him.*

[36:31] *Have they not seen how many generations We have destroyed before them, [and how] they never return?*

[36:32] *And indeed every one of them will be gathered before Us, arraigned.*

Q. 36:21

[36:33] *And a sign for them is the dead earth which We revive and out of which We bring forth grain, so that they eat thereof;* [36:34] *and We have placed therein gardens of date-palms and vines, and We have caused springs to gush forth therein,* [36:35] *that they might eat of its fruits; but it was not their hands that made it. Will they not then give thanks?*

[36:36] *Glory be to Him Who created all the pairs of what the earth produces, and of themselves, and of what they do not know.*]

[36:37] *And a sign for them is the night* of the darkness of the soul, *from which We strip the day* and the light of the sun of the spirit and variegation, *and, behold, they find themselves in darkness.*

[36:38] *And the sun* of the spirit *runs to its resting-place*: the station of truth at the end of the journey of the spirit. *That is the ordaining of the Mighty* Who prevents anything from reaching the presence of His Unity and overwhelms all things with power and annihilation, *the Knower* Who knows the limit of the perfection of every wayfarer, and the end of their journeys.

Q. 36:33

[36:39] *And the moon* of the heart *We have determined it*—determined its passage through its journey—*[to run] in phases* of fear, hope, patience, gratitude, and all the stations such as reliance and contentment, *until it returns* upon its annihilation in the spirit in the station of the mystery, *like an aged palm-bough* shortly before its complete waning, and the illumination of the side which faces the spirit before its total annihilation in it, and the veiling of its light from the soul and faculties. It only becomes a full moon in the place of the breast, when it faces the station of the mystery.

[36:40] *It does not behove the sun to catch up with the moon* in its journey, such that it would have the perfections of the breast, which are encompassment of the states of the worlds and manifestation with sublime character traits and attributes, *nor may the night outrun the day* by the moon catching the sun and transferring the darkness of the soul into the day of the heart's light; for when the moon rises to the station of the spirit, the spirit likewise reaches the presence of Unity, so that it does not catch it. At that point, the soul is illuminated in the station of the heart and there is no longer any darkness in it, so its darkness does not outrun its light, but rather disappears. Even if it did remain, it would not outrun the heart and its light, for they would already have moved on to the station of the spirit. *Each [of these] is in an orbit*, a designated circling path which it follows in its beginning and its end, whose set bounds it cannot transgress, *swimming* and journeying until God gathers them together in a limit, and the moon is eclipsed and the sun rises from the west, and the Resurrection begins.

[36:41] *And a sign for them is that We carried their seed in the laden Ark*: the ship of Noah. There is a subtle point of rhetorical eloquence here: He did not say 'their forefathers' to mean the people who were on the ship, but rather referred to their *seed*, who were carried in their loins; thus implying that their progeny must have also existed even then.

[36:42] *And We have created for them the like of it*—the like of Noah's Ark: meaning the Muḥammadan ship—*in which they ride.*

[36:43] [*And if We will, We drown them, whereat they have no one to call to, nor are they rescued,* [36:44] *except by a mercy from Us and for an enjoyment until some time.*

[36:45] *And when it is said to them,*] '*Beware of that which is before you* of the states of the Major Resurrection, *and that which is behind you* of the states of the Minor Resurrection, [*that perhaps you might find mercy*']: the former comes from the direction of the Real, the latter from the direction of the soul; the former is by annihilation in God, the latter by detachment from physical configurations and salvation from them.

Q. 36:42

[36:46] [*And never did a sign of the signs of their Lord come to them, but that they turned away from it.*

[36:47] *And when it is said to them, 'Expend of what God has provided you,' those who disbelieve say to those who believe, 'Are we to feed those whom, if God willed, He would feed? You are only in manifest error!'*

[36:48] *And they say, 'When will this promise be [fulfilled], if you are being truthful?'*

[36:49] *They await but a single Cry that will seize them while they are disputing.*

[36:50] *Then they will not be able to make any testament, nor will they return to their folk.*

[36:51] *And the Trumpet is blown*:] there will be two cries: one to call attention to the first blowing of the Trumpet, by the occurrence of its portents, and the agitation of all the faculties at once from their abodes; and the second when it actually occurs and they are all roused together, and the faculties are spread out in their places. [*And lo and behold, they will be scrambling out of their graves towards their Lord*:] their graves are the bodies in which they slumber.

[36:52] [*They will say, 'O woe to us! Who has raised us from our place of sleep? This is that which the Compassionate had promised and the messengers had spoken the truth.'*

[36:53] *It is but a single Cry, and, behold, they will all be arraigned before Us!*

[36:54] *'So today no soul shall be wronged in any way, and you shall not be requited, except what you used to do.*

[36:55] 'Indeed, today] the folk of Paradise are busy rejoicing in the lights of manifestations and witnessings of the Attributes—[36:56] they and their spouses: their assenting souls—beneath the shade of the lights of the Attributes, reclining upon couches: stations and ranks.

[36:57] 'They have fruits therein of all manner of perceptions and forms of inspirations and unveilings, and they have whatever they call for of witnessings.

[36:58] '"Peace!"—the word of the effusion of perfections and their absolution from all the kinds of deficiency which give rise to the impulses of desires, from a Lord [Who is] Merciful and grants all those wishes in His mercy.

[36:59] ['And stand apart, O you sinners, on this day!

[36:60] 'Did I not charge you, O children of Adam, that you should not worship Satan, for truly he is a manifest enemy to you:] the charge was the pledge of pre-eternity and the covenant of innate disposition, and the worship of Satan is to be veiled by multiplicity by heeding the impulses of delusion.

Q. 36:55

[36:61] ['And that [you should] worship Me—that is the straight path?] The straight path is the path of Unity.

[36:62] 'For verily he has led astray from among you many a creature. Did you not comprehend?

[36:64] 'Burn therein today [as chastisement] for that which you used to reject!'] Al-Ḍaḥḥāk said about the description of Hell, 'For each disbeliever in Hell there will be a pit in which he will dwell, neither seeing nor perceiving.' This alludes to the state of their veiling.

[36:65] [Today We shall seal up their mouths, and their hands shall speak to Us, and their feet shall bear witness concerning what they used to earn:] the meaning of the seal on their mouths and the speaking and witnessing of their hands and feet is that their forms will be changed, so that their tongues are prevented from speaking while their hands and feet will be turned into forms whose configurations and shapes will indicate their deeds, speaking with the language of their states to their propensities from the configurations of their deeds.

[36:66] [And had We wished We would have obliterated their eyes, then they [would have tried to] advance towards the path, but how would they have seen?

[36:67] And had We wished We would have transformed them in their place; then they would have neither been able to go ahead nor to return.

[36:68] And whomever We give long life, We cause him to regress in creation. Will they then not understand?

[36:69] And We did not teach him poetry, nor is it seemly for him. It is just

Remembrance and a Qur'ān that clarifies, [36:70] *that he may warn whoever is alive, and that the Word may be fulfilled against the disbelievers.*

[36:71] *Or have they not seen that We have created for them of what Our hands worked cattle, so that they are their owners?*

[36:72] *And We have subdued these* [cattle] *for them, so that some of them provide rides for them and some of them they eat.*

[36:73] *And there are other benefits for them therein and drinks. Will they not then give thanks?*

[36:74] *And they have taken besides God* [other] *gods that perhaps they might be helped.*

[36:75] *They cannot help them and they are their host, ever-present.*

[36:76] *So do not be grieved by their remarks. Indeed, We know what they conceal and what they proclaim.*

[36:77] *Or has man not seen that We created him from a drop? Then lo and behold, he is an open adversary.*

Q. 36:71

[36:78] *And he strikes for Us a similitude and forgets* [the manner of] *his creation; he says, 'Who will revive the bones when they are rot?'*

[36:79] *Say: 'He will revive them Who originated them the first time, and He is Knower of all creation.*

[36:80] *'It is He Who has made for you fire from the green tree, and, behold, from it you kindle.'*

[36:81] *'Is not He Who created the heavens and the earth able to create the like of them? And He is the Creator, the Knower.*]

[36:82] *'His command when He wills a thing is just* [*to say to it* "Be!" *and it is*]: when His will attaches to the engendering of a thing, its existence is determined by the attachment of that will to it simultaneously, without any interval of time between them.

[36:83] *'So glory be to Him:* transcendently exalted is He above incapacity and resemblance to material and corporeal things, in how both they and their acts are subject to time, *in Whose* [*hand*]—under Whose power and in the control of Whose grasp—*is the dominion of all things* of the souls and faculties, under His control; *and to Whom you will be returned'*: by annihilation in Him and the final arrival to Him. And God knows best.

37
THOSE WHO ARE RANGED IN RANKS
SŪRAT AL-ṢĀFFĀT

In the Name of God, the Compassionate, the Merciful

[37:1] *By those who are ranged in ranks*: He swears by the souls of the wayfarers who follow His path, the path of Oneness, who are ranged in their stations, the ranks of their manifestations and the levels of their witnessings, all orientated towards Him *in ranks*.

[37:2] *And the drivers who drive [away]* the impulses of devils and the empty egocentric hopes that arise from time to time, by means of lights, invocations and proofs.

[37:3] *And those who recite by way of* some kind of *remembrance* as determined by their states, whether by the tongue, the heart, the mystery or the spirit, as has been discussed before.

[37:4] [*Indeed, your God is certainly One*:] they remember the Unity of their God, so that they are kept stable in orientation towards Him and not swayed or led astray by the distractions of anything but Him.

[37:5] *Lord of the heavens* of the Seven Unseens in which they voyage *and the earth* of the body, *and all that is between them, and Lord of the sun's risings*: the risings of the manifestations of the lights of the Attributes. He describes Himself with Essential Unity throughout the states of lordship which reveal the facets of transmutations by the diversity of Names. Therefore, despite the diversity of the manifestations of the Attributes and the ranks of the stations, they are protected from being veiled by multiplicity.

[37:6] *We have indeed adorned the lowest heaven*—meaning the intellect, which is the nearest of the heavens of the spirit with respect to the heart—*with an adornment of the stars* of arguments and proofs, as He says, *And verily We have adorned the lowest heaven with lamps, and made them missiles against the devils* [Q. 67:5].

[37:7] *And [they are] to guard*—that is, We have guarded them—*against every rebellious devil* of the devils of estimations and the imaginative faculties, who refuse to obey the truth and the intellect, thereby preventing them from ascending to the horizon of the intellect by forming estimations and imaginations that give rise to errors and doubts.

[37:8] *They cannot listen in on the High Council* of heavenly spiritual beings and dominion because of those proofs, *[for they are pelted] from every side*: from every heavenly direction. No matter what facet of delusion or suggestion they might employ to construct an analogy in order to ascend, they are confronted with something to refute it, so that they are rebuffed and expelled:

[37:9] *[They are] repelled, and theirs is an everlasting chastisement*: in the form of constant spiritual discipline and all manner of rebukes for their transgressions.

[37:10] *[None of them can listen,] except him who snatches a fragment* by clothing his words in a noble guise and making them seem like truth, by means of a luminous image, which he took from a word of innate truth, *and who is then pursued by a piercing flame* in the form of a luminous intellectual proof, or a ray of holy light, which refutes his suggestion and expels it by annulling the delusional image he presented.

Q. 37:7

[37:11] *[So ask them: Are they stronger as a creation, or those [others] whom We created? Indeed, We created them from a viscous clay.*

[37:12] *Nay, but you marvel, while they engage in ridicule;* [37:13] *and [even] when they are reminded, they are not mindful;* [37:14] *and when they see a sign, they make it an object of ridicule.*

[37:15] *And they say, 'This is nothing but manifest sorcery.*

[37:16] *'When we are dead and have become dust and bones, shall we indeed be resurrected?*

[37:17] *'And our forefathers too?'*

[37:18] *Say: 'Yes, and you will be utterly humiliated!'*

[37:19] *For it will be only a single Cry and, lo and behold, they will be watching.*

[37:20] *And they will say, 'O woe to us!' 'This is the Day of Retribution.'*

[37:21] *'This is the Day of Judgement that you used to deny!*

[37:22] *'Gather those who did wrong together with their mates and what they used to worship* [37:23] *besides God and lead them to the path of Hell.*

[37:24] *'But [first] stop them, for they must be questioned.*

[37:25] *'"What is wrong with you that you do not help one another?"'*

[37:26] *Nay, but that day they offer complete submission.*

[37:27] *And some of them will turn to others, questioning each other.*

[37:28] *They will say, 'Indeed, you used to approach us from the right.'*

[37:29] *They say, 'On the contrary! You were [simply] not believers.*

[37:30] *'And we did not have any warrant over you. Nay, but you [yourselves] were a rebellious folk.*

[37:31] *'So our Lord's Words have become due against us. Indeed, we shall taste [the doom].*

[37:32] *'So we led you astray: Indeed, we [ourselves] were astray.'*

[37:33] *So they on that day will share in the chastisement.*

[37:34] *Indeed, so We deal with sinners.*

[37:35] *For truly it was they who, when it was said to them, 'There is no god except God,' used to be scornful,* [37:36] *and would say, 'Are we to abandon our gods for a mad poet?'*

[37:37] *Nay, but he has brought [them] the truth and confirmed the [earlier] messengers.*

[37:38] *'You shall certainly taste the painful chastisement,* [37:39] *and you will only be requited what you used to do.']*

Q. 37:29

[37:40] *Not so God's sincere servants*: this is a 'severed exception'.¹ What is meant is: but then there are those of God's servants whom He has singled out for additional nurture, whom God has purified from the dross of otherness, I-ness and the remnant of ego, and chosen sincerely for Himself by the annihilation of I-ness and duality.

[37:41] *For them there will be a distinct provision* known to God alone; and this is one of the things known to God that strengthen their hearts and nourish their spirits.

[37:42] *Fruits*: meaning extreme bliss, since fruit represents all that gives pleasure. They will experience the bliss of the unveiling of those things known to God that will come to them; *and they will be honoured* in *an abode of truth, before a King [Who is] Omnipotent* [Q. 54:55], [37:43] *[in the gardens of Bliss:]* in the three gardens, where they will enjoy nearness to the Real in His presence, which is the height of honour and favour.

[37:44] *[They will be reclining] upon couches* in ranks and levels, *facing one another* in the first row, visible to each other without being veiled from each other, nor being favoured above each other in their abodes.

[37:45] *They are served from all round with a cup* of the wine of love *from a spring (maʿīn)*² which is revealed to the folk of eye-witnessing (ʿayān); for its vessel is vision (muʿāyana), so how could it not be seen (yuʿāyan)?

---

1 A 'severed exception' (*istithnāʾ munqatiʿ*) is the use of the word 'except' (*illā*) in a context where what is excepted is wholly different in kind from the general term. See William Wright, *A Grammar of the Arabic Language*, Beirut: Librairie du Liban, 1996, vol. II, p. 336A.

2 Here Kāshānī engages in an extended play on words drawn from the root ʿ-y-n.

[37:46] [*It will be*] *white* and luminous from the source (*ʿayn*) of the Unity of *Kāfūr*,¹ neither blemished nor adulterated with any individuations (*taʿayyunāt*), *delicious to the drinkers*, [37:47] *wherein there is neither madness* which impairs the intellect, for they are folk of sobriety whom God has protected from impurities and veils, so that they are above reproach, *nor will they be spent by it* by the loss of mind, since otherwise they would not be inhabitants of the three gardens in the station of subsistence.

[37:48] *And with them will be maidens of restrained glances* from the folk of the realms of divine power, dominion and detached souls, standing beneath their ranks in the station of the manifestations of the Attributes and the pavilions of majesty, and in the venues of their witnessings beneath the domes of beauty, in the meadows of holiness and the presence of the Names; *with beautiful eyes* (*ʿīn*) because their essences are nothing but eyes (*ʿuyūn*) and they never look away from them because of their total love for them and devotion to them, for they are the objects of love, [37:49] *as if they were hidden eggs* in nests, because of their total purity in the chambers of holiness and their innocence of the matter of impurity.

Q. 37:46

[37:50] [*Some of them will turn to others,*] *questioning each other* and engaging in dialogue about the inhabitants of Paradise and Hell, and the description of the states of the saved and the damned, looking upon each group and the reward and retribution in which they find themselves. This was discussed in the commentary on the people of the Heights (*al-Aʿrāf*).

[37:51] [*One of them will say, 'Indeed, I had a comrade,* [37:52] *who used to say, "Are you really among those who affirm, as truth,* [37:53] [*that*] *when we are dead and have become dust and bones, we shall actually be called to account?"* '

[37:54] *He says, 'Will you have a look?'*

[37:55] *Then he will take a look and he will catch sight of him in the centre of Hell.*

[37:56] *He will say, 'By God! You very nearly destroyed me.*

[37:57] *'And had it not been for the favour of my Lord, I* [*too*] *would have been of those arraigned.'*

[37:58] [*Then he says to his companions,*] *'Do we then not die* [*anymore*], [37:59] *aside from our first death, and are we not to be chastised?*

[37:60] *Truly this is indeed the mighty success.'*

[37:61] *For the like of this let* [*all*] *the workers work.*

[37:62] *Is that a better hospitality or the Zaqqūm tree,* [37:63] [*whereby*] *We have indeed made it a trial for the wrongdoers?*]

---

1 A spring in Paradise.

[37:64] *Indeed, it is a tree that comes forth from the very source of Hell*: it is the tree of the impure veiled soul, growing from the pit of the hell of nature, its branches spreading through its awful terrible levels, bearing foul and revolting fruits of the utmost ugliness, wretchedness and horror.

[37:65] [*Its spathes are like*] *the heads of devils*: there sprout from it ruinous impulses and rebellious suggestions which encourage vile actions and evil deeds. These are the roots of devilry and the sources of evil and corruption, and thus they are the heads of devils.

[37:66] *And indeed they will eat of it*: drawing support, strength and nourishment from it, for evil people take nourishment from evil things and do not gain pleasure from anything else; *and will fill their bellies from it* with wicked configurations and dark attributes, like the one who is filled with anger, rancour and envy when they are stirred up in him.

Q. 37:64

[37:67] *Then, lo and behold, on top of it they will have a brew of* the *boiling water* of natural desires, base evil hopes and love for low things, while falling short of the truly heinous evils that alone can quench some of the thirst of the evildoers.

[37:68] *Then indeed their return shall be to Hellfire* because of the domination of avarice, lust, rancour, hatred, greed and the like, and the preponderance of their impulses despite the inability to attain their desires.

[37:69] [*Indeed, they found their fathers to be astray*, [37:70] *and so they are* [*also now*] *hurrying in their footsteps*.

[37:71] *And verily most of the ancients went astray before them*, [37:72] *and We certainly had sent among them warners*.

[37:73] *So behold how was the consequence for them who were warned*, [37:74] [*all*] *except God's sincere servants*.

[37:75] *And verily Noah called to Us, and how excellent were the Hearers of the prayer!*

[37:76] *And We delivered him and his family from the great distress*, [37:77] *and made his descendants the survivors*.

[37:78] *And We left for him among posterity*:

[37:79] *'Peace be upon Noah among the worlds!'*

[37:80] *Thus, indeed, We requite the virtuous*.

[37:81] *Indeed, he is one of Our faithful servants*.

[37:82] *Then We did drown the others*.

[37:83] *And truly of his adherents was Abraham*:] it is possible to read the story of Abraham (may God bless him and grant him peace) as a spiritual correspondence for the state of perfection of the innocent spirit:

222

[37:84] *When he came to his Lord,* by the prior knowledge of pre-eternity and the communion established at the original covenant, *with a heart that was* yet instilled with innate disposition and pure preparedness, and *pure* of flaws and blights, keeping to the innate covenant of Oneness, condemning those veiled from Unity by multiplicity, looking upon the stars of intellectual rational sciences and discursive arguments and proofs, perceiving by insight and consideration his own sickness caused by egocentric desires and veiling bodily preoccupations.

[37:85] [*When he said to his father and his folk, 'What do you worship?*

[37:86] *'Is it a calumny—gods other than God—that you desire?*

[37:87] *'What, then, is your supposition regarding the Lord of the Worlds?'*

[37:88] *And he cast a glance at the stars* [37:89] *and said, 'Indeed, I feel* [*I will be*] *sick.'*

[37:90] *So they went away, leaving him behind:*] his materialistic people turned away from him and his purpose and point of view, because of how he condemned them for yielding to created things and obeying Satan; and they went off to their festival, where they gathered regularly, to engage in their passions and pleasures.

[37:91] *Then he turned* [*to their gods*] *surreptitiously,* seeking to break their idols with the axe of Oneness and true remembrance; [*and said, 'Will you not eat?*

[37:92] *'What is wrong with you that you do not speak?'*

[37:93] *He then turned on them*] *striking* [*them with his right hand*]: the hand of the intellect.

[37:94] [*So they came running*] *towards him*: hoping to overcome him because of his weakness and put an end to his efforts.

[37:95] [*He said, 'Do you worship what you have carved,* [37:96] *when God created you and whatever you make?'*

[37:97] *They said, 'Build for him a structure,*] *then cast him* [*into the fierce fire*']: the fire of the heat of the womb. But God made it cool and peaceful for him: that is, He gave him repose and safety from blights, by the subsistence of the purity of his preparedness and the innocence of his innate disposition, and built over him the edifice of the body.

[37:98] [*So they sought to outwit him, but We made them the lowermost:*] God made his enemies—the evil-enjoining soul and the physical faculties that cast him into the fire—the lowermost, because of the wholeness of his preparedness. Then he went towards his Lord by wayfaring:

[37:99] *And he said, 'I shall indeed depart to my Lord; He will guide me*: he called to his Lord with the voice of perfect essential preparedness, and asked Him to grant him the son of the righteous heart; and He gave him tidings of that son, and granted it to him.

[37:100] ['*My Lord, grant me of the righteous.*'

[37:101] *So We gave him the good tidings of a forbearing son.*]

[37:102] *And when he was old enough to walk with him,* [*he said, 'O my dear son, I see in a dream that I shall sacrifice you. So see what you think.' He said, 'O my father, do whatever you have been commanded. You shall find me, God willing, of the steadfast'*]: when he was travelling the path of moral perfections and psychic virtues with him, God inspired him with the command to sacrifice him by annihilation in Oneness and to surrender to his true Lord, by detaching from the attributes of perfection. He told him of this, and he yielded and surrendered himself by annihilation in His Essence, rather than His Attributes.

[37:103] [*And when they had both submitted, and he had laid him down on his forehead,*

[37:104] *We called to him, 'O Abraham!*

[37:105] *'Verily you have fulfilled the vision.' So do We reward those who are virtuous.*

[37:106] *Indeed, this was indeed a clear test'.*

[37:107] *Then We ransomed him with a mighty sacrifice:*] He ransomed him by means of the Gabriel of the active intellect by sacrificing the noble soul, fattened by knowledge and possessing tremendous character traits and perfect virtues; and it was slaughtered by annihilation in Him, and the Ishmael of the heart was spared by veridical annihilation gifted through ransom from God.

[37:108] [*And We left for him among posterity:*] God left him (may God grant him peace) in the world among people who were short of his station, that he might guide them with his light and be an example to them through his faith and guidance.

[37:109] ['*Peace be upon Abraham!*'

[37:110] *So do We reward those who are virtuous.*

[37:111] *Indeed, he is one of Our faithful servants.*

[37:112] *And We gave him the good tidings of* [*the birth of*] *Isaac a prophet, one of the righteous.*

[37:113] *And We blessed him and Isaac. And among their descendants is he who is virtuous, and he who plainly wrongs his soul.*

[37:114] *And verily We favoured Moses and Aaron,* [37:115] *and We delivered them and their people from the great distress.*

[37:116] *And We helped them so that they became the victors.*

[37:117] *And We gave them the enlightening Book.*

Q. 37:100

[37:118] *And We guided them to the straight path,* [37:119] *and We left for them among posterity*:

[37:120] *'Peace be upon Moses and Aaron!'*

[37:121] *So do We reward the virtuous.*

[37:122] *Indeed, both were among Our faithful servants.*

[37:123] *And indeed Elias was one of the messengers,* [37:124] *when he said to his people, 'Will you not fear [God]?*

[37:125] *'Do you call on Baal and abandon the Best of Creators,* [37:126] *God, your Lord, and the Lord of your forefathers?'*

[37:127] *But they denied him. So they will indeed be arraigned*—[37:128] *[all] except God's delivered servants.*

[37:129] *And We left for him among posterity:*

[37:130] *'Peace be upon Elias!'*

[37:131] *So do We reward the virtuous.*

[37:132] *Indeed, he is one of Our faithful servants.*

[37:133] *And indeed Lot was one of the messengers,* [37:134] *when We delivered him together with all his family,* [37:135] *except an old woman among those who stayed behind.*

Q. 37:118

[37:136] *Then We destroyed [all] the others.*

[37:137] *And indeed you pass by them, [both] in the morning,* [37:138] *and at night: will you not then understand?]*

[37:139] *And indeed* the Jonah of the heart *was one of the messengers* sent to the flawed folk, veiled by the material, in thrall to Satan, engaged in open tyranny, [37:140] *when he fled to the [laden] ship* of the body, laden with the bodily faculties and their sensory perfections, floating on the sea of primordial matter.

[37:141] *Then he drew lots* with them for physical desires and their election by intellectual thoughts, *and was of those rejected*, veiled and led into error by arguments and proofs of certitude; for they were materialists and people of the sea and the ship, while he was a holy man removed from the folk of the divine presence, a runaway slave who had fled from his Master to the ship and hurled himself into destruction. And so he was cast into the sea.

[37:142] *Then the whale* of the womb *swallowed him* as an ovary swallows a sperm, *while he was blameworthy*: deserving of blame for attaching to the garb of the body, which was surely what had led him into that misfortune.

[37:143] *And had he not been one of those who glorify* and extol their Lord, by celebrating His holiness in the state of detachment and proclaiming

Oneness, [37:144] *he would have tarried in its belly* like the rest of the natural and egocentric faculties, trapped in the bellies of the whales of varied bodily images from the primordial natures, *until the day when they are raised*: the day when the detached ones are raised from the resting-places of their bodies, while remaining in his resting-place like the rest of the heedless ones. Or it means the day when his materialistic companions will be raised at the Minor Resurrection.

[37:145] *Then We cast him onto the barren land*, into the wide world by means of his birth, *and he was sick*, weak and beset by material accidents and natural circumstances.

[37:146] *And We made a gourd plant to grow above him*: a plant which does not stand upon a trunk but rather spreads over the ground, and its leaves gave him shade from the overwhelming faculties of the soul. In the exoteric exegeses, it has been said that his body weakened in the belly of the whale so that he became like a newborn baby.

[37:147] *And We sent him*—when he was perfected—*to a [community of a] hundred thousand or more*. And God knows best.

Q. 37:145

38
ṢĀD
SŪRAT ṢĀD

In the Name of God, the Compassionate, the Merciful

[38:1] *Ṣād.* [*By the Qur'ān bearing the Remembrance...!*

[38:2] *Nay, but those who disbelieve dwell in conceit and defiance:*] He swears by the Muḥammadan form (*ṣūra*), and by the total perfection that is remembered with honour and renown as the most complete of all perfections, namely the gathering Qur'ānic intellect which gathers all wisdoms and realities from the complete preparedness which is commensurate with that noble form. It is related from Ibn ʿAbbās, '*Ṣād* is a mountain in Mecca, upon which the Throne of the Compassionate sat for a year.' This is indicated by His Words *in conceit and defiance.*

The omission of the main clause of an oath is not uncommon. In this case, the implied main clause is: It must be followed and yielded to and accepted with submission and humility; *but those* who are veiled from the truth by their I-ness, and so oppose it, dwell in arrogance, wilfulness and defiance, because of how their souls have emerged with their falsehoods in opposition to the truth.

[38:3] [*How many a generation We have destroyed before them, and they cried out when it was no longer the time for escape!*

[38:4] *And they marvel that a warner has come to them from among themselves. And those who disbelieve say, 'This is a sorcerer, a liar.*

[38:5] *'Has he made the gods One God? Without doubt, that is indeed a curious thing.'*

[38:6] *And the council from among them go about, saying, 'Go! And stand by your gods! Without doubt, this is indeed a thing sought.*

[38:7] *'We never heard of this in the latter-day creed. This is surely [nothing] but an invention.*

[38:8] *'Has the Remembrance been revealed to him out of [all of] us?'* Nay, *but they are in doubt concerning My Remembrance. Nay, but they have not yet tasted My chastisement.*

[38:9] *Or do they possess the treasuries of your Lord's mercy, the Mighty, the Bestower?*

[38:10] *Or do they possess the kingdom of the heavens and the earth and whatever is between them? Then let them ascend by the means.*

[38:11] *A routed host [is all that they are], nothing more from among the factions.*

[38:12] *Before them the people of Noah denied, and [so did those of] ʿĀd and Pharaoh, he of the stakes, [38:13] and Thamūd and the people of Lot and the dwellers in the wood—those were the factions.*

[38:14] *Each one did not but deny the messengers. So My retribution was justified.*

[38:15] *And these do not await but a single Cry, for which there will be no revoking.*

[38:16] *And they said, 'Our Lord, hasten on for us the record of our deeds before the Day of Reckoning.']*

Q. 38:9

[38:17] *Bear patiently what they say*: maintain your firmness in upholding Oneness, and meet their persecution with patience in stability. Do not let your soul emerge in response to their persecution by variegation, for you stand with God and are realised through the Real, and you move only by Him. *And remember* the state of your brother, *Our servant*, singled out for Our timeless nurture, *David, the one of fortitude*: the one of strength, stability and mastery in religion, and how he fell from his state of uprightness into variegation. Let not your state be like his in how his soul emerged. He then describes the strength of David's state and his perfection (may God grant him peace): *Indeed, he was a penitent [soul]*, who returned to the Real from his attributes and deeds by annihilation in Him.

[38:18] *Truly We disposed the mountains* of the limbs *to glorify [God] with him* through submission and consistency in obedience at the times of worship: *at the evening* of concealment and the veiling of the sun of the spirit behind the soul, *and at the sunrise* of manifestation and the ascendance of the sun of the spirit over the soul. At both times, his state of worship was not ruled by the alternate rise and fall of resolve and lassitude, because of how perfectly trained his soul and body were for obedience.

[38:19] *And the birds* of the faculties in their entirety, *mustered* together dutifully in the configuration of temperance and allegiance to the paths of Unity, each with their own special glorifications, *each turning to him* and joining his glorifications with their own.

[38:20] *And We strengthened his kingdom* with aid and the gifts of might and

awe, and granted him glory and power, so that his soul was comforted with
the lights of the manifestations of divine power, might, grandeur and glory;
and he was adorned with Our Majestic Attributes, in order that all would
hold him in awe and reverence, and yield to his authority; *and We gave him
wisdom* because he was adorned with Our knowledge, *and decisive speech* and
eloquence to make the edicts plain: that is, practical and discursive wisdom,
gnosis and Divine Law. *Decisive speech* means rhetoric that is determined and
clarifying, pertaining to the Divine Laws. He then describes his variegation
and how his soul emerged with his error, and how the Real corrected him
by rebuking him for his fault and commanding him to repent of it:

[38:21] *Has there come to you the news of the disputants? When they climbed
over the wall of [his] prayer chamber,* [38:22] *[when they entered upon David, and
he was frightened by them. And they said, 'Do not fear two disputants. One of us
has infringed upon the [rights of the] other, so judge justly between us and do not
transgress, and guide us to the right path.'*

[38:23] *'Behold, this brother of mine has ninety-nine ewes, while I have a
single ewe; yet he said, "Entrust it to me," and he overcame me in speech.'*

Q. 38:21

[38:24] *He said, 'He has certainly wronged you by asking for your ewe that
he may add it to his sheep. And indeed many associates infringe upon [the rights
of] one other, except such as believe and perform righteous deeds, but few are they!']*
And David thought—that is, he was certain—*that We had indeed tried him*
with [Bathsheba], the wife of Uriah. *So he sought forgiveness of his Lord* by
renouncing his sin and seeking refuge with Him through spiritual exertion and breaking and taming the soul by disobeying it, *and fell down* by
erasing the attributes of the soul, *bowing* annihilated in the Attributes of
the Real, *and repented* to God by annihilation in His Essence.

[38:25] *So We forgave him that* variegation by covering his attributes
with the light of Our own, *and indeed he has [a station of] nearness with Us*
by veridical existence gifted in the state of subsistence after annihilation,
and a fair return because then he was adorned with Our Attributes rather
than his own I-ness, and so he attached to Us and ruled with Our Divine
Laws in the seat of divine vicegerency:

[38:26] *'O David! We have indeed made you a vicegerent on the earth; therefore, judge justly between people* with the rule of truth, nor your own self,
so that you are just and not tyrannical; *and do not follow desire* by allowing
your soul to emerge and act unjustly, straying from the way of the Real
to the way of Satan, *[that it then lead you astray from the way of God. Indeed,
those who go astray from the way of God—for them there will be a severe chastisement because of their forgetting the Day of Reckoning']*.

[38:27] *And We did not create the heavens and the earth and all that is between them* of creation *in vain*, such that there is no truth in them; but rather as truth veiled by their forms which do not exist independently, such that they could be purely vain. *That is the supposition of [those who disbelieve]*: the ones veiled from the Real by the images of existence. *So woe to the disbelievers from the Fire* of deprivation, veiling and turning about in the flames of nature and I-ness, which is the most terrible torment.

[38:28] Rather, *Shall We treat those who believe* by witnessing His beauty in the images of existence *and perform righteous deeds*—acts which are done for their own sake and connected to the righteousness of the world, emanating from His Names—*like those who cause corruption*: those who are veiled and who act by their souls and their attributes bestial, predatory and satanic deeds, *in the earth* of nature? *Or shall We treat the God-fearing* who are detached from their attributes *like the profligate* who are garbed with egocentric and satanic covers over their deeds?

Q. 38:27

[38:29] *[A Book that We have revealed to you, full of blessing,] that they may contemplate its signs* with intellectual consideration as long as they remain in the station of the soul, so that they shed themselves of their attributes in the pursuit of His, *and that those people of pith*—the people of pure realities detached from the husk of creation—*may remember* the state of the primal covenant and innate faith in Oneness upon detachment.

Then He mentioned the variegation of Solomon and his trial that confirmed his stabilisation and fortification in his straightness and stability:

[38:30] *[And upon David We bestowed Solomon]*—*what an excellent servant!* [This was] in terms of the appropriate preparedness to attain the specific human perfection and the station of prophethood. *Indeed, he was a penitent [soul]*: returning to Me through detachment.

[38:31] *When one evening there was displayed before him*, right before the setting of the sun of the spirit behind the bodily horizon, by the heart's inclination towards the soul and the emergence of its darkness by inclination towards wealth, and the ascendancy of the love and desire for material things, as God says, *Beautified for people is love of lusts—of women, children, stored-up heaps of gold and silver, horses of mark, cattle, and tillage* [Q. 3:14]. Inclination towards worldly treasures and sensory delights, and caprice for natural pleasures and base matters, cause the soul to turn away from the higher direction, and veil the heart from the divine presence. *[When one evening there were displayed before him] the prancing steeds* which he had called to be presented, and with which he was smitten.

[38:32] *He said, 'Indeed, I have loved the love of [worldly] good things*: I have loved wealth *over the remembrance of my Lord,'* for whom I ought to have been engrossed with love, for it befits one such as I to be engrossed with his Lord by remembrance and love. Yet instead of remembering and loving my Lord, I have loved wealth, and so become oblivious to Him. *Until it,* the sun of the spirit, *disappeared [behind the [night's] veil]* because of the veils of the soul.

[38:33] *'Bring them back to me!' Then he set about slashing [their] legs and necks:* he swung his sword around, hobbling some and slaughtering others, breaking the idols of the soul which it worships with its caprice, destroying its control and its faculties, lifting the veil between him and the Real, and asking forgiveness of Him and pledging repentance to Him through detachment and contrition.

[38:34] *And We certainly tried Solomon:* We tested him once more with an even more difficult variegation, namely the casting of the body upon his throne.

Q. 38:33

There are three different interpretations of this [aforementioned verse]. The first is that a son was born to him and the devils plotted to kill the child lest he tame them as his father had. He learned of this and attempted to hide the boy up in the clouds, but suddenly he saw the boy's body cast down upon his throne. With this he realised his error in not relying on his Lord.

The second interpretation is that one day he said, 'Tonight I shall lie with seventy women, each of whom will have a boy who one day will be a knight for God's cause.' Yet he forgot to add, 'God willing.' Then he lay with them all, but none of them became pregnant except for one woman who miscarried. According to these two interpretations, the nature of his trial pertained to love for a child and the soul's emergence by inclination towards it. This may have taken the form of extreme concern to protect and raise the child, and keep it safe from the devils of estimations and imaginations in the clouds of the active intellect, and to nourish it with intellectual wisdom. In all this he relied on the intellect and its object and the governance of its folk to perfect the child, rather than consigning its affair to God and relying on Him for its sake. Therefore, God tried him with the child's death, and he realised his error in his excessive love for other-than-God and the dominance of its folk. Or it may have taken the form of the emergence of the soul through planning, hope and overconfident expectation and assumption, so that he was veiled from faith in Providence by custom and action, and veiled from fate by planning, and thus was oblivious to the Real because of the dominance of the attributes of the soul. Hence, God tried him with a result that was exceptionally far from the outcome he had imagined and expected. He repented and returned to the Real when he realised how his soul had emerged, and he corrected the variegation by pleading for forgiveness and confessing his fault.

The third interpretation is that he invaded Sidon, a town on a peninsula by the sea, and killed its king, a great man, and took his beautiful daughter Jarāda for his wife after she converted to Islam. He loved her greatly, and when he saw how deeply she mourned for her father he commanded the devils to make a statue of him for her. She dressed the statue in his clothes and made trips to visit it every morning and evening with her chamber-maids, and they all prostrated to the statue as they had done to the king during his rule. Solomon's vizier Asaph told him of this, so he broke the statue and rebuked the woman, and then went out alone into the wilderness and made a bed for himself in the dirt, and sat down on it and repented humbly to God. He had an *umm walad* concubine[1] named Amīna, and whenever he went to perform ablutions or lie with a woman he would give her his ring for safekeeping. His kingship was bound to this ring. One day he left it with her and a demon of the sea named Ṣakhr came to her in the image of Solomon and said, 'Amīna, my ring!' He put on the ring and sat on Solomon's throne. When Solomon came back, his appearance had changed and Amīna did not recognise him, and threw him out. He realised that his sin had caught up with him, and so went around the houses begging; but whenever he tried to tell the people that he was the real Solomon, they hurled dust at him and cursed him. Then he went to the fishermen and worked for them for forty days, until the demon flew off and hurled the ring into the ocean, where a fish gobbled it up. Solomon caught the fish and opened its belly to find his ring inside. He put on the ring and fell down prostrate, and his kingdom returned to him. Then he trapped Ṣakhr in a stone jar (*ṣakhra*) and threw him into the sea.

Q. 38:34

If this [latter] tale was true, it would mean that he experienced a strong variegation and was tried with the like of the trials of Jonah and Adam (may God grant them peace). But in fact the tale is one of the fabrications (*mawḍūʿāt*) of the Jewish sages and clerics, like the many similar fables invented by sages, such as the tales of Absāl and Salāmān and others. Whether it is true or not—and God knows best—its interpretation is that Solomon went to the town of the Sidon of the body—a island in the sea of primordial matter—and killed its tyrant king, the evil-enjoining soul,

---

1 A concubine who has born her master a child.

with spiritual exertion in God's cause. Then he took his daughter Jarāda, the imaginative faculty which flies like a locust (*jarāda*) and feasts upon the crops of bodies and all things, stripping them bare (*tujarrid*) by wresting their forms from their matter, though she was fettered by their attachments and grieved over this. She was a great beauty, because of how she adorned and empowered her soul, and the things she imagined through its perceptions. She converted at his hand, yielding to the intellect and renouncing the religion of estimation, and thereby became a thinker. So he chose her for his bride and loved her because she was his only means of attaining perfection. Her grief for her father was her natural inclination towards the soul and her regret at the loss of its desires. His command to the devils to make a statue of her father, and how she dressed it in his clothes, symbolises how the origin of his variegation and trial was that he inclined towards the soul and became deluded by his perfection, becoming engrossed in the desires of the soul before the proper time. The Commander of the Believers said, 'We seek refuge with God from error after guidance.'

Q. 38:34

The obedience of the devils to him represents the subdual of the estimative faculties to him for the restoration of the soul to its first configuration, even if it did not regain its original strength or its life of caprice. This is because he was protected from being veiled, and was granted special nurture. The prostration of Jarāda and her maids to the old king, according to their custom in his kingdom, symbolises how the cognitive faculty and all the other bodily faculties worship the soul and seek to obey, serve and gratify it according to their custom in the original time of ignorance. How Asaph told Solomon of this represents how the intellect alerts the heart to its variegation when its death is nigh. The breaking of the idol and the rebuke of the woman represent his regret and repentance from that state, and how he took refuge with God and broke his soul with spiritual discipline. How he went out alone into the wilderness represents his detachment from the body at the fall of its faculties. The way he made a bed in the dirt and sat in it represents how his temperament altered and became sullied with adulterants, alongside the remnant of bodily attachment.

The *umm walad* concubine Amīna represents bodily nature, the mother of the egocentric faculties with whom he left the signet ring of his body when he engaged with natural matters and essential bodily functions, such as entering the privy, lying with a woman and the like. She was the one trusted (*amīna*) to protect it. The fact that his kingship was bound to the

233

ring symbolises how his spiritual and formal perfection depended on the body. The devil who came to her and took the ring from her represents elemental earthly nature, the master of the sea of lower primordial matter. He was named Ṣakhr ('rock') because he inclined towards the lower direction and remained stuck there like a heavy rock. His donning of the ring represents how he took it upon himself by joining it to him. His sitting on Solomon's throne refers to how God cast down his dead body upon his place and the seat of his power, as He says, *And We cast upon his throne a [lifeless] body.* The way Solomon's appearance changed represents the subsistence of corporeal configurations and primordial effects with the remnants of the egocentric attributes upon him after the bodily parting, and his change from the innate luminous nature and the original configuration. The way he went to Amīna to request the ring represents his inclination towards the body and his love and yearning for it. Her rejection and banishment of him represents how bodily nature does not accept life, because of the corruption of temperament.

The way he went around the houses begging represents his inclination towards corporeal desires and pleasures, and his attraction to them by yearning for egocentric configurations. The way they threw dust in his face and cursed him represents how he was deprived of those desires and pleasures, and lacked the means to attain those lusts. The way he went to the fishermen and served them represents inclination towards the vessel of the womb, which attaches to the sperm. The way he spent forty days working for the fishermen represents the words of the Prophet (may God grant him peace), quoting his Lord: 'I mixed the clay of Adam for forty days with My hand.'

The way the devil flew away represents the swiftness of elemental nature in composition. The way he threw the ring into the sea represents how the bodily composition vanishes in the sea of primordial matter. The fish swallowing the ring represents how the womb is attracted to the bodily matter of the sperm. The way the fish ended up in Solomon's hand represents his attachment to it in the womb, and his dominance over the womb by being nourished by it and controlling it. How he opened its belly, removed the ring from it and put it on his finger represents how the womb opened and the body came out of it. The way he put it on, fell down prostrate and received back his kingdom represents how he attained perfection through it, by yielding to God's command and becoming annihilated in Him. The way he put Ṣakhr in a stone jar and threw him into the sea represents how earthly nature remained as it was, confined within matter and inescapably bound by weight, inclining towards the lower direction in the sea of primordial matter as long as bodily nature was present. He left him there unable to overcome Amīna again and take the ring from her. *Then he repented* after all that to God with detachment and self-purification.

[38:35] *He said, 'My Lord, forgive me* for the sins of my attachments and configurations which covered my light and darkened and sullied my purity, with Your light; *and grant me a kingdom that shall not belong to anyone after me*: a perfection that befits my preparedness and behoves my ipseity, and would not be right for anyone but me because it is mine alone and is the farthest extent that can be reached. *Indeed, You are the Bestower'* of all preparednesses and every perfection I have requested, as He says, *And He gives you of all that you ask of Him* [Q. 14:34].

[38:36] *So We disposed for him the wind* of caprice, *which blew softly*, willingly, obediently and dutifully without struggling, or attempting to dominate, *at his command wherever he intended.*

[38:37] *And the devils*, the inner jinn of the egocentric faculties, *every builder* skilled in geometry and able to construct the edifices of practical wisdoms and the foundations of just laws (*qawānīn*), *and diver* in the seas of the holy and primordial realms, who brings out the pearls of universal and particular meanings and practical and discursive wisdoms.

[38:38] *And others too* of the egocentric and natural faculties, *bounded together in fetters* of the Divine Law and shackles of intellectual and outward human discipline from the workers who are disposed to work, and the profligate and sinners who are bound in chains.

[38:39] *'This is Our gift*, pure and simple. *So bestow or withhold*: unleash your will and choose whether to tie or untie, give or withhold, upon complete perfection and free power of bestowal, which is the existence granted in the state of subsistence after annihilation, however you see fit, *without any reckoning'* over you, for you exist through Us and choose by Our choosing, fully realised of Our Essence and Our Attributes. This is the meaning of His Words:

[38:40] *And indeed he has [a station of] nearness with Us and a fair resort.*

[38:41] *And mention also Our servant Job*: how We tried him when his soul emerged with variegation, upon his being pleased with his great wealth; or when he indulged the disbeliever of the soul in allowing it to emerge and failing to nourish it with spiritual discipline and exertion, because the livestock of his natural faculties were in the area. Alternatively, it was because he did not help the oppressed person of the discursive intellect

235

and the holy faculties, according to the differing narrations in the exoteric commentaries regarding the cause of his trial. One could even combine all of these narrations together. The nature of his trial was sickness and disease: he was infested with the worms of the natural faculties, and fell down upon the bed of the body when nothing was left of him but the heart and the tongue, meaning his original disposition and preparedness, and not any of the other perfections he had attained. *When he called out to his Lord* with the tongue of desperation and neediness in the core of preparedness, *'Indeed, Satan has afflicted me with hardship and suffering!'* [This means:] 'The estimative faculty has overcome me with its delusions, and this sickness has caused me suffering in the form of evil character traits and veiling.'

Q. 38:42

[38:42] *'Stamp your foot*: strike with your strength which is nearest the earth of the body, the aspect of the practical intellect that is called 'the breast of the earth of your body', and two springs of practical and discursive wisdom will gush forth. *This is a cool bath*, which is practical wisdom that purifies the soul and washes away the pollutants of natures, healing the ailments of vices, [by being] cool, relaxing and soothing, *and a drink,'* which is discursive wisdom, meaning the knowledge that bestows certitude and protects against the sickness of ignorance and debilitating illness that prevents wayfaring. Bathe and drink from it and by God's leave your inner and outer being will be healed and you will become fit and strong.

[38:43] *And We gave him [back] his family*: it is said that he had seven sons and seven daughters and that during his trial the house collapsed on them, killing them all. Then God revived them when the trial was over and returned the wealth of perfections to him. This symbolises how the spiritual and egocentric elements are ruined by variegation and the ascendance of bodily nature, reaching the point in the greater variegation where the body is ruined and infested with worms, until nothing remains of it but the heart and the tongue of innate preparedness. Thereafter God revived them upon repentance and contrition and returned them to health and strength, and the sickness and disease were cured by means of the drinking and bathing from the two springs; *along with others like them* by the acquisition of virtuous dispositions, praiseworthy traits and beautiful attributes, until the natural egocentric faculties became spiritual too at the second creation and the fashioning of the annihilated bodily faculties, *as a mercy from us* by the emanation of the perfections his preparedness requested, *and a reminder to people of pith*: the people of realities detached from the husks of corporeal matter who understand by the heart's hearing, so that they can consider their states in light of his, and recall the knowledge stored in their innate disposition.

[38:44] *And [We said to him], 'Take in your hand a bunch of twigs, [and smite therewith]*: it is said that during his illness he swore that he would strike his wife a hundred times if he recovered. There are different narrations regarding the reason for this oath. Some said that she was tardy when running an errand, while others argued that Satan tempted her to prostrate to him so that her lost wealth would be returned. It has also been said that she sold two locks of her hair, which Job had used to help pull himself up when he stood, in exchange for two pieces of bread; and others said that she had suggested to him that he drink wine. All of these symbolise the aforementioned variegation by the emergence of the soul, which is tardy and lazy in acts of worship; obedient to the Satan of estimation and submissive to it when desiring pleasures; neglectful of the support the heart requires to pull itself up from the bed of the body, rejecting the configurations that inspire it to seek beneficial knowledge and righteous deeds, and replacing them with paltry pleasures that are simple to acquire, in order to indulge in them or exalt in them for the soul's gratification; and which drinks the wine of caprice and inclines to that which impairs the intellect.

Q. 38:44

His oath symbolises his pledge to challenge his soul and engage in difficult spiritual disciplines and painful exertions. Or it symbolises how he concentrated in his preparedness on his love for detachment and self-purification by discipline, and his resolve to tame his soul with sublime character traits and etiquettes by engaging in painful challenges by the dictate of the primordial covenant and the rule of the pledge of innate disposition.

His grasping of the twigs and use of them to strike symbolises indulgence and the path of lenience and mercy, which is an aspect of balanced character; it means being confined to moderation and temperance in discipline and challenges, because of the purity of preparedness and the nobility of the soul and the dignity of its substance, rather than treating it with excessive hardship. He (may God bless him and grant him peace) said, 'I was sent with the way of the *ḥanīf*, which is tolerant and lenient.'

'And do not break [your] oath' by completely neglecting discipline, betraying the resolve of your pursuit of perfection and breaking your innate oath. *Truly We found him to be steadfast* in his trial and pursuit of perfection, so We had mercy on him. Not everyone who seeks is steadfast. *What an excellent servant! [Indeed, he was a penitent [soul]]* who returned to God with detachment, erasure and annihilation.

[38:45] *And mention [also] Our servants [Abraham, and Isaac and Jacob,]* who were singled out from the folk of divine nurture—*men of fortitude and insight:*[1] that is, action and knowledge, for the former pertains to hands, the latter to sight and vision. They were the masters of practical and discursive perfections.

[38:46] *Indeed, We purified them [with an exclusive [thought]]*: We cleansed them from the pollutants of the soul's attributes and the turbidity of I-ness, and made them solely for Us with true love, so that they had no concern for any but Us, and did not incline towards others with ephemeral conditional love, neither towards themselves nor towards any other, because of a special unadulterated trait instilled in them, namely *the remembrance of the Abode*: the eternal original home. We singled them out exclusively for Ourselves because of how they remembered the holy realm and turned away from the source of impurity, seeking Our lights and utterly disregarding the lower world and its darkness.

Q. 38:45

[38:47] *And indeed in Our sight*, in the presence of Unity, *they are of the elect* whom We have chosen to be near Us from among their species, *the excellent* who are purified from the pollutants of evil, possibility, nonbeing and temporality.

[38:48] *[And mention [also] Our servants Ishmael, and Elisha, and Dhū al-Kifl. Each was among the excellent.]*

[38:49] *This is a remembrance*: this is a special mention of the foremost of God's folk who have been singled out for nurture; *and indeed for the God-fearing* who are detached from the attributes of their souls, though they have not yet reached the carpet of nearness and nobility where they look upon Him in the garden of the spirit by witnessing, *there will truly be a fair return* in the station of the heart in the garden of the Attributes.

[38:50] *Gardens of Eden*—perpetual—*whose gates are [flung] open for them* with manifestations, so that they may enter through the paths of virtues and perfections.

[38:51] *Reclining therein* on the couches of stations; *therein they call for plenteous fruit* of delicious unveilings *and drink* of descriptive love.

[38:52] *And with them [there] will be maidens of restrained glances*—the holy brides and cosmic and human souls on their levels—*of a like age*: of an equal level.

[38:53] *['This is what you are promised for] the Day of Reckoning*: for the

---

1 *Ulū al-aydī wa'l-abṣār*, literally 'people of hands and sights'.

time of your recompense from the Divine Attributes, according to how far you are annihilated from human attributes.

[38:54] [*'This is indeed Our provision,*] *which will never be exhausted'* because it is not material and therefore cannot run out.

[38:55] *That* discourse on the description of Paradise and its inhabitants [*is so*]; *but for the insolent,* who transgress their bounds because of the attributes of the soul and its emergence, and therefore vie with the Real for His ascendancy and grandeur by their own desire for ascendancy and pride, *there will surely be an evil* [*place of*] *return* to the hell of the nature of effects and the fires of the darkness of primordial matter.

[38:56] [*Hell,*] *which they will enter* and suffer the loss of pleasures and the finding of torments; [*an evil resting place!*]

[38:57] *This, let them then taste it: burning hot water* of caprice and ignorance, *and pus* of darkened configurations and corporeal pollutants.

[38:58] *And other* [*kinds* [*of torment*] *resembling it*] of its type, or other experiences like it from the other forms of torment, degradation and deprivation, [*in pairs*].

Q. 38:54

[38:59] *'This is a horde* of your followers and fellows, the folk of evil natures and varied vices, *about to plunge with you'* into the narrow pits of humiliation and degradation. The insolent ones will say, *'No welcome* [*is there*] *for them* [*here*], due to the severity of their torment, and how they are squeezed together but disgusted by one another because of their vile appearance and evil condition. [*They will indeed roast in the Fire.'*]

[38:60] *They,* the followers, *say, 'Nay, but for you* [*there is*] *no welcome* because of your multiplied torment and the stubbornness of your configurations. *You prepared this for us* by misguiding us and goading us on. [*So what an evil abode!'*] These dialogues might be conducted with real speech, or they might be 'utterances of the state' (*lisān al-ḥāl*).

[38:61] [*They say, 'Our Lord, whoever prepared this for us, give him double his chastisement in the Fire!'*]

[38:62] *And they say, 'What is the matter with us that we do not see* [*here*] *people whom we used to count among the wicked?*

[38:63] *'Did we treat them mockingly?*] The ones they mocked were the poor folk who upheld God's Oneness and the paupers who attained realisation, to whom the evil folk were enemies in this world, because of how they refused to let them tempt them towards anything but God, or to turn away from their goals and abandon their traditions and the objects of their pursuit. *Or have* [*our*] *eyes missed them* [*here*]?' They did not see them because they were veiled by material coverings and natural matters from their true detached realities and their holy essences, just as they were veiled by common customs and ignorant ways from their paths. This is if we take the word *Or* here to be discontinuous.

[38:64] [*Indeed, that is true: the wrangling of the inhabitants of the Fire:*] the reason the wrangling of the inhabitants of Hell is true is that they are in a realm of opposition and a place of obstinacy, caught in the fetters of differing natures and the hands of conflicting faculties, contradictory caprices and mutually-exclusive inclinations.

[38:65] [*Say: 'I am only a warner:*] I do not call you to myself, nor do I have the power to guide you, for I am annihilated to myself and my power. I warn through God and His Attributes. *And there is no god* in existence *except God, the One* in His Essence, *the All-Compelling* Who overpowers all other things by annihilating them in His Unity.

Q. 38:64

[38:66] *'Lord [of the heavens and the earth and all that is between them*: the Lord] of all things Who lords over them in the presence of His Oneness with one of His Names; *the Mighty* Who overcomes the veiled one with His power, and torments him with the very thing that veils him in the covers of His majesty, because he deserves the emanations of lordship from the presence of the All-Compelling Avenger and the powers of the veiled torment; *the Forgiving'* Who conceals the darkness of the soul's attributes with the light of the manifestations of His beauty for those in whom remain the light of their innate disposition, so that they receive the light of forgiveness because there is still a trace of His luminousness in them.

[38:67] *Say: 'It*—my warning to you about the Oneness of Essence and Attribute—*is a tremendous tiding* [38:68] *from which you are turning away.*

[38:69] [*'I had no knowledge of the High Council when they disputed:*] he argues for the authenticity of his prophethood by citing his knowledge of the dispute of the High Council, which he could not have learned by any means other than revelation. He also makes a distinction between the dispute of the High Council and the dispute of the inhabitants of Hell, by saying about the latter that it is indeed true, while about the dispute of the High Council He says *when they disputed*, because the former is a true dispute that will never be resolved, while the latter was a passing dispute arising from their lack of knowledge of the perfection of Adam (may God grant him peace), which was above their own. Thus, it was resolved when they said, *Glory be to You! We know not except what You have taught us* [Q. 2:32], and when He said, *Did I not tell you that I know the Unseen in the heavens and the earth?* [Q. 2:33]. We commented on the interpretation of this story in [*sūrat*] al-Baqara [Q. 2].

[38:70] [*'It is revealed to me only that I may be a plain warner.'*

[38:71] *When your Lord said to the angels, 'Indeed, I am about to create a human being out of clay.*

[38:72] *'So when I have proportioned him, and breathed in him My spirit, then fall down in prostration before him!'*

[38:73] *Thereat the angels prostrated, all of them together,* [38:74] *except Iblīs:*] their prostration to Adam (may God grant him peace) was an expression of their respect, submission and humbleness before him at the reveal of his perfection, which was above their own. The refusal and pride of Iblīs symbolises how the Satan of estimation refuses to yield and submit, as a consequence of being veiled from its reality because of how it is trapped in matter, which is why He says *he was one of the disbelievers.*

[38:75] [*He said, 'O Iblīs, what prevents you from prostrating before that which*] *I have created with My own hands?* I created him with My Attributes of beauty and majesty, compulsion and kindness, and all My other complimentary Names that fall beneath My Attributes of compelling power and love, so that he would be made with this divine union (*al-jamʿiyya al-ilāhiyya*) in the Unitary Presence. This is not the case for the High Council: if one of them was created by the Attribute of compulsion, he is unable to be kind, and vice versa. *Are you being arrogant?* Have you chosen to be prideful and disdainful, *or are you of the exalted?* Are you higher than him and greater in rank?

[38:76] [*He said, 'I am better than him. You created me from fire and You created him from clay':*] the veiled one replied, 'Indeed, I am higher than him because of my origin,' since he was unaware of his detached reality and only saw his humanity. Without doubt, the animal fire spirit from which the Accursed was created is nobler than dense physical matter; but he was veiled from the divine union and the spiritual subtlety, and so refused to yield and held to his analogy, and disobeyed God's command to prostrate to humankind.

[38:77] [*He said, 'Then begone hence, for you are indeed accursed.*

[38:78] *'And indeed My curse shall be on you until the Day of Judgement.'*

[38:79] *He said, 'My Lord, then reprieve me until the day when they will be raised.'*

[38:80] *He said, 'Then you will indeed be among the reprieved* [38:81] *until the day of the known time':*] to be cursed means to be distanced from the holy presence, which is free of all base matter, and immersed in natural coverings and veiled by beings of primordial matter. This is why the curse was set until the Day of Judgement and ordained to come to an end then, since the time of the Resurrection is when the spirit is detached from the body and its matter. At that time he will have no further power over humankind, and he will yield and submit to him at the known time, which is the Major Resurrection, when he will no longer be cursed. He (may God grant him peace) said, 'My devil submitted at my hand.' His reprieve for temptation and his curse will end then.

[38:82] [*He said, 'Now, by Your might, I shall surely pervert them all,* [38:83] *except those servants of Yours among them who will be saved':*] those whom God chose for Himself, the folk of divine nurture whom He purified from the turbidity of psychic pollutants and the veils of humanity and I-ness, and cleansed their disposition from the adulterant of the darkness of creation, they cannot be perverted at all at the beginning, so how could they be at the end? Now, although the curse will be lifted by his submission and surrender at that time, he will still have to go to

Q. 38:82

Hell, because he adheres to primordial nature and corporeal matter and can never be detached. He can ascend to the heaven of the intellect and the spiritual horizons to insinuate and cast misgivings, and reach Adam in the garden of the soul to tempt him, but he will always be cast out: *Then begone hence, for you are indeed accursed* [Q. 38:77]. The reason he swore by God's might was that his situation was caused by his own claim to might, veiled as he was by the coverings of majesty and the curtains of pride. But he was kept from the reach of Iblīs because he was annihilated in the clouds of lights.

[38:84] [*He said, 'So the truth is—and the truth I [always] speak—*[38:85] *I shall assuredly fill Hell with you and with whoever of them follows you, all together':*] in return, God swore by the firm necessary truth, which never changes, that He would fill Hell with him and his followers because of that claim to might. They are doomed to remain in Hell perpetually and eternally in the same state, never changing or replacing, because detachment is by essence while attachment is by nature; and so this was dictated by essences, entities and realities in pre-eternity and is not a passing state that could ever end.

[38:86] *Say: 'I do not ask of you, in return for this, any reward:* I have no ulterior motive for this, for the utterances of the one who is perfected and realised in the Real exist for their own sake and are not occasioned by any outside motive; *nor am I an impostor*: a pretender who lays claim to perfections and manifests his soul and its attributes, claiming God's perfections as his own. Rather, I have become annihilated to my soul and its attributes, and God speaks with my voice.

[38:87] [*'It is only a reminder for all worlds.*]

[38:88] *'And you will assuredly come to know its tiding in [due] time'*: at the Minor or Major Resurrection, when its interpretation will become clear.

Q. 38:87

39
THE TROOPS
SŪRAT AL-ZUMAR

In the Name of God, the Compassionate, the Merciful

[39:1] *The revelation of the Book* of the discriminating intellect, by its manifestation upon you from the Unseen of Unseens, *is from God* and His Unitary Presence, *the Mighty* veiled by the coverings of majesty from the Unseen of His Unseen, *the Wise* Master of the wisdom hidden there and emergent in the levels of revelations.

[39:2] [*Indeed, We have revealed to you the Book*] *with the truth*: We revealed it with the manifestation of the truth in you after it was hidden. *So worship God*: single Him out for essential worship when He manifests to you with His Essence and none of His creatures remain, *devoting your religion purely to Him*: pure from the adulterants of otherness and duality. Worship Him through His witnessing of His own Essence, and the vision of the manifestations of His Attributes through His eyes, and the recitation of His Words through Him. With this, your wayfaring will be God's wayfaring, and your religion will be God's religion, and your disposition will be God's Essence.

[39:3] *Surely to God belongs pure religion*: pure from the adulterants of otherness and duality, so that you possess nothing because you are totally annihilated in Him, whereby you have no essence, no attribute, no act, no religion. Otherwise, the religion will not be truly pure, nor belong to God alone. *And those who* [*take besides Him patrons* [*say*], '*We only worship them so that they may bring us near to God*': they] became veiled by multiplicity from Unity, and took another as a patron with love in order to draw nearer to God by his mediation. *God will indeed judge between them* when their objects of worship are resurrected alongside them, *concerning that about which they differ* regarding their attributes, words and deeds. Each of them will be put with those whom they took as patrons, worshipper along with worshipped, and those who led astray will enter Hell along with those they misguided, just as those who guided to the truth will enter Paradise along with those they guided. Each will be requited according to his dominant attribute, what he stood by and what veiled him, which differs for each of them. *Truly God does not guide* to salvation and the world of light and manifestations of the Attributes and the Essence *one who is a liar, a disbeliever*, because of how far they are from Him and how they are veiled by the darkness of vices and the soul's attributes from the light, and how they refuse to accept it.

[39:4] [*Had God wanted to take a son, He could have chosen from what He has created whatever He wished.*] *Glory be to Him!* Declare Him transcendently above likeness, type and the taking of a son. Unity is necessary for His Essence, and He overwhelms all other things by His Unity; He has no likeness in existence, so how could there be one in necessity? [*He is God, the One, the All-Compelling.*]

[39:5] *He created the heavens and the earth with the truth*: by His manifestation in their loci and His veiling by their forms, directing all by His power and act. [*He turns the night into day, and turns the day into night,*] *and He has disposed the sun and the moon,* [*each running for an appointed term*] by His authority and dominion, so that nothing but Him possesses Essence, Attribute or act. This is proof of His Unity. *Verily it is He Who is the Mighty*: the All-Powerful Who compels all things with the authority of His compulsion, *the Forgiving* Who covers them with the light of His Essence and Attributes so that nothing remains alongside Him. Or the Mighty Untouchable One veiled from His creation by the forms of His creations, and the Forgiving Who covers for whom He chooses the sins of their existence and attributes by manifesting to them with His own.

[39:6] *He created you from a single soul*: the true Adam, namely the universal rational soul from which branched the particular souls; *then made from it its mate* the animal soul; *and He sent down for you* [*eight kinds of cattle*], because their forms were recorded in the Preserved Tablet, as was the descent of everything in the world of witnessing from the world of the Unseen. [*He creates you in your mothers' wombs,*] *creation after creation*: He creates you in the stages of creation through which you pass, *in a threefold darkness* from corporeal nature and the vegetative and animal soul. *That* Creator of your potential forms *is* [*God, your Lord*], Who directs by His power and disposes by His domination and authority, giving rise to multiplicity from His Unity by His Names and Attributes, sending down what He decreed and ordained by His acts. He is the Essence characterised by all His Attributes,

Q. 39:4

and He lords over you with His Names. *To Him belongs the kingdom* wherein He directs by His acts. *There is no god except Him* in existence. *Why, then, are you being turned away* from worshipping Him, worshipping others instead though they do not exist?

[39:7] *If you are ungrateful* and veiled by your own attributes and essences, *truly God* [*is Independent of you* and] does not need your essences and attributes for His manifestation and perfection, since in reality they are annihilated and would be nothing without Him, and He could not possibly need them. He is the Manifest by His Essence to His Essence, and the Hidden by His reality, and the Witness to His perfection by His sight. *Yet He does not approve* [*of ingratitude*, which means] veiling, *for His servants*, since it is the cause of their ruin and their fall into the captivity of the Hell-keeper Mālik and his attendant angels; and so that approval cannot attach to them, nor can they accept His light and enter Paradise. *And if you give thanks* by witnessing His favours and using them in His service, in order that you become prepared to receive His emanation, *He will approve of it for you* by manifesting His Attributes, so that you can adopt them and reach the station of approval, and enter Paradise. [*And no burdened soul shall bear the burden of another*:] ingratitude will harm no one but you, and gratitude will benefit no one but you. [*Then to your Lord will be your return, whereat He will inform you of what you used to do. Indeed, He is Knower of what is in the breasts.*]

[39:8] *And when distress befalls a person, he supplicates his Lord, turning to Him penitently. Then, when He bestows on him a grace from Himself, he forgets Him Whom he had supplicated before and sets up equals with God, that he may lead* [*others*] *astray from His way: 'Revel in your ingratitude for a while. You shall indeed be among the folk of the Fire.'*]

[39:9] Is this veiled ingrate better, *Or is he who devotes himself* [*in the watches of the night*], obedient in the station of the soul and the moments of the darkness of its attributes, *prostrating* by the annihilation of acts and Attributes, [*and standing*] by obedience and submission when the soul emerges with its attributes and acts, *apprehensive* [*of the* [*eventuality of the*] *Hereafter, and hoping for the mercy of his Lord*]? The wayfarer in the station of the soul cannot disengage from fear and hope. *Say: 'Are those* [*who know*] *equal* [*with those who do not know*]?' They are obviously not equal. The implication of this is that the obedient one in the station of the soul is the one who knows, while the ingrate is ignorant. The [reason for the superiority of the] first is because knowledge is what becomes deeply rooted in the heart and firmly established by its roots in the soul, so that its owner cannot contravene it; it takes control of the flesh and blood, and its effects manifest in the limbs, so that none of them contradict its dictate. As for that information which is merely held in the sphere of the intellect and the imagination, such that the soul can ignore it and disregard its dictate, it is not truly knowledge but rather a conceptual matter and an accidental imagination. If he really had knowledge, he would not be veiled by others from the Real. *Only people of pith*, whose minds are purified from the husks of imagination and estimation, *remember* and take heed of this remembrance, so that they can realise firm knowledge that takes effect on the outer being. As for those with minds tainted by estimation, they do not remember nor attain realisation of this knowledge, nor do they comprehend it, but merely babble about it for a moment before it departs them.

[39:10] *Say: 'O servants of Mine* singled out by Me as folk of My nurture, *who believe* with practical faith, *fear your Lord*: by erasing your attributes. *For those who are virtuous*, who adopt the Divine Attributes and worship Him through witnessing, *in this world there will be good*: whose nature cannot be comprehended until the Hereafter, namely the witnessing of the eternal countenance and its blessed beauty. *And God's earth [is vast]*: the tranquil soul—singled out by God because of its dutifulness to Him, its acceptance of His light and its tranquillity with Him—is an essence vast through its certitude which cannot be restrained by anything, nor does it languor in the confines of customs, norms or the dictate of any but the Real. *Truly the steadfast*, who were patient with God through the annihilation of their attributes, deeds and conduct in Him and traversing the stages of the soul made vast by certitude, *will be paid their reward* of the gardens of the Attributes *in full without any reckoning*. This is due to the fact that the reward paid in full according to deeds in the station of the soul commensurate with deeds in the garden of the soul is finite, because it is an instance of effects which are confined to matter, while the reward which is paid in full according to sublime character traits and states is infinite, because it is an instance of the manifestations of the Attributes in the garden of the heart and the realm of the holy, detached from matter.

Q. 39:10

[39:11] *[Say: 'Indeed, I have been commanded to worship God]* devoting *[my]* *religion purely to Him* without regard for any other, and journeying with the soul.

[39:12] *'And I have been commanded to be the first*, the foremost, *of those who submit'* and surrender their beings to God by annihilation in Him, and their leader in the first row, journeying to God, annihilated from the soul and its attributes.

KĀSHĀNĪ

[39:13] *Say: 'Indeed, should I disobey my Lord* by falling short of sincerity and paying regard to others, *I fear the chastisement of a tremendous day'* of veiling, deprivation and distance.

[39:14] *Say: 'God [alone] I worship, devoting [my] religion purely to Him* from the adulterants of I-ness and duality.

[39:15] [*'So worship whatever you wish besides Him'.*] *Say: 'Indeed, the losers* in reality—the sufferers of total loss—*are those* who stood with other-than-God and were veiled from the Real, *who [will] have lost their souls and their families [on the Day of Resurrection]*: by the ruining of souls and the squandering of families, which are the holy substances that attached to them and associated with them in their spiritual world, because they were veiled from them by primordial darknesses. *Truly that is the [manifest,] true, open, obvious loss!'*

Q. 39:13

[39:16] *Above them they will have canopies of fire, and beneath them [they will have [similar] canopies*, because of their immersion in primordial matter and their residence in the depths of the pit of dark nature. Above them are levels of natures, and below them are other levels, and they are in the depths of them. [*That is what God frightens His servants with: 'So, O servants of Mine, fear Me!'*]

[39:17] *As for those who steer clear [of the worship of false deities]*—the worship of other-than-God—*and turn penitently to God* with pure adherence to Oneness, *there are good tidings for them* of the meeting [with Him]. *So give [such] good tidings to My servants* who were chosen for My nurture, [39:18] *who listen to the words [of God]*, such as strict rulings and dispensations, obligations and recommendations, whether they be the words of the Real or others, *and follow the best [sense] of it*, such as the strict rather than the dispensation, the obligation rather than the recommendation, and only those words which are true and no others. *Those—they are the ones whom God has guided* to Him by the light of original guidance; *and those—they are the people of pith* who can differentiate between words by their detached piths, and receive the true meanings and no others.

[39:19] *He against whom the word of chastisement has been fulfilled—[will you deliver one who is in the Fire]?* Are their affairs in your hands, such that you could save one who has been destined for damnation? He cannot be saved at all.

[39:20] *But as for those who fear their Lord* by their deeds, attributes and essences with detachment (*tajrīd*) and seclusion (*tafrīd*)—[namely] the folk of faith in Oneness (*tawḥīd*)—*for them there will be lofty abodes with [other] lofty abodes built above them*: stations and states each above the

248

other, such as reliance through the annihilation of the acts, above which is contentment through the annihilation of the Attributes, above which is annihilation in the Essence, *with rivers* of the knowledge of unveilings *flowing beneath them*—[*a promise of God. God does not fail the tryst.*

[39:21] *Have you not seen that*] *God sends down water* of knowledge *from the heaven* of the spirit, *then conducts it as springs* of wisdoms in the grounds of souls, according to their levels of preparedness? *Then with it He brings forth crops* of deeds and character traits *of diverse* [*hues*, meaning] kinds, according to the differing faculties and limbs. *Then they wither* and are cut-off from their roots by the lights of manifestations, *and you see them turning yellow* as they fade away and disappear with the annihilation of the roots on which they stand, which are the faculties, souls and hearts. *Then He turns them into chaff* by removing them, breaking them and crumbing them when His Attributes manifest and become stable. *Truly in that there is a reminder for people of* [pith], realities detached from the husks of I-ness.

[39:22] *Is* [*there a comparison with*] *he whose breast God has opened to Islam by His light* in the state of subsistence after annihilation, and whose heart He has cleansed with the gift of veridical existence, so that his breast expands to accommodate the Real and creation without being veiled by either from the other, hence he witnesses differentiation in the heart of Unity and Oneness in the heart of multiplicity? [This is so as] Islam means annihilation in God and the surrendering of one's being to Him. In other words, is he whose breast God has expanded for him to surrender his being in the state of annihilation, *so that he follows a light from his Lord*, with which he sees Him, [*like he who disbelieves*]? *So woe to those whose hearts have been hardened against* the acceptance of *the remembrance of God*, because of their intense attraction to bodily pleasures and their disregard for holy perfections. *Such are in manifest error*: astray from the path of the Real.

Q. 39:21

[39:23] [*God has revealed the best of discourses: a Book,*] *consimilar* in truth and veracity, *in oft-repeated phrases* to be revealed to you in the station of the heart before and after annihilation, so that it is repeated with respect to the Real and to creation. Sometimes the Real recites it, and sometimes creation recites it; *whereat quiver the skins of* [*those who fear their Lord*]: the folk of God-fearing from those who know God, because they react to it by the luminous configurations that visit the heart and affect the body; *then their skins and their hearts* and their limbs *soften* with surrender, peace and tranquillity *to the remembrance of God* with illuminations of certitude. *That is God's guidance, by which He guides whomever He wishes* of the folk of His nurture; *and whomever God leads astray*, by veiling him from the light so that he does not understand His Words or see their meanings, *for him there is no guide.*

[39:24] *Is he who will be fending off with his face the awful chastisement,* though it is the noblest part of the body, because the rest of his limbs will be restrained by configurations so that he is unable to control them, and chained with fetters so that he cannot use them to defend himself or lift himself, [*on the Day of Resurrection*]—is he akin to the one who is safe from this chastisement? [*And it will be said to the wrongdoers, 'Taste* [*now*] *what you used to earn.'*

[39:25] *Those who were before them denied, and so the chastisement came on them whence they were not aware.*

[39:26] *Thus, God made them taste disgrace in the life of this world. And the chastisement of the Hereafter will surely be greater, had they known.*

[39:27] *And verily We have struck for people in this Qur'ān every* [*kind of*] *similitude, that perhaps they may remember:*

Q. 39:24

[39:28] *An Arabic Qur'ān without any deviation, that perhaps they may guard themselves.*

[39:29] *God strikes*] *a similitude* for the doctrine of Oneness and idolatry: [firstly,] *a person shared by several* [*masters*]*, quarrelling* with poor character traits so that they never come to terms about anything: one of them sends him off on an errand while another forbids him from going; one pulls him in one direction and another in the other, all arguing and jostling. This is the description of the one who allows the attracting attributes of his soul to overcome him, in which he is veiled by contradictory multiplicity, so that he dwells in total confusion, his resolve fractured and his heart unbalanced. [Secondly, in contrast to] this [latter] man: *and a person belonging exclusively to one person* who only sends him in one direction. This is the likeness of the one who upholds Oneness so that his inner being yields for him in the direction of the Lord. He has only one resolve and one purpose, and he dwells in the source of union (ʿayn al-jamʿiyya), gathered and collected, his mind at ease and his life and state mastered. [*Are the two equal in comparison? Praise be to God! Nay, but most of them do not know.*]

[39:30] *You will indeed die, and they* [*too*] *will indeed die*: the meaning of this is *Everything will perish except His countenance* [Q. 28:88]. All things are annihilated in God, and they are perished in your sight, having no existence of their own.

[39:31] *Then you will indeed be contending before your Lord on the Day of* the Major *Resurrection*, because of your differences concerning reality and the path, since they are veiled by the soul and its attributes, journeying in pursuit of its passions and pleasures, while you are contently journeying with the Real in pursuit of His countenance and approval.

[39:32] [*So who is a greater wrongdoer than he who imputes falsehood to God and [who] denies the truth when it reaches him? Is there not a [fitting] abode in Hell for the disbelievers?*

[39:33] *And he who brings the truth and [those] who confirm it, those—they are the ones who guard themselves.*

[39:34] *They shall have whatever they wish with their Lord. That is the reward of those who are virtuous,*] [39:35] *so that God may absolve them of the worst of what they did* from the attributes of their souls and the configurations of their vices, *and pay them their reward by the best of what they used to do*, with the manifestations of His Attributes and the gardens of His beauty, erasing the darknesses of their existences with the light of His countenance.

[39:36] *Does God not suffice [as the defender of] His servant*, who relies on Him through the Oneness of the acts, and as the source of all power and strength? *Yet they would frighten you with those besides Him* because they are veiled from Him by multiplicity, so that they attribute effect and power to beings that are intrinsically dead and possess no power or might. Of all people, you can be most hopeful that your Lord will defend you from their evil. *And whomever God leads astray* by veiling him from Him, *for him there is no guide*: for no one can turn back His decree or repel His ordainment.

Q. 39:32

[39:37] [*But whomever God guides, there is no one [able] to lead him astray. Is not God Mighty, a Lord of Retribution?*

[39:38] *And if you ask them, 'Who created the heavens and the earth?' they will surely say, 'God.' Say: 'Have you considered, then, those on whom you call, besides God, if God should desire some harm to befall me, would they [be able to] remove the harm imposed by Him? Or if He should desire some mercy for me, would they [be able to] withhold His mercy?' Say: 'God is sufficient for me. In Him do [all] the trusting put their trust.'*

[39:39] *Say: 'O my people, act according to your situation; I [too] am acting. For you will know* [39:40] *to whom will come a chastisement that will disgrace him and on whom there will descend a lasting chastisement.'*

[39:41] *Indeed, We have revealed the Book to you for [the sake of] people with the truth. So whoever is guided, then it is for [the sake of] his own soul; and whoever goes astray, goes astray only to the detriment thereof. And you are not [meant to be] a guardian over them.*

[39:42] *God takes the souls at the time of their death, and those that have not died in their sleep. Then He retains those for whom He has ordained death and releases the others until an appointed term. Truly in that there are signs for a people who reflect.*

[39:43] *Or have they taken besides God intercessors? Say: 'What! Even though they have no power whatsoever and are unable to comprehend?'*]

[39:44] *Say: 'All intercession belongs [solely] to God,* because it depends on His approval for the subject of the intercession by making him ready to receive it, and His permission to the intercessor by giving him stability in it and preparing him from His holiest emanation. The acceptance and the effect are from His side, and all dominion is His alone. *To Him belongs the kingdom of the heavens and the earth; then to Him you will be brought back':* to Him is the constant return.

[39:45] [*And when God is mentioned alone, thereat shrink the hearts of those who do not believe in the Hereafter; but when those [others] besides Him are mentioned, behold, they rejoice!*

[39:46] *Say: 'O God, Originator of the heavens and the earth, Knower of the Unseen and the visible, You will judge between Your servants concerning that wherein they used to differ.'*

[39:47] *And [even] if the evildoers possessed all that is in the earth, and as much of it besides, they would surely offer it to ransom themselves from the terrible chastisement on the Day of Resurrection. And there will appear to them from God]* that *which they had never reckoned:* they will witness the configurations of their deeds and the forms of their character traits, by which they became heedless because of their absorption in sensory distractions. Yet God recorded it all in their accounts, and in the four books: their souls, the heaven of this world, the Preserved Tablet, and the Mother Book.

[39:48] [*And there will appear to them the evils of what they had earned, and they will be besieged by that which they used to deride.*

[39:49] *So when some distress befalls man, he supplicates Us. Then, when We bestow on him a grace from Us, he says, 'I was given it merely by force of knowledge.' Nay, but it is a trial! But most of them do not know.*

[39:50] *Already the same was said by those who were before them. But what they used to earn did not avail them.*

[39:51] *So the evils of what they earned smote them. And the evildoers among these shall also be smitten by the evils of what they earned, and they will not be able to thwart it.*

[39:52] *Do they not know that God extends His provision for whomever He will, and restricts [for whomever He will?] Indeed, in that there are signs for a people who believe.*

[39:53] *Say [that God declares]: 'O My servants who have been prodigal against their own souls,] do not despair of God's mercy*: for despair is a sign of the fading of preparedness and the fall from innate disposition by veiling, and the severing of the tie to the Real and distancing from him. If even a hint of the original light remained in such a person, he would perceive the trace of His vast mercy, which intrinsically outpaces His wrath; and so would hope for that trace to reach him, even if he was guilty of excessively inclining towards the lower direction and neglecting the divine presence, since that remnant would keep him connected to the world of light. Despair only happens with total veiling and the blackening of the countenance by turning away from the higher world, and becoming enveloped by the material covering of creation. *Indeed, God forgives all sins* as long as the light of Oneness remains in the heart. This is why He singled out His servants in this regard, attributing them to Himself when He said, *O My servants.* This is why it has been said that He will forgive all of the sins of the Muḥammadan community alone among all the communities, as He said to the community of Noah (may God grant him peace), *That He may forgive you some of your sins* [Q. 71:4]. *Indeed, He is the Forgiving* of the configurations of vices, whether relating to negligence or excess, *the Merciful* by the emanation of the virtues.

Q. 39:54

[39:54] *'And turn [penitently] to your Lord* by renouncing the configurations of evil, *and submit* your beings *to Him* by detaching from the sins of deeds and attributes, *[before the chastisement comes on you, whereupon you will not be helped]*: before the door of forgiveness is closed to you by the occurrence of the chastisement you deserve upon death, when you will no longer be able to turn and submit because the instruments to do so will be lost and the doors will be closed.

[39:55] *['And follow the best of what has been revealed to you from your Lord before the chastisement comes on you suddenly while you are unaware,'* [39:56] *before any soul should say,] 'Alas for me for what I have neglected [of my duty to God]*: by failing to strive in pursuit of perfection, and being lax in obedience when I was in God's company, near to Him, because of the purity of my preparedness and my ability to travel in Him with all the bodily instruments at my disposal. *[Indeed, I was among those who ridiculed.'*

[39:57] *Or that it should say, 'If only God had guided me, I would have been among those who have feared.'*

[39:58] *Or that it should say, when it sees the chastisement, 'If only there had been a second chance, I would be among the virtuous.'*

[39:59] *'Yes, indeed! My signs came to you, but you denied them and were arrogant, and you were among the disbelievers.'*]

[39:60] *And on the Day of* Major *Resurrection you will see those who imputed lies to God*—the veiled ones who hold Him equal to created things by attributing a body to Him and ascribe attributes to Him that could not possibly be His, veiled as they are by matter—*with their faces blackened* by the perpetration of darkened configurations and the rooting of egocentric vices in their essences. *Is there not in* the *Hell* of primordial nature *a [fitting] abode for those who are arrogant?* [In other words,] those who were veiled by the attributes of their souls, which overpowered them.

[39:61] *And God will deliver those who fear* vices by detaching themselves from those attributes, *because of their triumph* and the means of their salvation, by the configurations of good deeds and the forms of virtues and perfections. *No evil will touch them,* for they are detached from painful negative configurations, *nor will they grieve* the loss of the perfections their preparedness occasioned.

[39:62] [*God is the Creator of all things and He is Guardian over all things.*]

[39:63] *To Him belong the keys of the heavens and the earth*: He alone possesses the treasures of their Unseens and the doors of their goodness and blessing, and He opens them to whomever He wills by His Beautiful Names. Each of His Names is a key to a particular treasure of His generosity, and its door can only be opened by it, after which He bestows it upon the person from the emanation of His universal and particular mercy, and His open and hidden favour. *And those who disbelieve in the signs of God*—those who are veiled from the lights of His Attributes and acts by the darkness of their natures and souls—*those*—*they are the losers* who will have no share of those treasures, because of how they have extinguished the original light that can receive them, and squandered their innate preparedness and the Name which would open it to them.

[39:64] *Say: 'Is it [something] other than God that you bid me to worship, [O you who are ignorant?*

[39:65] *'And certainly it has been revealed to you and to those before you [that] if you associate others [with God], your work shall surely fail and you shall surely be] among the losers'*: do you bid me to worship something other than God in ignorance, so that I am veiled from the emanation of His mercy and the light of His perfection, and thus become one of the losers?

[39:66] [*Rather, worship God*:] devote your worship to God alone and become annihilated in Him from seeing anything else, if you worship anything; *and be among the thankful* with Him and for Him.

[39:67] *And they do not esteem God as He should be esteemed*: they do not know Him as He should be known, for they esteem Him in their own souls and seek to imagine Him, but everything they imagine is a created thing, just like them. *And the entire earth will be in His grasp*, under His direction, the grasp of His power and the compulsion of His dominion [*on the Day of Resurrection*], *and the heavens will be [rolled up in His right hand]* in the grasp of His compulsion and the right hand of His power, so that He may direct them as He wills and do with them as He desires. He will roll them up and annihilate them from the vision of the witness on the Day of Major Resurrection and the annihilation in Oneness, for then all will be annihilated in the witnessing of Oneness. One will see that every direction is by His right hand, and that every Attribute is His, and that the world of power is in His right hand. Indeed, one will see everything as Him, and will see nothing besides Him but only His countenance, for there will be no essence or trace for anything but Him. *Glory be to Him! And exalted be He above what they associate* by affirming the existence of the other and attributing influence and power to it.

[39:68] *And the Trumpet will be blown* upon the dealing of death, when the spirit of the Real flows and manifests in all things, and He witnesses His Essence by His Essence, and all things are annihilated in Him; *and whoever is in the heavens and whoever is in the earth*, at the moment of annihilation in Oneness and the manifestation of ipseity with the blowing of the trumpet of the spirit, *will swoon* dead, *except whomever God wills* from the folk of subsistence after annihilation, whom God will revive after annihilation with veridical existence so that they will not die again at the Resurrection, because their life is through Him and they will already have been annihilated from their own souls. *Then it will be blown again* at the moment of subsistence after annihilation and the return to differentiation after unification; *and behold, they will rise up* through the Real, *looking on* through His eyes.

Q. 39:68

[39:69] *And the earth* of the soul then *will shine with the light of its Lord*, and be marked with the balance that is the shade of the sun of Oneness and the entire earth, in the time of the Mahdī (may God grant him peace), by the light of justice and truth. *And the Book shall be set in place*: the book of deeds will be presented to their doers so that each of them can read his deeds on his page, namely his soul upon which the forms of his deeds are inscribed; and those forms shall be imprinted on his body. *And the prophets and witnesses will be brought* from the foremost who will look upon their states, of whom God says, *On the Heights are men, who know each by their mark* [Q. 7:46]: that is, they will be brought to bear witness upon them because they are aware of their deeds. *And judgement will be made between them with truth*: when their deeds are weighed in the balance of justice and the rewards for them are given out in full with no subtractions; [*and they will not be wronged.*

[39:70] *And every soul will be paid in full for what it did,*] *and He is best aware of what they do*, because the forms of their deeds are established with Him.

[39:71] *And those who disbelieve*, the veiled ones, *will be driven to Hell in troops* by the driver of deeds and the leader of egocentric caprice and base inclination, [*until, when they reach it,*] *its gates are opened* because of its intense yearning for them and its acceptance of them, due to the correspondence between them. *And its keepers*, Mālik and the *Zabāniya*, or corporeal nature and the earthly dispositions assigned to the lower souls, *will say to them,* ['*Did there not come to you messengers from among yourselves, reciting to you the signs of your Lord, and warning you of the encounter of this day of yours?' They will say, 'Yes, indeed; but the word of chastisement against the disbelievers has been fulfilled.'*

[39:72] *It will be said, 'Enter the gates of Hell to abide therein. For evil is the abode of the arrogant!'*]

Q. 39:70

[39:73] *And those who feared* [*their Lord*] by shunning vices and the attributes of the soul *will be driven to Paradise in troops* by the driver of deeds and the leader of love, [*until, when they reach it and*] *its gates are* already *opened* before their arrival, because the doors of mercy and the emanation of the Real are always open, and are only missed on the side of reception, not the side of emanation, unlike the gates of Hell which only open when its denizens come to it, because matter is only prepared to receive souls when they move towards it. *Its keepers*—Riḍwān and the holy spirits and heavenly dispositions—*will say to them, 'Peace be to you!* Their greeting will be the Divine Attributes and the Sublime Names, by the emanation of perfection upon them and their absolution from blights and faults. *You are good*: free of the dross of egocentric attributes and configurations of primordial matter. [*So enter it, to abide therein forever*':] enter the spiritual garden of Paradise, granted perpetuity therein by the absolution of your essences from corporeal change.

[39:74] *And they will say, 'Praise be to God* by adopting His perfections and reaching the bliss of the manifestations of His Attributes, *Who has fulfilled His promise to us* by bringing us to what He assured us at the primal covenant, and [He is to be praised for] what He placed in us, and what He told us on the tongues of His messengers; *and has made us inherit* [*the land*], the garden of the Attributes, *that we may settle in Paradise wherever we wish*' according to our nobility and the dictate of our state. *So how excellent is the reward of those who worked*: those who acted on what they knew, so that they inherited the garden of the heart and soul from the lights and effects.

[39:75] *And you will see the angels* of the spiritual faculties in the garden of the Attributes *encircling all around the Throne* of the heart, *glorifying* by their disengagement from material attachments *with praise of their Lord* through spiritual perfections. *And judgement will be made between them with truth*: by their reconciliation and union (*ittiḥād*) of orientation towards perfection by the light of justice and Oneness, each of them singled out for what was justly ordained in His glorification, without any rivalry or dispute. *And it will be said*, with the tongue of Unity, that absolute *'Praise [be to God]*, in the Unitary Presence for the Divine Essence endowed with all its Attributes, *the Lord of the Worlds'* Who nourishes them according to the preparedness and states of things. Or the angels of the souls and heavenly spirits will circle in the garden of Paradise around the Throne of the supreme sphere, glorifying the praise of their Lord by adorning their detached essences with the lordly perfections. In addition, it will be said on the tongue of all, 'Total perfection is for God, the Lord of the Worlds.' Or if it is taken to apply to the Minor Resurrection, it means: the earth of the entire body is in His grasp, and He directs it with His power and restricts it from motion, and holds it back from the enjoyment of life at the moment of death. The heavens of the spirits and their faculties are rolled up in his right hand. The Trumpet is blown at the last breath, and all the spiritual faculties in the heavens and the egocentric natural faculties on earth will swoon, except whomever God wills from the spiritual reality and the human subtlety, which will not die. Then it will be blown again at the second creation with the light of life and balance, and the Book will be placed, meaning the tablet of the soul on which are engraved the forms of its deeds, dispersed upon it with the emergence of those souls. Thereafter the prophets and martyrs who are aware of their preparedness and states will be brought forth to be gathered with them. They will be requited for their deeds, and judgement will be made between them with truth, and they will not be wronged. The rest of the interpretation follows in the same way unto the end of the *sūra*. And God (Exalted is He) knows best.

Q. 39:75

40
THE BELIEVER OR THE FORGIVER
SŪRAT AL-MU'MIN OR GHĀFIR

In the Name of God, the Compassionate, the Merciful

This is [40:1] *Ḥā Mīm*: the truth (*ḥaqq*) veiled by Muḥammad, so that it is the truth in reality and Muḥammad in created form. He loved him, and so He manifested with his form, and His manifestation was through him.

[40:2] *The revelation of the* Muḥammadan *Book is from God*, from His Essence in which His Attributes are gathered, *the Mighty* in how His majesty was covered when the Book was a Gatherer (*Qur'ān*), *the Knower* Who manifested with His knowledge, so that it was a Criterion (*Furqān*). The meaning of *Ḥā Mīm* in reality is 'There is no god but God, and Muḥammad is His Messenger': that is, the hidden truth whose open reality was manifested in Muḥammad was the revelation of the Book, which was the source of unification that gathered all things, hidden by His might in the pavilions of His majesty, sent down in the stages of His Unseens and sublime loci in the Muḥammadan form, by which His knowledge was manifested in the locus of the discriminating intellect.

[40:3] *Forgiver of sins* by the manifestation of His light and His covering of souls and natures; *and Accepter of repentance* by the return of reality detached from the coverings of creation to Him; *Severe in retribution* to the veiled one who stands with other-than-God through idolatry rather than returning to Him with Unity; *One of [abundant] bounty*: the grace of emanating perfection which is added to the light of primal preparedness, if it be accepted. *There is no god except Him*: first and last, outward and inward, chastising and favouring; *to Him is the journeying* of everything in all circumstances, whether the returning repentant one or the halting punished one, and whether to His Essence, Attributes or acts. Whichever it may be, nothing is outside His encompassment such that it could be outside

258

His Essence and exist with an existence distinct from His. *Is it not sufficient that your Lord is witness to all things?* [Q. 47:53]

[40:4] *None dispute the signs of God, except those [who disbelieve]*: those who are veiled from the Real, because the non-veiled ones accept them by the light of their preparedness without denying His Attributes, while the veiled ones, because of the darkness of their substance and the impurity of their inner being, have essences which do not correspond to His signs, and so they deny them and dispute them. [*So do not be deceived by their bustle in the towns.*

[40:5] *The people of Noah denied before them and [also] the factions, [who came] after them. And every community sought to seize their messenger, and they argued] falsely [to rebut thereby the truth]*: attempting to blot out His signs with their disputes, and so chastisement was decreed for them: [*Then I seized them; so how [fitting] was My retribution!*

[40:6] *And thus was the word of your Lord fulfilled against those who disbelieve: that they shall be the folk of the Fire.*]

[40:7] *Those who bear the Throne*: the rational heavenly souls whose feet are planted on the lower earth by their influence upon it, and whose necks scrape the ceiling of the highest heaven by their detachment from it and their contemplation of it; or the spirits which are the objects of their yearning, *and those around it*: the detached holy spirits and celestial souls, *glorify with praise of their Lord*: declaring Him free of material connections by the detachment of their essences, and praising Him by displaying their perfections which are drawn from Him. They say with the voice of their state, 'O You whose Attributes these are, and whose gifts these are!' *And they believe in Him* with belief of true eye-witnessing, *and they ask forgiveness for those who believe* with supports of light and emanations of glory, because of how their essences correspond to theirs in the reality of faith. '*Our Lord, You embrace all things in [Your] mercy and knowledge*: Your mercy is encompassing, and Your knowledge covers all. *So forgive* by Your light *those who repent* to You by being detached from benighted configurations and darknesses of primordial matter, *and follow Your way* by travelling in You, following the footsteps of Your beloved in action, station and state, and renouncing the sins of their deeds, attributes and essences; *and shield them* with Your nurture *from the chastisement of the Hellfire* of nature.

[40:8] '*Our Lord, and admit them into the gardens* of Your Attributes and the meadows of Your holiness *of Eden which You have promised them, along with whoever were righteous* by detaching from material coverings and prepared for that purification and adornment [*among their fathers and their wives and their descendants*]: their relations who are connected to them by correspondence and spiritual kinship. *Indeed, You are the One Who is the Mighty*, the Conqueror Who is able to punish, *the Wise* Who only does what He does with wisdom; and one aspect of wisdom is fulfilling promises.

[40:9] *'And shield them from evil deeds*: by success through You, and the perfection of Your concern and protection; *for whomever You shield from evil deeds* [*that day, verily You will have been merciful to him*]: Your mercy will have been realised in him. *And that is indeed the supreme triumph'* because the one who is shown mercy is felicitous, while the veiled one will loath himself when he is shown his benighted configurations and their painful attributes, and the blackness of his bestial face and its hideous appearance, due to the lifting of the sensory distractions which used to keep him from perceiving his own essence. So he will be told:

Q. 40:9

[40:10] [*Indeed, to those who disbelieve it will be proclaimed*:] *'Surely God's loathing is greater than your loathing of yourselves*: for He is the light of lights; and the greater the luminosity and brightness of something, the further it is from the darkened impure substance, and thus it loathes it more. Their self-loathing also arises from the original light of preparedness, because the love for light is instilled therein. Indeed, light is intrinsically beloved, while darkness is intrinsically loathsome. *For you were called to faith but you used to disbelieve'*: His loathing of you was in the time of your veiling from Him and your refusal to accept the call to faith in Oneness, or how you and your fathers were veiled from the call of faith.

[40:11] *They will say, 'Our Lord, You have caused us to die twice*: You have created us dead twice; *and You have given us life* [*twice*]: at the two creations. *We confess our sins*: now that the retribution ordained for them has come and there is no escape from it. [*Is there any way to go out?'*]

[40:12] *That is because,* [*when God was invoked alone, you would disbelieve; but if partners were ascribed to Him, you would believe*]: the eternal chastisement and supreme loathing is because of your idolatry and how you were veiled from the Real by other than Him. *So the judgement* of your perpetual retribution *belongs to God,* [*the Exalted, the Great,*] and no other, and there is no chance of salvation because of His loftiness and might. No one can repel His judgement and retribution.

[40:13] *He it is Who shows you* [*His signs*]: the signs of His Attributes by His self-disclosures, *and sends down from the heaven* of the spirit *for you* true *provision* of a tremendous nature, namely the knowledge that gives the heart life and nourishment. *Yet no one remembers* their previous states by means of that provision, *except him who returns penitently* to Him by detachment and disregard of other-than-God.

[40:14] [*So supplicate God, devoting [your] religion purely to Him, however much the disbelievers be averse:*] so return to Him so that you remember, by devoting worship to Him and making your religion sincerely for Him and pure from the adulterants of otherness, and detaching your disposition from creation, however much the veiled ones condemn it and hate it.

[40:15] *Exalter of ranks*: raiser of the ranks of His Unseens, lifter of His heavens, the stations through which the wayfarers ascend; *Lord of the Throne*: [possessor of] the highest station, the Owner of all things. *He casts the Spirit*, the revelation and divinely-inspired knowledge that gives life to dead souls, *from* the realm of *His command upon whomever He wishes of His servants* whom He has chosen for His pre-eternal nurture, *that he may warn them of the Day of [Encounter]*: the Major Resurrection when the servant will meet his Lord by annihilation in Him, or the servants in the source of unification.

[40:16] *The day when they will emerge* from behind the veils of egos or the coverings or bodies, and *nothing about them will be hidden from God* of the deeds they concealed and hid from other people, imagining that they would never be seen; for they are apparent in their accounts and will be brought out into the open, as He says, *God has kept count of it, while they forgot it* [Q. 58:6]. *And they will say, 'O woe to us! What is it with this Book that it leaves out neither small nor great, but [instead it] has counted it?'* [Q. 18:49]. Nothing about them will be hidden from Him, for they will emerge from behind the veils of Attributes into the Essence of Being. *'To whom does the kingdom belong today?'* The Real will call this when all are annihilated in the source of unification, and then He alone will answer: *'To God, the One* besides whom there is nothing else, *the All-Compelling'* Who has annihilated all with His compelling power.

[40:17] [*Today every soul shall be requited for what it has earned; there will be no injustice today.*] *Indeed, God is swift at reckoning* because it will occur all at once, by the dictate of their evil deeds written in the accounts of their souls along with their consequences, as are their good deeds and their fruits.

[40:18] *And warn them of the Impending Day*, the near event which is the Minor Resurrection, *when the hearts will reach the throats* because of the intense fear, [*choking with anguish. The evildoers will not have any intimate [friend], nor any intercessor who might be heeded.*

[40:19] *He knows the treachery of the eyes and what the breasts hide.*

Q. 40:14

261

[40:20] *And God decrees with truth, while those on whom they call besides Him do not decree by any means [at all]. Indeed, God is the Hearer, the Seer.*

[40:21] *Have they not travelled in the land and beheld the nature of the consequence for those who were before them? They were more powerful than them in strength and in [their] vestiges on earth. Yet God seized them for their sins and they had none to shield them from God.*

[40:22] *That was because their messengers used to bring them clear signs, but they disbelieved. So God seized them. Indeed, He is Strong, Severe in retribution.*

[40:23] *And verily We sent Moses with Our signs and a clear warrant* [40:24] *to Pharaoh and Haman and Korah, but they said, 'A sorcerer, a [mere] liar!'*

[40:25] *So when he brought them the truth from Us, they said, 'Slay the sons of those who believe with him, and spare their women.' But the guile of the disbelievers is ever in error.*

[40:26] *And Pharaoh said, 'Let me slay Moses and let him call to his Lord. Indeed, I fear that he may change your religion, or that he may cause corruption to appear in the land.'*

[40:27] *And Moses said, 'Indeed, I seek refuge in my Lord and your Lord from every arrogant one who does not believe in the Day of Reckoning.'*

[40:28] *Then said a believing man from among Pharaoh's folk who had concealed his faith, 'Will you slay a man for saying, "My Lord is God," even though he has [also] brought you clear signs from your Lord? If he is lying, then his mendacity will be to his own detriment; but if he is truthful, then there will befall you some of that with which he is threatening you. Indeed, God does not guide one who is a prodigal, a liar.*

[40:29] *'O my people, today the kingdom is yours: [you are] dominant in the land. But who will help us against the might of God should it reach us?' Pharaoh said, 'I only point out to you what I see [to be best], and I am only guiding you to the path of rectitude.'*

[40:30] *Then said he who believed, 'O my people! Indeed, I fear for you [a day] like the day of the factions,* [40:31] *like the case of the people of Noah, and ʿĀd, and Thamūd, and those [who came] after them. And God does not desire to wrong [any of] His servants.*

[40:32] *'And O my people! Indeed, I fear for you a day of [mutual] calling:* [40:33] *a day when you will turn back to flee, not having anyone to defend you from God. And whomever God leads astray, for him there is no guide.*

[40:34] *'And verily Joseph brought you clear signs before, but you continued to be in doubt concerning what he had brought you until, when he died, you said, "God will never send any messenger after him."] So God leads astray one who is a prodigal, a sceptic'*: this—like His Words, *Indeed, God does not guide one who is a prodigal, a liar*—means that misguidance and forsaking are both occasioned by the two vices of knowledge and action. Lying and doubt are both vices of the rational faculty caused by the absence of certitude and honesty, while prodigality is a vice of the other two faculties and an excessive indulgence in their acts.

[40:35] *Those who dispute the signs of God without any warrant that has come to them—greatly hateful [is that] in the sight of God and in the sight of those who believe. So God sets a seal on the heart of every arrogant tyrant.*

[40:36] *And Pharaoh said, 'O Haman, build for me a tower that perhaps I may reach the routes:]* the tower that Pharaoh told Haman to build was the foundation of discursive wisdom from intellectual analogies. The people adhered to logic, but they were veiled by their estimation-tainted minds that were not illuminated by the light of guidance.

[40:37] *['The routes of the heavens, and look upon the God of Moses:]* he wanted to reach the paths of the heavens of Unseens and look upon the Unitary Presence, by means of rational thought, rather than travelling in God by detachment, erasure and annihilation, veiled as he was by his I-ness and knowledge. Thus, he said *for I truly think that he is lying.' And that arrogance and misguidance is how the evil [nature] of his conduct was made to seem fair to Pharaoh,* because of how he was veiled by the attributes of his soul and his vices; *and [that is how] he was barred from the [right] way* because of the error of his thought, and how his knowledge and logic were corrupted due to his intense inclination towards the world and his love for it, which was caused by the preponderance of caprice in him. [*And Pharaoh's guile ended only in ruin.*] This was in contrast to the one who believed, who began by warning against the world:

Q. 40:35

[40:38] [*And he who believed said, 'O my people, follow me. I will guide you to the way of rectitude.*]

[40:39] *'O my people, truly this life of the world is only an [ephemeral] enjoyment, whereas the Hereafter truly is the enduring abode,* because of how quickly the former ends and how enduring the latter is.

[40:40] [*'Whoever commits an evil deed shall not be requited except with the like of it; but whoever acts righteously, whether male or female, and is a believer—such shall be admitted into Paradise wherein they will be provided without any reckoning.*

[40:41] *'And O my people!]* [*How is it that*] *I call you to deliverance*—to Oneness and detachment, which will be the cause of your salvation—*when you call me to* idolatry, which only leads to *the Fire?*

[40:42] *'You call me [to disbelieve in God and] to associate with Him that whereof I have no knowledge* of its existence, for it does not exist, *whereas I call you to the Mighty* Who overcomes those who disobey Him, *the Forgiver* Who covers with His lights the darknesses of the souls of those who obey Him.

[40:43] *'No doubt that to which you call me has no call [that is heard] in this world or in the Hereafter,* because it has no existence of its own and thus cannot exist in either of them; *and indeed our return will be to God, and indeed the prodigal—it is they who will be the folk of the Fire.*

[40:44] *['For you will [soon] remember what I have said to you. And I entrust my affair to God. Indeed, God is Seer of [His] servants.'*

[40:45] *So God shielded him from the evils of what they had plotted, and there besieged the folk of Pharaoh a dreadful chastisement:]* [40:46] *the Fire, to which they are exposed morning and evening*: their spirits are roasted in the fire of natural configurations, being veiled from holy lights and deprived from sensory passions, yearning for them but unable to attain them. *And on the day when the Hour comes* with the gathering of bodies or the emergence of the Mahdī (may God grant him peace), it will be said to them, *'Enter [folk of Pharaoh] the most awful chastisement,'* because of the transformation of their configurations and forms, and the accumulation of darknesses and veils upon them, and the narrowness of their confinement and resting-place, if it be the former, or the domination of the Mahdī (may God grant him peace) over them and his chastisement of them for their denial of him and distance from him, and his knowledge of them by their marks, if it be the latter.

Q. 40:43

[40:47] *[And when they will be arguing [with one another] in the Fire, and the weak will say to those who were arrogant, 'Indeed, we were your followers; so will you [now] avail us against any portion of the Fire?'*

[40:48] *Those who were arrogant will say, 'Indeed, we are all [together] in it. God has indeed judged [fairly] between His servants.'*

[40:49] *And those who are in the Fire will say to the keepers of Hell, 'Call on your Lord that He relieve us of [at least] a day of the chastisement!'*

[40:50] *They will say, 'Did not your messengers bring you clear signs?' They will say, 'Yes indeed.' They will say, 'Then supplicate [God]!' But the supplications of the disbelievers can only be misguided.]*

[40:51] *Truly We shall help Our messengers and those who believe* with divine aid and holy light in the two abodes, *[in the life of this world and on the day when the witnesses rise up:* [40:52] *the day when their excuses will not benefit the evildoers, and theirs will be the curse, and theirs will be the ills of the [ultimate] abode.*

[40:53] *And verily We gave Moses the guidance, and We made the Children of*

Israel heirs to the Book, [40:54] *as a guidance, and as a remembrance for people of pith.*]

[40:55] *So be patient. Surely God's promise is true*: restrain the soul from emerging in reaction to their persecution, and know that you shall triumph in the moment of subsistence and stability, for We are ever triumphant. *And ask forgiveness for* the *sin* of your state by renouncing your deeds; *and glorify* through detachment *with praise of your Lord*, Who is ever endowed with His perfection, at all times, [*at night and in the early hours*]. As long as you are in the state of annihilation, do not feel safe from variegation by the emergence of the soul and its attributes. You must be patient, ask forgiveness and detach from the attributes by which the soul emerges, and become realised in God and His Attributes. When you attain the station of uprightness and stability in the state of subsistence after annihilation, that will be the time of triumph and the emergence of the soul, and the fulfilment of the promise.

[40:56] [*Truly those who dispute the signs of God without any warrant that has come to them—there is only vanity in their breasts which they will never attain* [*and satisfy*]. *So seek refuge with God. Indeed, He is the Hearer, the Seer.*

Q. 40:55

[40:57] *Assuredly the creation of the heavens and the earth is greater than the creation of people; but most people do not know.*

[40:58] *And the blind one and the seer are not equal; nor are those who believe and perform righteous deeds and the evildoer. Little do they reflect.*

[40:59] *Indeed, the Hour is coming; there is no doubt in it. But most people do not believe.*]

[40:60] *And your Lord has said, 'Call on Me and I will respond to you*: this means a call of state, because a call with the tongue without the knowledge of whether the one being called is good for it or not is the call of the veiled ones, as God says, *The call of the disbelievers goes only astray* [Q. 13:14]: that is, it is squandered. The call whose response is not delayed is the call of state, when the servant musters his preparedness to receive what he requests. The response to this call is not delayed. This is the call of the one who requests forgiveness by repenting to God and turning to Him penitently with asceticism and obedience, or the one who seeks arrival and chooses annihilation. Thus, He says, *Surely those who disdain to worship Me*—those who do not call upon Me with passion, humility and hopefulness, but rather manifest their souls with arrogance and haughtiness—*shall enter Hell* [*utterly*] *humiliated,'* because of how they called with the tongues of their states with pride and conceit, for the attribute of arrogance and vying with God for His grandeur warrants this.

[40:61] [*God it is Who made for you night that you may rest in it, and day for*

265

seeing. Indeed, God is a Lord of bounty to people, but most people are not thankful.]

[40:62] *That then is God, your Lord*: the One Who self-discloses with His acts and Attributes is God, to whom all Attributes belong, your Lord with His Names, each of which applies specifically to one of your states; *the Creator of all things*: by veiling Himself with them. *There is no god except Him* in existence, and He creates what He wills and manifests with His Attributes. *How, then, are you made to deviate* from obedience to Him, by affirming the existence of others and obeying them? An example of this was the blow you struck because of how you were veiled by multiplicity. The deniers of God's signs deviated when they did not recognise them, as a result of how He concealed them behind other-than-Him.

[40:63] [*Thus were deviated those who used to deny the signs of God.*

[40:64] *God it is Who made for you the earth as a* [*stable*] *abode and the heaven as a canopy. And He formed you and perfected your forms, and provided you with* [*all*] *the wholesome things. That, then, is God, your Lord, so blessed be God, the Lord of the Worlds.*

[40:65] *He is the Living; there is no god except Him. So supplicate Him, devoting* [*your*] *religion purely to Him. Praise be to God, the Lord of the Worlds.*

[40:66] *Say: 'I have been forbidden to worship those on whom you call besides God, since there have come to me clear signs from my Lord; and I have been commanded to submit to the Lord of the Worlds.'*

[40:67] *He it is Who created you from dust, then from a drop* [*of sperm*], *then from a clot, then He brings you forth as infants, then that you may come of age, then that you may become aged, though there are some of you who die earlier, and that you may complete an appointed term that perhaps you might understand.*

[40:68] *He it is Who gives life and brings death. So when He decides upon a matter, He only says to it 'Be!' and it is.*

[40:69] *Have you not regarded those who dispute the signs of God* [*and*] *how they are turned away?*]

[40:70] *Those who deny the Book*, because of the distance of their correspondence from it and how they are veiled by their darknesses from the light, [*and that wherewith We have sent Our messengers*]. *But they will come to know* the dire consequences of their affair, [40:71] *when,* [*with*] *fetters of* the restraints of differing natures *around their necks and chains of* endless accidents which prevents them from moving towards their goals, *they are dragged* [40:72] *into the boiling water* of ignorance and caprice; *and then in the Fire* of yearning for the sensory passions and pleasures they have lost, and the agonies of the painful configurations that have replaced them, *they are set aflame*: denied that with which they had been veiled and with

Q. 40:62

which they had halted, the forms of the multiplicity they worshipped.

[40:73] [*Then it will be said to them, 'Where are those whom you used to make partners* [40:74] *besides God?' They will say, 'They have forsaken us. Nay, but*] *we were not invoking anything before'*: they will say this in their knowledge that what they worshipped and wasted their lives serving was nothing at all, and certainly cannot do anything for them now. [*Thus does God lead astray the disbelievers.*]

[40:75] *'That* [*is because you used to exult in the earth without right and because you were insolent*: this] torment is the result of how you rejoiced in that ephemeral, passing falsehood in the lower direction, because of the soul and its engagement in it, due to the correspondence of your turbid, darkened souls to it, distant from the Real.

[40:76] *'Enter the gates of Hell, to abide therein,'* because of the rootedness of your vices and the firmness of your veils. *Evil then is the* [*ultimate*] *abode of the arrogant*, who manifest with the vice of arrogance.

Q. 40:73

[40:77] [*So be patient. Assuredly God's promise is true. And if We show you a part of what We promise them, or We take you unto Us* [*in death*], *then* [*in any case*] *to Us they will be returned.*

[40:78] *And verily We sent messengers before you. Of them are those whom We have recounted to you, and of them are those whom We have not recounted to you. And it was never* [*permitted*] *for any messenger to bring a sign except with God's permission. Hence, when God's command comes, judgement is passed justly; and it is thence that the advocates of falsehood become losers.*

[40:79] *God it is Who made for you cattle that you may ride some of them and eat of some.*

[40:80] *And there are* [*other*] *uses for you in them, and that by them you may satisfy any need that is in your breasts, and on them and on the ships you are carried.*

[40:81] *And He shows you His signs. So which of God's signs do you reject?*

[40:82] *Have they not travelled across the land to see the nature of the consequence for those before them? They were more powerful than them in might and in* [*their*] *vestiges on earth. But what they used to earn did not avail them.*]

[40:83] *And when their messengers brought them clear signs, they exulted in the knowledge they possessed,* [*and there besieged them that which they used to deride.*

[40:84] *Then, when they saw Our doom, they said, 'We believe in God alone, and we disavow what we used to associate with Him.'*

[40:85] *But their faith was of no benefit to them when they saw Our doom—God's way,* [*a precedent*] *which has passed among His servants, and it is thence that the disbelievers will be losers:*] they were veiled by minds tainted by estimation and their objects of cognition, devoid of the light of guidance and revelation. So when the messengers brought them teachings of reality and Oneness and veridical secrets of gnosis and unveiling, they rejoiced in their own knowledge and were veiled by it from accepting their guidance; and they mocked their messengers and belittled what they brought when they compared it to their own knowledge. Then the consequence of their mockery caught up with them, and they were utterly ruined. And God knows best.

Q. 40:85

41

EXPOUNDED

SŪRAT FUṢṢILAT

In the Name of God, the Compassionate, the Merciful

[41:1] *Ḥā. Mīm*: the manifestation of the Real in the Muḥammadan form.

[41:2] [*A revelation from the Compassionate, the Merciful.*]

[41:3] *A Book*: the universal book that gathers all realities from the Essential Unity attributed with the mercy of undiscriminating compassion (*raḥma raḥmāniyya*) for all by the emanation of existence and perfection to them, and the mercy of discriminating mercifulness (*raḥma raḥīmiyya*) for the Muḥammadan saints who are prepared to receive the special gnostic perfection and Essential Oneness, which is the book of the discriminating intellect, *whose signs have been expounded* by revelation after they were gathered in sum in the source of unification when it was *an* [*Arabic*] *Qur'ān*. They were expounded according to the manifestation of the Attributes and engendering of preparednesses at the time when it was a gathering book (*qirān*) of all; and [it is] *Arabic* because it was made to rise among the Arabs, *for a people who have knowledge* of the realities of its signs because of the nearness of their preparedness to it and the purity of their innate dispositions; [41:4] [*containing*] *good tidings* of the meeting for those who accept it and are prepared for perfection, seeing by its light; *and a warning* of the chastisement for those who are veiled by the darknesses of their souls. *But most of them turn away* because they are veiled by others and remain in the darknesses of concealment, *so that they do not hear* the speech of the Real because of the deafness of their hearts.

[41:5] [*And they say,*] '*Our hearts are veiled from that to which you call us, and in our ears there is a deafness*, because the coverings of nature and the veils of the soul's attributes blind the sight of hearts and deafen their hearing, placing them in concealment and secrecy and barring them from it; [*and between us and you there is a partition, so act. Indeed, we shall be acting!*]

269

[41:6] *Say: 'I am only a human being like you*: I am from your species, and I am like you in humanity and type, sent to humankind to live among you and show you the revelation that guides to Oneness and the path to follow. Attach to me by this correspondence of type and humanity, that you may be guided by the light of Oneness and revelation, so that your religion is made clear to you and you follow the path of the Real, which He has shown to me: [*It has been revealed to me*] *that your God is One God*: without any partner in existence. *So be upright* [*in your conduct*]: by holding true to faith, divine peace and certitude *before Him*, journeying towards Him without deviating towards falsehood or the wandering paths, nor straying by being distracted by other-than-God and inclining towards the soul. *And seek forgiveness from Him* by renouncing material configurations and detaching from human attributes, that the sins of your attributes be covered by the light of His. *And woe to* [*the idolaters*:] the ones who are veiled by other-than-God, [41:7] [*who do not pay* zakāt,] who do not purify themselves by erasing their attributes to lift the veil of otherness and attain realisation of Oneness; *and who are disbelievers in the Hereafter*, because they have covered the innate light which gives rise to yearning for the realm of holiness and the source of eternal life, with the darknesses of sense and the configurations of bodily nature.

Q. 41:6

[41:8] [*'Indeed, those who believe and perform righteous deeds shall have an enduring reward.'*]

[41:9] *Say: 'Do you* [*really*] *disbelieve in Him Who created the earth in two days,* [*and ascribe to Him associates? That is the Lord of* [*all*] *the Worlds': two days*] here means two events, since the term 'day' can be used to mean 'event', such as when people say 'in those days', meaning 'at the time of those events'; furthermore, an event resembles a day in the way that it emerges and then fades away. In this case, the two events were form and matter.

[41:10] [*And He set therein firm mountains* [*rising*] *above it,*] *and blessed it*—magnified its goodness—*and ordained therein* [*its sustenance*] *and provision in four days*: these were the four qualities and the four elements from which He created the composites, by means of composition and proportioning, *evenly* with temperance and balance [*for enquirers*]: for all seekers of provisions and means of sustenance, which He measured out for them.

[41:11] *Then He turned to the heaven*: that is, He directed His will to engendering it and then to making the distinction between the two creations, with regards to perfection or its absence and their differences in orientation and substance—but not with regards to the passage of time, since there was no time then; *when it was smoke*: that is, a subtle substance unlike the dense heavy substances of the earth; *and He said to it and to the earth, 'Come both of you willingly, or unwillingly!'* [*They said, 'We come willingly!'*] His command and will attached to their engendering, and they came into being instantly together, like an obedient servant responding to the command of an imposing master without delay. This is a metaphor, since there was no such thing as speech then.

[41:12] *Then He ordained them seven heavens in two days*: that is, matter and form, like for the earth; *and in each heaven He revealed its commandment*: that is, He indicated to them what He wanted from them, with regards to their motions and the influences of their dominions and directions, the special properties of their spheres, and everything relating to them. *And We adorned the lowest heaven*, meaning the ceiling closest to us containing the sphere of the moon, *with lamps*, meteors, *and* [*this was also*] *to guard them* against being burned by the rising of smoke to them, and to prevent the natural satanic faculties from reaching their angels. *That is the ordaining of the Mighty* Who manifests His commands however He pleases, *the Knower* Who perfects His work by His knowledge.

Q. 41:12

Alternatively, it means: do you really disbelieve? And are you really veiled by bodily coverings, from the One Who created the earth of the body and made it a veil for His countenance in two days, meaning two months or two events of form and matter? And do you set-up rivals for Him by halting with others, and attributing influence to that which possesses neither existence nor influence? That Creator is the One Who lords over the worlds with His Names, and Who placed therein the mountains of the limbs from above, or the mountains of natures which necessitate lower inclinations, namely the elemental faculties and material forms which cause it to remain firm as it is. He blessed it by preparing the instruments, means, temperaments and faculties by which its behaviours and deeds could be performed, and ordained its provisions for it by directing the nutritive faculty and its aids, and ordaining the digestive system and all related matters of nutrition and its means and materials. All this He did in exactly four even months, or in the matter of the four elements. Then He turned— that is, after that He directed His will without actually turning away from anything else—towards the heaven of the spirit and its balancing, when it was smoke, meaning a subtle material composed of the vapour and subtleties of the mixtures which rose from the heart. A *ḥadīth* says, 'The creation of each of you occurs by him being gathered in the belly of his mother for forty days as a drop, and then as a clot for the same term, and then as a morsel for the same term. After that God sends an angel to him with four words, and he writes his deeds, lifespan, provision and whether he will be damned or saved. Next He blows the spirit into him.' This is supported by another *hadīth* stating that the spirit is blown into the foetus four months after conception. Then He said to it and to the earth of the body, 'Come forth.' In other words, His will attached to their making and forming as one thing in a new creation, so that they would be in the form He desired for them. This is the meaning of why He left the earth uneven before the heaven, and then levelled it out afterwards. Although the material of the body was created before the spirit connected to it and was blown into it, the limbs were not stretched out or proportioned with each other until afterwards.

Afterwards He ordained them seven heavens, that is, the aforementioned Seven Unseens: the faculties, the soul, the heart, the mystery, the spirit, the hidden, and the truth whose ipseity is mixed into the ipseity of the given person, and which descends into these levels when he is engendered, after which it is veiled by them. Or if you would like to count the seven as created things, only so that this ipseity is excluded, then we would add the intellect as a fourth between the heart and the mystery. This is the lowest heaven because of how close it is to the heart, which makes a person a person. He ordained this in two days, which means another two months, extending the period of gestation to six months which is the time it takes for a human to be created. This is why if the child is born premature at the start of the seventh month, it can survive and live a normal life. Or the two days could mean two stages whether separate or joined, or two events meaning the spirit and body. And God knows best. Then in each heaven of the aforementioned levels He ordained its command and its specific role, in terms of deeds, perceptions, unveilings, witnessings, connections, inspirations and disclosures. Subsequently, He adorned the lowest heaven, the intellect, with lamps of arguments and proofs, and protected it from the domination of the devils of estimation and imagination through the speech of the High Council of spiritual beings, by ascension to the intellectual horizons and the summoning of analogical forms to repel their falsehoods and delusions from it.

Q. 41:13

[41:13] [*But if they turn away, then say, 'I warn you of a thunderbolt like the thunderbolt of ʿĀd and Thamūd.'*

[41:14] *When the messengers came to them from in front of them and from behind them, saying, 'Worship none but God,' they said, 'Had our Lord wished, He would have surely sent down angels; therefore we indeed disbelieve in what you have been sent with!'*

[41:15] *As for ʿĀd, they acted arrogantly in the earth without right, and they* said, *'Who is more powerful than us in might?'* Did they not see that God, He Who created them, was more powerful than them in might? And they used to deny Our signs.

[41:16] *So We unleashed upon them a raging wind during [some] ill-fated days that We might make them taste the chastisement of disgrace in the life of this world; yet the chastisement of the Hereafter is indeed more disgraceful, and they will not be helped.*

[41:17] *And as for Thamūd, We offered them guidance, but they preferred blindness to guidance. So the thunderbolt of the humiliating chastisement seized them on account of what they used to earn.*

[41:18] *And We delivered those who believed and feared.*

[41:19] *And [mention] the day when God's enemies are gathered to the Fire, for they will be driven [thereto],]* [41:20] *until, when they reach it, their hearing and their eyes and their skins will bear witness against them [concerning what they used to do]*: their body parts will be changed and transformed into the shapes of the deeds they did, and their skins and flesh will be replaced. Then they will speak with the tongue of their states and indicate with their shapes whatever it was that they used to do.

Q. 41:16

[41:21] *[And they will say to their skins, 'Why did you bear witness against us?' They will say,]* by their ability to speak with this tongue, *'God made us speak, Who gave speech to all things*: for everything possesses some kind of speech, but those who are oblivious to it do not understand it. [*And He created you the first time, and to Him you will be returned.*

[41:22] *'And you did not conceal yourselves, lest your hearing or your eyes or your skins should bear witness against you; but you thought that God did not know most of what you did.*

[41:23] *'And that supposition of yours, which you supposed of your Lord, has ruined you. So you have become among the losers.'*

[41:24] *So even if they endure, the Fire will [still] be their abode; and if they seek reconciliation, then they will not be among the reconciled.*]

[41:25] *And We have assigned them companions*: devils both human and jinn from the faculties of estimation and imagination, because of their distance from the High Council and their essential contradiction of holy souls and angelic lights, through their immersion in primordial matter, and their veiling with egocentric attributes, and their attraction to corporeal caprices and natural passions. They have corresponded to earthly souls which are foul, turbid and dark, and contradicted holy substances and detached essences, and so devils have been made their companions and they have been veiled from the light of the dominion. [Those devilish companions were the ones] *who have adorned for them that which is before them*: the bestial predatory pleasures and natural passions that are in their presence; *and that which is behind them*: the hopes and ambitions they have not yet attained. *And the word became due against them*—[meaning] the divine ordainment of their eternal damnation—*among communities that passed away before them* who denied the prophets and were veiled from the Real, [*of jinn and humankind,*] of the inward and the outward folk. *Truly they were losers* because of how they lost the light of innate preparedness and the opportunity to attain acquired perfection, and fell into perpetual perdition and eternal torment.

[41:26] [*And those who disbelieve say, 'Do not listen to this Qur'ān, and hoot it down that perhaps you might prevail.'*

[41:27] *But verily We will make those who disbelieve taste a severe chastisement, and We will verily requite them the worst of what they used to do.*

[41:28] *That is the requital of God's enemies—the Fire! Therein will be their everlasting abode as a requital for their denial of Our signs.*

Q. 41:26

[41:29] *And those who disbelieve will say,*] *'Our Lord, show us those who led us astray,* [*so that we may have them underneath our feet* [*to trample them*]*, that they may be among the lowermost'*]: when their chastisement comes, the veiled ones will become enraged at the members of both groups who led them astray, and will hope that they are punished even more severely and sent to an even lower level when they encounter the humiliation and pain of the fires, and the torment of deprivation and loss because of them. They will desire to attain closure by seeing them in the most awful state and lowest level. This is akin to how a person who gets into serious trouble because of the advice of a friend becomes enraged at him, and speaks furious words about him in his absence.

[41:30] *Indeed, those who say, 'Our Lord is God!'* declaring His Oneness by negating anything other than Him and knowing Him with certitude as He should be known, *and then remain upright* for Him by following His path and remaining firm upon it, devoting their deeds sincerely to Him alone and not giving regard to any other, *the angels descend upon them* because of the true correspondence between them in how they truly uphold Oneness and have true faith and firm action on the path of the Real and are upright in their journey to Him, without breaking their resolve, or straying from His direction, or erring in any deed. Likewise, the souls of the veil ones from the people of vice correspond to the devils because of the dark substances and foul deeds, and so they descend upon them too. [The angels say to them,] *'Do not fear* retribution, for your essences are illuminated by the lights and detached from the coverings of configurations, *nor grieve* the loss of the perfections that your preparedness merits, *and rejoice in the good tidings of the Paradise* of Attributes *which you were promised* when you had faith in the Unseen.

Alternatively, it means, *Indeed, those who say, 'Our Lord is God!'* by annihilation in Him, *and then remain upright* in Him through subsistence after annihilation when they attain stability, *the angels descend upon them* to revere them when they return to differentiation, for in the state of annihilation there are no angels nor anything else. [The angels say to them,] *'Do not fear* variegation, *nor grieve* for immersion in Oneness; for when the people of Unity return to differentiation and the vision of multiplicity, they are assailed with grief and emotion at first because of the loss of essential witnessing in the source of unification, and the veiling of differentiation. This lasts until they become stable in realisation of the Real, in the state of subsistence, and their breasts are expanded by the light of the Real, so that they are no longer veiled by multiplicity from Unity, nor by Unity from multiplicity. In the differentiation of the Attributes, they witness the reality of the Essence by the Essence. He said to His Prophet (may God grant him peace), speaking of this state, *Did We not expand your breast for you, and relieve you of your burden, that which weighed down your back?* [Q. 94:1–3]. *And rejoice in the good tidings of the Paradise* of the Essence, which contains all the levels of the gardens, *which you were promised* in the station of the self-disclosures of the Attributes.

Q. 41:31

[41:31] *'We are your friends* and loved ones [*in the life of this world and in the Hereafter*], because of the correspondence of attributes and the essential kinship between us and you, just as the devils are the friends of the veiled ones, because of the kinship and association of darkness and turbidity between them. *And therein you will have whatever your souls desire,* [*and therein you will have whatever you request*] of witnessings and self-disclosures, peace, comfort, and eternal bliss. When you reach the perfection which is the dictate of your preparedness, you will no longer yearn for what you do not have, but rather everything you desire and request will be yours the moment you desire it, in the three gardens.

[41:32] *'A hospitality* prepared for you *from* [*a Lord Who is*] *Forgiving*: Who covers with His light the sins of your effects, deeds, attributes and essences, *Merciful'*: Who graces you with the self-disclosures of His acts, Attributes and Essence, and replaces yours with them.

[41:33] *And who speaks better* with the tongue of state—since speech is often used to symbolise action and state, as before when He said, *Those*

who say, 'Our Lord is God!' [Q. 41:30], meaning those who choose faith
in Oneness as their religion; or the *ḥadīth*, 'Damned are the rich, save for
those who say such-and-such,' meaning those who give—*than him who
summons* [*others*] *to God, and acts righteously and says, 'Indeed, I am one of those
who submit* [*to God*]'? In other words, the one who submits his being to
God by faith in Oneness, and acts with uprightness and stability, and calls
others to the Real to perfect them. He mentioned calling others to the
Real and perfecting them first because it is the noblest level, as it requires
perfection of knowledge and action, since otherwise the call would not
be authentic; and even if it were authentic, it would not truly be a call to
God, meaning to His Essence endowed with all His Attributes. When the
one who has knowledge but not action calls, his call is to the Knower; and
when the one who has action but not knowledge calls, his call is to the
Forgiving Merciful One; but when the one who has knowledge, action
and perfect gnosis calls, his call is to God.

Q. 41:34

[41:34] *And they are not equal, the good deed and the evil deed*: for the former
is from the station of the heart and pulls its doer towards Paradise and the
company of the angels, while the latter is from the station of the soul and
pulls its doer towards Hell and the company of the devils. *Repel with that
which is better*: if you can repel the evil deed from your enemy with a good
deed which is best, then do not repel it with a good deed which is not as
good, never mind with an evil deed. Evil deeds do not repel evil deeds, but
only make them worse, just as a fire climbs higher when more kindling is
placed on it. If you repay it like-for-like, you will only be descending to the
station of the soul and following Satan, treading the path to Hell, as well
as pulling your fellow even further into sin, so that both of you become
evil folk and increase the sum total of evil while turning away from good.
If you repay it with a good deed, his evil will abate and his enmity will
be pacified, and you will remain firm in the station of the heart and the
side of good. You will be guided towards Paradise, and you will drive
Satan away. You will please the Compassionate and follow the path of His
dominion. You will erase your fellow's sin by inspiring regret in him. If
you repay it with that which is best, you will correspond to the presence
of mercifulness and the realm of divine mercy; and by adorning yourself
with His Attributes, you will become one of the folk of divine domination,
and emanate the emanation of mercy from yourself to your fellow: [*then,
behold, he between whom and you there was enmity will be as though*] *he were a dear
friend*. Thus, the Prophet (may God grant him peace) said, 'If the Maker
could appear, He would appear in the form of forbearance.'

[41:35] *But none is granted it*—this noble trait and tremendous virtue—*except those who are steadfast* with God, so that they are unchanged by the provocations of enemies, because of their awareness of Him and reliance on Him, and how they have adopted His forbearance, or obeyed His command; *and none is granted it except one with great fortune* from God by being adorned with His character traits.

[41:36] *And if some temptation from Satan should provoke you*: goading you into repaying with an evil deed, urging you to take revenge and rousing your anger, *then seek refuge in God*: by returning to Him and seeking refuge in His presence from Satan's evil insinuations and temptations. Do this through renouncing your own deeds and attributes by becoming annihilated in His from your own power and strength. *Indeed, He is the Hearer* of the thoughts of your soul and your words which disturb your mind, *the Knower* of your intentions and hidden states.

[41:37] *And among His signs are the night* of the soul's darkness by the emergence of its attributes which cover the light, causing you to fall into evil deeds and preparing you to receive satanic impulses, *and the day* of the spirit's light with the shining of its rays from the heart to the soul so that you engage in good deeds and repay evil deeds with them and refrain from accepting those impulses, and expose yourselves to the divine breezes, *and the sun* of the spirit *and the moon* of the heart. *Do not prostrate to the sun* by becoming annihilated in it and halting with it, veiled by it from the Real, *nor to the moon* by halting with virtues and perfections and inclining to the garden of the Attributes, *but prostrate to God Who created them* by becoming annihilated in the Essence, *if it is Him* alone *Whom you worship*, devoting your worship exclusively to Him without associating any others or being veiled.

Q. 41:35

[41:38] *But if they disdain* annihilation in Him by the emergence of I-ness, transgression and pride, through the soul's attributes and enmity, *still those who are with your Lord*—the foremost who are annihilated in Him—always *glorify Him* with detachment and transcendence from the veils of their essences and attributes, in the *night* of concealment in the station of differentiation and the *day* of self-disclosure in the station of unification; *and they tire not*: for they are sustained by God and invoke with essential love.

[41:39] [*And among His signs is that you see the earth desolate, but when We send down water upon it, it stirs and swells. Truly He Who revives it is indeed the Reviver of the dead. Surely He has power over all things.*]

[41:40] *Indeed, those who blaspheme Our signs*—those who incline and stray from the path of truth to falsehood regarding them, attributing them to other than the Real because of how they are veiled from Him, and reciting them with their souls so that all they understand from them is what corresponds to their own attributes—they *are not hidden from Us, though We are hidden from them. [Is one who is cast into the Fire better [off], or one who arrives secure on the Day of Resurrection? Act as you wish. Indeed, He is Seer of what you do.*

[41:41] *Truly those who disbelieve in the Remembrance when it comes to them [are not hidden from us],] and truly it is an unassailable Book*: guarded and protected from being touched and understood by impure, veiled souls who mean to change it, or viewed by workers of falsehood who seek to impugn it, for it is far beyond their minds and the false beliefs they hold.

[41:42] *Falsehood cannot approach it from [before it or from behind it or from]* any direction: not from the direction of truth, such that it could be refuted by something more eloquent or perfected, since it is real and true; nor from the direction of creation, such that they could refute it with blasphemous interpretations or change it with corruptions, for it is established in the Preserved Tablet on the side of the Real, as He says, *Indeed, it is We Who have revealed the Remembrance, and assuredly We will preserve it* [Q. 15:9]. [*A revelation from One Wise, Praised.*

[41:43] *Nothing is said to you, except what has already been said to the messengers before you. Indeed, your Lord is One of forgiveness and One of painful retribution.*

[41:44] *And had We made it a non-Arabic Qur'ān, they would have said, 'Why have its signs not been expounded [clearly]? What! Non-Arabic and an Arab?'] Say: 'For those who believe it is guidance and a healing*: for those who believe in the Unseen, it is guidance that guides them to the Real, gives them sight through gnosis, and heals the ailments of their hearts: vices such as hypocrisy and doubt. It shows them the way of consideration and action, teaching them and purifying them. *But as for those who do not believe*—the veiled ones—[*there is a deafness in their ears, and they are blind to it. Those—they are [as if they were being] called from a distant place'*]: they do not hear or understand; but rather it is confusing and strange to them, because of the grip heedlessness has over them, and how thoroughly natural coverings and bodily configurations have blocked the channels of their hearts' hearing and sight. Thus, it does not penetrate them or rouse them. They are like the one being called from a distant place, because of their distance from the source of the light by which the Real is perceived and seen. How lost they are in the darknesses of primordial matter!

Q. 41:41

[41:45] [*And verily We gave Moses the Book, but differences arose concerning it; and were it not for a Word that had [already] preceded from your Lord, judgement would have been made between them; for indeed they are in grave doubt concerning it.*

[41:46] *Whoever acts righteously, it is for [the good of] his own soul; and whoever does evil, it is to the detriment thereof. And your Lord is not [at all] a tyrant to His servants.*

[41:47] *To Him devolves [all] knowledge of the Hour. And no fruit emerges from its sheath, and no female bears [a child] or delivers except with His knowledge. And on the day when He will call out to them, 'Where are My associates?' they will say, 'We proclaim to You that there is no witness amongst us.'*

[41:48] *And what they used to call on before has forsaken them and they suppose that there is no refuge for them.*

[41:49] *Man never wearies of supplicating for good; but should any ill befall him, then he becomes despondent, despairing.*

[41:50] *And if We let him taste mercy from Us after the harm that had befallen him, he will surely say, 'This is my due! I do not think that the Hour will ever set in; and even if I am returned to my Lord, I will indeed have the best [reward] with Him.' But We will assuredly inform those who disbelieve of what they did, and assuredly We will make them taste a harsh chastisement.*

Q. 41:45

[41:51] *And when We bestow graces upon man, he is disregardful and turns aside; but when ill befalls him, he makes prolonged supplications.*

[41:52] *Say: 'Consider [this]: if it is from God, and you disbelieve in it, who will be further astray than one who is in extreme defiance?'*]

[41:53] *We shall show them Our signs in the horizons and in their own souls*: We shall rouse them to behold Our disposal of possibilities and their states, *until it becomes clear to them*, by means of rational reflection and proof-based certitude, *that it is the truth. Is it not sufficient* to those who have beheld Him, from the folk of witnessing, *that your Lord is witness to all things*, present and aware? Is it not enough to witness Him in the outward appearances of things through gnosis of Him and in the knowledge that He alone is the ultimate Real, such that it is necessary to adduce the proof of His acts or the intermediary of the self-disclosures of His Attributes? This is the state of the beloved recipient of unveiling by divine attraction before he even travels the path, while the other is the loving wayfarer who struggles in pursuit of arrival.

[41:54] *Nay, verily they are in doubt about the encounter with their Lord*, because of how they are veiled by things made by the Maker, and by creation from the Creator. *Nay, verily He encompasses all things*: nothing escapes His encompassment, otherwise it would not exist at all. The reality of all things is nothing other than His knowledge, and they all exist through it; and His knowledge is the entity of His Essence, and His Essence is the entity of His Being. Thus, nothing escapes His encompassment, for nothing but Him possesses Being, Entity or Essence: *Everything will perish except His countenance* [Q. 28:88]. *Everyone who is on it will perish, yet there will remain the countenance of your Lord,* [*the countenance*] *of majesty and munificence* [Q. 55:26–27].

Q. 41:54

42
COUNSEL[1]
SŪRAT AL-SHŪRĀ

In the Name of God, the Compassionate, the Merciful

[42:1] *Ḥā. Mīm*

[42:2] *ʿAyn. Sīn. Qāf*: the Real (*Ḥaqq*) manifested in Muḥammad by the manifestation of His knowledge (*ʿilm*) through the purity (*salāma*) of his heart (*qalb*). The Real is Muḥammad, outwardly and inwardly, and the knowledge is the purity of his heart from blemishes and blights: that is, his perfection and emergence from behind the veil when the heart was detached for the manifestation of knowledge.

[42:3] *Thus*, by means of such a manifestation upon your locus, and the manifestation of His knowledge upon your heart, *does He reveal to you and to those* prophets [*who were*] *before you*—God, endowed with all His Attributes, *the Mighty*, cloaked in the curtains of His majesty and the veils of His Attributes, *the Wise*, Who manifests His perfection according to preparednesses, and guides all His servants by means and appearances according to the receptivity of preparedness.

[42:4] *To Him belongs whatever is in the heavens and whatever is in the earth*: all of them are the loci of His Attributes, the forms of His domain, and the venues of His acts; *and He is the Exalted*: neither confined by their forms nor defined by their natures; *the Tremendous*: in whose dominion they shrink into insignificance, and in whose glory they disappear into annihilation.

[42:5] *The heavens are well-nigh rent asunder from above one another*: under the influence of the manifestations of His glory, vanishing beneath His power and authority; *and the angels* of detached intellects and contemplative souls *glorify* [*with praise of their Lord*]: glorifying His Essence by detaching their essences, and praising Him with the perfections of their

---

1 The Arabic copy gives this chapter its alternative title of *Ḥā Mīm ʿAyn Sīn Qāf*. [Ed.]

attributes, *and ask forgiveness for those on earth* by the emanation of lights upon their entities and beings, after first being bathed in them from the Unitary Presence. *Verily God is the Forgiving*: covering the darkness of the entities of all things, angels and people alike, with the light of His Essence; *the Merciful*: emanating perfections by the manifestations of His Attributes upon their beings, which none but He can do.

[42:6] [*And those who have taken besides Him guardians, God is watchful over them; and you are not a guardian over them.*

[42:7] *And thus have We revealed to you an Arabic Qurʾān, that you may warn the mother-town and those around it, and that you may warn of the Day of Gathering of which there is no doubt. A part will be in Paradise and a part will be in the Blaze.*]

[42:8] *And had God willed, He would have made them one community*: [such that] all of them were monotheists following natural disposition, as decreed by the divine omnipotence; but instead He based His command on wisdom, and made some of them righteous monotheists and others impious idolaters, as He said, *But they continue to differ* [Q. 11:118]. [This was] in order to differentiate the ranks, realise salvation and damnation, and fill the world, the Hereafter, Paradise and Hell with their inhabitants, so that each get what they merit, and order is established and fulfilled: [*but He admits whomever He will into His mercy, and the evildoers have neither guardian nor helper.*]

Q. 42:6

[42:9] *Or have they taken guardians besides Him* which have no real guardianship, since they have neither power, strength nor being? *But God, He* [*alone*] *is the Guardian*: for He had guardianship, authority and dominion over all things; *and He revives the dead, and He has power over all things*, so how could anything but Him possess guardianship?

[42:10] [*And whatever you may differ in, the verdict therein belongs to God. That, then, is God, my Lord;*] *in Him I have put my trust*: by the annihilation of the acts, and so I shall not counter your deeds with my own; *and to Him I turn penitently*: by the annihilation of my attributes, so I shall not manifest any attribute of mine to counter the attributes of your souls.

[42:11] [*The Originator of the heavens and the earth. He has made for you, from your own selves, pairs, and* [*also*] *pairs of cattle: He multiplies you by such* [*means*].] *There is nothing like Him*: all things are annihilated and reduced to nothingness in Him, and so nothing is alike to Him in 'thingness' (*shayʾiyya*) and being. *He is the Hearer*: through Who hears all that hear; *the Seer*: through Who sees all that see, in concentration and differentiation. He annihilates all things in His Essence and engenders them by His Attributes.

[42:12] [*To Him belong the keys of the heavens and the earth. He extends provision for whomever He will, and He restricts [it]. Indeed, He has knowledge of all things:*] in His hand are the keys to provisions and the treasuries of the kingdom and the dominion. He extends and restricts according to His knowledge to whom He will of His creatures, according to their interests of wealth or poverty.

[42:13] *He has prescribed for you as a religion [that which He enjoined upon Noah and that which We have revealed to you, and that which We enjoined upon Abraham, and Moses, and Jesus, [declaring], 'Establish religion and do not be divided in it']*: He has prescribed for you as absolute religion that which He charged all the prophets to establish, uniting them upon it and decreeing that they not be divided in it. This is the root of religion, which is Oneness, justice, and knowledge of the Resurrection, which is called faith in God and the Last Day. It does not mean the branches of Divine Laws wherein they differed according to their interests, such as the particular characteristics of acts of obedience, worship and transactions, as He says, *To every one of you We have appointed a Divine Law and a way* [Q. 5:48]. The enduring religion is that which pertains to the teachings and acts that are unchanging, and the Divine Law is that which pertains to the rulings and circumstances that are ever changing.

Q. 42:12

Dreadful is it for the idolaters, who are veiled from the Real by others, *that to which you summon them*: meaning Oneness, because they are the folk of enmity and loci for the manifestations of wrath and conquering power. They are not the beloved ones whom God has chosen for His pure nurture and His unadulterated will, nor the loving ones whom He has given the grace to turn to Him penitently by wayfaring and struggle, journeying to Him with yearning and neediness, so that He guided them to Him by the light of His countenance and the beauty of His Essence. He attracted the beloved ones to Him before they engaged in any wayfaring or discipline by destining their election, and chose the loving ones after giving them the grace to journey to Him and engage in the discipline of self-purification; and banished the veiled ones from His door and cast them far from His presence by the decree of destiny for their damnation. [*God chooses for it whomever He will, and He guides to it whomever turns penitently.*

[42:14] *And they did not become divided, except after the knowledge had come to them, out of [jealous] rivalry among themselves. And were it not for a Word that preceded from your Lord, until an appointed term, it would have [already] been judged between them. And indeed those who were made heirs to the Book after them are truly in grave doubt concerning him.*]

[42:15] *So for that* division in religion, *then, summon* to Oneness *and be upright* in realisation of God and true worshipfulness, *[just as you have been commanded,] and do not follow them in their desires*: be stable in this, and do not let your soul manifest with any attribute in the face of their denials and attempts to bring you over to their side. *And say: 'I believe in whatever Book God has revealed*: I have observed the perfections of all the prophets, and combined their teachings, stations, attributes and character traits, so that my upholding of Oneness has been perfected and I have become beloved because of the perfection of my love; and I have become stable in myself, so my righteousness has been completed. This is the meaning of His Words, *And I have been commanded to be just between you. God is our Lord and your Lord.* This refers to stability in the stations of Oneness and realisation. *Our deeds concern us, and your deeds concern you*: this refers to the form of uprightness and stability in righteousness. *There is no argument between us and you*: this refers to the perfection of love and purity, for the station of Oneness necessitated that they be viewed equally. *God will bring us together* at the Major Resurrection and annihilation, *and to Him is the [final] destination'* in the end for the requital.

Q. 42:15

[42:16] *And those who argue concerning God* because they are veiled by their own souls, *after His call has been answered* by surrender and submission to His religion and the acceptance of Oneness, by the purity of innate disposition, *their argument stands refuted [with their Lord]* because it comes from their own souls, and so is baseless in God's sight; *and [His] wrath shall be upon them*, which they deserve because of the manifestation of their own wrath, *and there will be a severe chastisement for them* because of their deprivation.

[42:17] *God it is Who has revealed the Book* of knowledge of Oneness *with the truth*, with the love that it merited and was its true due, *as well as the Balance* of justice. And when this knowledge and Oneness is attained in the spirit, and this love in the heart, and this justice in the soul, annihilation in God and the coming of the Major Resurrection is near: *[And what do you know—perhaps the Hour is near!*

[42:18] *Those who do not believe in it seek to hasten it, but those who believe are apprehensive of it and know that it is the truth. Nay, but verily those who are in doubt concerning the Hour are indeed in extreme error!]*

[42:19] *God is Gracious to His servants*, and kind to them in how He directs their perfections to them, facilitates their means and graces them with deeds that draw them closer to them. *He provides* ample knowledge *to whomever He will*: according to His nurture of them in the configuration of their preparedness for it. *And He is the Strong* Who conquers, *the Mighty* Who overwhelms, denying whomever He will according to His justice and wisdom. Each one has a share of this grace and power and none are bereft of them, but their shares differ according to their preparednesses, means, deeds and states.

[42:20] *And whoever desires the harvest of the Hereafter*: by the power of his will and the earnestness of his pursuit of a greater share of grace, and his determination to direct himself towards the Real and enter the sphere of nearness, *We will enhance for him [his harvest]*: his share, by making good his Hereafter and his worldly life as well, for this world is beneath the Hereafter, followed by its shadow, image and form. *And whoever desires the harvest of this world*: following his caprice towards the lower direction and attaching his aspiration to a greater share of power and distance from the Real, *We will give him of it*: whatever share was destined for him and apportioned to him, and no more; *but in the Hereafter he will have no share*, because of how he turned away from it and fixed his aspiration on the lower and clung onto it, so that it veiled him from the nobler and caused him to turn away from the ampler share. Thus, he will not be able to receive it, nor prepared to attain it, since the root does not follow the branch.

Q. 42:20

[42:21] [*Or have they associates who have prescribed for them a religion which God has not given permission for? And were it not for a [prior] decisive Word, it would have been judged between them. And indeed the wrongdoers will have a painful chastisement.*

[42:22] *You will see the wrongdoers apprehensive because of what they had earned; and it will surely befall them; but those who believe and perform righteous deeds will be in the lushest gardens. They will have whatever they wish near their Lord; that is the great favour.*

[42:23] *That is the good tidings which God gives to His servants who believe and perform righteous deeds.*] *Say: 'I do not ask of you any reward for it, except affection for the kinsfolk'*: this is a 'severed exception'. The implication of [*affection for*] *the kinsfolk* is 'the affection that already exists for the kinsfolk.' Thus, what it really means is that no reward is expected at all, since the affection they had for his kinsfolk would only benefit them, since it would be the cause of their salvation. Affection implies a spiritual correspondence that will cause them to be brought together at the Resurrection, as he (may God bless him and grant him peace) said, 'Every man will be resurrected alongside those he loves.' It would not make sense to call it a reward for him, given this. Nor is it possible for someone whose spirit is sullied and whose level is far from them to truly love them; nor for someone whose spirit is illuminated and who has gnosis of God and love for Him, being one of the folk of Oneness, not to love them. They are the folk of the prophetic household (*ahl bayt al-nubuwwa*) and the fonts of sainthood and chivalry, beloved in the primal divine nurture, raised up to the highest status, and no one loves them but he who loves God and His Messenger and is loved by God and His Messenger. Had they not been beloved to God from the beginning, the Messenger of God would not have loved them, for his love is identical with His love in formal differentiation after it was in the source of unification. They are the four mentioned in the upcoming *ḥadīth*. Nonetheless, note that he had many other children and relatives in their levels, yet did not refer them or encourage the community to love them in the same way he did for those ones whom he singled out for mention.

Q. 42:23

It was related that when this verse was revealed, someone said, 'Messenger of God, who are those kinsfolk of yours whom it is obligatory to love?' He replied, "ʿAlī, Fāṭima, al-Ḥasan and al-Ḥusayn, and their children.' Since kinship implies a temperamental correspondence that denotes spiritual affinity, their children who walked their path and followed their guidance shared their status, which is why he encouraged that they be treated well and loved absolutely; and he forbade that they be wronged or abused, and promised reward for the former and warned against the latter. The Prophet (may God bless him and grant him peace) said, 'Paradise is forbidden to those who wrong my household and offend me through my progeny. If anyone does an injury to any scion of ʿAbd al-Muṭṭalib and does not make amends for it, I shall make amends for it tomorrow when he meets me on the Day of Resurrection.' He (may God grant him peace) also said,

> Anyone who dies while having love for the family of Muḥammad (*āl Muḥammad*) will be forgiven. Indeed, anyone who dies while having love for the family of Muḥammad will die a true penitent. Indeed, anyone who dies while having love for the family of Muḥammad will die a true believer. Indeed, anyone who dies while having love for the family of Muḥammad will die a true witness with complete faith. Indeed, anyone who dies while having love for the family of Muḥammad will receive tidings of Paradise from the Angel of Death, and then from Munkar and Nakīr. Indeed, anyone who dies while having love for the family of Muḥammad will be carried to Paradise as the bride is carried to her husband's home. Indeed, anyone who dies while

having love for the family of Muḥammad will have two doors leading to Paradise opened inside his grave. Indeed, if someone dies while having love for the family of Muḥammad, God will make his grave a pilgrimage site for the angels of mercy. Indeed, anyone who dies while having love for the family of Muḥammad will die upon the Sunna and the Community. Indeed, anyone who dies while having hatred for the family of Muḥammad will come forth on the Day of Resurrection branded between the eyes, as one with no hope of God's mercy. Indeed, anyone who dies while having hatred for the family of Muḥammad will die a disbeliever. Indeed, no one who dies while having hatred for the family of Muḥammad will catch even a whiff of the scent of Paradise.

And whoever acquires a good deed by loving the Messenger's family, *We shall enhance for him its goodness* by helping him follow their path, for that love is due only to the purity of preparedness and the subsistence of innate disposition, which necessitates the grace to follow and receive guidance to the station of witnessing; hence, he becomes one of the folk of sainthood and is gathered alongside them at the Resurrection. *Indeed, God is Forgiving*: by illuminating the darkness of the attributes of those who love his family, *Appreciative* of the efforts of those who connect to them and love them, and by multiplying the rewards for their good deeds and emanating perfections upon them by the manifestation of His Attributes to correspond to them.

Q. 42:24

[42:24] [*Or do they say, 'He has invented a lie against God?'*] For if God wishes, *He can seal your heart*: for only those whose hearts are sealed like theirs invent lies against God. [*And God will efface the falsehood*:] for it is the nature of God to efface falsehood, *and vindicate the truth with His Words*. His decree is that when something is false, He effaces it and affirms its opposite, and so will He do to the falsehoods they speak. [*Indeed, He is Knower of what is in the breasts.*

[42:25] *And He it is Who accepts repentance from His servants, and pardons evil deeds, and knows what they do.*

[42:26] *And He answers those who believe and perform righteous deeds, and He enhances them of His bounty. And as for the disbelievers, for them there will be a severe chastisement.*

[42:27] *For were God to extend His provision to His servants, they would surely become covetous in the earth; but He sends down in the measure that He wishes. Indeed, He is Aware, Seer of His servants.*

[42:28] *And He it is Who sends down the rain after they have despaired, and unfolds His mercy, and He is the Patron, the Praised.*

[42:29] *And of His signs is the creation of the heavens and the earth and whatever He has scattered in them in the way of creatures. And He is able to bring them together, whenever He wishes.*

[42:30] *And whatever affliction may befall you is on account of what your hands have earned. And He pardons much.*

[42:31] *And you cannot escape on earth, and besides God you have neither protector nor helper.*

[42:32] *And of His signs are the ships [that run] on the sea [appearing] like landmarks.*

[42:33] *If He wishes He stills the wind, whereat they remain motionless on its surface. Indeed, in that there are signs for every steadfast, grateful [servant].*

[42:34] *Or He wrecks them because of what they have earned. And He pardons much.*

[42:35] *And that those who dispute concerning Our signs may know they have no refuge.*

[42:36] *So whatever you have been given is [but] the enjoyment of the life of this world.] But what is with God is better and more lasting,* because it is nobler and more enduring, *for those who believe* with true faith *and put their trust in their Lord* alone by the annihilation of the acts: that is, those whose knowledge is certitude and whose action is trust, by shedding their own deeds; [42:37] *and those who avoid grave sins* which are their own beings, the basest attributes of their souls that manifest in their deeds in the station of erasure, *and indecencies, and [who], when they are angry* in their variegations, *forgive:* that is, those who are singled out for mercy among others; [42:38] *and those who answer their Lord* with the voice of pure innate disposition when He calls them to Oneness by disclosing the light of Unity, *and establish* the *prayer* of witnessing and are not veiled by their opinions and intellects, but rather *whose courses of action are [a matter of] counsel between them* because of their knowledge that God has a task for each person, and a regard for them, and a secret in them, and no other shares that task, regard and secret; *and who, of what We have bestowed on them, expend* by instructing others in self-perfection; [42:39] *and those who, when they suffer aggression, defend themselves* with justice, avoiding humiliation and oppression because they are in the station of uprightness, upholding truth and justice, which casts its shadow in their souls.

[42:40] [*For the requital of an evil deed is an evil deed like it. But whoever pardons and reconciles, his reward will be with God. Indeed, He does not like wrongdoers.*

Q. 42:28

[42:41] *And whoever defends himself after he has been wronged, for such there will be no course [of action] against them.*

[42:42] *A course [of action] is only [open] against those who wrong people and seek [to commit] in the earth what is not right. For such there will be a painful chastisement.*

[42:43] *But verily he who is patient and forgives—indeed, that is constancy in [such] affairs.*

[42:44] *And whomever God leads astray has no protec or after Him. And you will see the wrongdoers, when they sight the chastisement, saying, 'Is there any way to return?'*

[42:45] *And you will see them being exposed to it, submissive by abasement, looking with a furtive glance. And those who believe will say, 'Indeed, the losers are those who have lost themselves and their families on the Day of Resurrection. Truly the wrongdoers will be in lasting chastisement.*

[42:46] *'And they have no guardians to help them besides God. And whomever God leads astray has no course [of action].'*

Q. 42:41

[42:47] *Answer your Lord before there comes a day for which there is no revoking from God. On that day you will have no refuge, and for you there will be no [way of] denying.*

[42:48] *But if they are disregardful, We have not sent you as a keeper over them. Your duty is only to deliver the Message. And indeed when We let man taste from Us some mercy, he exults in it; but if some ill befalls them because of what their [own] hands have sent ahead, then, lo and behold, humanity is ungrateful.*

[42:49] *To God belongs the kingdom of the heavens and the earth. He creates whatever He will; He gives to whomever He will females, and He gives to whomever He will males.*

[42:50] *Or He combines them, males and females; and He makes whomever He will infertile. Indeed, He is Knower, Powerful.]*

[42:51] *And it is not [possible] for any human that God should speak to him except by revelation*: that is, except by three modes: either by his reaching the station of Unity and annihilation in Him, and then realisation of his being in the station of subsistence, so that revelation comes to him without an intermediary, as God says, *Then he drew near and drew closer still, until he was within the length of two bows away or nearer, whereat He revealed to His servant what he revealed* [Q. 53:8–10]; *or from behind a veil*: by his being in the veil of the heart and the station of the self-disclosure of the Attributes, wherein He speaks to him by means of intimate discourse, communion, unveiling and conversation, but without vision because he is veiled by the veil of the Attributes, as was the situation of Moses (may God grant him peace); *or that He should send a messenger* from the angels who reveals to him in the form of casting and blowing inspiration into the heart, or a disembodied voice, or a dream, as he said (may God grant him peace), 'The Holy Spirit blew into my heart, telling me that no soul will die until its provision has been completed.' [*And he then reveals with His permission whatever He wishes.*] *Indeed, He is Exalted* above being faced and addressed; anything that faces Him becomes annihilated and disappears, for He is too exalted for anything to subsist with Him or share in His presence; *Wise:* He directs with wisdom the modes of discourse to manifest His knowledge in the details of the loci, and to perfect His servants so that they are guided to Him and to gnosis of Him. He then gives an example of this three-mode revelation:

Q. 42:52

[42:52] *And thus have We revealed to you a Spirit* to give life to dead hearts *from* the realm of *Our command,* transcendent beyond time and sanctified beyond space. *You did not know what the Book was,* the discriminating intellect which is the perfection that is yours alone, *nor faith,* the hidden faith that became yours upon subsistence after annihilation when you were veiled by the covers of your creation, and the state of your arrival at your annihilation and the vanishing of your being; *but We made it a light* at the moment of your uprightness *by which We guide whomever We wish of Our servants* singled out for pre-eternal nurture, whether they are the beloved ones or the loving ones. *And indeed you,* O beloved one, *guide* through Us whom you will *to a straight path,* whose nature cannot be perceived and whose character cannot be known.

[42:53] *The path of God,* [*to Whom belongs whatever is in the heavens and whatever is in the earth*]: the path that is His alone; the path of the affirmation of Essential Oneness that includes both Oneness of Attributes and Oneness of the acts, which is called the Oneness of Kingdom (*tawḥīd al-mulk*). By which I mean the path of Essential Unity with all the Attributes, outward and inward, by the kingdom of the heavens of the spirits and the earth of the absolute body. *Surely with God all matters end:* by annihilation in Him, when He calls out with His Essence, *'To whom does the kingdom belong today?'* And then He answers Himself: *'To God, the One, the All-Compelling!'* [Q. 40:16]. And God (Exalted is He) knows best.

43
ORNAMENTS OF GOLD
SŪRAT AL-ZUKHRUF

In the Name of God, the Compassionate, the Merciful

[43:1] [*Ḥā. Mīm.*

[43:2] *By the Book that clarifies:*] He swears by the first of all being, the Real (*Ḥaqq*), and the last of it, Muḥammad, which is the loftiest of all oaths for it is the root and perfection of all things. This is why the Testimony of Faith in these two is the foundation of Islam and the pillar of faith, and the unification of the two is the true path and the upright way. The Unity of Being and influence is compulsion (*jabr*), while the affirmation of differentiation in being and influence is free will (*qadar*); and the synthesis of the two in our words, 'There is no god but God, and Muḥammad is the Messenger of God', is the straight path and the firm faith. Or the oath may refer to something that corresponds to the Book, namely the Tablet (*lawḥ*) and the Pen (*qalam*), as in His Words, *Nūn. By the Pen and what they inscribe* [Q. 68:1]. [This is so] since one may allude to a word by its last letter just as one may with its first. According to the first reading, the Book could be taken to mean the soul of Muḥammad, because it explains the Real in concentration and differentiation and was sent down from God.

[43:3] [*Indeed, We have made it*] *an Arabic Qurʾān*—a synthesis of all the differentiations, combining all the Divine Attributes and levels of being and perfection—*that perhaps you may understand* that with which We address you.

[43:4] *And it is indeed in the Mother Book*: the root of being in the first degree, and the first dot of pristine, relative being by the first individuation from Absolute Being, reciting the pure ipseity alluded to by His Words [*which is*] *with Us,* [*and it is*] *indeed exalted* to the utmost heights beyond which there is nothing higher, *wise*, endowed with wisdom,

for by it were manifested the forms and realities of things, their entities and attributes, and the organisation and order of beings as they
are. According to the second reading, this interpretation would not be
congruent and the Book would be taken to refer to the Qur'ān, which
clarifies Oneness and the differentiation to which the oath alludes in
general. Then: *And it is indeed in the Mother Book*: the supreme spirit
that contains all knowledge, and indeed all things, which is with Us
and close to Us, closer than all the other teachings attained through all
levels of descent. Divinely-inspired knowledge is what was engraved in
the spirit, which was the first of spirits before its descent into the levels.
The meaning of the wisdom of the Qur'ān is that it contains discursive
wisdom which engenders true creeds, such as Oneness, prophethood,
the states of the Hereafter and the like. Practical wisdom consists of
explaining the rulings pertaining to the deeds of morally-responsible
individuals, such as Divine Laws and the proper method of progressing
through the levels and states of acquisitions and gifts.

Q. 43:5

[43:5] *Shall We turn away from you the Remembrance, [utterly, because you
are a profligate folk]?* Shall We neglect you and take the Remembrance from
you because of your profligacy, when the only reason you needed the
Remembrance was your profligacy? For if they were on the honest way
and the middle path, no reminder would have been needed. Reminders are
only needed in times of negligence or excess, which is why the prophets
were sent during times of stagnation. God says, *People were one community;
then God sent forth the prophets* [Q. 2:213].

[43:6] [*And how many a prophet did We send among the ancients!*

[43:7] *And never did a prophet come to them but that they used to deride him.*

[43:8] *So We destroyed those who were mightier than them in prowess, and
[already] there passed the example of the ancients.*

[43:9] *And if you ask them, 'Who created the heavens and the earth?' they
will surely say, 'The Mighty, the Knower created them.'*

[43:10] *He Who made the earth a cradle for you, and placed for you therein
ways, that perhaps you may be guided;* [43:11] *and Who sent down water from the
heaven in measure, and We revived with it a dead land. Thus will you be brought
forth;* [43:12] *and Who created the pairs, all of them; and made for you ships and
cattle on which you ride,* [43:13] *that you may sit upon their backs, and then remember your Lord's grace when you are settled on them, and say, 'Glory be to Him Who
has disposed this for us, and we [by] ourselves were no match for it.*

[43:14] *'And indeed it is to our Lord that we shall return.'*]

[43:15] *And they assign to Him from among His own servants a part*: they

acknowledged that He is the Creator of the heavens and earth and their
Designer and Maker, but they anthropomorphised Him and compartmentalised Him by asserting that He had a son, which is a part of the father
and shares its type. This was because they were people of the exoteric and
anthropomorphists who could not get past the level of materiality
and imagination; nor could they shed the garments of corporeal realities,
in order to perceive detached realities and sanctified essences, never mind
the essences of God. Thus, everything they depicted and imagined was
corporeal, and this is why they belied the prophets in their claims about
the Hereafter, the Resurrection and the Gathering, and everything else
relating to the afterlife. Their perception could not get past the lower
world; nor could their intellects, veiled from the light of guidance, move
beyond the affairs of their worldly lives. There was no correspondence
between their essences and the essences of the prophets, save for their
common external humanity, and they had no need for anything beyond
it. [*Indeed, man is a manifest ingrate.*

Q. 43:16

[43:16] *Or He has adopted, from all that He has created, daughters, and preferred you with sons?*] When they heard of how the sages from among their
forebears of old had spoken of the existence of angelic souls and referred
to them as feminine, whether with regards to the word[1] or because of
their passivity and receptivity to the holy intellectual spirits, as well as
how they described them as being close to the divine presence, they took
this to mean that they were literally females in the animal sense of the
counterpart to males; and since they were the chosen ones of God, they
took them to be His daughters. Indeed, common people usually imagine
angels to be ephemeral human forms of immense beauty.

[43:17] [*And when one of them is given the good tidings of that which he has
attributed to the Compassionate, his face becomes darkened, and he chokes inwardly.*

[43:18] *What! One that is brought up amid trinkets and is incoherent in a
dispute?*

[43:19] *And they have made the angels, who are themselves servants of the
Compassionate, females. Did they witness their creation? Their testimony will be
written down and they will be questioned.*]

[43:20] *And they say, 'Had the Compassionate [so] willed, we would not
have worshipped them'*: when they heard the prophets say that things are
contingent on God's will, they took advantage of this and made it an
excuse for their denial. They did not say this based on knowledge or

1 The word *nafs* ('soul') is a feminine noun.

certitude, but rather for the sake of obstinacy and belligerence. Therefore God answered them: *They do not have any knowledge of that*: for if they truly knew it they would be monotheists who attributed influence to none but God, and would find themselves bound to worship Him and no other, as they would see that benefit and harm come from Him alone. *They are only surmising*: they did not truly believe their own words, for they continued to revere and fear their idols and attempt to frighten the prophets with them, as the people of Hūd said, *We say nothing, save that one of our gods has possessed you in some evil way* [Q. 11:54]. When they attempted to frighten Abraham (may God grant him peace) with the same, he replied, *I have no fear of what you associate with Him, unless my Lord wills something. My Lord encompasses all things through His knowledge; will you not remember? How should I fear what you have associated, and you fear not, that you have associated with God that for which He has not revealed to you any warrant?* [Q. 6:80–81].

Q. 43:21

[43:21] [*Or have We brought them a Book before, so that they are holding fast to it?*

[43:22] *Nay, but they say, 'Indeed, we found our fathers following a [certain] creed and we are indeed in their footsteps rightly guided.'*

[43:23] *And thus We never sent a warner before you into any city without its affluent folk saying, 'Indeed, we found our fathers following a [certain] creed and [so] we are indeed following in their footsteps.'*

[43:24] *Say: 'What! Even if I bring you a better [means to] guidance than what you found your fathers following?' They say, 'Indeed, we disbelieve in what you are sent with.'*

[43:25] *So We took vengeance on them; behold then how was the sequel for the deniers.*

[43:26] *And when Abraham said to his father and his people, 'Indeed, I am innocent of that which you worship, [43:27] except Him Who originated me; for He will indeed guide me.'*

[43:28] *And he made it a word enduring among his posterity that perhaps they might recant.*

[43:29] *Nay, but I have let these and their fathers enjoy [life] until there came to them the truth, and a messenger who makes [things] clear.*

[43:30] *But when the truth came to them, they said, 'This is sorcery, and we are indeed disbelievers in it.'*]

[43:31] *And they said, 'If only this Qur'ān had been revealed to some great man from the two towns!'*

[43:32] [*Is it they who apportion the mercy of your Lord? We have apportioned among them their livelihood in the life of this world, and raised some of them above others by degrees, so that some of them may take others in service. And the mercy of your Lord is better than what they amass:*] since they were folk who did not understand meanings but recognised only external appearances, they did not perceive anything to revere in the Messenger of God (may God bless him and grant him peace) since he did not possess the kind of wealth, power and prestige they expected. They revered figures such as al-Walīd b. al-Mughīra, Abū Masʿūd al-Thaqafī and their ilk, because of their power, wealth and servants. Therefore, they scorned the Messenger of God (may God bless him and grant him peace) and said, 'His situation does not warrant that God should elect him and honour him. If this Qurʾān were truly from God, He would have chosen a great man for it such as al-Walīd or Abū Masʿūd and revealed it to him, since his situation befits the majesty of God.' So God answered them with the rebuttal that they did not apportion the mercy of religion and guidance, of which they had neither share nor knowledge; nor could they even apportion the things they did know and utilise: their livelihoods and worldly matters, which they had to struggle to acquire and with which they were solely concerned. How, then, could they hope to apportion that of which they had not the slightest knowledge?

Q. 43:33

[43:33] [*And were it not [for the danger] that people would be one community, We would have made, for those who disbelieve in the Compassionate, roofs of silver for their houses and stairs by which they ascend,* [43:34] *and doors for their houses, and couches on which they recline,* [43:35] *and ornaments of gold. Yet surely all that would be nothing but the [transient] enjoyment of the life of this world, and the Hereafter with your Lord is for the God-fearing.*]

[43:36] *And whoever is blind (yaʿsh) to the Remembrance of the Compassionate, We assign for him a devil, [and he becomes his companion]*: the verb can be read as *yaʿshu* or *yaʿsha*; the difference is that *yaʿshu* means 'to look away distractedly or wilfully without any impairment', while *yaʿsha* means 'to have impaired vision'. The former reading refers to one whose preparedness was pure and his disposition sound and ready to perceive the Remembrance of the Compassionate, meaning the Qurʾān revealed from Him, and to understand its meaning and recognise its truth, yet he turned a blind eye to it because of his worldly desire, iniquity and rancour, or failed to understand it and recognise its reality because he was veiled by natural coverings and preoccupied with sensory pleasures, or deluded by his religion and his false creeds and customs—for such a person, We assign a jinn-devil to lead him astray with temptations and embellishments of the pleasures in which he is plunged and the baubles he pursues, or with suggestions and false insinuations to keep him chasing his delusional capricious beliefs; or a human devil to delude him and join him, keeping him company on his path and leading him further from the Real. The latter reading refers to the one whose preparedness was impaired to begin with and who was damned before time began, his heart too blind to perceive the realities of the Remembrance and unable to understand its meaning—for such a person, We assign a devil from his own soul, or from his type, to accompany him in his error and delusion.

[43:37] *And indeed they bar them [from the way]*: the devils bar their companions from the path of Unity and the way of truth, *while they suppose that they are [rightly] guided* in what they do.

[43:38] *[It is so] until when he comes to Us, [he says, 'Oh, if only there were between me and you the distance of the two easts!'—What an evil companion then!]* When Our retribution arrives as an inevitable consequence of his beliefs and deeds, and the chastisement for his way of life and religion comes, he will wish to be as far away as possible from his devil, who deluded him from the truth and made the cause of his torment seemly to him. He will renounce his companion and blame him once the natural link or causal connection between them is severed by the destruction of the body.

Q. 43:37

[43:39] *And it will not benefit you [this day, given that you did wrong, that you will be sharing in the chastisement]*: this hope will not avail you when the chastisement comes and the retribution is rightfully dealt out, for you will both be guilty because of your shared responsibility for its cause. Or the fact that you share in the chastisement will not diminish its severity and torment.

[43:40] *[Can you, then, make the deaf hear, or can you guide the blind and one who is in manifest error?*

[43:41] *Either We shall take you away and then take vengeance on them,* [43:42] *or We shall show you that which We have promised them, for indeed We have power over them.*

[43:43] *So hold fast to that which has been revealed to you; surely you are on a straight path.*

[43:44] *And it is indeed a Reminder for you and for your people. And you will [eventually] be questioned.*

[43:45] *And ask those of Our messengers whom We sent before you: 'Did We [ever] appoint, besides the Compassionate, gods to be worshipped?'*

[43:46] *And verily We sent Moses with Our signs to Pharaoh and his council, and he said, 'I am indeed the messenger of the Lord of the Worlds.'*

[43:47] *But when he brought them Our signs, behold! they laughed at them.*

[43:48] *And We never showed them a sign, but it was greater than the one before it. And We seized them with chastisement, that perhaps they might recant.*

[43:49] *And they said, 'O sorcerer, supplicate your Lord for us by the covenant that He has made with you. Assuredly we will be guided.'*

[43:50] *But as soon as We relieved them from the chastisement, behold! they had broken their pledge.*

[43:51] *And Pharaoh proclaimed among his people, 'O my people, does not the kingdom of Egypt belong to me, and these rivers flowing beneath me? Do you not perceive?*

[43:52] *'Or am I not better than this one, who is contemptible, and who can scarcely speak clearly?*

[43:53] *'Why, then, have bracelets of gold not been cast on him or the angels not come with him one after the other?'*

[43:54] *Thus did he persuade his people and they obeyed him. Indeed, they were an immoral folk.*

[43:55] *So when they had angered Us, We took vengeance on them and drowned them all.*

[43:56] *And We made them a thing past, and an example for others.*

Q. 43:48

[43:57] *And when the son of Mary is cited as an example, behold! your people laugh at it.*

[43:58] *And they say, 'Are our gods better or he?' They only cite this to you for the sake of contention. Nay, but they are a contentious lot.*

[43:59] *He is only a servant [of Ours] on whom We bestowed favour, and We made him an exemplar for the Children of Israel.*

[43:60] *And had We willed, We would have appointed among you angels to be [your] successors in the earth.]*

[43:61] *And indeed he is a portent of the Hour, [so do not doubt it but follow Me. This is a straight path']*: Jesus (may God grant him peace) is one of the portents of the Major Resurrection, because his descent will be one of the portents of the Hour. A *ḥadīth* says that he will descend in a pass in the Holy Land called Afīq, holding a spear in his hand with which he will slay the Antichrist (*Dajjāl*). He will break the cross and demolish the monasteries and churches. He will enter Jerusalem as the people are performing the dawn prayer. The imam will step back for him, but Jesus (may God grant him peace) will push him forwards and pray behind him according to the religion of Muḥammad (may God bless him and grant him peace).

The pass called Afīq symbolises the locus in which he will be embodied. The Holy Land symbolises the pure matter from which his body will be constituted. The spear symbolises the form of the power and authority that will be manifested in it. The slaying of the Antichrist with the spear symbolises how he will overcome the deceiving pretender, in whose time he will emerge. The breaking of the cross and demolition of the monasteries and churches symbolises how he will abolish all the differing religions. His entry into Jerusalem symbolises how he will reach the station of essential sainthood in the divine presence, which is the station of the pole. The people performing the dawn prayer symbolises how the Muḥammadans will be united in the upright affirmation of Oneness at the rising of the dawn of the Major Resurrection, when the light of the sun of Unity appears. The imam stepping back symbolises how the guardian of the Muḥammadan faith in his time will sense his precedence over all others, because of his pole-hood. The way Jesus (may God grant him peace) will push him forward and follow him in prayer, according to the Muḥammadan Law, symbolises how he will follow the way of the Chosen Prophet, and not change any of its Laws, though he will teach them Essential Oneness and acquaint them with the states of the Major Resurrection and the rising of the enduring countenance. This interpretation applies to the view that the Mahdī will be Jesus son of Mary himself, according to the narrated *ḥadīth*, 'There is no Mahdī other than Jesus son of Mary.' If in fact the Mahdī is someone else, then his entry into Jerusalem symbolises his arrival at the locus of witnessing rather than the station of the pole, and the imam who steps back will be the Mahdī. He will step back, despite being the pole of the age, for the sake of good etiquette between the saint and the prophet. Then Jesus (may God grant him peace) will send him forward because he knows of his true precedence over him due to his pole-hood. His prayer behind him according to the Muḥammadan Law will be an act of deference to him, in realisation of the outward and inward emanation from him. And God knows best.

Q. 43:62

The reason He said, *Follow Me. This is a straight path*, is that the Muḥammadan way is the path of God because it will subsist after the annihilation. His religion is God's religion, and his path is God's path, and to follow him is to follow God. Hence, there is no difference between Him saying *Follow Me* and saying 'Follow My messengers.' This is why following him bequeaths God's love, for his way is the way of true Unity, without which there can be no uprightness. Thus, Jesus could do no more than follow him when he arrived at Unity. The transcendence of duality necessitates true love.

[43:62] [*And do not let Satan bar you. Indeed, he is a manifest enemy of yours.*
[43:63] *And when Jesus came with the clear signs, he said, 'Verily I have*

brought you wisdom, and [I have come] to make clear to you some of what you are at variance over. So fear God and obey me.

[43:64] *'Indeed, God is my Lord and your Lord; so worship Him—that is a straight path.'*

[43:65] *But the factions differed among themselves. So woe to those who do wrong from the chastisement of a painful day.]*

[43:66] *Are they awaiting anything but that the Hour should come upon them [suddenly]*—[meaning] that the Mahdī should emerge unexpectedly—*while they are unaware* of him?

[43:67] *Friends will, on that day, be foes of one another, except for the God-fearing*: friendship is either virtuous or otherwise. When it is virtuous, it is either in God or for God. When it is not virtuous, its cause is either egocentric pleasure or intellectual benefit.

Q. 43:64

The first type is spiritual essential love based on the correspondence of spirits in pre-eternity, because of their proximity to the divine presence and their equality in the Unitary Presence, about which he said, 'Those of them who recognise one another, bond with one another.' When they emerge into this realm of existence, they long for their homes in this proximity and direct themselves towards the Real, detaching from the garbs of sensory perception and base matter. When they meet, they recognise one another; and when they recognise one another, they love one another, because of their original homogeneity, circumstantial resemblance, fellowship of direction and path, similarity of purpose and instinct, and mutual detachment from corrupt desires and essential accidents, which are the cause of enmity. Each of them benefits from the other in their conduct, knowledge and recollection of their homes, and they rejoice in the meeting and draw purity from one another, and cooperate in the affairs of this life and the next. This is the friendship that is true and complete, and never ends. It is the friendship of the saints, prophets, elect ones (*aṣfiyā'*) and martyrs.

The second type is heart-centred love based on the correspondence of attributes, sublime character traits and virtuous conduct, arising from beliefs and righteous deeds. It is the love of the righteous and the pious among themselves, and the love of the gnostics and saints for them, and the love of the prophets for their communities.

The third type is egocentric love based on sensory pleasures and particular desires, such as love between spouses based on pure lust, or love between wicked and iniquitous folk who cooperate in the pursuit of desires and the amassing of wealth.

The fourth type is intellectual love based on the facilitation of means of livelihood and the attainment of worldly welfare, such as the love between merchants and manufacturers, or the love of the receiver of a kindness for the doer. Anything that is based on an ephemeral desire and a passing cause will end when it expires, and upon its loss will transform into enmity, because each party will have come to expect the usual pleasure and customary benefit it received from the other, though it can no longer be found because its cause is gone. Now since the folk of knowledge usually experience one of the latter two types, He spoke in absolute terms and said, *Friends will, on that day, be foes of one another, except for the God-fearing*, because the causes of the connection between them will be severed and their bodily functions will depart them, and they will no longer be able to attain sensory pleasure and corporeal benefit. Their former pleasures will be transformed into woe, pain, harm and loss; the pleasures and desires will be gone, while the chastisements and consequences will remain. Thus, each person will hate and despise his former friends, because he will deem them the cause of his present torment. He then exempted the God-fearing from this: those who experienced the other two types of love, because they are the minority, as He says, *But few are they!* [Q. 38:24]; *and few indeed of My servants are thankful* [Q. 34:13].

Q. 43:68

Upon my word, the first group are rarer than red sulphur; they are the folk of perfect God-fearing who have reached its far limit and attained all of its ranks. First they avoided sin, then curiosity, then deeds, then attributes, then essences, so that no remnant of them remained about which they could dispute and stray because of it from their Beloved and so ruin their love. Nothing remained of them but the love itself. The second group fell below the level of the first and sufficed with the external side of God-fearing, contentedly accepting the bliss they received in the Hereafter and happily relinquishing the world and its contents for the sake of that manifold grace. Therefore, the objects of their love remained among them because their causes remained, namely their common attributes and configurations for the pursuit of God's favour and reward, and the avoidance of God's wrath and chastisement. They are the approved servants—both these two groups—because they both sought God's approval and so He attributed them to Himself, saying:

[43:68] *'O My servants, there is no fear for [you this day, nor will you grieve]*: neither group will fear because they will be safe from chastisement, nor will they grieve for the loss of worldly pleasures because they enjoy a far more blissful and joyous state, although they will occupy an infinitely varied array of ranks of bliss, delight, contentment and peace, for each person's state will be greatly different from the other's; [43:69] [*those who believed in Our signs and had submitted themselves [to Me]*].

[43:70] '*Enter Paradise, you and your spouses, to be made joyful.*

[43:71] '*They will be served from all around with [large] dishes of gold and goblets and therein will be whatever souls desire and eyes delight in, and you will abide in it [forever]*:] the Paradise they will be commanded to enter is the garden of the soul, in which both groups will share, and not the gardens of the Attributes and Essence which are solely for the foremost, as is shown by His Words:

[43:72] '*And that is the Paradise which you have been given to inherit [as the reward] for what you used to do*: the Paradise that is the reward for deeds in the garden of the soul, for He says, *Therein will be whatever souls desire and eyes delight in* [Q. 43:71].

[43:73] ['*Therein are abundant fruits for you, from which you will eat.*'

[43:74] *Indeed, the guilty will abide in the chastisement of Hell*—[43:75] *it will not be lightened for them and they will be [utterly] despondent in it.*

[43:76] *And We never wronged them, but they themselves were the wrongdoers.*]

Q. 43:70

[43:77] *And they will call out, 'O Mālik*: the keeper of Hell is called Mālik ('Owner') because he deals solely with those who claimed ownership of the world and preferred it, as God says, *As for him who was rebellious, and preferred the life of this world, Hellfire will indeed be the abode* [Q. 79:37–39]. Likewise, the keeper of Paradise is called Riḍwān ('Contentment') because he deals solely with those with whom God is content and who are content with Him. It is said that contentment with fate is God's supreme door. [Mālik] is the corporeal nature to which are assigned the bodies of the world and dark primordial matter; or the universal animal soul to which is assigned influence on the animal bodies, which overcome the rational souls confined in the chains of sensory pleasures and base desires. The reason he is not tormented by the Fire himself is that he is made of the substance of that fire, so that it is a paradise for him but a fire for the inhabitants of Hell because of the clash of their substance with its. They will call to Mālik rather than to God because they will be completely veiled and distanced from God, and will direct their intentions and hopes worshipfully towards Mālik. The nature of the call will be that they direct themselves towards him and seek their aim from him.

Their call, '*Let your Lord finish us off!*' alludes to the hope for the complete end of preparedness and the death of innate instinct, so that they are no longer tormented by harmful configurations and rebellious flames. Or it is the hope for the numbing of the senses and the absence of sensation, because of the terrible pain of the bodily torment. *He will say, 'You will surely remain!'* This alludes to the temporary stay, which is commensurate with the stubbornness of the configurations and the sins and crimes they committed, if their preparednesses remain and their beliefs are sound, or to the perpetual stay if not. The concept of remaining can denote perpetuity, but it does not necessarily have to. Likewise, the guilty include both those who are inherently damned and those who are not. This is why the concept of abiding in His Words, *Indeed, the guilty will abide in the chastisement of Hell* [43:74], can be understood to mean a long stay and not necessarily an eternal one, and it is often used in this way in conventional speech in a figurative sense. This is based on the assumption that the class of guilty covers both the aforementioned groups of damned ones, in contrast to the class of God-fearing which covers both the aforementioned groups of saved ones. If we said that it applied only to those who are eternally damned and banished, we would take his Words, *You will surely remain*, to refer to perpetuity.

Q. 43:78

[43:78] ['*Verily We brought you the truth, but most of you were averse to the truth.'*

[43:79] *Or have they contrived some matter? For We [too] are indeed contriving.*

[43:80] *Or do they reckon that We do not hear their secret thoughts and their conspiring?*] *Yes, indeed! And Our messengers are with them keeping a record*: every evil thought that occurs to the mind is inscribed in the celestial souls, just as it is inscribed in the human souls, because of their connection to them. They are inscribed in the same way, whether in the imaginative faculties if they are particular or in the intellectual faculties if they are universal. Both of them are manifested upon the soul when it becomes oblivious to sensation and returns to its essence, and the things it had forgotten are reflected to it from the celestial souls upon this parting, so that it recalls them all at once. This is the meaning of His Words, *God has kept count of it, while they forgot it* [Q. 58:6]. The recording messengers are the celestial souls that correspond to each human being, according to the circumstance of the soul's connection to the body.

[43:81] [*Say: 'If the Compassionate had a son,*] *I would have been first among the worshippers* of that son. This either means to argue that God does not have a son, or to imply that the Messenger was not guilty of idolatry. The argument of the former is given in the Words:

[43:82] '*Glory be to the Lord of the heavens and the earth, the Lord of the Throne, above what they allege!'* This negates that he worshipped any such son, as though he were saying, 'I declare His Oneness and transcendence above what they allege about Him, namely that He could have any likeness, for He is Lord and Creator of all bodies, and could not be one of them.' This constitutes an argument that He could not have a son. As for the latter implication, his words *Glory be...* can be understood as the Words of God Himself rather than those of the Messenger, that is: declare the transcendence of the Lord of the heavens above what they allege. Thus, it would be a repudiation of the aforementioned hypothetical suggestion; and the conditional statement about the Messenger's worship would be a hypothetical description of an impossible situation, dependent on a condition that cannot be fulfilled, and therefore would serve to negate it. The rhetoricians say that a plain implication is more forceful than an outright statement. For example, when He denied the vision [to Moses] by saying, *Behold the mountain: if it remains in its place, then you shall see Me* [Q. 7:143]. And God (Exalted is He) knows best.

Q. 43:82

44
SMOKE
SŪRAT AL-DUKHĀN

In the Name of God, the Compassionate, the Merciful

[44:1] [*Ḥā. Mīm.*

[44:2] *By the Book that clarifies.*]

[44:3] *Indeed, We revealed it on a blessed night.* [*Indeed, We have been warning.*

[44:4] *In it every definitive matter is distinguished:*] the blessed night was the edifice of the Messenger of God (may God bless him and grant him peace), because it was a dark temporal creation that covered the light of the sun of the spirit. He described it as blessed because of how the mercy and blessing of guidance and justice were manifested in the world because of it, and how his rank and perfection were increased through it. Likewise, He called it the Night of Power because his power (may God grant him peace) was his self-knowledge, and his perfection was only manifested through it. (Consider how his Ascension could only have been bodily, because otherwise he could not have ascended through the levels to the affirmation of Oneness.)

The revelation of the Books on this blessed night symbolises how, on this night, the gathering Qur'ānic intellect which gathers all realities was sent down, together with the discriminating intellect which differentiates the levels of being, clarifies the details of the Attributes and the codes of their self-disclosures, and distinguishes the meanings of the Names and the codes of the acts. This is the meaning of His Words, *In it every definitive matter is distinguished.* Or it symbolises the sending down of the Muḥammadan spirit, which is the true reality of the clarifying Book in its form, or the Qur'ān. *Indeed, We have been warning* [Q. 43:3] the people of the world about its existence.

[44:5] *As a command from Us*: He noted that this command of wisdom was from Him, because every command that is based on wisdom and soundness—as all Divine Laws and juridical rulings should be—is in reality from Him and belongs to Him absolutely, due to its correspondence to reality. Otherwise, it would be a command based on nothing but caprice and whim. *Indeed, We have been sending,* [44:6] *as a mercy from your Lord*: complete and perfect to all the worlds, by sending him to rectify their religious and worldly affairs and put right their lives and afterlives, and manifesting goodness, perfection, blessing and guidance among them by means of him. Or We are sending you as a perfect comprehensive mercy to them.

Indeed, He is the Hearer of the different things they say about religious matters based on their caprices, *the Knower* of their false beliefs and corrupt opinions, and their imagined affairs and disorganised lives. Therefore, He had mercy on them by sending the Messenger to guide them to the truth in religion, and to organise their worldly affairs for their welfare, and to lead them to what is right, by showing the straight path and realising the affirmation of Oneness with sound arguments, and to deliver Divine Laws, traditions (*sunan*) and codes to establish order.

Q. 44:6

[44:7] [*Lord of the heavens and the earth and all that is between them, if you should be certain.*

[44:8] *There is no god except Him. He gives life and brings death. Your Lord and the Lord of your forefathers.*

[44:9] *Nay, but they linger in doubt, playing.*]

[44:10] *So watch out for the day when the heaven will produce a visible smoke* [44:11] *that will envelop the people*: this will be the time when the portents of the Minor or Major Resurrection appear, since smoke is one of these portents. Know that smoke is one of the subtle terrestrial particles that rise up from their centre because of their subtlety, as a result of heat. If we take it to refer to the Minor Resurrection, then the smoke is the drunkenness, swooning and constriction that appears in the heaven of the spirit upon death, because of the configuration of bodily attachment and the listlessness that builds up on its face, through contact with base affairs and the inclination towards sensory pleasures. He (may God grant him peace) said of this, 'The believer will be stricken with some dizziness, while the disbeliever will be like a drunkard, leaking from his nostrils, ears and backside.' The believer's reaction will be mild because he is less attached to bodily matters, and so this configuration from contact with base affairs will be weaker, and the state will leave him more easily, especially if he acquired the faculty of connection to the realm of illuminations. The disbeliever, on the other hand, will be totally overwhelmed by that configuration, because of his strong attachment and powerful love for corporeal things and his reliance on base things; and so it will confound him and surround him, until it encompasses his inward and outward senses and his higher and lower passages, and he will not be guided to any path, whether to the higher realm or the lower. *This is a painful chastisement!* Since he is usually either hoping or regretting, he will hope to return to the life and health he used to enjoy, and regret his former iniquity, sin, wickedness and transgression, and so he will say with the voice of his state:

[44:12] *'Our Lord, relieve us from the chastisement. Indeed, we have believed!'* Or he might even say it out loud, for sometimes sinners on their deathbeds proclaim their repentance and promise to return to righteousness.

[44:13] *How can there be a reminder for them?* How should they be counselled to return to faith, by merely the relief of the chastisement, *when already there has come to them* an even more obvious reminder in the form of *a manifest Messenger*, who showed them the way of truth with miracles and arguments, and called them to his way by the three means of wisdom, goodly counsel and fair debate?

Q. 44:12

[44:14] *But they [turned away from him and said, 'He has been taught; [he is] a madman!'* Thus, they]* accused him of two contradictory things, such was the degree of their veiling and obstinacy.

[44:15] *'Indeed, We will remove the chastisement a little*: by numbing the senses and perception. *[But] you will indeed revert'* to it.

[44:16] *The day when We shall assault with the most mighty assault*: when the time comes for the painful torment for those configurations and the realisation of perpetuity; *[then] indeed We shall take vengeance* and punish them truly. Or it means that even if they were to be returned to health and bodily life, they would revert to unbelief because they are so firmly rooted in it.

The day when We shall assault with the most mighty assault: by the end of preparedness and the extinguishing of the light of innate disposition, because of the rust that results from sin, and the total veiling that necessitates perpetual torment, as He says, *No, indeed! Rather, upon their hearts is the rust of that which they earned. Nay, they, on that day, will be veiled from their Lord* [Q. 83:14–15]: We shall take true vengeance on them by total deprivation, perpetual veiling and eternal torment.

If we take it to refer to the Major Resurrection, then the smoke is the veil of I-ness which covers people when the light of Oneness appears, because of the soul's transgression due to the transference of the Attributes of lordship and the overwhelming drunkenness of the day of unification which gives rise to permissiveness. It is a remnant of the subtle terrestrial soul which rises by the light of Unity to the locus of witnessing, produced by the heaven of the spirit through its illuminating influence upon it; for it is not completely burned by the fire of passion, but rather purified and made subtle so that it rises. Then the believer who has true faith in Oneness, complete preparedness and dominating love will be stricken with a kind of dizziness—the drunkenness which made Abū Yazīd[1] (may God sanctify his spirit) say, 'Glory be to me! How magnificent is my state!' and made al-Ḥusayn b. Manṣūr [al-Ḥallāj] (may God have mercy on him) say, 'I am the Real.' Then it will swiftly leave him thanks to the divine nurture and the power of innate preparedness and true love, and he will become aware of this and feel utterly tormented by it, and long with every fibre of his being for effacement in the source of unification. He will cry out, *This is a painful chastisement!* [Q. 44:11], and ask for total annihilation—as al-Ḥallāj (may God sanctify his spirit) said, 'Between me and you, the "me" is tormenting me; / By Your grace, remove the "me" from the between!' He will call out with the voice of humility and poverty, *Our Lord, relieve us from the chastisement. Indeed, we have believed* [Q. 44:12] with essential faith upon the lifting of the veil of I-ness. Yet *how can there be a reminder for them,* whence comes their mention of essence and essential faith in the station of the veil of I-ness, *when already there has come to them a manifest Messenger* [Q. 44:13]: the messenger of the intellect to make manifest their beings and attributes? They were only veiled by the veil of I-ness because of the manifestation of the intellect and its affirmation of their beings, so how could they be reminded of the Essence? How could such a reminder be of any use, when they are folk of intellect? Then He describes their passionate yearning by saying, *But they turned away from him* because of the strength of their love and the depth of their passion, *and said, 'He has been taught'* by God through the emanation of knowledge upon him; *[he is] a madman'* [Q. 44:14] whose perception is covered and veiled from the light of the Essence, as Gabriel (may God grant him peace) said, 'If I went any closer, I would be burned.' *Indeed, We will remove the chastisement* of veiling and deprivation *a little,* because of how they turned away from the Messenger because of the power of passion, by the rising of the light of the enduring countenance and the shining of its rays, which burn any of His creatures His gaze falls upon.

Q. 44:16

---

1 This is a correction of the original Arabic which has 'Abū Zayd'. [Ed.]

[*But*] *you will indeed revert* [Q. 44:15]: by variegation to the veil after the self-disclosure of the light of the Essence, because of the remnant of traces, until the time of stability. *The day when We shall assault with the most mighty assault*: the time of total annihilation and true effacement so that neither entity nor trace remain. *Indeed, We shall take vengeance*: with unitary power and total annihilation from their beings and remnants, purifying them from hidden idolatry with unitary being.

As for the disbeliever, meaning the one veiled from the light of the Essence, surrounded by the veils of the Attributes, deprived of effacement in the source of unification because of the delusion of perfection, he shall remain in the station of I-ness and become pharaonic behind the veil of I-ness, as the cursed one said: *I am your most high lord!* [Q. 79:24]; *I do not know of any god for you other than me* [Q. 28:38]. Then he will cast the chain of the Divine Law from his neck and follow the way of permissiveness, indulging in disobedience and wantonly committing sins and flouting obligations. He will become one of the most evil people of whom [the Prophet] said, 'The most evil of people will be those still alive when the Resurrection begins.' He will be bereft of discernment, unable to return to differentiation, plunged in natural impulses and steeped in pagan ignorance, like a drunkard whose intellect has been overwhelmed by caprice, surrounded by the veil on all sides, the deception having made a mark on his senses. This is a painful chastisement, but he does not sense it because of how steeped he is in his Pharaonism and how mired he is in his Satanism. Whenever the adherent of Oneness—who upholds the truth and is guided to the light of the Essence by absolute annihilation, aided by God with the gift of realised existence—calls him and warns him of his veiling, he proudly refuses and transgresses further, thinking himself to be self-sufficient, rooted in his deceit. Then when at last he falls into doubt and becomes aware of the veil when the door opens and he beholds his fate, he says, *Our Lord, relieve us from the chastisement. Indeed, we have believed!* [This is] just as Pharaoh said when he was about to drown, *I believe that there is no god save Him in whom the Children of Israel believe* [Q. 10:90].

How can there be a reminder for them of counsel and true faith, when they have opposed the truth and turned away from the upholder of the truth, and so they have been cursed and banished? *Indeed, We will remove the chastisement* when they realise their situation and how they have clung to the soul and neglected the rights of truth. [*But*] *you will indeed revert* because of how strong a grip caprice has on your souls, and how drunk your hearts are on love for them, and how their attributes have overwhelmed you,

Q. 44:16

and how powerful is your Satanism. *The day when We shall assault with the most mighty assault*: with true overwhelming power and total humiliation, rejection and banishment, We shall take vengeance upon them for their idolatry, self-worship and rebellion against Us by opposing Us and vying with Us for Our cloak of pride, as We said, 'Magnificence is My robe, and pride is My cloak; and anyone who vies with Me for either of them, I shall cast into Hell.' As for the account of Pharaoh's people, you may apply it analogously to the state of your own soul, so strive to understand this:

[44:17] *Verily We tried before them the people of Pharaoh*: the evil-enjoining soul, the Egyptians of the animal faculties; *when a messenger came to them, who was honoured*: the Moses of the heart, noble and detached; [44:18] *[saying]*, *'Give over to me the servants of God*: singled out for Him from the spiritual faculties, captives in the chains of your service, oppressed by your tyranny, enslaved to serve your needs and fulfil your desires for sensory pleasures and corporeal lusts. *Indeed, I am for you a messenger [who is] faithful*': by attainment of the knowledge of certitude, protected from its alteration.

[44:19] *And, 'Do not rebel against God*: by disobeying Him and arrogantly disdaining my call to you. *Indeed, I bring you [a clear warrant]*': a plain proof of intellectual arguments.

[44:20] *'And truly I seek refuge in my Lord and your Lord, lest you should stone me* with the rocks of base primordial matter, egocentric caprices and natural impulses, making me powerless to move in pursuit of spiritual perfections and merciful illuminations, and thereby destroy me.

[44:21] *'And if you do not believe me*—by obeying me and accompanying me on the journey to my Lord, seeking my perfection and illumination— *then stay away from me'* and do not bar me or prevent me from following my path.

[44:22] *So he called to his Lord*, with the voice of humility and poverty, *saying, 'These are indeed a guilty lot!'* who pursue sinful aims and sensory pleasures, and are totally plunged in them, never raising their heads from them.

[44:23] *So God said, 'Then set out with My servants*: the spiritual ones from among the intellectual, reflective, intuitive and holy faculties, and your attributes devoted to the presence of holiness beyond the sea of primordial matter; *by night*: when the sensory faculties were asleep and the corporeal faculties were stilled; *for you will assuredly be pursued*: they will seek you with the perfections of sense and attempt to attract you away from the presence of holiness.

[44:24] *'And leave the sea* of primordial matter and corporeal substance *[behind at rest]*, tranquil and calm, its waves pacified so that they do not

309

disturb you with their agitated states and inclemency, their channels vast and open for those faculties to pass through them and act in them. *Indeed, they will be a drowned host'*: destroyed by the rough seas when they swallow them up upon the ruination of the body.

[44:25] [*How many gardens and fountains did they leave behind,* [44:26] *as well as sown fields and many a glorious residence,* [44:27] *and the bounty in which they rejoiced!*

[44:28] *So [it was] and We made these an inheritance for another people.*

[44:29] *So neither the heaven nor the earth wept for them; nor were they reprieved.*

[44:30] *And verily We delivered the Children of Israel from the humiliating chastisement* [44:31] *from Pharaoh. Indeed, he was a tyrant of the wanton ones.*

[44:32] *And verily We chose them with a knowledge over all the worlds.*

[44:33] *And We gave them signs in which there was a manifest trial.*

[44:34] *Indeed, these ones say,* [44:35] *'It is nothing more than our first death, and we shall not be resurrected.*

[44:36] *'Bring us then our fathers, if you are being truthful.'*

[44:37] *Are they better, or the people of Tubbaᶜ and those before them? We destroyed [them]. Indeed, they were criminals.*

[44:38] *And We did not create the heavens and the earth and all that is between them [intending] to play.*

[44:39] *We did not create them, except with the truth; but most of them do not know.*

[44:40] *Indeed, the Day of Decision will be the tryst for all of them;* [44:41] *the day when a friend will not avail a friend anything, nor will they be helped,* [44:42] *except for him on whom God has mercy. He is indeed the Mighty, the Merciful.*

[44:43] *Indeed, the tree of Zaqqūm* [44:44] *will be the food of the sinful*: the *Zaqqūm* tree is the soul that seeks to dominate the heart with worship of desire and repeated indulgence in pleasures. It is called *Zaqqūm* because of its connection to pleasure, since *zaqm* and *tazaqqum* mean 'to eat butter and dates', and the name was derived from this concept because they are pleasurable foods to eat. None eat from this tree and draw from its power and desires except those who are engrossed in sin and immersed in caprice.

[44:45] *Like molten copper*: the word *muhl* can mean 'dregs of oil', which the soul resembles because of its thickness, and how it clumps together, how it quickly flows into the pores, and its heat, all of which resemble how the soul seeks what it desires. *Muhl* can also mean 'molten copper', which it resembles in how it inclines towards the lower direction, harms the heart with the fierceness of its impulse, and how it stirs up avarice and fans the flames of yearning in the face of deprivation; *it will boil inside the bellies*: agitating and shaking in the insides because of the fierce heat of the effort expended on the pursuit, shaking and burning of the heart with the fire of caprice and the clash of its darkness with its light. It will flow into it painfully because of how its configuration seeks to dominate it, and because of the subtlety of its caprice, which is the repose of the soul and the firmness of its love therein. This is why it is said, 'The tastes of sultans burn the lips.'

[44:46] [*There it will boil*] *as the boiling of boiling water* which flows boiling into the pores because of its subtlety. His Words *inside the bellies* [Q. 44:45] are akin to His Words, [*It is*] *the fire of God, kindled, which peers over the hearts* [Q. 104:6–7].

[44:47] [*'Seize him and drag him to the midst of Hellfire.*

[44:48] *'Then pour over his head the torture of boiling water!'*]

[44:49] *'Taste! Indeed, you are the mighty, the noble one!* This alludes to how their states will be reversed because of the violation of their innate disposition, for corporeal pleasure and might and egocentric nobility necessitate spiritual pain, humiliation and degradation.

Q. 44:46

[44:50] *'This is indeed that which you used to doubt'* because you imagined that pleasures and pains could only be sensory, and were veiled by them from their intellectual modes.

[44:51] *Assuredly the God-fearing* whose God-fearing was perfected because they avoided all remnant of the soul *will be in* [*a secure place*] [44:52], *amid* sublime *gardens* from among the three paradisiacal gardens, *and springs* of knowledge of states and gnostic secrets, and other such true blessings; [44:53] *dressed in fine silk* of subtle states and gifts, because of how they were adorned with their attributes, such as love, gnosis, annihilation and subsistence, *and* [*heavy*] *silk brocade* of virtuous character traits, such as patience, contentment, forbearance and generosity; *sitting face to face* in equal ranks in the first row of the rows of spirits, with no veil between them, because of the detachment of their essences and how they shed their own attributes for God.

[44:54] *So* [*shall it be*]; *and We shall pair them with houris of beautiful eyes*: We shall place them in the company of their dearest delight and the consolation of their hearts, for they will have reached their beloved and attained all that they sought.

[44:55] *They will call therein every fruit*—all of the pleasures of the three gardens—[*remaining*] *secure* from annihilation and from ever being deprived of those boons.

[44:56] *They will not taste death therein, other than the first death*: the natural bodily death, not the annihilation from the acts, Attributes and Essence, since although every annihilation from them is a voluntary death, it is also a purer, sweeter and more glorious life than what came before it; and all of them are in a garden. *And He will shield them from the chastisement of Hellfire*, even the hell of deprivation caused by the presence of the remnant, never mind forsaking them in the hell of nature; [44:57] *a bounty from your Lord*: a pure gift given freely from your Lord by veridical existence upon the disappearance of the egocentric functions. *That is the supreme triumph.* And God knows best.

Q. 44:56

45
LIFELESS
SŪRAT AL-JĀTHIYA

In the Name of God, the Compassionate, the Merciful

[45:1] *Ḥā. Mīm.*

[45:2] [*The revelation of the Book is from God, the Mighty, the Wise*]: the main clause of the oath is left unsaid, since the Words *The revelation of the Book...* clearly allude to it. In other words, He swore on the reality of ipseity (*ḥaqīqat al-hūwiyya*), [i.e.] Absolute Being, which is the root of all and the source of unification, and by Muḥammad, [i.e.] relative being, which is the perfection of all and the form of differentiation. 'By these two,' He swore, 'I shall reveal the Book which clarifies them both.'

Alternatively, one could read *Ḥā Mīm* as the subject of the sentence and *The revelation...* as its predicate, inferring an implied *iḍāfa* construction.[1] Thus, [the meaning is]: 'The manifestation of the reality of differentiated truth is the revelation of the Book.' In other words, [it is] the sending of the Muḥammadan being, or the revelation of the manifest Qur'ān which unveils the meaning of unification and differentiation in several places. For example, He speaks of unification when He says, *God bears witness that there is no god except Him* [Q. 3:18], and then speaks of differentiation by saying, *And so do the angels, and those of knowledge* [Q. 3:18]. *The revelation of the Book is from God*, from the source of unification, *the Mighty, the Wise* in the form of the differentiations of power and subtlety, which are the mothers of all the other Names and the source of the multiplicity of Attributes, since every Attribute pertains either to power or to subtlety.

[45:3] *Indeed, in the heavens and the earth*—in the universe—*there are signs*

---

1 An *iḍāfa* construction is one with the formula 'the *x* of *y*'. In this instance, the author reads *The manifestation of* as being implied but not said, and reads the letters *Ḥā Mīm* as representing *al-ḥaqq al-mufaṣṣal* ('differentiated truth').

for believers: signs of His Essence, for the universe is the locus of His Being, which is the entity of His Essence:

[45:4] *And in your creation, and what He has scattered of animals, there are signs for a people who are certain*: signs of His Attributes, for you and all other living creatures are loci for His Attributes in that He is endowed with life, knowledge, will, power, speech, hearing and sight, and by these Attributes you witness His Attributes.

[45:5] *And in the alternation of night and day, and what God sends down from the heaven [in the way] of provision with which He revives the earth after it is dead, and the circulation of the winds, there are signs for a people who understand* His acts; for these behaviours are His acts. The reason He distinguished between these three things by reference to belief, certitude and understanding is that the witnessing of the Essence is clearer, even if it is obscure, because of its immense clarity; and existence is more manifest, and those who believe in it are more numerous because it is self-evident; but witnessing the Attributes is more subtle and obscure than the other two, which is why He linked it to certitude.

Q. 45:4

Every person of certitude is a believer in His existence, but the inverse is not true; and it is possible for there to be certitude without faith in the Essence, in the sense that a believer in His existence could be certain about the Attributes but unable to witness the Essence, because he is veiled by multiplicity from Unity. As for the acts, knowledge of them can be attained by reasoning with the intellect, since the intellect realises that the changes that occur in things can only be the result of an active agent who changes them, since influence is impossible without an influencer.

The first is innate and spiritual, the second cognitive and heart-centred, [i.e.] drawn from unveiling and experiential realisation, and the third is intellectual. The beloved one who retains innate disposition believes first in the Essence, then is certain of the Attributes, and then intellectually understands the acts. The lover who is veiled from innate disposition by creation and matter is in the station of the soul, and so first understands His acts, then has certitude of His Attributes which are the originators of His acts, and then believes in His Essence. This is why when the Beloved of God (may God bless him and grant him peace) was asked how he came to know God, he replied, 'I came to know things through God.'

[45:6] *These*—the signs of the heavens of the spirits and the earth of the absolute body, [i.e.] the universe, and the signs of the living, created beings, and the signs of all other contingent things—*are the signs of God*: the signs of His Essence, Attributes and acts, [*which We recite to you with truth*]. *So in what* [*kind of*] *discourse then, after God and His signs*, and the signs of His Attributes and acts, *will they believe?* For there is no being beyond them, except that which is a word without meaning, or a name without a named, as He says, *These are nothing but names which you have named* [Q. 53:23]: names that signify nothing real.

[45:7] *Woe to every sinful liar*, engrossed in the lie of false delusional trumped-up existence, and the sin of idolatry by attributing acts to that existence, [45:8] *who hears the signs of God*, from every being speaking with the voice of state or speech, *being recited to him* on the voice of everything aside from the voice of the Prophet alone, *then persists arrogantly* by attributing them to other-than-God, veiled by his own being, pride and I-ness because of his fanatical Pharaonism or his delusion and obliviousness, *as if he had not heard them* because of their lack of effect on him. *So give him tidings of a* [*painful*] *chastisement*: the painful veiling and agonising deprivation.

[45:9] *And should he come to know anything of Our signs, he takes them in mockery*: by attributing them to something that has no being at all. *For such there is a degrading chastisement*: in the humiliation of contingence.

Q. 45:7

[45:10] [*Beyond them is Hell, and that which they have earned will not avail them in any way, nor those whom they took besides God as patrons. And for them there will be a great chastisement.*]

[45:11] *This is a guidance, and those who disbelieve in the signs of their Lord, for them there will be a torture of a painful chastisement.*

[45:12] *God it is Who disposed for you the sea so that the ships may sail upon it by His command, and that you may seek of His bounty, and that perhaps you may give thanks.*

[45:13] *And He has disposed for you whatever is in the heavens, and whatever is in the earth, all being from Him.*] *Indeed, in that there are signs for a people who reflect*: in other words, the way in which He disposed for you all that is in the heavens and the earth constitutes signs for the one who reflects on himself: who is he, and why did God dispose these things for him, even the realms of dominion and domination from Him and on His part? Thus, he will return to his own essence and recognise its reality, and the secrets of his being and the distinction with which he was ennobled and raised above them and made worthy of their being disposed for him. He will disdain to hold himself back from any rank other than that of the noblest among them, never mind being the lowliest among them, and so he will ascend to the purpose for which he was made.

[45:14] [*Tell those who believe to forgive those who do not anticipate the days of God that He may requite a people for what they used to earn.*

315

[45:15] *Whoever acts righteously, it is for [the benefit of] his own soul, and whoever does evil, it is to the detriment thereof; then to your Lord you will be returned.*

[45:16] *And verily We gave the Children of Israel the Book, and [the means of] judgement, and prophethood, and We provided them with the good things, and We favoured them above all the worlds.*

[45:17] *And We gave them clear illustrations of the commandment. And they did not differ, except after the knowledge had come to them, out of rivalry among themselves. Indeed, your Lord will judge between them on the Day of Resurrection concerning that in which they used to differ.*]

[45:18] *Then We set you upon a [clear] course*—a path—*of the command-*ment of the Real, which is the path of Oneness; *so follow it* by travelling upon it with clarity and insight, *and do not follow the desires*—the ignorant ways of the people of blind-following—*of those who do not know* with the knowledge of Oneness.

Q. 45:15

[45:19] *Indeed, they will not avail you in any way against God*: they cannot repel any harm from you with their deeds, for they have no ability to influence, nor can they repel any ignorance of veiling with their attributes, for they possess no strength, power or knowledge; for there can be no power or strength save through God. Nor can they alleviate any alienation with their presence, for there is no correspondence between you and them such that you could derive any consolation from them; your only consolation is in the Real. [*And indeed the wrongdoers are allies of one another.*] In the midst of your witnessing they are nothing at all, so there cannot be any allegiance between you and them. The allegiance of the wrongdoers can only be with other wrongdoers, because of their shared affinity and mutual veiling. *God is the ally [only] of the God-fearing*: He is the guardian of the affairs of those who fear His acts through reliance on Him in the witnessing of the Oneness of the acts. Or He is the succour of those who fear His Attributes in the station of contentment, through witnessing the self-disclosure of the Attributes. Or He is the beloved of those who fear His Essence in the witnessing of the Oneness of Essence. The word *walī* ('ally') can be used to mean all three of these concepts.

[45:20] *This* elucidation *is [a set of] insights [for people]*: clarifications for the hearts of those who behold the splendour of the Attributes, so that with each insight they behold a self-disclosure of an Attribute of His, *and guidance* for their spirits to the locus of witnessing of the Essence, *and mercy* for their souls from the torment of the veil of the acts, *for a people who have certitude* in these clarifications.

[45:21] [*Or do those who have perpetrated evil acts suppose that We shall treat*

316

them as those who believe and perform righteous deeds, equally in their life and in their death? How evil is that judgement which they make!

[45:22] *And God created the heavens and the earth with the truth and so that every soul may be requited for what it has earned, and they will not be wronged.*]

[45:23] *Have you then seen him who has taken as his god his [own] desire:* a god is a being that is worshipped; when they obeyed desire, they worshipped it and made a god of it, for everything that a person worships with his love and his obedience becomes his god, even if it is a stone; *and whom God has led astray [knowingly]:* knowing his state and how his preparedness has faded, and his face has turned towards the lower direction. Or it refers to how this worshipper of desire knows what the religion requires him to do. This applies if the word *knowingly* is read as referring to the object of *God has led astray*, rather than the Subject. If it was the latter, then it means that the leading astray was the result of how his deeds contravened his knowledge, and how he refused to contemplate—in order to allow his heart to drink its fill of love for the soul—and how desire was dominant. Such was the case of Balaam the son of Beor and his ilk, as he (may God grant him peace) said, 'Many a scholar went astray, taking his knowledge with him, though it availed him not.' Or it means that his knowledge was not beneficial because it pertained only to matters of idle curiosity and had nothing to do with conduct. [*God has led astray knowingly,*] *and set a seal upon his hearing and his heart:* by banishing him from the door of guidance and distancing him from the venue where the Word of the Real can be heard and comprehended, because of the rust on his heart and the density of the veil; *and laid a covering over his sight:* so that he cannot see His beauty or witness His meeting. *So who will guide him after God?* For nothing exists but Him, such that it could guide him. *Will you not then remember,* O you who affirm Oneness?

Q. 45:22

[45:24] [*And they say,*] *'There is only our life in this world:* [meaning] the sensory life. *We die* the natural bodily death *and we live* the corporeal, sensory life, and there is no other death or life but those, [*and nothing but time destroys us.' Of that they have no knowledge; they are only making conjectures.*] They attribute all this to nothing but the passage of time, for they are veiled from the true Influencer, Who holds the spirits in His grasp and emanates life to the bodies.

[45:25] [*And when Our signs are recited to them, being clear signs, their only argument is to say, 'Bring us our fathers, if you are being truthful.'*]

[45:26] *Say: 'God [is the One Who] gives you life, then makes you die,* not time, *then gathers you to* [the Day of Resurrection], the second life [*in which there is no doubt; but most people do not know'*]. Or it is God, and not time, Who gives you the eternal life of the heart after the life of the soul, and then makes you die with annihilation in Him, and then gathers you to Him with subsistence after annihilation and gifted existence, so that you can be with Him.

[45:27] *And to God belongs the kingdom of the heavens and the earth*, and there is no other owner alongside Him from the perspective of witnessing. *And on the day when the* Major Resurrection [*Hour*] *sets in,* [*on that day the followers of falsehood*] who affirm the existence of others *will be losers*, for everything besides Him is false, and anyone who affirms its existence and is veiled by it from Him is a sower of falsehood.

[45:28] *And you* affirmer of Oneness *will see every community lifeless*— bereft of movement because on its own it is dead and impotent—as He says, *You will indeed die, and they* [*too*] *will indeed die* [Q. 39:30]. Or you will see them lifeless at the first place of standing at the time of the Gathering before the Reckoning, in the condition they were in at the first creation when they were hidden. There is a mystery in this. *Every community will be summoned to its record*: the tablet wherein its deeds are recorded, its images embodied and inscribed therein in corporeal form. The recording of deeds is done in four tablets: the first is the lower tablet to which every community will be summoned. It will be presented to the right hands of those who are saved, and the left hands of those who are damned. The other three tablets are heavenly and high, and have already been discussed. The reason we say that the record meant here is the lower tablet is that this discourse is concerned with the requital for deeds, since He says, *'Today you will be requited for what you used to do*, and says:

Q. 45:27

[45:29] [*'This is Our book, which pronounces against you with truth.*] *Indeed, We used to write down what you used to do*': the scribes are the heavenly and earthly angels.

[45:30] *So as for those who believed* with unseen, blind faith, or faith of certain knowledge, *and performed righteous deeds* which rectified their state at the bodily Resurrection of all the forms of righteousness, *their Lord will admit them into His mercy*: the mercy of the reward for deeds in the garden of the acts. *That is the manifest triumph.*

[45:31] *But as for those who disbelieved*, veiled from the Real by original unbelief and immersion in criminal configurations, darkened by their criminality: [*'Were not My signs recited to you, but you were disdainful and were a guilty lot?*

[45:32] *'And when it was said, "God's promise is indeed true, and there is no doubt about the Hour,"* you said, *"We do not know what the Hour is. We only make conjectures and we are by no means certain."'*

[45:33] *And there will appear before them the evils of what they did, and they will be besieged by what they used to deride.*

[45:34] *And it will be said:*] '*Today We will forget you, just as you forgot the encounter of this day of yours*: We shall abandon you in the chastisement, just as you abandoned working for My encounter on this day of yours because you did not acknowledge it. Or We shall make you like a forgotten, abandoned thing, forsaken in the chastisement, just as you forgot the encounter of this day of yours by forgetting the pre-eternal covenant. [*And your abode will be the Fire, and you will not have any helpers.*

[45:35] '*That is because you took God's signs in mockery, and the life of this world deceived you.' So today they will not be brought out of it, nor can they make amends.*]

[45:36] *So to God belongs [all] praise*: perfect, absolute praise attained for all by how all things reach their destinations and attain their greatest possible degrees of perfection; *Lord of the heavens*: Completer and Director of the spirits; *and Lord of the earth*: Director, Owner and Discharger of the bodies; *the Lord of the Worlds*, Who directs the worlds to their perfections by His lordship over them.

Q. 45:33

[45:37] *And to Him belongs [all] supremacy [in the heavens and the earth]*: to Him belongs domination and the height of ascendancy and grandeur over all things, and the peak of loftiness and magnificence by His lack of need for all and their total need for Him. Everything praises Him by manifesting His perfection and declaring all His Attributes with the voices of their states; and they all magnify him by their changes, contingencies and movements along the chain of beings, which need Him and are annihilated in His Essence, unable to attain any perfections save those which are assigned to them. *And He is the Mighty*: the Omnipotent Who overwhelms all things with His influence on them and compels them to be what they are; *the Wise*: Who ordains the preparedness of each thing with subtlety, and readies them to receive what He wills for them from His Attributes, by His delicate craft and discreet wisdom.

46
THE WIND-CURVED SAND DUNES
SŪRAT AL-AḤQĀF

In the Name of God, the Compassionate, the Merciful

[46:1] [*Ḥā. Mīm.*

[46:2] *The revelation of the Book is from God, the Mighty, the Wise.*]

[46:3] *We have not created the heavens and the earth and all that is between them except in truth*: that is, with being that is absolute, firm, unitary, eternal and all-sustaining; or with justice, which is the shadow of Unity, whereby all multiplicity is ordered, as he said, 'The heavens and earth were made with justice'; *and for*, by the measure of, *an appointed term*: a specific perfection to which the perfection of existence leads, namely the Major Resurrection by the emergence of the Mahdī and the appearance of the All-Conquering One with Unitary Being, in Whom all things are annihilated as they were in the time before time. *Yet those who disbelieve* through being veiled from the Real *are disregardful of what they are warned* about concerning this Resurrection.

[46:4] *Say: 'Have you considered what you invoke besides God?* You give it a name and affirm existence and influence for it, whatever it may be. *Show me what* [*they have created of the earth. Or do they have any share in the heavens?* In other words: Show me] their influence on anything earthly by independence, or anything heavenly by partnership. *Bring me* [*a Book before this or some vestige of knowledge*]— some proof, whether traditional in the form of a Book, or rational in the form of well-reasoned knowledge—*if you are truthful.'*

[46:5] *And who is further astray than him who invokes, instead of God*, anything [*such as would not respond to him* [*even*] *until the Day of Resurrection and who are heedless of their supplication*]? Whatever it might be, such as how the slaves call upon their masters, for no one but God could answer him.

[46:6] *And when people are gathered, they will be enemies to them* [*and they will deny their worship*], because the worship which the people of this life devote to their masters, and the service they offer them, is only done for the sake of an egocentric goal; and likewise for how the masters enslave their servants. When these goals disappear and all causes and means are abolished, they will be enemies to them and will deny their worship, saying, 'You did not serve us, but only yourselves.' The same has been said about His Words, *Friends will, on that day, be foes of one another* [Q. 43:67].

[46:7] [*And when Our signs are recited to them, being clear signs, those who disbelieve say of the truth when it comes to them, 'This is plain sorcery!'*

[46:8] *Or do they say, 'He has invented it?' Say: 'If I have invented it, still you would have no power to avail me against God in any way. He knows best what you delve into* [*of gossip*] *concerning it. He suffices as a witness between me and you. And He is the Forgiving, the Merciful.'*

[46:9] *Say: 'I am not a novelty among the messengers. Nor do I know what will be done with me or with you. I only follow what is revealed to me. And I am only a plain warner.'*

Q. 46:7

[46:10] *Say: 'Have you considered: what if it is from God and you disbelieve in it? What if a witness from the Children of Israel has* [*already*] *testified to the like of it, and he has believed* [*in it*], *while you act with arrogance...? Indeed, God does not guide wrongdoing folk.'*

[46:11] *And those who disbelieve say of those who believe, 'Had it been* [*anything*] *good, they would not have attained it before us.' And since they will not be guided by it, they say, 'This is an ancient lie!'*

[46:12] *Yet before it,* [*there was*] *the Book of Moses, as a guidepost and a mercy, and this is a Book that confirms in the Arabic tongue to warn those who do wrong, and* [*as*] *good tidings for the virtuous.*]

[46:13] *Indeed, those who say, 'Our Lord is God'*: those who detach themselves from connections, refuse hindrances, and devote themselves to God, shunning all besides Him and sparing their eyes from any sight but Him, they can say truthfully, 'Our Lord is God,' for if any remnant of their souls remained, they would not be safe from variegations in the midst of annihilation, and would not be able to say it truthfully; *and then remain upright* with realisation of Him in their deeds, and in maintaining the proper conduct of the presence to protect them from slips and errors, so that their whole beings down to the tiniest detail exist through God and for God; *no fear will befall them*: for there is neither veil nor retribution; *nor will they grieve*: for they will have their every desire, and nothing will be lost to them. It is said that in God there is a consolation for every misfortune, and a recompense for every loss.

[46:14] *Those will be the folk of Paradise*: the absolute garden that contains all others, *abiding therein as a reward for what they used to do* in the state of wayfaring until arrival.

[46:15] [*And We have enjoined humanity to be kind to his parents. His mother carries him in travail, and gives birth to him in travail, and his gestation and his weaning take thirty months.*] *So that when he is mature and reaches forty years*: the soul is charged with the task of directing the body because its perfection depends on it; but is distracted by it from its perfection at the beginning of creation, because its insight is not yet open, nor is its perception purified, nor does it reach maturity, until the age of marriage, as He says about orphans: ...*until they reach the age of marrying; then, if you perceive in them maturity, deliver their property to them* [Q. 4:6]. This is the time of formal maturity.

Q. 46:14

Notice how, from the time of infancy until this point, the body does not expend energy on manufacturing reproductive matter, but only with attaining nourishment to make the body grow and replace itself, because of the weakness of the limbs and the need for development and strength. At that time the soul is immersed in the body and employs its nature for that end alone, and is oblivious to its perfection until it reaches that age. When the body parts are close to being perfected, and arrive at the point where they can be used for their purposes and no longer need fuel for their growth, the nature becomes ready to store up reproductive matter in the body, since it no longer needs that energy to fuel its growth. It is then that the insight of the intellect opens and the lights of innate disposition and preparedness appear, and it wakes from its infantile sleep of heedlessness, and becomes aware of the sanctity of its substance, and seeks out its centre and its end for two purposes: the rectitude of the body parts to be used for self-perfection, and the culmination of the body's special need for them so that it is now able to concentrate without much distraction. However, as long as the age of growth is still ongoing and the body parts are becoming stronger and more stable, they will not be able to direct themselves totally to the higher direction, nor detach themselves for the pursuit of intellectual perfections and spiritual goals, because of this distraction, even if it is only mild.

This goes on until two thirds of the lifetime are completed, as the medical sciences have explained. When it passes this point and reaches the age of halting, it turns to its world and the lights of its innate disposition shine forth, and it becomes devoted to the search for its perfection now that it is free to do so. It is then that the true guardian of orphans, the Holy

Spirit, senses that it is mature and the time has come to deliver to it its property of realities, gnostic secrets and teachings, now that it has reached the age of marriage to the brides of holy, immaterial realities and divine illuminations. This is the time when it travels through the Attributes of God to His Essence, until achieving total annihilation by immersion in the Essential Unity, because this journey in the Attributes becomes possible from the time of formal maturity to the culmination of this supra-sensory maturity, whose end comes at around the age of forty. This is why it is said that the one who becomes a Sufi after forty will be frigid, because he will not have prepared by turning, seeking and travelling in the divine acts by self-purification to receive that property and take ownership of it, since the Holy Spirit did not sense his maturity and deliver it to him.

If his journey to God is completed when that maturity comes by annihilation in Him, the time will arrive for subsistence after annihilation, and uprightness in action. He alludes to this by saying, *He says, 'My Lord, inspire me [to give thanks for Your favour with which You have favoured me and my parents]*: this is why all the prophets were sent after the age of forty, except for Jesus and John, who both halted in the heavens. And since such showers of blessings must be restrained with gratitude, he asked that he be inspired to give thanks for the blessing of perfection which itself was preceded by countless others, in order to preserve it so that he not be veiled by the consciousness of annihilation and so abandon obedience, through satisfaction in his state and reliance on his perfection. The blight of the station of annihilation is consciousness of annihilation, and the one afflicted with this blight will fall into variegation and be deprived of the blessing of stability. This is why he (may God grant him peace) said, 'Should I not be a grateful servant?' So he asked that the blessing of guidance and perfection be preserved for him by his being kept constant in acts of obedience, which express gratitude for the favour with which He favoured him and his parents, who were the immediate cause of his existence, since if there were no goodness, good character and a righteous secret in them, that perfection would not have been manifested in him, because he was their secret. This is why it is obligatory to be dutiful to parents and pray for them.

Q. 46:15

[*'Inspire me to give thanks for Your favour with which You have favoured me and my parents,*] *and that I may act righteously [in a way that will please You]*: by guiding prepared folk to perfection; for the obligation of the perfected one is first to preserve his perfection and then to guide others to their own. Action is a relative matter, and something that is righteous for one person could be bad for another, as he said, 'The good deeds of the pious are the sins of those drawn near.' Therefore, he continues, *And invest my seed with righteousness*: that is, my true children, whether biological or otherwise, for his righteous knowledge of imparting spiritual training and perfection to disciples can only succeed after their preparedness is readied, and their deeds and states are made righteous, which can only come from His holy emanation. If this God-given righteousness and total receptivity is not present, no spiritual guidance can have any effect, as He says, *You cannot guide whomever you like* [Q. 28:56]. These two things—preserving perfection through gratitude by fulfilling the dues of the Inspirer by acts of obedience, and imparting perfection to others—constitute the foundational act of uprightness, and the duty of the one who realises veridical existence in the station of subsistence.

'Indeed, I repent to You from the sin of consciousness of annihilation. This was the repentance of Moses (may God grant him peace), when he woke from his swoon, as He says, *And when he recovered his senses he said, 'Glory be to You! I repent to You...'* [Q. 7:143]; *and I am truly of those who submit* [*to You*]': those who yield and surrender in the journey of the servants to the place of uprightness.

Q. 46:16

[46:16] *Those*—the ones characterised by this repentance and uprightness—*are they from whom We accept the best of what they do*: by the manifestation of the effects of their spiritual training and their sound guidance of their disciples, because the perfecting of others is the best of their deeds. Notice how every perfected one who failed to stick to the way of adherence and the preservation of the Sunna had no followers, nor produced any perfected disciples, because of how their uprightness was impaired and they relied on their noble states. This is a sign that their righteous deeds were not accepted. As for the ones who gave thanks for the blessing of perfection, We accept their deeds *and overlook their misdeeds*, which are the remnants of their attributes and essences, by total effacement and true erasure in the station of stability, so that they do not fall into the sin of consciousness of annihilation nor the variegation of the manifestation of ego and I-ness; [*as they stand*] *among the folk of* absolute *Paradise*—[*this is*] *the true promise which they were promised* when He said, *We will make their descendants join them, and We will not deprive them of anything of their deeds* [Q. 52:21].

[46:17] [*As for him who says to his parents, 'Fie on you both. Do you threaten me that I shall be raised, when already generations have passed away before me?' And they call on God for succour, 'Woe to you. Believe! Indeed, God's promise is true.' But he says, 'This is nothing but the fables of the ancients.'*

[46:18] *Such are the ones against whom the Word is due concerning communities of jinn and humans that have passed away before them. Indeed, they are losers.*]

[46:19] *And for each one there will be degrees*: after mentioning the foremost and then their opposites, the rejected folk against whom the Word is due, and making clear how the first group are among the saved while the second are among the damned, the discourse then turns to the seven kinds of people described at the beginning of this book.[1] The first two kinds are mentioned explicitly, being as they are the roots of faith and unbelief, and then the other five kinds are mentioned in summary by the Words, [*And for each one there will be degrees* [*of status*],] *according to what they have done*: that is, for each kind of people there will be degrees of requitals for their deeds, from the highest of the high to the lowest of the low. These degrees are countless; indeed, every individual from every kind has a rank, station and foothold in one of the gardens of Paradise or levels of Hell; [*and that He may recompense them fully for their deeds, and they will not be wronged.*

Q. 46:18

[46:20] *And on the day when those who disbelieve are exposed to the Fire:*] '*You squandered your good things during your life of the world* [*and enjoyed them*]: He chastises them for squandering all their fortunes on the pleasures of the world, because everyone is granted perfection and imperfection commensurate with their original preparedness, and if it is utilised for ephemeral happiness there will be misery corresponding to it. Each person has, for both of the two creations, good things and fortunes which correspond to each of his two perfections. The one who directs himself towards enjoyment of the good things and fortunes of the world, and turns his heart away from the good things and pleasures of the Hereafter, will be denied the latter outright because of his immersion in dark matters and his veiling from luminous pursuits. God says, *There are some people who say, 'Our Lord, give to us in this world'; such people will have no part in the Hereafter* [Q. 2:200]. This is the meaning of His Words, *You squandered your good things during your life of the world*, because the fortunes of the Hereafter defined by his ipseity will have been squandered in this world, just as when the day gets longer the night gets shorter. As for the one who directs himself towards the Hereafter and transcends this world through asceticism and God-fearing, seeking gnostic realities, divine mysteries, sublime pleasures and holy lights, which are the true good things, he will be given his share of them; and he will not suffer the loss of his ephemeral fortunes like the first one will, but rather will

1 See Kāshānī's commentary on Q. 2:2.

receive them in full, as He says, *And whoever desires the harvest of the Hereafter, We will enhance for him his harvest; and whoever desires the harvest of this world, We will give him of it, but in the Hereafter he will have no share* [Q. 42:20]. This is because immersion in the world of holiness and direction towards the presence of the Real bequeath the soul strength and power which affect it in the sensory world; and so how should it be if it connects with the source of strength and power? Behold how the realm of the dominion affects the realm of the kingdom, and acts upon it and dominates it by God's leave and facilitation. Immersion in the sensory world extinguishes the power of innate disposition and blots out the light of the heart so that it no longer has strength, power or influence over anything. How should it be otherwise, when it has been influenced by that whose nature is pure influence, and subdued for that whose nature is total subdual and absolute reaction? This is why it is said that the world is like a shadow: it follows the one who turns away from it, and goes ahead of the one who pursues it. The Commander of the Believers (may God be pleased with him) said, 'When someone pursues it, it outruns him; and when someone turns away from it, it comes to him.'

Q. 46:21

'*So today you will be requited with the chastisement of humiliation*: degradation and disgrace, because of how you inclined naturally towards the lower direction and turned passionately towards worldly pursuits. You chose lowliness and humiliation by your tyranny and arrogance. This is why He says *in return for acting arrogantly*, in the station of the soul by the domination of the irascible faculty, whose nature is arrogance, *in the earth without right*: for had they detached themselves from the irascible and appetitive faculties, risen above the egocentric attributes and thrown off the robes of ego and I-ness, they would have been made proud through the Real in the heaven of the earth, and their pride would have been God's grandeur. Someone once said to al-Ṣādiq (may God grant him peace), 'You are endowed with every virtue and perfection, save that you are proud.' He replied, 'No, by God! I shed my pride, and so God's grandeur was thrown upon me.' Or he said words to that effect. This is the meaning of pride in the Real. [*So today you will be requited…*] *in return for that regarding which you used to act immorally*': by the dominance of the appetitive faculties whose nature is immorality and iniquity.

[46:21] [*And mention the brother of ʿĀd when he warned his people among the wind-curved sand dunes, and already warners had passed away before him and after him, saying, 'Do not worship anyone but God. Indeed, I fear for you the chastisement of a dreadful day.'*

[46:22] *They said, 'Have you come to divert us from our gods? Then bring us what you threaten us with, if you are of the truthful.'*

[46:23] *He said, 'The knowledge is with God only, and I am [merely] conveying to you what I have been sent with. But I see that you are an ignorant lot.'*

[46:24] *Then, when they saw it as a sudden cloud heading towards their valleys, they said, 'This is a cloud that will bring us rain!' Nay, but it is what you sought to hasten: a hurricane containing a painful chastisement,* [46:25] *destroying everything by the command of its Lord. So they became such that nothing could be seen except their dwellings. Thus do We requite guilty folk.*

[46:26] *And verily We had empowered them in ways in which We have not empowered you, and We had vested them with ears and eyes and hearts. But their ears and their eyes and their hearts did not avail them in any way since they used to deny the signs of God, and they were besieged by what they used to deride.*

[46:27] *And We certainly destroyed the towns [that were] around you, and We dispensed the signs so that perhaps they might return.*

Q. 46:22

[46:28] *So why did they not help them, those whom they had chosen besides God, as [a means of] nearness, to be gods? Nay, but they forsook them and that was their lie and what they used to invent.]*

[46:29] *And when We sent a company of jinn your way*: the jinn are earthly souls encased in subtle bodies composed of the subtle elements. The sages of Persia called them 'suspended forms' (*ṣuwar muʿallaqa*). [This was] because, like humans, they are earthly and encased in elemental bodies; hence, the two species are known collectively as 'the two weighty ones' (*thaqalayn*). Just as humans are capable of being guided by the Qurʾān, so too are the jinn. Their tales are so numerous, as told by the masters as well as others, that they cannot be denied, and too clear to brook any figurative interpretation.

If you would like a spiritual correspondence for this passage, then here it is: *And when We sent a company of jinn your way*: the spiritual faculties of intellect, cognition, imagination and estimation, as you were reciting in prayer. In other words, We dictated to them through you, and made them follow your secret by approaching you and sending them away from the soul and nature by subduing them and taming them for you, so that your aspiration could be mustered and your heart would not be disturbed or your mind distracted by their motions during your time of presence, when the dawn of the light of holiness broke; *to listen to the Qurʾān* being inspired to you from the holy realm; *and, when they were in its presence*: when they were in the presence of the gathering Qurʾānic intellect which gathers all perfections at the manifestation of the light

327

of discernment upon you, *they said, 'Listen carefully!'* They were silent, and bade one another be silent and cease their own speech, such as the monologues of the soul, imaginations, thoughts, misgivings, impulses, cognitive motions and imaginative transitions. This utterance of theirs was done in state, as has been discussed several times, since if they did not fall silent and listen carefully to the holy inspirations that were being emanated upon them, the inspiration would have had no effect, nor would it have been a true communication of the Unseen, nor a transmission of the holy meaning or a recitation of the Divine Word as it ought to be. Therefore, He said, *Indeed, rising in the night makes a deeper impression and sharpens speech* [Q. 73:6]. This is also why the revelation began with true dreams, because these faculties were silent and still during sleep, until he became strong enough to banish them from their labours and still them in his waking hours. *Then, when it was finished*—meaning the spiritual inspiration and holy disclosure of unveiling—*they went back to their people*, the egocentric and natural faculties, *to warn* [*them*] of the consequences of tyranny and transgression against the heart, by affecting them with virtuous dispositions and emanations of illuminated configurations, derived from the holy meanings disclosed to them, and preventing them from seeking to dominate the heart with subdual and taming.

Q. 46:30

[46:30] *They said, 'O our people! Indeed, we have heard a Book which has been revealed after Moses*: we have not felt an effect akin to this luminescence from the Muḥammadan being since the time of Moses; and from his time until this, we have not received such a meaning. This is because the ascension of Jesus (may God grant him peace) was not completed, and his state did not reach that of the other two prophets, Moses and Muḥammad, in his traversal of the path of holiness during his lifetime, such that all his faculties came under the sway of his inner mystery. His annihilation was not completed such that all his faculties realised veridical existence, which is why he remained in the fourth heaven and was veiled therein, unlike the two of them. When he descends, he will follow the Muḥammadan way in order for his state to be completed. *Confirming what was before it* because of how it corresponds to it in guidance to Oneness and uprightness, as He indicates by His Words, *It guides to the truth and to a straight way*.

[46:31] *'O our people, respond to God's summoner*: by obeying the heart in turning to God, adopting his etiquettes, yielding to His Divine Laws and surrendering to His commandments and prohibitions with obedience; *and believe in him*: by becoming enlightened by His light and following the path of His worship; *and He will forgive you some of your sins*: the base configurations and inclinations towards the lower directions, by following caprice and being veiled by the egocentric attributes; but not bodily attachments and natural preoccupations, since they cannot be detached from matter. Thus, He followed this by adding *and shelter you from a painful chastisement,'* because of the instinct and attraction towards pleasures and desires while being deprived of them, due to the absence of the physical means to attain them.

Some of the exegetes say that the jinn will receive no reward, and their conversion to Islam will only save them from punishment. If this is true, then the spiritual allusion of the verse would be that these bodily faculties will have no share of the universal intellectual meanings, luminous configurations and holy pleasures, but their submission and obedience to the inner mystery will repel their physical and emotional pain. And God (Exalted is He) knows best.

Q. 46:31

47
MUḤAMMAD
SŪRAT MUḤAMMAD

In the Name of God, the Compassionate, the Merciful

[47:1] [*Those who disbelieve and bar from the way of God, He has rendered their works void.*

[47:2] *But those who believe and perform righteous deeds and believe in what has been revealed to Muhammad—and it is the truth from their Lord—He will absolve them of their misdeeds and rightly dispose their mind.*] The spiritual correspondence of *Those who disbelieve...* is the egocentric faculties which bar the way to travelling the way of God, while *those who believe* symbolise the spiritual faculties which aid this journey. The symbolism of the rest of this passage is obvious based on what has already been said, so we need not repeat it.

[47:3] [*That is because those who disbelieve follow falsehood, and because those who believe follow the truth from their Lord. Thus, does God strike for people similitudes of themselves.*

[47:4] *So when you encounter [in battle] those who disbelieve, then [attack them with] a striking of the necks. Then, when you have thoroughly decimated them, bind. Thereafter either [set them free] by grace or by ransom, until the war lay down its burdens. So [shall it be]. And had God wished, He could have [Himself] taken vengeance on them, but that He may test some of you by means of others. And those who are slain in the way of God, He will not let their works go to waste.*

[47:5] *He will guide them and rightly dispose their minds.*

[47:6] *And He will admit them into Paradise, which He has made known to them.*

[47:7] *O you who believe! If you help God, He will help you and make your foothold firm.*

[47:8] *And as for those who disbelieve, wretchedness shall be their lot. And He will make their works go to waste.*

[47:9] *That is because they are averse to what God has revealed, so He has made their works fail.*

[47:10] *Have they not travelled in the land to see the nature of the consequence for those who were before them? God destroyed them; and [a fate] the like thereof will be for the disbelievers.*

[47:11] *That is because God is Patron of those who believe and because the disbelievers have no patron.*

[47:12] *Indeed, God will admit those who believe and perform righteous deeds into gardens underneath which rivers flow. As for those who disbelieve, they take their enjoyment and eat as the cattle eat; and the Fire will be their habitation.*

[47:13] *And how many a town mightier in power than your town, which expelled you, have We destroyed, and they had none to help them!*

[47:14] *Is he who follows a clear sign from his Lord like those whose evil deeds have been adorned for them, and who follow their desires?]*

[47:15] *A similitude of the Garden*: the similitude of the absolute Garden, which contains all the paradisiacal gardens, *promised to the God-fearing* from the aforementioned five kinds of people: *therein are rivers of water unpolluted*: that is, types of knowledge and gnostic realities which give life to hearts and nourish instincts, just as water gives life to the earth and nourishes living beings; *unpolluted*: unchanged by adulterants of estimations, doubts, divergent false doctrines and customs. It is for the God-fearing chosen ones from the egocentric attributes who have reached the station of the heart. *And rivers of milk unchanging in flavour*: beneficial knowledge pertaining to action and character, meant for the imperfect folk, who are prepared and fit for spiritual discipline and traversing the way-stations of the soul, before reaching the station of the heart, through a God-fearing avoidance of sins and base things. They include the sciences of the Divine Laws and practical wisdom, which are like the milk that is given to imperfect infants, *unchanging in flavour*: unaltered by the adulterants of caprice, heresy, the divergences of the partisans, and the fanaticisms of the adherents of religions and ideologies. *And rivers of wine*: of the different kinds of love of the Attributes and the Essence; *delicious to the drinkers*: the perfect ones who have reached the station of witnessing the radiance of the self-disclosures of the Attributes, and beholding the beauty of the Essence, and who passionately yearn for absolute beauty in the station of the spirit and immersion in the source of unification, through a God-fearing shedding of their own attributes and essences. *And rivers of [purified] honey*: the manifold sweetness of holy inspirations, luminous flashes and ecstatic pleasures in the states and stations of the wayfarers who become familiar with experiential realisation, and the seekers who direct themselves towards perfection before arriving at the station of love: those who have

Q. 47:10

a God-fearing aversion to curiosities. More people eat honey than drink wine, and not everyone who has tasted the sweetness of honey has tasted the pleasure of wine, though the inverse is not true. *And there will be for them therein every fruit*: all manner of pleasure from the self-disclosures of the acts, Attributes and Essence, as the poet said, 'I have attained every pleasure there is, / Save for the pleasure of my own torment'; for the witnessing experienced by the tormented one and the self-disclosure of the Attributes of overwhelming power to him is a special kind of pleasure for those who taste it. It is known to those who know it, while those who do not know it will deny it. *And forgiveness from their Lord* by the covering of the configurations of sins, and the expiation of the wickedness of depravities for those who consume the milk; and then the covering of deeds too for those who drink the water; and then the erasure of attributes for those who drink the honey and some of those who drink the wine; and then the effacement of the sins of states and stations, and the

Q. 47:16

annihilation of remnants and the masking of their manifestations, by illuminations and self-disclosures for the eaters of the fruits; and then the annihilation of the essence by immersion in the unification of Unity and destruction in the essence of ipseity for the drinkers of the pure wines. All of them are different kinds of God-fearing folk. [*Is such a one*] *like him who abides* [*in the Fire*]? Like one who is opposite them in the pits of the hell of nature, drinking the boiling water of caprice. [*And they will be given to drink boiling water which rips apart their bowels.*

[47:16] *And there are some among them who listen to you, until, when they go forth from you, they say to those who have been given knowledge, 'What was he saying just now?' Those are the ones on whose hearts God has set a seal and who follow their own desires.*

[47:17] *But those who are [rightly] guided, He enhances their guidance and invests them with fear [of Him].*

[47:18] *Do they, then, await anything except that the Hour should come upon them suddenly? For already its portents have come. So, when it has come upon them, for what [benefit] will their reminder be?*]

[47:19] *Know, then, that there is no god except God, [and ask forgiveness for your sin]*: attain certain knowledge of Oneness, and then follow His path. Asking forgiveness, which is the image of spiritual wayfaring, is preceded by faith that is rooted in knowledge and not mere supposition, because the one who is not granted stability of faith will not be able to travel the path, and stability is only attained through certitude. Blind faith can change, and every veil is a sin, whether it is caused by bodily configurations or attributes of the soul, heart or ego. As the saying goes, 'Your existence is a sin to which no other sin can be compared.' So the command for knowledge here is an encouragement to witness Oneness; and the command to ask forgiveness for sin is an encouragement to detach from the essence of manifestation of self-remnants and I-ness. [*Ask forgiveness for your sin*] *and for the believing men* [*and believing women*]: by imparting perfection to them, as well as leading and calling them to the Real, and guiding them along the path of Oneness. Such passages show that the majority of [the Prophet's] wayfaring to God occurred after the prophetic mission began. *And God knows your going to and fro*: your movements along the path from one stage to the next, and from one state to another; *and your place of rest*: the station in which you are, and He emanates lights upon you and sends down supports according to it.

[47:20] [*And those who believe say, 'Why has a sūra not been revealed?' But when a definitive* sūra *is revealed, and fighting is mentioned in it, you see those in whose hearts is a sickness looking at you with the look of someone fainting at* [*the point of*] *death. Yet more fitting for them* [47:21] *would be* [*to offer*] *obedience and honourable words. Then, when the matter has been resolved upon, if they are loyal to God, it will be better for them.*

[47:22] *May it not be* [*the case*] *with you that if you were to turn away, you would then cause corruption in the land and sever your kinship ties?*

[47:23] *Those are the ones whom God has cursed, so made them deaf and blinded their eyes.*

[47:24] *Do they not contemplate the Qur'ān? Or is it that there are locks on* [*their*] *hearts?*

[47:25] *Indeed, those who have turned their backs after the guidance has become clear to them, Satan has seduced them and has given them* [*false*] *hopes.*

[47:26] *That is because they said to those who were averse to what God revealed, 'We will obey you in some matters.' And God knows their secrets.*]

[47:27] *Then how will it be when the angels take them away,* [*beating their faces and their backs*]? The angels will take away the hopeless ones who languish in the station of the soul, ploughing along the path of the earthly dominion. What will their recourse be, or what will they do, when the earthly angels come to take them by seizing their spirits in that painful offensive way from their direction, veiling them from the holy lights from in front of their faces, and barring them from the sensory pleasures they desire from behind them? The soul's face is the direction towards which the heart inclines; and to beat it is to cause it pain on its

Q. 47:20

side, by veiling it from His lights and the delights of the self-disclosures of the Attributes. The soul's back is the direction to which the body inclines; and to beat it is to torment it on its side, by barring it from the lower direction and the sensory pleasures to which it is attracted by natural inclination and caprice, and to veil it from them by taking away the instruments that allow it to attain them.

[47:28] *That* beating and pain on both sides *is because they followed what angers God*: indulging in sins and corporeal desires that distanced them from Him, and so they deserved to be beaten on their backs; *and [because] they were averse to what pleases Him*: namely shedding their attributes in order to adopt His and directing themselves towards Him, which would have led them to the station of approval and nearness, and so they deserved to be beaten on their faces. [*Therefore, He has made their works fail.*]

Q. 47:28

[47:29] *Or did those in whose hearts is a sickness suppose [that God would not expose their rancour]?* [Did they suppose that] the configurations of the soul run to the body more quickly than the configurations of the body do to the soul, because they are from the dominion whose nature is to influence, while the body is from the earthly kingdom whose nature is to react? This is why it is not possible to conceal the egocentric states, as you can see by how the configurations of anger, discontent and happiness are manifested on the faces of the people who feel them. Ignorance, however, which is one of the most pernicious maladies of the heart, deludes and blinds the one who experiences it so that he thinks that he can conceal the rancour, malice and envy that are in his heart. Instead, God reveals them on the pages of his face and the twists of his tongue, as the Prophet (may God grant him peace) said, 'Whenever someone conceals something, God reveals it in the twists of his tongue and the pages of his face.' This is the meaning of His Words:

[47:30] [*And if We wish, We could show them to you,*] *then you would recognise them by their mark. And you will certainly recognise them by [their] tone of speech*: this is why it is said that if a person spends the night engaged in sin or obedience concealed behind seventy closed doors, in the morning the people will be chattering about it, because it will appear in his mark, his movements and stillnesses, and his dispositions will attest to it. [*And God knows your deeds.*]

[47:31] *And We will assuredly try you until We know [those of you who struggle [for God's cause] and those who are steadfast, and We will appraise your record]*: God's knowledge is of two types: the one that precedes its objects in general (*ijmālan*) in the Tablet of Decree (*lawḥ al-qaḍā'*) and in differ-entiation (*tafṣīlan*) in the Tablet of Destiny (*lawḥ al-qadar*); and the one that follows them in differentiated loci from human souls and heavenly-characteristic souls. The meaning of *until We know*, then is: until Our differentiated knowledge is manifested in the angelic and human loci by which the requital is affirmed. And God knows best.

Q. 47:31

48
VICTORY
SŪRAT AL-FATḤ

In the Name of God, the Compassionate, the Merciful

[48:1] *Indeed, We have given you a clear victory,* [48:2] [*that God may forgive you what is past of your sin and what is to come, and that He may perfect His favour to you and guide you to a straight path,* [48:3] *and that God may help you with mighty help:*] the victories of the Messenger of God (may God bless him and grant him peace) were three.

The first was the near victory to which He alluded when He said, [*He*] *assigned* [*you*] *before that a near victory* [Q. 48:27]. This was the opening[1] of the door of the heart by ascension from the station of the soul, which was facilitated by unveilings of the Unseen and illuminations of certitude. He was joined in this by most of the believers, as God says, *And another which you* [*all*] *love: help from God and a victory near at hand* [Q. 61:13], and His Words, *And He knew what was in their hearts, so He sent down the peace of reassurance upon them, and rewarded them with a near victory* [Q. 48:18]. This necessitated the glad tidings of angelic illuminations and self-disclosures of the Attributes, as He said [at Q. 61:13], and the attainment of gnostic certainties and unveiled holy realities, to which His Words *and abundant spoils which they will capture* [Q. 48:19] allude.

The second was the clear victory by the manifestation of the lights of the spirit and the heart's ascension to its station, when the soul ascends to the station of the heart so that the attributes that adhered to it before the heart's opening—the benighted configurations—are covered with the lights of the heart and utterly negated. This is the meaning of His Words *that God may forgive you what is past of your sin,* and likewise what would come after them of luminous configurations acquired through illumination by

---

1 The word *fatḥ* means both 'victory' and 'opening'.

the lights of the heart, which are manifested through it in variegations and conceal its state, namely the sins to which His Words *and what is to come* allude. This is not negated by the near victory, but the first is negated by it, because the station of the heart is not completed or perfected until after the ascension to the station of the spirit, when its lights overwhelm the heart. It is then that the heart's variegation manifests, and the variegation of the soul, which was in the station of the heart, is negated entirely and its matter is disconnected. In this victory the spoils of spiritual witnessings and mysterious communions are attained.

The third victory is the absolute victory, to which His Words *When the help of God comes together with victory* [Q. 110:1] allude. This is the opening of the door of Unity through absolute annihilation and immersion in the source of unification, by essential witnessing and the manifestation of the light of Unity. The victory mentioned here is the middle one, which pertains to four matters: the aforementioned forgiveness; the completion of the favour of the Attributes and witnessings of beauty and majesty, by the perfection of the station of the heart, as was described; and guidance to the path of Essential Unity by traversal of the Attributes, the rending of their veils of light and the uncovering of their subtle mysteries, until arrival at the annihilation of ego and the mighty help of gifted existence and veridical aid bequeathed after annihilation.

Q. 48:4

[48:4] *He it is Who sent down peace of reassurance [into the hearts of the believers]*: *peace of reassurance (sakīna)* is a light in the heart that gives peace and tranquillity to the one who beholds it. It issues from the eye of certitude after the knowledge of certitude, as though it were an experience of certitude accompanied by pleasure and joy. *That they might add* experiential, existential and essential *faith to their* cognitive *faith. And to God belong the hosts of the heavens*, the holy illuminations and spiritual assistances, *and the earth*, the egocentric attributes and earthly dominions, such as the human faculties and others, some of which dominate others according to His will, just as the heavenly dominions dominate the earthly, egocentric dominions in their hearts by the sending down of the peace of reassurance, and the earthly dominate the heavenly in the hearts of their enemies so that they fall into doubt and uncertainty. *And God is ever Knower* of their secrets and the dictates of their preparednesses, and the purity of the dispositions of the former group and the turbidity of the souls of the latter, *Wise* in what He does by allowing some to dominate others according to what is wise and right.

[48:5] *So that He may admit the believing men and believing women*, by the

337

sending down of the peace of reassurance, *into gardens [underneath which rivers flow*: the gardens] of the Attributes, under which flow the rivers of the teachings of reliance, contentment, gnosis and the other sciences of spiritual states, stations, realities and mysteries; [*wherein they will abide,*] *and that He may absolve them of their misdeeds* of the attributes of the soul; *for that, in God's sight, is a supreme triumph*: by the attainment of the degrees of the ones brought near, supreme in comparison to the gardens of the acts.

[48:6] *And so that He may chastise the hypocrites, men and women*: those who nullified their own preparedness and sullied their purity by their deeds and dispositions; *and the idolaters, men and women*: those who were cast out and expelled from the presence of the Real, the wretched ones who could not join the believers outwardly, because of the real opposition between them and the original, essential enmity between them, according to innate disposition; *and those who make evil assumptions about God* because of their doubt and uncertainty, and the darkness of their souls by veiling. *For them will be an evil turn of fortune*: through torment in this world by all manner of misfortunes, whether slaying, death or degradation, *and God is wroth with them* with overwhelming power and veils, *and He has cursed them* with banishment and expulsion in the Hereafter, *and has prepared for them* all manner of chastisements [in *Hell—and it is an evil destination*]!

Q. 48:6

[48:7] *And to God belong the hosts of the heavens [and the earth]*: He repeats this to indicate how He made the earthly hosts dominant over the heavenly in the case of the hypocrites and idolaters, in contrast to what He did with the believers; [*and God is ever Mighty, Wise*:] this time He says *Mighty* rather than 'Knower' to evoke the meaning of omnipotence and compulsion, because knowledge pertains to subtle kindness while might pertains to omnipotence.

[48:8] [*Indeed, We have sent you as a witness, and a bearer of good tidings, and a warner,* [48:9] *that you may believe in God and His Messenger, and that you may support Him, and revere Him, and glorify Him morning and evening.*]

[48:10] *Truly those who pledge allegiance to you,* [*in fact pledge allegiance to God*]: this pledge was the consequence of the original covenant taken with the servants at the beginning of innate disposition. The reason why pledging allegiance to him was pledging allegiance to God was that the Prophet could become annihilated to his own being, and realise God in his essence, attributes and acts, so that everything that came from him and was attributed to him was really from God and could be attributed to God. Thus, to pledge allegiance to him was to pledge allegiance to

God. The reason for us saying that this was a consequence of the covenant of innate disposition is that if there were not a primal connection and correspondence between them and him, this pledge would not have taken place because there would not have been the necessary affinity and love without the connection. This was a sign of how their innate disposition was still sound and had retained its primal purity.

The hand of God—manifest in the locus of His Messenger, who is His Supreme Name—*is above their hands*: His power manifested in the hand of the Messenger was above their power manifested in the forms of their hands, so that it would harm them if they reneged and benefit them if they held true. *So whoever reneges* against the covenant by sullying the purity of his innate disposition, and being veiled by the configurations of his creation and the dominance of the darkness of his soul's attributes from the light of his heart, which would cause him to break the covenant; *reneges against his own soul*: the harm of his reneging will befall him and no one else, because of his fall from the original innate disposition, his veiling by corporeal darknesses, his deprivation of spiritual pleasures, and his torment by egocentric pains. This is the true meaning of hypocrisy. *And whoever fulfils [the covenant which he has made with God]*, by preserving the light of his innate disposition, *He will give him a great reward*: by the lights of self-disclosures of the Attributes and the pleasures of witnessing. This is why this pledge was called the Pledge of Contentment (*bayʿat al-riḍwān*), since contentment means the annihilation of the will in His will, which is the perfection of the annihilation of the Attributes.

Q. 48:11

[48:11] [*Those of the Bedouins who were left behind will say to you, 'Our possessions and our families kept us occupied. So ask forgiveness for us!' They say with their tongues what is not in their hearts. Say: 'Who can avail you anything against God should He desire to cause you harm or desire to bring you benefit? Nay, but God is ever Aware of what you do.*

[48:12] *'Nay, but you thought that the Messenger and the believers would never return to their families, and that [thought] was adorned in your hearts, and you thought evil thoughts, and you were a ruined lot.'*

[48:13] *And whoever does not believe in God and His Messenger, We have prepared for the disbelievers a blaze.*

[48:14] *And to God belongs the kingdom of the heavens and the earth: He forgives whomever He will and chastises whomever He will; and God is ever Forgiving, Merciful.*

[48:15] *Those who were left behind will say, when you set forth after spoils, in order to capture them, 'Let us follow you.' They desire to change the Words of God. Say: 'You shall never follow us! Thus has God said beforehand.' Then they will say, 'Nay, but you are envious of us.' Nay, but they never understood, [all] except a few.*

[48:16] *Say to those of the Bedouins who were left behind: 'You shall be called against a people possessed of great might: you shall fight them, or they will submit. So if you obey, God will give you a good reward; but if you turn away like you turned away before, He will chastise you with a painful chastisement.'*

[48:17] *There is no blame on the blind, nor [is there] blame on the lame, nor [is there] blame on the sick. And whoever obeys God and His Messenger, He will admit him into gardens underneath which rivers flow; and whoever turns away, He will chastise him with a painful chastisement.]*

And because of the realisation of this reward [mentioned in Q. 48:10 above] due to God's awareness of the purity of their innate disposition, He said:

Q. 48:16

[48:18] *Verily God was pleased with the believers when they pledged allegiance to you under the tree. And He knew what was in their hearts* of sincerity and the resolve to fulfil the covenant and preserve that light, *so He sent down the peace of reassurance upon them*: shining with the light of self-disclosure of the Attributes, which is a light of perfection in addition to an essential light, and so they attained certitude; *and rewarded them with [a near victory]*: the victory described before. They attained the station of contentment and were content with Him for the reward He had given them; and had God not been content with them first, they would not have been content themselves.

[48:19] [He continues:] *and abundant spoils* of the knowledge of the Attributes and Names *which they will capture; and God is ever Mighty*: for His power was above their own; *Wise*: in that He concealed in the form of this mighty omnipotence the meaning of this subtle kindness, for the outward implication of His Words *The hand of God is above their hands* [Q. 48:10] is omnipotence, and a promise from which came the meaning of His Words *God was pleased with the believers* [Q. 48:18], which was pure kindness.

[48:20] *God has promised you abundant spoils which you will capture* from the teachings of the Oneness of the Essence. *So He has expedited this one for you, and withheld [people's hands]*—the hands of the people of your attributes—*from you, so that it may be a* guiding *sign for the believers* of the Oneness of the Essence, *and that He may guide you [on a straight path]*: along His path after knowledge of Him.

[48:21] *And others* of His teachings which are none other than His Essence, after your annihilation in Him and your realisation of Him in the state of subsistence after annihilation, *which you were not able to capture,* for they were His alone, *God* and no other *has verily encompassed these [already].* *And God has power over all things*: [namely] all objects of His knowledge. And God knows best.

Q. 48:21

49

THE APARTMENTS
SŪRAT AL-ḤUJURĀT

In the Name of God, the Compassionate, the Merciful

[49:1] *O you who believe, do not venture ahead of God and His Messenger*:
He commanded a combination of the etiquettes of the outward and the
inward from the people of presence, and forbade any venturing ahead in
the divine presence and the prophetic presence, which includes advancement in word, deed or thought, and manifesting the attributes and essence.
For the presence of every one of God's Names, there is a particular etiquette which must be observed by the one to whom God self-discloses
through that Name. Likewise, for every station and state there is an etiquette that must be observed. Venturing ahead of God in the station of
annihilation means to manifest I-ness in the presence of the Essence. In
the station of erasure, it means to manifest any attribute that opposes the
Attribute whose self-disclosure one witnesses in the presence of Names,
such as manifesting His will in the station of contentment and witnessing will in the presence of the self-disclosure of His Name the Willing,
or manifesting His knowledge by objecting in the station of submission
to the presence of the Knower, or by manifesting stout-heartedness in
the station of incapacity and witnessing the All-Powerful, or by allowing
idle thoughts in the station of vigilance and witnessing the Speaker, or
by acting in the station of reliance and shedding deeds in the presence of
the Doer. All of these violate the etiquette of the inner being with God.
As for violating the etiquette of the outer being with Him, this means
things such as seeking dispensatory allowances rather than adhering to
strict rules, indulging in lawful but frivolous matters of curiosity in words
and deeds, and the like.

As for venturing ahead of the Messenger by violating the etiquette of
the outward, it means things such as speaking before him, walking in front

of him, raising one's voice over his, calling to him from outside the chambers, sitting with him and fooling about and chatting idly, going into his room or leaving him without permission, and the like. Violating the etiquette of the inward with him means such things as desiring that the Messenger obey one about something, having bad thoughts about him, and the like. As for the breaches pertaining to commands and prohibitions, and doing anything before knowing God's ruling and the Messenger's ruling on it, such things are examples of the poor etiquette of the people of absence, not of presence, which is the subject at hand here.

And fear God in all these ventures, for the one who fears God as He truly ought to be feared will not commit such breaches in the manners described. *Indeed, God is Hearer* of the spoken ventures in matters of outward etiquette, and the thoughts of the soul in matters of inward etiquette, *Knower* of deeds, attributes and the manifestations of remnants.

[49:2] [*O you who believe, do not raise your voices above the voice of the Prophet, and do not shout words at him, as you shout to one another, lest your works should be invalidated without your being aware.*

[49:3] *Indeed, those who lower their voices in the presence of God's Messenger— they are the ones whose hearts God has tested for God-fearing. For them will be forgiveness and a great reward.*

[49:4] *Truly those who call you from behind the apartments—most of them do not understand.*

[49:5] *And had they been patient until you came out to them, it would have been better for them; and God is Forgiving, Merciful.*

[49:6] *O you who believe, if a reprobate should come to you with some tiding, verify [it], lest you injure a folk out of ignorance; and then become remorseful of what you have perpetrated.*]

[49:7] *And know that the Messenger of God is among you.* [*If he were to obey you in many matters, you would surely be in trouble. But God has endeared faith to you, adorning your hearts with it, and He has made odious to you disbelief and immorality and disobedience. Those—they are the right-minded*:] it would be an expression of the manifestation of the soul with its attributes if a believer was to hope for the Messenger to obey him, as well as showing that he was veiled from the virtue and perfection of the Messenger. This could only be the result of weak faith, a heart sullied by the soul's caprice, and the soul's dominance of the heart by inclination towards desires and pleasures because of the sway caprice holds over it.

Note how He placed the word *But* in between *If he were to obey you* and *God has endeared faith to you*, because of the purity of the spirit and how innate disposition has retained its original light, *adorning your hearts with it*: by the shining of the lights of the spirit over the heart and their illumination of it, and their preparedness for the angelic inspirations to submit and yield to His codes. *And He has made odious to you disbelief*, which means to be veiled from the religion, *and immorality [and disobedience]*, which means to incline towards following desires by caprice and following Satan by disobedience, because the soul is illuminated by the light of the heart and yields to it, so that it attains the disposition of protection from error by surrendering to its command. Protection is a configuration of light in the soul which prevents it from venturing towards sins. All of this is due to the power of the spirit and its domination of the heart and the soul by its innate light, just as the contrary state in those who hope for the Messenger to obey them is due to the power of the soul and its domination of the heart, veiling it from the light of the spirit. *Those* for whom faith was made beloved and adorned in their hearts, and disbelief was made odious, *they are the right-minded* who adhere to the straight path, unlike those who differ with them.

Q. 49:8

[49:8] [*That is*] *a favour from God*: by His nurture of them in pre-eternity, which led to spiritual guidance and preparation, from which all these perfections stretched out into eternity; *and a grace*: by how He blessed them to act according to that primal guidance and helped them by emanating perfections corresponding to their preparednesses, until they acquired the disposition of protection which led them to despise sin; *and God is Knower* of the states of their preparednesses; *Wise*: in how He emanates to them what suits them and corresponds to them, by His wisdom.

[49:9] *And if two parties of believers fall to fighting, make peace between them. And if one of them aggresses against the other, fight the one which aggresses until it returns to God's command. Then, if it returns, reconcile them, and act justly*: fighting only occurs because of inclination towards the world, reliance on caprice and attraction towards the lower direction and particular desires. Reconciliation can only come from the impulses of justice in the soul, which is the shadow of love, which in turn is the shadow of Unity. Thus, the believers in Oneness are commanded to make peace between them if they are both aggressors, or to fight the aggressor if only one of them aggressed until it desists, because the aggressor is opposed to the truth and resistant to it. Consider how ʿAmmār (may God be pleased with him) went out to fight the partisans of Muʿāwiya despite his old age, in order to make it clear that they were the aggressing party. Reconciliation is conditional for the second situation, namely when only one side is the aggressor, because aggression on both sides stirs up hearts and inflames souls towards injustice. And so He forbade this to them, for reconciliation is only significant when it occurs not only in the soul but in the heart as well according to pure justice, for the sake of bringing an end to injustice, and not for any other reason, such as protection, bias, worldly advantage or the like. Therefore, He says, *Indeed, God loves the just*: that is, the divine love is conditional on justice. So if the reconciliation is not done for justice, it is not done for love; and if it is not done for love, then God will not love them, because if God loved them, they would inevitably love Him, as He says, *He loves them, and they love Him* [Q. 5:54]. If they loved Him, they would love the believers and adhere to justice.

[49:10] [*The believers are indeed brothers. Therefore, [always] make peace between your brethren:*] He then made clear that faith, whose minimum level is affirmation of Oneness and action, necessitates that there be a true brotherhood among the believers, because of the primal correspondence and innate kinship that is infinitely beyond formal kinship and blood ties, as it implies heart-centred love that requires a spiritual connection in the source of unification, not mere egocentric love caused by material circumstance. At the bare minimum there must be the reconciliation that is one of the necessary results of justice and one of its traits; for if they had not strayed from innate disposition and been sullied by the coverings of creation, they would not have fought one another and fallen into conflict to begin with. Therefore, the folk of purity are obliged by the inherent mercy, compassion and empathy of true brotherhood to make peace between them and return them to purity.

Q. 49:10

And fear God when innate disposition is sullied and you are distanced from the primal light by the necessary consequences of creation, and when contentment is sullied by corruption, and when reconciliation fails because of the weakness of love, which indicates veiling from Unity, *so that perhaps you might receive mercy*: by the emanation of the light of perfection corresponding to the purity of preparedness. All of the prohibitions mentioned after this until the Words *Indeed, the noblest of you in the sight of God is the most God-fearing among you* [Q. 49:13] are different kinds of evildoing, which is the opposite of the justice that is required for faith in Oneness.

[49:11] [*O you who believe, do not let any people deride another people who may be better than they are; nor let any women deride [other] women who may be better than they are. And do not defame one another, nor insult one another by nicknames. Evil is the name of immorality after faith! And whoever does not repent, those—they are the evildoers.*

[49:12] *O you who believe, shun much suspicion. Indeed, some suspicions are* *sins. And do not spy, nor backbite one another. Would any of you love to eat the flesh* *of his brother dead? You would abhor it. And fear God. Indeed, God is Relenting,* *Merciful.*

[49:13] *O people, We have indeed created you from a male and a female, and* *made you nations and tribes that you may come to know one another.] Indeed,* *the noblest of you in the sight of God is the most God-fearing among you*: this means that there is no nobility among humankind inasmuch as they are all equally human with a common descent from male and female; the differentiation of nations and tribes only exists for the sake of identification by membership of them, not for jingoistic pride, since that is a vice, and nobility is only attained by avoiding vices, which is the root of God-fearing. Then, as God-fearing grows in degree, the person becomes more and more noble and esteemed in God's sight. The God-fearing person

Q. 49:12

who avoids those things the Divine Law prohibits, which are called 'sins' in the custom of the Law, is nobler than the iniquitous person. Then the one who avoids vices of character such as ignorance, stinginess, avarice, greed and cowardice is nobler than the one who avoids sins but is tainted by such traits. Then the one who avoids attributing influence and action to other-than-God, by relying on Him and witnessing the acts of the Real, is nobler than the virtuous one who is adorned with virtuous character traits but does attribute influence to other-than-God, and is veiled by beholding the acts of creation from the self-disclosures of the acts of the Real. Then the one who avoids the veils of the Attributes, by shedding them in the station of contentment and erasure of attributes, is nobler than the one who relies on God in the station of the Oneness of the acts but is veiled by the Attributes from the self-disclosures of the Attributes of the Real. Then the one who avoids his own particular being, meaning his ego which is the source of sin, through annihilation, is nobler than all the others. *Indeed, God is Knower* of the degrees of your God-fearing, *Aware* of your ranks of virtue.

[49:14] *The Bedouins say, 'We believe.' Say: 'You do not believe; but rather* *say, "We have submitted"; for faith has not yet entered into your hearts.' Yet if you* *obey God and His Messenger, He will not diminish for you anything of your deeds.* *Indeed, God is Forgiving, Merciful.*

[49:15] *The [true] believers are only those who believe in God and His* *Messenger, and then have not doubted*: after differentiating between faith and submission and explaining that faith is inward and heart-centred while submission is outward and body-centred, He then indicated that true, significant faith is the firm certitude that is established in the heart and unaccompanied by doubt, not that which comes and goes like a passing thought. The believers are the certain ones whose hearts dominate their souls by the power of the disposition of certitude, illuminating them with its lights, so that the dispositions of their hearts take firm root therein until their bodies are influenced by them, and can do nothing but obey their rule and yield to their configuration. This is the meaning of His Words *and who strive with their wealth and their souls for the cause of God*, after the negation of doubt from them, because to offer one's wealth and soul for the cause of the Real is the product of firm certitude, and its external effect. *It is they who are sincere* in faith, for the mark of sincerity is patent in their bodies and the truthfulness of their words and deeds, unlike those pretenders.

Q. 49:15

50
QĀF
SŪRAT QĀF

In the Name of God, the Compassionate, the Merciful

[50:1] *Qāf. By the Glorious Qur'ān*: the letter *Qāf* symbolises the Muḥammadan heart (*qalb*), which is the divine throne that encompasses all things, just as the letter *ṣād* symbolises his form (*ṣūra*), according to the allusion of Ibn ʿAbbās, who said that *Ṣād* is a mountain in Mecca on which the Throne of the Compassionate stood before there was such a thing as night and day. And because it is the throne of the Compassionate, he said, 'The heart of the believer is the throne of God'; and God said, 'Neither My earth nor My heaven can embrace Me, but the heart of My believing servant embraces Me.'

It is said that *Qāf* is the name of a mountain that surrounds the world, and that behind it is the phoenix, which encompasses all. It is the veil of the Lord, and no one knows of it except the one who reaches the station of the heart, and no one beholds it except the one who beholds this mountain.

Then He swore by *the Glorious Qur'ān*, meaning the perfect Qur'ānic intellect in it, which is the primal preparedness that gathers the differentiations of all existence. When it was manifested and came into action, it became a discerning intellect with patent glory and nobility, according to this meaning. Or it means the Glorious Qur'ān that was revealed to him, which is identical with the manifest Criterion to which we alluded before. He swore by these two together because of their correspondence. The main clause of the oath is omitted, as it is in *Ṣād* and other chapters, but it can be inferred as 'it is the truth', or 'it is an attested miracle', given what He says next:

[50:2] [*Nay, but they consider it odd that there should have come to them a warner from among themselves. So the disbelievers say, 'This is an odd thing!*

[50:3] *'What! When we are dead and have become dust? That is a far-fetched return!'*

[50:4] *We know what the earth diminishes of them, and with Us is a preserving Book.*

[50:5] *Nay, but they denied the truth, when it came to them, and so they are [now] in a confounded situation.*

[50:6] *Have they not then looked at the heaven above them, how We have built it, and adorned it, and how there are no cracks in it?*

[50:7] *And the earth We have spread it out, and cast in it firm mountains, and caused every delightful kind to grow in it,* [50:8] *as an insight and a reminder for every penitent servant.*

[50:9] *And We send down from the heaven blessed water with which We cause to grow gardens and the grain that is harvested,* [50:10] *and the date-palms that stand tall with piled spathes,* [50:11] *as provision for [Our] servants; and with it We revive a dead land. So shall be the rising.*

[50:12] *The people of Noah denied before them and [so did] the dwellers at al-Rass and Thamūd,* [50:13] *and ʿĀd, and Pharaoh, the brethren of Lot,* [50:14] *and the dwellers in the wood, and the people of Tubbaʿ. Each denied the messengers, and so My threat became due.]*

Q. 50:3

[50:15] *Were We then wearied by the first creation? Nay, yet they are in doubt about a new creation*: Did We not guide to the creation of realities and the engendering of the first things, such as the spirits and the heavens? On the contrary, they acknowledged this, and they are only in doubt and confusion about the fresh creation that is renewed in every instant. Concerning such, Satan confused them until they said, *We die and we live, and nothing but time destroys us* [Q. 45:24], attributing influence to time and being veiled from the meaning of His Words *Every day He is upon some matter* [Q. 55:29]. If they knew God as He should be known, and their recognition of His engendering of the first creation was based on knowledge and certitude, they would have witnessed the new creation in every moment. Thus, they would not have denied the Resurrection and would have been sincere worshippers over whom Satan held no sway.

[50:16] *And verily We created man and We know what his soul whispers to him, and We are nearer to him than his jugular vein*: this is a representation of a metaphysical concept with an observable, physical one. The reason He is closer, even though there is no distance at all between a thing and a part of it which is physically connected to it, is that the connection of the part to the whole is still observed as a distinction and duality and not a true union, while His with-ness and nearness to His servant is not like this, for His Ipseity and reality, inherent in his ipseity and realisation, is not something other than him; rather, his particular, individual being is nothing other than His reality, which is being as being itself, and without Him he would be total non-being and pure nothingness. So the jugular is of utmost formal nearness, meaning the connection of particularity which is the strongest bodily connection imaginable since it is the thing that keeps the person alive; yet this connection is more complete still, since it is enduring. He then proclaimed His greater nearness to make clear that He did not mean the nearness of connection and proximity, as the Commander of the Believers (may God grant him peace) said, 'He is with everything': not in the sense of being alongside it; for each thing is what it is because of Him, and it would not be anything at all without Him, such that it could be described as being alongside Him.

Q. 50:17

[50:17] *When the two Receivers receive, [seated on the right and on the left]*: He knows the thoughts of a man's soul which it whispers to him when the two Receivers receive, for He is closer to him than they are. Their reception is only for the purpose of establishing an argument against him, and recording his words and deeds in the illuminated pages for the requital. The Receiver who sits on the right is the faculty of practical intelligence, which inscribes the forms of good deeds and righteous words. The reason it sits on his right is that the right side is the side that is powerful, noble and blessed; it is the side of the soul that is nearest to the truth. The Receiver who sits on the left is the faculty of imagination, which inscribes the human, bestial and predatory deeds, satanic estimations and opinions, and foul corrupted words. The reason it sits on the left is that the left side is the side that is weak, base and ill-omened; it is the side that is closest to the body.

Human disposition is intrinsically good because it is from the realm of illuminations, and so it essentially and instinctively inclines to good things. Evil things are only presented to it from the direction of the body and its instruments and configurations.

The one on the right side is dominant over the one on the left. Whenever the person does a good deed, it writes it down immediately; however, when he does a bad deed it prevents the one on the left side from writing it down at once, awaiting a glorification: that is, waiting for him to transcend the corporeal coverings and natural configurations by returning to his primal home, true origin and instinctive state, to wipe away the mark of that ephemeral intrusion by bathing in the original light and seeking forgiveness—in other words, by being illuminated by the spiritual lights and turning to the divine presence to erase the mark of that transient evil by the inspiring light. He (may God bless him and grant him peace) said, 'The recorder of good deeds is on a man's right, and the recorder of evil deeds is on his left. The recorder of good deeds is the custodian of the recorder of evil deeds. When he does a good deed, the angel on the right records it tenfold. When he does an evil deed, the one on the right says to the one on the left, "Leave him for seven hours, in case he glorifies or seeks forgiveness."'

[50:18] [*He does not utter a word but that there is beside him a watcher,* [*who is*] *ready.*]

[50:19] *And the stupor of death*—its bewildering intensity which distracts the senses and startles the mind—*arrives with the truth*: with the reality of the thing which he ignored, [namely] the states of the Hereafter, reward and punishment. The stupor that prevented the dying man from utilising his outward perceptions to perceive the inner states arrives. *That is what you used to shun*, O dying man, when you inclined towards outward things and so ignored it.

Q. 50:18

[50:20] *And the Trumpet will be blown* to raise them all to life in a form that corresponds to them in the Hereafter. *That is* [*the Day of*] *the* realisation of the *Promised Threat*: by the witnessing of the deeds that they sent ahead of them.

[50:21] *And every soul will come, accompanied by a driver*, which is its knowledge, *and a witness*, which is its deeds, because every person is attracted to the object of his gaze and what he chose with his knowledge; and the inclination that drives him towards that thing arose only from his feelings about that thing and his judgement of it as appropriate for him, whether it is a lower corporeal matter towards which his caprice directed him and to which his estimation and faculties tempted him, or a higher spiritual matter to which his intellect and spiritual love led him and towards which his heart and innate disposition encouraged him. The knowledge that dominated him will be his driver towards its object, and his witness by inclination that dominates him and love that is rooted in him. The action written in his account will testify against him by its manifestation in the forms of his body parts and limbs, and his record will speak the truth against him, as will his limbs by the configurations of his body parts, shaped by his deeds.

[50:22] '*Verily you were oblivious of this*, veiled as you were by sense and sensations, distracted from it by your preoccupation with the external instead of the internal. *So* [*now*] *We have removed from you*, by death, *your covering,* the corporeal material covering that veiled you, *and so your sight on this day is acute':* your perception of that to which you were oblivious before, and that in which you did not truly believe, is now right there for you to see.

[50:23] *And his companion,* the devil of estimation that deluded him with externalities and veiled him from internalities, *will say, 'This is what I have ready with me':* prepared for Hell. In other words, it will become clear how the faculty of estimation controlled him by turning him towards the lower direction and enslaved him for the pursuit of bodily pleasures, until it prepared him for Hell in the pit of nature.

[50:24] *'Cast into Hell [every obdurate disbeliever,* [50:25] *hinderer of good, transgressor, sceptic,* [50:26] *who has set-up alongside God another god! Cast him then into the severe chastisement']*: these words are directed to the driver and the witness who will ruin him and cast him into the deepest depths of primordial, corporeal matter and the pits of dark nature, in the fires of deprivation. Or they are directed to Mālik, in which case the reason the imperative is in the dual form[1] is that the act is repeated, as though He said 'cast' to him twice, because of his power to banish and cast them towards the lower direction. The first reading is supported by the fact that this is the number of the ruinous vices, by which they deserved the torment of Hell and to be cast into its fires, and He made clear that they were from the nature of knowledge and action.

Disbelief and hindering good are both caused by the excess of the bestial and appetitive faculties, because of their engrossment in their pleasures and their improper utilisation of God's favours, by sinning and being veiled from the One Who provided them. These favours ought to have inspired them to remember Him and give thanks to Him, yet instead they pursued them avariciously because of their greed for them, and denied them to their rightful recipients. He named these vices by their emphatic active forms[2] to allude to how rooted they were in this person and how they utterly dominated him, and how deeply immersed he was in them, which caused him to fall from the level of innate disposition into the pit of the well of nature. Obduracy and transgression are both caused by the excess of the irascible faculty and its dominance, because of the preponderance of the satanic impulse and the breaching of the limits of justice. All four of them are forms of corruption of action. Scepticism

Q. 50:23

---

1 It is *alqiyā* ('Cast, you two…').
2 *Kaffār* and *mannāᶜ*: the emphatic forms of *kāfir* ('disbeliever') and *māniᶜ* ('hinderer') respectively.

and idolatry are both caused by the deficiency of the rational faculty and its fall from innate disposition, by its negligence of God and its failure to stay within the bounds of the intellectual faculty, which is a form of corruption of knowledge.

[50:27] *And his companion will say, 'Our Lord, I did not make him a rebel, [but he [himself] was in extreme error']*: these dialogues [narrated here and below] are all figurative, meant to provide an imaginative depiction of the concept so that the heart can perceive it by beholding the allegory in the imagination. When the disbeliever claims that the Devil made him rebel and the Devil denies it, this symbolises the inner conflict and struggle that goes on between his estimative and intellectual faculties, and between all of his opposing pairs of faculties, such as the irascible and the appetitive. This is why:

[50:28] *He will say, 'Do not dispute in My presence, [for I had already given you the threat]*: but since those two elements of his being are the intellectual and the estimative, the root of the dispute was between them. Likewise, all the other disputes between opposing sides over a given benefit or pleasure will continue, as long as their desired object still exists; but once they are deprived of it or fall into perdition and torment because of their pursuit of it, they will argue or blame each other for their fate, as a consequence of being veiled from Oneness. Each of them will disown their sin because of their self-love. This is why Ḥāritha (may God be pleased with him) said to the Prophet (may God bless him and grant him peace), 'I [dreamed I] saw the people of Hell quarrelling,' and he told him that this was the truth.

Q. 50:27

Satan's words here, *I did not make him a rebel, but he [himself] was in extreme error* [Q. 50:27], resemble what he said elsewhere: *Indeed, God promised you a promise of truth, whereas I promised you, then failed you, for over you I had no warrant, except that I called you and you responded to me. So do not blame me, but blame yourselves* [Q. 14:22]. If the person had not erred from the path of Oneness and gone far from innate disposition, by turning to the lower direction and becoming covered by dark natural coverings, he would not have accepted Satan's whisperings but would have heeded the inspirations of the angel instead. The sin is his alone because of his veiling from the light of innate disposition and his acquisition of affinity with Satan in darkness.

God's command to cease the dispute does not mean that they will stop, but only that it will be useless and He will not heed it, as though He has said, 'No dispute will be heard in My presence; for the warning was certainly given to you when you were able to benefit from it, because you still had the instruments at your disposal and your preparedness was intact. Yet you did not benefit from it, nor even raise a head to it, until the benighted configurations were firmly planted upon your souls, and the rust covered your hearts, and the veil was realised, and the word of chastisement was proclaimed.'

[50:29] *'The word [that comes] from Me cannot be altered* at that time, for the chastisement is inevitable when it occurs; *and I am not unjust [to the servants]'*: for I granted you preparedness and showed you the way to perfect it, and guided you to the path to acquire this perfection. It is you who have wronged yourselves by acquiring that which contradicted this perfection and squandering the preparedness, by placing the light into darkness and exchanging what is lasting for what is ephemeral.

[50:30] *On the day when We will say to Hell, 'Are you [now] full?' [it will say, 'Are there any more?'* This will be on the day when the inhabitants of Hell become so numerous that it seems there could not possibly be any more, yet it will have room for them all and its rage will not be abated. A *ḥadīth* says, 'Hell will continue to receive its denizens, saying, "Are there any more?" until the Lord of Might places His foot inside it, when it will say, "Enough, enough, by Your might and grace!"' In other words, humankind will continue to incline towards nature by desire and avarice, and nature will remain as it is, attracting that which corresponds to it and accepting those forms of theirs which suit it, and then casting what it accepts down to the lowest levels imaginable, until the mark of the light of perfection which visits the heart comes to it, whereupon it will be illuminated by it and cease what it is doing. He symbolised the shining of the divine light from the heart upon the soul with the foot of the Lord of Might, which has the power to dominate it, prevent it from acting and compel it to assent to the heart, so that it says, 'Enough, enough!'

Q. 50:29

[50:31] *And Paradise*—the garden of the Attributes—*will be brought near for the God-fearing* who shun the attributes of the soul, given how He then says *who fears the Compassionate in the Unseen* [50–33], because fear pertains to the self-disclosure of magnificence, and how He says *not far*: that is, not a distant place, for the garden of the Attributes is closer than the garden of the Essence in degree though not in manifestation, since the Essence is closer in manifestation, because in the world of lights everything that is further in loftiness and degree from a thing is closer to it in manifestation, due to the intensity of its illumination; and given how He says:

[50:32] *'This is what you were promised. [It is] for every penitent one* who returns to God by the [state of] annihilation of the Attributes, *who is mind-*

354

ful: who preserves the purity of his innate disposition and primal light so that it is not sullied by the darkness of the soul, [50:33] [*who fears the Compassionate*:] the one who is characterised by fear, so that fear becomes his station upon the self-disclosure of the Real with the Attribute of All-Compassionate compassion, for it is the greatest of His Attributes because of how it stands for the emanation of all good things and perfections to all, which are the most glorious and mighty of graces; *in the Unseen*: that is, when he is absent from the witnessing of the Essence, for the one veiled by the self-disclosure of the Attributes is absent to the beauty of the Essence; *and comes with a penitent heart'* to God, repenting of the sins of the soul's attributes through the ascensions of the Attributes of the Real, and not stopping idle in the station of fear without seeking to ascend further.

[50:34] *'Enter it [in peace!* whereby you are] absolved from the flaws of the soul, secure from its variegations. [*That is the day of immortality.'*]

[50:35] *Therein they will have whatever they wish* of the graces of self-disclosures of the Attributes and their illuminations, according to their intentions; *and with Us there is yet more* of the light of the self-disclosure of the Essence, which their hearts could scarcely imagine.

Q. 50:34

[50:36] *And how many [a generation] We destroyed before [them:* before] those God-fearing ones, by annihilation and burning with the rays of the Essence's self-disclosure, *who were mightier than these in prowess*: saints who were more strongly rooted in the attributes of their own souls. [This is] because preparedness is stronger when the attributes of the soul are stronger in the beginning. *And [they are those who] then searched throughout the land*: the stages and stations of the Attributes, [*wondering*]: *is there any escape* from annihilation by being veiled by some of them and concealed behind them, when the lights of the rays of the enduring countenance shone forth? Yet how could there be an escape, when there were no more Attributes left to hide behind?

[50:37] *Indeed, there is in that* concept *a reminder for him who has a heart* that is perfect and mature for ascension to the limit of its perfection, *or gives ear*: in the station of the soul to the heart, for understanding the meanings and unveilings for ascension, [*in [full] witness*:] present in his heart, turned towards it, bathed in its light, ascending to its station.

[50:38] *And verily We created the heavens and the earth, and all that is between them, in six days*: that is, six directions, if we take *the heavens and the earth* literally. Yet if we interpret *the heavens* to symbolise the spirits and *the earth* to symbolise the body, then it means the forms of the six contingencies, namely the realm of divine power, the realm of the dominion and the realm of the kingdom which are the sum of the substances, and the aspects of relativity, quantity and modality, which are the sum of accidents. These six cover all created beings, and the aforementioned six thousand years was the period of the cycle of concealment, as was discussed in [sūrat] al-Aʿrāf [Q. 7]; [and no weariness touched Us].

[50:39] *So endure patiently what they say*: by regarding them through annihilation and being unaffected by their words, and by shedding deeds and restraining the soul from manifesting with its deeds, if you do not restrain it from manifesting with its attributes; *and glorify with praise of your Lord*: by detaching from the attributes of the soul, praising your Lord by adorning yourself with His Attributes and manifesting His perfections that are written within you in the station of the heart; *before the rising of the sun* of the spirit and the station of witnessing, *and before the sunset* of annihilation in the Unity of the Essence.

Q. 50:39

[50:40] [*And glorify Him:*] declare His transcendence above the attributes of created beings, by detaching from the outward attribute of variegation; *at [some part of the] night*: at some moments of the darkness of variegation; *and after prostrations*: in the aftermath of every annihilation. This is so as the aftermath of annihilation from deeds requires that one cautiously avoid the variegation of the soul, and the aftermath of annihilation from the Attributes requires that one transcend the variegation of the heart, and the aftermath of annihilation of the Essence requires that one be sanctified above the manifestation of I-ness.

[50:41] *And listen on the day when the caller calls out [from a place that is near]*: when God Himself calls from the nearest place to you, just as He called to Moses from the tree of his own soul.

[50:42] *On the day [when they hear the call of truth]*: when the people of the Major Resurrection hear the call of overwhelming power and annihilation in the Real from the Real; *that is the day of coming forth*: from their own beings.

[50:43] *Indeed, it is We Who give life and bring death*: it is Our nature to give life and bring death; We give life first by the soul and then We bring death beyond it, and then We give life by the heart and then bring death beyond it, and then We give life by the spirit and then bring death beyond it by annihilation; *and to Us is the journey's end*: by subsistence after annihilation, and moreover in every annihilation, for there is nowhere else for them to go.

[50:44] *On the day when the earth* of the body *is split asunder from them, [they will come] hastening forth* to the creatures with whom they have affinity. *That is an easy gathering for Us*: We shall gather them with the one with whom they are allied through love, by attracting them to him all at once, without any input from anyone.

[50:45] *We know best what they say* because Our knowledge encompasses them and precedes them, as well as their words; *and you are not [to be] a coercer of them*: who forces them to do other than what their preparedness and state dictate. *For you are only an admonisher* [Q. 88:21]. Be steadfast, then, by witnessing that from Me, and restrain the soul from manifesting with variegation. [*So admonish by the Qur'ān*:] by that which was revealed to you of the gathering [Qur'ānic] intellect in all levels, *those who* are moved by the remembrance so that they *fear My threat*, because they are receptive to admonition and have affinity with you in preparedness, and are near to Me, not like the rejected ones who are not affected by it. And God (Exalted is He) knows best.

Q. 50:45

51
THE WINDS THAT WINNOW
SŪRAT AL-DHĀRIYĀT

In the Name of God, the Compassionate, the Merciful

[51:1] *By the winds that winnow as they scatter*: the divine breezes and holy draughts that scatter the dust of benighted configurations and the soil of egocentric attributes; [51:2] *and those that bear [a burden]*: the luminous inspirations that bear the burdens of veridical realities and true unveilings that are weighty in the balance, because of their permanence, not the light ephemeral ones, to the hearts of the people of gnosis and the receptive prepared souls that bear those realities and meanings; [51:3] *and those that run with ease*: the souls that run in the fields of interactions and the waypoints of devotions, by means of those breezes and inspirations, easily without the effort expended by those who are deprived of this, or the hearts that run upon the seas of the Attributes, by means of those breezes, with ease; [51:4] *and those that apportion by command*: the angels brought near from the inhabitants of the realms of divine power and dominion, who apportion each one a share of felicity and true provision, according to preparednesses.

[51:5] *Assuredly what you are promised* about the Major Resurrection and the attainment of absolute perfection *is true*.

[51:6] *And assuredly judgement*—the requital that is the emanation that comes according to efforts of spiritual wayfaring and action laying the ground for reception, or deprivation and torment by veiling and the pain of harmful benighted configurations because of reliance on nature—*will take place*, as He says, *But as for those who struggle for Our sake, We shall assuredly guide them in Our ways* [Q. 29:69]. And He says, *No, indeed! Rather, upon their hearts is the rust of that which they earned. Nay, they, on that day, will be veiled from their Lord. Then indeed they will be exposed to Hellfire* [Q. 83:14–16]. So He swears by the preparing entities, receiving entities and emanating entities that the dictate of their gathering must surely come to pass.

[51:7] *And by the heaven*—the spirit—*with all [its tracks]*: paths from the Attributes, for each Attribute is a path to the heaven of the spirit, leading anyone who travels it towards it[self], and every station and state is a door to it.

[51:8] *Indeed, you are of differing opinions*: from the discourse of the soul and its various concerns which prevent it from being focused in one direction of travel, or the corrupt beliefs and false ways of thought—of all manner of compounded ignorance—which bar the way to perfection.

[51:9] *He is turned away therefrom*, because of that differing opinion which is the chatter of the soul or false beliefs, *who has deviated*: the veiled one who was destined for a bad end unlike others. Or it means that the one destined for damnation in God's pre-eternal knowledge is turned away from the perfection that is promised to you all.

[51:10] *Perish the conjecturers*: cursed be the deniers with their divergent opinions; [51:11] *who are in a stupor*: immersed in ignorance; [*in an abyss*]: heedless of perfection and requital.

Q. 51:7

[51:12] *They ask, 'When is the Day of Judgement?'* because of how distant they are from this concept and how unlikely they deem it to be, veiled as they are. They say, 'When is this unlikely event supposed to take place?' So comes the answer:

[51:13] *On the day when they will be [tormented in the Fire]* of deprivation in the darknesses of configurations, by the corruption of bodies and the fall into perdition and ruin. Then it will be said to them:

[51:14] *'Taste this torment of yours*: your chastisement. [*This*] *is what you sought to hasten on!'* by immersing yourselves in corporeal pleasures and preferring immediate advantages and bestial, predatory perfections.

[51:15] *Indeed, the God-fearing*, who detached themselves from the configurations of nature and the attributes of the soul, *will be amid gardens* of the Attributes *and [springs]* of their knowledge, [51:16] *receiving*—in other words, accepting—*what their Lord has given them* of the lights of self-disclosures of the Attributes and rejoicing in them, *for formerly*, before they arrived at the station of the self-disclosures of the Attributes, *they had truly been virtuous*: by witnessing the acts in the station of worship and interaction, as he (may God grant him peace) said, 'Virtue is to worship God as though you see Him.'

[51:17] *Little of the night* of veiling in the station of the soul [*did they use to sleep*]: heedless of spiritual wayfaring; [51:18] *and in the hours before dawn*—the times of the rising of the lights of self-disclosures and the breaking of the darkness of the soul's attributes—*they used to seek forgiveness*: seeking to be illuminated by the lights, and for the attributes of the soul and the configurations of evil to be covered by them and erased; [51:19] *and there was a share in their wealth*—their veridical and beneficial knowledge—[*assigned*] *for the beggar*, the prepared seeker, *and the deprived*, the unprepared one or the one veiled from the light of his innate disposition by corporeal coverings and conventional ciphers, by conveying veridical knowledge and gnostic teachings of certitude to the former, and beneficial, inspirational teachings by means of spiritual discipline and exertion to the latter.

[51:20] *And in the earth*—the outward aspect of the body—*there are signs* of the manifestations of the Names and Attributes *for those who know with certitude*: who witness the Attributes of God in their loci; [51:21] *and in your souls* from the lights of their self-disclosures. *Will you not then perceive?*

Q. 51:19

[51:22] *And in the heaven* of the spirit *is your* supra-sensory *provision* of knowledge, just as in the heaven of the world is your formal provision, *and* [*there is also*] *what you are promised* of the lights and states of the Major Resurrection.

[51:23] [*So by the Lord of the heaven and the earth,*] *it is indeed true*: these signs of the earth, the souls, the aspects of provision and what was promised in heaven are as true *as* [*the fact*] *that you have* [*power of*] *speech*: for this is one of the Attributes of the true Speaker which is manifested on your tongues and in the earth of your bodies, and the true Speaker self-disclosed through it to your hearts when you were present to witness it; and through it descended the supra-sensory provision, which manifests gradually in the form of words from the heaven of your spirits upon you, if it is true speech and not merely a noise like the noises of the animals, which can only be called speech in a metaphorical sense. It was by this that your perfection was attained and His light shone out upon you to guide you to the states of the Hereafter.

[51:24] [*Has the story reached you of Abraham's honoured guests?*]

[51:25] *When they entered upon him and said, 'Peace!' He said, 'Peace!'* [*These are*] *an unfamiliar folk* [*he thought*].

[51:26] *Then he went aside to his family and brought a fat calf;* [51:27] *and he placed it near them, saying, 'Will you not eat?'*

[51:28] *Then he conceived a fear of them. They said, 'Do not be afraid!' And they gave him good tidings of* [*the birth of*] *a knowledgeable boy.*

[51:29] *Then his wife came forward clamouring and smote her face, and said, 'A barren old woman!'*

[51:30] *They said, 'So has your Lord said. Indeed, He is the Wise, the Knower.'*

[51:31] *He said, 'So what is your business, O you who have been sent [by God]?'*

[51:32] *They said, 'Indeed, we have been sent to a guilty folk,* [51:33] *that we may unleash upon them stones of clay,* [51:34] *marked by your Lord for [the destruction of] the prodigal.'*

[51:35] *So We brought forth those in them who were believers,* [51:36] *but We did not find therein other than one house of those who had submitted [to God].*

[51:37] *And We left therein a sign for those who fear the painful chastisement.*

[51:38] *And [a sign too] in Moses when We sent him to Pharaoh with a clear warrant.*

[51:39] *But he turned away to his supports, saying, 'A sorcerer, or a madman!'*

[51:40] *So We seized him and his hosts and cast them into the waters, for he was blameworthy.*

[51:41] *And [also] in ʿĀd [was another sign], when We unleashed against them a barren wind.*

Q. 51:29

[51:42] *It did not leave anything that it came upon without making it like decayed bones.*

[51:43] *And [also] in Thamūd, when it was said to them, 'Enjoy [yourselves] for a while!'*

[51:44] *Then they defied the command of their Lord; so the thunderbolt seized them as they were looking around.*

[51:45] *So they were unable to rise up, nor were they victors.*

[51:46] *And the people of Noah aforetime. Indeed, they were an immoral lot.*

[51:47] *And the heaven, We built it with might, and indeed We are powerful.*

[51:48] *And the earth, We spread it out: what excellent Spreaders then!*

[51:49] *And of all things We created pairs that perhaps you might remember:]* the story of Abraham's guests and what befell them was commented on in *sūrat Hūd* [Q. 11].

[51:50] [Say:] *'So flee unto God:* devote yourselves to Him and seek to be illuminated in His light; and draw strength from Him to combat the soul and Satan, and take refuge with Him from their enmity and tyranny; and do not turn to anything but Him, nor acknowledge existence or influence for anything but Him, lest Satan overpower you and make you obey and worship him. Do not allow the caprice of the soul to make you set-up another object of worship alongside Him, such as the soul and its desires, lest you associate partners with Him and be veiled by it from Him and fall into perdition. [*Indeed, I am a clear warner to you from Him.*

[51:51] *'And do not set-up another god alongside God. Indeed, I am a clear warner to you from Him.'*

[51:52] *Thus there did not come to those who were before them any messenger but they said, 'A sorcerer, or a madman!'*

[51:53] *Have they enjoined this upon one another? Nay, but they are an insolent folk.*

[51:54] *So shun them, for you will not be reproached.*

[51:55] *And remind, for reminding truly benefits believers.*]

[51:56] *And I did not create the jinn* of the souls *and the humankind* of the bodies, or the 'two weighty things' of lore, *except* [*that they may worship Me*]: that My Attributes and perfections be manifested upon them, so that they recognise Me and then worship Me; for worship depends on recognition, and the one who does not recognise cannot worship, as the realised gnostic (may God grant him peace) said, 'I would not worship a lord I had not seen.' In other words, I did not create them to be veiled by their own beings and attributes from Me so that they would make their own souls into gods alongside Me, nor to be veiled by My creation and the desire of their souls so that they would make it into a god alongside Me and worship it.

Q. 51:51

[51:57] *I do not desire from them any provision,* [*nor do I desire that they should feed Me*]: I created them by veiling them with My Essence and Attributes, so that they would manifest and adopt My character traits, and thus become veiled by Me and concealed by the annihilation of the acts and the Attributes. [This was] to ensure that they would not attribute provision, feeding and influence to themselves because of how they manifested those acts and attributes, usurping My acts and Attributes and laying false claim to them.

[51:58] *Indeed, it is God Who is the Provider, the Lord of Strength, the Firm*: His Essence, endowed with all the Attributes, is the sole source of subtle acts of kindness such as provision, as well as acts of overwhelming power such as influence over things.

[51:59] *And for those who have wronged* by attributing act and influence to any of God's creations, whether it be themselves or something else, *there will assuredly be* [*a lot*]—an ample share of God's chastisement—*like* [*the lot of their counterparts*]: those who are veiled by the Attributes. *So let them not ask Me to hasten on*: by further indulging in their deeds.

[51:60] *For woe to those who disbelieve*—veiled from the Real in any degree and by anything—*from that day of theirs which they are promised* at the Minor Resurrection. And God knows best.

362

52

THE MOUNT
SŪRAT AL-ṬŪR

In the Name of God, the Compassionate, the Merciful

[52:1] *By the Mount,* [[52:2] *and an inscribed Book,* [52:3] *on an unrolled parchment.*

[52:4] *By the [greatly] frequented House,* [52:5] *and the raised roof,* [52:6] *and the swarming sea:*] the Mount (al-Ṭūr) is the mountain on which Moses was spoken to, and it is the human brain which is the locus of the intellect and reason. He swore by this because of its honour and nobility, since the supreme sphere which defines the directions is to the world as the brain is to the human being. It could be that the Mount symbolises this sphere, in which case He swore by it due to its nobility, and how it is the locus of the divine command and the site of the pre-eternal decree.

The inscribed Book is the form of all things as they are, the acknowledged order engraved on the Tablet of Decree (*lawḥ al-qaḍāʾ*), which is the supreme spirit symbolised here by the *unrolled parchment*. They are assigned the indefinite article here to impart grandeur to them.

The frequented House is the heart of the world: that is, the universal rational soul. It is the Tablet of Destiny (*lawḥ al-qadar*), and it is frequented by the constant circling of the angelic realm around it.

The raised roof is the lowest heaven to which descend the forms and rulings from the Tablet of Destiny—namely the Preserved Tablet—which are then manifested in the world of witnessing by their indwelling in matter. It is the tablet of erasure and affirmation, akin to the place of imagination in the human being.

The swarming sea is primordial matter, filled with forms, upon which manifest everything that is affirmed in the aforementioned tablets.

[52:7] *Indeed, your Lord's chastisement will assuredly take place* with the manifestation of the Minor Resurrection. Or [it is understood] according to the first interpretation, namely that *the Mount* symbolises the brain, *the inscribed Book* would symbolise the objects of knowledge concentrated in the human spirit, which is called 'the Qur'ānic intellect', and the spirit would symbolise *the unrolled parchment*, whose unrolling is its manifestation and its effusion into the body. *The frequented House* would symbolise the human heart, *the raised roof* the platform of imagination engraved with particular forms, and *the swarming sea* the material of the body filled with forms. And God knows best.

[52:8] [*There is none that can avert it.*]

[52:9] *On the day when the heaven will heave with a great heaving*: the spirit will quake and sway to and fro when the confusions begin and it parts with the body; [52:10] *and the mountains move* [*with a great motion*]: the bones will depart and crumble into dust.

Q. 52:8

[52:11] *Woe then on that day to the deniers* who are veiled by the world from the Hereafter and so deny the requital; [52:12] *those who play around* [*in vain talk*]: those who plunge into the falsehood of sensory pleasures, corrupt beliefs and vainglorious words, and immerse themselves in the game that is the life of this world and its short-lived glories.

[52:13] *The day when they will be thrust* [*with a violent thrust*] *into* the Hell of deprivation and pain, in the pit of the well of iniquitous nature, chained in the shackles of attachments and the fetters of illicit configurations.

[52:14] [*'This is the Fire which you used to deny!*

[52:15] *'Is this, then, sorcery or is it that you do not see?*

[52:16] *'Burn in it! And whether you endure or do not endure will be the same for you. You are only being requited for what you used to do.'*]

[52:17] *Indeed, the God-fearing* who avoid vices and the attributes of the souls *will be amid gardens* [*and bliss*] from the gardens of the Attributes and pleasure, experiential realisation and bliss therein, [52:18] *rejoicing* bliss-fully *in what their Lord has given them* of the lights of self-disclosures and the gnostic secrets of ecstasies and unveilings; *and* [*that*] *their Lord has shielded them from the chastisement of* the Hellfire of natural configurations, and being veiled by bestial and predatory configurations.

[52:19] *'Eat* of the provisions of wisdom and veridical knowledge, which are the nourishment of hearts, *and drink* of the waters of beneficial knowledge and the wines of passion and love, eating and drinking *in full enjoyment*, not gulping for life, *for what you used to do,'* because of your deeds of asceticism, worship and spiritual exertion and struggle.

[52:20] [*They will be*] *reclining on ranged couches*, arranged ranks and stations, such as resignation, reliance, contentment; or facing one another, equal in their stations, as He says, *As brethren, [they shall recline] upon couches, facing one another* [Q. 15:47]. *And We will wed them to beautiful houris*: that is, We shall place them in the midst of what suits their ranks of sanctified forms and pure substances: spiritual realities of the highest beauty.

[52:21] [*And those who believed and whom We made to be followed by their descendants in faith, We will make their descendants join them, and We will not deprive them of anything of their deeds. Every man is subject to what he has earned.*]

[52:22] *And We will supply them with fruits* of pleasant inspirations, blissful ecstasies and wondrous illuminations, *and meat* of knowledge that strengthens hearts and wisdom that gives life to them, *such as they desire.* They yearn for it by the dictate of their preparednesses and states.

[52:23] *They will pass from one to another therein*, exchanging in their discourses, discussions and remembrances, *a cup* of delicious wine of gnosis, passion and ecstasy, *wherein is neither vain talk*—base chatter and pointless discourse—*nor cause for sin*, nor any words that incur sin on the part of the one who speaks them, such as backbiting, coarseness, swearing or lying.

Q. 52:21

[52:24] *And there will circulate from all around them youths of their own*: spiritual, angelic beings who will serve them spiritual realities, or the people of will and purity of preparedness from the young seekers, *as if they were*, because of their purity and luminescence, *hidden pearls*: protected from the changes of the soul's caprice and natural pollutants, preserved from the touch of the holders of base doctrines and blameworthy customs.

[52:25] *And some among them will turn to one another, questioning each other* about their beginnings and spiritual exertions in the realm of the soul and the home of the senses, which is this world.

[52:26] *They say, 'Indeed, before* arriving at the realm of the heart and the repose of the spirit in the Hereafter, *amid our families* of the corporeal faculties and the soul's attributes, *we used to be ever anxious*: timid from the remembrance of God and fearful of His chastisement.

[52:27] '*But God showed us favour* with the self-disclosures of the Attributes and the graces of unveilings, *and shielded us from the piercing chastisement* of the poison of the soul's caprice and the hell of nature.

[52:28] '*Indeed, before* this station *we used to call on Him*: invoking and worshipping Him. *Verily He is the Benign* Who is kind to the one who calls to Him by emanating knowledge and realisation, *the Merciful*' to those who worship Him and fear Him with guidance and grace.

[52:29] [*So remind. For by the grace of your Lord you are neither a soothsayer nor a madman.*

[52:30] Or do they say, 'A poet, for whom we may await the accidents of fate'?

[52:31] Say: 'Await! For I too will be with you awaiting.'

[52:32] Or do their faculties of understanding prompt them to [say] this? Or are they a rebellious lot?

[52:33] Or do they say, 'He has improvised it'? Rather, they do not believe.

[52:34] Then let them bring a discourse like it, if they are truthful.

[52:35] Or were they created out of nothing? Or are they the creators?

[52:36] Or did they create the heavens and the earth? Nay, but they are not certain.

[52:37] Or do they possess the treasuries of your Lord? Or are they the ones in control?

[52:38] Or do they have a ladder, whereby they eavesdrop? Then let their eavesdropper produce a manifest warrant.

[52:39] Or does He have daughters, whereas you have sons?

Q. 52:30

[52:40] Or are you asking them for a fee, so that they are weighed down with debt?

[52:41] Or do they have [access to] the Unseen, so that they can write it down?

[52:42] Or do they desire to outmanoeuvre? But those who disbelieve, they are the outmanoeuvred ones!

[52:43] Or do they have a god other than God? Glory be to God above any partners that they may ascribe!

[52:44] And if they were to see a fragment of the heaven falling, they would say, 'A heap of clouds!'

[52:45] So leave them until they encounter that day of theirs in which they will be thunderstruck: [52:46] the day when their guile will avail them nothing and they will not be helped.

[52:47] And indeed for those who do wrong, there is a chastisement beyond that, but most of them do not know.]

[52:48] And submit patiently [to the judgement of your Lord]: by preventing the soul from manifesting objection to this judgement, for surely you fare before Our eyes: We see you and observe you, so avoid the sin of manifesting the soul in Our presence. And glorify [with praise of your Lord]: declare God's transcendence by detaching from the garb of the soul's attributes, and praise your Lord by manifesting your perfections which are His Attributes, when you rise: at the Intermediate Resurrection, from the slumber of the heedlessness of the station of the soul, by returning to innate disposition.

[52:49] And glorify Him at night: in the times of darkness, when there is variegation because one of the soul's attributes manifest, so glorify Him by detaching from it and become illuminated by the light of the spirit; *and at the receding of the stars* of the Attributes and their fading by the appearance of the light of the sun of the Essence, and the rising of the dawn of the beginning of witnessing. And God (Exalted is He) knows best.

Q. 52:49

53

THE STAR
SŪRAT AL-NAJM

In the Name of God, the Compassionate, the Merciful

[53:1] *By the Star when it sets*: He swears by the Muḥammadan soul when it became annihilated and set from the place of manifestation, and fell from the level of relevance in manifestation and presence.

[53:2] *Your companion has neither gone astray*: by halting with the soul and deviating from the farthest goal by inclining towards it; *nor has he erred*: by becoming veiled by the Attributes and halting with them in the station of the heart.

[53:3] *Nor does he speak out of [his own] desire*: by manifesting the attribute of the soul in variegation.

[53:4] *It is but a revelation that is revealed* to him from the time of his arrival at the horizon of the heart, which is the heaven of the spirit, until he finally reached the highest horizon, which is the end of the station of the manifest spirit; [53:5] *taught to him by* the Holy Spirit, who is *one of awesome power* that overpowers all the levels underneath him and has a strong influence on them; [53:6] *[and who is] possessed of vigour*: endowed with fortitude and exactitude in his knowledge, which cannot be changed or forgotten. *And he stood upright* in his essential form, [53:7] *when he*, the Prophet, *was on the highest horizon*, because when the Prophet was on the clear horizon he did not come down in his form, since it is impossible for the pure spirit to appear in the station of the heart, except in a form which suits the forms represented in that station. This is why he used to take on the form of Diḥya al-Kalbī, who was one of the most physically beautiful people and the most beloved people to the Messenger of God (may God bless him and grant him peace). If he had not taken on a form that could be imprinted on the breast, the heart would not have understood his words nor beheld his form. As for his true form in which he was originally created, it only appeared to the Prophet (may God grant him peace) twice: when he ascended to the Unitary Presence and reached the station of the spirit on the way up, and when he returned to the first station by the lote-tree of the Ultimate Boundary on the way down.

[53:8] *Then he drew near*: the Messenger of God (may God bless him and grant him peace) drew near and ascended from the station of Gabriel by annihilation in Unity and rising to the station of the spirit. It was at this station that Gabriel (may God grant him peace) said, 'If I went any closer, I would be burned.' This is because there was nothing beyond his station but annihilation in the Essence and burning in the rays. *And came down*: he inclined towards the human direction, by returning from the Real to creation for subsistence after annihilation and gifted veridical existence, [53:9] *until he was within the length of two bows away*: he (may God grant him peace) became the measure of the circle of total existence for all things, divided by an imaginary line into two bows relative to the Real and creation. This imaginary line cuts the circle into two halves, which are defined by perspective: from the perspective of the beginning and the approach, creation is the first half-circle which veils ipseity in the entities of created things and their forms, and the Real is the latter half-circle which approaches it bit by bit so that it is erased and annihilated into it. From the perspective of the end and the descent, the Real is the first half-circle which remains in its state forever, and creation is the latter half-circle which comes to be after annihilation in the new existence which is gifted to it. *Or nearer* than two bow-lengths by the abolition of the illusory, separating duality, because of the connection of each half-circle to the other and the realisation of real Unity in the source of multiplicity, so that multiplicity itself vanished in it and the circle remained undivided in reality, one in essence and attributes.

Q. 53:8

[53:10] *Whereat He revealed to His servant*, in the station of Unity without the mediation of Gabriel (may God grant him peace), *what he revealed* of divine secrets that can only be disclosed to a person of prophethood.

[53:11] *The heart (fu'ād) did not deny what he saw* in the station of unification. The *fu'ād* is the heart that has ascended to the station of the spirit in witnessing: the witness of the Essence with all the Attributes, existing with veridical existence. This unification is the unification of existence (*jamʿ al-wujūd*), not the unification of Unity (*jamʿ al-waḥda*) in which there is neither heart nor servant because all is annihilated therein, which is what they call 'the source of unification of the Essence'. This unification is called 'the enduring countenance' (*al-wajh al-bāqī*): that is, the Essence that exists with all the Attributes.

[53:12] *Will you then dispute with him [concerning what he saw]?* Do you dispute with him about something you do not understand and which you cannot know or envisage? How could you possibly argue against it? Debate can only occur when it is possible to envisage the object of contention, and then produce arguments in support of it or against it. If it cannot be envisaged, there cannot be any real debate about it.

[53:13] *And verily he saw him*—Gabriel in his true form—*another time* when he returned from the Real and descended to the station of the spirit, [53:14] *by the lote-tree of the Ultimate Boundary*: it is said that this is a tree in the seventh heaven, and it is the furthest extent of the knowledge of the angels, and no one knows what lies beyond it. It is the final level of Paradise, to which the spirits of the martyrs return. It is the supreme spirit beyond which there is no further identity or level, and above which there is nothing except pure ipseity. For this reason he halted there on the return from pure annihilation to subsistence, and saw Gabriel (may God grant him peace) there in his true image.

Q. 53:12

[53:15] *Near which is the Garden of the Retreat* to which the spirits of the ones brought near return.

[53:16] *When there shrouded the lote-tree* of God's majesty and might *that which shrouded*: for he (may God bless him and grant him peace) could see it when he became realised with veridical existence in God's eye. Hence, he saw the Real self-disclosed it its form, and the lote-tree was shrouded by the divine self-disclosure which covered it and annihilated it; and he saw it with the eye of annihilation and was not veiled by it or its form—nor by Gabriel and his reality—from the Real. Therefore, He says:

[53:17] *The eye did not swerve* by looking towards other-than-God and seeing it, *nor did it go beyond [the bounds]* by regarding his own soul and being veiled by I-ness.

[53:18] *Verily he saw some of the greatest signs of his Lord*: he saw the Attribute of undiscriminating compassion in which all the Attributes are incorporated by His self-disclosure in it. Indeed, he saw the presence of the Supreme Name, which is the Essence along with all the Attributes, expressed by the word God (*Allāh*) in the source of the unification of existence. Thus, he was not veiled from the Essence by the Attributes, nor by the Attributes from the Essence.

[53:19] *[Have you considered al-Lāt and al-ʿUzzā,* [53:20] *and Manāt, the third, the other?*

[53:21] *Are you to have males, and He females?*

[53:22] *That, then, would indeed be an unfair division!*

[53:23] *These are nothing but names which you have named, you and your fathers. God has not revealed any warrant for them. They follow nothing but conjecture and that which [ignoble] souls desire, even though guidance has already come to them from their Lord.*

[53:24] *Or shall man have whatever he wishes for?*

[53:25] *Yet to God belong the Hereafter and the former [life].*]

[53:26] *And how many an angel there is in the heavens whose intercession cannot avail in any way except after God gives permission for whomever He wills, and He is satisfied*: intercession from the angels is the emanation of lights and supports to the supplicant when he requests this emanation, by seeking the mediation of the intercessor, who is the appropriate intermediary and means between the two. So their intercession for the human souls can only occur if those souls were originally prepared and receptive to the emanation of the angelic realm, and then became purified from human configurations and natural coverings, by turning towards the presence of holiness and shedding the garb of the sensory and the matter of impurity, seeking the emanation of its light, drawing support from its emanation, connecting with it and following its path, and so drawing nearer to God by means of it.

Q. 53:23

The original receptive preparedness is the permission to intercede, and the satisfaction of it is the growth and purity attained by striving and struggle. When both of these occur, the intercession takes place. If the preparedness was not there at the origin, or it was there but was subsequently changed by attachment and coverings and did not retain its purity, there will be neither permission nor satisfaction from God, and so no intercession. Thus, His Words *whose intercession cannot avail* really mean that there will be no intercession at all, not that it will exist but will be fruitless, since that is impossible in the angelic realm. It is like the expression, 'You do not see lizards going into their holes there.'[1]

[53:27] *[Indeed, those who do not believe in the Hereafter give the angels the names of females.*

[53:28] *But they do not have any knowledge thereof. They follow nothing but conjecture, and indeed conjecture can never substitute for the truth.*

[53:29] *So shun him who turns away from Our Remembrance, and desires nothing but the life of this world.*

[53:30] *That is the full extent of their knowledge. Truly your Lord knows best*

---

1 In other words, there are no lizards to be found there at all. This expression was commonly cited by scholars of classical Arabic rhetoric and exegesis to illustrate this principle.

those who have strayed from His way, and He knows best those who are [rightly] guided.

[53:31] And to God belongs whatever is in the heavens and whatever is in the earth, that He may requite those who do evil for what they have done, and reward those who are virtuous with the best [reward].

[53:32] [The latter are] those who avoid grave sins and abominations, excepting lesser offences. Indeed, your Lord is of vast forgiveness. He knows you best [from the time] when He produced you from the earth, and when you were hidden [fetuses] in the bellies of your mothers. So do not claim purity for yourselves. He knows best those who are God-fearing.

[53:33] Did you see him who turned away, [53:34] and gave a little, and was then grudging?

[53:35] Does he possess knowledge of the Unseen so that he sees?

[53:36] Or has he not been informed of what is in the scrolls of Moses,] [53:37] and Abraham who fulfilled the right of God over him, by surrendering his existence to Him in the state of annihilation in Oneness, and upholding the matter of servitude, and conveying the Message and prophecy in the station of uprightness; or completed the words with which God tested him, which were the mentioned attributes. The verb *waffā* ('fulfilled') can also be read as *wafā* ('redeemed'), meaning that he redeemed the pledge that was taken from him at the onset of innate disposition, which he vowed to uphold until he reached the station of Oneness alluded to by His Words, *Indeed, I have turned my face to Him Who originated the heavens and the earth* [Q. 6:79].

Q. 53:31

[53:38] That no burdened soul shall bear the burden of another, because retribution is occasioned by benighted configurations that become rooted in the soul by the repetition of evil deeds and words, which are sins; and likewise, reward is occasioned by their opposite: virtuous configurations, as He says:

[53:39] And that man shall have only what he [himself] strives for, unlike the case for the ephemeral fortunes doled out by fate, although that is also ultimately ordained by the decree and destiny of God, since what matters is the immediate cause for each of them; *[53:40] [and that his endeavour will be seen, [53:41] then he will be rewarded for it with the fullest reward, [53:42] and that the ultimate end is toward your Lord; [53:43] and that it is He Who makes one laugh and makes one weep; [53:44] and that it is He Who brings death and gives life, [53:45] and that He creates the two spouses—the male and the female—[53:46] from a drop [of semen] once it is emitted; [53:47] and that with Him rests the second genesis:]* the second genesis refers to three

things. The first is the return of spirits to bodies to be reckoned and requited, based on their good and evil deeds, and so sent to Hell or to the garden of the acts. The second is the return to innate disposition and the station of the heart. The third is the return to gifted veridical existence after total annihilation. The first is inevitable for all, whether the bodies are luminous or dark, unlike the other two.

[53:48] *And that it is He Who enriches and grants possessions;* [53:49] *and that it is He Who is the Lord of Sirius;* [53:50] *and that He destroyed ancient ʿĀd* [53:51] *and Thamūd, sparing not;* [53:52] *and the people of Noah before that—indeed, they were more unjust and more insolent.*

[53:53] *And the deviant [cities] He overturned,* [53:54] *so that there covered them that which covered [them].*

[53:55] *Then which of the bounties of your Lord do you dispute?*

[53:56] *This is a warner [in the tradition] of the warners of old.*

[53:57] *The Impending [Hour] is imminent*: if this is taken to mean the Minor Resurrection, then its nearness is obvious, and its disclosure would either be the clarification of its time or its postponement. If it is taken to mean the Major Resurrection, then its nearness has two aspects. One is supra-sensory nearness, since it is the nearest thing to every person because he is in the source of Unity, even if he seems distant from it because of his obliviousness of it and insensitivity to it. The second is that the existence and dispatching of Muḥammad (may God grant him peace) is the precursor to the cycle of manifestation and one of its requirements. This is why he said, 'The Hour and I were dispatched like this,' and put his index and middle fingers together. It will be manifested with the coming of the Mahdī (may God grant him peace).

Q. 53:48

[53:58] *None besides God can disclose it*, because nothing will then exist but Him and His knowledge.

[53:59] *[Do you then marvel at this discourse,* [53:60] *and laugh and not weep,* [53:61] *while you remain oblivious?]*

[53:62] *So prostrate to God* with annihilation *and worship Him* with subsistence afterwards. And God knows best.

54
THE MOON
SŪRAT AL-QAMAR

In the Name of God, the Compassionate, the Merciful

[54:1] *The Hour has drawn near and the moon has split*: the splitting of the moon is a sign of the imminence of the Major Resurrection, because the moon symbolises the heart since it has two sides: a dark side facing the soul, and a light side facing the spirit, and because it receives light from the spirit just as the moon receives its light from the sun. It splits because of the influence of the light of the spirit on it and the emergence of its sun from its west, meaning its appearance from the veil of the heart after being within it, symbolising the nearness of annihilation in Unity, because it is the station of witnessing which leads to essential witnessing.

If it is taken to symbolise the cycle of manifestation which is the time of the Mahdī sent in its wake, then the splitting of the moon means its branching from the manifestation of Muḥammad (may God grant him peace), because of his emergence during the cycle of the moon.

If it is taken to symbolise the Minor Resurrection, then the moon is the body, because of how it draws the light of consciousness and life from the sun of the spirit, and its darkness in its soul. This is supported by His Words *On the day when the Summoner summons* [Q. 54:6]: that is, the dictate of death appears and calls the fated one to something awful and terrible which all souls dread.

[54:2] [*And if they see a sign, they turn away and say, 'A powerful sorcery!'*

[54:3] *And they denied and followed their own desires, and every matter will be settled.*

[54:4] *And verily there has come to them such tidings as contain a deterrent—* [54:5] *wisdom [that is] far-reaching—but warnings are of no avail.*

[54:6] *So turn away from them! On the day when the Summoner summons to an awful thing,*] [54:7] *with their downcast looks* from humiliation, impotence, degradation and deprivation, *they will emerge from the graves* of the bodies *as though they were scattered locusts*: He likens them to locusts because of the multiplicity of departed souls; their humility, weakness and avarice; and how they gorge on the presence of the sensory essence and natural desires, and incline towards the lower direction. He also likens them to moths [Q. 101:4] because of how they go to their own destruction in the light of life.

Alternatively, in the first interpretation, *On the day when the Summoner* of the spirit and the heart *summons* the souls to something awful to them, namely parting with ephemeral fortunes and corporeal and sensory pleasures, which is the voluntary death by spiritual discipline, and accompanying the inner secret in turning towards the presence of the Real; *with their downcast looks*: humiliated and broken by the overwhelming power of the Summoner and its dominance of them; *they will emerge from the graves* of the bodies by detaching from them and shedding them, *as though they were scattered locusts* in their weakness, flying in the rays of the light of the sun of the spirit.

[54:8] *[They will be] scrambling toward the Summoner* in both interpretations, yielding whether willingly or unwillingly. *The disbelievers*—those who are veiled from the religion or the truth—*will say, 'This is a hard day!'* because of their desire for sensory pleasures and passions, and their yearning and greed for them. As for the unveiled one, both natural and voluntary deaths are the easiest of things for him.

[54:9] *[The people of Noah denied before them. Thus, they denied Our servant and said, 'A madman!' and he was reviled.*

[54:10] *And so he invoked his Lord, [saying,] 'I have been overcome, so help [me]!']*

[54:11] *Then We opened the gates of the heaven* of the intellect *with [torrential waters]*: knowledge poured down powerfully to the lower world. In other words, We turned their minds around towards the world, preoccupation with managing particular affairs and arranging sensory pleasures, and immersion in the matter of livelihood, so that their acts were directed towards it and they halted with it, and were veiled by it from the affairs of the Hereafter, which led to their ruin. This is akin to His Words, *And when We desire to destroy a town We command its affluent ones, and they fall into immorality therein* [Q. 17:16].

[54:12] *And We made the earth* of the soul *burst forth with springs* of particular sensory knowledge, attached to the acquisition of worldly trifles and enjoyment of their luxuries, as though their souls were nothing more than this pursuit, because of their intense attraction to them and their greed for them; *and the waters* of desire for the world and its attraction *met for a purpose that was preordained* by God, which was their ruin through immersion in passions because of ignorance.

[54:13] [*And We bore him on one,* [*made*] *of planks and nails:*] We bore Noah upon a Divine Law made of deeds and teachings to restrict those deeds, or codes and principles on which to base those codes; [54:14] *sailing before Our eyes*: proceeding upon Our protection atop the torrent of their ignorance which sought to rise above them, so that their ignorance could not overcome it and sink it, *as retaliation* [*for him who was rejected*]: for Noah (may God grant him peace), whose blessing was rejected by his people when they did not acknowledge him, when [he called them] to obey and revere him and attain salvation through him. Instead, they rejected him and disobeyed him, and so they met their ruin because of him.

[54:15] *And verily We left it*—the remnants of that Divine Law and that call unto the present day—*as a sign* for those who would reflect on it. *So is there anyone who will* [*remember* and] *take heed?* For the path of the Real is one, and the Divine Laws of the prophets all come from the same source.

Q. 54:13

[54:16] *How* [*dreadful*] *then were My chastisement* to his people, by drowning them in the deluge of ignorance and depriving them of true life and eternal bliss, *and My warnings* through the voice of Noah (may God grant him peace). There is another interpretation of this passage, which is that the opening of the heavens symbolises the sending down of mercy and revelation to Noah. In other words, We opened the doors of the heaven of Noah's spirit to a downpour of universal knowledge encompassing all particulars, and made the earth of his soul burst forth with springs of particular knowledge, as though his entire soul was this knowledge; and then the two waters of knowledge met by their merging, so that they became sound analogies and opinions on which his Divine Law was built, founded on practical and discursive matters. Then We bore him upon this by action that conformed to it and uprightness in it. Thus, he was saved by it while his people remained in the deluge of ignorance, and drowned in the sea of primordial matter and the waves of ignorance, and were destroyed.

[54:17] [*And verily We have made the Qur'ān easy to remember. So is there anyone who will remember?*

[54:18] *ʿĀd denied. How, then, were My chastisement and My warnings?*

[54:19] *Indeed, We unleashed upon them a clamorous wind on a day of prolonged ill fortune,* [54:20] *tearing people away, as if they were trunks of uprooted palm-trees.*

[54:21] *How, then, were My chastisement and My warnings?*

[54:22] *And verily We have made the Qur'ān easy to remember. So is there anyone who will remember?*

[54:23] *Thamūd denied the warnings,* [54:24] *and they said, 'Is it a mortal alone among us that we are to follow? Then indeed we would be in error and insanity!*

[54:25] *'Has the Reminder been cast upon him [alone] from among us? Nay, but he is a conceited liar.'*

[54:26] *'They will know tomorrow who is the conceited liar.*]

[54:27] *'Indeed, We are sending the She-camel* of his soul *as a trial for them* to distinguish the prepared receptive saved one from the ignorant denied damned one. *So watch them* to see how the first will be saved and the second damned, *and remain patient* in calling them.

[54:28] *'And inform them that the water* of knowledge *is to be divided between them:* the camel shall have the knowledge of the spirit that pours upon it, and they shall have the knowledge of the soul; it shall have the intelligibles, and they shall have the sensibles. *Every drinking will be attended':* it will attend to its own drinking, by turning to the spirit and receiving true and beneficial knowledge from it; and they will attend to their drinking, by heading towards the spring of imagination and estimation, and receiving estimations and imaginations from it.

Q. 54:22

[54:29] *[But they called their companion, and he took a sword in hand and hamstrung [her].*

[54:30] *How, then, were My chastisement and My warnings?*

[54:31] *Indeed, We unleashed upon them a single Cry, and they became like the chaff of a corral builder.*

[54:32] *And verily We have made the Qur'ān easy to remember. So is there anyone who will remember?*

[54:33] *The people of Lot denied the warnings.*

[54:34] *Indeed, We unleashed upon them a squall of pebbles, [all] except the family of Lot whom We delivered at dawn* [54:35] *as a grace from Us. This is how We requite him who gives thanks.*

[54:36] *And verily he had warned them of Our strike, but they disputed the warnings.*

[54:37] *And they had even solicited of him his guests. So We blotted out their eyes. 'So taste [now] My chastisement and My warnings.'*

[54:38] *And verily there greeted them in the early morning an abiding chastisement.*

[54:39] *'So taste [now] My chastisement and My warnings!'*

[54:40] *And verily We have made the Qur'ān easy to remember. So is there anyone who will remember?*

[54:41] *And verily there came to Pharaoh's folk the warnings.*

[54:42] *They denied Our signs, all of them. So We seized them with the seizing of One [Who is] Mighty, Omnipotent.*

[54:43] *Are your disbelievers better than those? Or have you [been granted] some immunity in the scriptures?*

[54:44] *Or do they say, 'We are a host that will be helped to victory'?*

[54:45] *The host will [truly] be routed and turn its back [to flee].]*

[54:46] *Nay, but the Hour is their tryst*: that is, the Minor Resurrection and their fall into eternal chastisement by the passing of preparedness and the downward turn of existence; *and the Hour will be more calamitous and more bitter* than the torment of slaughter and routing.

[54:47] *Indeed, the guilty* who acquired dark, base, corporeal configurations *are in error*: astray from the path of truth because their hearts are blinded by the darkness of the attributes of their souls, *and madness*, lunacy and deliriousness because of how their intellects are veiled from the light of the Real by the pollutants of delusion, plunged in the confusion of falsehood.

Q. 54:41

[54:48] *The day when they are dragged into the Fire on their faces*: mustered in the forms of their faces to the earth, and compelled in the overwhelming power of the earthly dominion and forced into all manner of chastisement, tormented by the fires of deprivation and told, *'Taste [now] the touch of Saqar.'*

[54:49] *[Indeed, We created everything in a measure.]*

[54:50] *And Our command is but one* word, *[like the twinkling of an eye]*: the attachment of the pre-eternal will to the existence of each thing, in a specific time and a specific way, is affirmed in the Tablet of Decree. It is known in the tradition as 'Be!' and obliges the existence of that thing in that time and that way instantaneously.

[54:51] *[And verily We have destroyed the likes of you. So is there anyone who will remember?*

[54:52] *And everything they have done is] in the scriptures*: the tablets of the souls; *[[54:53] and every small and great [thing] is inscribed.]*

[54:54] *Indeed, the God-fearing* in their entirety *will be amid gardens* from the levels of the three gardens, high and lofty, *and rivers* of knowledge arranged according to the aforementioned order of those gardens, [54:55] *in an abode of truth*: a place of goodness—and what could be better than the station of Unity?—*before a King [Who is Omnipotent]*: in the presence of the Names in the state of subsistence after annihilation, and the station of separation between the Essence and Attributes, existing with the Essence *in an abode of truth*, and with the Attributes *before a King* Who controls the domain of existence, according to wisdom and nurture in the best way and most perfect order, [*Who is*] *Omnipotent* and able to direct everything in His kingdom according to the decree of His will, and subdue it according to the dictate of His volition, without anything preventing Him.

Q. 54:55

55

THE COMPASSIONATE
SŪRAT AL-RAḤMĀN

In the Name of God, the Compassionate, the Merciful

[55:1] *The Compassionate* is one of the special Names of God, which relates to the emanation of the sources of all blessings, both the entities and their primal perfections, from the beginning. He invoked this here because of the universality of His attribution, which includes all the Attributes that fall under its meaning with respect to principality, so that all the other varied sources He mentioned after it would be linked back to it.

[55:2] *He has taught the Qur'ān*: that is, the perfect, human preparedness which is called 'the gathering Qur'ānic intellect' that gathers all things—their realities, attributes, rulings and everything else that can possibly exist or not—by framing it in the human disposition and planting it there. Furthermore, as its manifestation and emergence into action by the differentiation of what is gathered within it—so that it becomes a Criterion—only pertains to what happens at the end, He did not mention the Criterion here as He did when He said, *Blessed is He Who revealed the Criterion* [Q. 25:1], because that pertains to the compassion of discriminating mercifulness rather than undiscriminating compassion.

[55:3] *He created man*: when He framed his innate disposition and placed the Qur'ānic intellect therein, He brought it into existence in this world by creating it in this marvellous form; [55:4] *teaching him [coherent] speech*: that is, the reason which differentiated him from all other creatures, so that He could inform him about the Qur'ānic intellect that was within him.

[55:5] *The sun and the moon*: the spirit and the heart run therein, *follow a reckoning*: a defined measure of stations and levels which is set, and neither of them can transgress the measure and level that were ordained for it. They each have perfections and levels with defined limits for them to reach.

[55:6] *And the star*, the animal soul which is luminous by sensory consciousness in the night of the body, *and the trees*, the vegetable soul that gives it growth, *prostrate* by pressing their faces to the earth of the body, and placing their brows upon it by total inclination and attraction towards it, to instruct, guide and perfect it.

[55:7] *And He has raised the heaven* of the intellect to the place of the sun of the spirit and the moon of the heart, *and placed* [*the balance of*] *justice* upon the earth of the soul and the body. Justice is an egocentric configuration without which human virtue cannot be attained; and it causes balance in the body, without which it would not have existed and could not persist. And since the affairs of religion and worldly life are made upright by justice, and the perfections of the soul and body require it and they would be corrupted without it, He commanded that it be maintained and preserved before enumerating any of the other fundamentals, because of its crucial importance and necessity. This is why between mention of it and His Words *And the earth, He placed it for* [*all*] *creatures*, He said:

Q. 55:7

[55:8] *That you should not contravene with regard to the balance*: by transgressing the bounds of virtue and equilibrium, leading to tyranny and then corruption.

[55:9] *And observe the weights with justice*: by being upright on the path, as well as keeping within the bounds of virtue and the point of equilibrium in all things and all faculties; *and do not skimp the balance*: by falling short of the bounds of virtue. One of the sages said, 'Justice is God's balance. He placed it down for creation, and set it up for the truth.'

[55:10] *And the earth* of the body, *He placed it* [*for* [*all*] *creatures*]: for all of the aforementioned creations.

[55:11] *In it are fruits*: meaning all things that convey sensory pleasures derived from the perceptions of the senses and their objects; *and date-palms*, meaning the faculties which produce imaginative and estimative pleasures, that grow tall in the earth of the body in the caprice of the soul, *with sheaths*: coverings of material attachments; [55:12] *and grain*, meaning the faculty of nourishment, from which comes the pleasure of tasting, eating and drinking, *with husk*: meaning the many branches and leaves that spread out over the earth of the body—the powers of attraction, grasping, digestion, defence, alteration and abstraction that are necessary for the body, which dictate its special attributes and acts, and prepare it and make it able to preserve strength and growth, to replace what deteriorates and grow larger; *and fragrant herb*: meaning the faculty of procreation, which leads to sexual pleasure—the greatest of all corporeal pleasures—as well as the continuation of the species.

[55:13] *So which of your Lord's favours will you deny* of these enumerated blessings, O you outward and inward folk from jinn and humankind—the outward blessings, or the inward?

[55:14] *He created man*—meaning his outer being and his body, which perceives (*yuʿnis*)¹—*of dry clay*: a dense mixture of elemental substances in which the dominant trait is earthiness and dryness, *resembling the potter's*: the hard material that corresponds to the substance of the bones, which constitute the foundation and frame of the body.

[55:15] *And He created the jinn*—meaning his inner being and animal spirit which is concealed from the senses and is the father of the jinn: that is, the source of the animal faculties of which the strongest and noblest is estimation, namely the Devil called Iblīs, who is one of his progeny—*of a smokeless flame of fire*: a subtle, pure flame of fire: that is, a subtle mixture of elemental substances in which the dominant trait is fieriness and heat. The word *mārij* strictly means 'a flame that is agitated', for this spirit is constantly agitated and in motion.

Q. 55:13

[55:16] [*So which of your Lord's favours will you deny?*]

[55:17] *Lord of the two easts, and Lord of the two wests*: the easts and wests of the outward and inward, by the sunrise of the light of Absolute Being over the quiddities of outward bodies, and its setting behind them by being veiled by their quiddities and their identification with it. In His lordship over all beings, He has a sunrise by His engendering of them by the light of being and His manifestation in them, and a sunset by His concealment in them; and He sustains them by His lordship over them through both of these aspects.

[55:18] [*So which of your Lord's favours will you deny?*]

[55:19] *He has loosed the two waters*: the sea of corporeal, primordial matter which is salty and bitter, and the sea of the incorporeal spirit which is sweet and fresh; [*and so*] *they meet* in the human being.

[55:20] *Between them there is a barrier*, which is the animal soul that does not share the purity and subtlety of the incorporeal spirits, nor the turbidity and density of material bodies. *They do not overstep*: they do not transgress their boundaries so that one dominates the other by their special natures. The spirit does not detach the body and mix with it to make it its own kind, nor does the body solidify the spirit and make it material. Glory be to the Creator of creation, Who may do as He wills!

[55:21] [*So which of your Lord's favours will you deny?*]

---

1 The verb shares a common lexical root with the noun *insān* ('man').

[55:22] *From both of them*—by their composition and meeting—*is brought forth the pearl* of universal knowledge *and the coral* of particular knowledge: that is, the pearl of realities and gnostic secrets; and the coral of beneficial knowledge, such as ethics and Divine Laws.

[55:23] [*So which of your Lord's favours will you deny?*]

[55:24] *His are the crafted ships*—the vessels of the Divine Law and stations of the path, which the wayfarers embark on their journey to God through the waters of this lively sea, so that they are delivered safely to their destination—[*that sail*] *in the sea* [*appearing like landmarks*]: their comparison to *landmarks* alludes to how they are renowned and well-known, akin to how the pilgrimage rites are called 'the waymarks (*shaʿā'ir*) of God and the signposts (*maʿālim*) of the faith'. The ships are *crafted* in how their sails are raised up; the sails are the yearnings and desires that run when they are raised, and their attachment to the higher realm, by the power of the winds of divine breezes, which blow the vessel of the Divine Law and the path with its passengers to the destination of true perfection, namely annihilation in God. Therefore, He then says:

Q. 55:22

[55:25] [*So which of your Lord's favours will you deny?*]

[55:26] *Everyone who is on it will perish*: all of those who sail on the ships will reach the Real by annihilation in Him; or everyone on the earth of the body—all the differentiated entities, such as the spirit, intellect, heart, soul, and their abodes, stations and levels—will be annihilated upon arrival at the goal.

[55:27] *Yet there will remain the countenance of your Lord*, which will subsist after the annihilation of all creation: that is, His Essence with all His Attributes; [*the countenance*] *of majesty*: might and glory, veiled by the veils of light and dark, manifest with the Attributes of omnipotence and sovereignty; *and munificence*: by nearness and proximity in the forms of the self-disclosures of the Attributes, and at the manifestation of the Essence with the Attributes of subtle kindness and mercy.

[55:28] [*So which of your Lord's favours will you deny?*]

[55:29] *All who are in the heavens*: the inhabitants of the realms of dominion and divine power, *and the earth*: jinn and humankind, *implore Him*: everything implores Him. But He refers to sentient beings and let them stand for all, and used the word *who*: that is, all things constantly implore Him with the voice of preparedness and neediness. *Every day He is upon some matter*: by emanating to each preparedness what corresponds to it and what it deserves. In every instant, for every creature, He is upon some affair by the emanation of what it deserves and merits by its preparedness. For those who prepare by self-purification for perfections and illuminations, He emanates them upon them by the fulfilment of preparedness. For those who prepare by sullying the substance of their souls with benighted configurations, vices, corrupt doctrines and pollutants for evils, horrors and all manner of torments, misfortunes, chastisements and calamities, He emanates them upon them by the fulfilment of preparedness. This is the meaning of His Words *We will attend to you, O you two heavy ones* [Q. 55:31], which is a threat and a warning against the things that warrant punishment. He singled out the *two heavy ones* for mention because they are base beings, who incline towards the earth of the body.

[55:30] [*So which of your Lord's favours will you deny?*

[55:31] *We will attend to you, O you two heavy ones!*

[55:32] *So which of your Lord's favours will you deny?*]

[55:33] *O company of jinn and humans*: meaning inward and outward folk, *if you are able to pass through the confines of the heavens and the earth*: by detachment from corporeal configurations and bodily attachments, *then pass through* so that you penetrate through the paths of the angelic souls and spirits of divine power and reach the divine presence. *You will not pass through except with a sanction*: a manifest proof, which is Oneness (*tawḥīd*), detachment (*tajrīd*) and seclusion (*tafrīd*) by knowledge, action and annihilation in God.

[55:34] [*So which of your Lord's favours will you deny?*]

[55:35] *Against you will be unleashed a flash of fire*: you will be prevented from passing through their confines, and ascending through their ranks, by a pure flame unadulterated by smoke: that is, the authority of estimation and its rulings and perceptions, by sending estimations to the plain of the intellect and the heart, constantly preventing them from ascending; *and a flash of brass*: meaning smoke, a dark configuration sent by the animal soul by attraction to caprice and desires. The flash is a barrier on the side of knowledge, and the brass is a barrier on the side of action. *And you will not be able to seek help*: you will not be able to defend yourselves from them, or overcome them and pass through, without the grace of God and the authority of Oneness.

[55:36] [*So which of your Lord's favours will you deny?*]

[55:37] *And when the heaven is split open*: that is, the heaven of this world—namely the animal soul—which splits from the spirit when it leaves the body; for the human spirit is to the animal soul what the latter is to the body, and just as the body needs the soul to live, the soul needs the spirit. So [it is] when it [the animal soul] splits from it upon leaving

Q. 55:30

the body, *and it turns crimson*, [i.e.] red, because its colour is between the colour of the incorporeal spirit and the colour of the body. The spirit is white because of its light and its perception of pleasures, and the body is black because of its darkness and insensitivity to pleasures; and the middle colour between white and black is red. The reason He described it in *sūrat al-Baqara* as yellow[1] and here as red is that there it referred to the time of life, when it is still mostly luminous and prepared, while here it refers to the time of death and turbidity and the dominance of darkness over it, and the departure of preparedness. [*It turns crimson*] *like oil*: resembling oil in its colour, transparency and liquidity because it is on the way to annihilation and obliteration.

[55:38] [*So which of your Lord's favours will you deny?*]

[55:39] *Thus on that day no person* from the outward folk *will be questioned about his sin, nor any jinn* from the inward folk, since each will be attracted to his abode and the residence dictated by his state, and to which his dominant original or acquired preparedness corresponds. As for the halting and questioning described in His Words *But [first] stop them, for they must be questioned* [Q. 37:24] and similar passages, this refers to other moments of this long day which will last as long as fifty thousand years, in the state where neither of the two directions is dominant and neither side prevails. In the time when the original light dominates and the innate preparedness endures, or perfection and ascension of attributes is attained, or in the time when benighted configurations dominate and corporeal covers remain while the primal preparedness is lost, because of the rusting-over of the heart, they will not be asked. In the time when those configurations are not so persistent that the heart is rusted over entirely, but nevertheless they persist in the heart so that they cannot be sent back to their abode, they are halted and questioned until they have been chastised for their evil deeds according to how persistent they are. This could occur before the aforementioned moment of that day, as would be more usual in the manner just described, or it could occur after it. That is when the deeds fail and the acquired state overwhelms and dominates the essential state, to the point where the preparedness is entirely nullified, whereupon the primal preparedness resists it bit by bit and manifests in the form of torments and tribulations little by little, until the two sides are equal, like cold water being added to hot water until it becomes lukewarm. Such a person will be rejected at first when his preparedness is almost gone, but then he might

Q. 55:38

---

1 See Kāshānī's commentary on Q. 2:69. [Ed.]

be halted and questioned when the preparedness has almost returned to its original state, and can once again connect with the angelic realm. As for the damned rejected ones, they will not be questioned at all nor halted for questioning. Thus His Words *But [first] stop them, for they must be questioned* [Q. 37:24] and similar passages refer only to some of those who are punished, namely the damned ones who can still be saved later.

[55:40] [*So which of your Lord's favours will you deny?*]

[55:41] *The guilty* who are dominated by benighted configurations, because of their acquisition of vices that became rooted in them, *will be recognised by their mark*: by the marks of those configurations that are manifest on them and dominant over them. *So they will be seized by the forelocks* and chastised from above, and veiled and detained as prisoners from the direction of the vice of compounded ignorance and corrupt beliefs; *and the feet* and chastised from below, dragged upon their faces and cast into the pit of Hell. It is said that some of them will fall for seventy years because of how firmly corporeal configurations and practical vices are imprinted on him, as a consequence of the excess of avarice, greed, stinginess and lust, and the commitment of sins and iniquities of the nature of desire and anger.

[55:42] [*So which of your Lord's favours will you deny?*]

[55:43] *'This is Hell*: the pit of the well of the lowest lows of corporeal nature, [*which the guilty [were wont to] deny]!'*

[55:44] *They shall pass round between it and boiling, hot water* of the highest heat and burning because of their compounded ignorance. This is why it is said that the boiling water will be poured onto their heads, since the appropriate punishment relating to deeds is the fire of Hell from below, and the appropriate punishment relating to knowledge is boiling water from above.

[55:45] [*So which of your Lord's favours will you deny?*]

[55:46] *But for those who feared the station of their Lord*: that is, who feared His standing above their souls because of how He is ever watching, protecting and guarding it, as He says, *Who is it Who stands over every soul for what it has earned?* [Q. 13:33]. Or it means those who feared their Lord, such as when you say, 'I served the station of so-and-so,' meaning that you served them personally. [*But for those who feared the station of their Lord,*] *there will be two gardens*: one is the garden of the soul, the other the garden of the heart, because fear is one of the attributes and stations of the soul when it is illuminated by the light of the heart.

[55:47] [*So which of your Lord's favours will you deny?*]

Q. 55:40

386

[55:48] *Both with [abundant] branches* because of the diversity of their branches of faculties and attributes, adorned with the leaves of acts and sublime character traits and the fruits of knowledge and states. The word *afnān* strictly means the smaller branches that sprout from the main branches of a tree and bear its leaves and fruit.

[55:49] [*So which of your Lord's favours will you deny?*]

[55:50] *In both of them there are two flowing springs* of particular and universal perceptions, flowing to them from the garden of the spirit, producing in them the fruits of perceptibles and the self-disclosures of the Attributes.

[55:51] [*So which of your Lord's favours will you deny?*]

[55:52] *In both of them, of every fruit* of their delicious perceptibles *there are two kinds*: a particular kind that is known and familiar, and a universal kind that is strange. This is because all the universal meanings that the heart perceives have particular forms in the soul, and vice versa.

[55:53] [*So which of your Lord's favours will you deny?*]

Q. 55:48

[55:54] [*They will be*] *reclining upon couches*: the levels of their perfections and stations; *lined with [heavy] silk brocade* on the side which faces the lower, meaning the soul, composed of the configurations of righteous deeds such as virtuous character traits, noble attributes and goodly dispositions. Their front side, which faces the spirit, will be made of the silk of the self-disclosures of lights, and the subtleties of gifts and states attained from unveilings of knowledge and gnostic secrets, as was described in *sūrat al-Dukhān* [Q. 44]. *And the fruits* and perceptibles *of both gardens will be near*: so that whenever they desire them, no matter what state they are in, whether standing, seated or reclining, they will perceive them and pluck them, and they will instantly grow back, as has already been described.

[55:55] [*So which of your Lord's favours will you deny?*]

[55:56] *In them are maidens of restrained glances*: the angelic souls with which they connect, who are on their levels or below them, be they heavenly or earthly, pure and uncorrupted, unable to look beyond their levels nor to seek any perfection beyond their perfections, because their preparednesses are equal to theirs or below theirs. Otherwise, they would go beyond their gardens and rise above their levels, and so would not be *maidens of restrained glances*, nor would they be satisfied to dwell with them and enjoy their company. [*Maidens*] *who have not been touched by any man before them* from the human souls, because they were created solely for them and due to the sanctity of their essences, and the impossibility of their being touched by souls immersed in bodies, *nor any jinn* of the estimative faculties and earthly souls veiled by lower configurations.

[55:57] [*So which of your Lord's favours will you deny?*]

[55:58] *It is as though they are rubies and pearls*: the maidens of the garden of the soul are likened to rubies because—despite their beauty, purity and splendour—rubies have a red colour which corresponds to the colour of the soul. The maidens of the garden of the heart are compared to pearls because of their extreme whiteness and brightness. The word *marjān* strictly means 'small pearls', which are said to be purer and whiter than large ones.

[55:59] [*So which of your Lord's favours will you deny?*]

[55:60] *Is the reward of goodness* in action, namely worship with presence of mind, *anything but goodness* of reward, namely the attainment of perfection and admittance into these two gardens?

[55:61] [*So which of your Lord's favours will you deny?*]

[55:62] *And beside (dūn) these*: behind them in a place near to them. The word *dūn* here is used in the sense of 'near', not in the sense of 'opposite' with respect to their inhabitants; it means that it is after them, or other than them, as in God's Words, *Indeed, you and what you worship besides (dūn) God…*[Q. 21:98]; *there will be two [other] gardens* for the ones brought near and the foremost: the garden of the spirit and the garden of the Essence in the source of unification, where there is essential witnessing after the beholding in the station of the spirit.

[55:63] [*So which of your Lord's favours will you deny?*]

[55:64] *Deep green*: of the height of splendour, verdure and lushness.

[55:65] [*So which of your Lord's favours will you deny?*]

[55:66] *In both of them will be two gushing fountains*: the knowledge of the Oneness of Essence and the Oneness of Attributes: that is, the knowledge of annihilation and the knowledge of witnessing, which flow in these two gardens. Indeed, the two forms of knowledge that flow in the other two gardens have their source in these two gardens, and flow from one set into the others.

[55:67] [*So which of your Lord's favours will you deny?*]

[55:68] *In both of them will be fruits*—and what fruits! Fruits whose nature is unknowable and whose quality is inestimable, from the forms of witnessings, lights, self-disclosures and graces; *and date-palms*: that is, everything which imparts flavour and delight, namely the witnessing of lights and self-disclosures of beauty and majesty in the station of the spirit and its garden, along with the subsistence of the pith of I-ness which draws strength and pleasure from it; *and pomegranates*: that is, everything that imparts delight and health in the station of unification and the garden of the Essence: essential witnessing with total annihilation wherein there is no I-ness to experience flavour, but only pure pleasure and a cure for the malady of the manifestation of the soul's remnant with variegation. The pomegranate symbolises the form of unification that is hidden beneath the rind of the human form.

[55:69] [*So which of your Lord's favours will you deny?*]

[55:70] *In them are maidens [who are] good, beautiful*: that is, pure lights and graces, unadulterated by evil or contingency, and the beauties of the self-disclosures of beauty and majesty and the glories of the Attributes.

[55:71] [*So which of your Lord's favours will you deny?*]

[55:72] *Houris secluded in pavilions*: that is, sheltered in the presences of the Names. Nay, in the presence of Oneness and Unity, never emerging from it to be unveiled to anyone outside it, and having no bound or level beyond it to which they could ascend or to which they could lift their gazes, since they are secluded in it.

[55:73] [*So which of your Lord's favours will you deny?*

[55:74] *Untouched by any man or jinn before them.*

[55:75] *So which of your Lord's favours will you deny?*]

[55:76] *Reclining upon green cloths (rafraf)*: the word *rafraf* denotes a type of wide cloth that is extremely soft. Here it represents the light of the Essence, which is of the highest splendour and subtlety, or the light of the Attributes in the state of subsistence after annihilation, and reliance upon the self-sufficiency of Absolute Being and realisation of it; *and lovely fabrics (ʿabqarī)*: the word *ʿabqarī* denotes a marvellous type of fabric named after ʿAbqar, which the Arabs called the realm of the jinn. Here it represents the marvel of gifted veridical existence, adorned with His self-disclosed Attributes, which is of the utmost beauty, named after the realm of the Unseen—indeed, the Unseen of Unseens whose location is known to no one.

[55:77] [*So which of your Lord's favours will you deny?*]

[55:78] *Blessed be*—hallowed and exalted be—*the Name of your Lord*: the Supreme Name by which the rank of the travellers increases and ascends from the beginning to the end, until the ultimate arrival at Him and victory in Him; *He of Majesty and Munificence*: majesty in the form of beauty, and beauty in the form of majesty, neither of which veil the other in the state of subsistence after annihilation for the beloved ones and the lovers, who were the foremost to the ultimate level. This is distinct from

Q. 55:69

the majesty and munificence that were mentioned earlier, for there they veiled each other because the annihilated one had not yet realised veridical existence, and returned to the differentiation of the Attributes and their beholding in the source of unification.

Q. 55:78

56
THE EVENT
SŪRAT AL-WĀQIʿA

In the Name of God, the Compassionate, the Merciful

[56:1] *When the [imminent] Event comes to pass*: the Minor Resurrection, [56:2] *there will be no denying [its coming to pass]*: no soul will be able to belie God about the reality of the Resurrection and the states of the Hereafter, because every soul will witness its states of salvation and damnation.

[56:3] *[It will be] abasing [some], exalting [others]*—abasing the damned to the depths, and exalting the saved to the ranks—[56:4] *when the earth* of the body *is shaken with a violent shock* by the departure of the spirit, which agitates it and pulls everything out of it and demolishes all its parts; [56:5] *and the mountains* of the bones *are pulverised to [tiny] pieces* by being transformed into dust, or borne away, [56:6] *so that they become a scattered dust*, [56:7] *and you will be three kinds*:

[56:8] *[Those of the folk of the right hand—what of the folk of the right hand?* [56:9] *And the folk of the left hand—what of the folk of the left hand?]* The saved are the pious and righteous folk, and the damned are the evil, corrupting folk. The former are called *the folk of the right hand (al-maymana)* because they are the people of good omen (*yumn*) and blessing, or because they are turned towards the better and stronger of the two directions, which is the higher direction and the holy realm. The latter are called *the folk of the left hand (al-mash'ama)* because they are the people of ill omen (*shu'm*) and misfortune, or because they are turned towards the baser and weaker of the two directions, which is the lower direction and the sensory realm.

[56:10] *And the foremost*: the affirmers of Oneness who outstripped the other two groups and went beyond the two realms by annihilation in God; *the foremost*: those who cannot be praised any higher or have anything added to their attributes; [56:11] *they are the ones brought near [to God]*: in the state of realisation with veridical existence after annihilation; [56:12] *in the gardens of Bliss*: of all the levels of the gardens; [56:13] *a multitude from the former ones*: the beloved ones who are in the first row of the spirits, the folk of divine nurture in pre-eternity; [56:14] *and a few from the later ones*: the loving ones whose rank is behind that of the beloved ones, in the second row. They are said to be few because the loving one usually does not reach the level of the beloved one or his limit of perfection, and most of them are in the gardens of the Attributes, halted at the levels of the saved. The beloved ones, however, all enter the garden of the Essence and reach the farthest limits. This is why the Messenger of God (may God bless him and grant him peace) said, 'Both of them are from my community': that is, it is not that the former are from the previous communities while the latter are from his (may God grant him peace), but rather the reverse is true. Or it means that many are from the early generations of this community who saw the Prophet (may God bless him and grant him peace) and witnessed the unfolding of the revelation in his time, or lived shortly after him and saw those who kept his company, while the later ones are those who came long after when hearts had hardened, towards the end of the cycle and close to the time of the emergence of the Mahdī (may God grant him peace)—but not those of his time, since the foremost in his time will be the majority, because they will be the people of the Major Resurrection and the folk of unveiling and manifestation.

Q. 56:15

[56:15] *Upon encrusted couches*: in the midst of gifted, veridical existences meant especially for each one of them, as he (may God grant him peace) said, 'Upon pulpits of light.' Or it means in the levels of the Attributes.

[56:16] *Reclining on them*: existing in them outwardly, since they are their stations; *face to face*: equal in rank with no veil between them in the source of Unity, because of their realisation of the Essence and their freedom to manifest whichever of the Attributes they desire, united by the essential love, neither veiled by the Attributes from the Essence nor by the Essence from the Attributes.

[56:17] *They will be waited on by immortal youths*: served by their enduring spiritual faculties at the behest of their essences, or by the youthful, prepared ones from the folk of spiritual aspiration who reached them by the strength of their aspiration, as He says, *We will make their descendants join them* [Q. 52:21], or by the heavenly, angelic spirits; [56:18] *with goblets and ewers* of the wines of aspiration, gnosis, love, passion and experiential realisation, [*and a cup from a flowing spring*] of the waters of wisdom and knowledge, [56:19] *wherefrom they suffer no headache*: they impart only pleasure and no pain nor drunkenness, for they will have arrived and found the pleasure of the coolness of certitude, and will drink from the draught of camphor; for the love of arrival is pure and unsullied by the pain of yearning and the fear of loss; *nor any stupefaction*: their discernment and intellect will not be impaired by intoxication, nor will they drink to excess, for they are folk of sobriety not veiled by the Essence from the Attributes such that they would become drunk or overcome by an ecstatic state.

[56:20] *And such fruits* of experiences and unveilings of experiential realisation *as they prefer*: they may take them at will, because they will experience them all and choose the purest, noblest, loftiest and most glorious of them.

[56:21] *And such flesh of fowls as they desire* of the subtleties of wisdom and intricacies of meanings which nourish them.

[56:22] *And houris with wide eyes* of the self-disclosure of the Attributes and detached realities of divine power, and all the incorporeal spirits in their ranks, [56:23] *resembling hidden pearls* in their purity and luminescence, hidden in their shells or stored in the treasure-troves of the Unseen, concealed from the corrupting touch of the folk of the outward.

Q. 56:20

[56:24] *A reward for what they used to do* in the state of uprightness: the divine deeds done for their own sake which merited this reward. Or a reward for what they used to do in the state of wayfaring: the deeds of self-purification and spiritual growth.

[56:25] *They will not hear therein any vain talk*: any chatter or meaningless speech, for they are folk of realisation who maintain the courtesies of the spiritual folk; *or any sinful words*: foul speech which incurs sin for those who speak it, such as backbiting, lying and the like.

[56:26] *But only the saying, 'Peace!' 'Peace!'* In other words, speech that is peace itself, unsullied by flaws and innocent of curiosity and excess, and speech that safeguards the hearer from flaws and imperfections, gives him joy and nobility, and brings out his perfection and splendour; for their speech will be nothing but gnostic truths and realities, mutual love and subtle kindnesses of all manner of expression.

[56:27] *And the folk of the right hand—what of the folk of the right hand?* They are noble, glorious, exalted beings whose qualities of salvation are truly a thing of wonder.

[56:28] *Amid thornless (makhḍūd) lote-trees* in the garden of the Attributes, free of the thorns of the conflicts of faculties and natures and the struggles of caprices and impulses, detached from the configurations of their attributes by the light of the spirit and the heart; or, according to the other interpretation [of the word *makhḍūd*], it means that they are weighed down by the fruits of good deeds and righteous configurations.

[56:29] *And clustered plantains* in the garden of the heart, because the plantain is the banana tree, whose fruits are sweet, hearty and delicious and contain no piths, like the perceptibles of the heart and its meanings, which are detached from matter and sinful configurations. [This is] unlike the lote-tree which is very thorny, like the perceptibles of the soul, which are particular and attached to material qualities and sinful configurations. The plantains are clustered with fruit from bottom to top so that their trunks are barely visible, because of the endlessness of its multitude of perceptibles; [56:30] *and extended shade* from the expansive light of the spirit.

[56:31] *And cascading water*: knowledge that pours down upon them, in cascades from the realm of the spirit. The reason it cascades rather than flows is that the knowledge of the saved ones is scanty compared to their deeds, for their spiritual knowledge of experiences, gnostic realities, mysteries of Oneness and secrets of experiential realisation is scanty, though their beneficial knowledge is ample.

Q. 56:29

[56:32] *And abundant fruit* of delicious particular and universal perceptibles, such as the objects of sense, imagination and estimation, and universal, heart-centred meanings, [56:33] *neither unavailable* because it is infinite, *nor forbidden* because they are free to choose from all of it as they please.

[56:34] *And couches [that are] raised*: virtuous character traits and illuminated configurations of the soul acquired through good deeds, raised above the level of bodily configurations and the lower direction to the plain of the breast, which is the higher direction of the soul that is connected to the heart. Or it means houris: angelic females that are connected to them and share their level, depending on which interpretation [of the word *furush*] is followed.

[56:35] *Indeed, We have created them with an [unmediated] creation*: a wondrous, luminous creation detached from matter and purified from the dross of natures and the pollutants of elements; [56:36] *and made them virgins*: untouched by natural matters and naturalistic, outward beings from the folk of convention and the souls mixed with matter; [56:37] *amorous*: loving to them and beloved by them because of their purity, the beauty of their substance and the endurance of their connection to them; *of equal age* because they share the same level and are equal in rank and pre-eternal substance; [56:38] *for the folk of the right hand*: [56:39] *a multitude from the former [generations]*, because the beloved ones will visit the gardens of the folk of the right hand as they ascend the ranks, and as they descend for the return to the Attributes, mingling with them and crossing paths with them; [56:40] *and a multitude of the later ones*, because the loving ones will mostly be the folk of the right hand who halt with the Attributes and stop short of love of the Essence. Or if we take the former and later to mean the early and later generations of the Muḥammadan community, then the meaning is obvious, because there will be a multitude of the folk of the right hand in their later generations, rather than the foremost.

[56:41] *And the folk of the left hand—what of the folk of the left hand?* They are the ones whose states and attributes of damnation, misfortune, degradation and ruin are truly a thing of horror.

[56:42] *Amid a scorching wind* of rebellious caprices and iniquitous, harmful configurations *and scalding water* of false knowledge and corrupt beliefs; [56:43] *and the shade of pitch-black smoke*: the configurations of the soul blackened by dark attributes and black, foul configurations; [56:44] *neither cool nor pleasant*: possessing neither the attribute of shade which people seek out for comfort, nor the attribute of benefit for those who go to it for repose. On the contrary, it will be painful and harmful, and impart only hardship, heat and discomfort.

Q. 56:41

[56:45] *Indeed, before that they used to live at ease*: steeped in pleasures and desires, engrossed in natural matters and corporeal coverings, which is how they acquired these dreadful configurations and ruinous burdens.

[56:46] *And they used to persist in the great sin* of false words and corrupt beliefs, because of which they deserved eternal chastisement and perpetual punishment.

[56:47] *And they used to say* and believe in rejecting the Resurrection, [*'What! When we are dead and have become dust and bones, shall we indeed be resurrected?*

[56:48] *'What! And our forefathers too?'*

[56:49] *Say: 'Indeed, the former and the later* [*generations*] [56:50] *will be gathered for the tryst of a known day.*

[56:51] *'Then truly you,*] *the erring, the deniers*—the ignorant ones who wilfully persisted in their ignorance and denied the truth that contradicted their false beliefs—[56:52] *will assuredly eat from a Zaqqūm tree*: from the soul that worships pleasures and desires and is engrossed in them and attracted towards base, natural things, because of your habitual attachment to them and their benefits; [56:53] *and fill therewith*, with their horrific, burning fruits which are the configurations that negate perfection and lead to perdition, *your bellies*, because of your rapacious greed and desire for them as a result of your gluttony and sickness; [56:54] *and drink on top of that boiling water* of false estimations and deceitful doubts, which are forms of ignorance steeped in ruinous threats and calamities, making those satanic acts and bestial, dark deeds appear seemly; [56:55] *drinking like the drinking of thirsty camels'* afflicted with a disease that means they are never quenched no matter how much they drink, because of the intensity of your infatuation with them.

[56:56] [*This will be the hospitality for them on the Day of Judgement.*]

[56:57] *We created you* by manifesting Our existence in your forms. *Will you not then affirm* [*this*] *truth?*

[56:58] *Have you considered the sperm that you emit?*

[56:59] *Is it you who create it* by emanating the human form upon it, *or are We the Creators?*

[56:60] [*We have ordained death among you, and We are not to be outmanoeuvred from* [56:61] *replacing* [*you with*] *your likes and making you into what you do not know.*

[56:62] *For verily you have known the first creation, why then will you not remember?*

[56:63] *Have you considered what you sow?*]

[56:64] *Is it you who make it grow* by sending down the forms of growth to it, *or are We the Grower?*

[56:65] [*If We wish, We could surely turn it into chaff, and you would remain bemused:*

[56:66] '*We have indeed suffered anguish!*

[56:67] '*Nay, but we are deprived!*']

[56:68] *Have you considered the water* of knowledge *you drink* because of the thirst of your preparedness?

[56:69] *Is it you who cause it to come down from the* [*rain*] *clouds* of the primordial intellect, *or are We the Causer of its coming down?*

[56:70] *If We wished, We could make it bitter* by changing its life-giving nature on which the life of this world depends. *Why, then, will you not give thanks?*

[56:71] *Have you considered the fire* of holy meanings *that you kindle* with the flint of thought?

[56:72] *Was it you who created the tree thereof*—the intellectual faculty—*or were We the Creator?*

[56:73] *We made it a reminder* of the primal, pre-eternal covenant in the holy realm, *and a boon for* [*the desert-travellers*]: those who have no other provision of knowledge and action to take on their journey.

Q. 56:56

[56:74] [*So glorify the Name of your Lord, the Tremendous.*]

[56:75] *Nay, I swear by the setting-places of the stars*: that is, the times when the holy, Muḥammadan soul connected to the Holy Spirit, which were the times when the pieces of the Qurʾān were revealed to him, times of incredible sanctity and luminous connection. Or *the setting-places of the stars* represent the times when he was absent from his senses, which set behind the westerly horizon of the body, when they were rendered obsolete by the immersion of his inner secret in the Unseen and his traversal of the paths of holiness, whereby he was totally immersed in the Real and engrossed in Unity.

[56:76] *And indeed it is a tremendous oath, if you only knew*: yet how could they know, and whence could their knowledge of this come?

[56:77] *This is indeed a noble Qurʾān*: a gathering of knowledge endowed with ancient nobility and lofty status; [56:78] *in a Book guarded*: namely his heart, hidden from the senses and from all but the pure angels brought near; for the Qurʾānic intellect was stored in him, as he (may God grant him peace) said, 'Do not say that knowledge is in the heavens so that someone must bring it down, or in the depths of the earth so that someone must bring it up, nor over the seas so that someone must bring it across them. [Rather,] knowledge has been placed in your hearts. Have courtesy before God—the courtesy of the spiritual ones—and it will manifest to you.' Or it means the primal spirit, which is the locus of destiny and the home of the Muḥammadan spirit; indeed, they are one and the same.

Q. 56:74

[56:79] [*It is a Book*] *which none touch except the purified*: the incorporeal spirits purified from the dross of natures and the pollutants of material attachments; [56:80] *a revelation by the Lord of the Worlds*, because His knowledge was manifested in the Muḥammadan locus and so was sent down from Him gradually in stages.

[56:81] *Do you then belittle this discourse*: refusing to take it seriously, fulfil its due and understand its meaning, like the one who indulges himself and neglects his duties?

[56:82] *And for your livelihood you offer your denial?* Do you take the nourishment of your hearts and your true provision, only to deny it, veiled by your knowledge and denying anything that does not conform to it, like an ignorant man who denies what contradicts his beliefs, as though his knowledge is identical with his denial? Or do you make it your figurative livelihood? In other words, by your constant denial, you make denial into your nourishment, just as one says that a habitual liar has made lying his bread and butter.

[56:83] *Why, then, when it reaches the [dying person's] throat [[56:84] and you are at that moment looking—[56:85] and We are nearer to him than you are, but you do not perceive—[56:86] why, then, if you are not going to face a reckoning,* [56:87] *do you not bring it back]*: why do you not retrieve the spirit when it reaches the throat, *if you are truthful* about how you are not lorded over or ruled by a higher power? On the contrary, you are certainly compelled beneath the power of lordly omnipotence, for otherwise you would be able to repel the thing you hate the most: death.

[56:88] *Thus, if he be of those brought near,* [56:89] *[then repose, and a goodly provision, and a garden of Bliss]*: if he is from one of those three groups, he will have the repose of arrival at the garden of the Essence, and the provision of the garden of the Attributes and their glorious self-disclosures, and the garden of the acts and their bliss and delights.

Q. 56:83

[56:90] *And if he be [of the folk of the right hand,* [56:91] *then 'Peace be to you,' [a greeting] from the folk of the right hand*: if he is] one of the saved and righteous folk, he will have the joy of meeting the folk of the right hand, and being greeted by them with the security of innate disposition, salvation from torment, and absolution from the flaws of the attributes of the souls in the garden of the Attributes.

[56:92] *But if he be [of the deniers, the erring]*: the damned ones who opposed the foremost and denied their perfections and were veiled by compounded ignorance, and so they will endure the torment of the con-figurations of their false beliefs and dark ignorance poured down from above, as He says:

[56:93] *Then a welcome of boiling water*: and the torment of their cor-poreal configurations and consequences of their evil deeds from below, as He says:

[56:94] *And a roasting in Hellfire.*

[56:95] *This* reminder of the states of the three groups and their fates *indeed is [the certain truth]*: the plain fact of what will be experienced by the people of the Major Resurrection, who attain realisation of the Real by their certitude and witnessing. And God (Exalted is He) knows best.

57
IRON
SŪRAT AL-ḤADĪD

In the Name of God, the Compassionate, the Merciful

[57:1] *All that is in the heavens and the earth glorifies God*: every being manifests His transcendence beyond contingency and potential annihilation, through its relative existence and stability; *and He is the Mighty*: the Strong Who dominates and compels them; *the Wise* Who arranges their perfections; and they manifest His transcendence beyond incapacity through their contingency and change, and His transcendence beyond all flaws through the manifestation of the perfections of all beings, and their arrangement according to a wise order.

[57:2] [*To Him belongs the kingdom of the heavens and the earth; He gives life and He brings death, and He has power over all things.*]

[57:3] *He is the First* from Whom all relative existence originates from the perspective of His manifestation, *and the Last* with Whom it ends from the perspective of its contingency and the ultimate end of its need with Him; all things exist with Him and are annihilated in Him, so that He is their first and their last at the same instant from the two perspectives; *and the Manifest*: in the loci of beings through His Attributes and acts; *and the Hidden*: veiled by His quiddities and Essence. *And He has knowledge of all things*, because the very quiddity of each thing is one of the forms of the objects of His knowledge, since the forms of all things are in the Preserved Tablet, and He knows the Tablet with all those forms by the very quiddity of the Tablet on which those forms are engraved; and thus His knowledge of them is none other than His knowledge of His own Essence.

[57:4] *It is He Who created the heavens and the earth in six days*, meaning six divine days: that is, the six thousand from the time of Adam to the time of Muḥammad (may the peace of God be upon them both), spanning the entire duration of the cycle of concealment. In other words, He was veiled during them and creation appeared in front of Him, for creation was the veiling of the Real by created things, and this time was the time of veiling, as was discussed in [*sūrat*] *al-Aʿrāf* [Q. 7]; *then presided upon the Throne* of the Muḥammadan heart, by manifesting through all the Attributes, so that they were not veiled by one another nor by the Essence, nor did they veil the Essence; rather, all of them presided in manifestation on the seventh day. Or He created them in the forms of the six levels of substances and accidents mentioned in [*sūrat*] *Qāf* [Q. 50], and then presided over the throne of the supreme spirit by influence over all things in the All-Compassionate form, by ascending and manifesting with the Name of the Compassionate.

He knows what enters the earth of the corporeal world of archetypal forms, because they are the forms of the objects of His knowledge, *and what issues from it* of the spirits which depart it and the forms that separate from it, at the moment of annihilation and corruption, *and what comes down from the heaven and goes up into it*: meaning those spirits and forms. Or it means the knowledge and lights that come down from the heaven of the spirit and are emanated upon the heart, and the universalities drawn from tangible particulars and the configurations of purified deeds that go up into it. *And He is with you wherever you may be* because your existence is through Him and He is manifested in your loci; *and God is Seer of what you do* because of His prior knowledge of it, and how it is engraved in four tablets in the realm of His dominion in His presence.

Q. 57:5

[57:5] [*To Him belongs the kingdom of the heavens and the earth, and to Him* [*all*] *matters are returned.*]

[57:6] *He makes the night* of heedlessness *pass into the day* of mindfulness, *and makes the day* of mindfulness *pass into the night* of heedlessness; and He covers beauty with majesty and veils majesty with beauty. *And He is Knower of what is in the breasts*: of what He has placed there of His secrets and the intricacies and wisdoms of heedlessness and mindfulness, and the subtleties and purposes of concealment and self-disclosure, which are known to none but Him.

[57:7] *Believe in God* with certain faith in the Oneness of the acts, *and His Messenger,* [*and expend out of that of which He has made you successors*]: do not let your faith in the Oneness of the acts cause you to be veiled from the acts of creation by the acts of the Real, so that you fall into fatalism and are deprived of the reward. Rather, witness the acts of the Real through faith in Him, concentrated in the loci of differentiations by the rule of the Divine Law, so that you attain reliance and then find it easy to expend from the property of God, which you have in your possession and of which He has made you successors by putting you in the position to utilise it by the rule of the Divine Law; for all property belongs to God, and the permission to utilise it is governed by His rule in His Divine Law. *For those of you who believe* by witnessing the acts *and expend* from the station of reliance, *will have a great reward* in the garden of the acts.

[57:8] *And why should you not believe in God [when the Messenger is calling you to believe in your Lord, and a pledge has been taken from you]*: why should you not believe given these two grounds—one internal and the other external—which together ought to necessitate faith inherently? The external is the call of the Messenger, which is the active cause; and the internal is the taking of the pre-eternal pledge, namely innate preparedness, which is the passive cause, as well as the power of reasoning, *if you are believers* with conviction: that is, if the light of innate disposition and pre-eternal faith remains in you.

[57:9] *It is He Who sends down upon His servant clear signs*—the signs of the self-disclosures of the acts, the Attributes and the Essence—*that He may bring you forth from [the darkness to the light*: from] the darkness of the attributes of the soul and corporeal configurations derived from the senses to the illumination (*tanawwur*) of the heart, and from the darkness of the attributes of the heart to the light of the spirit, and from the darkness of your existences and egos to the light of the religion. These are the darknesses alluded to in His Words *manifold [layers of] darkness, one on top of another* [Q. 24:40]. *And indeed God is Kind, Merciful to you* in how He dispels the blight of imperfection from you by the gift of preparedness and the grace of guidance towards unveiling, by sending the Messenger and his teachings to you, and Merciful in how He emanates perfections with the attainment of receptivity by the purification of the soul and the cleansing of preparedness.

[57:10] *[And why should you not expend in the way of God when to God belongs the heritage of the heavens and the earth.] Not equal [to the rest of you] are those of you who expended and fought before the victory*: that is, who sacrificed their possessions and lives before the absolute victory that was granted to the Messenger of God (may God bless him and grant him peace), in the form of the perfect Ascension and arrival at the presence of Unity. *Such are greater in rank than those who expended and fought afterwards*, because of the strength of their preparedness and the power of the lights of their original inner beings; hence, they recognised him and welcomed him by the elevation of the spirit, and their perfections were manifested in them

Q. 57:8

without the intermediary of his influence on them. They were the ones who were whelmed in the holy power *whose oil would almost glow forth [of itself], though no fire touched it* [Q. 24:35]. As for those who expended later, the weakness of their preparedness and the dimness of its light meant that they required the power of his influence on them, and for their perfections to be manifested outwardly in action. *Yet to each God has promised the best reward* because of the attainment of certitude and the manifestation of perfection by whatever means, despite the countless levels this includes. [*And God is Aware of what you do.*

[57:11] *Who is it that will lend God a goodly loan so that He may multiply it for him, and [so that] there may be for him a generous reward?*

[57:12] *The day when you will see the believing men and believing women]* with their light shining forth before them and on their right: the latter group were those who attained perfection of character in the station of the soul, who loaned their possessions to God out of desire for multiplied reward and noble recompense, while the former were the foremost who detached themselves from them out of desire to please God and keep themselves firm on the path of truth. They are the believers whose light shines before them because they are on the straight path, directed towards God's countenance by the Oneness of the Essence, while the stragglers are those whose light shines on their right sides, since they are the folk of the right hand from among the believing men and women in the station of the heart and certitude. '*Good tidings for you on this day: [gardens underneath which rivers flow, wherein you will abide. That is the great success]* ': this is addressed to both groups but especially to the foremost because it mentions all three gardens. The reason for the success being called *great* (ʿaẓīm) is that *the great success* will be for the third group, while the success of the inhabitants of the other two gardens below them is called 'grand' (kabīr) or 'generous' (karīm).

[57:13] *The day when the hypocrites, men and women*: that is, the ones with strong preparedness and the ones with weak preparedness, veiled by the attributes of the souls and the configurations of the bodies, engrossed in the darkness of nature and the mire of sin, in whom there is still a faint glimmer of the light of innate disposition which has not yet been entirely snuffed out, so that they yearn for the light of perfection that the believers have attained, and therefore seek it out, wailing and moaning when they emerge from behind the veil of the body at the moment of death when the deprivation is manifested, confined and halted in the pit of imperfection, filled with regret when their loss becomes clear, while the believers pass

Q. 57:11

402

them by like a flash of lightning without noticing them. They *will say [to those who believe]*, *'Look at us that we may glean something of your light'* through the affinity of preparedness and the outward appearance of submission. *It will be said, 'Step back and seek light!'* Look behind you to the lower world, the place of acquisition, for light is only sought by means of the instruments of the body and the corporeal faculties—the outward and inward senses—and by good deeds and true knowledge.

Then there will be set-up between them a wall—the primordial isthmus by which they are veiled according to the degree of their benighted configurations—*with a gate*, which is the heart, since the realm of abomination can only be seen from the realm of holiness by means of the heart, *the inner side of which*—the realm of holiness—*contains mercy*: meaning light, repose, peace and the garden of bliss from the aforementioned levels; *and the outer side of which* that is nearest the soul—the realm of abomination and the seat of those darkened souls of the damned—*faces toward the chastisement* that they deserve because of their configurations in all their varieties. This door has no handle on the outside, which faces the damned, for it is closed and will never be opened to them. On the inside, whenever the foremost who dwell in Paradise wish, it is opened for them so they may look upon the inhabitants of Hell and their torments and go inside, whereupon the flames of the Fire are extinguished by their light. Indeed, their light burns the Fire for them but not for the denizens, and Hell itself calls out to them, 'Pass by, believers, for your light has extinguished my flames!'

Q. 57:14

[57:14] [*They will call out to them,*] *'Did we not use to be with you'* at the primal disposition and the source of unification of the Attributes? *They will say, 'Yes, indeed! But you caused your souls to fall into temptation*: you tempted them with sensory pleasures, corporeal desires, and bestial and predatory attributes, *and you awaited* by letting loose your imaginations of dominant hopes and wishes by the impulses of envy and greed, *and you doubted* by letting loose your estimations upon the intelligibles, and letting delusions overwhelm your intellects, *and [false] hopes deceived you* by the impulses of estimation and the dictate of imagination, *until God's command came* heralding death and punishment; [*and the Deceiver deceived you concerning God*.

[57:15] *'So on this day no ransom will be taken from you nor from those who disbelieved. Your abode will be the Fire: it will be your guardian, and an evil destination!'*

[57:16] *Is it not time for those who believe that their hearts should be humbled to the remembrance of God and [to] what has been revealed of the truth, and that they should not be like those who were given the Book before? For the stretch of time was too long for them and so their hearts became hardened, and many of them are immoral.*]

[57:17] *Know that God revives the earth after its death*: this symbolises how the reminder influences the heart and gives it life. [*We have certainly made clear for you the signs that perhaps you may understand.*]

[57:18] *Indeed, men who give charity and women who give charity* [*and* [*those of them*] *who have lent God a goodly loan, it will be multiplied for them and they will have a generous reward*]: this means those who believe in the Unseen in the station of the soul, since He says *a generous reward*.

[57:19] *And those who believe in God and His messengers—they are the truthful* by the power of certitude, *and the witnesses with their Lord*: the people of mindfulness and vigilance. This means the folk of certitude in the station of the heart, since He says *they will have their reward*, meaning the garden of the soul, *and their light*, meaning the garden of the heart by the self-disclosure of the Attributes. [*But those who disbelieve and deny Our signs*]—their opposites who were veiled from the Essence and the Attributes, and are neither people of faith in the Unseen nor people of certitude—*they will be the folk of the Hellfire* of nature.

Q. 57:17

[57:20] [*Know that the life of this world is merely play and diversion and glitter, and mutual vainglory in respect of wealth and children. [It is] as the likeness of rain whose vegetation the disbelievers admire; [but] then it withers, and you see it turn yellow, then it becomes chaff. And in the Hereafter there is a severe chastisement and forgiveness from God and beatitude; and the life of this world is but the comfort of delusion.*]

[57:21] *Vie with one another for forgiveness from your Lord*: after expressing disdain for the ephemeral egocentric sensory life and its forms by likening them to vegetation which quickly vanishes, He then invited them to the enduring intellectual, heart-centred life, saying, *Vie with one another for forgiveness from your Lord*: that is, cover the attributes of the soul with the light of the heart, *and a garden the breadth of which is as the breadth of the heaven and the earth*: meaning the entire corporeal world, because of how the heart encompasses it and its forms. Or He dissuaded them from human life and invited them to divine life: that is, vie with one another for forgiveness that will cover your essences and your beings, which are the root of the greater sin, by the light of His Essence and a garden the breadth of the heavens of all the spirits and the earth of all the bodies, meaning all of Absolute Being, which includes all relative beings; *prepared for those who believe in God and His messengers* with faith of certain knowledge for the former, and faith of essence and reality for the latter. [*That is the bounty of God, which He gives to whomever He will, and God is [dispenser] of tremendous bounty.*

[57:22] *No affliction befalls* [*in the earth or in yourselves*], of external corporeal or egocentric accidents, *but it is in a Book*: the universal heart which is called the 'Preserved Tablet', [*before We bring it about—that is indeed easy for God—*[57:23] *so that you may not grieve for what escapes you, nor exult at what He has given you*]: so that you may know with certitude that your acquisition, preservation, caution and vigilance play no role in what He gives you, nor do your impotence, negligence, heedlessness, witlessness, recklessness or carelessness play any role in what escapes you. Do not grieve for the loss of good or the befalling of evil, then, nor exult at the attainment of good or the avoidance of evil, since all of it is destined. *For God does not like any swaggering braggart*: one who swaggers about exulting in what He has given him, proud of it because he lacks certitude and is distant from the Real, due to his love for the world and his attraction to the lower direction, as a consequence of his negations of the divine presence and his veiling by manifold darkness from light; [57:24] *such as are miserly* because of excessive love for wealth, *and bid people to be miserly* because of the dominance of this vice over them. *And whoever turns away* from God by heading towards the lower world and the evil, dark substance, *still God, He is indeed the Independent* Who has no need for them because of His self-sufficiency, *the Praised* because of His independence through His own perfection, and so He will humiliate and debase them.

Q. 57:22

[57:25] *We have verily sent Our messengers with clear signs*, meaning gnostic teachings and wisdoms, *and We revealed with them the Book*, meaning writing, *and the Balance*, with justice, for that is its implement, [*so that people may uphold justice*]. *And We sent down iron*, [*wherein is great might, and [many] uses for people, and so that God may know those who help Him and His messengers through the Unseen. Indeed, God is Strong, Mighty*: iron] symbolises the sword because it is its material. All of these signify those things by which the perfection of the species is fulfilled and the universal order is maintained, leading to the welfare of worldly life and the Hereafter; for the crucial origin and first beginning is knowledge and wisdom, and the foundation of action and uprightness in the path of perfection is justice. After this, order cannot be maintained, nor can the welfare of all be preserved, save by the sword and the pen, by which the affairs of governance are fulfilled. These four together constitute the pillars of the perfection of the species and the welfare of the public.

It could also be that the *clear signs* symbolise gnostic teachings and discursive realities, *the Book* symbolises the Divine Law and practical wisdom, *the Balance* symbolises action according to justice and equality, and the *iron* symbolises power and defence against the evils of creation. It is also said that the *clear signs* represent the knowledge of reality and the other three represent the well-known three laws (*nawāmīs*, Greek *nomoi*) discussed in the books of wisdom, namely Divine Law, fair currency for trade, and the ruler.

Whichever it may be, they represent the things that guarantee perfection of the individual and the species in both lives, for the perfection of the individual cannot be attained without knowledge and action, nor can the perfection of the species be attained without the sword and the pen. The former is obvious, and the latter is because man is naturally social and requires interaction and cooperation, and he cannot live without company. Yet souls are either naturally good and free so that they follow the Divine Law, or naturally evil slaves who refuse the Divine Law. The first require nothing more than subtlety and the direction of the Divine Law to follow the path of perfection and act according to justice, while the latter require compulsion and the direction of the ruler.

 Q. 57:26

[57:26] [*And verily We sent Noah and Abraham and We ordained among their seed prophethood and the Book; and some of them are [rightly] guided, and many of them are immoral.*

[57:27] *Then We sent to follow in their footsteps Our messengers, and We sent to follow Jesus son of Mary, and We gave him the Gospel, and We placed in the hearts of those who followed him kindness and mercy. But [as for] monasticism, they invented it—We had not prescribed it for them—only seeking God's beatitude. Yet they did not observe it with due observance. So We gave those of them who believed their reward; but many of them are immoral.*]

[57:28] *O you who believe* with certain belief, *fear God* by detaching from your attributes and transcending your essences, *and believe in His Messenger* through uprightness in your deeds and states upon the path of emulation, *and He will give you a twofold portion of His mercy* in the garden of the soul; *and He will assign for you a light* from the lights of the spirit and the self-disclosures of the Attributes in the station of the heart—*by which you will walk* among the Attributes—*and forgive you* for the sins of your essences; *for God is Forgiving*: by the annihilation of remnants; *Merciful*: by the gift of veridical existence after the annihilation of I-ness.

[57:29] *So that the People of the Book*—the ones veiled by the rust of the heart from the truth, or the ones lost on the path of error and false religion, astray from the straight path and the true religion—*may know that they have no power over anything of God's bounty*, because it is gifted and cannot be acquired, *and that [all] bounty is in God's hand*: under His direction and beneath His power and possession. *He gives it to whomever He will* as a gift, not an acquisition; *and God is [dispenser] of tremendous bounty*, which is the culmination of perfection. And God (Exalted is He) knows best.

Q. 57:29

58

THE LADY DISPUTANT
SŪRAT AL-MUJĀDILA

In the Name of God, the Compassionate, the Merciful

[58:1] [*God has certainly heard the words of her who disputes with you concerning her husband and complains to God. And God hears your conversation. Indeed, God is Hearer, Seer.*

[58:2] *Those of you who repudiate their wives by ẓihār, they are not their mothers; their mothers are only those who gave birth to them, and indeed they utter indecent words and a calumny. Yet assuredly God is Pardoning, Forgiving.*

[58:3] *And those who repudiate their wives by ẓihār and then go back on what they have said, then [the penalty for them is] the setting free of a slave before they touch one another. By this you are being admonished; and God is Aware of what you do.*

[58:4] *And he who cannot find [the wherewithal], then [his redemption shall be] the fasting of two successive months before they touch one another. And if he is unable, then [the redemption shall be] the feeding of sixty needy persons. This, so that you may believe in God and His Messenger. And these are God's bounds; and for the rejecters there is a painful chastisement.*

[58:5] *Indeed, those who oppose God and His Messenger will be abased, just as those before them were abased. And verily We have revealed clear signs, and for those who disbelieve there is a humiliating chastisement.*]

[58:6] *The day when God will raise them [all together]* from the places where their bodies slumber, *He will then inform them of what they did* because of how the forms of their deeds are engraved on the tablets of their souls. *God has kept count of it*: by affirming it in the four aforementioned books, *while they forgot it* because of their obliviousness to it, distracted as they were by sensory pleasures and engrossed in corporeal diversions. *And God is Witness to all things*: present with them and observant of them.

[58:7] [*Have you not seen that God knows all that is in the heavens and all that is in the earth?*] *No secret conversation of three takes place but He is their fourth,* [*nor of five but He is their sixth, nor of fewer than that or more but He is with them wherever they may be*]: He is their fourth, not in the sense of number or company, but in the sense that they are differentiated from Him by their identities, veiled from Him by their quiddities and egos, separated from Him by the necessary contingency of their quiddities and ipseities, real-ised of the necessity of His Essence, and He is connected to them by His Ipseity which is mingled with theirs, and manifested in their loci yet con-cealed by their quiddities and personal existences which He upholds by His very being, necessitating them through His own necessity. From all these perspectives, He is the fourth to their three, while from the consid-eration of reality He is none other than their essence. This is why it is said that without perspectives, there would be no wisdom. The Commander of the Believers (may God grant him peace) said, 'All knowledge is a single dot, but ignorant folk have multiplied it.' [*Then He will inform them of what they did, on the Day of Resurrection. Indeed, God has knowledge of all things.*]

Q. 58:8

[58:8] *Have you not seen those who were forbidden from conversing in secret* [[*but*] *then returned to that which they had been forbidden, and* [*all the while*] *hold secret conversations* [*tainted*] *with sin and* [*plans for*] *enmity and disobedience to the Messenger? And* [*who*] *when they come to you, they greet you with that with which God never greeted you and they say within themselves, 'Why does God not chastise us for what we say?' Hell will suffice them! In it they will be made to burn—and* [*what*] *an evil journey's end!*] They were only forbidden because secret con-versation is a connection and unification of two parties about a given matter that concerns them both, in which no third party joins them. When souls join and connect, they engage in collaboration and cooperation so that they strengthen and support one another in the cause of their meeting, because of the peculiarity of the social configuration that is not found among indi-viduals. If the souls are evil, they will converse secretly about evil things and their evil will only grow, and the subject of their secret discourse will only grow stronger by their connection (*ittiṣāl*) and gathering (*ijtimāʿ*). This is why He then said *and* [*all the while*] *hold secret conversations* [*tainted*] *with sin*, which is the vice of the bestial faculties, *and enmity*, which is the vice of the irascible faculties, *and disobedience to the Messenger*, which is the vice of the rational faculty by ignorance and the dominance of satanic impulses. Note how after this verse He forbids the believers from engaging in secret conversation about these vices, and commands them to engage in secret conversation about good things, so that they are strengthened by the social configuration and so grow in goodness:

[58:9] [*O you who believe, if you do talk in secret,*] *then do not talk in secret sinfully and in enmity and disobedience to the Messenger, but talk secretly in piety*: meaning the virtues that are the opposites of those vices: righteous acts and good deeds pertaining to each of the three faculties; *and fear of God* through avoidance of all those types of vices. *And fear God* in the attributes of your souls, *to Whom you will be gathered* by proximity to Him when you become detached from them.

[58:10] [*Secret conversations are of [the work of] Satan that those who believe may end up grieving; but he cannot harm them in any way, except by God's leave. And in God let the believers put [all] their trust.*]

[58:11] *O you who believe, when it is said to you, 'Make room,' during the assembly,*] *then make room; God will make room for you*: escape from the constriction of competition for glory and pride, for they are egocentric configurations, and the dominance of the predatory faculties, and the soul's wallowing in the darkness of I-ness, veiled from the lights of the heart and the spirit. Transcend all these, and *God will make room for you* by detaching you from corporeal configurations and supporting you with illuminations, so that your breasts are expanded and enlarged, and your space in the realm of holiness is broadened. [*And when it is said, 'Rise up',*] *then rise up; God will raise those of you who have faith* of certitude *and those who have been given knowledge* of the blights of the soul and the intricacies of caprice, and knowledge of how to transcend them by detachment, *by degrees* of the attributes of the heart and the ranks of the dominion and power in the realm of lights. *And God is Aware of what you do*, and He will reward you and punish you for those configurations.

Q. 58:9

[58:12] [*O you who believe,*] *when you converse in secret with the Messenger, offer some charity before your secret talk*, because connecting with the Messenger about a specific concern can only occur when there is a spiritual proximity, a heart-centred correspondence, or a soul-centred affinity; and whichever it is, there must be charity. For the first and second, the talk must be preceded by a shedding of acts and attributes, and detachment from the externalities of means and possessions, and the cutting of ties, which is called 'renunciation'; and then the erasure of traces and enduring configurations from the heart, which is called 'detachment'; and then the disregarding of one's deeds and attributes and ascension to the station of the spirit for the first, or the station of the heart for the second, until one is purified for the station of secret, spiritual discourse with the Prophet about divine secrets, heart-centred mysteries and other matters of unveiling. For this reason Ibn ʿUmar (may God be pleased with him) said, "ʿAlī (may God grant him peace) had three things which I would rather have had than a treasure of fine, red camels: he married Fāṭima; he was given the banner on the day of Khaybar; and the verse about secret conversation was revealed about him.' As for the third [soul-centred affinity], the talk must be preceded by good deeds in the form of charitable donations by way of giving thanks for that blessing, so that it endures and grows. [*That is better for you and purer.*] But if you *find nothing* in the first two cases because you fall short of those two stations by halting with the soul, and in the third case because of the soul's stinginess and poverty, *then God is indeed Forgiving* of soul-centred attributes by the lights of His Attributes, *Merciful*: by emanating the lights of self-disclosures, witnessings, gnostic secrets and unveilings which lead to the experience of that charity for the first two; or He is *Forgiving* of the vice of stinginess and the misfortune of poverty, and *Merciful* by granting the grace of the acquisition of virtue and the giving of wealth for the third. The same applies to the fear and the relenting described in the next verse:

Q. 58:13

[58:13] [*Do you fear to offer alms before your secret talks? So, as you did not do this, and God relented to you, maintain prayer and pay* zakāt, *and obey God and His Messenger. For God is Aware of what you do*:] He then enjoined something to expiate the aforementioned shortcomings, the vice of stinginess, and extreme poverty; for the first is attained through the prayer of presence and vigilance in the station of the heart; the second is attained through the *zakāt* of renunciation and detachment; and the third is attained through obedience to God and the Messenger with virtuous deeds, because virtue is a habit, and the blessing of obedience nullifies poverty through the attainment of enrichment in God, as the saying goes, 'If someone sets his afterlife aright, God sets his worldly life aright.'

[58:14] *Have you not regarded those who fraternise with a folk at whom God is wrathful? They neither belong with you, nor with them, [and they swear falsely, while they know*]: fraternity is only firm and true when there is affinity and correspondence between the parties, and if such affinity exists it should be ended, or else it should be avoided lest it lead to companionship and fraternity. Fraternity can only exist without this affinity if it is caused by an external influence, such as a benefit or a pleasure, and such fraternity will end as soon as the external influence does since it cannot exist without it. This is why He negated that there can be true fraternity between them, saying, *They neither belong with you*, for their fraternisation is nothing but hypocrisy.

[58:15] [*God has prepared for them a severe chastisement. Evil indeed is that which they [are wont to] do.*

[58:16] *They have taken their oaths as a shield, and so they bar from the way of God. So for them there will be a humiliating chastisement.*

[58:17] *Neither their possessions nor their children will avail them in any way against God. Those—they are the folk of the Fire, wherein they will abide.*

[58:18] *The day when God will raise them all together, whereupon they will swear to Him, just as they swear to you [now], and suppose that they are [standing] on something. Yet assuredly it is they who are the liars!]*

[58:19] *Satan*—meaning delusion—*has prevailed upon them, and so he has caused them to forget the remembrance of God*: by tempting them with sensory pleasures and corporeal desires, and making the life of this world seem attractive to their eyes. [*Those are Satan's confederates. Yet it is indeed Satan's confederates who are the losers!*

[58:20] *Indeed, those who oppose God and His Messenger—they will be among the most abased.*

[58:21] *God has inscribed, 'I shall assuredly prevail, I and My messengers.' Indeed, God is Strong, Mighty.]*

[58:22] *You will not find a people who believe in God and the Last Day* with certain faith *loving those who oppose God and His Messenger, even though they were their fathers [or their sons or their brothers or their clan]*, because love is a spiritual matter. Hence, if they attained certitude and recognised the Real and His folk, it would overcome their hearts, spirits, souls and bodies and brand them with spiritual love. The only correspondence between them and the Real and His folk is natural love based on kinship and blood ties. The spiritual connection is stronger, firmer, sweeter and purer than the natural one. [*For*] *those He has inscribed faith upon their hearts*: by unveiling and certitude, reminding them of the primal covenant and uncovering it for them, *and reinforced them with a spirit from Him* because of their connection to the realm of holiness, or light of the self-disclosure of the Essence; *and He will admit them into gardens* of the three gardens *underneath which rivers* of the teachings of Oneness and Divine Law *flow, [wherein they will abide,] God being pleased with them*—by erasing their attributes with His own by the light of self-disclosure—*and they being pleased with Him*: by their connection to His Attributes. *Those [they] are God's confederates*: the foremost who pay no heed to anything but Him, nor acknowledge it. [*Assuredly it is God's confederates*] *who are the successful*: having attained absolute perfection.

59
EXILE
SŪRAT AL-ḤASHR

In the Name of God, the Compassionate, the Merciful

[59:1] [*All that is in the heavens and all that is in the earth glorifies God. And He is the Mighty, the Wise.*

[59:2] *It is He Who expelled those who disbelieved of the People of the Book from their homelands at the first exile. You did not think that they would go forth, and they thought that they would be protected by their fortresses from God. But God came at them from whence they had not reckoned,*] and He cast terror into their hearts: that is, He looked upon them with the gaze of overwhelming power and they reacted to it, [*destroying [as they did] their houses with their own hands and the hands of the believers. So take heed, O you who have eyes!*

[59:3] *And had God not prescribed banishment for them, He would have chastised them in this world, and in the Hereafter there is for them the chastisement of the Fire.*

[59:4] *That is because they defied God and His Messenger; and whoever defies God, indeed God is severe in retribution:*] they deserved this because of how they opposed the Beloved and defied him, and because of the doubt in their hearts and how they did not conduct themselves with insight or follow the clear signs of their Lord. Had they been people of certitude, the terror would not have been cast into their hearts and they would have recognised the Messenger of God (may God bless him and grant him peace), by the light of certitude, and believed in him instead of defying him.

[59:5] [*Whatever palm-trees you cut down or left standing on their roots, it was by God's leave, and in order that He might disgrace those who are immoral.*

[59:6] *And whatever spoils God has given to His Messenger from these, you did not spurn for it any horses or camels, but God gives His messengers sway over whomever He will, and God has power over all things.*

[59:7] *Whatever spoils God has given to His Messenger from the people of the towns, belong to God and to the Messenger and to the near of kin, and the orphans, and the needy, and the traveller, so that these do not become a thing circulating between the rich among you.*] *And whatever the Messenger gives you, take it; and whatever he forbids you, abstain*, because he is realised in God, so that whatever he commands is God's command, and whatever he prohibits is God's prohibition, as He says, *Nor does he speak out of [his own] desire; it is but a revelation that is revealed* [Q. 53:3–4]. [*And fear God. Indeed, God is severe in retribution.*]

[59:8] *It is for the poor Emigrants*—those who renounced, detached and emigrated from the station of the soul—*who were driven away*: it was God who drove them away, for had they left of their own accord they would have been veiled by their own souls and regard for their renunciation and detachment, thereby falling into the station of the soul because of the veil of pride, which is even worse than sin; *from their homes and their*

Q. 59:8

possessions: from where they were comfortable and from what they held dear, namely the attributes of their souls and the objects of their knowledge; *that they should seek bounty from God*: in the form of knowledge and virtuous character traits; *and beatitude*: in the form of spiritual states and sublime gifts from the lights of the self-disclosures of the Attributes; *and help God and His Messenger*: by sacrificing their souls by the power of certitude. *Those—they are the sincere* with certain faith, for their deeds confirm their claims; and the sign of the experience of certitude is the manifestation of its effect on the limbs, so that they can only move according to the knowledge they have attained.

[59:9] *And those who had settled in the hometown, and [had abided] in faith*: this means the original abode of innate disposition and the primal covenant, which is the home of faith, hence its connection to it here, for the soul is the abode of alienation. They settled there *before them*: meaning before the emigration there from the abode of alienation in the soul, because this abode is the original home that existed before their homes. This is why he (may God grant him peace) said, 'To love one's home is part of faith.' They are the ones who did not fall from innate disposition, nor were veiled by the soul in creation, but retained its purity, unlike the first ones who became sullied and changed and then returned to purity by means of spiritual wayfaring. They *love those who have emigrated to them*, because of the affinity of purity and the primal correspondence and true kinship between them, through honouring and remembering the primal covenant with faithfulness in religion and brotherhood; *and do not find in their breasts any need of that* fortune *which those* emigrants *have been given*, because their hearts are free of the blights of souls and pure from the impulses of avarice, having transcended the love of fortune and attained a true understanding of fate; *but prefer [others] to themselves,* because of their detachment and orientation towards the presence of holiness, and their elevation above base matter, so that virtue has become intrinsic to them, by the dictate of innate disposition and the overflowing love for their true brethren and helpers on the path, *though they be in poverty.* They prefer their fellows to themselves because of their chivalry and perfect integrity, and due to the power of their faith in Oneness and their aversion to the soul's fortune, fearing to return to particular desires after experiencing universal ones. *And whoever is saved from the avarice of his own soul* by God's protection and shelter, for the soul is the natural refuge of every evil and base attribute and the home of every imperfection and low trait, and avarice is part of the instinctual clay in which it was moulded, because of how it adheres to the lower direction and loves particular desires, and so it cannot be separated from it unless the soul itself is negated—God alone can protect people from these blights and evils—*those—they are the successful* who attain the perfections of the heart.

Q. 59:10

[59:10] *And those who will come after [them—*after*] those who emigrat*ed to innate disposition and set about travelling the path and traversing the way-stations of the soul—*say* humbly and penitently, with the voice of neediness, '*Our Lord, forgive us* for the configurations of vices and the attributes of souls, by the lights of the heart, *and our brethren who preceded us in [embracing] the faith* for the sins of variegations by the manifesting of those attributes and error after guidance; *and do not place any rancour in our hearts towards those who believe*: by the veil of predatory and satanic configurations and their establishment in our hearts. *Our Lord, You are indeed Kind* in how you cover those configurations with the lights of the Attributes, *Merciful*' by emanating perfections and displaying self-disclosures.

[59:11] [*Have you not considered the Hypocrites who say to their brethren who disbelieve from among the People of the Book, 'If you are expelled, we will assuredly go forth with you, and we will never obey anyone against you. And if you are fought against, we will certainly help you.' And God bears witness that they are truly liars.*]

[59:12] [*For] indeed if they are expelled, they would not go forth with them; and if they are fought against, they would not help them. And even if they were to help them, they would surely turn their backs [to flee], then they would not be helped.*]

[59:13] *You indeed arouse greater awe in their hearts than God.* [*That is because they are a people who do not comprehend:*] they are veiled by creation from the Real because of their ignorance of God and their failure to rec-

415

ognise Him; for if they recognised Him, they would know that there is no influencer but Him and would sense His might and power, and the might and power of creation would have no further value in their eyes. The Commander of the Believers (may God grant him peace) said, 'The might of the Creator in your eyes makes the creation seem small.'

[59:14] [*They will not fight against you together, except in fortified towns or from behind some wall.*] *Their might is great among themselves* because they are not compelled therein by God's compulsion, nor does the shade of the Messenger's power and awesomeness fall there, nor is the light of his aid and the illumination of his soul by the connection to the realm of holiness reflected upon them. *You* [*would*] *suppose them to be all together* because of their outward accord, *but their hearts are scattered* because they lack the true unification of the light of Oneness, and their impulses attract them to the temptations of their attachments to lower matters, and they are separated from the truth by falsehood, veiled as they are by multiplicity from Unity. *That is because they are a people who have no sense* such that they would choose the path of knowledge of Divine Oneness and keep away from the scattered paths of delusion; for the path of the intellect is one, while the paths of the Satan of estimation are many. The disunity of hearts weakens resolve and debilitates strength.

Q. 59:14

[59:15] [[*They are*] *as the likeness of those who recently before them tasted the evil consequences of their conduct. And for them there will be a painful chastisement.*]

[59:16] *Like Satan* [*when he says to man, 'Disbelieve!' So that when he* [*man*] *disbelieves, he says, 'Indeed, I am absolved of you. Indeed, I fear God, the Lord of the Worlds'*]: their brethren hypocrites who share in their temptations are like Satan, meaning human estimation, when it approaches man in innate disposition and attracts him towards sensory pleasures and corporeal desires, goading him to disobey the intellect by caprice and become veiled by nature so that he falls into depravity. Then when he is veiled by them from the Real and becomes immersed in the darkness of the soul, it repudiates him when it perceives the meanings beyond him and attempts to draw near to the Real, by ascending above the intellectual horizon and observing some of the Divine Attributes, evoking fear by perceiving the effects of His might and power and the lights of lordship.

[59:17] *So the sequel for both will be that they are in the Fire, therein abiding,* because they are both corporeal beings who cleave to nature and its various fires and assorted torments. *And that is the requital of the evildoers* who put worship in the wrong place, and worshipped the idol of caprice and the false god of the body, and took their desires as their gods.

[59:18] *O you who believe* with deferential blind faith in the Unseen, *fear God*: by avoiding sins, evil deeds and vices and by attaining good deeds, acts of obedience and virtues; *and let every soul consider what it has sent ahead for tomorrow*: what righteous deeds it has sent ahead for the afterlife. *And fear God*: by avoiding being veiled by accidents and desires, and using the Real as a pretext for attaining desires. *Indeed, God is Aware of what you do*, of your deeds and intentions, and will requite you according to them, as he (may God grant him peace) said, 'Each man shall have what he intends.' Or: believe with true faith, and fear God by avoiding being veiled from Him by your deeds and attributes; and let every soul consider what it has sent ahead for tomorrow of contemptible deeds and attributes, which are obstructive veils and blameworthy, rejected pretexts; and fear God by avoiding remnants of ego and variegations, for God is aware of what you do through your souls, and what you do through Him rather than your souls.

[59:19] *And do not be like those who forget God* by becoming veiled by corporeal desires and engrossed in egocentric pleasures, *so that He makes them forget their own souls* until they confuse the soul for the body and its composition and temperament, overlooking the holy substance and the illuminated disposition. *Those—they are the immoral* who have strayed outside the upright religion, namely the disposition of God in which He moulded humankind, and treacherously violated God's covenant and thrown it aside, thereby incurring tremendous loss.

Q. 59:18

[59:20] *Not equal are the folk of the Fire*, who forgot and reneged, *and the folk of Paradise*, who had true faith and God-fearing and held to their covenant. *It is the folk of Paradise who are the winners*, while the others are the losers because of their total heedlessness and lack of discernment, as though they cannot tell the difference between Paradise and Hell, since otherwise they would have acted according to their discernment.

[59:21] *[Had We sent down this Qur'ān]* upon a mountain, *[you would have surely seen it humbled, rent asunder by the fear of God]*: their hearts are harder than stone in their lack of reaction and receptivity, for the Divine Word is as moving as can be, and would even move a mountain to tremble and quake were it revealed upon it. *[And such similitudes do We strike for people, that perhaps they may reflect.]*

[59:22] *He is God, than Whom there is no other god*: since Islam is based on unification and differentiation, these two concepts are repeated often in the revelation. He implied unification by declaring that there is no god in existence but Him. Then He implied differentiation by saying, *Knower*

417

of the Unseen and the visible, since knowledge is the foundation of differentiation, and His knowingness is the identification of realities and the entities of quiddities in the midst of unification. In other words, the forms of the quiddities in the Unseen realm from His knowingness, and then their existence in the visible realm as beings, are one and the same; they were but manifested in material loci. It is not that they were transported from one realm to the other, but rather that they were manifested after being hidden, in the way that an already known form can be manifested on paper by means of writing. Everything that was manifested appeared from His prior knowledge. [*He is*] *the Compassionate*: by the emanation of the existences of quiddities and their archetypal forms upon the loci, from the perspective of the origin; *the Merciful*: by the emanation of their perfections in the end. He then repeats the declaration of Essential Oneness from the perspective of unification to show how this multiplicity, from the perspective of the differentiation of the Attributes, does not negate His Essential Unity, as is also true of the other relativities and apophatic qualities listed thereafter:

Q. 59:23

[59:23] [*He is God, than Whom there is no other god,*] *the King*: the absolutely Self-Sufficient whom all things need, the director of all things according to a wise order which could not be any more perfect or complete; *the Holy*: the One detached from matter and the impurities of contingency in all His Attributes, so that none of His Attributes depend on external power or can only be activated temporarily; *the Peace*: the One innocent of flaws such as incapacity; *the Securer* of the folk of certitude by the sending down of divine tranquillity; *the Guardian* Who keeps those whom He secures in a state of security from every terror; *the Mighty*: the Strong Who overwhelms and cannot be overwhelmed; *the Compeller* Who compels all things as He wills; *the Exalted*: too high to be reached or to share existence with any other. *Glorified be God above what partners they ascribe* by affirming the existence of other-than-Him.

[59:24] *He is God, the Creator*: the Measurer of loci according to whichever of His Names and Attributes He wishes to manifest; *the Maker* Who differentiates and identifies them from one another, by identifying configurations in the midst of His Essence; *the Shaper* of the form of the differentiations of the loci of His Attributes. *To Him belong the Most Beautiful Names*, manifested in the forms of formalised creations and hidden in the forms of unseen productions, so that they glorify His Essence with the voices of His Names and Attributes: [*All that is in the heavens and the earth glorify Him, and He is the Mighty, the Wise.*] And God knows best.

60
SHE WHO IS EXAMINED
SŪRAT AL-MUMTAḤANA

In the Name of God, the Compassionate, the Merciful

[60:1] [*O you who believe, do not take My enemy and your enemy for friends. You offer them affection when verily they have disbelieved in the truth that has come to you, expelling the Messenger and you because you believe in God, your Lord. If you have gone forth to struggle in My way and to seek My pleasure,* [*show them not affection*]. *You secretly harbour affection for them, when I know well what you hide and what you proclaim. And whoever among you does that has verily strayed from the right way:*] God's enemy is the one who violates His covenant and turns his heart away from Him, which necessarily must make him an idolater since he loves other-than-God, and an enemy to every monotheist who denies other-than-God, since there is natural enmity between them. Therefore, He said, *My enemy and your enemy*, and implied that the friendship between them is accidental, not essential, by saying, *You offer them affection*. Then He explained how it cannot be essential, because of the all-important contradiction between them and their lack of correspondence and affinity in all aspects, saying *when verily they have disbelieved*, and so on. He then indicated that this only occurs because of the emergence of an affinity and inclination towards idolatry, for they are the only explanation for its occurrence: *And whoever among you does that has verily strayed from the right way*: the path of Unity.

[60:2] [*If they were to prevail over you, they would be your enemies, and would stretch out against you their hands and their tongues with evil* [*intent*]; *and they long for you to disbelieve.*]

He then indicates that the people of realisation should never choose accidentality (ʿaraḍiyya), since its necessary cause is ephemeral matters whose benefit does not endure beyond this world. The intelligent person must choose what is enduring, not ephemeral:

419

[60:3] *Your relatives and your children will not avail you*: You will attain no benefit from those for whose sake you have chosen to ally with your true enemy, for the Minor Resurrection will divide you eternally because of the absence of a true connection between you that can survive death. This is the meaning of His Words, *On the Day of Resurrection you will be separated*: that is, God will separate you from your relatives and children, as He says, *The day when a man will flee from his [own] brother, and his mother and his father, and his wife and his sons* [Q. 80:34–36]. [*And God is Seer of what you do.*]

He then teaches them the path of Oneness by the example of the true patriarchal monotheist, Abraham the Prophet (may God grant him peace) and his companions:

[60:4] [*Verily there is for you a good example in* [*the person of*] *Abraham, and those who were with him, when they said to their people, 'Indeed, we are innocent of you and of what you worship besides God. We repudiate you. And between us and you there has arisen enmity and hate forever until you* [*come to*] *believe in God alone,' except for Abraham's saying to his father,*] '*I shall ask forgiveness for you*: I shall ask that you be forgiven by the erasure of your attributes and evil deeds by the divine light, [*but I cannot avail you anything against God*':] all I can do is ask, but the answer depends on God's will and nurture, as He says, *You cannot guide whomever you like, but* [*it is*] *God* [*Who*] *guides whomever He will* [Q. 28:56]. '*Our Lord, in You we put our trust* by renouncing our own acts through witnessing Yours, *and to You we turn* [*penitently*] by erasing our attributes through beholding Yours, *and to You is the journeying* by the annihilation of our essences and beings in Your Essence, which is the purest declaration of Oneness.

Q. 60:3

[60:5] '*Our Lord, make us not a temptation for those who disbelieve*: we do not fear them nor deem them to have any influence or existence, but we seek refuge in Your grace from Your punishment. Do not punish us through them, nor subject us to tribulation at their hands because of the evil deeds we have committed and how we have manifested our attributes; *and forgive us* for the sins of our excesses with clemency, not chastisement. [*Our Lord!*] *Indeed, You are the Mighty* with the power to punish us through them, as well as to protect us from them and overwhelm and restrain them, *the Wise*' Who chooses to do either of these two things according to the dictate of wisdom.

He then repeats the exhortation to emulate Abraham and his companions, affirming it for those who are in the beginning stage of the declaration of Oneness in the station of hope and expectation of perfection:

[60:6] [*Verily there is for you in them a good example, for those* [*of you*] *who*

anticipate God and the Last Day. And whoever turns away [should know that]
God is the Independent, the Worthy of Praise.]

[60:7] *It may be that God will bring about affection between you and those*
of them with whom you are at enmity: by removing the cause of the enmity,
which is disbelief; for veiling is not a matter of innate disposition, but
rather faith is, and disbelief only occurs when the person is veiled by
creation and engrossed in natural coverings. *For God is Powerful*: well able
to remove it; and when it is lifted, true affection emerges by the light of
Essential Unity and the dictate of fraternity rooted in faith; *and God is*
Forgiving: by covering those dark veiling configurations with the light of
His Attributes; *Merciful* to the people of imperfection by healing them
with the emanation of His perfections.

[60:8] [*God does not forbid you in regard to those who did not wage war against*
you on account of religion and did not expel you from your homes, that you should
treat them kindly and deal with them justly.] *Indeed, God loves the just*, because
justice is the shade of love, and love is the shade of Unity; and so if justice
is manifested in a locus, it must be that God's love attached to it first, for
there can be no shadow without essence. And God (Exalted is He) knows
best.

Q. 60:7

61
THE RANKS
SŪRAT AL-ṢAFF

In the Name of God, the Compassionate, the Merciful

[61:1] [*All that is in the heavens and all that is in the earth glorifies God, and He is the Mighty, the Wise.*]

[61:2] *O you who believe, why do you say what you do not do?* Among the marks of true faith are sincerity and firm resolve, for they are required in order for the innate disposition to be free of the impurities of creation. His Words *why do you say what you do not do* evoke deceit and the breaking of promises, and so the one who claims to have faith must avoid these two things by the dictate of his faith, for otherwise his faith would be meaningless. Therefore, He says:

[61:3] *It is greatly loathsome to God that you say what you do not do*, because lying is contrary to integrity, which is one of the principles of faith and certainly undermines its perfection. This is so because faith, at its core, means returning to innate disposition and the upright religion, which requires the attainment of all the types of virtue, the least of which is the decency that necessitates integrity. The liar has no integrity, and therefore has no real faith. The reason we say he has no integrity is that speech means the communication of an intelligible concept to another person using words that denote it, and the special quality that distinguishes humanity from other beings is speech; and if the communication does not conform to reality, the speech is useless, which takes the one who utters it outside the sphere of humanity. By uttering words that affirm the existence of something that does not actually exist, he has entered the sphere of Satanism, and so has incurred the supreme loathing of God by squandering his preparedness and acquiring its opposite. The same applies to breaking promises, since it is akin to lying and because being true to one's resolve is one of the requirements of courage, which is one of the necessary virtues for the preservation of innate disposition, and indeed the lowest of their ranks. If it is not present, faith itself is negated by the absence of its requirements, and so God's loathing is incurred.

[61:4] *Indeed, God loves those who fight for His cause in ranks, [as if they were a solid structure,]* because offering the soul for God's cause can only be done if the soul has pure love for God; for when a man loves anything other than God, he loves it for the sake of his own soul, and the root of idolatry and love for false gods is love for the soul. If he is prepared to sacrifice his soul, it can only be that he does not love it; and if he does not love it, then he must not love anything in the world. So if his self-sacrifice is for the sake of God and His cause, not for the soul—as he said, 'Leave the world for the world'—then the love for God in his heart must be greater than the love for anything else, and he must be one of those about whom He said, *But those who believe love God more ardently* [Q. 2:165]. And if that is true, then God must also love them, as He says, *He loves them, and they love Him* [Q. 5:54]. In reality, love for God is only from God.

Q. 61:4

[61:5] *[And when Moses said to his people, 'O my people, why do you harm me, when certainly you know that I am the messenger of God to you?']* So when *they deviated* from the dictate of their knowledge because of their excessive caprice and love for the world, *God caused their hearts to deviate* from the path of guidance, and veiled them from the light of perfection, because of how they turned towards the lower direction and inclined away from the dictate of innate disposition. *And God does not guide the immoral folk* who stray outside the dictate of innate disposition, which is the upright religion; He does not guide them to the light of perfection because they are no longer prepared for it or receptive to it.

[61:6] *[And when Jesus son of Mary said, 'O Children of Israel I am indeed God's messenger to you, confirming what is before me of the Torah and bringing good tidings of a messenger who will come after me, whose name is Aḥmad'. Yet when he brought them, they said, 'This is manifest sorcery!']*

[61:7] *And who does greater wrong than he who invents lies against God*: by placing His light in darkness and exchanging the goods of subsistence— meaning innate preparedness—for the wares of annihilation, *[when he is [actually] being summoned to submission [to God]]*? He does this despite being called by the herald from outside—[namely] the Prophet—to submission, which is the natural result of that primal light. *And God does not guide [the wrongdoing folk]*—those who are marked by this attribute—to the light of perfection: that is, the light of His Essence and the glorious rays of His countenance, for the same reason as He does not guide the immoral folk.

[61:8] [*They desire to extinguish the light of God with their mouths, but God will perfect His light, though the disbelievers be averse.*

[61:9] *It is He Who has sent His Messenger with the guidance and the religion of truth, that He may make it prevail over all [other] religions, though the disbelievers be averse.*]

[61:10] *O you who believe, [shall I show you a commerce that will deliver you from a painful chastisement?* This is addressed to the people who believe] with deferential blind faith, because the commerce that delivers from painful chastisement, to which he invited them, was only meant for those who are veiled from the light of God by the Attributes and configurations of their souls.

[61:11] *You should believe in God and His Messenger* with true faith or certitude and reason, *and* after you attain sound reasoning and strong certitude *struggle for the cause of God with your possessions and your lives*, because offering one's soul to God's cause can only result from certitude. *That is better for you* because they are only bound for annihilation in any case; and so if you trade them for pleasures that are enduring with sublimity, it would be better for you, *should you know* with certain knowledge.

Q. 61:8

[61:12] *He will [then] forgive you [your sins]:* your evil deeds and the benighted configurations of your souls, *and admit you into gardens* from the gardens of the soul, since they were merchants who offered their souls and possessions for recompense, acting according to His Words, *Indeed, God has purchased from the believers their lives and their possessions, so that theirs will be [the reward of] Paradise* [Q. 9:111]; *underneath which rivers* of the knowledge of reliance, the Oneness of the acts, the teachings of the Divine Law, and sublime character traits *flow and pleasant dwellings*, such as the station of reliance and the other waypoints and stations of the soul, *[in the gardens of Eden]. That is the supreme triumph* compared to those who do not reach those stations in those gardens, not the absolutely supreme triumph.

[61:13] *And another which you love:* another commerce even more profitable and beloved to you: *help from God* with angelic aid and luminous unveiling, *and a victory near at hand* by arrival at the station of the heart, beholding the self-disclosures of the Attributes and attaining the station of contentment. The reason He said *which you love* is that real love can only come after the station of the heart is reached. He called it *commerce* [Q. 61:10] because they are taking on God's Attributes in exchange for their own. [*And give good tidings to the believers.*

[61:14] [*O you who believe, be helpers of God, just as Jesus son of Mary said to the disciples*]—the disciples were those who rid themselves of the darkness of souls and the blackness of natural configurations, by reaching the station of the heart and becoming illuminated by the light of innate disposition, so that their true faces were made white by purification—'*Who will be my helpers unto God?*' [In other words,] 'Who will come with me towards God's help by travelling in His Attributes?' *The* pure *disciples said, 'We will be God's helpers* by manifesting the perfections of His Attributes in our loci.' So they travelled in His Attributes and manifested their lights until they reached perfection of the heart, and passed on this perfection to others: *So a group* [*of the Children of Israel*] *believed* in them because of the influence of their company, by the receptivity of their preparedness, *while a group disbelieved* because they were veiled by their own attributes. *Then We strengthened those who believed against their enemy* with luminous aid, *and so they became the triumphant* and overcame them with illuminating arguments and clear proofs. And God (Exalted is He) knows best.

Q. 61:14

62
THE DAY OF CONGREGATION
SŪRAT AL-JUMUʿA

In the Name of God, the Compassionate, the Merciful

[62:1] [*All that is the heavens and all that is in the earth glorifies God, the King, the Holy, the Mighty, the Wise.*

[62:2] *It is He Who sent to the unlettered [folk] a messenger from among them to recite to them His signs, and to purify them, and to teach them the Book and wisdom, though indeed before that they had been in manifest error.*

[62:3] *And [to] others from among them, who have not yet joined them; and He is the Mighty, the Wise.*

[62:4] *That is the bounty of God, which He gives to whom He will and God is [dispenser] of tremendous bounty.*

[62:5] *The likeness of those who were entrusted with the Torah then failed to uphold it is as the likeness of an ass carrying books. Evil is the likeness of the people who deny God's signs. And God does not guide the evildoing folk.*

[62:6] *Say: 'O you of Jewry, if you claim that you are the [favoured] friends of God, to the exclusion of other people, then long for death, if you are truthful.'*

[62:7] *But they will never long for it, because of what their hands have sent ahead; and God is Knower of the evildoers.*

[62:8] *Say: 'Assuredly the death from which you flee will indeed encounter you; then you will be returned to the Knower of the Unseen and the visible, and He will inform you of what you used to do.'*

[62:9] *O you who believe,] when you are called to the prayer on the day of congregation, [hasten to the remembrance of God, and leave aside [all] commerce]:* every situation whose cause cannot be observed by human minds is from a plane beyond the intellect tainted by estimation, because every particularisation requires a particulariser. Such situations include those of the letters of the alphabet and the days of the week, and indeed those of all languages, because in every place on earth there is a language whose first utterance must have been an inspired event, occasioned by a certain preparedness by the confluence of indefinable lower and higher matters. Even in the case of technical terminology, there must also have been a cause that necessitated the adoption of each term for the particular situation it signifies. The days of the week were established because of a parallelism between them and the divine days, which signify the duration of this world.

It is widely believed throughout the lands that the duration of this world is seven thousand years, corresponding to the number of the seven celestial spheres. Every thousand years amounts to a single one of the days of God, as He says, *And truly a day with your Lord is like a thousand years of your counting* [Q. 22:47]. This sevenfold duration of the world indicates that the entire duration of the cycle of absolute concealment was six thousand years. Subsequently, manifestation commenced on the seventh day with the emergence of Muḥammad (may God grant him peace), who said, 'The Hour and I were dispatched like this,' and he put his index and middle fingers together. This will then extend until seven thousand years have passed from the time of Adam (may God grant him peace), the first of the prophets, until the time of the Mahdī (may God grant him peace), whereupon the concealment will come to an end because of the total manifestation at the Hour and the Major Resurrection: the time of the annihilation of creation and the Resurrection and Reckoning. Thereafter the inhabitants of Paradise and Hell are made clear and the Throne of God is seen plainly, as Ḥāritha described in his account of his vision (may God be pleased with him), which will occur in the Hereafter.

Q. 62:9

The first six days were those wherein He created the heavens and the earth, because creation is the veil of the Real and the meaning of their creation is that He was concealed behind them—manifesting them and becoming hidden. The seventh day was the day of unification and the time of the ascension of the Throne, by manifestation with all the Attributes, and the incipience of the Day of Resurrection, whose dawn began with the sending of our prophet Muḥammad (may God bless him and his family and give them peace). The Muḥammadans are the people of Friday, and Muḥammad is its master and the Seal of Prophets. The reason it was called the Day of Unification (*yawm al-jamʿ* [i.e. *al-jumuʿa*]) is that it was the time of manifestation in the form of the Supreme Name of all the Attributes, and the time of His ascension through manifestation by all of them, so that there was no further differentiation of manifestation and concealment. This is the secret of why prayer is designated on Friday at the time of the sun's high point, while this is disliked on all the other days.[1] This manifestation is called 'the essence of unification', because of how all things are united in it; and this is why Friday is called *Jumuᶜa*.

The adherents of all the great traditions, including the Jews, agree that God rested from the creation of the heavens and the earth on the seventh day. However, the Jews say that this was Saturday and that creation began on Sunday, while according to our interpretation it would be Friday. The interpretation of Sunday (*al-aḥad*) as the first day of creation would be that the Unity (*aḥadiyya*) of the Essence is the source of multiplicity. If we said that Sunday was the first day and the beginning of creation, the cycle of prophethood would be the cycle of concealment. Hence, the sixth day would be the incipience of manifestation, which increased in spiritual power until it reached the peak of manifestation and the end of concealment at its final moments, when the Mahdī emerged and the manifestation became universal on the seventh day, Saturday. Now since this day—meaning Friday—was established parallel to this concept, people are encouraged on this day to halt their worldly pursuits, which are all veils, and to attend and gather for prayer. It is obligatory to hasten to the remembrance of God on this day and to leave aside all commerce, so that souls can manifest the configuration of the congregation (*ijtimāᶜ*) in the prayer of presence, which prepares the way for arrival at the presence of unification. By halting worldly pursuits, it may be that one of them might remember how to detach from the veils of creation, by hastening to the remembrance of God and following His path; and by praying with the congregation, he might arrive at the presence of unification, and thereby attain success. *That is better for you, should you know* the secret and reality of it.

[62:10] *And when the prayer is finished, disperse in the land and seek God's bounty*: the command to disperse in the land and seek bounty after the prayer ends symbolises the return to differentiation after annihilation in unification through true prayer; for halting at unification would amount to being veiled by the Real from creation, and by the Essence from the Attributes. Dispersal means to roam among the Attributes in the state of subsistence after annihilation by veridical existence, and to travel with God through creation. Seeking God's bounty means to seek the fortunes of the self-disclosures of the Names and the Attributes, and to return to

Q. 62:10

---

1 Traditionally the call for the midday prayer is sounded shortly after the sun passes its zenith, except on Fridays where it is sounded the very moment the zenith is reached.

the station of the earth of the soul and receive its fortunes through the Real. *And remember God frequently*: call to mind the Essential Unifying Unity in the form of attributional multiplicity, lest you be veiled by multiplicity from Unity and stray after being guided; and keep to the path of uprightness by fulfilling the dues of the Real and creation alike, and observing both unification and differentiation, *that perhaps you may be successful* and win the supreme success, which is the wisdom of the establishment of unification.

[62:11] *But when they sight some [opportunity for] commerce or a diversion, they scatter off towards it, and leave you standing*: how do they stand regarding this vocation? What part do they play in this interaction? They have strayed far and grown oblivious, and become veiled and diverted. *Say: 'That which is with God is better [than diversion and commerce]'*: if your aspiration will not rise as high as pursuing this vocation, then you should at least work for the enduring rewards from God, since they are better than those ephemeral things which you possess. Leave the matter of provision to Him by relying on Him, for *God is the best of providers.'* And God (Exalted is He) knows best.

Q. 62:11

63

THE HYPOCRITES
SŪRAT AL-MUNĀFIQŪN

In the Name of God, the Compassionate, the Merciful

[63:1] [*When*] *the Hypocrites* [*come to you they say, 'We bear witness that you are indeed the Messenger of God.' And God knows that you are indeed His Messenger, and God bears witness that the Hypocrites are truly liars.*

[63:2] *They have taken their oaths as a shield, and so they have barred from the way of God. Evil indeed is that which they are wont to do*: the hypocrites] are the erratic ones who are attracted to the light of faith by their innate preparedness, but also attracted to disbelief by their acquired preparedness which was created by natural configurations and base habits. The reason they were liars when they bore witness to the Message was that the true meaning of the Message is known only to God, and those who are firm in knowledge, who know God and through knowledge of Him know the Messenger of God; for to know the Messenger is only possible after one knows God, and the extent of one's knowledge of the Messenger is commensurate with one's knowledge of God. Thus, no one truly knows him except the one who sheds his own knowledge and participates in God's knowledge. The hypocrites, however, are veiled from God by the veils of their essences and attributes, and they have extinguished the light of their preparedness with corporeal coverings and benighted configurations; so how could they know the Messenger of God, and so bear witness to His Message?

[63:3] *That is because they believed* in God by the remnant of the light of innate disposition and preparedness, *then disbelieved* and covered that light with the veils of vices and the attributes of their souls; *therefore, their hearts have been stamped*: by the deep-rootedness of those configurations, and rusted over by those acquisitions, so that they have become completely veiled from their Lord. *Hence, they do not understand* the meaning of the Message, nor the knowledge of Oneness and religion.

[63:4] *And when you see them, their figures please you; [and if they speak, you listen to their speech. [Yet] they are like blocks of timber [that have been] propped-up. They assume that every cry is [directed] against them. They are the enemy, so beware of them. May God assail them! How can they deviate?]* The correspondence of their shapes, the beauty of their appearances, and the perfection and radiance of their images seemed to indicate that they were prepared in terms of chivalry and illuminated disposition. This is why the Messenger of God (may God bless him and grant him peace) paid heed to their words and listened to their speech, since radiance and beauty are the result of the original purity of disposition. But when he saw how their hearts were rusted over and the light of their preparedness had been snuffed out, and how corporeal, accidental configurations had nullified their original spiritual power, he lost hope in them and expressed his incredulity at their state: *How can they deviate?* How can they turn from light to darkness, and from truth to falsehood?

Q. 63:4

It is related that one of the sages once saw a young man with a handsome face and so asked him to speak, because he expected him to be intelligent and wise. When he realised that there was not a trace of this in him, he said, 'What a wonderful house this would be, if only it were inhabited!' This is the meaning of His Words *they are like blocks of timber*: that is, matter devoid of spirit which provides neither benefit nor fruit, like wood stacked against a wall when it dries out and the spirit of growth no longer resides in it; for the preparedness of true life and the human spirit had left them in the same way.

They assume that every cry is [directed] against them. They are the enemy, because courage is simply the product of certitude, and certitude comes from the light of innate disposition and the purity of the heart. But they are engrossed in the darknesses of the soul's attributes and veiled by pleasures and desires, [being] folk of doubt and uncertainty, and so they are overwhelmed by cowardice and timidity. *So beware of them,* for their preparedness has been nullified and they will not follow your guiding light or be moved by your company.

[63:5] *[And when it is said to them, 'Come, and God's Messenger will ask forgiveness for you,']* they twist their heads because of their greed for benighted things and their habitual indulgence in predatory and bestial perfections, so that they are unaccustomed to light and have no desire for it, nor for human perfections due to the perversion of the essential form. *And you see them turning away* because of their attraction to the lower direction and worldly trifles, bereft of any natural inclination towards the higher direction and spiritual meanings, *disdainful* because of the preponderance of Satanism and the domination of the estimative faculty, and their veiling by I-ness and lack of virtue.

[63:6] [*It will be the same for them, whether you ask forgiveness for them or do not ask forgiveness for them:*] God will never forgive them because of the firmness of the benighted configurations in them, and the lack of receptivity of their preparedness for guidance, as a result of their immorality and how they have strayed from the upright religion of innate disposition. [*Indeed, God does not guide the immoral folk.*]

[63:7] *They are the ones who say, 'Do not expend on those who are with the Messenger of God, until they scatter off.'* [*Yet to God belong the treasuries of the heavens and the earth, but the hypocrites do not understand,*] because they are veiled by their acts from seeing God's act, and veiled by what is in their hands from what is in God's treasuries, so that in their ignorance they imagine they are the ones who expend. Likewise, they imagine that power and glory are theirs, veiled as they are by their attributes from God's:

Q. 63:6

[63:8] [*They say, 'Surely if we return to Medina,*] the powerful will [*soon*] expel from it the weaker.' [*Yet* [*the real*] might belongs to God and to His Messenger, and to the believers, but the hypocrites do not know:*] they do not sense that glory, power and might are all lights of the Essence of God and the Attributes inherent to His Essence, which are manifested upon the human loci the nearer one gets to Him and is annihilated in Him and erased in His Attributes; and no one is nearer to Him than the Messenger of God (may God bless him and grant him peace), and then the true believers of certitude. Thus, there are none in all creation mightier than him (may God grant him peace), and then the believers closest to him.

But the Hypocrites do not know because of how veiled and doubtful they are. And indeed He destined that the very one who uttered these words was expelled, detained and forbidden from entering Medina, until he had acknowledged that true might belongs to God and to His Messenger and the believers. It is narrated that the one who said it was ʿAbd Allāh b. Ubayy, and that when they returned to Medina his son drew his sword and prevented his father from entering and detained him, until the Messenger of God (may God bless him and grant him peace) permitted him to enter and he attested to the might of God and His Messenger and the believers.

[63:9] [*O you who believe,*] do not let your possessions and your children divert you from the remembrance of God; [*for whoever does that—it is they who are the losers*]: do not let this happen if you are true believers, for faith means that love for God overwhelms love for everything else; so do not let your love for them and for the world, because of your strong attachment to them and to your possessions, gain ascendancy in your hearts over your love for God, whereby they veil you from Him and you plummet towards Hell, and lose the light of innate preparedness by squandering it on that which quickly fades away.

[63:10] [*And expend of that with which We have provided you before death comes to any of you, whereat he will say, 'My Lord, if only You would reprieve me for a short time so that I might give charity and become one of the righteous!'*] Detach yourselves from your possessions by expending them when you are healthy and have need of them, so that they will become a virtue in your souls and a luminous confirmation for them. Spending is only useful when it comes from a disposition of generosity and a configuration of detachment in the soul. If it is only done when a person is at death's door, the possessions really belong to the heir and not the dying person, so it will do him no good to spend them and he will only feel loss and regret, and express a vainglorious wish to have more time. If his claim to faith had been sincere and he had been certain of the Hereafter, he would have known beyond doubt that death was inevitable and that its time was destined by God, according to His wisdom, and that it cannot be delayed.

Q. 63:10

[63:11] [*But God will never reprieve a soul when its term has come.*] *And God is Aware* [*of what you do*]: aware of your deeds and intentions. Thus, there is no use in spending at that time, nor in hoping for a reprieve and promising to spend and be righteous, since He would know that such spending was not done out of generosity, detachment or a desire for purity, but only out of stinginess and love for wealth, as though he had imagined that he could take his possessions with him when he died. He would recognise such a wish and promise to be nothing but a lie and an expression of love for immediate gratification, because of the presence of the configuration that contradicts charity and righteousness in the soul, and the inclination towards the world, as He says, *Even if they were sent back, they would return to that which they were forbidden. Indeed, they are liars* [Q. 6:28]. And God knows best.

64

DISPOSSESSION
SŪRAT AL-TAGHĀBUN

In the Name of God, the Compassionate, the Merciful

[64:1] [*All that is in the heavens and all that is in the earth glorifies God. To Him belongs the kingdom and to Him belongs [all] praise, and He has power over all things.*

[64:2] *It is He Who created you. Then some of you are disbelievers and some of you are believers; and God is Seer of what you do.*

[64:3] *He created the heavens and the earth with the truth, and He shaped you and made your shapes excellent; and to Him is the journey's end.*

[64:4] *He knows all that is in the heavens and the earth, and He knows what you hide and what you disclose, and God is Knower of what is in the breasts.*

[64:5] *Has there not come to you the tidings of those who disbelieved before and thus tasted the evil consequences of their conduct? And there will be for them a painful chastisement?*

[64:6] *That is because their messengers used to bring them clear signs,*] but they said, 'Shall [mere] humans be our guides?' Since they were veiled by the attributes of their souls from the light which made him immeasurably superior to them, and sensed only his human nature, they denied his guidance. Every cognisant person only knows the object of his knowledge according to the meaning that is in him; the light of perfection can only be perceived by the light of innate disposition, and only a perfect one can recognise a perfect one. This is why it is said that only God knows God. Every seeker who finds what he seeks finds it in a way that reflects the manner in which he approached it; and likewise, everyone who believes in something experiences the concept in which he believes in a way that reflects the way that this concept exists in his own soul. Now since there was nothing of the light of innate disposition left in them, they did not recognise the perfection in him and so denied him. Nor did they recognise anything of the truth such that they would be moved to seek guidance, and therefore they rejected his guidance. *So they disbelieved* [*and turned away*]: they were veiled from the Real, the religion and the Messenger, and turned towards the sensory things they experienced instead of the intellectual things; *and God was independent* in His perfection, because He experiences His own perfection and witnesses His own Essence, whether they recognise it or not. *And God is* inherently *Independent* of their faith, and none of His perfections are contingent on them nor on their recognition of Him; *Praised* and perfect in Himself by His perfections which are manifested, in the loci of the atoms of existence, to His allies even if not to them. In other words, even if they do not see Him or praise Him for those perfections because of how they are veiled from them, He is nonetheless praised by every being through the special perfections that are His in each of them.

[64:7] [*Those who disbelieve claim that they will never be resurrected. Say: 'Yes indeed, by my Lord, you will be resurrected; then you will be informed of what you did. And that is easy for God.'*

[64:8] *So believe in God and His Messenger and the Light, which We have revealed. And God is Aware of what you do.*

[64:9] *The day when He will gather you for the Day of Gathering*]—*that will be the Day of Dispossession*: true dispossession does not apply to worldly things, since they are ephemeral and short-lived and none of them can remain for anyone; and so if any of them were lost, or someone lost it— even if it were his own life—it would be nothing more than the loss of something whose loss was always inevitable, and consequently it would not be any kind of wronging or injustice. The true wronging and dispossession is to lose something that, had it not been lost, would have remained forever and been a perpetual benefit to its owner, namely the light of perfection and preparedness. Thus, the loss and dispossession there will be real, because of the squandering of profit and capital in the commerce of triumph and salvation, as He says, *Their commerce has not profited them, nor are they guided* [Q. 2:16]. The one who squanders his preparedness and the light of his innate disposition will be utterly dispossessed, like a man whose light is taken from him, leaving him in darkness. So, too, the one who retains the light of his disposition but does not acquire the perfection that befits it as merited by his preparedness, or acquires some but not all of it, will be dispossessed compared to the one who reaches full perfection, as though he won his station and his prize from him and left him bewildered in his imperfection.

Q. 64:7

435

And [as for] those who believe in God according to the light of their preparedness, *and act righteously* according to the dictate of their faith, since action is commensurate with reflection, *He will absolve them of their misdeeds* for which they feared God after doing them, *and admit them into gardens [underneath which rivers flow wherein they will abide],* according to the degrees of their deeds. If they believed with blind faith based on following authority and avoided sins and did good deeds, He will absolve them of the misdeeds of their sins and admit them into the gardens of the soul, according to the degree of their deeds and God-fearing. If they believed with realisation, shunned their own attributes and acted by traversing the Attributes and approvals of God, He will absolve them of the misdeeds of the attributes of their souls and admit them into the gardens of the heart, according to the degrees of their deeds and stations. If they believed with certain faith and acted through witnessing, and feared God by shunning their own existence, He will admit them into the gardens of the spirit by absolving them of the misdeeds of the existence of their hearts and attributes. If they believed with true faith and feared God by shunning their I-ness and refraining from regarding their annihilation, He will absolve them of the misdeeds of their remnants and variegations by manifesting His own I-ness, and admit them into the gardens of the Essence. [*That is the supreme triumph.*]

Q. 64:10

[64:10] *And [as for] those who disbelieved*: the veiled ones in contrast to the believers and their ranks, [*and denied Our signs]—those—they will be the folk of the Fire* of the level by which they were veiled, [*wherein they will abide*] in chastisement. *And [what] an evil journey's end!*

[64:11] *No affliction strikes* of these veiling afflictions as well as others, *except by the leave of God*: by His ordainment and will, according to His wisdom. *And whoever believes in God* with any of the aforementioned levels of faith, *He will guide his heart* towards acting in accordance with his faith until he experiences the perfection of the Being he seeks by his faith, and reaches the venue of His beholding. *And God is Knower of all things*: He knows the levels of your faith, the secrets of your hearts, and the states of your deeds and whether they are tainted by imperfections or not.

[64:12] *And obey God and obey the Messenger* according to your knowledge of God and the Messenger; for the failure to attain perfection and the fall into loss and imperfection is usually the result of laxity in action and lack of effort, not the absence of reflection. [*But if you turn away, then the Messenger's duty is only to communicate [the Message] clearly.*

[64:13] *God—there is no god except Him. And in God let [all] believers put their trust.*

[64:14] *O you who believe!] Indeed, among your wives and children there are enemies for you*: that is, some of them, because of how you are veiled by them and are so devoted and attached to them that you associate them with God by loving them as much as Him, and worship them instead of Him by preferring them to Him. *So beware of them*: guard yourselves against being so devoted and attached to them that you are veiled by them, and chide them if they demand this of you by asking you to put their rights before God's rights in all things, whether love or otherwise. *And if you pardon* with kindness, *and overlook* their faults with forbearance, *and forgive* their transgressions with mercy, then there is no sin or harm. The only sin is that you be veiled by them and excessively devoted and attached to them, not that you conduct yourselves with justice and virtue and treat them kindly and pleasantly; for not only is that recommended, but it is part of adorning oneself with the Attributes of God. *Indeed, God is Forgiving, Merciful*, and so you must adorn yourselves with His character traits.

Q. 64:13

[64:15] *Your possessions and your children are only a trial*: a tribulation and a test from God to you; *and God—with Him is a great reward*: for those who are patient in the station of tribulation and observe God's rights therein, and make up for the obligations wherein they were remiss, by having poor conduct and contravening God's command concerning the wealth they amassed, denying God's right and committing the sins of stinginess and disobedience; and for how they went to excesses in their worldly love and connections, thereby squandering God's due and becoming veiled by their kin from Him, and likewise for their love for possessions, thereby falling into ignominy and loss; and for what they wasted by expending it on sinful things, thereby showing ingratitude for God's favours and failing to give thanks for them. If they were granted goodly wealth and children, they gave thanks and did not fall into prideful exultation nor arrogant ingratitude; and if they were deprived of them, they held steadfast and were not driven by grief into hopelessness, which leads only to ruin and perdition.

[64:16] *So fear God* with regards to these sins and blights to which the person undergoing tribulation is prone, *as far as you can*: according to your station and ability to bear your situation; *and listen and obey*: understand these commands and follow them; *and expend* your possessions with which God has tested you on things that please Him; *that is better for your souls*: seek for your children and possessions what is best for you. *And whoever is shielded* by God's protection [*from the avarice of his own soul*]—from this vice that is mixed into the clay of his soul—*such are the successful* who win the station of the heart and the reward of virtue.

Q. 64:16

65
DIVORCE
SŪRAT AL-ṬALĀQ

In the Name of God, the Compassionate, the Merciful

[65:1] *[O Prophet, when you [men] divorce women, divorce them by their prescribed period. And count the prescribed period, and fear God your Lord. Do not expel them from their houses, nor let them go forth, unless they commit a blatant [act of] indecency. And those are God's bounds; and whoever transgresses the bounds of God has verily wronged his soul. You never know: it may be that God will bring something new to pass afterwards.*

[65:2] *Then, when they have reached their term, retain them honourably, or separate from them honourably. And call to witness two just men from among yourselves, and bear witness for the sake of God. By this is exhorted whoever believes in God and the Last Day.]* And whoever fears God according to his station and how he avoids the sin of his state, *He will make a way out for him* from the confines of stations and acquisitions to the broad expanse of states and gifts. Whoever fears Him by refraining from disobeying Him, He will make for him a way out of the confines of benighted configurations and the punishing fires of nature.

[65:3] *And He will provide for him* the reward of the garden of the soul and the lights of virtues from the Unseen realm, *from whence he never expected*, because he did not halt with them. And whoever fears Him by shunning the acts of his own soul, He will make for him a way out to the station of reliance, and provide him with the self-disclosures of the acts from whence he never expected. And whoever fears Him by shunning the attributes of his soul, He will make for him a way out to the station of contentment, and provide him with the spirit of certitude and the fruits of the self-disclosures of the Divine Attributes in the garden of the heart, from whence he never expected, because he did not sense them. And whoever fears Him by shunning and transcending his own existence, He

439

will make for him a way out of the confines of his I-ness to the expanse of absolute existence, and provide him with gifted existence from whence he never expected nor imagined.

And whoever puts his trust in God by disregarding means and devoting himself to Him directly, *He will suffice him* by sending him what was destined for him and directing to him the fortunes of the world and the Hereafter that were apportioned for him. *Indeed, God fulfils His command*: He fulfils His will, and nothing can prevent Him or impede Him. The one who is certain of this will have nothing to fear or hope of anyone, and will surrender his affairs to God and find salvation. *Verily God has ordained for everything a measure*: He has specified a limit and a time for each thing pre-eternally, which cannot be increased by anyone's effort or decreased by anyone's sabotage, nor delayed or brought forward from its appointed time. The one who is certain of this, and who bears witness to it, is the truly reliant one.

Q. 65:4

[65:4] [*And [as for] those of your women who no longer expect to menstruate, if you have any doubts, their prescribed period shall be three months, and [also for] those who have not yet menstruated. And those who are pregnant, their term shall be when they deliver.*] *And whoever fears God* by being constantly vigilant and avoiding the sin of his state, *He will make matters easy for him* in his spiritual journey: that is, when he adheres to the courtesies of his station and avoids the sins of his state, in whatever stage he is in, He will make it easier for him to ascend to a higher one.

[65:5] *That* ease in each level, based on God-fearing, *is God's command* ordained by Him alone; it is grace according to preparedness, and emanation according to receptivity, *which He has revealed to you.* He then repeats to add emphasis and detail to what was stated in general terms before: *And whoever fears God, He will absolve him of his misdeeds*: his impediments and the configurations of his soul which veiled him from the emanation and prevented its increase, *and magnify the reward for him*: by emanating what suits his state according to the new perfection of receptivity and preparedness.

[65:6] [*Lodge them where you dwell in accordance with your means and do not harass them so as to put them in straits. And if they are pregnant, then maintain them until they deliver. Then, if they suckle for you, give them their wages, and consult together, honourably. But if you both make difficulties, then another woman will suckle [the child] for him.*]

[65:7] *Let the affluent man expend out of his affluence. And let he whose provision has been straitened for him expend of what God has given him. God does not charge any soul save except with what He has given it. God will assuredly bring about ease after hardship.*

[65:8] *And how many a town disobeyed the command of its Lord and His messengers, then We called it to a severe reckoning and chastised it with a dire chastisement.*

[65:9] *So it tasted the evil consequences of its conduct, and the consequence of its conduct was [utter] loss.*

[65:10] *God has prepared for them a severe chastisement.] So fear God, O people of pith, who believe!* Reflect on the state of the nations of old who denied and opposed, and the chastisement and calamity that was sent down upon them; and fear God by observing His commandments and prohibitions, if your intellects are untainted by the adulterants of delusion. The pith is the intellect untainted by the impurities of delusion, which is achieved when the heart is untainted by the impurities of the attributes of the soul, so that it returns to innate disposition. When the intellect is untainted by delusion and the heart is untainted by the soul, faith becomes certain, which is why He describes them as people *who believe*, meaning people of true faith. *God has certainly revealed to you a [source of] remembrance*: a criterion containing remembrance of the Essence, Attributes, Names, acts and the afterlife.

Q. 65:8

[65:11] *A messenger*: the Holy Spirit who brought it down; He treated the Message as interchangeable with the messenger, because the sending down of the remembrance meant sending it down by the connection to the prophetic spirit and the inspiring of meanings in the heart; *reciting to you the clear signs of God*: showing you His Attributes and revealing their Unity to you, clearly disclosing the lights of the Essence; *that He may bring forth those who believe* with certain faith *[and perform righteous deeds] from the darkness* of the attributes of the heart *to the light* of the spirit and the station of witnessing. *And those who believe in God* with vision-based faith of certitude *and act righteously* by travelling in God and with God, *He will admit them into gardens* of the witnessing of the self-disclosures of His Attributes and the beholding of their lights, *underneath which rivers* of the teachings of the Unity of the acts, Attributes and Essence *flow, wherein they will abide forever. God has verily made a good provision for him* in the form of those teachings.

[65:12] *God it is Who created seven heavens, and of earth the like thereof*: if we take the *heavens* literally, then the seven earths refer to the well-known strata of elements, which are the vessels for the causes and thus function as the earth upon which descend from them the existential forms, namely: pure fire; the mixed stratum of fire and air called 'ether', from which come meteors, comets and the like; the stratum of bitter cold (*zamharīr*); the stratum of wind (*nasīm*); the stratum of plateau (*ṣaʿīd*) and water (*māʾ*)

which is contained in air, and itself contains the stratum of clay which is the sixth stratum; and the stratum of pure earth which is at the centre.[1] If we take the *heavens* to represent the levels of the aforementioned Seven Unseens—namely the Unseens of the faculties, soul, intellect, secret, spirit, hidden, and Unseen of Unseens, [i.e.] the source of the unification of the Essence—then the earths are the well-known seven limbs of the body. *The command* of God for creation, engendering, ordering and perfecting *descends between them* [*that you may know that God has power over all things and that God encompasses all things in knowledge*]. And God (Exalted is He) knows best.

Q. 65:12

1 This closely corresponds to the meteorology of the Ikhwān al-Ṣafāʾ, which itself was highly influenced by Aristotle. See Seyyed Hossein Nasr, *An Introduction to Islamic Cosmological Doctrines*, New York: SUNY Press, 1993, pp. 85–88.

66
PROHIBITION
SŪRAT AL-TAḤRĪM

In the Name of God, the Compassionate, the Merciful

[66:1] [*O Prophet, why do you prohibit what God has made lawful for you, seeking to please your wives? And God is Forgiving, Merciful.*

[66:2] *Verily God has prescribed for you* [*when necessary*] *the absolution of your oaths. And God is your Protector, and He is the Knower, the Wise.*

[66:3] *And when the Prophet confided to one of his wives a certain matter, but she divulged it and God apprised him of it, he announced part of it, and passed over part. So when he told her about it, she said, 'Who told you this?' He said, 'I was told by the Knower, the Aware.'*

[66:4] *If the two of you repent to God...for your hearts were certainly inclined, and if you support one another against him, then* [*know that*] *God, He is indeed his Protector, and Gabriel, and the righteous among the believers, and the angels, furthermore, are his supporters.*

[66:5] *It may be that, if he divorces you, his Lord will give him in* [*your*] *stead wives better than you—women submissive* [*to God*]*, believing, obedient, penitent, devout, given to fasting, previously married and virgins.*

[66:6] *O you who believe,*] *guard yourselves and your families against a Fire*: the true family are those with whom a man has a spiritual bond and a loving connection, whether they are biologically related to him or not. Everything to which he has a bond of love will necessarily be with him in this life and the next, and therefore he must guard it and protect it from the Fire just as he guards himself. If he purifies himself from benighted configurations, but still feels an inclination towards and love for certain souls who are engrossed in them, then he has not truly purified himself, because by that love he will be attracted to them and so he will fall into perdition alongside them and be veiled by them. This is true whether they are natural faculties within his own constitution, or human souls immersed in the world of nature outside his own essence. This is why the sincere one must love the pure folk and the saints, so that he will be resurrected alongside them; for each man will be resurrected with those he loves.

[*Guard yourselves and your families against*] *a Fire whose fuel is people and stones*: that is, a particular fire from among the many fires, fuelled only by people and stones, because it is a spiritual fire from the attributes of God's power, which overwhelms souls that are tied to lower matters and attached to earthly base substances by chains of spiritual love; hence, when those souls bonded themselves to them with love, they were raised alongside them in perdition; *over which stand* to maintain them *angels, stern*, powerful and harsh of substance: they are the faculties of heaven and the dominion who actively engage with earthly matters, who are the spiritual beings of the seven celestial bodies and the twelve constellations, known as The Nineteen *Zabāniya* (aside from Mālik). They are the corporeal nature assigned to the lower world and all the faculties and dispositions that influence the bodies, and which, if they detached from human souls, would rise from their levels and connect with the realm of divine power and come to influence these angelic faculties; but since they are immersed in corporeal matters and attached to the primordial substrata that here is referred to as *stones*, they have become influenced by them and confined where they are, tormented by their hands. [In addition, they are] *mighty*: strong and bereft of leniency, compassion and mercy because they are created with a nature of compulsion and derive no joy from anything besides it; *who do not disobey God in what He commands them*, because of how they are compelled and bent to His will and to obedience and subservience to Him, since although they are powers of compulsion and influence, with respect to the substances and faculties of this world beneath them, they are in turn compelled and influenced by the divine presence, and if they were not naturally subservient to the divine command they would have no influence over this world; *but do what they are commanded*, because of their constant influence and the infinitude of their faculties and powers.

Q. 66:7

[66:7] [*'O you who disbelieve,*] *do not make any excuses today*: for after the destruction of the body and the permanence of configurations, all that remains is requital for deeds, and there is no more hope for perfection. [*You are only being requited for what you used to do.'*]

[66:8] *O you who believe, repent to God*: by returning to Him in all of your states, for the levels of repentance are like the levels of God-fearing; and just as the first level of God-fearing is to avoid what the Divine Law prohibits and its final level is to shun I-ness and any remnant of ego, likewise the first level of repentance is to renounce sin and its final level is to renounce the sin of existence, which is the source of all enormities, according to the folk of realisation. [*Repent to God*] *with sincere repentance*: repentance that mends all fissures, repairs all breaches and corrects all corruptions, for the corruption of every station can only be repaired and put right by repentance in the form of ascension to the station above it. When one repents from it by ascending above it and emerging from behind the veil of regard for that station, its flaws are healed and it is completed. The word *naṣūḥ* ('sincere') is from *nuṣḥ*, meaning 'to sew'. Or it means repentance that is free from the impurity of inclination towards the station from which one has repented and regard for it, which is achieved by turning away from it and disregarding it. In that case, it is from *nuṣūḥ*, meaning 'purity' (*khulūṣ*).

Q. 66:8

It may be that your Lord will absolve you of your misdeeds: the sins, veils and blights of the station from which you have repented to Him, as well as regard for it, esteem for it, inclination towards it and recognition of it, or any variegation that occurs after ascension from it, such as the manifestation of the soul in the station of the heart, or manifestation of the heart in the station of the spirit, or the manifestation of I-ness in the station of Unity; *and admit you into gardens* arrayed according to the levels of repentance [*underneath which rivers flow,*] *on the day when God will not let down the Prophet and those who believe with him*: by manifesting the veil in the station of nearness. *Their light will be running before them*: the light which is theirs through reflection and intellectual perfection; *and on their right*: the light which is theirs through action and its perfection, since intellectual light is from the wellspring of Unity while active light is from the side of the heart, which is to the right of the soul. Or the light of the foremost among them will run before them while the light of the righteous among them will run on their right.

They will say, 'Our Lord, perfect our light for us: they will seek refuge with Him and rush to His protection from the manifestation of the remnant of ego, for it would darken their vision, and so they seek the permanence of light through total annihilation. Or it means: make this perfection endure for us by Your being and the enduring shining of the rays of Your countenance. They will say this out of their great yearning even while they are in the midst of witnessing, as the poet said, 'He weeps even as he draws nearer, fearing ever to be parted.' Or it means that some of them will say this, namely those who have not yet reached essential witnessing.

[*Perfect our light for us,*] *and forgive us* for the manifestation of remnants after annihilation, or the presence of affirmation before it. [*Indeed, You have power over all things.'*

[66:9] *O Prophet,*] *struggle against the disbelievers and the Hypocrites* because of the true contrariety between you and them, *and be stern with them* because your strength through God is the wellspring of faculties and powers, and the source of potency and might. Perhaps their resistance will break and their obstinacy will falter, so that their souls yield and surrender, reacting to the light of divine power and being guided, in order that the form of power will become the very essence of kindness. *For their abode will be Hell—and* [*what*] *an evil journey's end!—*as long as they remain as they are and retain their attributes, or forever in perpetuity because of the dissolution or absence of their preparedness.

Q. 66:9

[66:10] [*God has struck a similitude for those who disbelieve: the wife of Noah and the wife of Lot. They were under two of Our righteous servants, yet they betrayed them. So they did not avail the two women in any way against God, and it was said, 'Enter, both of you, the Fire along with the incomers.'*

[66:11] *And God has struck a similitude for those who believe: the wife of Pharaoh when she said, 'My Lord, build for me a home near You in Paradise, and deliver me from Pharaoh and his work, and deliver me from the evildoing folk.'*

[66:12] *And Mary daughter of ʿImrān, who preserved* [*the chastity of*] *her womb, so We breathed into it of Our Spirit, and she confirmed the Words of her Lord and His Books, and she was of the obedient:*] He then explains that natural kinship and formal connections are of no account when it comes to the affairs of the Hereafter, but rather real love and spiritual connections are all that matter. The formal connections of blood, cohabitation and proximity will not have any further effect after death, nor do they take any form in this world except one of the two similitudes described here. The relevant concern regarding the merit of perfection with God is righteous action and true belief, like the chastity of Mary and how she confirmed the Words of her Lord and obeyed Him, which prepared her to receive the breath of God's Spirit into her. The difference between them is that the treacherous soul that does not obey the spirit or the heart, nor lives alongside them amiably or heeds their commands and prohibitions, nor keeps their secrets, but permits that they be defied and lives a life of licentiousness by seeking to usurp the word of Oneness and violating perfection, it will enter the hell of deprivation and the fire of banishment alongside the other veiled ones; and the guidance of the spirit of the heart will not avail it in any way in terms of its punishment, though they will avail it when it comes to the question of perpetually abiding therein. Likewise, the heart languishing under the domination of the evil-enjoining, pharaonic soul, seeking to be free and turning to the Real for refuge, strong in love for God because of its purity but too weak to overcome the heart and Satan because of its incapacity and weakness, it will not remain in punishment forever; but it will be freed from it and admitted into perpetual bliss, though it must be punished therein for a spell and tormented for its deeds for a brief time. Yet the soul that is beautified with the virtue of chastity—alluded to here by the guarding of the womb—is receptive to the emanation of the Holy Spirit, carrying the Jesus of the heart, illuminated by the light of the spirit, confirming the words of the Lord which are doctrines of wisdom and Divine Laws, absolutely obedient to God with knowledge and action, privately and publicly, following the path of Oneness in unification and differentiation, inwardly and outwardly. And God (Exalted is He) knows best.

Q. 66:12

67
THE KINGDOM
SŪRAT AL-MULK

In the Name of God, the Compassionate, the Merciful

[67:1] *Blessed is He in Whose hand is the kingdom (mulk)*: the *mulk* is the realm of bodies, just as the *malakūt* ('dominion') is the realm of souls. This is why He described Himself, with respect to how He directs the realm of the kingdom according to His will, as blessed, since this is the peak of magnificence and the culmination of increase in sublimity and blessing. Likewise, He described Himself with respect to how He bends the realm of dominion to His will as transcendent, such as when He said, *So glory be to Him in Whose hand is the dominion of all things* [Q. 36:83]. They are each appropriate because magnificence, increase and blessing corresponds to bodies, while transcendence corresponds to things that are detached from matter. The meaning of *blessed (tabārak)* is: Sublime and Magnificent is the One Who directs the realm of the kingdom with the hand of His power, and no other has any hand in it; all of the bodies therein are in His hand and no other, and He may direct them as He wills; *and He has power over all things*: the power to bring any non-existent, contingent thing into being as He wills. The divine power makes a thing contingent when it attaches to it, so that it is said to be the object of His power because it is contingent.

[67:2] [*He*] *Who created death and life,* [*that He may try you* [*to see*] *which of you is best in conduct*]: death and life pertain to non-being and habitude (*malaka*), for life is sensation and motion, whether voluntary or involuntary (such as breathing), while death is the absence of this in something that would usually possess it. The absence of habitude is not a pure absence, since there is still a trace of existence in it, for otherwise the potential locus of existence would not be recognised in it, and thus it can be said that He 'created' death just as He did life.

448

The purpose of their creation was to test humanity in terms of good and evil deeds: that is, the knowledge which conforms to its object and is judged and requited accordingly. This is the knowledge that is manifested upon the human loci after the occurrence of its object, for it is nothing other than God's knowledge hidden in the Unseen and manifested by the manifestation of its object. Life is what makes action possible, and death is what inspires and encourages righteous action, and that through which the consequences of deeds are manifested, just as their roots are manifested through life. Through the two of them, souls are arrayed in ranks of virtue and degrees of damnation and salvation. He mentioned death before life because, in the realm of the kingdom, death is essential while life is ephemeral. *And He is the Mighty*: the Overwhelmer Who conquers those who act evilly; *the Forgiving* Who covers those who act righteously with the light of His Attributes.

[67:3] [*He*] *Who created seven heavens in layers.* [*You do not see in the Compassionate's creation any irregularity. Then cast your eyes again: do you see any fissure?*] The culmination of the perfection of the realm of the kingdom is in the creation of the heavens, and you will not see anything with a wiser creation or a more beautiful order or composition than them. He attributes their creation to the Compassionate because they are among the sources of manifest favours and the origins of all other worldly blessings. He negates irregularity in them because of their simplicity and circularity and how each of them conforms to the other, and the beauty of their order and correspondence. He negates any fissure in them because of how they cannot be torn or disharmonised.

Q. 67:3

[67:4] [*Then cast your eyes yet again and your sight will return to you, humbled and wearied:*] the reason He says *cast your eyes yet again* is that repeated regard and reflection solidifies realities in the mind. Since that is their reality, any attempt to find fissures and flaws in them will only result in failure, for it is a wearisome pursuit to seek that which is impossible.

[67:5] *And verily We have adorned the lowest heaven* of the supra-sensory heavens, meaning the human intellect, *with lamps* of arguments and proofs, *and made them missiles against the devils* of estimation and imagination; *and We have prepared for them the chastisement of the Blaze* of veiling in the pit of nature, and perdition in the chasm of corporeal nature and the dark impenetrable isthmus. Or it means the physical heaven that is closer to us than the intellectual one, which He has adorned with the lamps of the celestial spheres and made them missiles to pelt the souls who are distant from the realm of light, because of how their substance has been darkened by association with corporeal coverings. [The] foul substances [of the latter] contradict the holy substances which have been overwhelmed by the darkness of the world and the rusting-over of the heart, and sullied by direct contact with natural desires, and polluted by the impurities of corporeal attachments with which they have mixed, so that benighted configurations have become rooted in them, changing their natures. Then they are affected by the higher bodies whenever they yearn instinctively for their realm. Thereafter they are pelted by the spiritual beings of the celestial spheres and banished to the hell of the lower realm, and forced to dwell among the bodies that correspond to their configurations and the isthmuses that conform to their natures, cast into the torment of the contrariety of natures and the hell of the ascendance of the natures of those coverings.

Q. 67:6

[67:6] *And for those who [disbelieve in their Lord*—those who] are veiled from Him in general, both the devils who are at the extremity of distance, contradiction and evil, and the other weak veiled ones who are not so evil—*there is the chastisement of Hell*: the lower realm which is covered and naturally contrary to the realm of light; *and [what] an evil journey's end* is that dark, burning, ruinous pit!

[67:7] *When they are flung into it they hear it [blaring]* with the voices of its inhabitants which deny and negate the voices of the humans and the spiritual beings, or their own voices as they cry out therein with the sounds of animals with hideous images and vile voices, *as it seethes*: boiling and rising above them, [67:8] *almost exploding with rage*: it almost breaks apart because of how powerfully it is dominated by contrariety and its extreme opposition to the substances of souls. Upon my word, the extreme aversion that natures have for one another engenders extreme enmity and rancour among them that leads to extreme rage and fury; and because of this—the extreme natural contradiction between that pit and the realm of light—the detached substance and the source of the soul's innate disposition will inflame its terrible rage towards them, so that it burns them with the fire of its wrath. May God save us from that! [*Whenever a host is flung into it, its keepers ask them, 'Did there not come to you a warner?'*] Its keepers are the earthly and heavenly souls assigned to the realm of lower nature.

[67:9] [*They will say, 'Yes, a warner did indeed come to us, but we denied and said, "God has not revealed anything; you are assuredly in great error."'*]

[67:10] *And they will say, 'Had we listened or comprehended, we would not have been among the folk of the Blaze.'*

[67:11] *Thus, they will confess their sin. So away with the folk of the Blaze!*]
Their questioning expresses how they bar and prevent them from escaping Hell, because of how they denied the messengers and how their beliefs contradicted their teachings, and how they resisted them and refused to acknowledge God and His Words, and were deaf to the truth and refused to hear it, and how they failed to comprehend God's communications and signs and the proofs of His Oneness. Had they listened and understood, they would have recognised the truth and obeyed, and so been saved and sent to the realm of light and the presence of the Real instead of being the inhabitants of the Blaze.

[67:12] *Indeed, those who fear their Lord [in secret]* by envisaging His magnificence, though they are absent from the witnessing of the Attributes, in the station of the soul by assenting with belief, *there will be for them forgiveness* for the attributes of the soul *and a great reward* of the lights of the heart and the garden of the Attributes. Or those who fear their Lord by observing the attributes of magnificence in the station of the heart, though absent from the essential witnessing, will be forgiven for the attributes of the heart and granted a great reward of the lights of the spirit and the garden of the Essence.

Q. 67:11

[67:13] *[And [whether you] keep secret your speech or proclaim it,]* He indeed *is Knower of what is in the breasts*: for their consciences are none other than His knowledge, and how could He not know their contents when He created them and shaped them and made them the witnesses of His secrets?

[67:14] *[Will He Who has created not know?]* And He is the Subtle Whose knowledge is hidden in them and can penetrate their unseen depths, *the Aware* of what manifests of their states. He encompasses the inner and outer beings of what He created, so in reality He is them inwardly and outwardly [in a sense], and there is no differentiation except through necessity and contingency, absoluteness and delimitation, and the veiling of ipseity with haecceity,[1] and reality with individuality.

[67:15] *It is He Who made the earth* of the soul *tractable for you, so walk* upon the feet on innate disposition *[in its flanks]*, in the heights of its attributes and the glories of its expanses and directions, and subdue it for yourselves; *and eat of His provision* which is attained from its direction, namely knowledge derived from the senses. This is the nourishment from beneath the feet to which He alluded when He said, *They would surely have received nourishment from above them and from beneath their feet* [Q. 5:66]. *And*

1 *Hūwiyya* (literally 'is-ness') and *hādhiyya* (literally 'this-ness') respectively.

to Him is the Resurrection: by ascension to the station of sainthood and the presence of unification.

[67:16] *Are you secure [in thinking] that [He Who is in the heaven]*—He Whose authority dominates the heaven of the spirit and Whose light outshines the sun of the intellect with influence and illumination—*will not cause the earth* of the body *to swallow you*: by turning it and moving it upon you, so that it overwhelms and overpowers you and takes away your light, ruining you and making you the lowest of the low, *while it quakes* and agitates, bereft of stability and tranquillity through divine peace because of its natural state of wavering and agitation?

[67:17] *Or are you secure [in thinking] that [He Who is in the heaven]*—the Sublime All-Conquering One—*will not unleash upon you a squall of pebbles* of the attributes of the soul and its pleasures and desires, which overcome the heart by the winds of caprice in the air of hopes and wishes, destroying you just as were destroyed the deniers whose souls were moved by God's overwhelming power, so that they were veiled by their darknesses from the light of the messengers' guidance, and swallowed up and annihilated? Their situation was certainly incredible, yet they came to see the terrible thing of which they were warned. [*But you will [soon] come to know the nature of My warning.*

[67:18] *And verily those who were before them denied, then [see] how was My rebuttal!*]

[67:19] *Or have they not seen the birds* of gnostic secrets and realities, illuminations and holy meanings *above them* in the heaven of the spirit, *spreading their wings*—their beings which are ordered and arrayed therein—*and closing* from descent to the heart? *Nothing sustains them except the Compassionate*, Who shapes their preparedness and readies their receptivity and places it within them, and arranges them according to the breadth of His vast compassion which envelops all that He creates and measures, and grants each thing its creation. Nor are they sent forth by any but the Merciful, Who emanates perfection to all that He measures according to the preparedness that is manifested for all the meanings and attributes that He ordained in the Unseen. *Indeed, He is Seer of all things* in the treasury of His Unseen, giving them what is apt for them, shaping them according to His will, and placing in them what He wills according to His wisdom, and then guiding them to it by His grace.

[67:20] *Or who is it that will be an army for you*: who is it other than God whose help can be sought, whether limbs, instruments, faculties or any other medium to which influence and aid are attributed, such that it

Q. 67:16

could be called *an army for you to help you besides the Compassionate*, and send to you the inward and outward blessings which He withheld from you, or withhold the supra-sensory and formal blessings which He sent, or attain for you what He denied you and did not destine for you, or deny you what He sent you and destined for you? *Indeed, [the disbelievers]*—the veiled ones whose light of innate disposition is covered—*are in nothing but delusion*: [deluded] by such intermediaries.

[67:21] *Or who is it that will provide for you if He*—the Compassionate—*withholds His provision*, whether supra-sensory or formal? *Nay, but they persist in disdain*, obstinacy and transgression because of how they oppose truth with falsehood, and light with the darkness of their souls, *and aversion* because of the distance of their natures from Him.

[67:22] *Is he who walks cast down on his face*—turning his face towards the lower direction, in love with sensory pleasures and attracted to natural matters—*more rightly guided, or he who walks upright on [a straight path]*: the path of Oneness, which is completely straight in a manner whose nature cannot be known or measured?

Q. 67:21

[67:23] *[Say: 'It is He Who created you and endowed you with hearing and sight and hearts. Little do you thank!'*

[67:24] *Say: 'It is He Who multiplied you on earth, and to Him you will be gathered.'*

[67:25] *And they say, 'When will this promise be [fulfilled], if you are truthful?'*

[67:26] *Say: 'The knowledge is only with God, and I am but a plain warner.'*

[67:27] *But when they see it near at hand, the faces of those who disbelieved will be awry, and it will be said, 'This is that which you used to make claims about.'*

[67:28] *Say: 'Have you considered: if God destroys me and those with me, or has mercy on us, who then will protect the disbelievers from a painful chastisement?'*

[67:29] *Say: 'He is the Compassionate. We believe in Him, and in Him we put our trust. And assuredly you will [soon] know who is in manifest error.'*

[67:30] *Say: 'Have you considered: if your water were to sink deep into the earth, who then will bring you running water?'*] After describing the difference between the two groups—the errant ones and the guided monotheists— He alludes to the Oneness of the Attributes by saying, *Say: 'It is He Who created you'* [Q. 67:23], and invoking His acts of engendering and returning, describing how although the veiled ones acknowledge the engendering, they deny the return, and so it is inevitable that their faces will be awry when they see what they had denied, and that they will be stricken with disappointment. Then indescribably painful torment will come to them, and they will not be protected from it by the things that veiled them from the Real and to which they attributed influence, because those things will be incapable and powerless. Nor will the Compassionate protect them from it, because they did not rely on Him, by bearing witness to how all acts are from Him and how nothing but Him has any influence. They did not believe in Him with true faith, and so He countered their disbelief and idolatry with His Words, *He is the Compassionate. We believe in Him, and in Him we put our trust*: that is, we do not trust in anything but Him, because we have witnessed the presence of undiscriminating compassion from which all things proceed; and our true faith prevented us from attributing any act to anything but Him, and so He will protect us and not you. And God knows best.

Q. 67:30

68
THE PEN
SŪRAT AL-QALAM

In the Name of God, the Compassionate, the Merciful

[68:1] *Nūn. By the Pen and what they inscribe*: the letter *Nūn* signifies the universal soul (*nafs kulliyya*), and *the Pen* signifies the universal intellect. The former is an instance of signifying a word by reference to its first letter, the latter of signifying by similitude, since the forms of beings are inscribed on the soul by the influence of the intellect, just as forms are inscribed on the Tablet by the Pen. What they inscribe are the forms, quiddities and states of things as they are destined to occur. The subjects of the verb *inscribe* are the intermediary intellect-scribes and sanctified spirits, although in reality the Scribe is God Himself; in the presence of the Names, however, the act is attributed to them figuratively. He swears by them and by what issues through them from the principles of existence and the forms of divine decree, and the principle of His command and the treasury of His Unseen, because of their nobility and how they contain everything in existence from the first level of influence and reaction, and how they correspond to the object of the oath, which is:

[68:2] *You are not, by the grace of you Lord, a madman*: your intellect is not covered or impaired when you are in the blessed state of witnessing what is inscribed with them, for no one is more sane than the one who beholds the secret of destiny and perceives the realities of things as they are.

[68:3] *And indeed you will have an unfailing reward* from the lights of witnessing and unveiling from these two worlds, unfailing and uninterrupted because it is perpetual and immaterial and so will never end. Yet those materialists are veiled from it and opposed to you in their state and orientation, which is why they call you mad, for their intellects and minds are confined to material concerns.

[68:4] *And assuredly you possess a magnificent nature*: for you are adorned with the character traits of God and assisted by holy aid. So you are not moved by their insinuations nor harmed by their persecution, for your patience is by God, not by yourself, as He said, *Your patience is only by [the help of] God* [Q. 16:127].

[68:5] *Then you will see and they will see,* when the veil is lifted upon death, [68:6] *which of you is the* true *madman*: whether it is you to whom the secrets of destiny were unveiled and to whom was given the sum of all excellent speech, or they who are veiled from the signs and admonitions of God that are right in front of them, and deluded by the worship of idols.

[68:7] *Indeed, your Lord knows best those who stray from His way, [and He knows best those who are guided]*: He knows the identity of those who are truly mad and veiled from the religion, and those who are sane and guided. No one knows the true nature of their madness and misguidance except for God because of its extremity, and likewise no one knows the true nature of your guidance and that of those who follow your guidance but Him.

Q. 68:5

[68:8] [*So do not obey the deniers.*

[68:9] *They desire that you should be pliable, so that they may be pliable [towards you].*

[68:10] *And do not obey any mean oath-monger,* [68:11] *backbiting, scandal-monger,* [68:12] *hinderer of good, sinful transgressor,* [68:13] *coarse-grained, moreover ignoble,* [68:14] *[only] because he has wealth and sons.*

[68:15] *When Our signs are recited to him, he says, 'Fables of the ancients!']* Do not conform to them outwardly, just as you do not conform to them inwardly, for outward conformity has an effect on inward conformity; and the same is true for divergence, since otherwise it would be a short-lived hypocrisy and an ephemeral affectation. As for them, they are so engrossed in vices and immersed in variegation and inconstancy—because of their divergent caprices, scattered hopes, biased faculties and multifaceted souls—that they put on an act, adding one more vice to their list of many, hoping to fool you into affecting a false camaraderie with them. Do not allow yourself to be deceived by the wealth of the wealthiest of them and his many relatives and followers, so that you obey him and affect camaraderie with him despite his many vices. Continue to keep your outward aspect in conformity with your inward, enriched by God and content in Him, true to those who believe in you, amiable to those who accord with you, friendly to your faithful companions who are ascetic in this world.

[68:16] *We shall brand him on the snout*: We shall change his face at the

Minor Resurrection and make the instrument of his avarice conform to the shape of the configuration of his soul, like the trunk of an elephant for example, and transform the noblest part of his body to a mark of the utmost humiliation because of the disgrace of his soul, which is attracted to the lower direction and in turn attracts base matter to itself.

[68:17] *Indeed, We have tried them, just as We tried the owners of the garden, when they vowed that they would pluck [its fruit] in the morning.*

[68:18] *And they did not make any exception.*

[68:19] *Then a visitation from your Lord visited it while they slept.*

[68:20] *So by the morning it was like the darkness of night.*

[68:21] *They then called out to one another in the morning,* [68:22] *[saying],* 'Go forth early to your tillage if you are going to pluck.'

[68:23] *So off they went, whispering to one another,* [68:24] *'No needy person shall today come to you in it.'*

[68:25] *And they went forth early, able to prohibit.*

Q. 68:17

[68:26] *But when they saw it, they said, 'Indeed, we have strayed!*

[68:27] *'Nay, but we have been deprived!'*

[68:28] *The most moderate among them said, 'Did I not say to you, "Why do you not glorify?"'*

[68:29] *They said, 'Glory be to God, our Lord! Indeed, we have been wrongdoers.'*

[68:30] *They then turned to one another, blaming each other.*

[68:31] *They said, 'O woe to us! We have indeed been unjust.*

[68:32] *'It may be that our Lord will give us in its place one that is better than it. Truly we turn humbly to our Lord.'*

[68:33] *Such will be the chastisement; and the chastisement of the Hereafter is assuredly greater, did they but know.*

[68:34] *Verily for the God-fearing there will be the gardens of Bliss near their Lord.*

[68:35] *Are We then to treat those who submit [to Us] as [We treat] the sinners?*

[68:36] *What is wrong with you? How do you judge?*

[68:37] *Or do you have a Book, wherein you learn,* [68:38] *that you will indeed have in it whatever you choose?*

[68:39] *Or do you have oaths, binding on Us until the Day of Resurrection that you will indeed have whatever you decide?*

[68:40] *Ask them, which of them will aver that?*

[68:41] *Or do they have partners? Then let them produce their partners if they are truthful.*

[68:42] *The day when the shank is bared*: remember the day when things will intensify beyond the limits of description, because of the parting from corporeal familiarities and sensory pleasures, and the emergence of

457

psychological horrors and pains by means of terrifying configurations and offensive forms; *and they are summoned*, by the voice of the dominion through primal affinity and innate correspondence, *to prostrate themselves* in an expression of surrender and submission to receive the divine lights and glorious illuminations, *but they will not be able* to submit and surrender to receive them because their original preparedness will have been erased by benighted configurations, and they will have become veiled by corporeal coverings and garments of primordial matter.

[68:43] *With humbled gazes*—humiliated and bewildered because of how their luminous faculties have departed, and they are unable to look towards the realm of light, and how distant they are from perceiving the rays that bring happiness—*they will be overcast by abasement*: reliant on lower things, mired in the degradation of reactive things and adherence to natural things. *For they had indeed been summoned*, when their preparedness yet remained and they had the necessary instruments, *to prostrate themselves* out of submission by the configuration of preparedness to receive support from the realm of lights, *while they were yet sound* of preparedness and able to attain salvation in the Hereafter.

Q. 68:42

[68:44] [*So leave Me [to deal] with those who deny this discourse. We will draw them on by degrees, whence they do not know.*

[68:45] *And I will grant them respite. Indeed, My devising is firm.*

[68:46] *Or are you asking them a fee, so that they are weighed down with debt?*

[68:47] *Or do they possess [access to] the Unseen, so that they are writing down?*]

[68:48] *So await patiently the judgement of your Lord*: for the felicity of the felicitous, the damnation of the damned, the salvation of the saved, the ruin of the ruined, the guidance of the guided, and the error of the errant; *and do not be like the One of the Whale*—in how the attributes of the soul overwhelmed him and he was overcome by confusion and irascibility, and veiled from the rule of the Lord, until he was banished from the holy presence into the abode of nature and gobbled up by the whale of lower nature in the station of the soul, and swallowed up for gestation in the belly of the whale of the womb—*who called out* to his Lord for his people to be overwhelmed and destroyed because of his extreme wrath in the station of the soul, not by his Lord's permission, *choking with [grief and filled with] rage.*

[68:49] *Had it not been for a* perfect *grace from his Lord that reached him* with guidance to perfection, because a trace of sound preparedness still remained in him and the irascible configuration was not irrevocably rooted in him, and so he was able to repent from the excesses of the soul and detach from its attributes, *he would have surely been cast into the wilderness*, out into the realm of the senses and totally banished from the holy presence to wander the valley of the soul, *while he was blameworthy*: marked by vices and deserving of humiliation and degradation, veiled from the Real, afflicted with deprivation.

[68:50] *But his Lord chose him* for His mercy, because of the soundness of his innate disposition and the remnant of original light in him. Thus, He brought him near to Him and united him with His Essence, by inspiring the word of Divine Oneness in him and connecting him to the station of unification; *and made him one of the righteous*: for the station of prophethood, by placing him upright in the state of subsistence after annihilation in the source of unification. And God (Exalted is He) knows best.

Q. 68:49

69
THE REALITY
SŪRAT AL-ḤĀQQA

In the Name of God, the Compassionate, the Merciful

[69:1] *The Reality!*

[69:2] *[What is the Reality?*

[69:3] *And how would you know what the Reality is?]* The Reality is the Hour which must come to pass without doubt, if it refers to the Minor Resurrection. Or it means the thing that makes all things real, [i.e.] recognised and realised, if it refers to the Major Resurrection. It means, 'The Hour! What is it? What could tell you what the Hour is?' For the first interpretation, this would mean that its intensity and horror and the states that will appear in it cannot be known, while for the second interpretation it would mean that its reality, lofty status, illuminated signs and all that shall appear in it cannot be known by anyone but God. Both Resurrections will alarm humanity and bring about their annihilation and destruction with explosive power and might.

[69:4] *[Thamūd and ʿĀd denied the Clatterer:]* their denial of the first was due to how they cleaved to the world and failed to work for the Resurrection, and were rendered oblivious and deluded by the sensory life. Their denial of the second was due to their lack of knowledge of it, their ignorance of it and how they were veiled from it. The example of the deniers could also be applied to the extremists, whether the extremely negligent or the extremely transgressive, as follows:

[69:5] *As for Thamūd*—the people who lacked water, signifying the people who have outward knowledge but are veiled from the knowledge of realities—*they were destroyed by the [overwhelming] Roar*: the event that uncovered the inward aspect and the world of detachment, crashing upon their knowledge and annihilating it; this means the destruction of the body.

[69:6] *And as for ʿĀd*—the extremists who transgressed the bounds of the Divine Laws with heresy and licentious interpretations of Oneness—*they were destroyed by a [deafening violent] wind*: the caprice of the soul chilled by the cold of nature and the absence of the warmth of passion and yearning, which overwhelmed them and bore them away to the valleys of perdition.

[69:7] *He*—God—*forced it upon them [for seven nights and eight days successively]* in the levels of the Seven Unseens which were nights to them because of how they were veiled from them, and the eight external attributes which were like days for them, namely existence, life, knowledge, power, will, hearing, seeing and speech, according to what was revealed from them and what was within them, cutting them down and obliterating them; *so that you might have seen the people therein lying prostrate*: dead with no real life in them because they lived through the soul instead of God, as He says, *They are like blocks of timber [that have been] propped-up* [Q. 63:4]; *as if they were the hollow trunks of palm-trees*: strong in appearance but devoid of meaning and life, fallen from the rank of relevance and real existence, since they do not live through God.

Q. 69:7

[69:8] *So do you see any remnant of them?* In other words, any subsistence or a remaining soul, for they are entirely annihilated.

[69:9] *And Pharaoh*, the evil-enjoining soul, *and those of his followers*, its faculties and helpers, *and the deviant [cities]*, the spiritual faculties changed from their nature by inclination towards the outward and turned from the intelligible to the sensory, *brought iniquity* in the form of the trait that was error, namely transgression from internalities to externalities.

[69:10] *Then they disobeyed the messenger of their Lord*—the intellect which guides to the truth—*so He seized them with a [devastating] blow*: by drowning them in the sea of primordial matter and the earthquake of the disturbance and destruction of the body's temperament.

[69:11] *Indeed, when the waters* of the flood of primordial matter *rose high, We carried you in the sailing vessel* of the Divine Law, constructed from perfections of knowledge and action.

[69:12] *So that We might make it a reminder for you* of the realm of holiness and the presence of the Real, which is your original home and your true abode, *and that receptive ears might remember it*: in order that preserving ears might safeguard it when they heard it from God at the beginning of disposition and so remain in their dispositional state, instead of forgetting His covenant and Oneness and the secrets He placed in them, by listening to vain speech in this creation and preserving falsehood from Satan and turning away from the presence of the Compassionate. Therefore, when this was revealed, the Prophet (may God bless him and grant him peace) said to ʿAlī (may God grant him peace), 'I asked God to make it your ear, ʿAlī.' For he was the preserver of those secrets, as he said, 'I was born upon innate disposition, and was the first to believe and emigrate.'

[69:13] *Thus, when the Trumpet is blown with a single blast*: this is the first blast to herald death at the Minor Resurrection, since it cannot be interpreted to refer to the Major Resurrection because of how He later says, *As for him who is given his book in his right hand* [Q. 69:19], and the other details which follow. This blast symbolises the influence of the Holy Spirit through the mediation of the spirit of Isrāfīl, who is assigned with the task of removing the spirit from the human form at the moment of death, whereupon the spirit of Azrael seizes it. All of this happens in a single instant, which is why He described it as a single blast.

[69:14] *And the earth* of the body *and the mountains* of the limbs *are lifted and levelled with a single levelling* and made into separate elemental parts, [69:15] [*then, on that day, the [imminent] Event will come to pass,*] [69:16] *and the heaven* of the animal soul *will be rent asunder* and split as the spirit is wrenched from it; *for it will be very frail on that day*: unable to act, move or perceive during the moment of death.

Q. 69:13

[69:17] *And the angels*—the faculties that succour it and give it refuge and support for perception, and whose perceptibles are gathered with it, or by means of which it perceives, or through which its perceptibles are manifested—*will be [all] over its borders*: its sides—which are the spirit, the heart, the intellect and the body—and they will be parted from it and dispersed to the directions from which they came originally. *And above them, on that day, eight will carry the Throne of your Lord*: meaning the human heart. The eight of them who carry it will be the overpowering lights, the lords of the elemental bodies from the archetypal forms, who will carry it together on both sides, the higher and the lower, four bearers on each side at the Resurrection. Therefore, the Prophet (may God bless him and grant him peace) said, 'There are four of them now, but on the Day of Resurrection God will aid them with another four, so there will be eight.' However, those angels will have differing realities according to their differing elemental types. Some say that they will have different forms, and the way they dominate and overwhelm those bodies will make them resemble mountain goats. Others say that they will take the form of mountain goats because of how the bodies resemble mountains, since they will cover them all over their entire surface. Then there are those who say that there will be eight angels with their feet planted in the seven earths and the Throne above their heads, bowing their heads and glorifying. But God knows the realities of these matters best.

[69:18] *On that day you will be exposed* to God, with all the configurations of deeds and forms of acts that your souls harbour. *No hidden thing of yours will remain hidden.*

[69:19] *As for him who is given his book,* the bodily tablet containing the forms of his deeds, *in his right hand,* on his stronger, divine side which is the intellect, so that he rejoices in it and looks to survey his states of goodly configurations and harbingers of felicity, and therefore *he will say, 'Here, read my book!*

[69:20] *'I was truly certain that I would encounter my account,'* because of his faith in the Resurrection, the Gathering, the Reckoning and the Requital.

[69:21] *So he will enjoy a pleasant living*: a true life that is perpetual and eternal, [69:22] *in a lofty Garden* of the gardens of the heart and spirit, [69:23] *whose clusters* of the meanings and realities perceived by the heart and spirit *are in easy reach*: so that whenever they desire them they may have them.

Q. 69:18

[69:24] [*'Eat and drink in enjoyment for what you did in advance in former days.'*]

[69:25] *But as for him who is given his book in his left hand*: on his weaker, egocentric, animal side, so that he feels regret, sorrow and adversity towards those loathsome forms and configurations and all the ugliness which he had forgotten, though God accounted for it all; and he shrinks from them and longs that he had died before them, certain now that all the wealth, power and might that he spent his life acquiring were not benefitting him at all but only harming him, and therefore *he will say, 'O would that I had not been given my book,* [69:26] *and not known what my account were!*

[69:27] *'O would that it had been the [final] end!*

[69:28] *'My wealth has not availed me.*

[69:29] *'My authority has gone from me'*: then the call will come with the voice of glory and authority to the powers assigned to the realm of being and corruption, those heavenly and earthly souls:

[69:30] *'Seize him, then fetter him*: restrain him with the forms that correspond to the configurations of his soul, and confine him in the prison of nature with bodies that prevent him from moving according to his will; [69:31] *then admit him into Hellfire* of deprivation and the fires of pain; [69:32] *then in a chain* of infinite accidents [*whose length is seventy cubits*] *insert him* to be tormented with all manner of chastisements. The number 'seventy' is conventionally used to denote an unfathomably large number, rather than that specific amount.

[69:33] *'Indeed, he never believed in God [the Tremendous]*: all of this is because of his disbelief and veiling from God and His magnificence, and his ardent love for possessions; [69:34] *[and never urged the feeding of the needy;]* [69:35] *therefore, here today he has no [loyal] friend*, because he is alienated even from his own soul, so how could he not be alienated from others? He is repulsive to everyone, even himself.

[69:36] *'Nor any food except pus* emitted by the inhabitants of Hell. We once had a waking vision of them consuming it.

[69:37] *['Which none shall eat but the sinners.']*

[69:38] *So indeed I swear [by all that you see,* [69:39] *and all that you do not see]*: by the outward and the inward of the corporeal and spiritual realms, and by all of existence, inward and outward:

[69:40] *[It is indeed the speech of a noble messenger.*

[69:41] *And it is not the speech of a poet. Little do you believe!*

[69:42] *Nor [is it] the speech of a soothsayer. Little do you remember!*

[69:43] *A revelation from the Lord of the Worlds.*

[69:44] *And had he fabricated any lies against Us,* [69:45] *We would have assuredly seized him by the Right Hand,* [69:46] *then We would have assuredly severed his life-artery,* [69:47] *and not one of you could have defended him.*

[69:48] *And indeed it is a reminder for the God-fearing.*

[69:49] *And assuredly We know that some of you are deniers.*

[69:50] *And assuredly it is a [cause of] anguish for the disbelievers.]*

Q. 69:33

[69:51] *And indeed it is the truth of certitude* (ḥaqq al-yaqīn): that is, pure certitude, [which is] speech issuing from the source of unification; for had it issued from the station of the heart, it would have been the knowledge of certitude (ʿilm al-yaqīn), and had it issued from the station of the spirit it would have been the eye of certitude (ʿayn al-yaqīn). But since it issued from the station of Unity, it was the truth of certitude: that is, pure, certain truth unsullied by any trace of the falsehood that is anything other than it. He attributed the speech first to the Messenger and then to the Real in order to allude to Essential Oneness, and then said:

[69:52] *So glorify the Name of your Lord, the Tremendous*: declare God's transcendence and detachment from the stain of other-than-Him with your essence, which is His Supreme Name that contains all the other Names, so that no variegations from the soul or the heart emerge in your witnessing, veiling you with acknowledgement of duality or I-ness; for then you would be comparing Him, not glorifying Him. And God (Exalted is He) knows best.

70
THE ASCENSIONS
SŪRAT AL-MAʿĀRIJ

In the Name of God, the Compassionate, the Merciful

[70:1] [*A petitioner petitioned an impending chastisement*—[70:2] *which in the case of the disbelievers none can avert*—[70:3] *from God,*] *Lord of the Ascensions*: the ascensions (*maʿārija*) are the ladders that form the stages of ascension from the station of natures to the station of minerals with equilibrium, and then to the station of plants, then to animals, then to humanity through the steps of arrayed transferrals, each above the other. Then there is ascension through the halting-places of wayfaring such as alertness, wakefulness, repentance, contrition and so on, as described by the masters of wayfaring; the halting-places of the soul; and the waterholes of the heart. Then there is ascension through the levels of annihilation in the deeds and the acts to annihilation in the Essence, which are beyond enumeration. With each Attribute He has a ladder, after all those ladders which precede the station of annihilation in the Attributes.

[70:4] *To Him ascend the angels* of the earthly and heavenly faculties in the human being, *and the* human *Spirit*, to His essential, unifying presence at the Major Resurrection, *in a day whose span is fifty thousand years*: that is, long cycles and extended epochs throughout eternity without beginning or end, not that actual number. Note how He said elsewhere about the very same ascension, *Then it ascends to Him in a day whose measure is a thousand years by your reckoning* [Q. 32:5].

[70:5] *So be patient with a graceful patience*: for the chastisement will fall during this extended period.

[70:6] *Indeed, they see it as [being] far off* because they are veiled from it, [70:7] *while We see it [to be] near* and present in the moment. The veiled ones imagine that it is delayed until a future time because of their obliviousness, while We see it as present.

[70:8] *The day when the heaven* of the short-lived, doomed, animal soul *will be as molten silver*, just as He said before that it will turn *crimson like oil* [Q. 55:37]; [70:9] *and the mountains* of the limbs *will be as flakes of wool*: scattered like dust in the wind according to their various colours.

[70:10] *And no friend will inquire about his friend* because of the intensity and gravity of the moment, so that people will be concerned only for themselves and the tribulations that assail them from the configurations of their souls and the terrors of the situation, even though they are visible to one another.

[70:11] [*They will* [*however*] *be made to see them. The guilty one will desire to ransom himself from the chastisement of that day at the price of his children,* [70:12] *and his companion, and his brother,* [70:13] *and his kin that had sheltered him,* [70:14] *and all who are on earth, if it might then deliver him.*]

Q. 70:8

[70:15] *Nay*, this is a denial of this desire for self-ransom and salvation, for he deserves his chastisement because of the configuration of his constituents; hence, because of the correspondence between his soul and Hell, he will be dragged there. *Indeed,* [*for him*] *it will be the Churning Fire* [70:16] *ripping out the scalp.*

[70:17] *It will call him who turned his back and ignored* [70:18] [*and amassed* [*wealth*], *then hoarded* [*it*]]: for the flames of the hell of lower nature call only to those who turn their backs from the Real, and shun the presence of holiness and the realm of light, turning their faces towards the mine of darkness and choosing to devote their love to corrupt, low, benighted substances. Thus, they are attracted by their natures to the material of the fires of nature, which call them and attract them to themselves because of the affinity between them, and then burn them with their spiritual fires which rise over the hearts. How could they be saved from them when they sought them with their natural impulse, and cried out to them with the voice of their preparedness?

[70:19] *Indeed, humanity was created restless*: the soul by its nature is a mine of evil and a refuge of impurity because it is from the realm of darkness. So the one who inclines to it with his heart, and is overcome by the dictate of his constitution and creation, will correspond to lower things and become characterised by the vices that suit them, the lowest of which are cowardice and greed:

[70:20] *When evil befalls him,* [*he is*] *anxious,* [70:21] *and when good befalls him,* [*he is*] *grudging*, because of his love for the body and its comforts, and his pursuit of its desires and pleasures. The reason they are the lowest of them is that they attract the heart to the lowest level of existence. The

466

Prophet (may God bless him and grant him peace) said, 'The most evil attributes a person can possess are anxious greed and shameless cowardice.'

[70:22] *Except those who pray*: man by his constitution and the nature of his soul is a mine of vices, except for those who strive for God as He ought to be striven for, and shed the garments of the soul and transcend its attributes, [namely] the arrived ones who are the people of essential witnessing: [70:23] *those who maintain their prayers*: for witnessing is the prayer of the spirit. In the constancy of their witnessing, they become oblivious to the soul and its attributes and from everything besides the One they witness.

[70:24] [*And those in whose wealth there is an acknowledged due* [70:25] *for the beggar and the deprived*:] the detached ones who detach from their formal and supra-sensory possessions of beneficial and real knowledge, and donate it to deserving recipients who are prepared to pursue it, and to deprived ones who are kept from seeking it by distractions.

[70:26] *And those who affirm* [*the truth of the Day of Judgement*]: the people of proof-based certitude and faithful belief in the states of the Hereafter and the Resurrection; these are the middlemost, the masters of hearts.

Q. 70:22

[70:27] *And those who are apprehensive of the chastisement of their Lord*: the people of fear from the novices in the station of the soul who travel from it by the light of the heart, not those who halt with it; or those who are apprehensive of the chastisement of deprivation and veiling in the station of the heart from among the wayfarers, or of variegation in the station of witnessing, for as long as a remnant of the self remains there cannot be security from veiling, as He says:

[70:28] *Indeed, there is no security from the chastisement of their Lord*.

[70:29] *And those who guard their private parts*: the people of chastity and the masters of chivalry, [70:30] [*except from their wives and those whom their right hands own, for in that case they are not blameworthy;* [70:31] *but whoever seeks beyond that, those are the infringers.*]

[70:32] *And those who are keepers of their trusts*—the intellectual, gnostic secrets to which they were drawn by their innate disposition—*and their covenant* which God took from them in pre-eternity. In other words, those who kept their dispositions sound and did not sully them with natural coverings and egocentric caprices.

[70:33] *And those who give their testimony*, who act according to the knowledge they witness, so that when they witness something they uphold its ruling and proceed according to what they witness, and nothing else.

[70:34] *And those who preserve their prayers*: the prayer of the heart, which is vigilance; or the prayer of the soul, in the literal sense.

[70:35] *Those will be in gardens, honoured* according to their differing levels. The first will be in all three gardens, the middlemost masters of hearts will be in two of them, and the rest will be in the gardens of the soul alone.

[70:36] [*So what is wrong with those who disbelieve that they keep staring towards you* [70:37] *to the right and to the left in droves?*

[70:38] *Does each one of them hope to be admitted into a Garden of Bliss?*

[70:39] *No, indeed! We created them from what they know.*]

[70:40] *For verily I swear by the Lord of the rising-places and the setting-places* of the things He brought into being by raising His light over them, and set in them by His identity with them; or which He annihilated by raising His light over them, and brought into being by setting in them; *that indeed We are able* [70:41] *to replace* [*them*] *with* [*others*] *better than them*: by withdrawing Our light from them and thereby destroying them, and then making it set on others who are better than them, thereby bringing them into being; [*and We are not to be outmanoeuvred.*

[70:42] *So leave them to indulge and to play, until they encounter that day of theirs, which they are promised:*]

[70:43] *The day when they will come forth from the graves* of the bodies, *hastening* to the abode of forms that correspond to their configurations. And God (Exalted is He) knows best.

Q. 70:34

468

71
NOAH
SŪRAT NŪḤ

In the Name of God, the Compassionate, the Merciful

[71:1] [*Indeed, We sent Noah to his people* [*saying*]: '*Warn your people before there comes upon them a painful chastisement.*'

[71:2] *He said, 'O my people, I am indeed a plain warner to you,*] [71:3] *that* [*you should*] *worship God*: by struggle and spiritual discipline in His cause; *and fear Him*: by detaching from everything but Him, even your attributes and essences; *and obey me* with uprightness, [71:4] *that He may forgive you some of your sins*: the sins of the traces of your deeds, attributes and essences, *and defer you, until an appointed term* after which there is no other term, namely annihilation in Oneness. *Indeed, when God's term comes*: when He personally comes to you with death, *it cannot be deferred* by the existence of anything other than Him, for everything but Him will be annihilated, *if only you knew.*'

[71:5] *He said, 'My Lord, I have summoned my people* [*night and day*] in the station of unification, between darkness and light, to Oneness, [71:6] *but my summons has only increased their evasion* because they were materialists and externalists, who could not see any light except corporeal reflections, nor any existence except dark, corporeal substances, and so they were averse to the affirmation of pure, detached light which made their own light seem like darkness.

[71:7] '*And indeed whenever I summoned them, so that You might forgive them* and cover them with Your light, *they* [*put their fingers in their ears and*] feigned deafness to it because of their lack of understanding and the paucity of their preparedness, or its total absence, *and drew their cloaks over themselves*: covering themselves with their own bodily forms and wrapping up in them, because of their intense inclination towards them, attachment to them and veiling by them; *and they persisted* in this and did not resolve to become detached, *and acted in great arrogance*: by allowing the ascendance of the attributes of their souls and the dominance of their irascibility.

[71:8] *'Then indeed I summoned them aloud*: I descended from the station of Oneness and called them to the station of the intellect and the realm of light.

[71:9] *'Then assuredly I proclaimed to them* with external intelligibles, *and I confided to them [secretly]* in the station of the heart with internal secrets, so that they would reach them by means of intelligibles.

[71:10] *'I said, "Ask your Lord for forgiveness*: ask that your Lord cover you with His light, so that your hearts become illuminated, and divine realities and secrets of the Unseen are revealed to you. [*Indeed, He is ever Forgiving.*]

Q. 71:8

[71:11] *'"He will release the heaven* of the spirit *for you in torrents*: showers of gifts and states, [71:12] *and furnish you with wealth* of acquisitions and stations, *and sons* of holy assistance from the realm of dominion, *and assign to you gardens* of the Attributes in the station of the heart, *and assign to you rivers* of knowledge.

[71:13] *'"What is wrong with you that you do not hope for dignity from God*: esteem that dignifies you with ascension through the levels to the realm of lights, [71:14] *when verily He created you in stages*: each stage nobler than the last, so that your state continued to improve and grow nobler the more you ascended? Why do you not use the visible world as an analogue for the invisible world, and the sensory for the intelligible, and the past for the future, and thereby ascend to the heaven of the spirit on the ladder of the Divine Law, knowledge and action, just as you ascended through the stages of creation on the ladder of nature, wisdom and power?

[71:15] *'"Have you not seen how God created seven heavens in layers* of the levels of the aforementioned Seven Unseens, layered atop one another, [71:16] *and made the moon* of the heart *therein as a light* in addition to the light of the soul and the stars of the faculties, *and made the sun* of the spirit *as a lamp* of dazzling brightness?

[71:17] *'"And God has caused you to grow from the earth* of the body.

[71:18] *'"Then He will make you return into it*: by your inclination towards it and your donning of the garb of its passions and pleasures, and by the corporeal configurations of your souls and coverings of primordial matter, *and bring you forth* from it at the Resurrection in the station of the heart upon voluntary death.

[71:19] *'"And God has made the earth a flat [open] expanse for you, [71:20] so that you may follow* the paths of the senses *throughout it spacious routes"*:

[meaning] broad tracks; or from its direction, the paths of the heaven of the spirit to Oneness, as the Commander of the Believers (may God grant him peace) said, 'Ask me about the roads of heaven, for I know them better than the roads of the earth.' He meant the roads that lead to perfection, the stations and states, such as asceticism, worship, reliance, contentment and the like. This is why the Ascension of the Prophet (may God bless him and grant him peace) had to be bodily.

[71:21] [*Noah said, 'My Lord, they have disobeyed me*] *and followed those whose wealth and children only add to their loss*: their leaders whom they followed, the folk of wealth and might, the ruined ones who were veiled from the Real having lost the light of their preparedness, by being veiled by them and by their children and followers; or the ones veiled by the wealth of knowledge acquired through the satanic intellect tainted by estimation, and the results of their ideas, which led them to love of the body and wealth.

[71:22] [*'And they have devised a mighty plot*, [71:23] *and have said,*] *"Do not abandon your gods*, [*and do not abandon Wadd nor Suwāʿ, nor Yaghūth and Yaʿūq and Nasr"*]: the objects of your worship to which you came to be devoted through your caprice: the Wadd of the body which you worshipped and loved for your passions, the Suwāʿ of the soul, the Yaghūth of the family, the Yaʿūq of wealth, and the Nasr of avarice.[1]

[71:24] [*'And they have certainly led astray many. And do not* [*O God*] *increase the evildoers except in error!'*

[71:25] *Due to their iniquities*, their deeds which contradicted what is right, *they were drowned* in the sea of primordial matter, *then made to enter a Fire*: the fire of nature. [*And they did not find for themselves besides God any helpers*.

[71:26] *And Noah said, 'My Lord, do not leave from among the disbelievers a single dweller upon the earth.*]

[71:27] *'Indeed, if You leave them, they will lead Your servants astray, and will beget only disbelieving profligates*: he grew weary of calling his people and was overcome with sorrow and anger. So he called upon his Lord to destroy them and overwhelm them, judging according to the outward appearance of the situation: that a veiled man overwhelmed by disbelief will only beget another like him, for the drop issued from the foul, veiled soul and raised by its benighted configuration will only become another soul like it, just as a seed only grows into the species and variety

Q. 71:21

---

1 These names refer to various Arabian pagan gods.

of plant from which it came. However, he overlooked the fact that the son is the secret of his father, meaning the state of his that dominates his inner being. Therefore, a disbeliever can still retain sound preparedness and pure innate disposition within him—a pure root according to innate preparedness—even while his outer being is dominated by the custom and religion of his forefathers and the people among whom he was raised, so that he followed their religion outwardly but his inner being was sound. Thus, he might beget a believer in his luminous state, just as the father of Abraham begat him (may God grant him peace). Without doubt, his inner being was overcome by this irascible, benighted configuration and it veiled him [Noah] in the moment he uttered these words such that the substance of his son Canaan was begotten; and this was the consequence of the sin of his state.[1]

Q. 71:28

[71:28] *'My Lord, forgive me*: cover me with Your light by annihilation in Oneness, [*and my parents*:] my spirit and soul, which are the parents of the heart, *and whoever enters my house*: my station in the presence of holiness, *as a believer* with practical affirmation of Oneness, *and* [*the believing men and believing women*]: the spouses of those who believe in me, which are their souls—deliver them to the station of annihilation in Oneness; *and do not increase the evildoers* who squandered their fortune, by becoming veiled by the darkness of their souls from the realm of light, *except in ruin'*: by drowning in the sea of primordial matter and total veiling. And God (Exalted is He) knows best.

---

1 See Kāshānī's explanations of Q. 11:42–3 and Q. 11:45–6 for further discussions on Canaan and Noah's relation to him. [Ed.]

72

THE JINN
SŪRAT AL-JINN

In the Name of God, the Compassionate, the Merciful

[72:1] [*Say: 'It has been revealed to me that a company of the jinn listened, then said, "We have indeed heard a marvellous Qur'ān, [72:2] which guides to rectitude. Therefore, we believe in it and we will never associate anyone with our Lord*:] as has been discussed, there exist powerful, earthly souls which do not share the coarseness, density and lack of perception of predatory and bestial souls, nor the configurations and preparednesses of human souls so that they are attached to dense bodies and dominated by earthliness, nor the purity and subtlety of detached souls so that they are connected to the higher realm. These [powerful, earthly souls] detach from, or attach to, certain heavenly bodies pertaining to the bodies of subtle elements dominated by the nature of air, fire or smoke, according to their differing states. Some of the sages called them 'suspended forms'. They possess knowledge and perception akin to our own, but their natural proximity to the heavenly dominions allows them to receive some knowledge of the Unseen from there. Thus, it is not beyond the realm of possibility for them to ascend to the horizon of heaven and steal a listen to the discourse of the angels, [i.e.] the detached souls. However, since they are earthly and weak compared to the heavenly faculties, they are pelted by the power of those faculties and prevented from reaching them to perceive the full extent of their knowledge. Nor is it far-fetched that their smoke-based bodies might be ignited by the rays of the celestial bodies and burn up, or be prevented from ascending to the horizon of heaven and forced to descend. Indeed, such things are not beyond the realm of possibility, and the truthful people of unveiling and witnessing from among the prophets and saints have spoken of them, not least the most perfect of them, our prophet Muḥammad (may God bless him and grant him peace).

If you would like a spiritual correspondence for this, then know that when the heart is prepared to receive revelation and the discourse of the Unseen, the egocentric faculties of imagination, estimation, thought, discursive and practical intellect, and all the other inward perceptions, which are the jinn of the human being, listen in on it. And since the divine discourse that visits the heart by means of the Holy Spirit shares an affinity of type with discourse that is created and communicated by thought and imagination, or composed of intellectual analogies and estimative and imaginative premises, they said, *We have indeed heard a marvellous Qur'ān, which guides to rectitude*: that is, to what is right. This was how they were affected by the light of the spirit and invigorated by the meanings of the revelation, illuminated by its light, and how they in turn affected the other faculties—the irascible, appetitive and all the other corporeal faculties. *Therefore, we believe in it*: we are illuminated by its light and guided to the presence of holiness; *and we will never associate anyone with our Lord*: we will not liken Him to any of the things we perceive, thereby comparing Him to other-than-Him, but rather we will share the secret of orientation towards the presence of Unity. Nor will we plummet towards the realm of multiplicity to worship passions through the soul's caprice, or seek its desires from the realm of baseness, thereby worshipping other-than-Him.

Q. 72:3

[72:3] *'"And [we believe] that exalted be the majesty of our Lord* beyond our imagining Him as a perceptible thing restricted by a modality, such that He could be categorised in a type; *He has taken neither spouse* from a type beneath Him, *nor a son* of a type like His own.

[72:4] *'"And that the foolish among us*, which is estimation, *used to utter atrocious lies against God*: by imagining that He exists in a physical place and treating Him as a class of beings subject to material contexts, as though He resembled created things in class or type.

[72:5] *'"And we thought that* the *humans* of the external senses *and* the *jinn* of the internal faculties *would never utter a lie against God* concerning what they perceived of Him. We imagined that sight could perceive His shape and colour, and that hearing could perceive his voice, and that estimation and imagination could estimate and imagine Him as He truly is, before our guidance and illumination; but then we learned from revelation that nothing can perceive Him, but rather He perceives all things, and perceives what they perceive and what they perceive not.

[72:6] *'"And that certain individuals of humankind used to seek the protection of [certain individuals of the jinn:]* the external faculties used to rely on the internal faculties and draw strength from them, *so that they increased them in oppressiveness*: the coverings of forbidden things and indulgence in prohibited deeds, because of estimative impulses, appetitive and irascible whims, and egocentric thoughts.

[72:7] *"And they thought just as you thought*—before becoming illuminated by the light of guidance—*that God would never raise anyone*: that He would not raise the intellect upon them, illuminated by the light of the Divine Law, to refine, purify and educate them in matters of virtuous conduct, and so they did whatever they desired according to their natures, and followed their instincts and caprices, not bothering with any discipline or effort.

[72:8] *"And we made for the heaven*: we sought the heaven of the intellect to benefit from its perceptions in order to reach our own pleasures, and to steal any of them that could help us attain our desires, just as it was before we were educated by the Divine Laws; *but we found it filled with mighty guards*: meanings that barred us from reaching our goals, and powerful wisdoms that prevented us from attaining our desires; *and meteors*: holy lights and illuminations that prevented us from perceiving the meanings that were purified from the pollutants of estimation, and from reaching the plain of the intellect illuminated by the light of holiness; for until it became guided, the intellect was sullied by estimation, halted near the horizon of imagination and thought, restricted to attaining a livelihood as befitted the soul and its faculties. Then when it became illuminated by the light of holiness, it went far beyond the halting-places of the faculties and the limits of their knowledge and perception. This is the meaning of His Words:

Q. 72:7

[72:9] *"And we used to sit in [certain] places therein to listen in; but anyone listening now will find a meteor lying in wait for him*: that is, a light of the dominion and an intellectual proof, which expels us from the intellectual horizon and protects the intellect from inclining to the soul and mixing with us, lest it descend to the places to which we ascended, such that we could acquire analogical opinions from it that would lead to the body's indulgence and the soul's safety.

[72:10] *"And we do not know whether ill is intended for those who are in the earth*: the faculties in the earth of the body, so that they remain in struggle and discipline, denied their pleasures, veiled from their desires and wants, *or whether their Lord intends*, by means of legal rulings, religious prohibitions and moral requirements, *for them good*: uprightness and rectitude and all that is good for them; for the purpose of the Divine Law and the perfection of the soul are beyond the reach of the perception of these faculties.

[72:11] *"And that among us some have become righteous*, such as the faculties that manage the affairs of livelihood and the body's welfare, *and some of us are otherwise*: the corrupting faculties such as estimation, irascibility and appetite, which conform to the soul's caprice, and the middlemost ones such as the vegetable and natural faculties; *we are [made up of] [different sects]*: contrasting ways of life, each with its own path and direction which God assigned and entrusted to it.

[72:12] *"And we assume [that we will never be able to elude God in the earth, nor will we be able to elude Him by fleeing]*: we are certain that God is ascendant over us and we could never outdo Him, confined as we are to the earth of the body and unable to flee to the heaven of the spirit. We cannot even resist one another, never mind the Creator of all faculties and powers.

Q. 72:11

[72:13] *"[And that when we heard] the guidance*: the Qur'ān, *[we believed in it]* and we were illuminated by it, and we expressed our belief in it by obeying its commandments and prohibitions, just as he (may God grant him peace) said, 'Everyone has a devil, but my devil submitted [to God] at my hands.' *[For whoever believes in his Lord] shall not fear [loss nor oppression]*: he shall not fear that any of the rights and perfections that were destined for him will be denied him, nor any of his fortunes; for even when the soul becomes tranquil and its faculties are illuminated, so that it does not vie with the inner secret or seek to dominate the heart, it is not denied its fortunes, but rather given them in full, so that it and its faculties can draw strength from them to obey God and engage in divine acts in the state of uprightness, just as the Prophet (may God grant him peace) indulged his soul by marrying nine women and enjoying other things. Nor shall he fear the oppression of humiliation and the domination of discipline. Or he shall not fear the loss of perfection nor the oppression of any vice, or the attachment of any tormenting configuration leading to deprivation and banishment.

[72:14] *"And that among us some have submitted*: yielding to obedience of the heart and the command of the Lord by nature, such as the intellect, *while some of us are unjust*: transgressing beyond the path of rectitude, such as the estimation. *So whoever [has submitted]*: yielded and deferred, *those are the ones who seek right guidance* and uprightness.

[72:15] *"And as for [those who are unjust]*: the transgressors, *they will be [firewood for Hell]!"'* [Meaning] fuel for the hell of corporeal nature.

[72:16] *And [it has been revealed to me] that if they adopt [the [right] path]*: this is a continuation of the revelation, not the words of the jinn. In other words, if the jinn all become upright and walk the path to the Real, following the inner secret towards Oneness, *We will give them abundant water to drink*: We will provide them with comprehensive knowledge, as was described in connection with Adam's address to the angels.

[72:17] *That We may try them therein*: to test whether they give thanks by acting in accordance with it and using it correctly in ways that please God, or not, as He said elsewhere, *And We tried them with good things* [Q. 7:168]. *And whoever turns away from the remembrance of his Lord* and is stingy with His favour, or uses it for ill deeds and forgets the dues of His favour, *We will admit him into a torturous chastisement*: by means of hard spiritual discipline and deprivation from fortune, until he repents and is upright, or with a painful, contradictory configuration so that he is tormented severely and unbearably.

[72:18] *And* [*it has been revealed to me*] *that the places of prayer*—the station of the perfection of each faculty, namely the configuration of its submission and surrender to the heart, which is its prayer; or the perfection of each thing including the heart and spirit—*belong to God*: the right of God is stamped on that thing; indeed, the Attribute of God is manifested in its locus; *so do not invoke anyone along with God*: by attaining the desires of the soul, worshiping caprice, and seeking pleasures and passions according to your natures, thereby associating partners with God and worshipping them alongside Him.

Q. 72:17

[72:19] *And that when the servant of God*: the heart directed towards the Real with humility and obedience, *rose to invoke Him*: by turning to Him and asking for light from Him, and magnifying and glorying Him, *they were almost upon him in heaps*: crowding around it to dominate and veil it with manifestation and defiance.

[72:20] *He said, 'I invoke only my Lord*: declaring His Oneness, [*and I do not associate anyone with Him'*]: I do not pay regard to anything but Him, lest I become an idolater.

[72:21] *Say: 'Indeed, I have no power to bring you any harm or any good'*: that is, misguidance or guidance, for they come only from God. If He gives me authority over you, you shall be guided by my light; and if not, you shall remain in error. I do not have the power to force you to be guided.

[72:22] [*Say: 'Indeed, none shall protect me*:] this is an emphatic declaration of his lack of power over them. In other words, none shall protect me [*from God*] if either He wills any harm or misguidance upon me by giving you or anyone else power over me; *and I shall never find besides Him any refuge*: [meaning that I shall not find] any place to flee to for protection if He destroys me or torments me by your hands or the hands of any others; and if I do not have the power to benefit, harm, guide or misguide even myself, then how could I do anything for you?

[72:23] *But only* to convey unto you *a communication from God and* convey unto you *His Messages*, the meanings of the revelation and the codes of the Real. In other words, *I have no power* [Q. 72:21] to do that, but only to convey the Messages. *And whoever disobeys God and His Messenger* from among you, not accepting His light of listening to what the messenger of the intellect conveys, *indeed there will be for him the Fire of Hell*—the burning fire of nature—*abiding therein forever* when it comes to dominate him.

[72:24] [*It shall be thus*] *until when they see*—that is, they will be upon it in heaps, crowding around it in an effort to dominate it—*what they are promised* in the Messages, namely the occurrence of the Minor Resurrection with death, the Intermediate Resurrection with the manifestation of the light of innate disposition and the ascendance of the heart over them, or the Major Resurrection with the manifestation of the light of Unity, they will realise their weakness and lack of numbers, and how their fire has faded and gone out, and how their blade has been dulled by the occurrence of any of these three states, and how they cannot support one another because of how totally defeated, incapacitated and annihilated they are. Then *they will know who is weaker in supporters* than the heart, *and fewer in numbers*, even if they almost overwhelmed it by multiplicity and deemed that it was scanty when compared to their numbers; for a single one aided by God is more powerful and numerous: *And verily Our Word has gone beforehand in favour of Our servants, the messengers, that indeed they shall be helped* [Q. 37:171–172]. *If God helps you, then none can overcome you* [Q. 3:160].

[72:25] *Say: 'I do not know if what you are promised is near*: at the Minor Resurrection, namely annihilation and entrance into the hell of nature upon the arrival, because I am unaware of what God has destined; or for the other two Resurrections of voluntary death and true annihilation, because I am unaware of the strength and weakness of preparedness; I do not know if it will occur presently, *or if my Lord has set a* [distant] *length for it.*

[72:26] *'Knower of the Unseen is He alone, and He does not disclose His Unseen to anyone,* [72:27] *except to a messenger of whom He approves*: a messenger of the holy faculty whom He prepared, refined and purified at the primordial disposition. *Then, He despatches before him* on the divine side *and behind him* on the bodily side *watchers*: guardians either from the side of God towards which his face is turned, in which case they are the Holy Spirit and the angelic and lordly lights; or from the side of the body,

Q. 72:23

in which case they are virtuous character traits and luminous configurations attained from the forms of obedience and worship, which guard him from the sabotage of the jinn and then prevent their insinuations, estimations and imaginations from mixing with their gnostic certainties, holy meanings, Unseen inspirations and unveiled realities; [72:28] *so that He may know that they have conveyed [the Messages of their Lord]*: so that His knowledge may be manifested in the loci of the messengers after having been hidden in their preparedness, in order that they are perfected and convey the Messages charged to them as perfectly as they possibly can; *and that He encompasses all that is with them*: meaning the discriminating intellect and the meanings hidden in their disposition in pre-eternity, which He then manifests; *and keeps count of all things'*: He ordains all things with the discriminating intellect, and brings to light total perfection in concentration and differentiation, universally and particularly; or that He ordains the number of all things absolutely in His decree and destiny, universally and particularly. And God (Exalted is He) knows best.

Q. 72:28

479

73

THE ENWRAPPED ONE
SŪRAT AL-MUZZAMMIL

In the Name of God, the Compassionate, the Merciful

[73:1] *O enwrapped one [in your garment]!* O you wrapped in the coverings and garments of the body!

[73:2] *Stand in vigil [through the night, except a little, [73:3] a half of it, or reduce of it a little]*: rise from the sleep of heedlessness and travel the path of God, traversing the plains of the soul and the way-stations of the heart towards God, through the night of the station of the soul and the dominance of nature, except a little for the necessity of rest, eating, drinking and tending to the welfare and needs of the body without which it cannot live. That amounts to *half of it*: that is, half of the entire duration of time in the station of nature, so that a quarter of the full twenty-four hour cycle is for rest, another quarter for the needs of the body. Or reduce of it *a little* if you are one of the strong ones, so that a third remains, a sixth for rest and another sixth for the needs of life.

[73:4] *Or add to it* a little, if you are one of the weak ones, so that it is two thirds: a third for rest, another third for needs, and the final third for engaging with God and travelling His path. *And recite the Qur'ān [in a measured tone]*: differentiate the meanings and realities that are synthesised in your disposition and hidden in your preparedness, by manifesting them and bringing them into the open through spiritual growth and self-purification.

[73:5] *Indeed, [soon] We shall cast on you*: by aiding you with the Holy Spirit and emanating His light upon you, until He brings out the meanings and wisdoms within you into action by force, *a weighty word* of substance and import.

[73:6] *Indeed, rising in the night*—rousing the soul from the station of nature and the slumber of heedlessness—*makes a deeper impression*, in conformity to the heart, *and [sharpens speech]*: speech that issues from knowledge rather than imagination, supposition and estimation.

[73:7] *[For] assuredly during the day* of the station of the heart, when the sun of the spirit rises, *you have extended engagements*: movements and turns within the Divine Attributes and stations of the path that stretch out infinitely.

[73:8] *And mention the Name of your Lord*, which is [a reference to] you: recognise yourself and remember it and do not forget it, lest God forget you, and strive to attain its perfection after recognising its reality; *and devote yourself [to Him with complete devotion]*: devote yourself to God completely by turning away from everything besides Him and relying on Him alone.

[73:9] *Lord of the east and the west*: He whose light has been manifested upon you, rising from the horizon of your being by bringing you into existence, and the Lord of the west who concealed your existence and whose light set in you and was veiled by you; *there is no god* in existence *except Him*; there is nothing in existence to be worshipped but Him; He is the First and the Last, the Manifest and the Hidden; *so take Him for a Guardian*: shed your action and planning by regarding all acts as from Him, so that your affair is entrusted to Him and He plans for you and acts through you as He wills, and you are His executor.

Q. 73:7

[73:10] *And bear patiently what they say*: restrain yourself from worry, agitation and movement towards the pursuit of provision and concern for it, because of what the faculties of your soul whisper to you, and the thoughts of estimation, impulses of desire and instigations of caprice that they send your way, lest they goad you and burden you with your needs; *and part with them* by turning away from them *in a gracious manner* based on canonical and intellectual knowledge, not on caprice and frivolousness.

[73:11] *And leave Me [to deal] with the deniers, those enjoying affluence*: leave them to Me, for they deny the station of reliance and how I see to your needs, because they are veiled from Me by the favours I have granted them—the favours of perception, power and will—and so they sense only by their faculties and powers and do not believe My Words; *and respite them a little* as I wrest from them their power and strength by the self-disclosure of My Attributes, manifesting their incapacity.

[73:12] *[For] indeed with Us are heavy fetters* of the Divine Law and responsibilities, which prevent them from their acts, *and Hellfire* of the flames of the toil of pursuit, [73:13] *and a food that chokes*, by the contradictions of their nature and their duties in place of their fortunes, *and a painful chastisement* of all manner of spiritual disciplines and exertions.

[73:14] *On the day when the earth* of the soul *and the mountains* of its configurations and attributes *will quake*, and crumble, at the ascendance of the lights of self-disclosures over the heart, making them tremble and quiver, *and the mountains will be like heaps of shifting sand* that fade into nothingness. Or: respite them a little as the whirlwinds of the breakdown of temperament and the conflicts of modalities rage; for with Us are fetters of evil configurations and harmful, tormenting forms, and a fire of the flames of nature, and choking food that gives no pleasure from all manner of vile pus, *Zaqqūm* and cactus; and a painful chastisement in those flames and forms, on the day when the earth of the body and the mountains of the limbs will quake at the exit of the spirit and the pangs of death, and the mountains will crumble into shifting sand. And God knows best.

Q. 73:14

74

THE ENVELOPED ONE
SŪRAT AL-MUDDATHTHIR

In the Name of God, the Compassionate, the Merciful

[74:1] *O enveloped one [in your mantle]!* O you dressed in the garb of the body, veiled by its form!

[74:2] *Arise* from that on which you have come to lean, and the occupations of nature which you have come to wear, and wake from the slumber of heedlessness; *and warn* your soul and faculties as well as all others of the chastisement of a terrible day.

[74:3] *And magnify your Lord*: if you magnify and laud anything, then let it be your Lord alone, and let nothing but Him be magnified in your eyes, and let everything else be belittled in your heart by witnessing His magnificence.

[74:4] *And purify your clothes*: purify your external being first before the purification of your inner being, from impure character traits, vile deeds and blameworthy customs.

[74:5] *And shun [all] defilement*: the defilement of primordial matter which leads to chastisement. Disengage your inner being from material attachments, dark corporeal configurations and benighted, primordial coverings.

[74:6] *And do not grant a favour seeking greater gain*: do not give wealth while you are detached from it to curry favour and seek compensation and great reward from it, for that would amount to being veiled by the favour from the Favourer and having low aspiration. Rather, be sincerely devoted to God alone, and do what you do for the steadfast purpose of being virtuous for Him and for no other reason. This is the meaning of His Words:

[74:7] *And endure steadfastly for the sake of your Lord*. Or it means: do not give what you give through asceticism, obedience, renunciation and detachment with an attitude of mindful munificence, while deeming what you give to be great, for you will become veiled by regard for your virtue and suffer the tribulation of self-satisfaction. The sin of regard for one's own virtue is even worse than the sin of vice, as he (may God grant him peace) said, 'If none of you ever sinned, I would fear for you something worse than sin: self-satisfaction, self-satisfaction, self-satisfaction!' Rather, endure steadfastly to virtue that is sincere for your Lord alone and not for any other motive, and flee from what is a vice by nature and possesses no inherent virtue at all. Do not exult in regarding the beauty of the virtuous soul, but rejoice only in God's grace towards you and be humble and lowly, not proud and self-righteous.

Q. 74:8

[74:8] *For when the Trumpet is sounded,* [74:9] *[that day will be a harsh day* [74:10] *for the disbelievers, not at all easy]*: when the spirit is wrested from the body and the spiritual configurations, formal beauties, pleasures and perceptions are blown from it, so that the vessel from which they are blown is affected by this parting and severing. This refers to the first blast of the Trumpet which heralds death. Or it means that the resurrected body is engraved with the damning configurations it acquired which lead to chastisement, or the beautiful, salvific configurations which lead to reward, in which case it refers to the second blast of the Trumpet heralding the revival, which is more likely. That day will be difficult for the veiled ones in particular, though its ease will be concealed from others, except for the realised ones from the folk of unveiling and eye-witnessing.

[74:11] *[Leave Me [to deal] with him whom I created lonely,* [74:12] *and [then] assigned him ample means,* [74:13] *and sons present [by his side],* [74:14] *and facilitated for him greatly.*

[74:15] *Still he is eager that I should give [him] more.*

[74:16] *Nay, he is indeed stubborn to Our signs.*

[74:17] *[Soon] I shall burden him with a trying chastisement.*

[74:18] *Indeed, he pondered and decided.*

[74:19] *Perish he, how he decided!*

[74:20] *Again, perish he, how he decided!*

[74:21] *Then he contemplated.*

[74:22] *Then he frowned and scowled.*

[74:23] *Then he turned his back in disdain,* [74:24] *and said, 'This is nothing but handed-down sorcery;* [74:25] *this is nothing but the speech of humans.']*

[74:26] *I shall [soon] admit him into Saqar!* This refers back to His Words, *I shall burden him with a trying chastisement (saʿūd)* [Q. 74:17]. The word *saʿūd* means an obstacle that is difficult to climb over. It is related that the

Prophet (may God bless him and grant him peace) said that it is a mountain of fire which such a person must climb for seventy years, and then
fall from it for the same duration, repeating this forever. And God knows
best, but it may be an allusion to the mountain of the soul which is its
highest peak, namely its horizon which is beside the human disposition.
He must climb it for many long years through the forms of chastisement
and isthmuses of veiling, being ruined and burned therein, as he (may
God grant him peace) said, 'He is burdened with the task of climbing
a mountain of fire. Every time he places his hand upon it, it melts; and
when he lifts it, it returns. Every time he places his foot upon it, it melts;
and when he lifts it, it returns. Then he plummets from it to the deepest
depth.' Just so, he moves from one level to another through manifold
isthmuses for eternity. This climb is the *Saqar* of nature, from its highest
level to its deepest depth.

[74:27] [*And how would you know what is Saqar?*]

[74:28] *It neither spares nor leaves behind*:] I shall admit him into it, and
nothing will remain therein without being destroyed and annihilated;
and when he is destroyed, it will not leave him destroyed, but will bring
him back and destroy him again and again in perpetuity.

[74:29] *It burns away the flesh*: it changes the externalities of bodies to
the colour of the blackness of their sins and the configurations of their
misdeeds. This is one of the special properties of that fire, just as corporeal
fire changes colours and configurations.

[74:30] *There are nineteen [keepers] standing over it*: they are the earthly
angelic powers that accompany matter—the spiritual beings of the seven
celestial spheres and the twelve constellations—assigned to manage the
lower world and influence it. They will scourge them with whips of influence and return them to its torments.

[74:31] *And We have appointed only angels as wardens of the Fire* because
of their dominating and conquering power, for the realm of the kingdom
is under the compulsion and power of the realm of the dominion; *and
We have made their number only [as a stumbling-block for those who disbelieve]*:
to test and chastise the veiled ones and increase their veiling and doubt,
*so that those who were given the Book may be certain, and that those who believe
may increase in faith, [and that those given the Book and the believers may not be
in doubt]*: so that those who were given the book of the discriminating
intellect may be certain, and that those who believe with faith of certain knowledge may increase in faith by unveiling and eye-witnessing,
in order that they do not doubt like the ignorant ones who suffer from

simple ignorance and the veiled ones; or so that the blind-faith believers who were given the Book may become certain, and that the realised ones may increase in realisation and not doubt like the ignorant ones who have no belief at all, whether blind faith or realisation; *and that those in whose hearts there is a sickness* of hypocrisy or doubt, the ignorant ones who suffer from simple ignorance, *and the disbelievers*, the ones veiled by their corrupt doctrines who suffer from compound ignorance, *may say, 'What did God mean by this* incredible and unusual *similitude?'* In other words, We only mentioned their number, and made them that way, in order for it to be a cause for the manifestation of the error of the errant and the guidance of the guided, just like all the other means that cause the error of those who err and the guidance of those who are guided. *Thus,* in this way, *God leads astray whom He will* of the folk of original damnation *and guides whom He will* of the folk of pre-eternal salvation. *And none knows the hosts of your Lord*—their numbers, quantities, modes and realities—*except Him*, because His knowledge encompasses all quiddities and states. *And it*—meaning *Saqar*—*is nothing but a reminder for humans*: this refers back to His Words, *I shall [soon] admit him into Saqar*, and completes the description of it, while His Words *And We have appointed only angels…except Him* are a digression concerning the *Zabāniya*.

Q. 74:32

[74:32] *Nay* is a denial of it being a reminder to them all in an absolute sense, since most of them are unprepared, heart-sealed and destined for damnation, and so they will not pay any heed to it. Then He swears *by the moon*, meaning by the heart that is prepared, pure and receptive to the warning, and so pays heed to it and benefits from the reminder, by way of expressing esteem for it.

[74:33] *And by the night* of the soul's darkness *when it departs*: when its darkness is removed from the heart by the shining of the spirit's light upon it and the radiance of its rays.

[74:34] *And by the dawn when it appears*: the dawn of the rising of that light when it appears, so that the darkness is entirely banished and the heart is illuminated.

[74:35] *Indeed, it is one of the enormities*: the *Saqar* of nature is one of the great calamities, unique and without counterpart among them. This is akin to the expression, 'He is a man among men' or 'She is a woman among women,' meaning unique among them.

[74:36] *A warning to humans*: [74:37] [*to those of you who wish to advance or linger behind*:] a unique warning to them, yet not to all of them but to those who are prepared and receptive, so that if they willed they could advance to the station of the heart and spirit by acquiring virtues, merits and perfections, or likewise if they willed they could regress by inclining to the body and its passions and pleasures, thereby falling into it.

[74:38] *Every soul is held to ransom [by what it earns]*: held captive before God, unable to escape because of the dominance of the configurations of its deeds and the effects of its actions upon it, which adhere to it and cannot be separated from it; [74:39] *except the folk of the right hand*: the saved ones who detached from corporeal configurations and devoted themselves to the station of innate disposition, thereby freeing themselves from their captivity.

[74:40] They shall be *in gardens* from among the gardens of the Attributes, *questioning one another* [74:41] *about the guilty*: for they will be able to see their state, enquiring as to how they came to be chastised and kept in the *Saqar* of nature. The ones they ask will reply by questioning them about their states, saying:

[74:42] *'What has landed you in Saqar?'*

[74:43] *They will say* with the voice of state, or with real words, [*'We were not of those who prayed.*

[74:44] *'Nor did we [ever] feed the needy.*

[74:45] *'And we used to delve along with those who delved,* [74:46] *and we used to deny the Day of Judgement*:] such were our vices. We preferred bodily comforts, loved wealth, neglected worshipful action and comportment and spiritual discipline, indulged in false talk, ridicule and idiocy, and denied the Reckoning and the Resurrection.

Q. 74:38

These are the vices of the three faculties which lead to immersion in the fire of primordial nature.

[74:47] *'Until [finally] the inevitable came to us'*: that is, death, when at last we saw with our own eyes what we had denied before.

[74:48] *Thus, the intercession of the intercessors will not avail them*, whether the intercession of a prophet or an angel, even if it were offered to them, for they will be unable to receive it; but in any case, no permission to intercede will be given, and so there will be no intercession or avail. Intercession at that time will be the emanation of light and succour, and this is only possible when the locus for it is pure enough to receive it.

[74:49] [*So what is wrong with them that they turn away from the Reminder*, [74:50] *as if they were wild asses* [74:51] *fleeing from a lion?*

[74:52] *Nay, but everyone of them desires to be given unrolled scrolls.*

[74:53] *No, indeed! Rather, they do not fear the Hereafter.*

[74:54] *No, indeed! Assuredly it is a Reminder.*

[74:55] *So whoever wills shall remember it.*

[74:56] *And they will not remember unless God wills [it]. He is [the One] worthy of [your] fear, and [the One] worthy to forgive:*] He then describes why they are unable to receive this or benefit from intercession, which is that they turned away from the Reminder with hearts as foolish as the hearts of wild asses, harbouring vainglorious hopes because of their obstinacy, stubbornness and lack of fear of the Hereafter, which is due to their absence of faith; and all of this is by God's will and ordainment. And God (Exalted is He) knows best.

Q. 74:55

75

THE RESURRECTION
SŪRAT AL-QIYĀMA

In the Name of God, the Compassionate, the Merciful

[75:1] [*Nay, I swear by the Day of Resurrection.*

[75:2] *And, nay, I swear by the self-reproaching soul:*] He swears by the Resurrection and the self-reproaching soul together to stress their monumental importance and the correspondence between them; for the self-reproaching soul is the soul that believes in the Resurrection and is certain that it will come to pass, and is readying itself to meet it. It constantly reproaches itself for its shortcomings and failures to do good, even if it is virtuous, because it always strives to be better and to do more righteous deeds, certain as it is of the requital. Naturally, its self-reproach is even more severe when it errs and slips into moments of heedlessness and forgetfulness. He omitted the main clause of the oath because it is implied by His Words:

[75:3] *Does man suppose that We shall not assemble his bones?* In other words, you shall certainly be resurrected. These Words also make it clear that the Resurrection meant here is the Minor one.

[75:4] *Yes, indeed! We are able to reshape [even] his fingers:* to remake his bodily constitution with all its extremities, exactly as they were. Some of the exoteric commentaries say that it means: We are able to reshape his fingers so that they are stuck fast to one another as though they are a single object, like the hoof of a donkey or the pad of a camel.

[75:5] *Nay, but man desires [to deny what lies ahead of him:* he desires] to continue in his iniquity through inclination to corporeal pleasures and bestial passions, plunging his head into them for the time that lies ahead of him, both the present and the future; and so he is oblivious to the Resurrection, because his gaze does not reach as far as it should due to his absorption and excessive indulgence in immediate gratifications, which veil him from the long-term future. Thus, he asks about it incredulously and scornfully:

[75:6] [*He asks,*] *'When is the Day of Resurrection?'*

[75:7] *But when the eyes are dazzled*—bewildered and shocked by the panic of death— [75:8] *and the moon* of the heart *is eclipsed* because the light of the intellect leaves it, [75:9] *and the sun* of the spirit *and the moon* of the heart *are brought together* and made into a single thing that rises from the west of the body, no longer having two separate levels as it was during life, but now united into a single spirit, [75:10] *on that day humanity will say, 'Where is the escape?'* He will look for a place to flee and seek refuge.

[75:11] *No, indeed!* But his search for escape will be rebuffed. *There is no refuge.*

[75:12] *On that day the recourse will be to your Lord*: the abode of Hell or Paradise will be decided by Him alone and no other. Or the destination will be with Him and the return to Him, as He says elsewhere, *Indeed, to your Lord is the return* [Q. 96:8].

[75:13] *On that day man will be informed of what he has sent ahead* of the righteous good deeds of his that necessitate salvation and reward, *and left behind*: by being negligent and failing to do them.

[75:14] *Rather, man has insight into his [own] soul*: a clear proof in the form of the configurations of his deeds which are written in his soul and fixed in his essence, and how his limbs will be transformed into the shapes of his attributes, so that there will be no need for him to be informed from outside himself; [75:15] *though he should offer his excuses*: even if he lowered his coverings and hid behind them when he performed those deeds, or even if he proffered his excuses and attempted to defend himself with any kind of justification.

[75:16] *Do not move your tongue with it to hasten it*: humanity is hasty by nature, as He says, *Humanity was created of haste* [Q. 21:37], which is why he prefers instant gratification and is veiled by it from the long-term future. See how, despite your perfect tranquillity and confidence in God, you still act hastily when We convey the revelation to you, thereby manifesting your soul to grasp at it, which is the sin of your state and the veil of your existence. This is the meaning of His Words, *No, indeed! Rather, you [all] love the transitory [life] and forsake the Hereafter* [Q. 75:20–21]. Be not so, and move not your tongue with it, for the manifestation and agitation of your soul is hastiness, when your faculties ought to be calm, your soul absent from the visitation of the revelation, and your heart free of the soul's attributes and purified from its motions.

[75:17] *Indeed, it is for Us to bring it together* within you *and to recite it*: let

Q. 75:6

its gathering in the station of Unity, and your recitation of it therein, be through Us, and become annihilated from your own essence, and enter the source of unification so that you have no existence, remnant, essence or trace.

[75:18] *So when We recite it*—when We bring it into existence at the moment of your annihilation in Us—*follow its recitation*: by returning to the station of subsistence after annihilation and the manifestation of the heart and soul through Me.

[75:19] *Then*, when you enter the station of differentiation, *it is for Us to explain it* and manifest its meanings in your heart and soul, differentiated and elucidated.

[75:20] *No, indeed! Be not hasty! Rather, you [all] love the transitory [life]*: your state is akin to theirs because of your common humanity and the dictate of nature and the restless soul, [75:21] *[and forsake the Hereafter]*.

[75:22] *Some faces on that day will be radiant*: illuminated by the light of holiness and connection to the realm of light, grace and perpetual bliss, basking in the beauty of their gnostic secrets and configurations, made radiant by the radiance of their essences, traversing the paths of the realms of the dominion and power; [75:23] *looking upon their Lord*: beholding only the presence of the Essence, turned expectantly towards perfect mercy in the station of the lights of the Attributes. Or radiant by His light, looking upon His countenance and beholding Him alone without looking to anything but Him, witnessing the beauty of His Essence and the rays of His countenance, or looking upon the beauty of His Attributes without being distracted by anything but Him.

Q. 75:18

[75:24] *[And other faces on that day will be]* scowling, because of the gloominess of its configurations and the darkness of the fires and flames therein, and all the terrors and forms of chastisement and torment that they will behold therein, [75:25] *certain that a spine-crushing calamity will fall on them*: a disaster that will break the back because of its severity and the vileness and awfulness of its state. What a difference between these two conditions! And God (Exalted is He) knows best.

76
MAN
SŪRAT AL-INSĀN

In the Name of God, the Compassionate, the Merciful

[76:1] *Has there [ever] been for man a period of time in which he was a thing unmentioned?* In other words, there certainly has been such a time: he was unmentioned in the sense that he was not yet affirmed; he was a thing in God's knowledge and existed objectively because of the beginninglessness of his spirit, but he had not been mentioned among the people since he was in the realm of the Unseen, and the people in the realm of witnessing did not sense him.

[76:2] [*Indeed, We created man from a drop of mixed fluid, so that We may test him. So We made him hearing, seeing.*]

[76:3] *Indeed, We have guided him to the way* of truth with proofs of the intellect and the hearing, *whether he be grateful* and guided by employing the gifts of the senses, instruments and means, as they ought to be employed by performing acts of obedience and using them to reach the Giver, *or ungrateful*: by being veiled as a result of the gifts from the Giver and employing them in a way He does not approve by sinning.

[76:4] *We have assuredly prepared for the disbelievers*—those veiled by gifts—*chains* of inclinations and devotions to corporeal passions, which cause them to be restrained by them and deprived of the true goals, confined in the flames *and fetters* of forms and configurations that prevent motion for the pursuit of the goal, *and Hellfire* of chastisement in the pit of nature and the chasm of deprivation.

[76:5] *Truly the righteous*—the saved ones who emerged from behind the veil of effects and deeds, and were veiled by the veils of the Attributes but did not halt with them, and headed towards the source of the Essence while remaining in the realm of the Attributes, who are the middlemost among the wayfarers—*will drink from a cup whose mixture is Kāfūr* ('camphor'): a cup of love for the beauty of the Attributes whose draught is not pure but rather mixed with the pleasure of the love of the Essence, which is the spring of camphor that provides the bliss of the coolness of certitude and the whiteness of luminescence, and exhilarates and strengthens to the heart that is enflamed with the heat of yearning. Camphor possesses the properties of coolness, whiteness and exhilaration.

[76:6] *Kāfūr is a spring from which the servants of God drink* exclusively: His elites from among the folk of Essential Unity whose love is solely for the Essence and not the Attributes, who do not distinguish between power and subtlety, gentleness and violence, tribulation and ease, but whose love persists through these contrarieties and whose bliss continues through bliss and hardship, mercy and pain. [They are] as the poet said, 'My love for Him must be, whether He is kind or distant; / His draught is sweet whether it is pure or mixed; / I have resigned all my affairs to the Beloved, / Whether He wills that I live or die.' As for the righteous, although they love the Giver, the Subtly Kind, the Merciful, their love does not remain the same upon the self-disclosure of the Omnipotent, the Afflicter, the Avenger, nor does their bliss persist, but rather are averse to it. [So *the servants of God drink,*] *making it gush forth plenteously* because they are identical with its springs and there is no duality or otherness there. Likewise, the camphor of the wrongdoers is the veil and blackness of I-ness and duality.

Q. 76:6

[76:7] *They fulfil their vows and fear a day the evil of which will be widespread*: the righteous uphold the covenant they made with God on the morning of the day of pre-eternity, when they vowed that when they became stable with their instruments and means, they would manifest the realities, gnosis, knowledge and virtues hidden in their preparednesses and dispositions, and bring them into action by means of self-purification and spiritual growth. And they fear the day of the self-disclosure of the Attributes of omnipotence, wrath and vengeance because they are folk of the Attributes; *a day the evil of which will be widespread* to the utmost extent imaginable, by the dominance of benighted configurations and veils that cover the light from the attributes of the soul over the heart, which is the farthest extent of evil.

[76:8] *And they give food, despite [their] love of it [to the needy, and the orphan, and the prisoner]*: they detach from benefits of possession and purify themselves of vices, especially avarice, because love for wealth is the densest veil. Thus, they acquire the virtue of selflessness and give food, despite their own need for it, to satiate the hunger of its rightful recipients, pre-

493

ferring others to themselves. Consider the well-known story of ʿAlī and his household (upon them be blessings and peace) with regards to the revelation of this verse, and how they selflessly helped these three categories of worthy recipients to break the fast, and patiently bore their own hunger and went three days and nights with nothing but water. Alternatively, such people [under discussion in this verse] purify themselves from the vice of ignorance by giving spiritual food of wisdoms and Divine Laws, which is beloved in its own right, for the sake of love for God to *the needy one* who perpetually relies on the soil of the body, *the orphan* who is cut-off from the guidance of his true father the Holy Spirit, *and the prisoner* confined in the cell of nature and the chains of the soul's attributes.

[76:9] *'We feed you only for the sake (wajh) of God*: they say this to themselves by way of expressing their intention to give food to earn God's favour, for the righteous do good deeds to seek God's favour, not reward, since they have come from behind the veil of the acts to the Attributes. Or they do it for God's Essence and out of love for It, since the word *wajh* can mean the Essence along with the Attributes, for they are wayfarers travelling through the plains of the Attributes to the destination of the Essence, and do not halt at them. *We do not desire any reward from you, nor any thanks*: neither recompense nor praise, for we are not veiled by desires or accidents.

[76:10] *'Indeed, we fear from our Lord a day of frowning, [calamitous]'*: the day of the self-disclosure of wrath and anger and its manifestation in the Attributes of frowning and overwhelming power.

[76:11] *God has therefore shielded them from the evil of that day* by self-disclosing to them in the form of contentment and kindness, *and has granted them radiance* of contentment *and joy* of endless bliss.

[76:12] *And He has rewarded them [for their patience with a Garden and silk]*: He has rewarded them for their steadfast renunciation of egocentric pleasures and satanic allures in the gardens of the acts with the lights of the Attributes, with the garden of the Essence and the silk of the garments of the illuminated, subtle Divine Attributes.

[76:13] *[They will be] reclining therein*, in that garden, *upon couches* of the Names, which are the Essence with the Attributes, according to their stations, ranks and levels therein. *They will not find therein either sun or bitter cold*: neither the sun of the heat of yearning for it, despite deprivation, nor the cold of halting with created beings; for halting with creation is bitterly cold and unbearably heavy.

[76:14] *And close over them will be its shades, and its clusters [of fruits] will hang low*: the shades of the Attributes will be near to them, covering them

Q. 76:9

because of how they adopted them and now dwell in their repose; and the fruits of the knowledge of the Oneness of the Essence and the Oneness of the Attributes, states and gifts will hang perfectly low for them, so that whenever they wish to pluck them and enjoy them they will be able to.

[76:15] *And they will be waited upon from all around them with vessels of silver,* which are the external manifestations of the beauty of the attributes from the beauties of forms; they are silver because of their luminescence, whiteness, beauty and splendour; *and goblets of crystal,* which are the forms of the attributes of subtle detached essences and holy substances, because they lack a direct attachment to matter and so cannot be grasped directly without connecting to their essences; and because they are from the realm of the Unseen, they do not have open tops like other vessels. They are made of crystal because of their purity and how the light of the Essence shines from behind them and makes them glimmer, as He said about the likeness of the heart to glass, *The glass as it were a glittering star* [Q. 24:35], with regards to the purity of glass and the brilliance of the star. Therefore, He says here:

Q. 76:15

[76:16] *Crystal of silver,* as pure and limpid as glass and as white and gleaming as silver, *which they have measured in a precise measure,* according to their preparednesses and the extent of their imbibing, which is commensurate with their yearning and their desire. However they measure it in themselves, such is how they will find it, neither half-full nor overflowing.

[76:17] *And they will be given to drink therein a cup whose mixture is ginger*: the ginger of the bliss of nostalgia; for they will not experience such yearning that their drink would be pure ginger, which symbolises the limit of the heat of desire, since they will have arrived. However, they will still feel nostalgia as they travel among the Attributes while being unable to reach them all at once, and so their love will not be entirely devoid of the bliss of the heat of desire, unlike the love of the ones immersed in the spring of the entire Essence, whose drink will be from the spring of pure camphor.

[76:18] [*It will be from*] *a spring therein*: that is, the ginger is a spring in Paradise, because the heat of yearning is nothing other than the love that arises from the source of Unity along with disassociation (*hijrān*); *named Salsabīl* because of its smoothness (*salāsa*) in the throat and pleasant taste. The separated lovers who seek and follow the path of arrival experience incomparable experiential realisation and intoxication, because of the heat of their passion.

[76:19] *And they will be waited upon by immortal youths* from the emanations of the Divine Names that are disclosed to them in the realm of holiness, which are the lights of the dominion and the divine power that are revealed to them in the presences and gardens of the Attributes. If they were in the gardens of the acts, then it would be the houris who waited upon them rather than the youths, because the Names affect the acts while the Attributes are their origin and the sources of effects and configurations. They are immortal because they endure perpetually in detachment. *When you see them you will suppose them to be scattered pearls* because of the luminousness, purity and the simplicity of their substance.

[76:21] *Upon them will be garments of fine, green silk and [heavy] silk brocade*: they will be donned with garments of the silk of subtle states and gifts from the lights of the splendid Attributes, and the brocade of divine character traits. Green symbolises splendour and radiance. *And they will be adorned with bracelets of silver*: they will be bedecked with the decorations of intelligible meanings illuminated by the light of ecstasy. *And their Lord will give them a pure drink to imbibe*: of the bliss of the love of the Essence and true, pure passion, free from the pollutants of otherness and duality of attributes, and the impurities of the manifestation of I-ness and ego.

[76:22] *'Indeed, this*—the garden, vessels, youths and drinks—*is a reward for you* for how you fulfilled the dues of the self-disclosures of the Attributes; *and your endeavour*—your deeds of heart in their stations (such as fear and dread) at the self-disclosure of magnificence, humility and comfort at the self-disclosure of mercy, sincerity when seeking the self-disclosure of Oneness, and the like—*has been appreciated'* with this reward.

[76:23] *Assuredly We have revealed the Qur'ān to you* Ourselves, not through any other, [*as a gradual revelation*].

[76:24] *So submit patiently to your Lord's decree*: the decree of the self-disclosure of Essential Unity in the station of annihilation, alongside the tribulation of the manifestation of I-ness and ego; for the Lord in the station of the descent of the Attributes is the Essence alone; *and do not obey of them any sinner* veiled by attributes and states, or by his own essence from the Divine Essence and by his own attributes and their configurations from the Divine Attributes, *or disbeliever* veiled by the acts and effects and halting with them, and by his own deeds and acquisitions from the divine acts, lest you be veiled by association with them.

[76:25] *And mention the Name of your Lord* which is your own essence, the Supreme Name among His Names, by fulfilling His dues and manifesting His perfections, *at dawn and with the declining of the sun*: at the beginning and the end, by the attributes of innate disposition from the time of the rising of the divine light, by its engendering in pre-eternity and the instilling of His perfections in it, and its setting by its individuation when He became veiled by it and manifested it with its perfections.

[76:26] *And prostrate to Him for a portion of the night*: single out the station of the soul or the heart, in the time of subsidence after annihilation and the return to creation to uphold the Divine Law, with the prostration of annihilation and veridical worship; for the call cannot be carried out without the veil of the heart and the existence of the soul. Prostrate to Him with the prostration of annihilation, by beholding your own subsistence through the Real and the annihilation of humanity in totality, so that you exist through Him, not it. Declare Him transcendent beyond with-ness, duality, I-ness and the manifestation of ego; *and glorify Him the length of the night*: perpetually and ceaselessly, as long as you remain in that station.

[76:27] *Assuredly these* ones who are veiled by effects, acts or attributes *love the transitory [life]* and experience nothing but the present moment of imperfect, experiential realisation, *and leave behind them [a burdensome day]*: the day of essential self-disclosure, which is the Major Resurrection, a day so weighty that none can bear it.

[76:28] *We created them* by individuating their preparednesses *and made firm their frames*, strengthening them with the pre-eternal covenant and the real connection, *and, whenever We will, We can completely replace them with others like them*: by replacing their acts with Ours, erasing their attributes with Ours and annihilating their essences with Ours, so that they are replaced.

Q. 76:26

[76:29] *This is indeed a reminder* for traversing My path and travelling to Me. *Let him who will, then, choose [a way to his Lord]*: a path to Me.

[76:30] *But you will not, [unless God wills]*: except by My will, if I desire them and they desire Me; for their desire is preceded by My own. Indeed, their desire is My desire, manifested in their loci. *Assuredly God is ever Knower* of the knowledge He instilled in them, *Wise*: in the way He instilled it and brought it to light in them by manifesting their perfection.

[76:31] *He admits whomever He will into His mercy*: by emanating that instilled perfection upon them and manifesting it; *and as for the evildoers* who squandered their due and negated their share of it by becoming veiled from it, or who placed the light of their disposition—which is the original divine light attained from His Name the Originator—in the wrong place by loving opposites, becoming veiled by effects and worshipping others, *He has prepared for them a [painful] chastisement*: by standing before the Lord because of how they stood with other than Him, and then in Hell because of how they halted with effects, which brings tremendous pain.

77

THOSE SENT FORTH
SŪRAT AL-MURSALĀT

In the Name of God, the Compassionate, the Merciful

[77:1] *By those sent forth in succession.*

[77:2] [*By the raging hurricanes*:] He swears by the lights of domination and subtlety which necessitate perfection and herald the states of the Resurrection. Thus, He says, *By those sent forth*, referring to the dominating lights that are sent to the human souls *in succession* (ʿurfan), meaning consecutively and regularly, and are then bolstered and strengthened like hurricane winds that rage against the egocentric attributes and corporeal and spiritual faculties, with the self-disclosures of the attributes of divine might and domination, overwhelming and scattering them. Or if the word ʿurfan is understood in the sense of 'rightfully', then it means those sent for the sake of virtue, because this compulsion bears within it a hidden subtle kindness, as He said [in the *ḥadīth qudsī*], 'My mercy outstrips My wrath.' The Commander of the Believers (may God grant him peace) said, 'His mercy to His saints is vast, even in the midst of His terrible wrath.'

[77:3] *By the sweeping spreaders.*

[77:4] [*By the decisive discriminators.*

[77:5] *By the casters of the remembrance*:] by the lights that spread and give life to what was destroyed and annihilated by the hurricanes from the self-disclosures of love and mercy, discriminating them by setting each one in its station to distinguish them from one another and to differentiate truth from falsehood in their deeds. Thus, they cast remembrance, which means knowledge and wisdom, because knowledge necessitates an outward existential claim and so cannot be emanated in the state of annihilation by the self-disclosure of domination, nor before it, for otherwise it would be discursive, deduced by the intellect tainted by

498

estimation, and consequently would be a satanic suggestion and a doubt in which truth and falsehood are mixed.

[77:6] *To excuse or to warn*: both of these refer back to the remembrance. In other words, to excuse those who seek forgiveness and are connected, by erasing their misdeeds and the configurations of their souls and attributes, and to warn those who are immersed in the garb of nature and the body and veiled by their coverings, pleasures and desires from the Real. Or it can be read as: to erase the misdeeds of the former and the sins of their attributes and deeds, and to warn the latter. Or it can be read as: they cast remembrance, acting as excusers and warners.

[77:7] *Surely that which you are promised*—the states of the Minor and Major Resurrections—*will befall*.

[77:8] *So when the stars*, the senses, *are obliterated* and erased by death, [77:9] *and when the heaven*, the animal spirit, *is rent asunder*, split and severed from the human spirit, [77:10] *and when the mountains*, the limbs, *are blown away*, annihilated and scattered, [77:11] *and when the time is set for the [testimony of the] messengers*, when the appointed time for the angels of reward and punishment comes, either for the communication of tidings, joy and repose, or for the conveyance of torment, woe and degradation, [77:12] *for what day has it been appointed?* [Such is] for a tremendous day that was delayed so that the reward and punishment were not dealt out in the very instant of the deeds. Or it means the human messengers, the prophets, and their appointed time to differentiate the obedient from the sinful, the saved from the damned; for the messengers recognise them all by their marks.

Q. 77:6

[77:13] *For the Day of Decision*: between the saved and the damned. Or if it is taken to mean the Major Resurrection, then it means: when the stars of the egocentric faculties are blotted out by the hurricanes, and when the heaven of the intellect is split and rent asunder by the influence of the light of the spirit on it, and when the mountains of the soul's attributes are blown away by the self-disclosures of the Attributes at the Intermediate Resurrection—and indeed, when the mountains of the soul, heart, intellect, spirit and everything upon them are blown away by the self-disclosure of the Essence; and when the sweeping messengers bringing life in the state of subsistence after annihilation come for the appointed time of separation after unification, which is the state of subsistence—that is the time of the return from unification to differentiation which is called the Day of Decision, delayed until after the time of unification which is annihilation.

[77:14] [*And how would you know what the Day of Decision is?*]

[77:15] *Woe to the deniers on that day*, who deny either of the Resurrections and are veiled from the requital. His Words *Woe to the deniers on that day* and what follows them indicate that the Minor Resurrection is what is meant by *Surely that which you are promised*.

[77:16] [*Did We not destroy the ancients,* [77:17] *then made the latter folk follow them?*

[77:18] *So will We deal with the guilty.*

[77:19] *Woe to the deniers on that day!*

[77:20] *Did We not create you from a base fluid,* [77:21] *then lodged it in a secure abode* [77:22] *for a known span?*

[77:23] *Thus, We were able; so* [*how*] *excellent are We as able ones!*

[77:24] *Woe to the deniers on that day!*

[77:25] *Have We not made the earth a receptacle* [77:26] *for the living and the dead,* [77:27] *and set therein soaring mountains and give you sweet water to drink?*

[77:28] *Woe to the deniers on that day!*

[77:29] *Depart to that which you used to deny!*]

Q. 77:14

[77:30] *Depart to a triple-forked shadow*: that is, the shadow of the *Zaqqūm* tree, which is the impure, cursed human soul when it is veiled by its attributes and cut-off from the light of Oneness by the darkness of its essence, so that it remains firmly planted in the earth of the body, growing in the hell of nature and spreading its branches to the branches of the three souls: bestial, predatory and satanic. These are the angelic faculties which have been overwhelmed by active estimation, according to the caprice of the soul.

[77:31] *Neither shady* like the shade of the *Ṭūbā* tree, which provides rest and repose unlike this tree; it is the goodly soul illuminated by the light of Unitary Unity in its acts which issue from the intellect, and does not branch out into contradictory opposed branches; *nor of any avail against the flame* of the fire of caprice and the toil of pursuing that which does not endure.

[77:32] *Indeed, it throws up sparks*, tremendous impulses and false hopes, [[*huge*] *like palace edifices,*] like mountains of fire, despite the impossibility of attaining those hopes; [77:33] [*as if they were* [*dark*] *yellow camels.*

[77:34] *Woe to the deniers on that day!*

[77:35] *This is the day in which they will not utter*, because they will lack the instruments of speech and permission for it, their mouths sealed so that they are unable to make excuses; [77:36] [*nor will they be given permission, and so offer excuses:*] that day will be unendingly long and many different events will occur during it. In some of these they will be unable to speak, while in others they will be able.

[77:37] [*Woe to the deniers on that day!*]

[77:38] '*This is the Day of Decision. We have brought you and the ancients together* at the universal gathering in the source of the unification of existence; and *then* We have separated the saved from the damned among you; or We have decided among you by distinguishing you from the saved, and brought you and the ancient damned ones who died before you together in Hell.

[77:39] '*So if you have any stratagems, try your stratagems against Me!*' This is a declaration of their incapacity, and of how they are utterly dominated and unable to employ any ruse to evade the chastisement.

[77:40] [*Woe to the deniers on that day!*]

[77:41] *Indeed, the God-fearing*—those who purified themselves from the attributes of the soul and the configurations of deeds, and detached from them—*will be amid shade* of the Divine Attributes *and springs* of knowledge, gnosis, wisdom and realities attained from their self-disclosures; [77:42] *and fruits* of the pleasures of loves and perceptions *such as they desire*, according to their will. It will be said to them:

Q. 77:37

[77:43] '*Eat and drink* [*in* [*full*] *enjoyment*] *for what you used to do*': eat of those fruits and drink from those springs joyfully and contentedly, on account of the purifying deeds and spiritual disciplines of the heart and outward form in which you used to engage.

[77:44] *So do We reward the virtuous* who worship God in the station of witnessing the Attributes and the Essence beyond them, as he said, 'Virtue is to worship God as though you see Him.'

[77:45] [*Woe to the deniers on that day!*

[77:46] '*Eat and enjoy for a little. Indeed, you are guilty!*'

[77:47] *Woe to the deniers on that day!*]

[77:48] *For when it is said to them, 'Bow down!'* [*they do not bow down*]: when they are told to be humble and contrite with selflessness, and to lower themselves to receive the emanation by renouncing pride and arrogance, they decline and refuse to yield; and this is the offence that brings about their destruction.

78

THE AWESOME TIDING
SŪRAT AL-NABA'

In the Name of God, the Compassionate, the Merciful

[78:1] [*About what are they questioning one another?*

[78:2] *About the awesome tiding,* [78:3] *concerning which they are at variance:*] *the awesome tiding* is the Major Resurrection, which is why a poet said of the Commander of the Believers (may God grant him peace), 'He is the Awesome Tiding, and the Ark of Noah.' In other words, [he is] the unification and differentiation from the perspective of reality and Divine Law, since he combines them.

[78:4] [*No, indeed! They will come to know.*

[78:5] *Again, no, indeed! They will come to know!*

[78:6] *Have We not made the earth a cradle,* [78:7] *and the mountains pegs,* [78:8] *and created you in pairs,* [78:9] *and made your sleep for rest,* [78:10] *and made the night a cloak,* [78:11] *and made the day for livelihood?*

[78:12] *And* [*did We not*] *build above you seven mighty ones,* [78:13] *and set a radiant lamp,* [78:14] *and send down from the rain-clouds cascading water,* [78:15] *that with it We may bring forth grains and plants,* [78:16] *and gardens of intertwining foliage?*]

[78:17] *Indeed, the Day of Decision*—the day on which people are differentiated and the saved are separated from the damned, and then each of the two groups is divided according to the ranks of their configurations, forms, character traits and deeds and their correspondences—*is the tryst:* the set limit and appointed time to which all creation will arrive, held with God in His knowledge and decree.

[78:18] *The day the Trumpet is blown* for the connection of spirits with bodies and their return to life, *and you come forth in droves:* in different groups, each with their leader according to their differing doctrines and deeds. It is related that Muʿādh (may God be pleased with him) asked the

Messenger of God (may God bless him and grant him peace) about this. He replied, 'Mu'ādh, you have asked about a tremendous matter indeed.' Then he looked him in the eyes and said,

> Ten types will be gathered from my community: some in the forms of apes, some in the forms of swine, some turned feet upwards and dragged on their faces, some blind, some deaf and dumb, some chewing on their tongues which loll upon their breasts while pus drips from their mouths so that all detest them, some with their hands and feet cut-off, some fixed to trunks of fire, some more putrid than a corpse, some clothed in garments doused in pitch that adheres to their bodies. Those in the forms of apes are the talebearers. Those in the forms of swine are the people who indulge in bribery. Those dragged on their faces are the consumers of usury. The blind are the people who judge unjustly. The deaf and dumb are the people who are pleased with their own deeds. The tongue-chewers are the scholars and sages whose deeds contradict their words. Those whose hands and feet are cut-off are the people who harm their neighbours. Those fixed to the trunks of fire are the people who bring false charges to the authorities. Those who are more putrid than corpses are the people who pursue desires and pleasures but refuse God's share of their wealth. Those who wear the [pitch-doused] garments are the people of pride, arrogance and conceit.

Q. 78:19

The Messenger of God (may God bless him and grant him peace) spoke true.

[78:19] *And the heaven* of the spirit *is opened* at the return to the body through the gates of the external and internal senses, *and becomes as gates*: a thing of many gates which are the passages of the senses, so numerous that they appear as gates.

[78:20] *And the mountains* of the veils that cover their configurations and attributes from the entities and block their manifestation, meaning the bodies and limbs that get in the way of those configurations which are manifested at the Gathering, *are set in motion, and become as a mirage*, just as He said elsewhere, *So that they become a scattered dust* [Q. 56:6]: that is, they become like nothing because of how they crumble and their parts are scattered.

[78:21] *Indeed, Hell lurks in ambush*: the hell of nature is a destination that awaits for everyone, and the angels lie in wait by it for them—even for the saved folk, since they will also pass by it and go over it, as He says,

There is not one of you, but he shall come to it. That is an inevitability [already] decreed by your Lord. Then We will deliver those who were wary [Q. 19:71–72]. It is related that al-Ṣādiq (may God grant him peace) was asked about this verse, 'Will you also come to it?' He replied, 'We passed by it, but its flames died down.' As for the damned, it lies in wait for them because it is their destined abode, as He says:

[78:22] *For the rebellious [it is] a resort*, and as He says, *And We shall leave those who did wrong crouching therein* [Q. 19:72]; [78:23] *to remain therein for ages*: for long successive aeons, whether endlessly if their beliefs are false and corrupt, or eventually ending depending on how firmly fixed their configurations are if it was a matter of evil deeds and no belief, or evil deeds but true belief.

Q. 78:22

[78:24] *Tasting in it neither coolness*—peace and tranquillity as the result of certitude—*nor drink* of the experiential realisation and pleasure of love, [78:25] *but only boiling water* as the result of compound ignorance *and pus* from the darkness of the configurations of love for iniquitous substances and inclination towards them; [78:26] *as a fitting requital* that corresponds to the deeds they did and the beliefs and character traits they sent ahead.

[78:27] *Indeed, they never feared any reckoning,* [78:28] *[and they denied Our signs mendaciously]*: that chastisement is because they were characterised by these vices, and how they had no expectation of consequences and denied the signs and Attributes. In other words, it is because of the corruptions of action and knowledge: they did not act righteously in expectation of reward, nor did they seek knowledge and believe in the signs.

[78:29] *And everything [have We kept count of in a Book]*: We have record-ed all of the forms of their deeds and the configurations of their beliefs in writing, in the pages of their souls as well as the pages of the heavenly souls.

[78:30] *'So [now] taste! For We will increase you in nothing but chastise-ment'*: because of them you must taste chastisement which is equal to them and not any greater, for they are already torment enough for you on their own. What it means is: taste their chastisement, for We shall not increase you in anything, except for the chastisement of them of which you were unaware before.

[78:31] *Indeed, for the God-fearing*—those who are opposed to the rebel-lious and who adhered to the limit of justice in their deeds, as defined by the Divine Law and the intellect; the ones who purified themselves from vices and the configurations of evil deeds—*there will be a triumph*: salvation from the Fire that will be the abode of the rebellious.

[78:32] *Gardens* of the gardens of sublime character traits *and vineyards* of the fruits and confirmations of deeds, [78:33] *and buxom maidens* of the forms of the effects of the Names in the garden of the acts, *of equal age*, equal in status, [78:34] *and a [brimming] cup* of the pleasure of the love of effects mixed with ginger and camphor; for the inhabitants of the garden of effects and acts do not desire anything beyond it, for they are veiled by effects from the Effecter and by gifts from the Giver.

[78:35] [*They will not hear in it any vain talk or lies*—[78:36] [*this will be*] *a reward from your Lord,*] *a gift that is sufficing*: it will be sufficient to meet their aspirations and the farthest reach of their gazes, for because of their diminutive preparednesses they will not yearn for anything beyond that, and nothing will seem sweeter to their tastes than what they already have.

[78:37] *Lord of the heavens and the earth and all that is between them, the Compassionate*: their Lord, Who gives them this gift, is the Compassionate, because their gifts are external, manifest favours, not internal, subtle favours, and so they partake in the Name of the Compassionate particularly; *Whom they will not be able to address*, because they will not reach the station of the Attributes and so will have no share in communion.

Q. 78:32

[78:38] *On the day when the* human *spirit and the angels* of the faculties *stand arrayed* in their ranks, each in his station, as He says *there is not one of us, but he has a known station* [Q. 37:164]. *They will not speak, except him whom the Compassionate permits* and assists by preparing him for communion in pre-eternity, and giving him the grace to bring that preparedness into action by self-purification; *and who says what is right*: what is true and not what is false.

[78:39] [*That is the True Day. So whoever wishes [to], let him seek resort with his Lord.*]

[78:40] *Indeed, We have warned you of a chastisement [that is near, the day when a person will behold what his hands have sent ahead and the disbeliever will say, 'O would that I were dust!'*] The near chastisement is the chastisement of iniquitous configurations from corrupt deeds, not the farther chastisement of domination and wrath, which is what their hands have sent ahead. And God (Exalted is He) knows best.

79
THOSE THAT WREST VIOLENTLY
SŪRAT AL-NĀZIʿĀT

In the Name of God, the Compassionate, the Merciful

[79:1] [*By those that wrest violently;* [79:2] *by those that draw out (nāshiṭāt) gently;* [79:3] *by those that glide serenely;* [79:4] *by those that race forward;* [79:5] *and by those that direct the affair:*] He swears by the yearning souls overcome with restless desire for the presence of the Real, drowning in the sea of yearning and love, which creep out of the abode of the soul and the prison of nature, escaping from the chains of its attributes and the attachments of the body, from the word *nāshiṭ*, meaning an animal which has fled or a prisoner who has escaped; and by those that glide through the waters of the seas of the Attributes, racing towards the source of the Essence and the station of annihilation in Unity. Then by the return to multiplicity, they direct their thought to the affair of the call to the Real and guidance, and the affair of order in the station of differentiation after unification. He swears also by the celestial spheres that wrest from east to west, dispersed in their paths to the farthest west, exiting from one constellation to another, gliding in their orbits, each one racing with the other in their journey, directing the affair and passage of the world as they are charged to do. Or He swears by the angels of the celestial souls who wrest the human spirits from the bodies at the moment of death, from the extremities of the body, its fingertips and nails, and which draw them out of the body as a pail is drawn out of a well, and which glide in their courses as they are commanded to, racing to them and directing what they are commanded to do just as they are commanded to do it. The main clause of the oath is omitted, as has been noted before, but it can be inferred as: you shall certainly be resurrected. This is indicated by the Words:

[79:6] *The day when the Tremor quakes*: when the reality occurs which shakes the earth of the body and the mountains of the limbs, which is the first blast of the Trumpet or the moment when the spirit leaves the body.

[79:7] *Followed by the Aftershock*: the second blast of the Trumpet for revival at the Resurrection.

[79:8] *On that day hearts will be trembling*—agitated when the quake occurs at the moment of death—[79:9] *their eyes humbled.*

[79:10] *They*—the veiled ones who deny the Resurrection—*will say* scornfully, *'Are we indeed being restored [as before?*

[79:11] *'What! When we have been decayed bones?'*

[79:12] *They will say, 'That then would be a ruinous return!']* Will we be returned to the original mode of life after we have become dry bones? We would certainly be losers if that were so.

[79:13] *But it*—the quake of return to life for the Resurrection—*will be only a single blast*: the influence of the spirit of Isrāfīl on the attachment of this departed spirit to matter receptive to it will take place in a single instant, and it will come to life. This is the day of the Minor Resurrection.

Q. 79:7

[79:14] *Behold, then, when they will be upon the surface of the earth (sāhira)*: at the moment of this blast. The blast and their appearance on the earth will occur at the same instant. The word *sāhira* means 'land that is flat and white'. Here it means the realm of the departed, imperfect, human spirit, which is an earth compared to the heaven of the realm of holiness (the abode of the perfected ones). It is called *sāhira* because of its luminescence and simplicity. Or it means the animal spirit because of the connection of the imperfect human spirit to it at the Resurrection; it is bound to remain with it because of its attraction to matter. It could also be an allusion to the locus to which the spirit connects at the Resurrection, because of its whiteness and the balance of its parts.

[79:15] *[Have you received the story of Moses,]* [79:16] *when his Lord called out to him in the holy valley of Ṭuwā?* The holy valley is the realm of the detached spirit, too holy to attach to matter. It is called *Ṭuwā* because of how all bodies and souls are rolled up (*inṭiwā*) beneath it and how it dominates them. It is the realm of the Attributes, and the station of communion is one of its self-disclosures. This is why He called out to him in this valley. The end of this realm is the highest horizon where the Messenger of God (may God bless him and grant him peace) saw Gabriel in his true form.

[79:17] *['Go to Pharaoh; he has indeed become] rebellious*: that is, he has manifested his I-ness. Pharaoh possessed a powerful soul and was wise and learned. He trod the valley of the acts and traversed the valley of the Attributes, but became veiled by his I-ness and so [made a claim to have] usurped the Attributes of lordship and claimed them as his own. This was his Pharaonism, tyranny and rebellion, and thus he became one of those about whom the Prophet (may God bless him and grant him peace) said, 'The most evil of people are those who are alive when the Resurrection rises over them.' He persisted on living through his own soul and its caprice in the station of the Oneness of the Attributes, which is one of the most powerful veils.

[79:18] ['And say,] "Would you purify yourself by becoming annihilated from your I-ness, [79:19] and allow me to guide you [to your Lord]—to Essential Unity by means of true gnosis—so that you may have fear [of Him] and that your I-ness might soften and become annihilated?"'

[79:20] So he showed him the greatest sign: the true ipseity by knowledge of Oneness and veridical guidance, but he did not see it because of the strength of his veil and the fixedness of his estimation.

Q. 79:18

[79:21] But he denied that there could be any other level beyond the station he had reached, and disobeyed His command because of his Pharaonism and obstinacy.

[79:22] Then he turned his back from the station of Oneness of the Attributes in which he was because of the sin of his state, and directed himself entirely towards the station of the soul because of his stubbornness and the dominance of his soul and its strong manifestation and claim, going about in haste to repel Moses with satanic ruses and egocentric plots. Therefore, he was banished from the holy presence and became even more veiled.

[79:23] [Then he gathered, and proclaimed,] [79:24] and said, 'I am your lord most high!' With these words he manifested himself or sought to vie with the Real, because of how intensely his I-ness was manifested, for the cloak of pride, but he was defeated and cast into Hell, accursed. For He said, 'Magnificence is My robe, and pride is My cloak; and anyone who vies with Me for either of them, I shall cast into Hell'; or another narration has, 'I shall break him.' This defeat is the meaning of His Words:

[79:25] So God seized him [in order to place emphasis on him] as exemplary punishment for the latter and for the former.

[79:26] Indeed, in that there is a moral for him who fears and becomes humble, so that his soul softens and breaks instead of manifesting.

[79:27] [Are you harder to create or the heaven which He has built?

[79:28] *He made it rise high and levelled it,* [79:29] *and darkened its night, and brought forth its day;* [79:30] *and after that He spread out the earth;* [79:31] *from it He has brought forth its waters and its pastures,* [79:32] *and has set firm the mountains* [79:33] *as a [source of] sustenance for you and your flocks.]*

[79:34] *So when the Greatest Catastrophe befalls*: when the light of Essential Unity is disclosed, destroying and erasing everything in its wake; [79:35] *the day when man will remember his efforts*: in all the stages from the beginning of his disposition to his annihilation, and his voyage through the stations and ranks until he reached his final destination, and gives thanks for it.

[79:36] *And Hellfire*—the fire of effective nature—*is revealed for all to see*: for those who can see by the light of God and emerge from behind the veil for God, but not for the blind veiled ones who will burn in His fire but not see it; for on that day humankind will be divided into two groups with regards to the beholding of it.

[79:37] *As for him who was rebellious*, who transgressed the bounds of human disposition and went beyond the limit of justice and the Divine Law to the bestial or predatory level and went to excess in his transgression, [79:38] *and preferred the life of this world*—preferred the sensory life to the real life through love for lower pleasures—[79:39] *Hellfire will indeed be the abode*: the place to which he returns.

Q. 79:28

[79:40] *But as for him who feared the stance before his Lord* by ascending to the station of the heart and witnessing His sustainment of his soul, *and forbade the soul from [pursuing] desire*—fearing His punishment or His power—[79:41] *Paradise will indeed be the abode* according to His level.

[79:42] *[They will ask you about the Hour: when will it set in?*

[79:43] *What have you to do with the mention of it?]*

[79:44] *With your Lord it belongs ultimately*: what could you possibly know about it or its mention? Knowledge of it belongs only to your Lord; for the one who knows the Resurrection is the one whose knowledge is erased by His knowledge first, and then whose essence is annihilated in His Essence. How could he know it, then, when he has neither knowledge nor essence? How could you or anyone else know it? No one knows it but God alone.

[79:45] *You are only a warner for the one who fears it* because he believes in it with blind faith.

[79:46] *[The day they see it,] it will be as if they had only tarried for an evening or the morning thereof*: when the light of the Real sets in the bodies, or when it rises from the west—that is, when they see the Resurrection by annihilation in Unity—they will be certain that they never had any existence at all, except for the delusion of tarrying in the realm of bodies and being veiled by the senses, or tarrying in the realm of spirits and being veiled by the intellect. This is what is meant by the saying, 'Just two steps, and you will arrive.' In other words, if you can pass through these two planes of being, you will arrive. And God knows best.

Q. 79:46

80
HE FROWNED
SŪRAT ʿABASA

In the Name of God, the Compassionate, the Merciful

[80:1] *He frowned and turned away,* [80:2] *[because the blind man came to him.*
[80:3] *And how would you know? Perhaps he would cleanse himself* [80:4] *or
be admonished, and so the reminder might benefit him.*

[80:5] *But as for the one [who thinks himself] self-sufficient,* [80:6] *to him
you [do] attend:]* the Prophet (may God bless him and grant him peace) was
in the lap of his Lord's upbringing, because he was beloved. So when his
soul manifested with an attribute, veiling the light of the Real from him
so that he moved through his soul instead of through his Lord, he was
rebuked and corrected for this—as he said, 'My Lord has trained me, and
trained me well'—until he took on the character traits of his Lord. Taking
on His character traits comes after arrival, annihilation and realisation
of Him in the state of subsistence, which is uprightness at the time of
stability and the negation of variegation. When he looked towards the
powerful ones in the outward state and was impressed by the wealth of
the wealthy ones, and turned away from the pauper—hoping that Islam
would be strengthened by those people if they came to have faith, and dis-
regarded the faith of the pauper—he was alerted to how one such as him
should never base his viewpoint on the outward state, and so be distracted
by the powerful wealthy man from the seeker who is prepared but weak.
Rather, he must look only to preparedness and receptivity to faith, and
take that into account alone, and not be veiled by the outward from the
inward. It could be that the pauper he overlooked was one who acted with
self-purification and adornment, and had reached the limit of perfection,
and so could become one who was guided and could guide others, while
the rich one to whom he paid attention did not have faith because of his
lack of preparedness or his obstinacy and pride.

[80:7] *Yet it is not your concern [if he does not cleanse himself]*: it will not harm you if he refuses to embrace Islam.

[80:8] *[But as for him who comes to you hurrying, [80:9] fearful, [80:10] to him you pay no heed.]*

[80:11] *No, indeed!* Be not so! It is related that after this verse was revealed, he never frowned at a poor person again, nor attempted to woo a rich person. *[Indeed, it is a reminder, [80:12] so let whoever will, remember it, [80:13] on leaves [that are] honoured* with God in the tablets of the heavenly souls to which the Qur'ān was first sent down from the Preserved Tablet, as was described; [80:14] *elevated* in status and position, *purified* from the pollutant of natures and their changes; [80:15] *in the hands of scribes*, which are the sanctified intellects that influence those tablets; [80:16] *noble* because of their dignity and proximity to God, *pious* because of their sanctity and purity from matter and the transcendence of their substance beyond attachments.

Q. 80:7

Thereafter, having explained how the Qur'ān is a reminder to the mindful, He expresses incredulity at man's ingratitude and how he is so veiled that he needs to be reminded at all. He then lists the outward gifts which ought to be seen as signs of the Giver: the foundations of his creation and the states of his soul, and the things external to him without which he could not live:

[80:17] *[Perish man! What has made him ungrateful?*

[80:18] *From what thing has He created him?*

[80:19] *From a drop of sperm did He create him then proportion him.*

[80:20] *Then He made the way easy for him; [80:21] then He makes him die and buries him; [80:22] then, when He wills, He will raise him.*

[80:23] *No, indeed! He has not accomplished what He commanded him:]* He then affirms that despite these two proofs—namely reflecting on these states, which ought to lead to recognition of the Giving Creator and gratitude to Him, and paying heed to the admonition and reminder imparted by the revelation of the Qur'ān—*he has still not accomplished*, in all this time, *what He commanded him*, which was to give thanks for His gifts by using them to bring out his perfections into action and employing them as a means of reaching the Giver. Instead, he was veiled from Him by them and by his own soul.

[80:24] *[So let humanity consider his [source of] food: [80:25] that We pour down water plenteously, [80:26] then We split the earth into fissures, [80:27] and cause the grains to grow therein, [80:28] and vines and herbs, [80:29] and olives and date-palms, [80:30] and gardens of dense foliage, [80:31] and fruits and pastures, [80:32] as sustenance for you and your flocks.]*

[80:33] *So when the [deafening] Cry comes*—the first blast of the Trumpet which does away with the mind and the senses—[80:34] *the day [when a man will flee from his [own] brother,* [80:35] *and his mother and his father,* [80:36] *and his wife and his sons,* [80:37] *every person that day will have a matter to preoccupy him:* the day] when each one will be concerned for himself alone and pay no heed to anyone else, because of the horror of his situation and his preoccupation with his own affairs.

[80:38] *[On that day some faces will be shining,* [80:39] *laughing, joyous.*

[80:40] *And some faces on that day will be covered with dust,* [80:41] *overcast with gloom:*] people will be divided into two groups: the saved ones whose faces will be shining, radiant and bright because of the luminescence of their essences and their purity, rejoicing when they encounter the configurations of their deeds and the bliss of their gardens; and the damned ones whose faces will be blackened by the blackness of their disbelief and the darkness of their essences, covered with the dust of the configurations of their iniquity and the pitch of the effects of their deeds.

Q. 80:33

[80:42] *Those are the disbelievers, the profligates:* the combination of their disbelief and their profligacy will be the reason for the mixture of blackness and dust on their faces.

81
THE ENFOLDING
SŪRAT AL-TAKWĪR

In the Name of God, the Compassionate, the Merciful

[81:1] *When the sun is folded away*: when the sun of the spirit is folded away by the rolling-up of its light, which is life, and its wresting from the body; [81:2] [*and when the stars scatter*:] and when the stars of the senses are scattered by the departure of their light; [81:3] [*and when the mountains are set in motion*:] when the mountains of the limbs are set in motion by their crumbling into dust; [81:4] [*and when the pregnant camels are neglected*:] when the feet which provide the benefit of travel are neglected: prevented from being used for walking and thereby rendered useless, or when the most prized possessions are no longer of any use—for camels were the most prized possessions of the Arabs; [81:5] [*and when the wild beasts are mustered*:] when the beasts of the animalistic faculties are mustered by being destroyed and annihilated—from the expression 'age has mustered them', meaning that it has utterly ruined them—or when they are mustered by revival for the Resurrection; [81:6] [*and when the seas boil over*:] when the seas of the elements fill to overflowing, so that they flow into one another and each part connects with its source, hence becoming one single sea; [81:7] [*and when the souls are coupled*] so that each soul is gathered with the types that resemble it, forming groups of the saved and damned, each with their peers; [81:8] [*and when the girl buried-alive asks*] [81:9] *for what sin she was slain*: when the rational soul, buried and destroyed by the weight of the animal soul in the grave of the body, asks to see the sin by which the animal soul came to dominate the rational, whether irascibility, desire or another, barring it from its special properties and deeds and destroying it. So it manifests, and its pursuit of manifestation is symbolised here by its question. This is why he (may God grant him peace) said, 'Both the one who buries the infant and the infant will be in Hell,' because the rational soul will be chastised right alongside the animal soul. There is another secret to this *ḥadīth*, but this is not the place for discussing it.

[81:10] *And when the scrolls are unrolled*: when the pages of the faculties and souls, containing the configurations of deeds, are rolled up upon death alongside the sun of the spirit, and then unrolled at the Resurrection when it returns to the body; [81:11] *and when the heaven is stripped off*: when the animal spirit or the intellect is removed and taken away; [81:12] *and when Hellfire is set ablaze*: when the fire of the effects of wrath and power in the hell of nature is lit for the veiled ones; [81:13] *and when Paradise is brought near*: when the bliss of the effects of approval and kindness are brought near to the righteous; [81:14] *[then] a soul will know [what it has presented*: every soul will know] what it has prepared and sent ahead, after having forgotten about it and been oblivious to it.

[81:15] *So I swear by the receding [planets]*, the celestial bodies that come and go in their orbits, [81:16] *[the movers,] the setters* that enter their constellations like beasts that enter their nests, or the souls that return to the bodies and run to their destinations; [81:17] *and the night as it approaches*: by the night of the dead body when it recedes, as its darkness begins to be beaten back by the light of life when the spirit connects to it and the light of its sun rises above it; [81:18] *and the dawn as it breathes*: and by the effect of the light of the rising of that sun when it breathes and spreads through the body giving life.

Q. 81:10

[81:19] *Indeed, this is the word of a noble messenger*: the Holy Spirit which breathes into the human heart; [81:20] *[powerful, eminent in the presence of the Lord of the Throne; [81:21] obeyed there, trustworthy.*

[81:22] *And your companion is not a madman.]*

[81:23] *For verily he saw him on the clear horizon*: at the end of the plain of the heart bordering on the spirit, which is the place where the holy breath is blown; [81:24] *and he is not to be accused regarding the Unseen*: he is above reproach regarding the reports he conveys from the Unseen, for the Satan of estimation and the jinn of imagination cannot overcome him to make him err in his words, or mix up the holy meanings with estimations and imaginations; for his intellect is not covered, but rather purified from the taint of estimation.

[81:25] *And it is not [the word of an accursed Satan*: it is not] cast by the Satan of estimation, who is pelted by the light of the spirit, such that it would be rendered into a delusional estimation.

[81:26] *So where are you going?* After all this, why do you still claim that this discourse is a delusion, or mixed, and accuse its conveyor of being a madman, when the truth ought to be obvious to anyone? Someone who follows these paths and makes any of these three accusations has fallen so distant from the truth that there is barely any hope for him, like a traveller who has wandered so far from his course that one can only exclaim, 'Where are you going?'

[81:27] [*It is only a reminder for all the worlds,*] [81:28] *for those of you who wish* [*to go straight*]: for anyone from the worlds who wishes to be upright and follow the straight path, which is the path of the Real, as He says, *Indeed, my Lord is on a straight path* [Q. 11:56].

[81:29] [*But you will not* [*wish*] *unless God, the Lord of the Worlds, wills:*] none will choose to follow it unless God wills so, for His path can only be followed by His will. And God (Exalted is He) knows best.

Q. 81:27

82
THE SPLITTING
SŪRAT AL-INFIṬĀR

In the Name of God, the Compassionate, the Merciful

[82:1] *When the heaven is split open*: when the heaven of the animal spirit splits upon being rent from the human spirit and departs it; [82:2] *and when the stars are dispersed*: when the senses are dispersed by death and taken away; [82:3] *and when the seas are burst forth*: when the elemental bodies burst into one another, upon the disappearance of the isthmus barriers that prevent everything from returning to its source, namely the animal spirits which prevent the destruction of the body and the return of its parts to their origin; [82:4] *and when the tombs are overturned*: when the bodies are summoned and the spirits and faculties they contain are brought out of them, [82:5] [*a soul will know what it has sent ahead and left behind.*

[82:6] [O man,] *what has deceived you [with regard to your generous Lord]?* It was wrong of you to be deceived by His generosity; for although His generosity made it easy for you to become deceived, He gave you such plentiful gifts and tremendous, perfect favours that you ought to have not done so, and they were more plentiful than what they encouraged you to do [of bad].

[82:7] [*He Who created you, then made you upright, then proportioned you,* [82:8] *assembling you in whatever form He wishes?*

[82:9] *No, indeed! Rather, you deny the Judgement.*

[82:10] *Yet indeed, there are above you watchers,* [82:11] *noble, writers,* [82:12] *who know whatever you do*:] the noble writers are the heavenly souls and celestial faculties who engrave their deeds. In other words, cease being deceived by generosity, for the reason you sin at all is because you deny the requital, which is ever more heinous than deception. The noble ones who are ennobled above being and corruption preserve your deeds and write them down against you, in addition to the two angels who are assigned to you, as He says, *Seated on the right and on the left* [Q. 50:17]. How could you dare indulge in sins, when they are written against you in the heavens and the earth? And God (Exalted is He) knows best.

Q. 82: 12

83
THE DEFRAUDERS
SŪRAT AL-MUṬAFFIFĪN

In the Name of God, the Compassionate, the Merciful

[83:1] *Woe to the defrauders:* [83:2] *[those who,] when they take measure from people, demand [it] in full;* [83:3] *but when [they measure for them
or weigh for them, they cause [them] loss]*: the defrauders are those who
violate people's rights of weighing and measuring. Aside from the literal understanding, it could be interpreted to mean violations of the
true scale—justice—in which are weighed character traits and deeds.
Furthermore, the defrauders are those who, when they judge their own
perfections compared to those of others, act as though their virtues are
many, and seek more than their due by claiming to possess more intellectual and practical virtues than they truly do, out of self-satisfaction
and pride. Then, when they measure the perfections of others compared
to their own, they diminish them and belittle them. So in neither case
do they uphold justice, because of their pride and love of lording it over
other people, as He says, *They love to be praised for what they have not done*
[Q. 3:188].

[83:4] *Do such [individuals]*—those who are guilty of this vice, which
is one of the worst forms of injustice—*not suspect* at the very least and so
desist, even if they do not know for sure, *that they will be resurrected,* when
the virtues and vices of their soul will be laid bare and they will be reckoned, [83:5] *for an awful day*: when no one will be able to display anything
that is not within him, nor to conceal anything that is, for his inner being
will become outward and his attribute will become his form, and he will
be exposed and experience the consequence of his vice.

[83:6] *A day when people will rise* from the beds of their bodies *before
the Lord of the Worlds*: manifest before Him with no part of them invisible
to Him.

[83:7] *Nay, desist from that vice! The record of the profligates is in Sijjīn*: the deeds of the indulgers in vice who were profligate, by transgressing beyond the bounds of justice as determined by the Divine Law and the intellect, are written in *Sijjīn*.

[83:8] [*And what would tell you what Sijjīn is?*]

[83:9] [*It is*] *a sealed book*: *Sijjīn* is a level of existence in which its inhabitants are imprisoned (*masjūn*) in dark confined cells, crawling upon their bellies like lizards, snakes and scorpions, debased and disgraced in the lowest level of nature and its pits. It is also the record of the deeds of the people of evil, which is why He calls it *a sealed book*; it is the place where their deeds are recorded, written and sealed with the configurations of their vices and evils.

[83:10] [*Woe to the deniers on that day,* [83:11] *who deny the Day of Judgement.*]

Q. 83:7

[83:12] *And none deny it but every sinful transgressor* who strays outside the bounds of human disposition, by transgressing the limit of justice and indulging in negligence and excess, veiled by the sins of the configurations of his attributes.

[83:13] [*When Our signs are recited to him, he says, '[Mere] fables of the ancients!'*]

[83:14] *Nay, indeed:* this is a warning against these two vices. *Rather, upon their hearts is the rust of that which they earned*: their hearts have become rusted by the fixity of those attributes in them, which has sullied their substance and changed their nature. The rust is a result of the compounding of sins upon sins until they became fixed, so that the veil was realised and the door to forgiveness was closed. We seek God's refuge from such a thing! Therefore, He says:

[83:15] *Nay,* endeavour to prevent that rust! *They, on that day, will be veiled from their Lord*, because their hearts will be unable to receive the light or return to the original purity of disposition, like water mixed with sulphur which cannot return to the cool water-nature no matter how much it is filtered or boiled, since its substance has been changed, unlike heated water which has only changed its mode, not its nature. Thus, they deserve to dwell in chastisement forever, and so He passes judgement upon them by saying:

[83:16] *Then indeed they will be exposed to Hellfire,* [83:17] [*then it will be said, 'This is that which you used to deny!'*]

[83:18] [*Nay,*] *the record of the pious is in 'Illiyyūn*: the record of the forms of the deeds of the saved, and the configurations of their illuminated souls and virtuous qualities, is written in *'Illiyyūn*, which is the opposite of *Sijjīn* in its loftiness and high status; it is the record of the deeds of the good people, as He says:

[83:19] [*And what will tell you what 'Illiyyun is?*]

[83:20] [*It is*] *a sealed book*: a noble site sealed with the forms of their deeds, with a substance that is heavenly or elemental and human; [83:21] *witnessed by those brought near*: that site is attended by God's elite folk, the folk of Essential Oneness.

[83:22] *Indeed, the pious*—the saved folk who shunned the attributes of the soul—*will be amid bliss* in the gardens of the Attributes and the acts; [83:23] *upon couches* which are their stations from the Divine Names, in the privacy of the realm of holiness, concealed from human eyes, *gazing* at all the levels of existence, beholding the inhabitants of Paradise and Hell and their bliss and torment, not veiled from anything in their privacy while all others are veiled from them.

[83:24] *You will perceive in their faces the radiance of bliss*—its splendour and luminescence and the effects of its joys—[83:25] *as they are given to drink a nectar* [*that is*] *sealed*: a pure wine of spiritual love not mixed with the soul's love for corporeal substances, sealed by the Divine Law so that it is not mixed with the satanic impurities of forbidden, delusional love and egocentric passions; [83:26] *whose seal is musk. So for such*—for the drinking of the pure nectar of spiritual love, defined by the Divine Law, and its pure bliss—*let the ones who vie* [*go ahead and*] *vie*: for it is more precious than red sulphur.

[83:27] *And whose mixture is of Tasnīm*: the wine of the righteous is mixed with the *Tasnīm* of true, pure devotion, which is the love of the Essence that is called *Kāfūr* with respect to its special property in the state of unification, and *Tasnīm* with respect to its level in the state of differentiation; for it is in the highest level of existence and is said to flow in the air, rather than over the ground, because of how it is detached from any locus and unidentified by any fixed form. So alongside the love of the Attributes in their station, they will also have the pure love of the Essence, which will be mixed with their drink as they behold the Essence from behind the veils of the Attributes.

[83:28] *A spring from which those brought near will drink*: *Tasnīm* is a spring from which those brought near will drink alone; they are the perfected ones who arrived at the Oneness of the Essence from among the folk of stability, who stand through God in the station of differentiation as a result of uprightness. He set apart the folk of uprightness in the sta-

Q. 83:19

521

tion of differentiation from the folk of immersion (*istighrāq*) in the station of unification with respect to their different names, and the names of their drinks, while evoking their reality and the reality of their drinks, by calling them *those brought near*, which evokes separation despite nearness. He called their drink *Tasnīm* [literally 'to scale a peak'] to evoke the loftiness of their rank compared to the other ranks. He called the folk of immersion *the servants of God*[1] to evoke how they are dominated by the overwhelming divine power, which opens the way for annihilation, and called their drink *Kāfūr* to evoke pure Unity and whiteness without any attribution or separation.

Q. 83:28

---

1 *Truly the righteous will drink from a cup whose mixture is Kāfūr; a spring from which the servants of God drink, making it gush forth plenteously* [Q. 76:5–6].

84
THE SUNDERING
SŪRAT AL-INSHIQĀQ

In the Name of God, the Compassionate, the Merciful

[84:1] *When the heaven is rent asunder*: this is akin to His Words, [*When the heaven is*] *split open* [Q. 82:1]; [84:2] *and heeds its Lord*: yields to His command by splitting from the human spirit with dutiful deference; *as it should*: for it is only right that it yield to the command of the Absolutely Omnipotent and that it not disobey, and this is what makes it real.

[84:3] *And when the earth* of the body *is stretched out* and flattened by the wresting of the spirit from it, [84:4] *and casts out all that is in it*—meaning the spirit and faculties—*and empties itself* of all the effects and accidents it contains, such as life, temperament, composition and shape, which is the necessary consequence of it being emptied of the spirit, [84:5] [*and heeds its Lord, as it should*.

[84:6] *O humanity!] Indeed, you are labouring toward your Lord* [*laboriously*]: working your way studiously towards Him through death, moving closer with every breath, for it is said that your breaths are but the steps you take towards your fate; or you are engaged in the labour of your deeds, whether good or bad, and headed towards your Lord; *and you will encounter Him* inevitably. Or it can be read as 'encounter it', the pronoun referring either to the Lord or to the labour.

[84:7] *Then as for him who is given his book in his right hand*—by being made one of the folk of the right hand in human form, taking the book of his soul or his body with the right hand of his intellect, reading what it contains of the meanings of the Qur'ānic intellect—[84:8] *he will receive an easy reckoning*: by having his misdeeds erased and pardoned and being rewarded for his good deeds all at once, for his disposition retains its innate purity and original luminescence; [84:9] *and return to his family*—to those who correspond to him and resemble him, his fellow folk of the right hand—*joyful* and delighting in their company and in the fortunes he has been granted.

[84:10] *But as for him who is given his book from behind his back*: from the side closest to the darkness, the animal spirit and the body; for a man's face is directed towards the Real, while his back is directed towards the benighted body, so that he is returned to the darknesses in the forms of the animals; [84:11] *he will pray for annihilation*, because of how he finds himself in the calamity of the spirit's ruin and the body's torment; [84:12] *and he will enter the Blaze*: the blazing fire of effects in the chasms of nature.

[84:13] *Indeed, among his folk he used to be joyful.*

[84:14] [*Indeed, he thought that he would never return*:] he will meet this fate because among his folk he enjoyed his gifts and was veiled by them from the Giver, and thought that he would never return to his Lord or to life through the Resurrection, believing that he would simply live and die, and that nothing but time would be his ruin.

Q. 84:10

[84:15] *Nay, they will indeed be brought to life! Indeed, his Lord is ever Seer of him*, and will requite him according to his state.

[84:16] *So I swear by the twilight*: by the luminescence that endures from human innate disposition after it sets and is veiled by the horizon of the body, mixed with the darkness of the soul. He honours it by swearing by it here because it is the means for acquiring perfection and ascending through the stages.

[84:17] *And [by] the night* of the darkness of the body *and what [it envelops]*: the faculties, instruments and preparednesses combined in it, by means of which it is able to acquire knowledge and virtue, ascend through stations, and attain gifts and perfections.

[84:18] *And [by] the moon when it is at the full*: by the moon of the pure heart free from the eclipse of the soul, when it is gathered and its light is completed so that it is perfected.

[84:19] *You will surely journey from stage to stage*: through levels and degrees arranged in ranks, through death and what follows it of the way-stations of the Resurrection.

[84:20] *So what is wrong with them that they do not have faith* in it, [84:21] *and that when the Qur'ān is recited to them*, reminding them of these stages and levels, [*they do not prostrate*:] humbling themselves and yielding?

[84:22] *Nay, [but the disbelievers deny]*: those who are veiled from the Real are necessarily veiled from the religion.

[84:23] *And God knows best what they are amassing* in the container of their souls and inner beings, where false beliefs and iniquitous configurations are amassed.

[84:24] *So give them tidings of a painful chastisement* of the fires of effects and deprivation of lights, which is exceedingly painful.

[84:25] *But those who believe* with faith of knowledge, their hearts purified from the turbidity of the attributes of the soul, *and perform righteous deeds* by acquiring virtues, [they] *will have an unfailing reward*: the reward of effects and attributes in the garden of the soul and the heart, uninterrupted because it is free from contingency and iniquity and detached from matter. And God (Glorious and Exalted is He) knows best.

Q. 84:24

85
THE CONSTELLATIONS
SŪRAT AL-BURŪJ

In the Name of God, the Compassionate, the Merciful

[85:1] *By the heaven of the constellations*: the human spirit which ascends through stations and levels; [85:2] *and [by] the promised day*: the Major Resurrection, which is the last of its levels, [namely] the unveiling of Essential Oneness; [85:3] *and [by] a witness* who beholds essential witnessing in the essence of unification, *and a witnessed*: the Essential Unity. The indefinite form here [for *a witnessed*] is used to impart grandeur to the nouns, as in: a witness that no one but God could know or appraise, due to his annihilation in Him and the extinction of his individuality and ego. For how could he be known, given this? In addition, he is an object of witnessing also known only to Him, which in fact is identical with the witness, and there is no distinction between them except that of perspective. The main clause of the oath is left unsaid, but is suggested by the next verse and can be inferred as 'you all are veiled' or 'you all are cursed'.

[85:4] *Perish the men of the ditch*: cursed be the materialists, veiled by the attributes of the soul in the chasms and pits of the earth of the body; [85:5] *of the fire abounding in fuel*: this describes the ditch with which the fire is inextricably bound; it is causal nature, which burns its folk with desires and hopes; [85:6] *when they sat by it*: by that fire, settled there with no inclination to leave it for the expanses of the plain of holiness to taste the repose of the divine breezes.

[85:7] *And they themselves, to what they did to those who believed*—how they mocked, insulted and humiliated the monotheists and folk of unveiling and witnessing—*were witnesses* who could testify against one another about this.

[85:8] *And they had nought against them*—no reason to condemn them—

save that they believed in God, the Mighty Who overcomes His enemies with irresistible power, vengeance, veiling and deprivation, *the Praised* Who blesses His saints with guidance and grace.

[85:9] *To Whom belongs the kingdom of the heavens and the earth*: veiling Himself behind them from the wretched and disclosing Himself in them to the righteous; *and God is Witness to all things*: present, manifesting and self-disclosing to His saints in every atom, which is why the believers believe and the deniers deny.

[85:10] *Indeed, those* veiled ones *who persecute believing men and believing women* from the hearts and souls of the folk of witnessing, by denying and humiliating them, *then do not repent* but remain veiled and do not see and so desist, *there will be for them the chastisement [of Hell]*, the influence of the fire of lower nature, [*and there will [also] be for them the chastisement of burning*]: the burning of the fire of attributes in addition to the fire of influences. This will be caused by their yearning, at the destruction of the body, for the lights of the Attributes in the realm of holiness and their deprivation and banishment by the power of the Real, so that they will be tormented by both fires together.

Q. 85:9

[85:11] *Indeed, those who believe* with true first-hand faith *and perform righteous deeds* in the station of uprightness—divine deeds that lead to the perfection of creation and the order of the universe—*for them there will be gardens* from the three gardens *underneath which rivers flow*: rivers of the knowledge of the Oneness of the acts, the Attributes and the Essence, and the codes of their self-disclosures. *That is the supreme triumph*: the complete triumph beyond which there is no greater victory.

[85:12] *Assuredly your Lord's assault* with true domination and annihilation *is severe*: leaving no trace or remnant.

[85:13] *Assuredly it is He Who originates* the assault *and restores*: repeats it; originates it first by the annihilation of the acts, and then repeats it with the annihilation of the Attributes, then the Essence.

[85:14] *And He is the Forgiving* Who covers the sins of the existences and remnants of the lovers with His light, *the Loving* of the beloved ones by leading them to His presence and blessing, and honouring them with His perfections without any spiritual discipline.

[85:15] *Lord of the Throne*: presiding over the throne of the hearts of His loved ones from among the gnostics; *the Glorious*: the Mighty Who self-discloses with the Attributes of perfection of beauty and majesty.

[85:16] *Doer of what He desires*: through their loci because of their uprightness, so that they choose what He chooses for their deeds; or He veils those He will with His majesty, such as the deniers, and self-discloses to those He will with His beauty, such as the gnostics.

[85:17] *Have you received the story* [*of the hosts,* [85:18] *Pharaoh and Thamūd*]? [In other words,] of those veiled either with I-ness such as Pharaoh and those who follow his religion, or veiled by effects, and others such as Thamūd and those who connected with them.

[85:19] *Nay, but the disbelievers*—those who are veiled in any way, in any station, and by anything—*are* [*engrossed*] *in denial* of the folk of truth, because of how they remain in their state.

[85:20] *And God is behind them*: above their state and their veil; *All-Encompassing*: He encompasses all things, and they have restricted Him to that which they witness, but have not witnessed His encompassment, which is why they deny Him.

[85:21] *Nay, but it*—this knowledge—*is a glorious Qur'ān*: in which all knowledge is gathered, glorious in its magnificence and its encompassment; [85:22] *in a tablet*: the Muḥammadan heart; *preserved* from substitution, alteration and the tampering of devils by suggestion or falsification. All of the aforementioned is [understood] if the promised day is taken to refer to the Major Resurrection.

Q. 85:17

If it is interpreted to signify the Minor Resurrection, then it means:[1]

By the spirit of the bodies, for bodies are to the spirit like constellations (*burūj*). Or it means the senses, for they come out of them like doves flying out of dovecots (also *burūj*). Also by the witness of his knowledge, and how he acts on it. The main clause of the oath is: the materialists shall be ruined. Perish the men of the ditch—the egocentric faculties which cleave to the ditch of the body—as they sit around it, all the while witnessing what they do to the believers of the spiritual faculties, by dominating them and veiling them from their noble goals and precious perfections, and enslaving them to do the bidding of their caprices and desires. They bear witness to all this with the voices of their states. And the only complaint that these veiled faculties have against the supra-sensory perfections of the spiritual ones is that they have faith in God, Who is Detached from where-ness and direction and Dominant over the veiled ones with praiseworthy power, the Giver of guidance to those who follow it, the One veiled by the external manifestations of the kingdom of heaven and earth, and the Manifest Witness over all things.

These persecutors who enslave and enthral the faithful men of the

---

1 Kāshānī now provides an alternative verse-by-verse commentary on the *sūra*.

intellects and the faithful women of the souls, and then do not desist through spiritual discipline and the acquisition of virtuous character traits and so yield to them, they shall have the chastisement of the hell of effects and nature, and the torment of the fire of yearning for familiar comforts, while being deprived of them. And those spiritual ones who believe with the faith of knowledge, and who do righteous deeds of [various] virtues and praiseworthy character traits, they shall have gardens from the gardens of the acts and the Attributes, which are the gardens of the souls and hearts; and that is the supreme triumph, which is salvation from Hell and arrival at the goal that is supreme, relative to the first state. Your Lord's assault—His taking to task of the veiled ones by destruction and chastisement—is severe indeed. He it is Who originates them and destroys them, and then restores them for chastisement. He is the Forgiver of the spiritual ones who believe and repent, covering for them the sins of the configurations of evil with the light of mercy, the Loving Who loves them with pre-eternal love and so honours them with the emanation of perfections and virtues. He is the Lord of the Throne Who presides over the heart, the Glorious One Who illuminates all the faculties with His light, the Doer of what He desires, the Self-Discloser upon the loci of the kingdom to the heart, so that the station of reliance is realised through annihilation in the Oneness of the acts. And God knows best.

Q. 85:22

86

THE NIGHT-VISITOR
SŪRAT AL-ṬĀRIQ

In the Name of God, the Compassionate, the Merciful

[86:1] *By the heaven and the night-visitor.*

[86:2] [*And what will tell you what the night-visitor is?*

[86:3] *The piercing star!*] By the human spirit and the intellect which manifests in the darkness of the soul, which is the star that pierces its darkness and penetrates it so that its light may be followed and used as a guide, as He says, *And by the star they are guided* [Q. 16:16].

[86:4] *Over every soul there is a keeper*: a guardian who watches over it and protects it. This means God if *every soul* here means the human totality; or if it refers to the technical meaning of soul—the animal faculty—then it is protected by the human spirit.

[86:5] [*So let humanity consider from what he was created.*

[86:6] *He was created from a gushing fluid,* [86:7] *issuing from between the loins and the breast-bones.*]

[86:8] *Indeed, He* [*is able to bring him back*]: God is able to bring back man at the second creation, just as He was able to originate him at the first creation.

[86:9] *On the day when* [*all*] *secrets are inspected*: when the hidden things of the minds are manifested and made known by the separation from the body, and the inward is made outward; [86:10] *whereat he will have neither strength* to defend himself by his own power, *nor any helper* to protect him and help him defend himself.

[86:11] *By the heaven of returns*: the spirit that returns at the second creation; [86:12] *and* [*by*] *the earth* of the body *of fissures*: meaning the split from the spirit at the moment of death, or the joining when it reconnects to it.

[86:13] *Indeed, it*—the Qurʾān—*is a decisive word* that differentiates between truth and falsehood; a discriminating intellect that manifested after it had been a Qurʾānic intellect.

[86:14] *And it is not a jest*: it is not discourse that lacks a basis in innate disposition or a meaning in the heart. And God knows best.

Q. 86:14

87
THE MOST HIGH
SŪRAT AL-AʿLĀ

In the Name of God, the Compassionate, the Merciful

[87:1] *Glorify the Name of your Lord, the Most High*: His Names the Most High and the Most Magnificent denote the Essence along with all the Attributes. In other words, make your own essence transcendent by detaching from everything but the Real, and disregard all that are other than Him, so that all the veridical perfections might be manifested in it. This was the Prophet's special glorification in the station of annihilation, because he alone possessed complete preparedness and receptivity for all the Divine Attributes. His essence was the Most High Name when he reached his perfection. Everything has its own special glorification with which it glorifies a particular Name of its Lord.

[87:2] [He] *Who created*—made your outward being—*and proportioned*: shaped your body, so that its special temperament accepted the spirit that was completed and prepared for all perfections; [87:3] *and Who determined* total perfection of type in you, *and guided* to its manifestation and emergence into action by means of purification and spiritual nurture; [87:4] *and Who brought forth the pasture*: the allure of the life of this world and its benefits, food and drink, which are the pasture of the animal soul and the meadow of the beasts of the faculties; [87:5] *then made it blackened stubble*: made it quick to annihilation and perpetually on the brink of departure, like straw and empty, black chaff. Therefore, do not pay attention to it or be absorbed by it, lest it prevent you from your special glorification and keep your essence from transcending and detaching, so that you are veiled by it from your perfection which was measured out for you. Do not let your gaze turn from Him to it, for it is headed for annihilation while He will endure forever without end.

[87:6] *We will have you recite* [*so that you will not forget*]: We will make you a reciter of what is in the book of your preparedness, which is the Qurʾānic intellect from the Qurʾān that gathers realities, and you will remember it and never forget it, [87:7] *except what God may will* to make you forget and disregard, saving it for the praised station in which you were raised. *Indeed, He knows what is overt*—the perfection that manifested in you—*and what is hidden* afterwards by force.

[87:8] *And We will ease your way to the easy way*: We will grace you with guidance to the easy path: the indulgent, tolerant Divine Law which is the easiest of all paths to God. This refers back to *We will have you recite* [Q. 87:6]: that is, We will perfect you with perfection of both knowledge and action that is complete and beyond complete, in the sense of imparting perfection to others, which is far-reaching wisdom and perfect strength.

[87:9] *So remind, in case the reminder should be of benefit*: perfect crea-tion by calling to them, if they are receptive and prepared to receive the reminder, that it might benefit them. Although the reminder is universal, it will not benefit all of creation but rather depends on their preparedness; those who were already prepared will benefit from it, while the rest will not. Thus, after speaking in general terms by saying *in case the reminder should be of benefit*, He then speaks specifically and says:

Q. 87:8

[87:10] *He who fears will be reminded*: the one whose heart is soft and whose innate purity is sound will be reminded, and take admonition and benefit from it, for he is prepared to receive it and will react to it because of his luminescence and purity.

[87:11] *But the most wretched one will shun it*: the one who is veiled from his Lord, bereft of preparedness and hard of heart will be averse to it. He is more wretched than the one who was prepared, but then lost his pre-paredness and became veiled by the darkness of the attributes of his soul.

[87:12] *He who will be roasted in the greater Fire*, which is the fire of veil-ing from the Lord by idolatry and halting with other than Him, and the fire of dominating power in the station of the attributes, and the fire of wrath and rage in the station of the acts, and the fire of the hell of effects in the four stopping-places of the kingdom, the dominion, the realm of divine power and the presence of the Essence, for all eternity. How great is his fire! As for the other, he will only be roasted in the fire of effects.

[87:13] *Then he will neither die therein*—since he will never cease to exist—*nor live* truly, because of his spiritual destruction. He will be perpetu-ally and ceaselessly tormented in a state wherein he will wish for death; but whenever he is burned and destroyed, he will he brought back to life and tormented again, so that he is neither absolutely alive nor absolutely dead.

[87:14] *Successful indeed is he who purifies himself*: triumphant is he who becomes purified from the attributes of his soul and the darknesses of his body after attaining his preparedness; [87:15] *and mentions the Name of his Lord and prays*: he mentions the special Name by which He sustains him by emanating his perfection through which he may ask his Lord with the voice of his preparedness, such as the Knower for the ignorant one, or the Guide for the lost one, or the Forgiving for the sinner. In reality, it is nothing other than his essence, to which he has become oblivious because of the veil of effects and configurations, the attributes of the soul and all other darknesses, as He says, *They forget God, so He makes them forget their own souls* [Q. 59:19]. So he mentions Him, recognises Him and requests the perfection that is specially intended for him by lordly aid and divine grace, and prays, worshipping his God, the Real, Who self-discloses to him in the form of that special Name by which he knows his Lord after seeing Him, by means of the perfection that was destined for him.

Q. 87:14

[87:16] *Nay, but you prefer the life of this world*, [87:17] [*whereas the Hereafter is better and more lasting*]: you are oblivious and veiled from the remembrance of that Name and the prayer of the Lord by sensory life and its pleasures and delights, because of the lack of self-purification; and you prefer to devote your love to it instead of the real, eternal, spiritual life, though it is better and more enduring.

[87:18] *Indeed, this* concept—concerning how the prepared person benefits from the reminder, while the unprepared person does not and is tormented by the greater fire; and how the prepared people of purification and adornment will succeed, while those who prefer the sensory life will be ruined—*is in the* [*former*]—ancient—*scrolls,* [87:19] [*the scrolls of Abraham and Moses,*] which are protected from substitution and alteration, preserved with God on the detached tablets of light, upon which those two prophets gazed and which was manifested and sent down to them. And God knows best.

88
THE ENVELOPER
SŪRAT AL-GHĀSHIYA

In the Name of God, the Compassionate, the Merciful

[88:1] [*Has there come to you the tiding of the Enveloper?*] The Enveloper is the catastrophe that will envelop humankind with its disasters; it is the Major Resurrection that will envelop essences and annihilate them with the light of essential self-disclosure. On the day when it envelops those whom it envelops, the people will be uncovered and divided into the damned and the saved. It is also the Minor Resurrection that envelops the mind with the calamity of drunkenness and whose horrors will confuse man, so that on the day it envelops them people will either be damned or saved.

[88:2] *Some faces*—meaning essences—*on that day will be humbled*: fearful and lowly; [88:3] *toiling, weary*: working under the burden of difficult tasks that exhaust them, like those who plummet into the pits of Hell and must climb its ravines, carrying the burden of the heavy forms and configurations of the effects of their deeds. Or they toil under the yoke of the *Zabāniya*, who drive them in awful, burdensome labours that are akin to the deeds they did in the world. This toiling therein does not benefit them in the least, and earns them nothing but weariness and torment.

[88:4] *Roasting in a scorching fire* of the fires of the effects of nature, which is harmful and painful, commensurate with the things they did in the world.

[88:5] *Made to drink from a boiling spring* of compound ignorance, which is their drink, and harmful corrupt beliefs.

[88:6] *They will have no food except cactus*, which resembles the harmful and useless knowledge they amassed, such as contentions, arguments, sophistries and the like; [88:7] *neither nourishing*—giving no nourishment to the soul—*nor availing against hunger*: nor abating the impulse of the

535

soul and its avarice to learn and pursue such things [namely, contentions, arguments, sophistries and the like]. Perhaps some of the damned will be raised in the forms of their thorny dry food: that of the *Zaqqūm* tree for some, that of the *Ghislīn* tree for others.

[88:8] *Other faces on that day will be delicate*: the radiance of bliss visible in them as softness and luminescence because of their detachment; [88:9] *pleased by their efforts*: grateful and free of regret or remorse, not seeking to renounce their deeds like the first, content with how they strove on the path of righteousness and the acquisition of virtues, and how they travelled in God.

[88:10] *In a lofty Garden* of the garden of the Attributes and the presence of holiness, of high status and sublime position; [88:11] *in which they will not hear any vanity*, because their speech will be wisdom, gnosis, glorification and praise.

[88:12] *Therein is a running spring*: from the springs of the waters of gnosis, experiential realisation, unveiling, ecstasy and Oneness.

[88:13] *Therein are lofty couches*: of the levels of the Divine Names that they reached by adopting His Attributes, which are above the degree of the corporeal levels; [88:14] *and goblets set*: goblets of the qualities and beauties of detached essences, which are the containers for the wine of love, set in how they adhere to their state and position; [88:15] *and cushions arrayed*: cushions of their states and sitting-places in the levels of the Attributes, arrayed in levels. Every Attribute—from the onset of its self-disclosure and the shining forth of its lights, and in how it leads towards perfection of attribution by it, and in how it is a disposition and a station—has footholds and sitting-places; and when the wayfarer attains his share of it, according to his preparedness, and reaches his farthest extent until his journey in it is complete, and it becomes a disposition for him, his station in it is a cushion on the couch which is the site of that Attribute alongside the Essence.

[88:16] *And [there shall be] carpets spread out*: carpets of the stations of the self-disclosures of the acts, which are beneath the stations of the Attributes, such as how reliance is beneath contentment, spread out beneath them.

[88:17] *Will they not consider [the camels, how they are created?*

[88:18] *And the heaven, how it was raised?*

[88:19] *And the mountains, how they were set?*

[88:20] *And the earth, how it was laid out flat?* Will they not consider]* the outward effects with their senses and reflect on them, and through them reach the self-disclosure of arrival at the self-disclosure of the Attributes?

[88:21] *So remind.* [*For you are only an admonisher;* [88:22] *you are not a taskmaster over them*: remind,] and perhaps among them there will be those who are prepared to take heed and ascend the ladder to the presence of the Real, while others turn away and are veiled by these effects from the Effecter:

[88:23] [*But he who turns away and disbelieves,*] [88:24] *God will chastise him with the greater chastisement,* which is the greater fire alluded to in *sūrat al-Aʿlā* [Q. 87], prepared for those who are totally veiled in all the levels of existence. His Words *For you are only an admonisher; you are not a taskmaster over them* are an aside: that is, your role is only to remind, not to compel or force, as He says, *You cannot guide whomever you like* [Q. 28:56]; *you are not* [*to be*] *a coercer of them* [Q. 50:45].

[88:25] *Indeed, to Us will be their return,* [88:26] *then truly with Us will lie their reckoning*: to Us alone will be their return, and to no other, and We shall reckon them and chastise them with the greater chastisement; for compulsion and force are for Us, not you.

Q. 88:21

89
THE DAWN
SŪRAT AL-FAJR

In the Name of God, the Compassionate, the Merciful

[89:1] [*By the dawn*:] He swears by the commencement of the manifestation of the light of the spirit upon the matter of the body at the first effect of its attachment to it.

[89:2] *And* [*by*] *the ten nights*: the loci of the ten external and internal senses which were actualised upon its attachment to it, since they are the means by which perfection is attained and the instruments of attaining it.

[89:3] *And* [*by*] *the even*: the spirit and the body when they meet, and the completion of man's existence by which arrival is possible; *and the odd*: the detached spirit when it departs.

[89:4] *And* [*by*] *the night in motion*: the darkness of the body when it departs and ends through the detachment of the spirit. Thus, the oath is sworn on the beginning and the end.

Alternatively, it might mean the Major Resurrection and its effects: *by the dawn*, which is the commencement of the rising of the light of the Real and His influence in the night of the soul. *And* [*by*] *the ten nights* of the senses which are still, calm, benighted and incapacitated from their tasks upon the self-disclosure of the divine light. *And* [*by*] *the even* which is the witness and the witnessed before the self-disclosure of total annihilation at the state of witnessing in the station of the Attributes; *and* [*by*] *the odd* which is the Essential Unity upon total annihilation and the lifting of duality. *And* [*by*] *the night*: the darkness of I-ness when it departs and ends by the ceasing of remnants.

On the other hand, it could signify the Minor Resurrection: *by the dawn* of the beginning of the manifestation of the light of the sun when it rises from its west; *and* [*by*] *the ten nights* of the turbid, benighted senses upon death; *and* [*by*] *the even* of the spirit and body, *and* [*by*] *the odd* of the departed spirit when it detaches; *and [by] the night* in motion: the body when its darkness disperses from the spirit and it ends in death.

[89:5] *Is there in that an oath for one of sense?* This is a condemnation worded as a question. In other words, is there any intelligent person who would be guided to the oath upon these things, and to the reason they are honoured with this oath, and to the wisdom of their arrangement in a single oath, and their correspondence? The minds of the folk of the world are tainted by estimation, and so they will not be guided to this. The main clause of the oath can be inferred as 'the veiled ones will be tormented', based on how He then says:

[89:6] *Have you not seen how your Lord dealt with ʿĀd,* [89:7] *Iram of the towering ones,* [89:8] *the like of which was not created in the land,* [89:9] *and Thamūd, who hollowed the rocks in the valley,* [89:10] *and Pharaoh, the one of the tent-pegs—*[89:11] *those who were rebellious in the land,* [89:12] *and caused much corruption therein?*

[89:13] *So your Lord poured on them a scourge of chastisement.*

[89:14] *Indeed, your Lord is ever watchful.*

Q. 89:5

Alternatively, the question might be meant as an affirmation that only people with sound minds, pure of the taint of estimation, will be guided to this, and the main clause of the oath could be inferred as 'the intelligent ones who reflect on the state of the veiled ones will be rewarded'.

[89:15] *And as for man, whenever his Lord tests him [and honours him, and is gracious to him, he says, 'My Lord has honoured me.'*

[89:16] *But when he tests him and restricts his provision for him, he says, 'My Lord has humiliated me.'*

[89:17] *No, indeed! Rather, they do not honour the orphan,* [89:18] *and they do not urge the feeding of the needy;* [89:19] *and they devour inheritance greedily;* [89:20] *and they love wealth with abounding love:]* humanity ought to be in the station of gratitude or patience, for as he said, 'Faith has two halves: one half patience, the other half gratitude.' This is because God is always trying him: either with favours and ease, in which case he should give thanks to Him by using His favours correctly, such as by helping orphans, feeding the poor and other things that please Him, rather than showing ingratitude to His favours by displaying pride and conceit and saying, 'God gave me this because I deserved it and was worthy in His sight,' and wasting it on extravagant food and being veiled by love for wealth, denying the rights of worthy recipients; or else He tries him with poverty and straitened provision, in which case he ought to be patient and not panic or say, 'God has disgraced me!' for perhaps it is meant to honour him, by preventing him from being distracted by gifts from the Giver. He should use it as a way of turning to the Real and travelling His path through his lack of attachment. Likewise, if he were given what the first man was, it might only lead him on.

[89:21] *No, indeed! When the earth* of the body *is pulverised* by death *repeatedly* and smashed into pieces, [89:22] *and your Lord comes*: when He manifests in the form of overwhelming power to those who emerge from behind the veil of the body at the departure from it; *and the angels rank on rank*: when the influence of the angels of the heavenly and earthly souls is manifested, arranged in their levels, to torment him after he was veiled from them by the distractions of the body; [89:23] *and Hell on that day is brought [near]*: when the fire of nature appears and is brought forth for those who are to be tormented; *on that day humanity will remember* differently to how he believed in the world, and what became a configuration in his soul because of the dictates of his disposition; for the manifestation of the Maker in the Attribute of overwhelming power, and the angels in the ranks of chastisement, will only be for those who believed in something contrary to what appeared before them in the moment, as with Munkar and Nakīr; *but how will remembering avail him [now]?* It will not benefit him now, for his firm belief will prevent the reminder from having any benefit.

Q. 89:21

[89:24] [*He will say, 'O would that I had sent ahead for my life!'*

[89:25] *Then on that day none shall mete out chastisement as He will;* [89:26] *and none shall bind as He shall bind.*]

[89:27] *'O soul at peace*—upon which divine tranquillity has descended and which has become illuminated by the light of certitude, so that it has found peace with God from all that commotion—[89:28] *return to your Lord, [pleased, pleasing]*: in a state of contentment. When the perfection of the Attributes is completed for you, do not halt with it, but rather return to the Essence in the state of contentment, which is the perfection of the station of the Attributes. The soul can only be pleased with God after God is pleased with it, as He says, *God is well pleased with them, and they are well pleased with Him* [Q. 5:119].

[89:29] *'Then enter among My servants*: join the ranks of My servants who are Mine alone, from the folk of Essential Oneness.

[89:30] *'And enter My Paradise'* which is Mine alone: the garden of the Essence. This can also be read as 'Enter into My servant' [in the singular], and also as 'into the body of My servant', in which case it refers to the moment of the Resurrection when the spirits are returned to the bodies. And God knows best.

90
THE LAND
SŪRAT AL-BALAD

In the Name of God, the Compassionate, the Merciful

[90:1] [*I swear by this land*:] He swears by the sacred land, which was the holy land that the Messenger of God (may God bless him and grant him peace) visited, namely the highest horizon and the sanctified valley.

[90:2] *And you have free disposal of this land*: you may do as you please, for you are not restricted by the fetters of the soul's attributes and customs.

[90:3] *And* [*by*] *the begetter and that which he begat*: by the Holy Spirit which is the true father of human souls, as Jesus (may God grant him peace) said, 'I am going to my heavenly father and yours.' He also said, 'Be like your heavenly father and your soul which he begat.' In other words, the Holy Spirit and your rational soul.

[90:4] *Verily We created humanity in travail* (*kabad*): meaning toil and difficulty from his soul and caprice, or an inner malady and corruption of the heart and dense veiling; for *kabad* means a swelling and corruption of the liver, which is the origin of the natural faculty, and the veiling and corruption of the heart comes from this faculty. Thus, the swelling of the liver is used as a metaphor for the density of the heart's veil and the malady of ignorance.

[90:5] *Does he suppose*—due to the density of his veil and the sickness of his heart, because of how he is veiled by nature—*that no one will have power over him?*

[90:6] *He says, 'I have exhausted vast wealth'*: on luxurious things for the purpose of vanity and boasting. The Arabs would speak of 'losing wealth' to mean spending it lavishly and excessively on people in order to curry their favour, and would deem this to be a virtue because of how they were veiled from true virtue and ignorant of it. Thus, He says:

[90:7] *Does he suppose that no one has seen him?* Does he imagine that

God cannot see his inner being and intention when he spends his money for the sake of vanity, ostentation and boastfulness, rather than spending it rightfully on things that please God? This is one vice atop another, so how could it be a virtue?

[90:8] *Have We not given him two eyes,* [90:9] *[and a tongue, and two lips,]* [90:10] *and guided him [to the two clear ways]?* Have We not blessed him with corporeal instruments by means of which he can attain perfection by seeing that which matters, and asking about what he does not know and discussing it? Furthermore, have We not guided him to the two paths of good and evil?

[90:11] *Yet why does he not assault the obstacle?* Why does he not assault the obstacle of the soul and its caprice, which veil the heart, by means of spiritual discipline and exertion?

[90:12] *[And what will show you what the obstacle is?]* What a challenging obstacle it is, whose difficulty can barely be known.

Q. 90:8

[90:13] *The freeing of a slave*: the obstacle that must be assaulted is to rescue the enslaved heart held captive in the fetters of the soul's caprice, and to free it from captivity by detaching completely from natural impulses; and if the freeing is not fulfilled by means of spiritual discipline, the slaying of the faculties and the overwhelming of the soul, then it should at least take the form of affecting virtues, adhering to their path and acquiring them until the affectation becomes second nature. This is the meaning of His Words [90:14] *or to give food on a day of hunger,* [90:15] *[to an orphan near of kin* [90:16] *or a needy person in misery;*

[90:17] *and then is one of those who believe and enjoin one another to steadfastness]* *and enjoin one another to compassion*: giving food to worthy recipients, especially when one has dire need for it, is an aspect of the virtue of temperance and indeed is the best type of it. Belief is from the virtue of wisdom and the noblest and most eminent of its types; it is faith based on certain knowledge. Steadfastness in times of tribulation is one of the greatest types of courage. He mentioned it after belief because the virtue of courage cannot be attained without certitude. Compassion—meaning mutual mercy and empathy—is one of the best types of justice.

Note, then, how He listed the four kinds of virtue by which the perfection of the soul is attained. He began with temperance, which is the first of the virtues, and expressed it by reference to its predominant type and most special trait, which is generosity. He thereafter mentioned belief, which is the root and the foundation; and He used the word *then* because of how distant its level is from the first in terms of elevation and sublimity. He used it to express wisdom, because it is the mother of all its other degrees and types. Then He mentioned steadfastness after it, since it cannot be attained without certitude. He left justice until the end because it is the last of them and let compassion—the Attribute of the Compassionate—stand for all its other types, just as He let steadfastness stand for all the other types of courage.

[90:18] *Those are the folk of the right hand*: those who possess these virtues are the saved, the folk of the right hand and the denizens of the realm of holiness.

[90:19] *But those who disbelieve in Our signs*—those who are veiled from these attributes, which are God's true signs by which His Essence can be known—*they are the folk of the [left hand]*: the ill-fated denizens of the realm of impurity.

[90:20] *Over them will be [an enclosing Fire]*: the fire of causal nature will surround them and its gates will close around them, confining them therein and barring them from repose and its ranks, forever. And God knows best.

Q. 90:18

543

91
THE SUN
SŪRAT AL-SHAMS

In the Name of God, the Compassionate, the Merciful

[91:1] *By the sun [and her morning light]*: He swears by the sun of the spirit and its light which spreads in the body and shines over the soul.

[91:2] *And [by] the moon [when it follows her]*: by the moon of the heart when it follows the spirit by being illuminated by it, and turns in its direction and borrows its light instead of following the souls and being eclipsed by its darkness.

[91:3] *And [by] the day when it reveals her*: by the day of the ascendancy of the spirit's light, the rise of its authority and the presiding of its light, when it reveals it and manifests it as clear as daylight at noon when the sun is shining high.

[91:4] *And [by] the night when it enshrouds her*: by the night of the soul's darkness when it covers the spirit; for the existence of the heart, which is the locus of gnosis and the throne of the Compassionate, cannot be without the balance of the light of the spirit and the darkness of the soul, as though it is a being composed of the two of them, birthed from their congregation. If not for the darkness of the soul, the meanings would not be clearly visible in the heart; they would not be discernible as they are in the spirit, because of its total purity and luminescence. Yet, in reality, all these three are but one single thing, whose names differ according to its differing levels.

[91:5] *By the heaven and the One Who built it*: by the animal spirit which is the heaven of this existence, and the All-Powerful Who built it.

[91:6] *And [by] the earth and the One Who spread it*: by the body and the Creator Who shaped it.

[91:7] *And [by] the soul and the One Who proportioned it*: by the animal faculty imprinted in the animal spirit, which in the language of the Divine

544

Law and Sufism is called 'the soul' in general terms, or 'the human total-ity', or 'the rational soul'; and the Wise Who balanced it between the directions of lordship and lowliness—neither in the darkness and density of the body nor the light and subtlety of the spirit, as He says, *Neither of the east nor of the west* [Q. 26:36]—if it refers to the first; or Who balanced its temperament and composition, if it refers to the second; or Who prepared it to receive perfection and placed it in the middlemost position among the worlds, if it refers to the third.

[91:8] *And He inspired it to discern its vices and piety*: He made it under-stand them and sense them by angelic inspiration, and gave them stability in recognition of them and of the beauty of righteousness and the ugliness of iniquity, by the primordial intellect.

[91:9] *Successful indeed will be the one who purifies it*: the one who puri-fies and cleanses it will attain the triumph of arrival at perfection and the fruition of innate disposition; [91:10] *and he who eclipses it will indeed have failed*: who buries it beneath the dust of the body, concealing it from the light and mercy of the Real.

[91:11] [*Thamūd denied because of their rebellious nature*, [91:12] *when the most wretched of them was dispatched.*

[91:13] *But then the messenger of God said to them, '[This is] the she-camel of God, so let her have her drink!'*

[91:14] *But they denied him, then hamstrung her. So their Lord closed in on them because of their sin, and meted it equally [among them].*

[91:15] *And He does not fear the consequence of it*:] the main clause of the oath is omitted but can be inferred as: the veiled ones who deny the Prophet in their tyranny will be destroyed, just as Thamūd were destroyed for denying their prophet in their tyranny; for they did not accept that inspiration, but clung to their iniquity so that the intellect was veiled and the darkness of the soul was ascendant. The symbolism of the she-camel and its watering has already been discussed.[1] And God (Exalted is He) knows best.

Q. 91:8

---

1 See the commentary on Q. 54:28 above.

92

THE NIGHT
SŪRAT AL-LAYL

In the Name of God, the Compassionate, the Merciful

[92:1] [*By the night as it enshrouds*:] He swears by the night of the darkness of the soul when it covers the light of the spirit.

[92:2] [*And* [*by*] *the day*] *as it unveils*: by the day of the light of the spirit
when it manifests, upon their meeting, the existence of the heart which
is the throne of the Compassionate; for the heart is manifested by the
meeting of these two, and has one facet which faces the spirit and is called
'the inner-heart' (*fu'ād*), with which it receives gnostic secrets and realities,
and another facing the soul which is called 'the breast' (*ṣadr*), with which
it preserves thoughts and in which meanings are represented.

[92:3] *And* [*by*] *the One*—by the Almighty, Omnipotent Wise One of
overwhelming wisdom—*Who created the male*, the spirit, *and the female*, the
soul, so that the heart was begotten.

[92:4] *Indeed, your efforts are dissimilar*: different because of how some of
you are attracted towards the spirit and goodness because of the preponderance of light, while others incline towards the soul and indulgence in
evil because of the preponderance of darkness. This is explained further
by His Words:

[92:5] *As for him who gives and is fearful*: who prefers abstention and
detachment and so refuses anything that would distract him from the Real,
and renounces it easily and is fearful of the configurations of the soul and
so detaches it from inclination towards what he refused, and from looking
towards it; [92:6] *and affirms the truth of the best* [*word*]: the virtue that is the
level of perfection with knowledge-based faith; for if he were not certain of
the existence of the perfection of a Perfect Being, he would not be able to
ascend; [92:7] *We shall surely ease his way to* [*the abode of*] *ease*: We shall prepare
him and give him the grace to follow the easy path, which is to travel

in God, by the severing of his ties and the strength of his certitude.

[92:8] *But as for him who is miserly, and deems himself self-sufficient*: who prefers to love wealth and amass it and then withhold it, and deems that it frees him of the need to acquire virtue, because he is veiled by it from the Real; [92:9] *and denies the best [word]*: denies the existence of the level of perfection and virtue, because he deems the life of this world to be sufficient and is veiled by it from the realm of light and the Hereafter; [92:10] *We shall surely ease his way to hardship*: We shall prepare him with degradation for the difficult path, which is the fall from the level of innate disposition into the chasm of nature and the pits of the lowest of the low, the abode of insects and worms, dividing him from his desires with deprivation.

[92:11] *And his wealth*, which he wore himself out attaining and spent his whole life maintaining, *shall not avail him when he perishes*: when he plummets into the pit of Hell and the depths of perdition.

[92:12] *Indeed, with Us lies [all] guidance*: by direction to Us with the light of the intellect and the senses, and the combination of intellectual and scriptural proofs, and stability of reasoning and insight.

Q. 92:8

[92:13] *And truly to Us belong the Hereafter and the first [life]*: We give them to those who approach Us. We do not deny the abstinent, detached man the rewards of the world alongside the rewards of the Hereafter, for the one who prefers what is noble will surely find that what is base is beneath his feet, as He says, *They would surely have received nourishment from above them and from beneath their feet* [Q. 4:66].

[92:14] *So I have warned you of a raging fire*: a tremendous fire whose rage reaches all the levels of existence; it is the greater fire which contains the veil, overwhelming power, wrath, and chastisement with effects, which is why He says:

[92:15] *None shall enter it but the wretched one*: the one bereft of preparedness and foul of substance, who associates partners with God in the four halting-places; [92:16] *he who denies* God in his idolatry *and turns away* from the religion in his obstinacy.

[92:17] *The God-fearing one shall be spared it*: protected from it and taken distant from it in all its levels; [92:18] *he who gives his wealth to purify himself*: he who avoids everything other than God: his own essence, attributes and acts as well as all others and traces by immersion in the source of unification. This is the absolutely God-fearing one, who does not halt with anything other than God such that he would have to stand before God and be chastised by any of the fires. The ordinary God-fearer, on the other hand, might not avoid all of its levels, such as the one who detaches from configurations and acts but halts with the Attributes; for although his sins are forgiven, he is denied the repose of the Essence and the bliss of the ones brought near because of the veil of his existence. The one who gives his wealth to purify himself is the one who gives it while in a state of self-purification from the pollution of love for rivals, attachments to others, and concern for anything but God, thereby purifying himself from hidden idolatry.

[92:19] *And no one has any favour [outstanding] with him that must be requited*: it is not given to them as payment or reimbursement; [92:20] *but only seeking the pleasure of his Lord the Most High*: by avoiding everything but Him and by being at the highest level of God-fearing. God has, for each of His Names, a face through which He self-discloses to those who call to him with the voice of their state by that Name, whereby they worship Him with their preparedness; and the highest face is the one which corresponds to His Name the Most High, which contains all the other Names. If it is made a descriptor of his Lord, then the Lord is that Name.

Q. 92:19

[92:21] *And verily [soon] he shall [himself] be pleased*: when he reaches Him in the source of unification and essential witnessing, and then witnesses that face in the station of differentiation in the state of subsistence after annihilation, for his very being with that Attribute necessitates that he be pleased. And God (Exalted is He) knows best.

93

THE FORENOON
SŪRAT AL-ḌUḤĀ

In the Name of God, the Compassionate, the Merciful

[93:1] [*By the forenoon,* [93:2] *and* [*by*] *the night when it is still:*] He swears by light and pure, untouched darkness—which together are the root of human existence and the meeting-place of the two worlds—that your Lord has not left you or bidden you farewell in the realm of light and the presence of holiness, along with the enduring of the love and yearning, in the station of the Attributes, [whereby you are] veiled from the Essence; for the one who bids farewell does so with love and yearning.

[93:3] [*Your Lord has neither forsaken you,*] *nor does He hate you*: He has not abandoned you in the realm of darkness, to halt with creation without love or yearning, in the station of the soul, veiled from the Lord and His Attributes and acts, in the manner of one who abandons because of hate. When the beloved one, whose unveiling comes before his struggle, is shown the Essential Oneness, and his cover is lifted so that he may partake in passion, he is then returned to the veil; and his path to the presence of the Essence's self-disclosure is blocked, so that his yearning becomes intense and his inner secret is softened, and his I-ness is melted by the fire of yearning. Then his path is opened once more and the veil is entirely lifted, and he is shown the pure truth, in order that his experiential realisation be more complete and his unveiling more perfect. During this veiling, the Prophet (may God bless him and grant him peace) would climb the mountains to see for himself, and when his energy was expended the veil was lifted and he came down.

[93:4] *And verily the last*—the final state which is self-disclosure after veiling and intense yearning—*shall be better for you than the first* state.

[93:5] *And verily your Lord shall give you* veridical existence to guide people and call to the Real after this pure annihilation, *and you shall be satisfied* with Him: for you were not satisfied with human existence, and satisfaction can only be in the state of existence.

[93:6] *Did He not find you an orphan*: alone and veiled by the attributes of the soul from the light of your true father the Holy Spirit, cut-off from him and lost; *and shelter you*: in His presence, and raise you in the lap of His nurture and education, replacing your father in order to teach you and purify you?

[93:7] *And did He not find you erring*: from Essential Oneness when you were in the world of your father and veiled by the attributes from the essence; *and guide you* Himself to the source of the Essence?

[93:8] *And did He not find you needy*: poor and annihilated in Him with the poverty which is blackness of countenance in the two worlds, namely pure annihilation after poverty, that was his pride, meaning the annihilation of the Attributes, as he said, 'Poverty is my pride'; *and enrich you* with the gifted existence He gave you, endowed with the attributes of veridical perfection and adorned with lordly character traits? So since your perfection is complete, adorn yourself with My character traits and do with My servants what I did with you, that you may be a grateful servant who gives thanks for My favours:

Q. 93:6

[93:9] *So as for the orphan*—the isolated broken-hearted one cut-off from the light of holiness and veiled by the veil of the soul—*do not oppress* [*him*]: but be kind to him and show him compassion and gentleness, and draw him to yourself by calling to him with wisdom and goodly counsel, just as I drew you.

[93:10] *And as for the beggar*—the one who is prepared but veiled and astray from the path to his goal, though he seeks it—*do not drive* [*him*] *away* or prevent him from asking, but guide him as I have guided you.

[93:11] *And as for your Lord's grace*—the knowledge and wisdom He emanated upon you in the station of subsistence—*proclaim* [*it*]: by teaching the people and enriching them with true goodness, just as I enriched you. And God (Exalted is He) knows best.

94
SOLACE
SŪRAT AL-INSHIRĀḤ

In the Name of God, the Compassionate, the Merciful

[94:1] *Did We not expand your breast for you,* [94:2] *[and relieve you of your burden*—[94:3] *that which weighed down your back?*

[94:4] *Did We not exalt your mention?]* This is a rhetorical question meant to discount any negation of the expansion (*sharḥ*), thereby emphasising its affirmation, [meaning] 'We expanded your breast for you.' This is because the monotheist in the station of annihilation is veiled by the Real from creation because of his annihilation; the annihilated man is restricted from all things, for non-being cannot accept being, just as before the annihilation he was veiled by creation from the Real, because of the constriction of his existential container and his inability to receive the existence of the divine, essential self-disclosure. So when he was sent back to creation with gifted veridical existence and returned to differentiation, his breast became broad enough for the Real and creation together, because it was true existence. This is the meaning of the expansion of the breast. In other words, We expanded it with Our light that you might engage in the call and uphold the realities of the Message.

The burden which his back carried and which weighed it down, making it creak under the weight, was the burden of prophethood and the upholding of its duties; for when he was in the station of witnessing, he was not aware that creation possessed any existence at all, never mind action, and he made no distinction between one act and another because of his witnessing of God's acts. In such a state, how could he affirm good and evil, and issue commands and prohibitions, when he could see nothing but the Real alone? So when he was returned to the station of prophethood from the station of sainthood and veiled by the veil of the heart, this weighed heavily upon him and almost broke his back because of how he was veiled from essential witnessing at that time. Therefore, he was granted stability in the station of subsistence, so that he was not veiled by multiplicity from Unity and was able to behold unification in the midst of differentiation, and was not distracted from his witnessing by the Message. This is the meaning of the expansion of the breast, and it was this expansion that relieved the burden and exalted the mention; for the annihilated man in unification is not a thing at all, never mind a thing of mention. Had he remained in the source of unification, it would not have been right to follow 'There is no god but God' with 'Muḥammad is the Messenger of God' (may God bless him and grant him peace), because of his annihilation. Islam was not complete until both statements were true.

[94:5] *Indeed, with hardship comes ease*: with the hardship of the first veiling by creation from the Real comes the ease of the unveiling of the Essence and the station of sainthood.

Q. 94:5

[94:6] *Truly with hardship comes ease*: with the hardship of the second veiling by the Real from creation comes the ease of the expansion of the breast, by gifted veridical existence and the station of prophethood.

[94:7] *So when you are finished* with your journey with God, in God and from God, *toil* on the path of uprightness, and travel to God and strive to call creation.

[94:8] *And seek your Lord* alone by calling to Him. Do not seek anything but His Essence—not reward or other motives—so that your call and your guidance is with Him and to Him; for otherwise you will not subsist through Him and be upright for Him, but will stray from Him and subsist through the soul. And God (Exalted is He) knows best.

95
THE FIG
SŪRAT AL-TĪN

In the Name of God, the Compassionate, the Merciful

[95:1] *By the fig and the olive*: The fig represents the universal mean-ings removed from particularities, which are the perceptibles of the heart. He likens them to *the fig* because they are not material but purely intelligible, and correspond to their particularities, and nourish the soul, and are delicious, like the fig which has no pit but rather is nothing but core, and contains seeds like particularities which are the content of universalities, and nourishes the body with nutrition as well as having a pleasant taste.

The olive represents the particular meanings which are the percep-tibles of the soul. He likens them to the olive because of how they are material and prepare the soul to perceive universalities, just as the olive has a pit and changes the colour of the instruments of consumption to its own colour.

[95:2] *And [by] the Mount Sinai*: the brain which is the source of sensation and imagination, raised above the earth of the body like a mountain.

[95:3] *And [by] this secure land*: the heart which protects the universal meanings it contains, or which is secure from corruption and annihila-tion because of its detachment from change, depending on whether *amīn* ('secure') here comes from *amāna* ('protection') or *amn* ('safety'). So He swears by that through which human perfection and existence are attained, the universal and particular meanings, and the heart and soul: that is, by the perceivers and their perceptibles. This serves to honour man and acknowledge his nobility, for:

[95:4] *Verily We created man in the best of forms*: meaning a balance between darkness and light wherein opposites are combined and reconciled. He made him an intermediary between the worlds and a meeting-place for them, and balanced his creation and form and beautified his image. *The best of forms* means the most balanced of temperaments, the most perfect of types and the soundest of creations.

[95:5] *Then We reduced him,* because of how he was veiled by darkness from light, and how he halted with base qualities and turned away from virtues, *to the lowest [of the low]*: to the depths of creation, the level of the folk of the pits, the ugliest of forms and vilest of shapes and appearances, namely the folk of the fire in the hellish prison of nature.

[95:6] *Except those who believe* by the dominance of the light of the heart over the darkness of the soul, and the universal over the particular, *[and perform righteous deeds]*: acquiring virtue and goodness—those who attain perfection of knowledge and action, for they are in the high ranks of the realm of holiness; *for they shall have an unfailing reward*: the reward of the gardens of hearts and souls which is unfailing, because of its nourishing connection to the realm of holiness, its freedom from contingency and corruption, and its eternal existence.

Q. 95:5

[95:7] *[So what makes you deny thereafter the Judgement?]* Why do you deny the cause of the requital, O humanity, making yourself a liar with your denial, despite your awareness of this wondrous creation which contains all the levels of existence from the lowest to the highest, and encompasses all the perfections of the two worlds from the noblest to the basest?

[95:8] *Is not God the fairest of all judges?* He will judge him by halting him in whichever rank He chooses, whether rewarding him in the highest or punishing him in the lowest.

96
THE CLOT
SŪRAT AL-ʿALAQ

In the Name of God, the Compassionate, the Merciful

[96:1] *Recite in the Name of your Lord Who created*: this was revealed in the first level of his return (may God grant him peace) from unification to differentiation. This is why it is said that it was the first *sūra* of the Qurʾān to be revealed. The meaning of the *bi* in *in the Name* (*bi-ism*) is 'to seek assistance', in the same way as one says 'I wrote with the pen' (*bi'l-qalam*), meaning with the assistance of the pen. This is because when he returned to creation from the Real, he existed with veridical existence after being annihilated from his existence and attributed with His Attributes, thereby becoming one of His Names, since the Name is the Essence along with the Attribute. So it means, 'Recite with essential existence which is His Supreme Name.' He was the commander from the perspective of unification, and the commanded from the perspective of differentiation. This is why the Lord is described as the One *Who created*, or in other words became veiled by the form of creation. 'You have been manifested in your form, so arise through Me in the form of creation and return from reality to creation, and be a creature realised through the Real.' So when He returned him to creation in the form of the human union and commanded him to be veiled by it, for the stability of the revelation, inspiration and prophethood, He singled out the creation of humanity specifically after having first mentioned creation in general, and said:

[96:2] *Created humanity from a clot.*

[96:3] *Recite* in the Name: *and your Lord is the Most Generous*, Whose generosity is infinitely great and cannot be surpassed. In the largesse of His Essence and Attributes, He has gifted you His Essence and Attributes, for He is too generous to leave you annihilated in the source of unification without replacing your personal existence with something else. If

He were to leave you in the state of annihilation, none of His Attributes would be manifested, whether generosity or any other. And His generosity dictated that He bequeath you the noblest of His Attributes, which is knowledge, and that He not withhold any of His perfections from you. Thus, He describes the Most Generous by saying:

[96:4] *Who taught by the pen*: meaning the supreme pen which is the first and greatest spirit; He taught through it and by means of it. Yet since he was in the first state of subsistence and had not yet reached stability, He wanted to make him stable and protect him from variegation by the manifestation of his I-ness and the transference of the Attribute of God, and therefore said:

[96:5] *Taught man what he did not know*: He did not have knowledge, so He gave him His own knowledge and gifted him the attribute of His knowingness, lest he see his own essence as possessing the attribute of perfection and thus rebel by manifesting his I-ness. Therefore, He kept him away from the station of rebellion by saying:

Q. 96:4

[96:6] *Nay, but verily man is [wont to be] rebellious*, [96:7] *when he sees it to be self-sufficient*: that is, because of how he sees himself as self-sufficient due to his perfection.

[96:8] *Indeed, to your Lord is the return*: by essential annihilation; for you have no essence or attribute of your own. So he (may God grant him peace) desisted and maintained the proper courtesy of his state and said, 'I am not a reciter.' In other words, 'It is not I who recites, but You.'

[96:9] *Have you seen him*—the veiled ignorant one who deems himself free of need for the Real because of his situation, wealth and family—*who forbids* [96:10] *a servant*, any servant, *[when he prays]* the prayer of presence and worship in the station of uprightness, due to his rebellion?

[96:11] *[Have you considered] if he is upon [a path of] guidance*, [96:12] *or bidding [others] to fear of God* in the midst of his idolatry and his call to idolatry, for the sake of argument, as he claims?

[96:13] *[Have you considered what if he should be denying [God's guidance] and turning away?]*

[96:14] *Is he not aware that God sees* him either way, and will requite him?

[96:15] *No, indeed!* This is a command to desist from forbidding prayer, and an affirmation of the second clause of the conditional sentence that follows, if the warning in the first clause is not heeded: *assuredly if he does not desist* from this and from attributing deceit and error to him in the most emphatic way, [*We shall seize him by the forelock*, [96:16] *a lying, iniquitous forelock!*

[96:17] *Let him, then, call upon* [*the henchmen of*] *his council.*

[96:18] *We shall call the Zabāniya*:] this describes how he is veiled by his people and reliant on their strength, while oblivious to the overwhelming power and wrath of the Real, Who will unleash upon him the heavenly and earthly dominions which act in the realm of nature, and which none can resist.

[96:19] *No, indeed! Do not obey him*: do not go along with him, but adhere to your stance of defying him by holding to Oneness; *and prostrate yourself* with the obeisance of annihilation in the prayer of presence, *and draw near* to Him by annihilation in the acts, and then the Attributes, and then the Essence. Remain in your state of total annihilation in the station of uprightness and the call until you are in the state of subsistence with Him, annihilated from yourself. Do not let any variegation manifest in you by the existence of a remnant of any of the three. Thus, he recited in this prostration (may God grant him peace), 'I seek refuge in Your clemency from Your chastisement,' meaning refuge in a deed of Yours from a deed of Yours; 'and I seek refuge in Your contentment from Your wrath,' meaning refuge in an Attribute of Yours from an Attribute of Yours; 'and I seek refuge in You from You,' meaning refuge in Your Essence from Your Essence. This is the meaning of his drawing near with prostration. A *ḥadīth* says, 'The nearest a servant ever is to his Lord is when he prostrates.' And God (Exalted is He) knows best.

Q. 96:17

557

97

THE NIGHT OF POWER
SŪRAT AL-QADR

In the Name of God, the Compassionate, the Merciful

[97:1] *Indeed, We revealed it on the Night of Power*: the Night of Power is the Muḥammadan edifice in his state of veiling (may God grant him peace), in the station of the heart after the essential witnessing. This is because the revelation could only visit this edifice in this state. The power is his might and his nobility (may God grant him peace), for his worth was not manifest or recognisable to him except in that state. He then follows this by saying:

[97:2] *And what will show you what the Night of Power is?* What could make you recognise the nature of its worth and nobility?

[97:3] [*The Night of Power is*] *better than a thousand months*: we have seen that a day represents an event, as in God's Words, *And remind them of the Days of God* [Q. 14:5]. Every being is a day, and in the same sense every species is a month, because of how a month contains days and nights just as a species contains individuals. Then every genus is a year because of how a year contains months, just as a genus contains species. One thousand is the complete number beyond which there is no greater multiplicity except by repeating it and adding to it, and so it is used to symbolise the totality; that is, this single individual is greater than all species. He then explains the nature of its superiority by saying:

[97:4] *The angels and the Spirit*—meaning the spiritual and egocentric faculties and all the heavenly and earthly angelic forces, as well as the Spirit—*descend in it by the leave of their Lord with every command*: from the direction of every command. This refers to the recognition of all things and their existences, essences, attributes, qualities, rulings, states, management and control.

[97:5] *It is peace*—security from all flaws and imperfections—*until* [*the rising of*] *the dawn* of the sun from its west shortly before death, whereupon it will no longer be secure. Or it means that it is peace itself because of the abundant peace invoked upon it by God, the angels and all people.

98
THE CLEAR PROOF
SŪRAT AL-BAYYINA

In the Name of God, the Compassionate, the Merciful

[98:1] *The disbelievers [from among the People of the Book and the idola-ters]*—those who were veiled, either from the religion and the path of arrival to the Real such as the People of the Book, or from the Real as well like the idolaters—*were not going to leave off* their error *until the clear proof should come to them*: the plain sign that leads to the goal. What this means is that the divergent groups veiled by their caprices and errors—whether the Jews, Christians or idolaters—all argued with one another, each faction claiming that they possessed the truth and calling the others to it, and dismissing the religions of the others as false. Then they agreed that they would never leave off their own way until the coming of the prophet who was promised in both Books, and whom they were bound to obey, whereupon they would follow him and agree upon a single word of truth. This is exactly the same as the present situation, where all the adherents of the different schools of thought are awaiting the coming of the Mahdī at the end of time, and promise that they will follow him and agree on a single word. I do not expect that they will do anything differ-ent to what those others did when he finally does come, though we seek God's refuge from that. So God relates their words here and shows that they only became strongly divided and conflicted after the clear proof came to them with his emergence, since each faction—and indeed each individual—imagined that he would confirm their caprices and approve of their opinions, veiled as they were by their own religions. When this did not happen, their disbelief and obstinacy only grew, and their rage and hatred only intensified.

[98:2] *A messenger*—this refers back to *the clear proof* [Q. 98:1], mean-ing a manifest plain sign—*from God reciting scrolls* from the tablets of the heavenly intellects and souls, because of his connection to them due to his detachment, *purified* from the pollutant of natures, the turbidity of elements, the impurity of matter, and the corrupt alterations of servants; [98:3] *wherein are upright precepts*: writings which are firm, timeless and upright, proclaiming truth and justice, never altered or replaced. They are the foundations of the upright religion.

[98:4] [*And those who were given the Book did not become divided, except after the clear proof had come to them.*]

[98:5] *And they were only commanded*—those People of the Books who were veiled by their caprices from the religion and what they were commanded therein—*to worship God, devoting religion purely to Him*: to single Him out for worship free from the taint of falsehood and regard for anything but Him; *as ḥanīfs*: turned away from any path that does not lead to Him, and from everything other than Him; [*and to establish prayer and pay zakāt*:] to head towards Him with acts of worship from their bodies and possessions. They were only commanded with this in order to establish the three foundations of upholding Oneness with sincerity; and to disregard everything but Him for obedience, and to turn away from all but Him; and to perform bodily acts of worship, meaning such purifying deeds as prayer, which is the mainstay of them all, as he (may God grant him peace) said, 'Prayer is the pillar of the religion'; and to uphold the realities of asceticism such as renunciation and detachment, of which paying *zakāt* is one of the major foundations. [*That is the upright religion*:] none other than the religion of the upright Books which this messenger recites. The true *ḥanīfī* religion has been one and the same from the time of Adam to this day, and it is to adhere to Oneness and follow the path of justice, which includes the other two foundations. Had they not been veiled by their caprices, nor corrupted their Books and become divided into factions, because of the manifestation of their predatory souls, nor halted with their passions, nor become veiled by their estimations and imaginations, because of the externalities of their situations, customs, wishes and desires, from the realities of what their Books contained, their religion would have been nothing other than this religion.

[98:6] [*Indeed, the disbelievers from among the People of the Book and the idolaters shall be in the fire of Hell, to abide therein—those are the worst of creatures.*] The result of this is that the veiled ones from whichever faction they may be are the worst of creatures, dwelling in the fire of the hell of effects, the pit of nature.

[98:7] [*Indeed, those who believe and perform righteous deeds*]—the monotheists who uphold Oneness with knowledge and action according to

Q. 98:3

the laws (*qānūn*) of justice for the acquisition of virtues—*they are the best of creatures.*

[98:8] [*Their reward with their Lord will be gardens of Eden underneath which rivers flow, wherein they shall abide forever:*] they shall dwell in gardens of eternity according to their ranks, in the gardens of the acts and the Attributes. Their highest rank is the station of perfection of attributes, which is contentment: [*God is pleased with them, and they are pleased with Him.*] *That is* [*the reward*] *for him who fears his Lord*: that station is only for those who were overcome with lordly fear when He self-disclosed with the Attribute of magnificence; for when the Lord self-discloses to the heart with the Attribute of magnificence, fear overcomes the servant. This fear does not contradict the station of contentment, but rather is the consequence of the self-disclosure and its effect on the soul. And just as He affirmed the common ground among the veiled ones in the fire—but not the greatest fire which is for the most wretched of all—He also affirmed the common ground between the monotheists in the garden, but not the most high garden which is for the righteous gnostics alone, which is why the highest of its levels is that of contentment and peace.

Q. 98:8

99

THE EARTHQUAKE
SŪRAT AL-ZALZALA

In the Name of God, the Compassionate, the Merciful

[99:1] *When earth is shaken with its [final] quake*: when the earth of the body is shaken upon the wresting of the human spirit from it, by the agitation of the animal spirit and the faculties, with the quake that necessarily visits it in that moment, heralding its destruction and the collapse of its edifice.

[99:2] *And the earth brings forth its burdens (athqāl)*: its effects which give it value, namely the faculties, spirits, and configurations of deeds and beliefs rooted in the heart. The word *athqāl* is the plural of *thaql*, meaning 'household effects'.

[99:3] *And humanity says, 'What is wrong with it?'* Why does it shake and agitate so? How can it be cured, and what is its ailment? Has its temperament been disturbed, or has it become overcome with confusion?

[99:4] *On that day it shall relate its chronicles* with the voice of its state; [99:5] *for its Lord will [have inspired it]*: commanded it to agitate and collapse and to discharge its burdens upon the exit of the spirit and the realisation of death.

[99:6] *On that day people shall issue forth* from their sleeping places and the exits of their bodies to their meeting-places and the site of their reckoning and requital, *in separate groups*, divided into the saved and the damned, *to be shown their deeds*: their requitals according to the forms and configurations of their deeds, recorded in the pages of their souls.

[99:7] *So whoever* of the saved *does an atom's weight of good shall see it*, [99:8] *and whoever* of the damned *does an atom's weight of evil shall see it*: this specific reading of the general import of *whoever* can be inferred from the previous words *in separate groups* [Q. 99:6], for the good deeds of the damned will be annulled by disbelief and veiling, while the evil deeds of the saved will be effaced by faith, repentance, good deeds and sound, innate disposition.

100
THE CHARGERS
SŪRAT AL-ʿĀDIYĀT

In the Name of God, the Compassionate, the Merciful

[100:1] *By the chargers [snorting]*: the souls striving on the path of God, snorting from the arduousness of their labours and disciplines, like charging horses, heaving and panting with yearning.

[100:2] *By the strikers of sparks* which kindle a fire with the flint of effects and engagement with the light of the active intellect, and the steel of consideration and composition of information by reflection.

[100:3] *By the dawn-raiders* who raid what is connected with them: both the possessive matters external to them and outside them, and the configurations of attributes of souls, effects of deeds, inclinations, desires and pleasures, and insinuations of estimation and imagination which are internal to them and within them, by the light of the dawn of divine self-disclosure, the effect of the rays of light, and the origins of arrival through renunciation and detachment.

[100:4] *Raising therein*—by the light of that self-disclosure and the dawn of the day of Major Resurrection—*a trail of dust*: the dust of the body, by exhausting it, weakening it and emaciating it with spiritual discipline and denying it its desires, by concentrating intensely on the Real and approaching Him with ardour; and disturbing the faculties by drawing the heart and spirit away from the side of the body, and keeping them from it by the transmission of lights. It is like the expression 'he reduced it to dust', meaning that he annihilated and destroyed it so completely that it disappeared like dust.

[100:5] *Cleaving therewith a host*: cleaving with that dawn and its light the host of the source of the Essence, so that they were immersed into it. They softened the density of the earth of the body so that it became like dust, and then plunged through that dust into the host of the Essence.

Arrival must be with the body, just as the Ascension of the Prophet (may God grant him peace) was bodily. They are the forces of knowledge and action, renunciation and detachment by the light of self-disclosure, which assail the bodies with spiritual discipline and thus arrive.

[100:6] *Indeed, man is ungrateful to his Lord*: He swears, by the sanctity of those who give thanks for His favours and reach Him by their efforts, that man is ungrateful to his Lord due to how he is veiled from Him by His favours, and halts with them instead of using them as they ought to be used in order to reach Him.

[100:7] *And indeed to that he is a witness*: for he knows that he is veiled, and his intellect and the light of his disposition bear witness that he is not fulfilling the duties of God's favours, and that in his ingratitude he is failing to honour God's due.

Q. 100:6

[100:8] *And indeed in the love of good things he is avid*: he is a miser because of his avid love for wealth, or for the sake of his love for wealth. Therefore, he is veiled by it and plants his head in the pursuit, preservation, amassing and protection of it, distracted by it from the Real so that he turns away from His presence. Or it means that he is constricted and closed to love for the goodness that leads to the Real, instead of being open to it and welcoming of it.

[100:9] *Does he not know*—has this veiling and defiance of the intellect rendered him incapable of knowing, by the light of his disposition and the power of his intellect—*that when that which is in the graves is strewn*, when the souls and spirits that lie in the graves of their bodies are brought out, [100:10] *and that which is in the breasts is obtained*, when the configurations of their deeds, attributes, secrets and intentions that are hidden in their hearts are brought out, [100:11] *on that day their Lord will indeed be Aware of them?* He knows their secrets, thoughts, deeds and externalities, and will requite them according to them.

101
THE CLATTERER
SŪRAT AL-QĀRIʿA

In the Name of God, the Compassionate, the Merciful

[101:1] *The Clatterer*: the catastrophe that will clatter the people and destroy them. This means either the Major or Minor Resurrection. If it is the Major, then it means the state wherein the clattered one will be annihilated by the self-disclosure of the Essential Unity and humanity will be utterly annihilated. This is a state whose nature and immensity cannot be known, which will clatter into them.

[101:2] [*What is the Clatterer?*

[101:3] *And what will show you what the Clatterer is?*]

[101:4] *The day people will be like scattered moths*: in that witnessing, they will be as humble and dispersed as scattered moths. [In fact, they will be] even more lowly and debased than that, for they will have no value or esteem in the sight of the monotheist, as he said, 'A man's faith is not perfected until all of people are like gnats to him.' Or they will be like scattered moths when they flutter into a fire and are burned, when He fixes the eye of annihilation upon them.

[101:5] *And the mountains*—the contingencies and levels of existence in their various types and species—*will be like tufts of wool* when they become like dust in the wind and shrink and disappear into the self-disclosure. Or if *people* [Q. 101:4] here means those who are clattered by the Major Resurrection, then it means that they will be like scattered moths that burn in the light of self-disclosure and disappear, and the mountains of their essences and attributes in their different levels and variegations will disappear like tufts of wool. However, this interpretation is not supported by His Words *as for him whose scales weigh heavy* [Q. 101:6], and *as for him whose scales weigh light* [Q. 101:8], since there will be no differentiation at that time. Know also that the balance of the Real is not like the balance of people, for in His balance heavy things rise while light things fall, because His balance is justice. The things that weigh heavy in it are those which are sound and good in His sight, and have value and weight in His judgement, namely the enduring, righteous matter; and there is nothing heavier than eternal subsistence. In addition, the things that weigh light in it and have no weight or value in His sight are the ephemeral, corrupt matters: sensory pleasures and passions; and there is nothing lighter than pure annihilation.

[101:6] *Then as for him whose scales weigh heavy*—for they contain real knowledge, soul-centred virtues, and heart and spirit-centred perfections— [101:7] *he will enjoy a [pleasant] life* of contentment: a true life in the gardens of the Attributes above the gardens of the acts.

[101:8] *But as for him whose scales weigh light*—for they contain evil deeds and soul-centred vices—[101:9] *his home will be the Abyss*: the pit of the hell of corporeal nature into which its denizens plummet.

[101:10] *And what will show you [what it is]*: its reality and nature?

[101:11] *A scorching fire* as hot as can be. The meaning of his home being the Abyss is that he is headed for ruin. Yet what will show you the nature of this calamity that will be his ruin? It will be *a scorching fire*. If it refers to the Minor Resurrection, then it is the state whose severity will clatter people, namely death. [This shall be] on the day when people will be like scattered moths, in how they will depart their bodies, and will be raised from their slumbering places, and how they will head towards the luminosity of the realm of light, and how they will be humbled and fearful, and how they will have disparate goals and be perplexed, according to the disparity of their beliefs and caprices. The mountains of the limbs will be like tufts of wool, in their differing colours and types and the dispersion of their parts, and how they will be scattered and become like dust in the wind. The rest of the *sūra* can be interpreted the same way. And God knows best.

Q. 101:6

102
RIVALRY
SŪRAT AL-TAKĀTHUR

In the Name of God, the Compassionate, the Merciful

[102:1] *Rivalry [in worldly things] distracts you,* [102:2] *until [you visit the graves]:* you are distracted by sensory, imaginative, ephemeral pleasures from the bliss of the life of this world, which have veiled you, and you have buried your perfection in them and squandered your good things from the light of preparedness, and the purity of innate disposition, and the intellect and its objects, instead of the intellectual pleasures and enduring, supra-sensory perfections from the bliss of the next life. Your pride and exultation in these ephemeral things, such as the proliferation of wealth and children, and the honour of forefathers and ancestors, have led you astray, to the point where you are not content with what you presently have of them; but you also exult in those of them which have come and gone and been reduced to bare bones. This is because of the density of the veil, the dominance of the pleasure of imagination and the ascendancy of the Satan of estimation. Or all of this distracts you until you die, and you waste your whole lives on it, never once paying heed to the means of your salvation.

[102:3] *No, indeed!* You ought not to be distracted by it, and you ought to wake up and become aware of its dire consequences. *You will come to know* when the body is destroyed and the veil of contingencies is lifted; but this knowledge will not avail you then, because death will spell the end of the means and instruments with which you might pursue perfection. You will come to know the dire consequences of being distracted by sensory matters and short-lived delusions; and their consequences are dire indeed, for their effects will remain, and their configurations will torment you, and the fire of their traces will overwhelm you.

[102:4] *Again, no, indeed! You will come to know:* He repeats the warning.

[102:5] *No, indeed! If you only knew with certain knowledge*: if you tasted the true pleasures of certain knowledge and the luminous perceptions that transcend these ephemeral sensory and imaginative pleasures, then you would feel indescribable regret and would mourn how you squandered your precious lives on them, and were distracted by them from the others.

[102:6] *You will surely see Hellfire*: by God, you will see the fire of the hell of causal nature because of how you are veiled by these sensory things.

[102:7] *Again, you will surely see it with the eye of certitude*: you will taste it first-hand with the certitude of experiential realisation and experience, which is above knowledge.

[102:8] *Then, on that day, you will assuredly be questioned about bliss*: what is it? The bliss and ephemeral pleasure of the world, of which this is the consequence and result, or the eternally enduring bliss of the Hereafter which you used to deny? It could also be that His Words *You will surely see Hellfire* [Q. 102:6] function as a main clause to the conditional *If you only knew with certain knowledge* [Q. 102:5], since it is possible for an oath and a conditional to share the same main clause, as in His Words, *And if you obey them, you are truly idolaters* [Q. 6:121]. In that case it would mean: by God, if you knew with certain knowledge and reached its level, then you would see the fire of the hell of nature that is intended for the ones veiled by these vices, immersed in passions and pleasures of estimation and imagination, and sensory and corporeal perfections, in which you have planted your heads and worn yourselves out indulging, reaching the furthest extent of them. Hence, you would not stop at the level of certain knowledge, for you would be acquainted with its taste and recognise its pleasure, permanence, beauty, nobility and splendour, as well as the permanence of the consequence of your present state and its temporality, vileness, lowliness and baseness; and so you would ascend to the level of first-hand beholding and witnessing, and would behold the realities as they truly are—the holy lights and Divine Attributes—and by the light of witnessing you would behold the reality of Hell and the consequence of these pleasures and their painful configurations, and the torment of flames and deprivation. Then, on that day, you would assuredly be questioned about bliss: what is it? Is it the bliss of the Hereafter which you are currently experiencing, or is it that worldly bliss?

Alternatively, it means: if you knew with certain knowledge, you who are veiled by these allures and vanities, then you would surely see Hellfire because of the intensity of yearning and the overwhelming fire of passion, and then through this yearning you would ascend to the level of the eye of

Q. 102:5

certitude and witnessing and see the reality of the fire of passion first-hand; and then after this experiential realisation you would be questioned about the bliss which is the reality of certitude, and what it is. In other words, then you would be acquainted with the experiential realisation of arrival and the effect of the level of the truth of certitude, and you would be able to speak about it. And God (Exalted is He) knows best.

Q. 102:8

103
TIME
SŪRAT AL-ʿAṢR

In the Name of God, the Compassionate, the Merciful

[103:1] [*By time!*

[103:2] *Indeed, humanity is in* [*a state of*] *loss*:] He swears *by time*, meaning the extension of the subsistence of duration, and all that it contains, and all that occurs with it; by their originator and cause, which is time. People consider it to be the reason why circumstances and situations change and attribute influence to it, so that in their minds *nothing but time destroys us* [Q. 45:24]. Yet the true Influencer is God, as the Prophet (may God grant him peace) said, 'Curse not time, for God is time.' So He swears here *by time* in order to venerate it because of how He manifests in its locus with His Attributes and acts, that the man who is veiled by it from Him is in a state of loss because of how he has lost his capital—which is the light of innate disposition and original guidance from pre-eternal preparedness—by choosing the life of this world and ephemeral pleasures, and becoming veiled by them and by time, squandering the eternal for the ephemeral.

[103:3] *Except those who believe* in God with faith of certain knowledge, and recognise that the only Influencer is God, thereby emerging from behind the veil of time, *and perform righteous deeds* of enduring virtues and good actions, acquiring them and thereby attaining the light of perfection to compliment the light of preparedness which is their capital, *and enjoin one another to* [*follow*] *the truth*, meaning that which is constant and enduring and remains in the same state perpetually, which is Oneness and justice—Oneness of Essence, Attribute and Act—for that alone is the firm truth; *and enjoin one another to steadfastness* with Him and by Him, resisting everything but Him, with stability and uprightness; for it is easy to reach the Real, but remaining with Him steadfastly by righteousness in servitude is rarer than red sulphur or a white crow. In sum, the human species is in a state of loss, except for those who attain perfect knowledge and action and impart their perfections to others.

One could also read the word *ʿaṣr* ('time') to be the gerund of the verb *ʿaṣara/yaʿṣiru* ('to press, to squeeze'), as in: by God's pressing of man with tribulation, struggle and spiritual discipline until he is purified, verily the man who remains with the dregs and halts with the veil of humanity is in a state of loss; except for those who become characterised by knowledge and action, and enjoin one another to the firm truth, meaning the certain belief that leads to enduring purity after the disposal of the dregs, and who enjoin one another to be steadfast throughout this pressing and to bear the squeeze of tribulation and discipline patiently. Thus, he (may God grant him peace) said, 'Tribulation is assigned to the prophets, and then the saints, and then those who most resemble them, and then those who most resemble them.' And he said, 'Tribulation is one of God's whips, with which He drives His servants towards Himself.'

Q. 103 : 3

571

104
THE BACKBITER
SŪRAT AL-HUMAZA

In the Name of God, the Compassionate, the Merciful

[104:1] *Woe to every backbiter, [who is a] slanderer*: everyone who habitually engages in these two vices. The morphological form of the nouns used here denotes habit. Backbiting means to violate other people's privacy, and slander means to speak ill of them. Both are vices composed of ignorance, irascibility and pride, because they involve offence and the desire to raise oneself above other people. The one who engages in them wishes to be deemed superior to others; but he does not find any virtue within himself that would merit this, and so instead he attributes flaws and vices to them to make himself look better than them, not realising that this act is itself a vice. In any case, the absence of vice does not equal virtue. Thus, he is deceived by both his ego and his devil, guilty of the two vices of the rational and irascible faculties. He then adds mention of the vice of the appetitive faculty, saying:

[104:2] [He] *who amasses wealth and counts it over*: the counting over also alludes to ignorance, because the one who saves up wealth for emergencies does not realise that this wealth is the very thing that causes emergencies to occur, as God's wisdom dictates that it be dispersed on them. How, then, could he hope to repel them? Likewise, He says:

[104:3] *He thinks that his wealth will make him immortal*: he does not sense that the acquisitions that give immortality are knowledge and enduring virtues of the soul, not ephemeral accidents and corporeal treasures. He is deceived by his high hopes and deluded by the Satan of estimation, so that he overlooks the reality of the unexpected moment of death. In sum, ignorance, which is the vice of the angelic faculty, is the root and cause of all other vices; and therefore it is only right that the one immersed in it should deserve perpetual chastisement, which overwhelms the heart and nullifies its substance.

[104:4] *Nay*, the impossible cannot happen. *He will surely be flung into the Crusher.*

[104:5] [*And what will show you what the Crusher is?*

[104:6] [*It is*] *the fire of God, kindled,* [104:7] *which peers over the hearts:*] he will fall from the level of his innate disposition to the level of overwhelming nature, which is the crusher whose nature is to break everything that falls into it by losing its power upon it; it is the spiritual fire that nullifies the substance of the heart, causing it unfathomable pain, overwhelming it and penetrating its noble facet and interior, the highest part of it which is the inner-heart that connects to the spirit.

[104:8] *Indeed, it will be closed in on them*: its gates shut closed because of how the heart within it is veiled by corporeal matter and controlled by benighted configurations, material attachments and bestial, predatory and satanic forms, preventing its escape to the realm of holiness; [104:9] *in outstretched columns*: stretching from the expanse of the sphere of the moon to the centre, which are the elemental natures that have become tied to it because of the connection and the chains of inclination and love. And God knows best.

Q. 104:4

105

THE ELEPHANT
SŪRAT AL-FĪL

In the Name of God, the Compassionate, the Merciful

[105:1] *Have you not considered the way in which your Lord dealt with the Folk of the Elephant?*

[105:2] *[Did He not make their stratagem go astray]* [105:3] *and unleash upon them swarms of birds,* [105:4] *pelting them with stones of baked clay,* [105:5] *thus making them like devoured blades?* The story of the Folk of the Elephant is well-known. The incident occurred shortly before the time of the Messenger of God (may God bless him and grant him peace), and was one of the signs of God's power and the manifestations of His wrath upon those who dared defy Him by threatening His Sanctuary. The inspiring of birds and beasts was more direct than the inspiring of man, since their souls are more naturally subservient. Nor was the influencing of the stones, by means of a special power that God placed in them, an impossible feat. Anyone who beholds the realm of divine power and looks behind the veil of wisdom will recognise the potency of such things. In fact, even in our own times there have been instances of it, such as the plague of mice that fell upon the city of Abivard and ruined their crops, and then returned to the countryside via the banks of the Oxus, each of them taking a piece of wood from the nearby forest and crossing the river atop it. Such events brook no figurative interpretation, just like the states of the Resurrection and similar matters.

As for the spiritual correspondence of it, it is that the Abraha of the Abyssinian soul set out to destroy the Kaʿba of the heart, which is the true house of God, by overwhelming it, and sought to divert the pilgrims of the spiritual faculties to the mock temple of corporeal nature which he had constructed, desiring that it be venerated. But the Qurashī of the practical intellect defiled his temple, by discarding the refuse of intellec-

tual nourishment into it, in the form of chastisement specially designed
for natural matters, such as beautiful customs and praiseworthy character
traits. This kindled flames of the fire of yearning which were stoked by
the caravan of the Quraysh of the spiritual faculties, burning it with spiritual discipline. So he mustered his hosts and sent forth his armies—the
egocentric faculties and their naturally benighted attributes (irascibility,
passion, and the like)—and dispatched the elephant of the Satan of estimation, which does not shrink from the forces of the intellect but wages
war against them. Satan often takes the form of an elephant, as Muʿādh
witnessed during the time of the Messenger of God (may God bless him
and grant him peace), who said, 'Satan places his trunk upon the heart of
the son of Adam; but when he remembers God, he slinks away.'

But God made their plot go awry, and unleashed upon them the birds
of thoughts and remembrances, bright and illuminated by the light of the
spirit, which swarmed against them in groups with the forms of analogies and manifold remembrances. They pelted them with stones of baked
clay—spiritual disciplines set down in stone and specially designed for
each of them—each engraved with the name of its target by the pen of
the Divine Law and the intellect, so that each discipline was intended for
a particular faculty and sent to destroy it: subdual and restraint for irascibility, fasting for desire, lowliness for arrogance, humility for pride, and
so on. Thus, He made them ruined and motionless like devoured blades,
identical to the vegetative faculties which were slain, their strength and
power depleted, incapacitated through being weakened by spiritual discipline. And God knows best.

Q. 105:5

106
QURAYSH
SŪRAT QURAYSH

In the Name of God, the Compassionate, the Merciful

[106:1] *[In gratitude] for the security of Quraysh*: the spiritual faculties and the granting of their comfort, correspondence and safety in the acquisition of virtues, and unifying their orientation towards perfection in the two journeys: [106:2] *[their security] for the journey of winter*, when the sun of the spirit is distant from the zenith point above their heads and they seek refuge in the depths of the body, to tend to the needs of life and rectify the states of the body and see to its needs, *and the journey of summer*, when that sun nears the zenith point above their heads, and they ascend to the plains of the realm of holiness and receive the spirit of certitude; [106:3] *let them worship the Lord of this House*: by affirming His Oneness and devoting worship to Him alone and turning in His direction after recognising Him; [106:4] *Who has fed them* the food of meanings of certitude, gnostic secrets and divine realities *against hunger*: the hunger of the impulse of preparedness and the urge of innate disposition in the midst of the famine of simple ignorance; *and made them secure from fear* of the dominance of the Abyssinians of the egocentric faculties, guarding them from them and preventing them from yielding and joining the attempt to destroy the temples, or falling captive to them willingly and being utterly destroyed and wiped out. All grace is from God.

In the Qur'ān manuscript of Ubayy, *al-Fīl* [Q. 105] and *Quraysh* were written as one single *sūra*, and some of the elder Companions used to recite them together in the second cycle of the sunset prayer.

107
AID
SŪRAT AL-MĀʿŪN

In the Name of God, the Compassionate, the Merciful

[107:1] *Have you seen him who denies the Judgement?* Do you know of the ignorant one who is veiled from the requital, or do you not know him?

[107:2] *That is he who repels the orphan* [107:3] *and does not urge the feeding of the needy*: he is the one who commits all kinds of vices and becomes engrossed in them; for ignorance and veiling together constitute the vice of the rational faculty, which is the root of all other vices. He repels the orphan, harming the weak, rebuffing them violently and harshly because of the dominance and excess of the predatory soul. He does not urge his kin to feed the needy, and denies kindness to those who deserve it because of the dominance of the bestial soul, his love for wealth, and the ascendancy of the vice of stinginess in his soul.

[107:4] *So woe to them who pray,* [107:5] *those who are heedless of their prayers*: woe to those who possess these attributes and who, if they pray at all, are oblivious to their prayer, because they are veiled from its reality by their ignorance and lack of mindfulness. He calls them people *who pray* in order to draw attention to their inward state by reference to their outward appearance, condemning them by showing how their noblest actions and the forms of their good deeds are in reality sins and misdeeds, because they are bereft of the mindfulness and sincerity which is essential to them. He refers to them in the plural because the meaning of *him who denies* [Q. 107:1] is the entire class of such people.

[107:6] *Those who make a pretence* because of how they are veiled by creation from the Real, [107:7] *and deny aid* to help and assist their fellow creatures with property, goods and anything else that might benefit them; for the veil has doomed them to prefer to help themselves, and they are deprived of the perspective of Oneness, veiled by particular desires from universals and bereft of faith in the Reckoning. They have no love for the Real because they rely on the realm of contrariety, and have fallen to the nature of contingency and corruption, and are veiled from the reality of Unity. There is no justice in their souls because they are characterised by vices and are distant from virtues. They possess neither fear nor hope, oblivious as they are to perfection and ignorant as they are of the Resurrection. They offer no help to anyone, and so they shall never find salvation. And God knows best.

Q. 107:7

108
ABUNDANCE
SŪRAT AL-KAWTHAR

In the Name of God, the Compassionate, the Merciful

[108:1] *We have assuredly given you Abundance*: gnosis of multiplicity through Unity and differentiated knowledge of Oneness, and witnessing of Unity in multiplicity itself by the self-disclosure of the One and Abundant, and the Abundant and One. *Kawthar* ('Abundance') is a river in Paradise; the one who drinks from it will never thirst again.

[108:2] *So pray to your Lord and sacrifice*: when you witness the One in multiplicity, pray the perfect prayer uprightly with witnessing of spirit, presence of heart, surrender of soul and obedience of body, moving through all the forms of worship; for that is the perfect prayer which fulfils all the duties of unification and differentiation. Offer the sacrificial animal of your I-ness, lest it manifest in the midst of your witnessing by variegation and wrest you from the station of stability. Be with the Real through total annihilation, and subsist eternally through His subsistence, so that you never become severed from your arrival and your state, and so that your community—who are your progeny—remain connected to you.

[108:3] *Indeed, [it is your antagonist] who is the severed one*:[1] the one who hates you and occupies a contrary state to yours, and who is cut-off from the real, is the true severed one, not you, for you are the one who will subsist through His subsistence so that your true progeny—the folk of faith—will remain connected to you forever. You will forever be remembered among them, while he will be the one who is truly annihilated and destroyed, never to be found again, nor remembered, nor having any true progeny attributed to him. And God knows best.

1 *Abtar*, literally 'childless'.

109
THE DISBELIEVERS
SŪRAT AL-KĀFIRŪN

In the Name of God, the Compassionate, the Merciful

[109:1] *Say: 'O disbelievers!* You whose light of original preparedness is covered by the darkness of the attributes of souls and effects of nature, veiling them from the Real by other-than-Him.

[109:2] *'I do not worship*—nor will I as long as I bear witness to the Real with essential witnessing—*what you worship*: the gods made by your caprice, fashioned by your imagination, and formed by your minds because of how veiled you are.

[109:3] *'And you do not worship what I worship*: nor will you ever, for you will remain the same and retain your current state of veiling; for those whose hearts are sealed with rust cannot possibly recognise the Real.

[109:4] *'Nor will I worship what you have worshipped*: nor have I ever in the past—before perfection and the ultimate arrival according to primal preparedness and innate disposition, meaning the detached essence alone—worshipped what you have worshipped according to your own primal preparedness before becoming veiled and rusted, because my preparedness was perfect in pre-eternity, and oriented towards the Real innately, while your preparedness was always imperfect.

[109:5] *'Nor will you worship*—according to that preparedness—*what I worship*: you are not able to worship what I worship because of the inherent imperfection of your disposition. In sum, the notion that I could worship what you worship, or that you could worship what I worship, given our current state of secondary preparedness which is my perfection and your veiling, is impossible on both sides in the present and the future. And likewise, before this preparedness in the state of primal preparedness according to essences and entities, it was impossible in pre-eternity too because of how my preparedness was complete while yours was lacking.

The meaning of this is a negation of possibility applying to the future, to the Attribute, to the Essence and to pre-eternity, implying the necessity of pre-eternal negation.

[109:6] '*You have your religion* of worship to the things you worship, *and I have my religion*' of worship to what I worship. Since there can be no correspondence between us, I have left you alone with your religion, so leave me alone with mine. And God knows best.

Q. 109:6

110
HELP
SŪRAT AL-NAṢR

In the Name of God, the Compassionate, the Merciful

[110:1] *When the help of God*—the angelic succour and holy aid through the self-disclosures of the Names and Attributes—*comes together with victory*: the absolute victory beyond which there is no other; the opening of the door of Unitary Presence and essential unveiling after the manifest victory in the station of the spirit by witnessing; [110:2] *and you see people entering God's religion*—namely the affirmation of Oneness and traversal of the straight path, thanks to the influence of your light upon them after you finished perfecting yourself—*in throngs*: gathered together like a single soul receiving the emanations of your essence and standing in the station of your soul. They are the prepared ones whose souls were connected to his (may God grant him peace) by a correspondence and affinity which linked them to him, so they could receive his emanation.

[110:3] *Then glorify*—absolve your essence from being veiled by the station of the heart, which is the source of prophethood, by cutting the ties of the body and ascending to the station of the truth of certitude, which is the source of sainthood—*with praise of your Lord*: praise Him by manifesting His perfections and His complete Attributes when you detach with active praise; *and seek forgiveness from Him*: ask Him to cover your essence with His own, just as it was in the state of annihilation before the return to creation, for ever more. *Indeed, He is ever ready to relent*: ever welcoming of those who return to Him by annihilating them with His light.

When the religion was completed and the call for which he was sent had been made, He commanded him to return to the station of the truth of certitude, which only continues after death. Therefore, when this was revealed and the Messenger of God (may God bless him and grant him peace) recited it, the Companions rejoiced, yet Ibn ʿAbbās wept. He (may

God bless him and grant him peace) said, 'Why do you weep?' He replied,
'Your soul has been called home.' He (may God grant him peace) said,
'This lad has been granted much knowledge.' It is also narrated that when
it was revealed, the Messenger of God (may God bless him and grant him
peace) gave a sermon, saying, 'God has called a servant to choose between
the world and the meeting with Him, and he has chosen to meet God.'
Abū Bakr (may God be pleased with him) knew what this meant and said,
'We would give our lives, our possessions, our fathers and our sons as
ransom for you!' Then he called Fāṭima (may God grant her peace), and
said, 'My daughter, my soul has been called home.' She wept, and he said,
'Weep not, for you shall be the first of my family to join me.' At this she
smiled. This *sūra* is known as the Farewell Chapter on account of this.
It is also narrated that he lived another two years after it, and that it was
revealed during the Farewell Pilgrimage.

Q. 110:3

111
PERISH
SŪRAT TABBAT

In the Name of God, the Compassionate, the Merciful

[111:1] *Perish the hands of Abū Lahab and perish he!* The means of his foul labours, on account of which he earned Hell and the fire of perdition, will be ruined, and so will his foul essence which deserves this by the dictate of its preparedness. He deserved Hell by his essence and his attributes, fire upon fire, which is why He called him by his nickname Abū Lahab ('Father of Flames'), which evokes this fate.

[111:2] *His wealth will not avail him, nor what he has earned*: neither his original wealth—the knowledge of innate preparedness—will avail him, nor will what he acquired thereafter, because his belief does not correspond to reality. Neither will aid him in his torment, nor will either of them be of any use to him.

[111:3] *He will [soon] enter a Fire*—a tremendous fire due to his veiling with idolatry—*of flames* in addition to his origin, because of the foulness of his acts and their configurations, roasted by corrupt beliefs and evil deeds.

[111:4] Both him *and his wife* will be there together, *the carrier of firewood*: carrying the burdens of her sins and the configurations of her foul deeds, which are the fuel of Hellfire; [111:5] *with a rope [of palm-fibre] around her neck*: a strong braid tightly wound from the chains of Hell because of her love for vices and iniquities, so that her configurations and sins will be tied to her neck with that rope to chastise her with a torment that corresponds to her crimes. And God knows best.

112
SINCERITY
SŪRAT AL-IKHLĀṢ

In the Name of God, the Compassionate, the Merciful

[112:1] *Say: 'He, God, is One.* The word *Say* is a command from the source of unification, issued to the locus of differentiation. *He* is an expression of the pure unitary reality, meaning the Essence as it is without consideration for any Attribute, which is known only to Him. Then *God* also refers to this; it is the Name of the Essence along with all the Attributes, and so this construction indicates that His Attributes are not an addition to His Essence, but rather they are the Essence itself, and there is no distinction between them except on the level of the intellectual perspective. This is why this *sūra* is called *al-Ikhlāṣ* ('Sincerity'), since 'sincerity' means a pure expression of the unitary reality unsullied by multiplicity, as the Commander of the Believers (may God grant him peace) said, 'Perfection of sincerity to Him means to negate Attributes from Him.' This is because every Attribute attests that it is not the object of attribution, and every object of attribution attests that it is not the Attribute. This is what is meant by those who say that His Attributes are neither Him nor other than Him: they are not Him from the perspective of the intellect, nor other than Him from the perspective of reality.

Is One (aḥad) is the predicate of the sentence. The difference between *aḥad* and *wāḥid*[1] is that *aḥad* means the Essence alone without regard for any multiplicity in it: that is, the pure reality that is the font of the spring of *Kāfūr* and indeed is identical with it; it is existence inasmuch as it is existence, without the restriction of universality or specificity or the stipulation of accidents or their absence. *Wāḥid*, conversely, means the Essence with consideration for the multiplicity of Attributes; it is

---

1 They both broadly mean 'one'.

the Name-presence, because the Name is the Essence with the Attribute. Thus, He represented the pure reality known only to Him with *He*, and then referred to it again as the Essence with all the Attributes in order to express how it is the Essence itself, alone in reality. Then He referred to its Oneness to indicate that the multiplicity of perspective is not a thing in reality, and thus does not impinge on His Unity or affect His Oneness. Rather, the presence of Oneness (*wāhidiyya*) is identical with the presence of Unity (*ahadiyya*) in reality, just as one might imagine that the sea is composed of drops of water.

[112:2] *'God, the Self-Sufficient, Besought of all*: the Essence in the presence of Oneness, from the perspective of the Names, is the absolute support for all things, because of how every contingent being needs It and exists through It. He is the Absolutely Independent on which all things depend, as He says, *For God is the Independent, while you are the needy* [Q. 47:38]. Since everything but Him exists through His existence, it is not a thing in itself, because the contingency that is necessary for quiddity does not entail existence. Thus, there is nothing that shares His genus or likeness in existence.

Q. 112:2

[112:3] *'He neither begot*: for the objects of His knowledge do not exist alongside Him but rather in Him; they exist in Him, but in themselves they are nothing; *nor was He begotten*, because of His absolute self-sufficiency; He was never in need of anything in existence. And since His unique Ipseity does not accept multiplicity or division, and the Essential Unity is not accompanied by any other, for everything besides Absolute Being is pure nothingness, there can be nothing equal to Him:

[112:4] *'Nor is there anyone equal to Him'*: for pure nothingness cannot be equal to pure existence. Accordingly, this *sūra* is also known as the Foundation Chapter, since the foundation (*asās*) of religion—indeed, the foundation of all existence—is the affirmation of Oneness. It was related through Anas that the Prophet (may God bless him and grant him peace) said, 'The seven heavens and the seven earths were built on *Say: "He, God, is One."'* This is the meaning of His absolute self-sufficiency.

113
THE DAYBREAK
SŪRAT AL-FALAQ

In the Name of God, the Compassionate, the Merciful

[113:1] *Say: 'I seek refuge in the Lord of the Daybreak*: I seek the shelter of the Name of the Guide, and refuge in Him by adopting His Attribute and connecting to the Holy Spirit in the Name-presence; for daybreak is the light of dawn that precedes the rising of the sun. In other words, I seek refuge in the Lord of the light of the dawn of the self-disclosure of the Attributes, which comes before the rising of the light of the Essence, and the Lord of the light of the dawn of the Attributes, which is the Name of the Guide. This is always the meaning of seeking refuge with one's Lord from any evil, for it means to seek refuge with a particular Name that is connected to that thing. When the sick man seeks refuge in his Lord, he seeks refuge in the Healer; and the ignorant man seeks refuge from his ignorance in the Knower.

[113:2] *'From the evil of what He has created*: from the evil of being veiled by creation and their influence; for the one who connects to the realm of holiness in the presence of the Names and adopts God's Attributes will influence every other creature, without being influenced by any of them, as they are in the realm of effects and the station of the acts, while he has ascended from the station of the acts to their originators from the Attributes.

[113:3] *'And from the evil of darkness when it gathers*: from the evil of being veiled by the benighted body, when its darkness enters all things and dominates and influences by alterations to its states and disturbances to its balance in the heart, due to the heart's love for it, inclination to it and attraction towards it.

[113:4] *'And from the evil of the women-blowers* [*on knots*]: the egocentric faculties of estimation, imagination, irascibility, appetite and the like, which blow on the knots of the resolutions of the wayfarers by weakening them with satanic impulses, and untying and blowing upon them with insinuations and suggestions.

[113:5] *'And from the evil of an envier when he envies'*: the soul when it *envies* the illumination of the heart, and so usurps its attributes and gnostic secrets by grasping the attention of the hearing, transgressing and manifesting upon it and veiling it. This is the meaning of variegation in the station of the heart. The *darkness* [Q. 113:3] could also be interpreted as the dominating soul that veils the heart with the darkness of its attributes, and the *envier* as the heart when in manifests in the station of witnessing; for the variegation of the station of witnessing is caused by the presence of the heart, just as the variegation of the station of the heart is caused by the presence of the soul. He singles out these three things for the seeking of refuge, after first mentioning seeking refuge from the evil of creation in general, because among all creatures they are the most frequent causes of veiling, due to their connection to it and its attachment to them. And God (Exalted is He) knows best.

Q. 113:5

114
PEOPLE
SŪRAT AL-NĀS

In the Name of God, the Compassionate, the Merciful

[114:1] *Say: 'I seek refuge in the Lord of people*: the *Lord of people* is the Essence along with all the Attributes. Due to the fact that man is the universal being who contains all the levels of existence, his Lord Who created him and emanated his perfection is the Essence from the perspective of all the Names at the beginning, which is expressed by the Name God (*Allāh*). Therefore, He says, *What prevents you from prostrating before that which I have created with My own hands* [Q. 38:75], meaning with pairs of opposing Attributes, such as subtlety and power, beauty and majesty, which cover all of them. He sought refuge in His countenance after seeking refuge in His Attributes, which is why this *sūra* comes after the first *sūra* of refuge, since that one described seeking refuge in the station of the Attributes in His Name the Guide, whereupon He guided him to His Essence.

He subsequently clarifies that the *Lord of people* is also:

[114:2] *'The King of people*, because the King is the One Who has sovereignty (*mulk*) over their lives and affairs from the perspective of their annihilation in Him, as He says, *To whom does the kingdom belong today? To God, the One, the All-Compelling!* [Q. 40:16]. The King in reality is the One, the All-Compelling, Who compels everything by His manifestation.

[114:3] *'The God of people*: He adds this to clarify the state of their subsistence after annihilation, because God is the absolute object of worship, which is the Essence along with all the Attributes from the perspective of the end. He sought refuge in His absolute presence, and so was annihilated in Him, whence His nature as King was manifested. Then He returned him to existence for the station of servitude, so that He was worshipped perpetually, and his search for refuge in Him was fulfilled.

[114:4] *'From the evil of the [slinking (khannās)] whisperer (waswās)*: whispering implies an existential locus, as He says: [114:5] *who whispers in the hearts of people*: and there is no existence in the state of annihilation, and so no hearts, nor any whispering, nor any whisperer. But if any variegation is manifested there through the existence of I-ness, then say, 'I seek refuge in You from You.'

Besides, when He became worshipped through the existence of the worshipper, Satan manifested through the manifestation of the worshipper, just as in the beginning he had existed through his existence.

The word *waswās* actually means 'whisper', but it became a name for the whisperer because he is always whispering, as though he himself is a whisper. The reason he sought refuge from him in [the Name] God rather than in any of His other Names—as is described in the first *sūra*—is that Satan is the one who opposes the Compassionate and seeks to dominate the universal human form, and manifest himself in the forms of all Names and adopt their image, except for the Name of God. Thus, it is not sufficient to seek refuge from him in [other Names like] the Guide, or the Knower, or the Powerful or any other. This is why, when he sought refuge from veiling and error, he sought refuge in *the Lord of daybreak* [Q. 113:1], while here he sought refuge in *the Lord of people* [Q. 114:1]. This allows us to understand the meaning of his words (may God grant him peace), 'The one who sees me has truly seen me, for Satan cannot take on my form.' *Khannās* means 'the one who returns', for he only whispers when there is heedlessness. Yet whenever the servant becomes alert and remembers God, he slinks away. Slinking is his nature, just as whispering is.

Q. 114:4

[114:6] *'Of the jinn and people'*: these words explain the identity of the whisperer. The whispering devils are of two kinds: the intangible jinn, such as estimation, and the tangible human, such as people who lead others astray. Sometimes they come in the guise of the Guide, as He says, *Indeed, you used to approach us from the right* [Q. 37:28]. At other times, they come in the guise of other Names, and so the only way to seek refuge from them properly is to seek it in God. God is the Protector.

APPENDIX
PERSONS CITED IN THE TEXT[1]
(Excluding prophets)

ʿABD ALLĀH B. UBAYY (d. 9/631). One of the leading men of Medina when the Prophet emigrated to the city. He would become the leader of the Hypocrites, apparently after leading three hundred men to abandon the Prophet before the battle of Uḥud. Nonetheless, his son, ʿAbd Allāh, was a faithful Muslim, who was willing to kill his father for opposing the Prophet. (Ṭabarī, *History*, VII.XXIV, XXXI and 159 (notes by Watt); Ṭabarī, *History*, IX.73)

ʿABD AL-MUṬṬALIB (d. ca. 578). The grandfather of the Prophet. After the death of the Prophet's mother, ʿAbd al-Muṭṭalib took him into his care until his own death two years thereafter. (Ghazālī, *Condemnation of Pride*, 154 (note by Rustom).)

ABRAHA. An Abyssinian ruler of Yemen who constructed a temple in Sanaʾa with the intention of rivalling the Kaʿba, and attempted to divert the pilgrims there. In response, a man of the Quraysh tribe defiled the temple, enraging Abraha. In response, he led the march with elephants against Mecca shortly before the birth of the Messenger of God. As recounted in Q. 105, God repelled them with *swarms of birds pelting them with stones of baked clay.* (Kāshānī on Q. 105; Shafi, *Maʿariful*, VIII. 877–884.)

ABSĀL. The name of a main character conveyed in varying fables by, for example, the philosopher Ibn Sīnā and the poet Jāmī. (Dehghan, 'Jāmī's *Salāmān and Absāl'*.)

ABŪ BAKR al-Ṣiddīq b. Abī Quḥāfa al-Taymī (d. 13/634). A businessman of Mecca who personally accompanied the Prophet on his emigration to Medina. Abū Bakr became the Prophet's closest advisor, and after his death became the first Caliph. He narrated 142 ḥadīth. (*Disciplining*, 210; Ṣiddīqī, *Ḥadīth Literature*, 17.)

ABŪ MASʿŪD AL-THAQAFĪ. He was a Hijazi notable. It is narrated that when Abraha al-Ashram attacked Mecca in the Year of the Elephant in ca. 552 CE, he accompanied ʿAbd al-Muṭṭalib, along with other chieftains, to Mount Ḥirāʾ to supplicate for God's protection. (However, it is possible that Kāshānī meant ʿUrwa b. Masʿūd al-Thaqafī or Masʿūd b. ʿAmr al-Thaqafī, who have been mentioned, among others, in reference to Q. 43:31.) (Ṭabarī, *History*, V. 207, 220 (Bosworth's note) and 234; Ibn Kathīr, *Tafsīr*, 1679.)

---

1 Any references to *Disciplining* refer to the notes, often slightly amended, from T. J. Winter in Ghazālī, *On Disciplining the Soul*.

ABŪ YAZĪD al-Basṭāmī, Ṭayfūr b. ʿĪsā (d. 261/874 or 264/877–8). Al-Junayd is reported as saying that ʿAbū Yazīd holds the same rank among us as Gabriel among the angels.' A Sufi of Central Asia famous for his ecstatic and enigmatic utterances (shaṭaḥāt). In addition, he was regarded as a reliable Traditionist. (Disciplining, 212.)

ʿALĪ b. Abī Ṭālib (d. 40/661). The cousin and son-in-law of the Prophet, having married his daughter Fāṭima. He lived a life of austerity and piety. Upon the death of ʿUthmān (35/656) he accepted, with some reluctance, the office of Caliph, which he held for five years disturbed by several rebellions, including that of Muʿāwiya, the governor of Syria. He was assassinated at Kufa by a member of the extreme Khārijī sect, which repudiated him for having agreed to negotiate with Muʿāwiya. Only ten Companions narrated more than his 536 ḥadīth. (Disciplining, 213; Ṣiddīqī, Ḥadīth Literature, 18.)

AMĪNA. She is narrated to be the umm walad concubine of Prophet Solomon. The legend relates that Solomon would leave his ring of kingship with her when he went to perform ablutions. Then, on one occasion, when she was in possession of the ring, the demon of the sea, Ṣakhr, tricked her into giving her the ring. (Kāshānī on Q. 38:34.)

ʿAMMĀR b. Yāsir (d. 37/657). A Companion and one of the earliest Muslims. His mother Sumayya was the first martyr of Islam. He narrated sixty-two ḥadīth. (Ghazālī, Condemnation of Pride, 156 (note by Rustom); Ṣiddīqī, Ḥadīth Literature, 17.)

ANAS b. Mālik (d. 91–3/709–712]. He was the Prophet's favourite servant, from the age of ten until the Prophet passed away. He participated in the wars of conquest after the Prophet's death. During the reign of Caliph Abū Bakr, he was appointed as the tax-collector for Baḥrayn. He is the third most prolific narrator of ḥadīth amongst the Companions, who transmitted 2,286 traditions. (Disciplining, 213; Ṣiddīqī, Ḥadīth Literature, 18 and 20–1.)

ASAPH. Legend portrays him as either the vizier of Prophet Solomon or the latter's scribe (kātib). It is said that Solomon highly valued his counsel, and he had open access to Solomon. The tafsīr tradition shows him to be The one who had knowledge of the Scripture (Q. 27:40), who knew God's Greatest Name. (Kāshānī on Q. 38:34; Ibn Kathīr, Tafsīr, 1396 (on Q. 27:39); Ṭabarī, History, III. 167 (with Brinner's note).)

ĀSIYA. The Islamic tradition names her as the wife of Pharaoh referred to at Q. 28:9, whereby she pleads for baby Moses' life. A ḥadīth refers to her being one of the most saintly women of humankind. (Kaltner & Mirza, The Bible and the Qurʾan, 144; SQ, 143 and 948.)

BALAAM THE SON OF BEOR. The tafsīr tradition asserts that he was a spiritually enlightened person who lived at the time of Moses. It is narrated that his supplications were answered, and that he knew God's Greatest Name. He was either forced or bribed to try and supplicate against Moses, whereby he forsook the faith. (Ṭabarī, as cited in *SQ*, 469–470.)

[Bathsheba], THE WIFE OF URIAH. Uriah was Prophet David's leading officer. Whilst Muslim scholars never accepted the Biblical account that David committed adultery with Bathsheba, Muslim exegesis before the thirteenth century—although the Biblical story is not present in the Qur'ān—did accept the Judeo-Christian narrative that David sought Uriah's death in order to marry Bathsheba. Some early Muslim sources accepted that she did eventually marry David and was the mother of Prophet Solomon, whereas some later authorities denied her being Solomon's mother, but accepted her marriage to David. (Mohammed, *David in the Muslim Tradition*, 2, 42–4, 118 and 187; Shafi, *Ma'ariful*, VII. 504–9.)

BILQĪS (or Bilqays). She was the Queen of Sheba (*Saba'*) at the time of Prophet Solomon. Her people prostrated to the sun, but she converted to Islam upon Solomon's invitation to the faith. (Q. 27:22–44; *SQ*, 932 and 1046–7.)

CANAAN (Kanʿān). Muslim exegetes often name him as the son of Noah referred to in Q. 11:42–3 and Q. 11:45–6 (although Yām is an alternative name that is proposed). He is said to have been Noah's fourth son (whereas the Bible mentions three sons of Noah that do not include a Canaan, and relates that Noah's son Ham had a son called Canaan). (Shafi, *Ma'ariful*, IV.635; *SQ*, 574; *EQ*, III.541 [Brinner].)

AL-ḌAḤḤĀK b. Muzāḥim (d. 102–106/720–25). A Successor from Balkh, who settled in Kufa and was famous for his Qur'ānic commentary, which he almost certainly did not acquire directly from Ibn ʿAbbās. His reputation was mixed, with Yaḥyā b. Saʿīd al-Qaṭṭān evaluating him as 'weak', but Ibn Ḥanbal and Ibn Maʿīn saying that he was 'reliable'. Al-Ḍaḥḥāk is one of Ṭabarī's most frequently-cited interpreters in his *Tafsīr*, and his *ḥadīth*s are found in Abū Dāwūd, Tirmidhī, Nasāʾī and Ibn Māja. (Ṭabarī, *Selections*, I. 518 (note by Lucas).)

DIḤYA AL-KALBĪ. A Companion of the Prophet. He converted before the battle of Badr, but did not participate in it. The Prophet entrusted him to deliver the letter of invitation to Islam to Heraclius, via the governor of Buṣrā. After the Prophet, he participated in the battle of Yarmouk. He lived until the time of Muʿāwiya. (Dhahabī, *Siyar*, II. 550–554 (with Arnaʾūṭ's notes).)

FĀṬIMA (d. 11/632). The youngest and best-loved of the daughters of the Prophet. He once told her that 'God is angry when you are angry, and glad when you are glad.' In the year 2 AH she married ʿAlī b. Abī Ṭālib in the union which was to produce al-Ḥasan and al-Ḥusayn. Her piety made her greatly revered by later generations. (*Disciplining*, 215.)

ḤABĪB [b. Murā]. Some Muslim sources assert that he lived in Antioch when the city received disciples from Jesus, including Simon (see the below entry). Upon having his sick son healed by Jesus' disciples, he became a believer, and helped spread the faith amongst his people. He was meticulous in giving a significant proportion of his wage in charity. (Ṭabarī, *Selections*, I. 408–9; Bayḍāwī, *Tafsīr*, VII. 60; Shafi, *Ma'ariful*, VII. 376–8.)

HAMAN. During the time of Moses, he was a key member of Pharaoh's court, perhaps in a military capacity. He was instrumental in opposing Moses and his followers. The Qur'ān explains that his fate was to be drowned in the sea with Pharaoh. Muslim scholarship has rejected that he is the Haman of the Biblical book of Esther. There is also the assertion that it was a title, and not a personal name. (Kaltner & Mirza, *The Bible and the Qur'an*, 60–1.)

ḤĀRITHA. Unidentified. From the Companions there was Ḥāritha b. al-Nuʿmān, who participated in the battle of Badr and lived until the time of Muʿāwiya. Yet the narration included by Kāshānī might be a variant of a famous, but unauthenticated, tradition related from another Companion called al-Ḥārith b. Mālik al-Anṣārī. In the latter, as proof for asserting that he is 'a believer', al-Ḥārith says, 'O Messenger of God, I have ordered my soul to turn away from this world, and it has [obeyed] calmly; I have abstained from drinking during daylight and have spent the nights awake. It is as if I look at the throne of the Lord and at Paradise's dwellers paying visits to one another and at Hell's dwellers howling at one another.' A similar conversation is also narrated in relation to ʿAwf b. Mālik. (Dhahabī, *Siyar*, II. 378–380; Ṭabarī, *History*, XXXIX. 154; Ibn Abī Shayba, *Īmān*, 43 (with Albānī's notes).)

AL-ḤASAN b. ʿAlī b. Abī Ṭālib (d. ca. 50/670–1). Grandson of the Prophet, and second Imām of the Shīʿa. Until the reign of ʿAlī he lived a secluded life at Medina, which was interrupted by a short period in which he claimed the Caliphate. (Ghazālī, *Remembrance*, 292–3 (note by Winter).)

AL-ḤUSAYN b. ʿAlī b. Abī Ṭālib (d. 61/680). A grandson of the Prophet, who, although he acquiesced in the Caliphate of Muʿāwiya, refused to recognise his son al-Yazīd upon his accession in 60 AH (680 AD). Against the advice of Ibn ʿAbbās and ʿAbd Allāh b. ʿUmar, al-Ḥusayn marched with a handful of supporters to Kufa, where he believed that he could muster support. The Kufans, however, intimidated by al-Yazīd's governor, met him in battle at nearby Karbala, where he was slain. (Ghazālī, *Remembrance*, 293–4 (note by Winter).)

AL-ḤUSAYN B. MANṢŪR AL-ḤALLĀJ (d. 309/922). He was a Persian-born, Iraqi Sufi executed by the authorities, apparently for the controversy caused by some of his ecstatic, or theopathic, statements (*shaṭaḥāt*)—famously, 'I am the Truth' (*anā al-Ḥaqq*); but his execution was most likely for political reasons connected to the intrigues of the viziers at the Abbasid court and the rivalry between the various dominant Sunni schools in Baghdad. (*EI²*, III. 99 [L. Massignon and L. Gardet]; Massignon, *Hallāj*; Sulamī, 236.)

IBN ʿABBĀS, ʿAbd Allāh (d. 68/687–8). A cousin and close Companion of the Prophet respected for his piety, and commonly acknowledged as the greatest scholar of the first generation of Muslims, the fifth most prolific narrator of *ḥadīth* amongst the Companions (with 1,660 traditions) and the founder of the science of Qurʾānic exegesis. He fought alongside ʿAlī at Ṣiffīn, and died at Taʾif, where the site of his grave is still visited. (*Disciplining*, 216; Ṣiddīqī, *Ḥadīth Literature*, 18.)

IBN AL-ʿARABĪ, Muḥyī al-Dīn (d. 638/1240). Born in Muslim Spain, he went on to travel the world, eventually coming to rest in Damascus. He is arguably the most famous, or infamous, Sufi philosopher, who is revered by some as 'the Greatest Spiritual Master' (*al-shaykh al-akbar*). He was educated in a wide array of Islamic sciences, and was a jurist. Although he wrote many books, his most famous ones are *Fuṣūṣ al-ḥikam, al-Futūḥāt al-Makkiyya* and *Tarjuman al-ashwāq*. (Chittick, *Ibn ʿArabi: Heir to the Prophets*; Winkel, *Islam and the Living Law*.)

IBN MASʿŪD, ʿAbd Allāh al-Hudhalī (d. 32/652). Of Bedouin origin, Ibn Masʿūd is said to have been either the third or the sixth convert to Islam. He became one of the most erudite Companions. He was particularly well versed in the recitation and interpretation of the Qurʾān, and was an expert in matters of Law. His narration of 848 *ḥadīth* places him eighth on the list of Companion narrators. (*Disciplining*, 216; Ṣiddīqī, *Ḥadīth Literature*, 18.)

IBN ʿUMAR (d. 73/693–4). The son of the second Caliph and a Companion of the Prophet who, at the age of fourteen, asked to be permitted to fight at Uḥud, although permission was denied. However, he later participated in numerous battles during the Prophet's lifetime. Possessed of high moral qualities, he commanded universal deference and respect. Although it is said that he was offered the Caliphate on three separate occasions, he kept himself aloof from politics and occupied himself instead with study and instruction. He is the second most prolific narrator of *ḥadīth* amongst the Companions, with 2,630 traditions, despite it being narrated that he was very cautious about transmitting. (*Disciplining*, 217; Ṣiddīqī, *Ḥadīth Literature*, 18 and 20.)

JĀBIR B. ʿABD ALLĀH (d. 68–78/688–698). A Companion of the Prophet who was an early Medinan convert. His father died at the battle of Uḥud. He participated in nineteen of the expeditions of the Prophet, and related a sizeable number of *ḥadīth* (1,540 traditions, placing him sixth on the list of Companions). (Ghazālī, *Remembrance*, 299 (note by Winter); Ṣiddīqī, *Ḥadīth Literature*, 18 and 22.)

JARĀDA. Kāshānī argues that Jewish legend portrays her as the beautiful daughter of the king of Sidon, who is taken as a wife by Prophet Solomon upon his conquering of her father's land and her conversion to Islam. The tale asserts that she fell into worshipping an image of her father which Solomon arranged for her. (Kāshānī on Q. 38:34.)

KORAH. He is named three times in the Qurʾān, and in two of them he is mentioned alongside Pharaoh and Haman as enemies of Moses. He mistreated people, sought to divide them and attributed his vast wealth to his own ability. His worldly end occurred with him being swallowed up by the earth. (Kaltner & Mirza, *The Bible and the Qur'an*, 105.)

MUʿĀDH b. Jabal (d. *c* 18/639–40). An early convert to Islam, be became well versed in *fiqh* in a short space of time. He was the Prophet's governor of the Yemen, and died in Syria. He narrated 157 *hadīth*. (Ghazālī, *Remembrance*, 301 (note by Winter); Ṣiddīqī, *Hadīth Literature*, 18.)

MUʿĀWIYA b. Abī Sufyān (*regn.* 40–60/661–80). A Companion and first Caliph of the Umayyad dynasty. He was able and astute, and continued the conquests of his predecessors. He narrated 163 *hadīth*. (Ghazālī, *Remembrance*, 301 (note by Winter); Ṣiddīqī, *Hadīth Literature*, 18.)

MUJĀHID b. Jabr al-Makkī (d. 104/722–3). Sometimes considered the most learned authority among the 'Followers' (*tābiʿūn*) on the exegesis of the Qur'ān, which he learnt from Ibn ʿAbbās, he was particularly concerned to establish the circumstances under which each verse had been revealed. He was also respected for his austere and pious lifestyle. (Ghazālī, *Remembrance*, 303 (note by Winter).)

NŪR AL-DĪN ʿABD AL-ṢAMAD Naṭanzī (d. 691/1292). He was a spiritual master of the Suhrawardī order in Natanz, near Isfahan. There is no documentation of his writings, but it is recorded that he lived and taught in Natanz. Upon his death, a disciple who was an Īlkhānid amir established a complex around his tomb in Natanz, which is still visited today and includes a masjid and a Sufi lodge. (Lory, "Abd al-Razzāq al-Kāshānī'; Blair, 'Sufi Saints and Shrine Architecture', 35 and 40.)

PHARAOH. He was the ruler of Egypt who is mentioned almost seventy-five times in the Qur'ān. His name is mostly cited in relation to Moses and the latter's liberation of the Israelites from Pharaoh's tyrannical rule. Around the time of Moses' birth, Pharaoh had ordered that all the male children of the Israelites were to be killed; but Moses escaped this fate upon the intervention of Pharaoh's female family. When Moses invited Pharaoh to faith in God, he rejected the call and claimed divinity for himself. After Moses and the Israelites were given a route of escape through the miraculously parted sea, Pharaoh was drowned with his army as the sea was brought down upon them. (Kaltner & Mirza, *The Bible and the Qur'an*, 141–2.)

QATĀDA b. Diʿāma al-Sadūsī (d. 117/735). A Basran Successor, who was famous for his Qur'ānic interpretation. He is one of the most frequently-cited interpreters in Ṭabarī's *Tafsīr*. Qatāda was considered 'reliable', even though he was also associated with the advocates of free will (Qadariyya). He studied with al-Ḥasan al-Baṣrī for twelve years and had a reputation for having a prodigious memory. His *hadīth*s are found in all Six Books. (Ṭabarī, *Selections*, 1. 522 (note by Lucas).)

AL-ṢĀDIQ, Jaʿfar b. Muḥammad (d. 148/765). A major authority on Law and *Hadīth*, he taught both Abū Ḥanīfa and Mālik. His austere and saintly life made him an important ideal for the Sufis, who gathered large numbers of sayings attributed to him. He was regarded as the seventh Imām of the Shīʿa: the Jaʿfariyya sect is named after him. (*Disciplining*, 217–8.)

SALĀMĀN. The name of a main character conveyed in varying fables by, for example, the philosopher Ibn Sīnā and the poet Jāmī. (Dehghan, 'Jāmī's *Salāmān and Absāl*'.)

SHIHĀB AL-DĪN Abū Ḥafṣ AL-SUHRAWARDĪ (d. 632/1234). The famous Sufi master who is considered to be the founder of the Suhrawardī order. He authored the famed Sufi manual *ʿAwārif al-maʿārif*, after studying in Baghdad under his Sufi master uncle Abū al-Najīb. His spiritual sermons were popular and noted for their forcefulness. He is not to be confused with Shihāb al-Dīn Yaḥyā al-Suhrawardī, who is associated with the School of Illumination (*al-ishrāq*), and was executed in 587/1191 on charges of heresy, on the order of Ṣalāḥ al-Dīn Ayyūbī. (Hanif, *Biographical Encyclopaedia of Sufis*, 461–3; *SQ*, 1732.)

SIMON. Unidentified. The Muslim traditions that name him as the third disciple sent by Jesus to Antioch do not specify whether it is Simon Peter or Simon the Zealot, although the former is more likely intended. While some Muslim commentators of the Qurʾān question the veracity of the story, many have accepted it and talk of Simon performing miracles before the ruler. (McDowell, *Fate of the Apostles*, 25–6, 55 and 245; Bayḍāwī, *Tafsīr*, vii. 60; Qurṭubī, cited in Ṣābūnī, *Ṣafwāt*, iii. 7; Shafi, *Maʿariful*, vii. 372–3 and 378.)

UBAYY b. Kaʿb (d. 19–32/640–53). A Companion among the Helpers, who was present at the Second ʿAqaba pledge with the Prophet. He fought at Badr and the subsequent campaigns, although he is famous primarily for his knowledge, especially regarding the Qurʾān. He was a scribe, who wrote down much of the Qurʾān during the Prophet's lifetime. The Prophet recited the Qurʾān to him twice in the last year of his life, including once after the Prophet's last reading with Gabriel. He was a member of the committee established by ʿUthmān to agree on an authorised copy of the Qurʾān. He narrated 164 *ḥadīth*. (Ṭabarī, *Selections*, i. 524 (note by Lucas); Ṣiddīqī, *Ḥadīth Literature*, 18; Al-Aʿzamī, *History*, 52 and 89.)

AL-WALĪD B. AL-MUGHĪRA (d. 2/624). He was one of the Meccan chieftains most bitterly opposed to the Prophet. A number of Qurʾānic verses refer to him and his enmity to Islam. (Ghazālī, *Condemnation of Pride*, 164 (note by Rustom).)

BIBLIOGRAPHY

Abdel Haleem, M. A. S., *The Qur'an: A New Translation*, New York: Oxford University Press, 2005, repr. 2008.

Aigle, Denise, 'The Mongol Invasions of Bilād al-Shām by Ghāzān Khān and Ibn Taymīyah's Three "Anti-Mongol" Fatwas', *Mamlūk Studies Review*, vol. xi, no. 2, 2007, pp. 89–120.

Al-Aʿẓamī, Muḥammad Muṣṭafā, *The History of the Qur'ānic Text from Revelation to Compilation: A Comparative Study with the Old and New Testaments*, Leicester: UK Islamic Academy, 2003.

Arberry, Arthur J., *The Koran Interpreted*, Oxford & New York: Oxford University Press, 1998.

Bayḍāwī, ʿAbd Allāh b. ʿUmar al-, *Tafsīr*, with the *Ḥāshiya* of Shaykh Zādah, ed. Muḥammad ʿAbd al-Qādir Shāhīn, 8 vols., Beirut: Dār al-Kutub al-ʿIlmiyya, 1999.

Blair, Sheila S., 'Sufi Saints and Shrine Architecture in the Early Fourteenth Century', *Muqarnas*, vol. vii, 1990, pp. 35–49.

Brinner, William M., s.v. 'Noah', in Jane Dammen McAuliffe, ed., *Encyclopaedia of the Qur'ān (EQ)*, 6 vols., Leiden: Brill, 2001–6.

Chittick, William C., *Ibn ʿArabi: Heir to the Prophets*, Oxford: Oneworld, 2005.

——, 'Ibn al-ʿArabī's Hermeneutics of Mercy', in Steven T. Katz, ed., *Mysticism and Sacred Scripture*, Oxford: Oxford University Press, 2000, pp. 153–168.

——, *Imaginal Worlds: Ibn al-ʿArabi and the Problem of Religious Diversity*, Albany, NY: SUNY Press, 1994.

——, 'Rūmī and *waḥdat al-wujūd*', in Amin Banani et al., eds., *Poetry and Mysticism in Islam: The Heritage of Rūmī*, Cambridge: Cambridge University Press, 1994, pp. 70–111.

——, *The Sufi Path of Knowledge: Ibn al-ʿArabi's Metaphysics of Imagination*, Albany, NY: SUNY Press, 1989.

Chodkiewicz, Michel, *Un Océan sans rivage. Ibn ʿArabī, le Livre et la Loi*, trans. David Streight as *An Ocean Without Shore: Ibn ʿArabī, the Book and the Law*, Albany, NY: SUNY Press, 1993.

——, *Le Sceau des Saints, Prophétie et Sainteté dans la doctrine d'Ibn ʿArabī*, trans. Liadain Sherrard as *Seal of the Saints: Prophethood and Sainthood in the Doctrine of Ibn ʿArabī*, Cambridge: Islamic Texts Society, 1993.

Coppens, Pieter, *Seeing God in Sufi Qur'an Commentaries: Crossings between This World and the Otherworld*, Edinburgh: Edinburgh University Press, 2018.

Dehghan, Iraj, 'Jāmī's *Salāmān and Absāl*', *Journal of Near Eastern Studies*, vol. xxx, no. 2, 1971, pp. 118–126.

Dhahabī, Shams al-Dīn al-, *Siyar aʿlām al-nubalāʾ*, ed. Shuʿayb al-Arnaʾūṭ et al., 2nd ed., 25 vols., Beirut: Muʾassasat al-Risāla, 1982.

Edaibat, Omar, 'Muḥyī l-Dīn Ibn ʿArabī's Personalist Theory of the *Sharīʿa*: An Examination of His Legal Doctrine', *Journal of Sufi Studies*, vol. XI, 2017, pp. 1–46.

Elias, Jamal J., *The Throne Carrier of God: The Life and Thought of ʿAlāʾ ad-dawla as-Simnānī*, Albany, NY: SUNY Press, 1995.

Esposito, John L., ed., *The Oxford Dictionary of Islam*, New York: Oxford University Press, 2003.

Ghazālī, Abū Ḥāmid al-, *On Condemnation of Pride and Self-Admiration* (Book XXIX of *The Revival of the Religious Sciences*, translated by Mohammed Rustom), Cambridge: Islamic Texts Society, 2018.

——, *On Disciplining the Soul & on Breaking the Two Desires* (Books XXII & XXIII of *The Revival of the Religious Sciences*, translated by T. J. Winter), Cambridge: Islamic Texts Society, 1995, repr. 1997.

——, *On the Remembrance of Death and the Afterlife* (Book XL of *The Revival of the Religious Sciences*, translated by T. J. Winter), Cambridge: Islamic Texts Society, 1989, repr. 1995.

Gruber, Christiane, *The Ilkhanid Book of Ascension: A Persian-Sunni Devotional Tale*, London & New York: Tauris Academic Studies, 2010.

Hanif, N., *Biographical Encyclopaedia of Sufis: Central Asia & Middle East*, New Delhi: Sarup & Sons, 2002.

Hashtroodi, Fatemeh Tayefeh Aghakhan, 'Concept of Chivalry (*Futuwwah*) According to Abd al-Razzaq Kashani: Analysis of His Tuhfah al-Ikhwan Fi Khasais al-Fityan', PhD thesis, University of Malaya, 2015.

Hoover, Jon, 'Ibn Taymiyya between Moderation and Radicalism', in Elisabeth Kendall and Ahmad Khan, eds., *Reclaiming Islamic Tradition: Modern Interpretations of the Classical Tradition*, Edinburgh: Edinburgh University Press, 2016, pp. 177–203.

Hope, Michael, *Power, Politics, and Tradition in the Mongol Empire and the Īlkhānate of Iran*, Oxford: Oxford University Press, 2016.

Ibn Abī Shayba, *Kitāb al-īmān*, ed. Muḥammad Nāṣir al-Dīn al-Albānī, 7 vols., 2nd ed., Beirut & Damascus: al-Maktab al-Islāmī, 1983.

Ibn ʿArabī, Muḥyī al-Dīn, *Fuṣūṣ al-ḥikam*, Beirut: Dār al-Kutub al-ʿIlmiyya, n.d.

Ibn Kathīr, *Tafsīr al-Qurʾān al-ʿaẓīm*, Beirut: Dār Ibn Ḥazm, 1420/2000.

Jackson, P., s.v. 'Abū Saʿīd Bahādor Khan', in Ehsan Yarshater et al., eds., *Encyclopædia Iranica*, Leiden: Brill, 1985–.

Jackson, Peter, *The Mongols and the Islamic World: From Conquest to Conversion*, New Haven & London: Yale University Press, 2017.

Kaltner, John and Younus Y. Mirza, *The Bible and the Qurʾan: Biblical Figures in the Islamic Tradition*, London and New York: Bloomsbury, 2018.

Kāshānī, ʿAbd al-Razzāq al-, *Kitāb iṣṭilāḥāt al-ṣūfiyya*, trans. Nabil Safwat as *A Glossary of Sufi Technical Terms*, London: Octogan Press, 1991.

Bibliography

——, *Rashḥ al-zulāl fī sharḥ al-alfāẓ al-mutadāwala bayna arbāb al-adhwāq wa'l-aḥwāl*, ed. Saʿīd ʿAbd al-Fattāḥ, Cairo: al-Maktaba al-Azhariyya li'l-Turāth, 1995.

——, *Ta'wīlāt al-Qur'ān*, published as *Tafsīr Ibn ʿArabī*. Beirut: Dār al-Kutub al-ʿIlmiyya, n.d.

Knysh, Alexander D., *Ibn ʿArabi in the Later Islamic Tradition: The Making of a Polemical Image in Medieval Islam*, Albany, NY: SUNY Press, 1999.

Lala, Ismail, *Knowing God: Ibn ʿArabī and ʿAbd al-Razzāq al-Qāshānī's Metaphysics of the Divine*, Leiden & Boston: Brill, 2020.

Lipton, Gregory A., *Rethinking Ibn 'Arabi*, New York: Oxford University Press, 2018.

Lory, Pierre, s.v. "ʿAbd al-Razzāq al-Kāshānī', in Kate Fleet, Gudrun Krämer et al., eds., *Encyclopaedia of Islam*, 3rd ed. (*EI³*), 6 vols., Leiden: Brill, 2007–.

Maḥallī, Jalāl al-Dīn al- & Jalāl al-Dīn al-Suyūṭī, *Tafsīr al-Jalālayn*, Beirut: Dār al-Maʿrifa, 1403/1983.

Massignon, Louis, *La passion de Hussayn Ibn Mansûr an-Hallâj*, trans. Herbert Mason as *Hallāj: Mystic and Martyr*, Princeton: Princeton University Press, 1982.

Massignon, Louis & Louis Gardet, s.v. 'Al-Ḥallādj', in P. J. Bearman, Th. Bianquis et al., eds., *Encyclopaedia of Islam*, 2nd ed. (*EI²*), 12 vols., Leiden: Brill, 1960–2007.

McDowell, Sean, *The Fate of the Apostles: Examining the Martyrdom Accounts of the Closest Followers of Jesus*, Farnham, Surrey & Burlington, VT: Ashgate, 2015.

Michot, Yahya, *Ibn Taymiyya: Mardin: Hégire, fuite du péché et demeure de l'Islam*, trans. Jamil Qureshi as *Ibn Taymiyya: Muslims Under Non-Muslim Rule*, Oxford & London: Interface Publications, 2006.

Mohammed, Khaleel, *David in the Muslim Tradition: The Bathsheba Affair*, Lanham, MD: Lexington Books, 2015.

Morris, James Winston, 'Ibn ʿArabi and His Interpreters Part II (Conclusion): Influences and Interpretations', *Journal of the American Oriental Society*, vol. cvii, no. 1, 1987, pp. 101–119.

Muslim b. al-Ḥajjāj, *Ṣaḥīḥ Muslim*, trans. Nasiruddin al-Khattab, 7 vols., Riyadh: Darussalam, 2007.

Nadwi, S. Abul Hasan Ali, *Ta'rīkh-i-daʿwat awr ʿazīmat*, trans. Mohiuddin Ahmad as *Saviours of the Islamic Spirit*, 4 vols., Lucknow: Academy of Islamic Research and Publications, 1986–1997.

Nasr, Seyyed Hossein, *The Garden of Truth: The Vision and Promise of Sufism, Islam's Mystical Tradition*, New York: HarperOne, 2007.

——, *An Introduction to Islamic Cosmological Doctrines*, New York: SUNY Press, 1993.

Nasr, Seyyed Hossein et al., eds., *The Study Quran: A New Translation and Commentary* (*SQ*), San Francisco: HarperOne, 2015.

Ott, Sandra, 'Aristotle Among the Basques: The "Cheese Analogy" of Conception', *Man* (New Series), vol. xiv, no. 4, 1979, pp. 699–711.

Pagani, Samuela, 'Ibn ʿArabi, Ibn Qayyim al-Jawziyya, and the Political Functions of Punishment in the Islamic Hell', in Christian Lange, ed., *Locating Hell in Islamic Traditions*, Leiden & Boston: Brill, 2016, pp. 175–207.

Pfeiffer, Judith, 'Conversion Versions: Sultan Öljeytü's Conversion to Shi'ism (709/1309) in Muslim Narrative Sources', *Mongolian Studies*, vol. XXII, 1999, pp. 35–67.

——, 'Reflections on a "Double Rapprochement": Conversion to Islam among the Mongol Elite During the Early Ilkhanate', in Linda Komaroff, ed., *Beyond the Legacy of Genghis Khan*, Leiden & Boston: Brill, 2006, pp. 369–389.

Pickthall, Mohammed Marmaduke, *The Meaning of the Glorious Qur'an: An Explanatory Translation*, New Delhi: Idara Ishaat-e-Diniyat, n.d.

Post, Arjan Antonius Johannes, 'The Journey of a Taymiyyan Sufi: Sufism Through the Eyes of ʿImād al-Dīn Aḥmad al-Wāsiṭī (d. 711/1311)', PhD thesis, Utrecht University, 2017.

Qurṭubī, Abū ʿAbd Allāh Muḥammad b. Aḥmad al-, *al-Jāmiʿ li-aḥkām al-Qur'ān*, ed. ʿAbd Allāh b. ʿAbd al-Muḥsin al-Turkī et al., Beirut: Muʾassasat al-Risāla, 2006.

Ṣābūnī, Muḥammad ʿAlī al-, *Ṣafwāt al-tafāsīr*, Beirut: Dār wa Maktabat al-Hilāl, 2002.

Saleh, Walid, 'Quranic Commentaries', in Seyyed Hossein Nasr et al., eds., *The Study Quran: A New Translation and Commentary (SQ)*, San Francisco: HarperOne, 2015, pp. 1645–1658.

Sands, Kristen Zahra, *Ṣūfī Commentaries on the Qur'ān in Classical Islam*, Abingdon, Oxon and New York: Routledge, 2006.

Shafi, Muhammad, *Maʿariful Qur'an: A Comprehensive Commentary on the Holy Quran*, trans. Muḥammad Shamīm et al., Karachi: Maktaba-Darul-Uloom Karachi, 1998–2004.

Ṣiddīqī, Muḥammad Zubayr, *Ḥadīth Literature: Its Origin, Development & Special Features*, ed. Abdal Hakim Murad, Cambridge: Islamic Texts Society, 1993.

Sulamī, Abū ʿAbd al-Raḥmān al-, *Ṭabaqāt al-ṣūfiyya*, ed. Muṣṭafā ʿAbd al-Qādir ʿAṭā, Beirut: Dār al-Kutub al-ʿIlmiyya, 1998.

Ṭabarī, [Abū Jaʿfar Muḥammad b. Jarīr] al-, *Jāmiʿ al-bayān ʿan ta'wīl āy al-Qur'ān*, cf. partial translation by Scott C. Lucas as *Selections from The Comprehensive Exposition of the Interpretation of the Verses of the Qur'ān*, 2 vols., Cambridge: The Royal Aal al-Bayt Institute for Islamic Thought and the Islamic Texts Society, 2017.

——, *Tārīkh al-rusul wa'l-mulūk*, extract trans. William M. Brinner as *The History of al-Ṭabarī: An Annotated Translation, Volume III: The Children of Israel*, New York: SUNY Press, 1991.

——, *Tārīkh al-rusul wa'l-mulūk*, extract trans. C. E. Bosworth as *The History of al-Ṭabarī: An Annotated Translation, Volume V: The Sāsānids, the Byzantines, the Lakmids, and Yemen*, New York: SUNY Press, 1999.

——, *Tārīkh al-rusul wa'l-mulūk*, extract trans. M.V. McDonald and annotated by W. Montgomery Watt as *The History of al-Ṭabarī: An Annotated Translation, Volume VII: The Foundation of the Community*, New York: SUNY Press, 1987.

——, *Tārīkh al-rusul wa'l-mulūk*, extract trans. Ismail K. Poonawala as *The History of al-Ṭabarī: An Annotated Translation, Volume IX: The Last Years of the Prophet*, New York: SUNY Press, 1990.

Bibliography

——, *Tārīkh al-rusul wa'l-mulūk: dhayl al-mudhayyal*, trans. Ella Landau-Tasseron as *The History of al-Ṭabarī: An Annotated Translation, Volume XXXIX: Biographies of the Prophet's Companions and Their Successors*, New York: SUNY Press, 1988.

Winkel, Eric, *Islam and the Living Law: The Ibn al-Arabi Approach*, Karachi: Oxford University Press, 1997.

Woerner-Powell, Tom, *Another Road to Damascus: An Integrative Approach to ʿAbd al-Qādir al-Jazāʾirī (1808–1883)*, Berlin & Boston: De Gruyter, 2017.

Wright, William, *A Grammar of the Arabic Language*, 2 vols. in 1, Beirut: Librairie du Liban, 1996.

Yaman, Hikmet, 'Ḥanbalīte Criticism of Sufism: Ibn Taymiyya (d. 795/1328), a Ḥanbalīte Ascetic (*Zāhid*)', *Ekev Akademi Dergisi*, vol. XIII, no. 43, 2010, pp. 37–56.

Zarrabi-Zadeh, Saeed, *Practical Mysticism in Islam and Christianity: a Comparative Study of Jalal al-Din Rumi and Meister Eckhart*, Abingdon, Oxon and New York: Routledge, 2016.

INDEX

298, 328; path of the Essence,
63; path of God, 290; path of
Oneness, 56, 80, 93, 112, 135,
146, 210, 218, 316, 333, 353, 420,
447, 453; path of Unity, 113, 114,
226, 296, 419; The Pilgrimage
(Q. 22), 63; The Prophets
(Q. 21), 56–7; straight path, 37,
56, 70, 80, 93, 131, 142, 146, 210,
216, 225, 290, 291, 296, 297–8,
305, 336, 340, 344, 402, 407,
453, 516, 582; upright way, 291
patience, 41, 456, 465, 481; faith
and, 539
peace (salām), 111; absolute peace,
137–8; Divine Name, 191, 210,
418; divine peace, 51, 52, 55, 58,
70, 92, 99, 107, 143, 172, 270;
greeting/speech of 'Peace!',
10, 109–10, 191, 256, 393, 398;
Mary (Q. 19), 7, 10; The Night
of Power (Q. 97), 558; soul at
peace, 540; Yā Sīn (Q. 36), 216
peace of reassurance (sakīna), 336,
337–8, 340
Pen (qalam), 291, 405, 455, 555, 575
The Pen (Sūrat al-Qalam, Q. 68):
deniers, 456–8; Divine Names,
455; guidance, 456; madness,
455–6; outward/inward
conformity, 456; the Pen, 455;
preparedness, 458; reward, 455;
the Scribe is God Himself, 455;
submission, 458; the Tablet,
455; unveiling, 455; veiled/
veiling, 455; wealth, 456;
witnessing, 455
People (Sūrat al-Nās, Q. 114):
annihilation, 589, 590; evil, 590;

jinn, 590; Satan, 590; seeking
refuge in God, 589–90
People of the Book, 165–6, 189; The
Clear Proof (Q. 98), 559–60;
Exile (Q. 59), 413, 415–16; Hell,
560; Iron (Q. 57), 406–407;
terror in their hearts, 413;
veiled/veiling, 559, 560; see also
Christians; Jews; Sabaeans
people of pith, 230, 236, 247, 248,
249, 265, 441
perfection, 477; absolute perfection,
59, 104, 137, 358, 412; Adam,
240, 241; The Angels (Q. 35),
208, 209; believers, perfection
of, 185; character, perfection
of, 402; creation, perfection
of, 449; deed, perfection of,
133; defrauders, 519; Divine
Attribute, 144, 145, 155, 159,
172, 188, 197, 281, 319, 435;
emanation of perfections, 192,
193, 195, 401, 418, 421, 452, 497,
529; experiential realisation,
perfection of, 133; Gardens
of Eden, 209; God's will of
perfection, 2; gratitude and,
323–4; human perfection, 45,
211, 230, 431, 553; I-ness and,
158; Iron (Q. 57), 402, 405–406,
407; knowledge, perfection of,
34, 66, 164, 276, 461, 554; level
of, 149, 152, 210–11; limit of,
214; love, perfection of, 284;
Moses, 149, 150; The Most
High (Q. 87), 532, 533, 534;
Noah (Q. 71), 471; perfect faith,
565; perfection of the soul and
virtues, 542–3; perfection of the